Application Environment Specification (AES) User Environment Volume

Revision B

Open Software Foundation

Prentice Hall, Englewood Cliffs, New Jersey 07632

This book was formatted with troff

Cover design
and cover illustration: BETH FAGAN

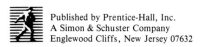
Published by Prentice-Hall, Inc.
A Simon & Schuster Company
Englewood Cliffs, New Jersey 07632

Printed in the United States of America
10 9   8   7   6   5   4   3   2

ISBN   0-13-043530-9

Prentice-Hall International (UK) Limited, *London*
Prentice-Hall of Australia Pty. Limited, *Sydney*
Prentice-Hall Canada Inc., *Toronto*
Prentice-Hall Hispanoamericana, S.A., *Mexico*
Prentice-Hall of India Private Limited, *New Delhi*
Prentice-Hall of Japan, Inc., *Tokyo*
Simon & Schuster Asia Pte. Ltd., *Singapore*
Editora Prentice-Hall do Brasil, Ltda., *Rio de Janeiro*

Contents

List of Tables

Preface

Part of the charter of the Open Software Foundation™ (OSF™) is to foster the development of portable software that will run on a variety of hardware platforms. The Application Environment Specification (AES) specifies the interfaces that support such software.

Specifically, this document (the Application Environment Specification (AES) User Environment Volume, Revision B) specifies interfaces for the user environment portion of OSF's Applications Environment.

Chapter 1 describes the purpose of the Application Environment Specification, incorporating a document originally published by itself as "The AES Definition." It provides a detailed description of the relationship of the AES to:

- Formal (de jure) standards and specifications.

- Implementations; for example, operating systems like OSF's operating system component (OSC).

- Portable applications software.

Audience

This document is written for:

- Software engineers developing AES-compliant applications to run on AES-compliant implementations.

- Software engineers developing AES-compliant implementations on which AES-compliant applications can run.

- Organizations (for example, standards-setting bodies) for whom the AES (or some part of it) is an appropriate part of the formal, de jure process.

Contents

This document is organized into two chapters.

- *Chapter 1* introduces the AES, providing the general AES definition, and the general rationale for inclusion and specification of interfaces in the AES. This chapter includes the AES Service Outline.

- *Chapter 2* contains manual pages for all of the AES/UE interfaces. They are ordered alphabetically within commands and functions.

Typographical Conventions

This volume uses the following typographical conventions:

- **Boldfaced** strings represent literals; type them exactly as they appear.

- *Italicized* strings represent variables (for example, function or macro arguments).

- Ellipses (...) indicate that additional arguments are optional.

Interface Definition Manual Page Format

The manual pages for interface definitions in this volume use the following format:

Purpose
This section gives a short description of the interface.

AES Support Level
This section indicates whether the interfaces's AES support status is full-, trial-, or temporary-use.

Compatibility
This section lists the standards and industry specifications in which the interface exists.

Synopsis
This section describes the appropriate syntax for using the interface.

Description

This section describes the behavior of the interface. On widget man pages there are tables of resource values in the descriptions. Those tables have the following headers:

Name   Contains the name of the resource. Each new resource is described following the new resources table.

Class   Contains the class of the resource.

Type   Contains the type of the resource.

Default   Contains the default value of the resource.

Access   Contains the access permissions for the resource. A **C** in this column means the resource can be set at widget creation time. A **S** means the resource can be set anytime. A **G** means the resource's value can retrieved.

Return Value

This lists the values returned by function interfaces.

Errors

This section describes the error conditions associated with using this interface.

Related Information

This section provides cross references to related interfaces and header files described within this document.

Chapter 1

Introduction

This chapter introduces the user enviromnent volume of the AES. Section 1.1 defines the AES. Section 1.2 is the AES/UE service outline. Section 1.3 is a table of AES support levels ordered by functional area.

1.1 The Application Environment Specification Definition

This section provides a detailed description of the Application Environment Specification (AES).

1.1.1 Introduction to the AES Definition

Part of the charter of the Open Software Foundation (OSF) is to foster the development of portable software applications that will run on a wide variety of hardware platforms. The software required to support such applications is an "application environment" provided by systems or software vendors. An application environment is a set of programming and user interfaces and their associated semantics, available to applications and users.

The AES is a specification for a consistent application environment across different hardware platforms. This definition uses the term "implementation" to describe the application environment that vendors supply to application developers, because such software is an implementation of the AES.

The AES specifies the following:

- Application-level interfaces that an implementation must provide in order to support portable applications

- Semantics or protocols associated with each of these interfaces

This definition describes the purpose, contents, and organization of the AES. It also discusses the meaning of AES compliance for applications and implementations, the relationship of the AES to other industry documents (standards and specifications) and to implementations. Finally, the document describes the AES development process and the support levels used to characterize interfaces within the AES.

1.1.2 Purpose of the AES

The primary purpose of the AES is to provide a common definition of application interfaces that both systems providers and systems users can rely on in the development of portable applications. The composite AES defines the stable, reliable, application-level interfaces in several functional areas. Systems sellers who comply with the AES know exactly what interfaces they must provide, and how each element of those interfaces must behave. Systems buyers who look for AES conformance know unequivocally the interfaces they can rely on.

A secondary purpose of the AES is to take advantage of OSF's organizational charter to expedite the specification of application environments. Unlike specifications and standards bodies, OSF also provides vendor-neutral, hardware-independent implementations. The task of providing these implementations gives practical experience and feedback that enables the AES to expand faster than standards documents can. Also, OSF's technical staff is chartered to provide an expeditious resolution of the conflicts that can delay the decision process in other types of organizations.

By integrating functionality that is already standardized with newer functionality that is suitable for eventual standardization, the AES provides material that contributes to future standards. Because of OSF's timely, vendor-neutral decision process, this newer functionality can be added relatively quickly.

1.1.3 Contents of the AES

As previously stated, the AES is a set of specifications for programming and user interfaces and their associated semantics. The library routines, user commands, and data objects specified in the AES have the following characteristics:

- They provide valuable services to portable applications.

- They can be implemented on a wide variety of hardware platforms and support hardware-independent applications.

- They are stable (they are not likely to need to change).

- They are reliable (because they are tightly specified, applications writers can rely on consistent behavior across applications platforms).

We call AES-specified program and user interfaces "portability interfaces" because they provide support for portable (hardware-independent) applications.

In order to be useful for applications development within these criteria, the AES must provide the richest possible function set. Development of the AES requires a balance between expansion to provide richer functionality, and conservatism to guarantee the stability of included interfaces.

Internal interfaces are interfaces that are not visible to applications. Internal interfaces are not part of the AES. The AES specifies only application-level portability interfaces (as previously defined).

1.1.4 Organization of the AES

The AES is an evolving set of *area specifications*. Each area specification describes portability interfaces for one *functional area* of the application environment. OSF has identified the following functional areas:

- Operating System Programming Interfaces
- Operating System Commands and Utilities
- Network Services
- User Environment Services
- Graphics Services
- Database Management Services
- Programming Languages (BASIC, Fortran, Pascal, C, COBOL, Ada, and Lisp)

In certain functional areas, OSF publishes its own area specifications, which add to or extend existing standards and specifications. This definition focuses on the development process for the specifications that OSF publishes. In other areas, the AES just points to widely known existing standards and specifications.

The initial AES area specifications for OSF publication are in three functional areas.

- The *AES/Operating System* area specification describes the programming interfaces that an AES-conforming operating system must provide.

- The *AES/Network Services* area specification describes protocol-independent and protocol-specific interfaces to network services.

- The *AES/User Environment* area specification describes the programming interfaces that an AES-compliant user interface must provide.

An area specification can consist of one or more volumes, and the term "AES Volume" describes the document that contains all or part of an area specification.

OSF's goal is to promote usability and coherence of the AES documents themselves; therefore, document titles are as descriptive as possible. Also, OSF uses revisions, rather than supplements, to add functions to existing AES volumes.

Each revision of an AES Volume includes, for reference, the complete list of standards and specifications that make up the Application Environment. (This list first appeared as "AES Level 0" in May, 1988.) Because, unless otherwise stated, the standards and specifications that comprise the Application Environment are independent of one another, this list is provided only for user reference. Any direct dependencies that an area AES has on specifications in another area are listed within the AES Volume for the first area.

1.1.5 The Meaning of AES Conformance

This section provides a brief, general discussion of AES conformance for implementations and applications. This document does not discuss the specific means of measuring or proving conformance or such issues as validation, compliance, branding, and waivers.

Implementations and applications that conform to the AES do so on the basis of *area functionality.* An implementation or application that conforms to one AES area is considered to be AES-conforming for that area.

Implementations and applications conform to the AES differently, since implementations *provide* services and applications *use* interfaces specified in the AES to access these services. A conforming implementation provides *at least* the interfaces defined in the AES. A conforming application uses *only* the interfaces defined in the AES and those defined in any standards or specifications that the AES depends on. Such dependencies are called out explicitly in AES area specifications.

1.1.5.1 AES Conformance for Implementations

For an implementation to be AES conforming in a functional area, it must implement each interface element as specified by the AES volume for that functional area.

AES area-conforming implementations may offer additional interfaces not specified in the AES, or extensions to AES interfaces, provided they do not affect the conformance of any element of the AES-specified interfaces.

Unless specifically called out within the area specification, an implementation that conforms to one functional area need not provide services from other functional areas, or to conform to other functional areas.

1.1.5.2 Conformance Document

Vendors of AES-conforming implementations should make available to their customers a conformance document that describes:

- The AES area and revision the implementation conforms to

- The values of all implementation-defined variables and limits that the implementation supports

- The actual behavior of all features described in the AES as implementation defined

If the implementation supports any nonstandard extensions that change the behavior of interfaces specified in the AES, the conformance document must specify how to create an environment that provides the AES-specified behavior. If conformance information exists in other documents provided with the implementation, the AES conformance document can provide a reference to that information rather than repeat it.

1.1.5.3 AES Conformance for Applications

For an application to be AES conforming in a functional area, it must use only the interfaces in the relevant AES area specification or those in other standards and specifications the area specification depends on. Standards or specifications included by reference are considered to be part of the AES for conforming applications.

The application must depend only on AES-specified behavior for AES interfaces. An application should not depend on any behavior that the AES describes as unspecified, undefined, or implementation defined.

1.1.5.4 AES Support Levels and Conformance

Each AES interface element has a support level, which specifies the commitment OSF makes to its definition. The higher the support level, the longer the warning period required before OSF can delete the element, or make an incompatible change in the element's definition. (An incompatible change is one that might require conforming applications to be rewritten.)

Conforming implementations will provide all AES interfaces for the relevant area at all support levels. Developers of conforming applications can choose to use or not use elements at any support level. Support levels serve as advisories for application developers because they indicate the length of time that an interface specification is guaranteed to remain stable.

During the AES development process, OSF staff members propose support levels for interface elements, based on criteria defined later in this document. OSF members review and comment on these support levels along with the rest of the document.

Section 1.1.9 provides detailed information about AES support levels.

1.1.6 Relationship of the AES to Standards and Other Specifications

The AES incorporates relevant industry standards and selected industry specifications. When an AES area specification incorporates an industry standard or specification, the area specification either points to that standard or specification, or includes the text. (Document revision schedules, source availability, and document usability influence the decision to use pointers or text.)

The AES may extend or further specify interface elements derived from an included standard or specification, and when such extensions occur, they are clearly marked as such within the appropriate AES Volume.

An AES-conforming implementation of an interface should also conform to all included standards and specifications that contain the interface. If this is not possible, because of conflicts between definitions in included standards, the AES resolves conflicts based on a defined precedence order of standards. AES Volumes define, in an introductory chapter, the order of precedence of any included standards and specifications.

Inclusion of whole standards and specifications in the AES sometimes results in inclusion of interfaces or interface elements that might not have been selected for inclusion on their own merit. In such cases, OSF still includes the element because it is in the standard and the standard takes precedence. However, the AES interface definition notes any problems and discourages applications' use of the problematic interface. OSF also works within the standards or specification bodies to remove or modify such interfaces.

1.1.7 Relationship of the AES to Implementations

The AES is a specification to which vendors can build implementations. OSF itself provides implementations for some of the AES functional areas. These OSF implementations include the portability interfaces defined in the AES, and may also include interfaces not specified in the AES, or extensions to AES-specified interfaces. These extensions may be obsolete interfaces provided for support of existing applications, or they may be experimental, new interfaces. Only those interfaces that are recommended for use by new portable applications will be included in the AES. Some of the interfaces that are not in the AES may be candidates for inclusion in a subsequent AES revision.

1.1.8 The AES Development Process

This section describes the processes for development of the AES, for document revision control, and for membership review cycles.

For each functional area, OSF produces one or more AES area specification drafts for its membership to review (see Section 1.1.8.3). After incorporating review comments, OSF produces a final AES area specification. A final AES area specification for a particular revision includes the interface definitions for a stable set of portability interfaces in one functional area of the OSF-supported Application Environment.

1.1.8.1 Document Control and the AES

OSF labels the AES for each functional area with a *revision letter*. As the collection of revisions grows, OSF may group the existing revisions into an *AES Level*. For example, an AES Level might include AES/UE Revision B, AES/OS Revision A, and so on.

1.1.8.2 The Service Outline

A Service Outline is a document that lists all the elements in each AES interface for a functional area and indicates the support level for each element without giving detailed descriptions. OSF makes two uses of Service Outlines.

- In some functional areas, a Service Outline may be a draft document that precedes a full AES volume. (A full AES volume provides complete interface definitions or pointers to other information or conceptual descriptions.) A draft Service Outline proposes the interfaces to be included in a full AES volume. In this case, the full AES volume draft, when complete, supersedes the Service Outline draft.

- In other functional areas, a Service Outline may become a permanent document. If all the interfaces for a functional area are completely specified, with no conflicts, in industry standards or other specification documents, the AES area specification for that functional area may remain as a Service Outline and never evolve into a full AES volume.

When appropriate, a Service Outline also contains a table that shows each element and lists relevant industry standards, specifications, and implementations that include the element.

Complete AES documents (not Service Outlines) provide complete interface definitions and pointers to other information or conceptual descriptions.

1.1.8.3 The Membership Review

In general, membership review proceeds as follows:

1. OSF prepares a draft Service Outline and/or AES Volume for a functional area, and circulates it to OSF members. This review period may last from one to several months.

2. Members submit comments using a prescribed comment template.

3. OSF responds to members' comments in the next version of the document, or in a discussion that takes place in an electronic news group or at a meeting.

OSF considers all review comments during the development of AES documents and brings important or controversial issues up for further discussion. However, the review process is not a voting process, and OSF does not wait for consensus among the membership before adding new interfaces to the AES or making other technical decisions.

1.1.9 AES Support Levels

This section defines the support levels assigned to each AES interface element. As previously mentioned, support levels define OSF's commitment to interface definitions by indicating the warning period required to make an incompatible modification or deletion of the definition.

New AES revisions may introduce upwardly compatible changes at any time, regardless of the support level. Any such changes will be noted in the associated **Specification Context** section.

The support levels are:

- Full use

- Trial use

- Temporary use

Typically, elements in the AES have full-use or trial-use support levels. Conforming implementations must provide them, and application developers can use them freely (with the knowledge that trial-use elements are subject to more rapid change than full-use elements). The temporary-use support level appears only rarely in area specifications; it is for special cases, as described below. Implementations must provide temporary-use elements too, when they appear.

The following sections explain each support level. Section 1.1.9.4 describes how elements move from proposed status (in draft specifications) to final status (in published specifications).

1.1.9.1 Full Use

A full-use element has the highest support level, so it is the most protected from incompatible modification or deletion from the AES.

OSF assigns a support level of full use to elements for reasons such as the following:

- The element already exists in an approved de-jure standard. (A de-jure standard is one that is set by an official standards body.)

- The element as specified in the AES is considered stable and already in widespread use in applications.

- The element has been upgraded to full-use status after a period of trial-use status in an earlier AES revision.

There should rarely be a need to remove a full-use element, or make incompatible modifications to it. However, if this ever becomes necessary, a full-use element keeps its full-use status, but a warning describing the proposed future change must be published in at least two successive revisions of the AES area volume before the change can be made. This provides time for applications to be altered to deal with a different behavior, and for implementations to prepare for the change.

For example, suppose it becomes necessary to modify a full-use element that appeared in Revision A of an AES Volume. The draft for Revision B shows the element as "proposed-for-modification/removal." Assuming the review concludes that this change is appropriate, the element in Revision B still has full-use status, but is accompanied by a warning. The warning states that the element is scheduled for modification after Revision C, and describes the modified behavior. Application developers can now allow for either the original or the modified behavior. Revision C contains the same warning. Revision D provides the modified definition only. The **Specification Context** section of the interface element definition documents the history of such changes.

1.1.9.2 Trial Use

A trial-use element is easier to modify or delete than a full-use element. There are several reasons that OSF classifies elements as trial use instead of full use. An element may be under consideration for inclusion in a de-jure standard and so may possibly change as a result of the standards process. Or, OSF may perceive that the element is new compared to other included elements and, therefore, the implementation and use of the element may suggest revisions in its definition.

If it becomes necessary to modify or delete a trial-use element, it keeps its trial-use status, with warnings about its removal or incompatible change, for one full revision of the AES. In the example above, if the element to be modified were a trial-use element, Revision B would include the unmodified definition with a warning and description of the change, and Revision C would include the modified definition only.

1.1.9.3 Temporary Use

A temporary-use element is a special case. Because it is limited in use, not sufficiently general, or faulty in some other way, it is likely to be changed. As such, it does not meet the criteria for inclusion in the AES with a full-use or trial-use support level, but it provides necessary functionality not available through other full-use or trial-use interface elements. Conforming applications may use these elements as necessary; an application containing a temporary-use element should be labeled as such. The AES replaces temporary-use interface elements when appropriate full- or trial-use elements become available.

Giving an element temporary-use status makes it clear from the outset that OSF intends to replace it. In the meantime, the element provides necessary and clearly specified functionality. Compliant implementations must provide services classified as temporary use, and applications can use them, although it is clear that the element will eventually be replaced. Once a replacement exists, the AES includes a warning in the temporary-use element's definition and lists the removal date. As in the case of a trial-use element, the warning exists for one revision only.

For example, certain network interfaces provide a general service using a protocol-specific algorithm. These might be candidates for temporary-use status, because as time passes, interfaces based on protocol-independent algorithms will become available to replace them.

1.1.9.4 Proposed Usage Levels

Draft versions of specifications give newly added or changed elements a "proposed-for-*level*" status, where *level* is one of those defined previously. In final versions, these elements move from "proposed-for-*level*" status to *level* status.

In the review draft of the first revision of an AES area specification, all elements are at "proposed-for-*level*" status. In review drafts of subsequent revisions, the elements may have one of several statuses. Most existing elements retain their support level from the existing revision. A few may carry a proposed-for-*change* status (described below). New elements carry a proposed-for-*level* status.

The following list defines more exactly the AES proposed-for-inclusion and proposed for-change levels.

Proposed-for-*level*-use

A review level leading to *level*-use inclusion on acceptance, and no change in status otherwise. This status may be used to propose a new element for *level*-use, or to move an existing element to a higher status.

Proposed-for-modification/removal

A review level for existing elements that OSF proposes to make an incompatible modification in or remove from the AES. If this proposal is accepted during the review process, a full-use element remains as is, with a warning, for two revisions; a trial-use or temporary-use element remains as is with a warning, for one revision. If the proposal is rejected, the element remains as is.

Proposed-for-correction

> A review level for elements of any support level in which OSF wishes to correct a specification error. OSF will propose correcting an element if a definition was obviously wrong (and implementations and applications could never follow the specification as it is written), if clarification of an unclear section is required, or if an error makes a definition clearly internally inconsistent or inappropriate. Elements proposed for correction return to their original status, in corrected form, on acceptance of the correction. They return to their original status in uncorrected form on rejection of the correction. (Proposal for correction is not required for OSF to fix a typographical error.)

Proposed-for-enhancement

> A review level for elements in which OSF wants to make an upwardly compatible change in definition. If accepted, the definition change is effective in the published revision after the draft in which the proposal for enhancement occurred.

1.2 Service Outline

This service outline lists all the services included in the AES/UE.

- The first column is the name of the service. The table is organized alphabetically by this column. All services that are new in the implementation for this revision are marked by an asterisk (*).

- The second column is the type of the service. The type is widget, function, command, data type, or file format.

- The third column is the AES support level.

Table 1-1. Service Outline

Service Name	Service Type	AES Level
ApplicationShell	widget	full-use
Composite	widget	full-use
Constraint	widget	full-use
Core	widget	full-use
MrmCloseHierarchy	function	trial-use
MrmFetchColorLiteral	function	trial-use
MrmFetchIconLiteral	function	trial-use
MrmFetchLiteral	function	trial-use
MrmFetchSetValues	function	trial-use
MrmFetchWidget	function	trial-use
MrmFetchWidgetOverride	function	trial-use
MrmInitialize	function	trial-use
MrmOpenHierarchy	function	trial-use
MrmRegisterClass	function	trial-use
MrmRegisterNames	function	trial-use
MrmRegisterNamesInHierarchy*	function	trial-use
Object	widget	full-use
OverrideShell	widget	full-use
RectObj	widget	full-use
Shell	widget	full-use
TopLevelShell	widget	full-use
TransientShell	widget	full-use
Uil	function	trial-use
VendorShell	widget	full-use
WMShell	widget	full-use
XmActivateProtocol	function	trial-use
XmActivateWMProtocol	function	trial-use
XmAddProtocolCallbacks	function	trial-use

Service Name	Service Type	AES Level
XmAddProtocols	function	trial-use
XmAddTabGroup	function	full-use
XmAddWMProtocolCallbacks	function	trial-use
XmAddWMProtocols	function	trial-use
XmArrowButton	widget	full-use
XmArrowButtonGadget	widget	full-use
XmBulletinBoard	widget	full-use
XmCascadeButton	widget	full-use
XmCascadeButtonGadget	widget	full-use
XmCascadeButtonGadgetHighlight*	function	trial-use
XmCascadeButtonHighlight	function	full-use
XmClipboardCancelCopy	function	full-use
XmClipboardCopy	function	full-use
XmClipboardCopyByName	function	full-use
XmClipboardEndCopy	function	full-use
XmClipboardEndRetrieve	function	full-use
XmClipboardInquireCount	function	full-use
XmClipboardInquireFormat	function	full-use
XmClipboardInquireLength	function	full-use
XmClipboardInquirePendingItems	function	full-use
XmClipboardLock	function	full-use
XmClipboardRegisterFormat	function	full-use
XmClipboardRetrieve	function	full-use
XmClipboardStartCopy	function	full-use
XmClipboardStartRetrieve	function	full-use
XmClipboardUndoCopy	function	full-use
XmClipboardUnlock	function	full-use
XmClipboardWithdrawFormat	function	full-use
XmCommand	widget	full-use
XmCommandAppendValue	function	full-use

Service Name	Service Type	AES Level
XmCommandError	function	full-use
XmCommandGetChild	function	full-use
XmCommandSetValue	function	full-use
XmConvertUnits	function	trial-use
XmCreateArrowButton	function	full-use
XmCreateArrowButtonGadget	function	full-use
XmCreateBulletinBoard	function	full-use
XmCreateBulletinBoardDialog	function	full-use
XmCreateCascadeButton	function	full-use
XmCreateCascadeButtonGadget	function	full-use
XmCreateCommand	function	full-use
XmCreateDialogShell	function	full-use
XmCreateDrawingArea	function	full-use
XmCreateDrawnButton	function	full-use
XmCreateErrorDialog	function	full-use
XmCreateFileSelectionBox	function	full-use
XmCreateFileSelectionDialog	function	full-use
XmCreateForm	function	full-use
XmCreateFormDialog	function	full-use
XmCreateFrame	function	full-use
XmCreateInformationDialog	function	full-use
XmCreateLabel	function	full-use
XmCreateLabelGadget	function	full-use
XmCreateList	function	full-use
XmCreateMainWindow	function	full-use
XmCreateMenuBar	function	full-use
XmCreateMenuShell	function	full-use
XmCreateMessageBox	function	full-use
XmCreateMessageDialog	function	full-use
XmCreateOptionMenu	function	full-use

Service Name	Service Type	AES Level
XmCreatePanedWindow	function	full-use
XmCreatePopupMenu	function	full-use
XmCreatePromptDialog	function	full-use
XmCreatePulldownMenu	function	full-use
XmCreatePushButton	function	full-use
XmCreatePushButtonGadget	function	full-use
XmCreateQuestionDialog	function	full-use
XmCreateRadioBox	function	full-use
XmCreateRowColumn	function	full-use
XmCreateScale	function	full-use
XmCreateScrollBar	function	full-use
XmCreateScrolledList	function	full-use
XmCreateScrolledText	function	full-use
XmCreateScrolledWindow	function	full-use
XmCreateSelectionBox	function	full-use
XmCreateSelectionDialog	function	full-use
XmCreateSeparator	function	full-use
XmCreateSeparatorGadget	function	full-use
XmCreateWorkArea*	function	trial-use
XmCreateText	function	full-use
XmCreateToggleButton	function	full-use
XmCreateToggleButtonGadget	function	full-use
XmCreateWarningDialog	function	full-use
XmCreateWorkingDialog	function	full-use
XmCvtCTToXmString*	function	trial-use
XmCvtXmStringToCT*	function	trial-use
XmDeactivateProtocol	function	trial-use
XmDeactivateWMProtocol	function	trial-use
XmDestroyPixmap	function	full-use
XmDialogShell	widget	full-use

Service Name	Service Type	AES Level
XmDrawingArea	widget	full-use
XmDrawnButton	widget	full-use
XmFileSelectionBox	widget	full-use
XmFileSelectionBoxGetChild	function	full-use
XmFileSelectionDoSearch	function	full-use
XmFontList*	data type	trial-use
XmFontListAdd	function	trial-use
XmFontListCreate	function	trial-use
XmFontListFree	function	trial-use
XmForm	widget	full-use
XmFrame	widget	full-use
XmGadget	widget	full-use
XmGetAtomName	function	full-use
XmGetColors*	function	trial-use
XmGetMenuCursor	function	full-use
XmGetPixmap	function	full-use
XmGetPostedFromWidget*	function	trial-use
XmInstallImage	function	full-use
XmInternAtom	function	full-use
XmIsMotifWMRunning	function	full-use
XmLabel	widget	full-use
XmLabelGadget	widget	full-use
XmList	widget	full-use
XmListAddItem	function	full-use
XmListAddItems*	function	trial-use
XmListAddItemUnselected	function	full-use
XmListDeleteAllItems*	function	trial-use
XmListDeleteItem	function	full-use
XmListDeleteItems*	function	trial-use
XmListDeleteItemsPos*	function	trial-use

Service Name	Service Type	AES Level
XmListDeletePos	function	full-use
XmListDeselectAllItems	function	full-use
XmListDeselectItem	function	full-use
XmListDeselectPos	function	full-use
XmListGetMatchPos*	function	trial-use
XmListGetSelectedPos*	function	trial-use
XmListItemExists	function	full-use
XmListItemPos*	function	trial-use
XmListReplaceItems*	function	trial-use
XmListReplaceItemsPos*	function	trial-use
XmListSelectItem	function	full-use
XmListSelectPos	function	full-use
XmListSetAddMode*	function	trial-use
XmListSetBottomItem	function	full-use
XmListSetBottomPos	function	full-use
XmListSetHorizPos	function	full-use
XmListSetItem	function	full-use
XmListSetPos	function	full-use
XmMainWindow	widget	full-use
XmMainWindowSep1	function	full-use
XmMainWindowSep2	function	full-use
XmMainWindowSep3*	function	trial-use
XmMainWindowSetAreas	function	full-use
XmManager	widget	full-use
XmMenuPosition	function	full-use
XmMenuShell	widget	full-use
XmMessageBox	widget	full-use
XmMessageBoxGetChild	function	full-use
XmOptionButtonWidget	function	full-use
XmOptionLabelWidget	function	full-use

Service Name	Service Type	AES Level
XmPanedWindow	widget	full-use
XmPrimitive	widget	full-use
XmProcessTraversal*	function	trial-use
XmPushButton	widget	full-use
XmPushButtonGadget	widget	full-use
XmRemoveProtocolCallbacks	function	trial-use
XmRemoveProtocols	function	trial-use
XmRemoveTabGroup	function	full-use
XmRemoveWMProtocolCallbacks	function	trial-use
XmRemoveWMProtocols	function	trial-use
XmResolvePartOffsets	function	full-use
XmRowColumn	widget	full-use
XmScale	widget	full-use
XmScaleGetValue	function	full-use
XmScaleSetValue	function	full-use
XmScrollBar	widget	full-use
XmScrollBarGetValues	function	full-use
XmScrollBarSetValues	function	full-use
XmScrolledWindow	widget	full-use
XmScrolledWindowSetAreas	function	full-use
XmSelectionBox	widget	full-use
XmSelectionBoxGetChild	function	full-use
XmSeparator	widget	full-use
XmSeparatorGadget	widget	full-use
XmSetMenuCursor	function	full-use
XmSetProtocolHooks	function	trial-use
XmSetWMProtocolHooks	function	trial-use
XmString*	data type	trial-use
XmStringBaseline	function	trial-use
XmStringByteCompare	function	trial-use

Service Name	Service Type	AES Level
XmStringCompare	function	trial-use
XmStringConcat	function	trial-use
XmStringCopy	function	trial-use
XmStringCreate	function	temporary-use
XmStringCreateSimple*	function	temporary-use
XmStringDirection*	data type	trial-use
XmStringDraw	function	trial-use
XmStringDrawImage	function	trial-use
XmStringDrawUnderline	function	trial-use
XmStringEmpty	function	trial-use
XmStringExtent	function	trial-use
XmStringFree	function	trial-use
XmStringHasSubstring*	function	trial-use
XmStringHeight	function	trial-use
XmStringLength	function	trial-use
XmStringLineCount	function	trial-use
XmStringNConcat	function	trial-use
XmStringNCopy	function	trial-use
XmStringSeparatorCreate	function	trial-use
XmStringTable*	data type	trial-use
XmStringWidth	function	trial-use
XmText	widget	full-use
XmTextClearSelection	function	full-use
XmTextCopy*	function	trial-use
XmTextCut*	function	trial-use
XmTextGetBaseline*	function	trial-use
XmTextGetEditable	function	full-use
XmTextGetInsertionPosition*	function	trial-use
XmTextGetLastPosition*	function	trial-use
XmTextGetMaxLength	function	full-use

Service Name	Service Type	AES Level
XmTextGetSelection	function	full-use
XmTextGetSelectionPosition*	function	trial-use
XmTextGetString	function	full-use
XmTextGetSource*	function	trial-use
XmTextGetTopCharacter*	function	trial-use
XmTextInsert*	function	trial-use
XmTextPaste*	function	trial-use
XmTextPosToXY*	function	trial-use
XmTextPosition*	data type	trial-use
XmTextRemove*	function	trial-use
XmTextReplace	function	full-use
XmTextScroll*	function	trial-use
XmTextSetAddMode*	function	trial-use
XmTextSetEditable	function	full-use
XmTextSetHighlight*	function	trial-use
XmTextSetInsertionPosition*	function	trial-use
XmTextSetMaxLength	function	full-use
XmTextSetSelection	function	full-use
XmTextSetSource*	function	trial-use
XmTextSetString	function	full-use
XmTextSetTopCharacter*	function	trial-use
XmTextShowPosition*	function	trial-use
XmTextXYToPos*	function	trial-use
XmToggleButton	widget	full-use
XmToggleButtonGadget	widget	full-use
XmToggleButtonGadgetGetState	function	full-use
XmToggleButtonGadgetSetState	function	full-use
XmToggleButtonGetState	function	full-use
XmToggleButtonSetState	function	full-use
XmTrackingLocate*	function	trial-use

Service Name	Service Type	AES Level
XmUninstallImage	function	full-use
XmUpdateDisplay	function	full-use
mwm	command	full-use

1.3 Overview of Services by Type and Function

All the services are broken into four types in the tables below.

- Window manager
- Widgets and widget functions
- Toolkit functions
- User interface language

Within each table components are organized by function.

1.3.1 Window manager

Table 1-2. Window Manager Services

Service Name	Service Type	AES Level
mwm	command	full-use

1.3.2 Widgets and Widget Functions

This table organizes widgets by hierarchy. Position in the hierarchy is shown by the indentation of the service name. The functions for each widget immediately follow the widget.

Table 1-3. Widget Services

Service Name	Service Type	AES Level
Core	widget	full-use
Object	widget	full-use
RectObj	widget	full-use
XmPrimitive	widget	full-use
XmArrowButton	widget	full-use
XmCreateArrowButton	function	full-use
XmLabel	widget	full-use
XmCreateLabel	function	full-use
XmCascadeButton	widget	full-use
XmCreateCascadeButton	function	full-use
XmCascadeButtonHighlight	function	full-use
XmDrawnButton	widget	full-use
XmCreateDrawnButton	function	full-use
XmPushButton	widget	full-use
XmCreatePushButton	function	full-use
XmToggleButton	widget	full-use
XmCreateToggleButton	function	full-use
XmToggleButtonGetState	function	full-use
XmToggleButtonSetState	function	full-use
XmList	widget	full-use
XmCreateList	function	full-use
XmListAddItem	function	full-use

Service Name	Service Type	AES Level
XmListAddItems*	function	trial-use
XmListAddItemUnselected	function	full-use
XmListDeleteAllItems*	function	trial-use
XmListDeleteItem	function	full-use
XmListDeleteItems*	function	trial-use
XmListDeleteItemsPos*	function	trial-use
XmListDeletePos	function	full-use
XmListDeselectAllItems	function	full-use
XmListDeselectItem	function	full-use
XmListDeselectPos	function	full-use
XmListGetMatchPos*	function	trial-use
XmListGetSelectedPos*	function	trial-use
XmListItemExists	function	full-use
XmListItemPos*	function	trial-use
XmListReplaceItems*	function	trial-use
XmListReplaceItemsPos*	function	trial-use
XmListSelectItem	function	full-use
XmListSelectPos	function	full-use
XmListSetAddMode*	function	trial-use
XmListSetBottomItem	function	full-use
XmListSetBottomPos	function	full-use
XmListSetHorizPos	function	full-use
XmListSetItem	function	full-use
XmListSetPos	function	full-use
XmScrollBar	widget	full-use
XmCreateScrollBar	function	full-use
XmScrollBarGetValues	function	full-use
XmScrollBarSetValues	function	full-use
XmSeparator	widget	full-use
XmCreateSeparator	function	full-use

Service Name	Service Type	AES Level
XmText	widget	full-use
XmCreateText	function	full-use
XmTextClearSelection	function	full-use
XmTextCopy*	function	trial-use
XmTextCut*	function	trial-use
XmTextGetBaseline*	function	trial-use
XmTextGetEditable	function	full-use
XmTextGetInsertionPosition*	function	trial-use
XmTextGetLastPosition*	function	trial-use
XmTextGetMaxLength	function	full-use
XmTextGetSelection	function	full-use
XmTextGetSelectionPosition*	function	trial-use
XmTextGetSource*	function	trial-use
XmTextGetString	function	full-use
XmTextGetTopCharacter*	function	trial-use
XmTextInsert*	function	trial-use
XmTextPaste*	function	trial-use
XmTextPosToXY*	function	trial-use
XmTextRemove*	function	trial-use
XmTextReplace	function	full-use
XmTextScroll*	function	trial-use
XmTextSetAddMode*	function	trial-use
XmTextSetEditable	function	full-use
XmTextSetHighlight*	function	trial-use
XmTextSetInsertionPosition*	function	trial-use
XmTextSetMaxLength	function	full-use
XmTextSetSelection	function	full-use
XmTextSetSource*	function	trial-use
XmTextSetString	function	full-use
XmTextSetTopCharacter*	function	trial-use

Service Name	Service Type	AES Level
XmTextShowPosition*	function	trial-use
XmTextXYToPos*	function	trial-use
Composite	widget	full-use
Shell	widget	full-use
OverrideShell	widget	full-use
XmMenuShell	widget	full-use
XmCreateMenuShell	function	full-use
WMShell	widget	full-use
VendorShell	widget	full-use
XmGetAtomName	function	full-use
XmInternAtom	function	full-use
TopLevelShell	widget	full-use
ApplicationShell	widget	full-use
TransientShell	widget	full-use
XmDialogShell	widget	full-use
XmCreateDialogShell	function	full-use
Constraint	widget	full-use
XmManager	widget	full-use
XmBulletinBoard	widget	full-use
XmCreateBulletinBoard	function	full-use
XmCreateBulletinBoardDialog	function	full-use
XmForm	widget	full-use
XmCreateForm	function	full-use
XmCreateFormDialog	function	full-use
XmMessageBox	widget	full-use
XmCreateMessageBox	function	full-use
XmCreateErrorDialog	function	full-use
XmCreateInformationDialog	function	full-use
XmCreateMessageDialog	function	full-use
XmCreateQuestionDialog	function	full-use

Service Name	Service Type	AES Level
XmCreateWarningDialog	function	full-use
XmCreateWorkingDialog	function	full-use
XmMessageBoxGetChild	function	full-use
XmSelectionBox	widget	full-use
XmCreateSelectionBox	function	full-use
XmCreatePromptDialog	function	full-use
XmCreateSelectionDialog	function	full-use
XmSelectionBoxGetChild	function	full-use
XmCommand	widget	full-use
XmCreateCommand	function	full-use
XmCommandAppendValue	function	full-use
XmCommandError	function	full-use
XmCommandGetChild	function	full-use
XmCommandSetValue	function	full-use
XmFileSelectionBox	widget	full-use
XmCreateFileSelectionBox	function	full-use
XmCreateFileSelectionDialog	function	full-use
XmFileSelectionBoxGetChild	function	full-use
XmFileSelectionDoSearch	function	full-use
XmDrawingArea	widget	full-use
XmCreateDrawingArea	function	full-use
XmFrame	widget	full-use
XmCreateFrame	function	full-use
XmPanedWindow	widget	full-use
XmCreatePanedWindow	function	full-use
XmRowColumn	widget	full-use
XmCreateRowColumn	function	full-use
XmCreateMenuBar	function	full-use
XmCreateOptionMenu	function	full-use
XmCreatePopupMenu	function	full-use

Service Name	Service Type	AES Level
XmCreatePulldownMenu	function	full-use
XmCreateRadioBox	function	full-use
XmCreateWorkArea*	function	trial-use
XmGetMenuCursor	function	full-use
XmGetPostedFromWidget*	function	trial-use
XmMenuPosition	function	full-use
XmOptionButtonWidget	function	full-use
XmOptionLabelWidget	function	full-use
XmSetMenuCursor	function	full-use
XmScale	widget	full-use
XmCreateScale	function	full-use
XmScaleGetValue	function	full-use
XmScaleSetValue	function	full-use
XmScrolledWindow	widget	full-use
XmCreateScrolledWindow	function	full-use
XmCreateScrolledList	function	full-use
XmCreateScrolledText	function	full-use
XmScrolledWindowSetAreas	function	full-use
XmMainWindow	widget	full-use
XmCreateMainWindow	function	full-use
XmMainWindowSep1	function	full-use
XmMainWindowSep2	function	full-use
XmMainWindowSep3*	function	trial-use
XmMainWindowSetAreas	function	full-use
XmGadget	widget	full-use
XmArrowButtonGadget	widget	full-use
XmCreateArrowButtonGadget	function	full-use
XmLabelGadget	widget	full-use
XmCreateLabelGadget	function	full-use
XmCascadeButtonGadget	widget	full-use

Service Name	Service Type	AES Level
XmCascadeButtonGadgetHighlight*	function	trial-use
XmCreateCascadeButtonGadget	function	full-use
XmPushButtonGadget	widget	full-use
XmCreatePushButtonGadget	function	full-use
XmToggleButtonGadget	widget	full-use
XmCreateToggleButtonGadget	function	full-use
XmToggleButtonGadgetGetState	function	full-use
XmToggleButtonGadgetSetState	function	full-use
XmSeparatorGadget	widget	full-use
XmCreateSeparatorGadget	function	full-use

1.3.3 Toolkit Functions

Table 1-4. Toolkit Services

Service Name	Service Type	AES Level
XmActivateProtocol	function	trial-use
XmActivateWMProtocol	function	trial-use
XmAddProtocolCallbacks	function	trial-use
XmAddProtocols	function	trial-use
XmAddTabGroup	function	full-use
XmAddWMProtocolCallbacks	function	trial-use
XmAddWMProtocols	function	trial-use
XmClipboardCancelCopy	function	full-use
XmClipboardCopy	function	full-use
XmClipboardCopyByName	function	full-use
XmClipboardEndCopy	function	full-use

Service Name	Service Type	AES Level
XmClipboardEndRetrieve	function	full-use
XmClipboardInquireCount	function	full-use
XmClipboardInquireFormat	function	full-use
XmClipboardInquireLength	function	full-use
XmClipboardInquirePendingItems	function	full-use
XmClipboardLock	function	full-use
XmClipboardRegisterFormat	function	full-use
XmClipboardRetrieve	function	full-use
XmClipboardStartCopy	function	full-use
XmClipboardStartRetrieve	function	full-use
XmClipboardUndoCopy	function	full-use
XmClipboardUnlock	function	full-use
XmClipboardWithdrawFormat	function	full-use
XmConvertUnits	function	trial-use
XmCvtCTToXmString*	function	trial-use
XmCvtXmStringToCT*	function	trial-use
XmDeactivateProtocol	function	trial-use
XmDeactivateWMProtocol	function	trial-use
XmDestroyPixmap	function	full-use
XmFontList*	data type	trial-use
XmFontListAdd	function	trial-use
XmFontListCreate	function	trial-use
XmFontListFree	function	trial-use
XmGetColors*	function	trial-use
XmGetPixmap	function	full-use
XmInstallImage	function	full-use
XmIsMotifWMRunning	function	full-use
XmProcessTraversal	function	trial-use
XmRemoveProtocolCallbacks	function	trial-use
XmRemoveProtocols	function	trial-use

Service Name	Service Type	AES Level
XmRemoveTabGroup	function	full-use
XmRemoveWMProtocolCallbacks	function	trial-use
XmRemoveWMProtocols	function	trial-use
XmResolvePartOffsets	function	full-use
XmSetProtocolHooks	function	trial-use
XmSetWMProtocolHooks	function	trial-use
XmString*	data type	trial-use
XmStringBaseline	function	trial-use
XmStringByteCompare	function	trial-use
XmStringCompare	function	trial-use
XmStringConcat	function	trial-use
XmStringCopy	function	trial-use
XmStringCreate	function	temporary-use
XmStringCreateSimple*	function	temporary-use
XmStringDirection*	data type	trial-use
XmStringDraw	function	trial-use
XmStringDrawImage	function	trial-use
XmStringDrawUnderline	function	trial-use
XmStringEmpty	function	trial-use
XmStringExtent	function	trial-use
XmStringFree	function	trial-use
XmStringHasSubstring*	function	trial-use
XmStringHeight	function	trial-use
XmStringLength	function	trial-use
XmStringLineCount	function	trial-use
XmStringNConcat	function	trial-use
XmStringNCopy	function	trial-use
XmStringSeparatorCreate	function	trial-use
XmStringTable*	data type	trial-use
XmStringWidth	function	trial-use

Service Name	Service Type	AES Level
XmTextPosition*	data type	trial-use
XmTrackingLocate	function	trial-use
XmUninstallImage	function	full-use
XmUpdateDisplay	function	full-use

1.3.4 User Interface Language

Table 1-5. User Interface Language Services

Service Name	Service Type	AES Level
MrmCloseHierarchy	function	trial-use
MrmFetchColorLiteral	function	trial-use
MrmFetchIconLiteral	function	trial-use
MrmFetchLiteral	function	trial-use
MrmFetchSetValues	function	trial-use
MrmFetchWidget	function	trial-use
MrmFetchWidgetOverride	function	trial-use
MrmInitialize	function	trial-use
MrmOpenHierarchy	function	trial-use
MrmRegisterClass	function	trial-use
MrmRegisterNames	function	trial-use
MrmRegisterNamesInHierarchy*	function	trial-use
Uil	function	trial-use

Chapter 2

Reference Pages

This chapter contains the reference pages for the Application Environment Specification User Environment Volume. Each supported service is described on a separate manual page.

mwm

Purpose

The Motif Window Manager

AES Support Level

Full-use

Synopsis

mwm [*options*]

Description

mwm is an X Window System client that provides window management
functionality and some session management functionality. It provides
functions that facilitate control (by the user and the programmer) of
elements of window states such as placement, size, icon/normal display, and
input-focus ownership. It also provides session management functions such
as stopping a client.

Options

-display *display*
> This option specifies the display to use; see *X(1)*.

-xrm *resourcestring*
> This option specifies a resource string to use.

-multiscreen

This option causes **mwm** to manage all screens on the display. The default is to manage only a single screen.

-name *name*

This option causes **mwm** to retrieve its resources using the specified name, as in *name*resource*.

-screens *name [name [...]]/fP*

This option specifies the resource names to use for the screens managed by **mwm**. If **mwm** is managing a single screen, only the first name in the list is used. If **mwm** is managing multiple screens, the names are assigned to the screens in order, starting with screen 0. Screen 0 gets the first name, screen 1 the second name, and so on.

Appearance

The following sections describe the basic default behaviors of windows, icons, the icon box, input focus, and window stacking. The appearance and behavior of the window manager can be altered by changing the configuration of specific resources. Resources are defined under the heading "X DEFAULTS."

Screens

By default, **mwm** manages only the single screen specified by the **-display** option or the DISPLAY environment variable (by default, screen 0). If the **-multiscreen** option is specified or if the **multiScreen** resource is True, **mwm** tries to manage all the screens on the display.

When **mwm** is managing multiple screens, the **-screens** option can be used to give each screen a unique resource name. The names are separated by blanks, for example, **-screens** mwm0 mwm1. If there are more screens than names, resources for the remaining screens will be retrieved using the first name.

Windows

Default **mwm** window frames have distinct components with associated functions:

Title Area
In addition to displaying the client's title, the title area is used to move the window. To move the window, place the pointer over the title area, press button 1 and drag the window to a new location. A wire frame is moved during the drag to indicate the new location. When the button is released, the window is moved to the new location.

Title Bar
The title bar includes the title area, the minimize button, the maximize button, and the window menu button.

Minimize Button
To turn the window into an icon, click button 1 on the minimize button (the frame box with a *small* square in it).

Maximize Button
To make the window fill the screen (or enlarge to the largest size allowed by the configuration files), click button 1 on the maximize button (the frame box with a *large* square in it).

Window Menu Button
The window menu button is the frame box with a horizontal bar in it. To pull down the window menu, press button 1. While pressing, drag the pointer on the menu to your selection, then release the button when your selection is highlighted. Alternately, you can click button 1 to pull down the menu and keep it posted; then position the pointer and select.

Default Window Menu		
Selection	**Accelerator**	**Description**
Restore	Alt+F5	Restores the window to its size before minimizing or maximizing
Move	Alt+F7	Allows the window to be moved with keys or mouse
Size	Alt+F8	Allows the window to be resized
Minimize	Alt+F9	Turns the window into an icon
Maximize	Alt+F10	Makes the window fill the screen
Lower	Alt+F3	Moves window to bottom of window stack
Close	Alt+F4	Causes client to terminate

Resize Border Handles

To change the size of a window, move the pointer over a resize border handle (the cursor changes), press button 1, and drag the window to a new size. When the button is released, the window is resized. While dragging is being done, a rubber-band outline is displayed to indicate the new window size.

Matte

An optional matte decoration can be added between the client area and the window frame. A matte is not actually part of the window frame. There is no functionality associated with a matte.

Icons

Icons are small graphic representations of windows. A window can be minimized (iconified) using the minimize button on the window frame. Icons provide a way to reduce clutter on the screen.

Pressing mouse button 1 when the pointer is over an icon causes the icon's window menu to pop up. Releasing the button (press + release without moving mouse = click) causes the menu to stay posted. The menu contains the following selections:

Icon Window Menu		
Selection	**Accelerator**	**Description**
Restore	Alt+F5	Opens the associated window
Move	Alt+F7	Allows the icon to be moved with keys
Size	Alt+F8	Inactive (not an option for icons)
Minimize	Alt+F9	Inactive (not an option for icons)
Maximize	Alt+F10	Opens the associated window and makes it fill the screen
Lower	Alt+F3	Moves icon to bottom of icon stack
Close	Alt+F4	Removes client from **mwm** management

Note that pressing button 3 over an icon also causes the icon's window menu to pop up. To make a menu selection, drag the pointer over the menu and release button 3 when the desired item is highlighted.

Double-clicking button 1 on an icon normalizes the icon into its associated window. Double-clicking button 1 on the icon box's icon opens the icon box and allows access to the contained icons. (In general, double-clicking a mouse button is a quick way to perform a function.) Double-clicking button 1 with the pointer on the window menu button closes the window.

Icon Box

When icons begin to clutter the screen, they can be packed into an icon box. (To use an icon box, **mwm** must be started with the icon box configuration already set.) The icon box is a **mwm** window that holds client icons. It includes one or more scroll bars when there are more window icons than the icon box can show at the same time.

Icons in the icon box can be manipulated with the mouse. The following table summarizes the behavior of this interface. Button actions apply whenever the pointer is on any part of the icon. Note that invoking the **f.raise** function on an icon in the icon box raises an already open window to the top of the stack.

Button Action	Description
Button 1 click	Selects the icon
Button 1 double-click	Normalizes (opens) the associated window
Button 1 double-click	Raises an already open window to the top of the stack
Button 1 drag	Moves the icon
Button 3 press	Causes the menu for that icon to pop up
Button 3 drag	Highlights items as the pointer moves across the menu

Pressing mouse button 3 when the pointer is over an icon causes the menu for that icon to pop up.

Icon Menu for the Icon Box		
Selection	Accelerator	Description
Restore	Alt+F5	Opens the associated window (if not already open)
Move	Alt+F7	Allows the icon to be moved with keys
Size	Alt+F8	Inactive
Minimize	Alt+F9	Inactive
Maximize	Alt+F10	Opens the associated window (if not already open) and maximizes its size
Lower	Alt+F3	Inactive
Close	Alt+F4	Removes client from **mwm** management

To pull down the window menu for the icon box itself, press button 1 with the pointer over the menu button for the icon box. The window menu of the icon box differs from the window menu of a client window: The "Close" selection is replaced with the "PackIcons Shift+Alt+F7" selection. When selected, PackIcons packs the icons in the box to achieve neat rows with no empty slots.

Pressing [Shift][Escape] when the icon box has the input focus causes the window menu of the icon box to pop up. Pressing F4 (the pop-up menu key) causes the window menu of the currently selected icon to pop up.

Input Focus

mwm supports (by default) a keyboard input focus policy of explicit selection. This means when a window is selected to get keyboard input, it continues to get keyboard input until the window is withdrawn from window management, another window is explicitly selected to get keyboard input, or the window is iconified. Several resources control the input focus. The client window with the keyboard input focus has the active window appearance with a visually distinct window frame.

The following tables summarize the keyboard input focus selection behavior:

Button Action	Object	Function Description
Button 1 press	Window / window frame	Keyboard focus selection
Button 1 press	Icon	Keyboard focus selection

Key Action	Function Description
[Alt][Tab]	Move input focus to next window in window stack
[Alt][Shift][Tab]	Move input focus to previous window in window stack

X Defaults

mwm is configured from its resource database. This database is built from the following sources. They are listed in order of precedence, low to high:

/usr/lib/X11/app-defaults/Mwm
$HOME/Mwm
RESOURCE_MANAGER root window property or $HOME/.Xdefaults
XENVIRONMENT variable or $HOME/.Xdefaults-*host*
mwm command line options

The file names /usr/lib/X11/app-defaults/Mwm and $HOME/Mwm represent customary locations for these files. The actual location of the system-wide class resource file may depend on the XFILESEARCHPATH environment variable and the current language environment. The actual location of the user-specific class resource file may depend on the XUSERFILESEARCHPATH and XAPPLRESDIR environment variables and the current language environment.

Entries in the resource database may refer to other resource files for specific types of resources. These include files that contain bitmaps, fonts, and **mwm** specific resources such as menus and behavior specifications (for example, button and key bindings).

Mwm is the resource class name of **mwm** and **mwm** is the resource name used by **mwm** to look up resources. (For looking up resources of multiple screens, the **-screens** command line option specifies resource names, such as "mwm_b+w" and "mwm_color".) In the following discussion of resource specification, "Mwm" and "mwm" (and the aliased **mwm** resource names) can be used interchangeably, but "mwm" takes precedence over "Mwm".

mwm uses the following types of resources:

Component Appearance Resources:

These resources specify appearance attributes of window manager user interface components. They can be applied to the appearance of window manager menus, feedback windows (for example, the window reconfiguration feedback window), client window frames, and icons.

Specific Appearance and Behavior Resources:

These resources specify **mwm** appearance and behavior (for example, window management policies). They are not set separately for different **mwm** user interface components.

Client Specific Resources:

These **mwm** resources can be set for a particular client window or class of client windows. They specify client-specific icon and client window frame appearance and behavior.

Resource identifiers can be either a resource name (for example, foreground) or a resource class (for example, Foreground). If the value of a resource is a filename and if the filename is prefixed by "~/", then it is relative to the path contained in the HOME environment variable (generally the user's home directory).

Component Appearance Resources

The syntax for specifying component appearance resources that apply to window manager icons, menus, and client window frames is

> **Mwm****resource_id*

For example, **Mwm*foreground** is used to specify the foreground color for **mwm** menus, icons, client window frames, and feedback dialogs.

The syntax for specifying component appearance resources that apply to a particular **mwm** component is

> **Mwm*[menu|icon|client|feedback]****resource_id*

If *menu* is specified, the resource is applied only to **mwm** If *menu* is specified, the resource is applied only to MWM menus; if *icon* is specified, the resource is applied to icons; and if *client* is specified, the resource is applied to client window frames. For example, **Mwm*icon*foreground** is used to specify the foreground color for **mwm** icons, **Mwm*menu*foreground** specifies the foreground color for **mwm** menus, and **Mwm*client*foreground** is used to specify the foreground color for **mwm** client window frames.

The appearance of the title area of a client window frame (including window management buttons) can be separately configured. The syntax for configuring the title area of a client window frame is

> **Mwm*client*title****resource_id*

For example, **Mwm*client*title*foreground** specifies the foreground color for the title area. Defaults for title area resources are based on the values of the corresponding client window frame resources.

The appearance of menus can be configured based on the name of the menu. The syntax for specifying menu appearance by name is

Mwm*menu*_menu_name_*****_resource_id_

For example, **Mwm*menu*my_menu*foreground** specifies the foreground color for the menu named **my_menu**.

The following component appearance resources that apply to all window manager parts can be specified:

Component Appearance Resources — All Window Manager Parts			
Name	**Class**	**Value Type**	**Default**
background	Background	color	varies†
backgroundPixmap	BackgroundPixmap	string††	varies†
bottomShadowColor	Foreground	color	varies†
bottomShadowPixmap	BottomShadowPixmap	string††	varies†
fontList	FontList	string†††	"fixed"
foreground	Foreground	color	varies†
saveUnder	SaveUnder	T/F	F
topShadowColor	Background	color	varies†
topShadowPixmap	TopShadowPixmap	string††	varies

†The default is chosen based on the visual type of the screen.
††Image name. See XmInstallImage(3X).
†††X11 R4 Font description.

background (class **Background**)
This resource specifies the background color. Any legal X color may be specified. The default value is chosen based on the visual type of the screen.

backgroundPixmap (class **BackgroundPixmap**)

This resource specifies the background Pixmap of the **mwm** decoration when the window is inactive (does not have the keyboard focus). The default value is chosen based on the visual type of the screen.

bottomShadowColor (class **Foreground**)

This resource specifies the bottom shadow color. This color is used for the lower and right bevels of the window manager decoration. Any legal X color may be specified. The default value is chosen based on the visual type of the screen.

bottomShadowPixmap (class **BottomShadowPixmap**)

This resource specifies the bottom shadow Pixmap. This Pixmap is used for the lower and right bevels of the window manager decoration. The default is chosen based on the visual type of the screen.

fontList (class **FontList**)

This resource specifies the font used in the window manager decoration. The character encoding of the font should match the character encoding of the strings that are used. The default is "fixed."

foreground (class **Foreground**)

This resource specifies the foreground color. The default is chosen based on the visual type of the screen.

saveUnder (class **SaveUnder**)

This is used to indicate whether "save unders" are used for **mwm** components. For this to have any effect, save unders must be implemented by the X server. If save unders are implemented, the X server saves the contents of windows obscured by windows that have the save under attribute set. If the saveUnder resource is True, **mwm** will set the save under attribute on the window manager frame of any client that has it set. If saveUnder is False, save unders will not be used on any window manager frames. The default value is False.

topShadowColor (class **Background**)

> This resource specifies the top shadow color. This color is used for the upper and left bevels of the window manager decoration. The default is chosen based on the visual type of the screen.

topShadowPixmap (class **TopShadowPixmap**)

> This resource specifies the top shadow Pixmap. This Pixmap is used for the upper and left bevels of the window manager decoration. The default is chosen based on the visual type of the screen.

The following component appearance resources that apply to frame and icons can be specified:

Frame and Icon Components			
Name	**Class**	**Value Type**	**Default**
activeBackground	Background	color	varies†
activeBackgroundPixmap	BackgroundPixmap	string ††	varies†
activeBottomShadowColor	Foreground	color	varies†
activeBottomShadowPixmap	BottomShadowPixmap	string††	variesfR†
activeForeground	Foreground	color	varies†g
activeTopShadowColor	Background	color	varies†
activeTopShadowPixmap	TopShadowPixmap	string††/fP	varies†

†The default is chosen based on the visual type of the screen.
††See XmInstallImage(3X).

activeBackground (class **Background**)

> This resource specifies the background color of the **mwm** decoration when the window is active (has the keyboard focus). The default is chosen based on the visual type of the screen.

activeBackgroundPixmap (class **ActiveBackgroundPixmap**)

> This resource specifies the background Pixmap of the **mwm** decoration when the window is active (has the keyboard focus). The default is chosen based on the visual type of the screen.

activeBottomShadowColor (class **Foreground**)
> This resource specifies the bottom shadow color of the **mwm** decoration when the window is active (has the keyboard focus). The default is chosen based on the visual type of the screen.

activeBottomShadowPixmap (class **BottomShadowPixmap**)
> This resource specifies the bottom shadow Pixmap of the **mwm** decoration when the window is active (has the keyboard focus). The default is chosen based on the visual type of the screen.

activeForeground (class **Foreground**)
> This resource specifies the foreground color of the **mwm** decoration when the window is active (has the keyboard focus). The default is chosen based on the visual type of the screen.

activeTopShadowColor (class **Background**)
> This resource specifies the top shadow color of the **mwm** decoration when the window is active (has the keyboard focus). The default is chosen based on the visual type of the screen.

activeTopShadowPixmap (class **TopShadowPixmap**)
> This resource specifies the top shadow Pixmap of the **mwm** decoration when the window is active (has the keyboard focus). The default is chosen based on the visual type of the screen.

Specific Appearance and Behavior Resources

The syntax for specifying specific appearance and behavior resources is

> **Mwm***resource_id

For example, **Mwm*keyboardFocusPolicy** specifies the window manager policy for setting the keyboard focus to a particular client window.

The following specific appearance and behavior resources can be specified:

Specific Appearance and Behavior Resources			
Name	**Class**	**Value Type**	**Default**
autoKeyFocus	AutoKeyFocus	T/F	T
autoRaiseDelay	AutoRaiseDelay	millisec	500
bitmapDirectory	BitmapDirectory	directory	/usr/include/\ X11/bitmaps
buttonBindings	ButtonBindings	string	"DefaultBut\ tonBindings"
cleanText	CleanText	T/F	T
clientAutoPlace	ClientAutoPlace	T/F	T
colormapFocusPolicy	ColormapFocusPolicy	string	keyboard
configFile	ConfigFile	file	.mwmrc
deiconifyKeyFocus	DeiconifyKeyFocus	T/F	T
doubleClickTime	DoubleClickTime	millisec.	multi-click time
enableWarp	enableWarp	T/F	T
enforceKeyFocus	EnforceKeyFocus	T/F	T
fadeNormalIcon	FadeNormalIcon	T/F	F
frameBorderWidth	FrameBorderWidth	pixels	5
iconAutoPlace	IconAutoPlace	T/F	T
iconBoxGeometry	IconBoxGeometry	string	6x1+0-0
iconBoxName	IconBoxName	string	iconbox
iconBoxSBDisplayPolicy	IconBoxSBDisplayPolicy	string	all
iconBoxTitle	IconBoxTitle	XmString	Icons
iconClick	IconClick	T/F	T
iconDecoration	IconDecoration	string	varies
iconImageMaximum	IconImageMaximum	wxh	50x50
iconImageMinimum	IconImageMinimum	wxh	16x16

Specific Appearance and Behavior Resources (Continued)			
Name	**Class**	**Value Type**	**Default**
iconPlacement	IconPlacement	string	left bottom
iconPlacementMargin	IconPlacementMargin	pixels	varies
interactivePlacement	InteractivePlacement	T/F	F
keyBindings	KeyBindings	string	"DefaultKey\ Bindings"
keyboardFocusPolicy	KeyboardFocusPolicy	string	explicit
limitResize	LimitResize	T/F	T
lowerOnIconify	LowerOnIconify	T/F	T
maximumMaximumSize	MaximumMaximumSize	wxh (pixels)	2X screen w&h
moveThreshold	MoveThreshold	pixels	4
multiScreen	MultiScreen	T/F	F
passButtons	PassButtons	T/F	F
passSelectButton	PassSelectButton	T/F	T
positionIsFrame	PositionIsFrame	T/F	T
positionOnScreen	PositionOnScreen	T/F	T
quitTimeout	QuitTimeout	millisec.	1000
raiseKeyFocus	RaiseKeyFocus	T/F	F
resizeBorderWidth	ResizeBorderWidth	pixels	10
resizeCursors	ResizeCursors	T/F	T
screens	Screens	string	varies
showFeedback	ShowFeedback	string	-kill
startupKeyFocus	StartupKeyFocus	T/F	T
transientDecoration	TransientDecoration	string	system title

Specific Appearance and Behavior Resources (Continued)			
Name	**Class**	**Value Type**	**Default**
transientFunctions	TransientFunctions	string	-minimize -maximize
useIconBox	UseIconBox	T/F	F
wMenuButtonClick	WMenuButtonClick	T/F	T
wMenuButtonClick2	WMenuButtonClick2	T/F	T

autoKeyFocus (class **AutoKeyFocus**)

This resource is available only when the keyboard input focus policy is explicit. If autoKeyFocus is given a value of True, then when a window with the keyboard input focus is withdrawn from window management or is iconified, the focus is set to the previous window that had the focus. If the value given is False, there is no automatic setting of the keyboard input focus. The default value is True.

autoRaiseDelay (class **AutoRaiseDelay**)

This resource is available only when the focusAutoRaise resource is True and the keyboard focus policy is pointer. The autoRaiseDelay resource specifies the amount of time (in milliseconds) that **mwm** will wait before raising a window after it gets the keyboard focus. The default value of this resource is 500 (ms).

bitmapDirectory (class **BitmapDirectory**)

This resource identifies a directory to be searched for bitmaps referenced by **mwm** resources. This directory is searched if a bitmap is specified without an absolute pathname. The default value for this resource is /usr/include/X11/bitmaps.

buttonBindings (class **ButtonBindings**)

This resource identifies the set of button bindings for window management functions. The named set of button bindings is specified in the **mwm** resource description file. These button bindings are *merged* with the built-in default bindings. The default value for this resource is "DefaultButtonBindings".

cleanText (class **CleanText**)

This resource controls the display of window manager text in the client title and feedback windows. If the default value of True is used, the text is drawn with a clear (no stipple) background. This makes text easier to read on monochrome systems where a backgroundPixmap is specified. Only the stippling in the area immediately around the text is cleared. If False, the text is drawn directly on top of the existing background.

clientAutoPlace (class **ClientAutoPlace**)

This resource determines the position of a window when the window has not been given a user-specified position. With a value of True, windows are positioned with the top left corners of the frames offset horizontally and vertically. A value of False causes the currently configured position of the window to be used. In either case, **mwm** will attempt to place the windows totally on-screen. The default value is True.

colormapFocusPolicy (class **ColormapFocusPolicy**)

This resource indicates the colormap focus policy that is to be used. If the resource value is explicit, a colormap selection action is done on a client window to set the colormap focus to that window. If the value is pointer, the client window containing the pointer has the colormap focus. If the value is keyboard, the client window that has the keyboard input focus has the colormap focus. The default value for this resource is keyboard.

configFile (class **ConfigFile**)

The resource value is the pathname for an **mwm** resource description file.

If the pathname begins with "~/", **mwm** considers it to be relative to the user's home directory (as specified by the HOME environment variable). If the LANG environment variable is set, **mwm** looks for $HOME/$LANG/*configFile*. If that file does not exist or if LANG is not set, **mwm** looks for $HOME/*configFile*.

If the **configFile** pathname does not begin with "~/", **mwm** considers it to be relative to the current working directory.

If the **configFile** resource is not specified or if that file does not exist, **mwm** uses several default paths to find a configuration file.

If the LANG environment variable is set, **mwm** looks for the configuration file first in $HOME/$LANG/.mwmrc. If that file does not exist or if LANG is not set, **mwm** looks for $HOME/.mwmrc. If that file does not exist and if LANG is set, **mwm** next looks for /usr/lib/X11/$LANG/system.mwmrc. If that file does not exist or if LANG is not set, **mwm** looks for /usr/lib/X11/system.mwmrc.

deiconifyKeyFocus (class **DeiconifyKeyFocus**)

This resource applies only when the keyboard input focus policy is explicit. If a value of True is used, a window receives the keyboard input focus when it is normalized (deiconified). True is the default value.

doubleClickTime (class **DoubleClickTime**)

This resource is used to set the maximum time (in ms) between the clicks (button presses) that make up a double-click. The default value of this resource is the display's multi-click time.

enableWarp (class **EnableWarp**)

The default value of this resource, True, causes **mwm** to "warp" the pointer to the center of the selected window during keyboard-controlled resize and move operations. Setting the value to False causes **mwm** to leave the pointer at its original place on the screen, unless the user explicitly moves it with the cursor keys or pointing device.

enforceKeyFocus (class **EnforceKeyFocus**)

If this resource is given a value of True, the keyboard input focus is always explicitly set to selected windows even if there is an indication that they are "globally active" input windows. (An example of a globally active window is a scroll bar that can be operated without setting the focus to that client.) If the resource is False, the keyboard input focus is not explicitly set to globally active windows. The default value is True.

fadeNormalIcon (class **FadeNormalIcon**)

If this resource is given a value of True, an icon is grayed out whenever it has been normalized (its window has been opened). The default value is False.

frameBorderWidth (class **FrameBorderWidth**)

This resource specifies the width (in pixels) of a client window frame border without resize handles. The border width includes the 3-D shadows. The default value is 5 pixels.

iconAutoPlace (class **IconAutoPlace**)

This resource indicates whether the window manager arranges icons in a particular area of the screen or places each icon where the window was when it was iconified. The value True indicates that icons are arranged in a particular area of the screen, determined by the iconPlacement resource. The value False indicates that an icon is placed at the location of the window when it is iconified. The default is True.

iconBoxGeometry (class **IconBoxGeometry**)

This resource indicates the initial position and size of the icon box. The value of the resource is a standard window geometry string with the following syntax:

$$[=][\textit{width}\mathbf{x}\textit{height}][\{+\text{-}\}\textit{xoffset}\{+\text{-}\}\textit{yoffset}]$$

If the offsets are not provided, the iconPlacement policy is used to determine the initial placement. The units for width and height are columns and rows.

The actual screen size of the icon box window depends on the iconImageMaximum (size) and iconDecoration resources. The default value for size is (6 * iconWidth + padding) wide by (1 * iconHeight + padding) high. The default value of the location is +0 -0.

iconBoxName (class **IconBoxName**)

This resource specifies the name that is used to look up icon box resources. The default name is "iconbox".

iconBoxSBDisplayPolicy (class **IconBoxSBDisplayPolicy**)

This resource specifies the scroll bar display policy of the window manager in the icon box. The resource has three possible values: all, vertical, and horizontal. The default value, "all", causes both vertical and horizontal scroll bars always to appear. The value "vertical" causes a single vertical scroll bar to appear in the icon box and sets the orientation of the icon box to horizontal (regardless of the iconBoxGeometry specification). The value "horizontal" causes a single horizontal scroll bar to appear in the icon box and sets the orientation of the icon box to vertical (regardless of the iconBoxGeometry specification).

iconBoxTitle (class **IconBoxTitle**)

This resource specifies the name that is used in the title area of the icon box frame. The default value is "Icons".

iconClick (class **IconClick**)

When this resource is given the value of True, the system menu is posted and left posted when an icon is clicked. The default value is True.

iconDecoration (class **IconDecoration**)

This resource specifies the general icon decoration. The resource value is label (only the label part is displayed) or image (only the image part is displayed) or label image (both the label and image parts are displayed). A value of activelabel can also be specified to get a label (not truncated to the width of the icon) when the icon is selected. The default icon decoration for icon box icons is that each icon has a label part and an image part (label image). The default icon decoration for stand alone icons is that each icon has an active label part, a label part, and an image part (activelabel label image).

iconImageMaximum (class **IconImageMaximum**)

This resource specifies the maximum size of the icon *image*. The resource value is *width***x***height* (for example, 64x64). The maximum supported size is 128x128. The default value of this resource is 50x50.

iconImageMinimum (class **IconImageMinimum**)

This resource specifies the minimum size of the icon *image*. The resource value is *width***x***height* (for example, 32x50). The minimum supported size is 16x16. The default value of this resource is 16x16.

iconPlacement (class **IconPlacement**)

This resource specifies the icon placement scheme to be used. The resource value has the following syntax:

primary_layout secondary_layout

The layout values are one of the following:

Value	Description
top	Lay the icons out top to bottom.
bottom	Lay the icons out bottom to top.
left	Lay the icons out left to right.
right	Lay the icons out right to left.

A horizontal (vertical) layout value should not be used for both the *primary_layout* and the *secondary_layout* (for example, don't use top for the *primary_layout* and bottom for the *secondary_layout*). The *primary_layout* indicates whether, when an icon placement is done, the icon is placed in a row or a column and the direction of placement. The *secondary_layout* indicates where to place new rows or columns. For example, top right indicates that icons should be placed top to bottom on the screen and that columns should be added from right to left on the screen. The default placement is left bottom (icons are placed left to right on the screen, with the first row on the bottom of the screen, and new rows added from the bottom of the screen to the top of the screen).

iconPlacementMargin (class **IconPlacementMargin**)
This resource sets the distance between the edge of the screen and the icons that are placed along the edge of the screen. The value should be greater than or equal to 0. A default value (see below) is used if the value specified is invalid. The default value for this resource is equal to the space between icons as they are placed on the screen (this space is based on maximizing the number of icons in each row and column).

interactivePlacement (class **InteractivePlacement**)
This resource controls the initial placement of new windows on the screen. If the value is True, the pointer shape changes before a new window is placed on the screen to indicate to the user that a position should be selected for the upper-left hand corner of the window. If the value is False, windows are placed according to the initial window configuration attributes. The default value of this resource is False.

keyBindings (class **KeyBindings**)

> This resource identifies the set of key bindings for window management functions. If specified, these key bindings *replace* the built-in default bindings. The named set of key bindings is specified in **mwm** resource description file. The default value for this resource is "DefaultKeyBindings".

keyboardFocusPolicy (class **KeyboardFocusPolicy**)

> If set to pointer, the keyboard focus policy is to have the keyboard focus set to the client window that contains the pointer (the pointer could also be in the client window decoration that **mwm** adds). If set to explicit, the policy is to have the keyboard focus set to a client window when the user presses button 1 with the pointer on the client window or any part of the associated **mwm** decoration. The default value for this resource is explicit.

limitResize (class **LimitResize**)

> If this resource is True, the user is not allowed to resize a window to greater than the maximum size. The default value for this resource is True.

lowerOnIconify (class **LowerOnIconify**)

> If this resource is given the default value of True, a window's icon appears on the bottom of the window stack when the window is minimized (iconified). A value of False places the icon in the stacking order at the same place as its associated window. The default value of this resource is True.

maximumMaximumSize (class **MaximumMaximumSize**)

> This resource is used to limit the maximum size of a client window as set by the user or client. The resource value is *width***x***height* (for example, 1024x1024) where the width and height are in pixels. The default value of this resource is twice the screen width and height.

moveThreshold (class **MoveThreshold**)

> This resource is used to control the sensitivity of dragging operations that move windows and icons. The value of this resource is the number of pixels that the locator is moved with a button down before the move operation is initiated. This is used to

prevent window/icon movement when you click or double-click and there is unintentional pointer movement with the button down. The default value of this resource is 4 (pixels).

multiScreen (class **MultiScreen**)

This resource, if True, causes **mwm** to manage all the screens on the display. If False, **mwm** manages only a single screen. The default value is False.

passButtons (class **PassButtons**)

This resource indicates whether or not button press events are passed to clients after they are used to do a window manager function in the client context. If the resource value is False, the button press is not passed to the client. If the value is True, the button press is passed to the client window. The window manager function is done in either case. The default value for this resource is False.

passSelectButton (class **PassSelectButton**)

This resource indicates whether or not to pass the select button press events to clients after they are used to do a window manager function in the client context. If the resource value is False, then the button press will not be passed to the client. If the value is True, the button press is passed to the client window. The window manager function is done in either case. The default value for this resource is True.

positionIsFrame (class **PositionIsFrame**)

This resource indicates how client window position information (from the WM_NORMAL_HINTS property and from configuration requests) is to be interpreted. If the resource value is True, the information is interpreted as the position of the MWM client window frame. If the value is False, it is interpreted as being the position of the client area of the window. The default value of this resource is True.

positionOnScreen (class **PositionOnScreen**)

This resource is used to indicate that windows should initially be placed (if possible) so that they are not clipped by the edge of the screen (if the resource value is True). If a window is larger than the size of the screen, at least the upper-left corner of the window is on-screen. If the resource value is False, windows are placed in the requested position even if totally off-screen. The default value of this resource is True.

quitTimeout (class **QuitTimeout**)

This resource specifies the amount of time (in milliseconds) that **mwm** will wait for a client to update the WM_COMMAND property after **mwm** has sent the WM_SAVE_YOURSELF message. This protocol is used only for those clients that have a WM_SAVE_YOURSELF atom and no WM_DELETE_WINDOW atom in the WM_PROTOCOLS client window property. The default value of this resource is 1000 (ms). (Refer to the f.kill function for additional information.)

raiseKeyFocus (class **RaiseKeyFocus**)

This resource is available only when the keyboard input focus policy is explicit. When set to True, this resource specifies that a window raised by means of the f.normalize_and_raise function also receives the input focus. The default value of this resource is False.

resizeBorderWidth (class **ResizeBorderWidth**)

This resource specifies the width (in pixels) of a client window frame border with resize handles. The specified border width includes the 3-D shadows. The default is 10 (pixels).

resizeCursors (class **ResizeCursors**)

This is used to indicate whether the resize cursors are always displayed when the pointer is in the window size border. If True, the cursors are shown, otherwise the window manager cursor is shown. The default value is True.

screens (class **Screens**)

This resource specifies the resource names to use for the screens mananged by **mwm**. If **mwm** is managing a single screen, only the first name in the list is used. If **mwm** is managing multiple screens, the names are assigned to the screens in order, starting with screen 0. Screen 0 gets the first name, screen 1 the second name, and so on. The default screen names are 0, 1, and so on.

showFeedback (class **ShowFeedback**)

This resource controls when feedback information is displayed. It controls both window position and size feedback during move or resize operations and initial client placement. It also controls window manager message and dialog boxes.

The value for this resource is a list of names of the feedback options to be enabled or disabled; the names must be separated by a space. If an option is preceded by a minus sign, that option is excluded from the list. The *sign* of the first item in the list determines the initial set of options. If the sign of the first option is minus, **mwm** assumes all options are present and starts subtracting from that set. If the sign of the first decoration is plus (or not specified), **mwm** starts with no options and builds up a list from the resource.

The names of the feedback options are shown below:

Name	Description
all	Show all feedback (Default value)
behavior	Confirm behavior switch
kill	Confirm on receipt of KILL signal
move	Show position during move
none	Show no feedback
placement	Show position and size during initial placement
quit	Confirm quitting **mwm**
resize	Show size during resize
restart	Confirm **mwm** restart

The following command line illustrates the syntax for showFeedback:

Mwm*showFeedback: placement resize behavior restart

This resource specification provides feedback for initial client placement and resize, and enables the dialog boxes to confirm the restart and set behavior functions. It disables feedback for the move function. The default value for this resource is all.

startupKeyFocus (class **StartupKeyFocus**)

This resource is available only when the keyboard input focus policy is explicit. When given the default value of True, a window gets the keyboard input focus when the window is mapped (that is, initially managed by the window manager).

transientDecoration (class **TransientDecoration**)

This controls the amount of decoration that **mwm** puts on transient windows. The decoration specification is exactly the same as for the **clientDecoration** (client specific) resource. Transient windows are identified by the WM_TRANSIENT_FOR property, which is added by the client to indicate a relatively temporary window. The default value for this resource is menu title (that is, transient windows have resize borders and a titlebar with a window menu button).

transientFunctions (class **TransientFunctions**)

This resource is used to indicate which window management functions are applicable (or not applicable) to transient windows. The function specification is exactly the same as for the **clientFunctions** (client specific) resource. The default value for this resource is -minimize -maximize.

useIconBox (class **UseIconBox**)

If this resource is given a value of True, icons are placed in an icon box. When an icon box is not used, the icons are placed on the root window (default value).

wMenuButtonClick (class **WMenuButtonClick**)

This resource indicates whether a click of the mouse when the pointer is over the window menu button posts and leaves posted the window menu. If the value given this resource is True, the menu remains posted. True is the default value for this resource.

wMenuButtonClick2 (class **WMenuButtonClick2**)

When this resource is given the default value of True, a double-click action on the window menu button does an f.kill function.

Client Specific Resources

The syntax for specifying client specific resources is

Mwm**client_name_or_class*resource_id*

For example, **Mwm*mterm*windowMenu** is used to specify the window menu to be used with mterm clients.

The syntax for specifying client specific resources for all classes of clients is

Mwm*resource_id

Specific client specifications take precedence over the specifications for all clients. For example, **Mwm*windowMenu** is used to specify the window menu to be used for all classes of clients that don't have a window menu specified.

The syntax for specifying resource values for windows that have an unknown name and class (that is, windows that do not have a WM_CLASS property associated with them) is

Mwm*defaults*resource_id

For example, **Mwm*defaults*iconImage** is used to specify the icon image to be used for windows that have an unknown name and class.

The following client specific resources can be specified:

Client Specific Resources			
Name	**Class**	**Value Type**	**Default**
clientDecoration	ClientDecoration	string	all
clientFunctions	ClientFunctions	string	all
focusAutoRaise	FocusAutoRaise	T/F	varies
iconImage	IconImage	pathname	(image)
iconImageBackground	Background	color	icon background
iconImageBottomShadowColor	Foreground	color	icon bottom shadow
iconImageBottomShadowPixmap	BottomShadow-Pixmap	color	icon bottom shadow pixmap
iconImageForeground	Foreground	color	varies
iconImageTopShadowColor	Background	color	icon top shadow color
iconImageTopShadowPixmap	TopShadow-Pixmap	color	icon top shadow pixmap
matteBackground	Background	color	background
matteBottomShadowColor	Foreground	color	bottom shadow color
matteBottomShadowPixmap	BottomShadow-Pixmap	color	bottom shadow pixmap
matteForeground	Foreground	color	foreground

Client Specific Resources (Continued)			
Name	**Class**	**Value Type**	**Default**
matteTopShadowColor	Background	color	top shadow color
matteTopShadowPixmap	TopShadow-Pixmap	color	top shadow pixmap
matteWidth	MatteWidth	pixels	0
maximumClientSize	MaximumClientSize	wxh	fill the screen
useClientIcon	UseClientIcon	T/F	F
windowMenu	WindowMenu	string	"Default-Window-Menu"

clientDecoration (class **ClientDecoration**)

This resource controls the amount of window frame decoration. The resource is specified as a list of decorations to specify their inclusion in the frame. If a decoration is preceded by a minus sign, that decoration is excluded from the frame. The *sign* of the first item in the list determines the initial amount of decoration. If the sign of the first decoration is minus, **mwm** assumes all decorations are present and starts subtracting from that set. If the sign of the first decoration is plus (or not specified), then **mwm** starts with no decoration and builds up a list from the resource.

Name	Description
all	Include all decorations (default value)
border	Window border
maximize	Maximize button (includes title bar)
minimize	Minimize button (includes title bar)
none	No decorations
resizeh	Border resize handles (includes border)
menu	Window menu button (includes title bar)
title	Title bar (includes border)

clientFunctions (class **ClientFunctions**)

> This resource is used to indicate which **mwm** functions are applicable (or not applicable) to the client window. The value for the resource is a list of functions. If the first function in the list has a minus sign in front of it, then **mwm** starts with all functions and subtracts from that set. If the first function in the list has a plus sign in front of it, then **mwm** starts with no functions and builds up a list. Each function in the list must be preceded by the appropriate plus or minus sign and separated from the next function by a space.

The table below lists the functions available for this resource:

Name	Description
all	Include all functions (default value)
none	No functions
resize	f.resize
move	f.move
minimize	f.minimize
maximize	f.maximize
close	f.kill

focusAutoRaise (class **FocusAutoRaise**)

When the value of this resource is True, clients are raised when they get the keyboard input focus. If the value is False, the stacking of windows on the display is not changed when a window gets the keyboard input focus. The default value is True when the keyboardFocusPolicy is explicit and False when the keyboardFocusPolicy is pointer.

iconImage (class **IconImage**)

This resource can be used to specify an icon image for a client (for example, "Mwm*myclock*iconImage"). The resource value is a pathname for a bitmap file. The value of the (client specific) useClientIcon resource is used to determine whether or not user supplied icon images are used instead of client supplied icon images. The default value is to display a built-in window manager icon image.

iconImageBackground (class **Background**)

This resource specifies the background color of the icon image that is displayed in the image part of an icon. The default value of this resource is the icon background color (that is, specified by "Mwm*background or Mwm*icon*background).

iconImageBottomShadowColor (class **Foreground**)

This resource specifies the bottom shadow color of the icon image that is displayed in the image part of an icon. The default value of this resource is the icon bottom shadow color (that is, specified by Mwm*icon*bottomShadowColor).

iconImageBottomShadowPixmap (class **BottomShadowPixmap**)

This resource specifies the bottom shadow Pixmap of the icon image that is displayed in the image part of an icon. The default value of this resource is the icon bottom shadow Pixmap (that is, specified by Mwm*icon*bottomShadowPixmap).

iconImageForeground (class **Foreground**)

This resource specifies the foreground color of the icon image that is displayed in the image part of an icon. The default value of this resource varies depending on the icon background.

iconImageTopShadowColor (class **Background**)
This resource specifies the top shadow color of the icon image that is displayed in the image part of an icon. The default value of this resource is the icon top shadow color (that is, specified by Mwm*icon*topShadowColor).

iconImageTopShadowPixmap (class **TopShadowPixmap**)
This resource specifies the top shadow Pixmap of the icon image that is displayed in the image part of an icon. The default value of this resource is the icon top shadow pixmap (that is, specified by Mwm*icon*topShadowPixmap).

matteBackground (class **Background**)
This resource specifies the background color of the matte, when **matteWidth** is positive. The default value of this resource is the client background color (that is, specified by "Mwm*background or Mwm*client*background).

matteBottomShadowColor (class **Foreground**)
This resource specifies the bottom shadow color of the matte, when **matteWidth** is positive. The default value of this resource is the client bottom shadow color (that is, specified by "Mwm*bottomShadowColor or Mwm*client*bottomShadowColor).

matteBottomShadowPixmap (class **BottomShadowPixmap**)
This resource specifies the bottom shadow Pixmap of the matte, when **matteWidth** is positive. The default value of this resource is the client bottom shadow pixmap (that is, specified by "Mwm*bottomShadowPixmap or Mwm*client*bottomShadowPixmap).

matteForeground (class **Foreground**)
This resource specifies the foreground color of the matte, when **matteWidth** is positive. The default value of this resource is the client foreground color (that is, specified by "Mwm*foreground or Mwm*client*foreground).

matteTopShadowColor (class **Background**)
This resource specifies the top shadow color of the matte, when **matteWidth** is positive. The default value of this resource is the client top shadow color (that is, specified by "Mwm*topShadowColor or Mwm*client*topShadowColor).

matteTopShadowPixmap (class **TopShadowPixmap**)
This resource specifies the top shadow pixmap of the matte, when **matteWidth** is positive. The default value of this resource is the client top shadow pixmap (that is, specified by "Mwm*topShadowPixmap or Mwm*client*topShadowPixmap).

matteWidth (class **MatteWidth**)
This resource specifies the width of the optional matte. The default value is 0, which effectively disables the matte.

maximumClientSize (class **MaximumClientSize**)
This is a size specification that indicates the client size to be used when an application is maximized. The resource value is specified as *width*x*height*. The width and height are interpreted in the units that the client uses (for example, for terminal emulators this is generally characters). If this resource is not specified, the maximum size from the WM_NORMAL_HINTS property is used if set. Otherwise the default value is the size where the client window with window management borders fills the screen. When the maximum client size is not determined by the maximumClientSize resource, the maximumMaximumSize resource value is used as a constraint on the maximum size.

useClientIcon (class **UseClientIcon**)
If the value given for this resource is True, a client-supplied icon image takes precedence over a user-supplied icon image. The default value is False, giving the user-supplied icon image higher precedence than the client-supplied icon image.

windowMenu (class **WindowMenu**)
This resource indicates the name of the menu pane that is posted when the window menu is popped up (usually by pressing button 1 on the window menu button on the client window frame). Menu panes are specified in the MWM resource description file. Window menus can be customized on a client class basis by

specifying resources of the form
Mwm*client_name_or_class***windowMenu** (see "Mwm
Resource Description File Syntax"). The default value of this
resource is "DefaultWindowMenu".

Resource Description File

The MWM resource description file is a supplementary resource file that
contains resource descriptions that are referred to by entries in the defaults
files (.Xdefaults, app-defaults/Mwm). It contains descriptions of resources
that are to be used by **mwm**, and that cannot be easily encoded in the
defaults files (a bitmap file is an analogous type of resource description file).
A particular **mwm resource description file** can be selected using the
configFile resource.

The following types of resources can be described in the **mwm** resource
description file:

Buttons   Window manager functions can be bound (associated)
with button events.

Keys   Window manager functions can be bound (associated)
with key press events.

Menus   Menu panes can be used for the window menu and other
menus posted with key bindings and button bindings.

mwm Resource Description File Syntax

The **mwm** resource description file is a standard text file that contains items
of information separated by blanks, tabs, and newline characters. Blank
lines are ignored. Items or characters can be quoted to avoid special
interpretation (for example, the comment character can be quoted to prevent
it from being interpreted as the comment character). A quoted item can be
contained in double quotes ("). Single characters can be quoted by
preceding them by the backslash character (\). All text from an unquoted #
to the end of the line is regarded as a comment and is not interpreted as part
of a resource description. If ! is the first character in a line, the line is
regarded as a comment. Window manager functions can be accessed with

button and key bindings, and with window manager menus. Functions are indicated as part of the specifications for button and key binding sets, and menu panes. The function specification has the following syntax:

> *function =*   *function_name [function_args]*
> *function_name =*   *window manager function*
> *function_args =*   *{quoted_item | unquoted_item}*

The following functions are supported. If a function is specified that isn't one of the supported functions, then it is interpreted by **mwm** as *f.nop*.

f.beep   This function causes a beep.

f.circle_down [icon | window]

This function causes the window or icon that is on the top of the window stack to be put on the bottom of the window stack (so that it no longer obscures any other window or icon). This function affects only those windows and icons that obscure other windows and icons, or that are obscured by other windows and icons. Secondary windows (that is, transient windows) are restacked with their associated primary window. Secondary windows always stay on top of the associated primary window and there can be no other primary windows between the secondary windows and their primary window. If an **icon** function argument is specified, the function applies only to icons. If a **window** function argument is specified, the function applies only to windows.

f.circle_up [icon | window]

This function raises the window or icon on the bottom of the window stack (so that it is not obscured by any other windows). This function affects only those windows and icons that obscure other windows and icons, or that are obscured by other windows and icons. Secondary windows (that is, transient windows) are restacked with their associated primary window. If an *icon* function argument is specified, the function applies only to icons. If a *window* function argument is specified, the function applies only to windows.

f.exec or **!**   This function causes *command* to be executed (using the value of the MWMSHELL environment variable if it is set, otherwise the value of the SHELL environment variable if it is set, otherwise */bin/sh*). The **!** notation can be used in place of the **f.exec** function name.

f.focus_color

This function sets the colormap focus to a client window. If this function is done in a root context, the default colormap (set up by the *X Window System* for the screen where MWM is running) is installed and there is no specific client window colormap focus. This function is treated as *f.nop* if colormapFocusPolicy is not explicit.

f.focus_key   This function sets the keyboard input focus to a client window or icon. This function is treated as *f.nop* if keyboardFocusPolicy is not explicit or the function is executed in a root context.

f.kill   This function is used to terminate a client. If the WM_DELETE_WINDOW protocol is set up, the client is sent a client message event, indicating that the client window should be deleted. If the WM_SAVE_YOURSELF protocol is set up and the WM_DELETE_WINDOW protocol is not set up, the client is sent a client message event, indicating that the client needs to prepare to be terminated. If the client does not have the WM_DELETE_WINDOW or WM_SAVE_YOURSELF protocol set up, this function causes a client's X connection to be terminated (usually resulting in termination of the client). Refer to the description of the quitTimeout resource and the WM_PROTOCOLS property.

f.lower [-*client*]

This function lowers a client window to the bottom of the window stack (where it obscures no other window). Secondary windows (that is, transient windows) are restacked with their associated primary window. The *client* argument indicates the name or class of a client to lower. If the *client* argument is not specified, the context that the function was invoked in indicates the window or icon to lower.

f.maximize   This function causes a client window to be displayed with its maximum size.

f.menu   This function associates a cascading (pull-right) menu with a menu pane entry or a menu with a button or key binding. The *menu_name* function argument identifies the menu to be used.

f.minimize   This function causes a client window to be minimized (iconified). When a window is minimized when no icon box is used, its icon is placed on the bottom of the window stack (so that it obscures no other window). If an icon box is used, the client's icon changes to its iconified form inside the icon box. Secondary windows (that is, transient windows) are minimized with their associated primary window. There is only one icon for a primary window and all its secondary windows.

f.move   This function causes a client window to be interactively moved.

f.next_cmap This function installs the next colormap in the list of colormaps for the window with the colormap focus.

f.next_key [**icon** | **window** | **transient**]
This function sets the keyboard input focus to the next window/icon in the set of windows/icons managed by the window manager (the ordering of this set is based on the stacking of windows on the screen). This function is treated as *f.nop* if keyboardFocusPolicy is not explicit. The keyboard input focus is moved only to windows that do not have an associated secondary window that is application modal. If the **transient** argument is specified, transient (secondary) windows are traversed (otherwise, if only **window** is specified, traversal is done only to the last focused window in a transient group). If an **icon** function argument is specified, the function applies only to icons. If a **window** function argument is specified, the function applies only to windows.

f.nop   This function does nothing.

f.normalize This function causes a client window to be displayed with its normal size. Secondary windows (that is, transient windows) are placed in their normal state along with their associated primary window.

f.normalize_and_raise

This function causes the corresponding client window to be displayed with its normal size and raised to the top of the window stack. Secondary windows (that is, transient windows) are placed in their normal state along with their associated primary window.

f.pack_icons

This function is used to relayout icons (based on the layout policy being used) on the root window or in the icon box. In general this causes icons to be "packed" into the icon grid.

f.pass_keys This function is used to enable/disable (toggle) processing of key bindings for window manager functions. When it disables key binding processing, all keys are passed on to the window with the keyboard input focus and no window manager functions are invoked. If the *f.pass_keys* function is invoked with a key binding to disable key-binding processing, the same key binding can be used to enable key-binding processing.

f.post_wmenu

This function is used to post the window menu. If a key is used to post the window menu and a window menu button is present, the window menu is automatically placed with its top-left corner at the bottom-left corner of the window menu button for the client window. If no window menu button is present, the window menu is placed at the top-left corner of the client window.

f.prev_cmap

This function installs the previous colormap in the list of colormaps for the window with the colormap focus.

f.prev_key [icon | window | transient]

This function sets the keyboard input focus to the previous window/icon in the set of windows/icons managed by the window manager (the ordering of this set is based on the stacking of windows on the screen). This function is treated as *f.nop* if keyboardFocusPolicy is not explicit. The keyboard input focus is moved only to windows that do not have an associated secondary window that is application modal. If the *transient* argument is specified, transient (secondary) windows are traversed (otherwise, if only *window* is specified, traversal is done only to the last focused window in a transient group). If an *icon* function argument is specified, the function applies only to icons. If an *window* function argument is specified, the function applies only to windows.

f.quit_mwm This function terminates **mwm** (but NOT the X window system).

f.raise [-*client*]

This function raises a client window to the top of the window stack (where it is obscured by no other window). Secondary windows (that is, transient windows) are restacked with their associated primary window. The *client* argument indicates the name or class of a client to raise. If the *client* argument is not specified, the context that the function was invoked in indicates the window or icon to raise.

f.raise_lower

This function raises a client window to the top of the window stack if it is partially obscured by another window, otherwise it lowers the window to the bottom of the window stack. Secondary windows (that is, transient windows) are restacked with their associated primary window.

f.refresh This function causes all windows to be redrawn.

f.refresh_win

This function causes a client window to be redrawn.

f.resize This function causes a client window to be interactively resized.

f.restart This function causes **mwm** to be restarted (effectively terminated and re-executed).

f.send_msg *message_number*

This function sends a client message of the type _MOTIF_WM_MESSAGES with the *message_type* indicated by the *message_number* function argument. The client message is sent only if *message_number* is included in the client's _MOTIF_WM_MESSAGES property. A menu item label is grayed out if the menu item is used to do *f.send_msg* of a message that is not included in the client's _MOTIF_WM_MESSAGES property.

f.separator   This function causes a menu separator to be put in the menu pane at the specified location (the label is ignored).

f.set_behavior

This function causes the window manager to restart with the default behavior (if a custom behavior is configured) or revert to the custom behavior. By default this is bound to **Shift Ctrl Meta <Key>!**.

f.title   This function inserts a title in the menu pane at the specified location.

Each function may be constrained as to which resource types can specify the function (for example, menu pane) and also what context the function can be used in (for example, the function is done to the selected client window). Function contexts are

root   No client window or icon has been selected as an object for the function.

window   A client window has been selected as an object for the function. This includes the window's title bar and frame. Some functions are applied only when the window is in its normalized state (for example, *f.maximize*) or its maximized state (for example, *f.normalize*).

icon   An icon has been selected as an object for the function.

If a function's context has been specified as **icon|window** and the function is invoked in an icon box, the function applies to the icon box, not to the icons inside.

If a function is specified in a type of resource where it is not supported or is invoked in a context that does not apply, the function is treated as *f.nop*. The following table indicates the resource types and function contexts in which window manager functions apply.

Function	Contexts	Resources
f.beep	root, icon, window	button, key, menu
f.circle_down	root, icon, window	button, key, menu
f.circle_up	root, icon, window	button, key, menu
f.exec	root, icon, window	button, key, menu
f.focus_color	root, icon, window	button, key, menu
f.focus_key	root, icon, window	button, key, menu
f.kill	icon, window	button, key, menu
f.lower	icon, window	button, key, menu
f.maximize	icon, window(normal)	button, key, menu
f.menu	root, icon, window	button, key, menu
f.minimize	window	button, key, menu
f.move	icon, window	button, key, menu
f.next_cmap	root, icon, window	button, key, menu
f.next_key	root, icon, window	button, key, menu
f.nop	root, icon, window	button, key, menu
f.normalize	icon, window(maximized)	button, key, menu
f.normalize_and_raise	icon, window	button, key, menu
f.pack_icons	root, icon, window	button, key, menu
f.pass_keys	root, icon, window	button, key, menu
f.post_wmenu	root, icon, window	button, key
f.prev_cmap	root, icon, window	button, key, menu
f.prev_key	root, icon, window	button, key, menu
f.quit_mwm	root	button, key, menu (root only)
f.raise	icon, window	button, key, menu
f.raise_lower	icon, window	button, key, menu
f.refresh	root, icon, window	button, key, menu
f.refresh_win	window	button, key, menu
f.resize	window	button, key, menu

Function	Contexts	Resources
f.restart	root	button, key, menu (root only)
f.send_msg	icon, window	button, key, menu
f.separator	root, icon, window	menu
f.set_behavior	root, icon, window	button, key, menu
f.title	root, icon, window	menu

Window Manager Event Specification

Events are indicated as part of the specifications for button and key-binding sets, and menu panes.

Button events have the following syntax:

button =   [*modifier_list*]<*button_event_name*>
modifier_list =   *modifier_name* {*modifier_name*}

All modifiers specified are interpreted as being exclusive (this means that only the specified modifiers can be present when the button event occurs). The following table indicates the values that can be used for *modifier_name*. The [Alt] key is frequently labeled [Extend] or [Meta]. Alt and Meta can be used interchangeably in event specification.

Modifier	Description
Ctrl	Control Key
Shift	Shift Key
Alt	Alt/Meta Key
Meta	Meta/Alt Key
Lock	Lock Key
Mod1	Modifier1
Mod2	Modifier2

Modifier	Description
Mod3	Modifier3
Mod4	Modifier4
Mod5	Modifier5

The following table indicates the values that can be used for *button_event_name*.

Button	Description
Btn1Down	Button 1 Press
Btn1Up	Button 1 Release
Btn1Click	Button 1 Press and Release
Btn1Click2	Button 1 Double-Click
Btn2Down	Button 2 Press
Btn2Up	Button 2 Release
Btn2Click	Button 2 Press and Release
Btn2Click2	Button 2 Double-Click
Btn3Down	Button 3 Press
Btn3Up	Button 3 Release
Btn3Click	Button 3 Press and Release
Btn3Click2	Button 3 Double-Click
Btn4Down	Button 4 Press
Btn4Up	Button 4 Release
Btn4Click	Button 4 Press and Release
Btn4Click2	Button 4 Double-Click
Btn5Down	Button 5 Press
Btn5Up	Button 5 Release
Btn5Click	Button 5 Press and Release
Btn5Click2	Button 5 Double-Click

Key events that are used by the window manager for menu mnemonics and for binding to window manager functions are single key presses; key releases are ignored. Key events have the following syntax:

key =   [*modifier_list*]<**Key**>*key_name*
modifier_list =   *modifier_name* {*modifier_name*}

All modifiers specified are interpreted as being exclusive (this means that only the specified modifiers can be present when the key event occurs). Modifiers for keys are the same as those that apply to buttons. The *key_name* is an X11 keysym name. Keysym names can be found in the keysymdef.h file (remove the *XK_* prefix).

Button Bindings

The **buttonBindings** resource value is the name of a set of button bindings that are used to configure window manager behavior. A window manager function can be done when a button press occurs with the pointer over a framed client window, an icon, or the root window. The context for indicating where the button press applies is also the context for invoking the window manager function when the button press is done (significant for functions that are context sensitive).

The button binding syntax is

Buttons *bindings_set_name*
{
   button   *context*   *function*
   button   *context*   *function*
             .
             .

   button   *context*   *function*
}

The syntax for the *context* specification is

> *context* =   *object*[|*context*]
> *object* =   **root** | **icon** | **window** | **title** | **frame** | **border** | **app**

The context specification indicates where the pointer must be for the button binding to be effective. For example, a context of **window** indicates that the pointer must be over a client window or window management frame for the button binding to be effective. The **frame** context is for the window management frame around a client window (including the border and titlebar), the **border** context is for the border part of the window management frame (not including the titlebar), the **title** context is for the title area of the window management frame, and the **app** context is for the application window (not including the window management frame).

If an *f.nop* function is specified for a button binding, the button binding is not done.

Key Bindings

The **keyBindings** resource value is the name of a set of key bindings that are used to configure window manager behavior. A window manager function can be done when a particular key is pressed. The context in which the key binding applies is indicated in the key binding specification. The valid contexts are the same as those that apply to button bindings.

The key binding syntax is

> **Keys** *bindings_set_name*
> {
>   *key   context   function*
>   *key   context   function*
>   .
>   .
>   *key   context   function*
> }

If an *f.nop* function is specified for a key binding, the key binding is not done. If an *f.post_wmenu* or *f.menu* function is bound to a key, **mwm** will automatically use the same key for removing the menu from the screen after it has been popped up.

The *context* specification syntax is the same as for button bindings. For key bindings, the **frame**, **title**, **border**, and **app** contexts are equivalent to the **window** context. The context for a key event is the window or icon that has the keyboard input focus (**root** if no window or icon has the keyboard input focus).

Menu Panes

Menus can be popped up using the *f.post_wmenu* and *f.menu* window manager functions. The context for window manager functions that are done from a menu is *root*, *icon* or *window* depending on how the menu was popped up. In the case of the *window* menu or menus popped up with a key binding, the location of the keyboard input focus indicates the context. For menus popped up using a button binding, the context of the button binding is the context of the menu.

The menu pane specification syntax is

> **Menu** *menu_name*
> {
>   *label* [*mnemonic*] [*accelerator*] *function*
>   *label* [*mnemonic*] [*accelerator*] *function*
>
>   .
>
>   .
>   *label* [*mnemonic*] [*accelerator*] *function*
> }

Each line in the *Menu* specification identifies the label for a menu item and the function to be done if the menu item is selected. Optionally a menu button mnemonic and a menu button keyboard accelerator may be specified. Mnemonics are functional only when the menu is posted and keyboard traversal applies.

The *label* may be a string or a bitmap file. The label specification has the following syntax:

label =	*text* | *bitmap_file*
bitmap_file =	**@**file_name
text =	*quoted_item* | *unquoted_item*

The string encoding for labels must be compatible with the menu font that is used. Labels are greyed out for menu items that do the *f.nop* function or an invalid function or a function that doesn't apply in the current context.

A *mnemonic* specification has the following syntax

mnemonic = _character

The first matching *character* in the label is underlined. If there is no matching *character* in the label, no mnemonic is registered with the window manager for that label. Although the *character* must exactly match a character in the label, the mnemonic does not execute if any modifier (such as Shift) is pressed with the character key.

The *accelerator* specification is a key event specification with the same syntax as is used for key bindings to window manager functions.

Environment

mwm uses the environment variable HOME specifying the user's home directory.

mwm uses the environment variable LANG specifying the user's choice of language for the **mwm** message catalog and the **mwm** resource description file.

mwm uses the environment variables XFILESEARCHPATH, XUSERFILESEARCHPATH, XAPPLRESDIR, XENVIRONMENT, LANG, and HOME in determining search paths for resource defaults files.

mwm reads the $HOME/.motifbind file if it exists to install a virtual key bindings property on the root window.

mwm uses the environment variable MWMSHELL (or SHELL, if MWMSHELL is not set), specifying the shell to use when executing commands via the *f.exec* function.

Files

/usr/lib/X11/$LANG/system.mwmrc   /usr/lib/X11/system.mwmrc
/usr/lib/X11/app-defaults/Mwm $HOME/Mwm $HOME/.Xdefaults
$HOME/$LANG/.mwmrc $HOME/.mwmrc $HOME/.motifbind

Related Information

VendorShell(3X), **X(1)**, and **XmInstallImage(3X)**.

ApplicationShell

Purpose

The ApplicationShell widget class

AES Support Level

Full-use

Synopsis

```
#include <Xm/Xm.h>
#include <X11/Shell.h>
```

Description

ApplicationShell is used as the main top-level window for an application. An application should have more than one ApplicationShell only if it implements multiple logical applications.

Classes

ApplicationShell inherits behavior and resources from **Core**, **Composite**, **Shell**, **WMShell**, **VendorShell**, and **TopLevelShell**.

The class pointer is **applicationShellWidgetClass**.

The class name is **ApplicationShell**.

New Resources

The following table defines a set of widget resources used by the programmer to specify data. The programmer can also set the resource values for the inherited classes to set attributes for this widget. To reference a resource by name or by class in a .Xdefaults file, remove the **XmN** or **XmC** prefix and use the remaining letters. To specify one of the defined values for a resource in a .Xdefaults file, remove the **Xm** prefix and use the remaining letters (in either lowercase or uppercase, but include any underscores between words). The codes in the access column indicate if the given resource can be set at creation time (**C**), set by using **XtSetValues** (**S**), retrieved by using **XtGetValues** (**G**), or is not applicable (**N/A**).

ApplicationShell Resource Set		
Name	**Default**	**Access**
Class	**Type**	
XmNargc	0	CSG
XmCArgc	int	
XmNargv	NULL	CSG
XmCArgv	String *	

> **XmNargc**   Specifies the number of arguments given in the **XmNargv**
> resource. The function **XtInitialize** sets this resource on the
> shell widget instance it creates by using its parameters as the
> values.
>
> **XmNargv**   Specifies the argument list required by a session manager to
> restart the application, if it is killed. This list should be
> updated at appropriate points by the application if a new state
> has been reached which can be directly restarted. The
> function **XtInitialize** sets this resource on the shell widget
> instance it creates by using its parameters as the values.

Inherited Resources

ApplicationShell inherits behavior and resources from the following
superclasses. For a complete description of each resource, refer to the
manual page for that superclass.

TopLevelShell Resource Set		
Name	**Default**	**Access**
Class	**Type**	
XmNiconic	False	CSG
XmCIconic	Boolean	
XmNiconName	NULL	CSG
XmCIconName	String	
XmNiconNameEncoding	XA_STRING	CSG
XmCIconNameEncoding	Atom	

VendorShell Resource Set		
Name	**Default**	**Access**
Class	**Type**	
XmNdefaultFontList	dynamic	C
XmCDefaultFontList	XmFontList	
XmNdeleteResponse	XmDESTROY	CSG
XmCDeleteResponse	unsigned char	
XmNkeyboardFocusPolicy	XmEXPLICIT	CSG
XmCKeyboardFocusPolicy	unsigned char	
XmNmwmDecorations	-1	CSG
XmCMwmDecorations	int	
XmNmwmFunctions	-1	CSG
XmCMwmFunctions	int	
XmNmwmInputMode	-1	CSG
XmCMwmInputMode	int	
XmNmwmMenu	NULL	CSG
XmCMwmMenu	String	

WMShell Resource Set		
Name Class	**Default** Type	**Access**
XmNbaseHeight XmCBaseHeight	XtUnspecifiedShellInt int	CSG
XmNbaseWidth XmCBaseWidth	XtUnspecifiedShellInt int	CSG
XmNheightInc XmCHeightInc	XtUnspecifiedShellInt int	CSG
XmNiconMask XmCIconMask	NULL Pixmap	CSG
XmNiconPixmap XmCIconPixmap	NULL Pixmap	CSG
XmNiconWindow XmCIconWindow	NULL Window	CSG
XmNiconX XmCIconX	-1 int	CSG
XmNiconY XmCIconY	-1 int	CSG
XmNinitialState XmCInitialState	NormalState int	CSG
XmNinput XmCInput	True Boolean	CSG
XmNmaxAspectX XmCMaxAspectX	XtUnspecifiedShellInt int	CSG
XmNmaxAspectY XmCMaxAspectY	XtUnspecifiedShellInt int	CSG
XmNmaxHeight XmCMaxHeight	XtUnspecifiedShellInt int	CSG
XmNmaxWidth XmCMaxWidth	XtUnspecifiedShellInt int	CSG

Name
    Class
	Default
	    Type
		Access

XmNminAspectX
    XmCMinAspectX
	XtUnspecifiedShellInt
	    int
		CSG

XmNminAspectY
    XmCMinAspectY
	XtUnspecifiedShellInt
	    int
		CSG

XmNminHeight
    XmCMinHeight
	XtUnspecifiedShellInt
	    int
		CSG

XmNminWidth
    XmCMinWidth
	XtUnspecifiedShellInt
	    int
		CSG

XmNtitle
    XmCTitle
	dynamic
	    String
		CSG

XmNtitleEncoding
    XmCTitleEncoding
	XA_STRING
	    Atom
		CSG

XmNtransient
    XmCTransient
	False
	    Boolean
		CSG

XmNwaitForWm
    XmCWaitForWm
	True
	    Boolean
		CSG

XmNwidthInc
    XmCWidthInc
	XtUnspecifiedShellInt
	    int
		CSG

XmNwindowGroup
    XmCWindowGroup
	dynamic
	    Window
		CSG

XmNwinGravity
    XmCWinGravity
	dynamic
	    int
		CSG

XmNwmTimeout
    XmCWmTimeout
	5000 ms
	    int
		CSG

Shell Resource Set		
Name	**Default**	**Access**
Class	Type	
XmNallowShellResize	False	CG
XmCAllowShellResize	Boolean	
XmNcreatePopupChildProc	NULL	CSG
XmCCreatePopupChildProc	(*)()	
XmNgeometry	NULL	CSG
XmCGeometry	String	
XmNoverrideRedirect	False	CSG
XmCOverrideRedirect	Boolean	
XmNpopdownCallback	NULL	C
XmCCallback	XtCallbackList	
XmNpopupCallback	NULL	C
XmCCallback	XtCallbackList	
XmNsaveUnder	False	CSG
XmCSaveUnder	Boolean	
XmNvisual	CopyFromParent	CSG
XmCVisual	Visual *	

Composite Resource Set		
Name	**Default**	**Access**
Class	Type	
XmNchildren	NULL	G
XmCReadOnly	WidgetList	
XmNinsertPosition	NULL	CSG
XmCInsertPosition	(*)()	
XmNnumChildren	0	G
XmCReadOnly	Cardinal	

Core Resource Set		
Name	**Default**	**Access**
Class	**Type**	
XmNaccelerators	dynamic	CSG
XmCAccelerators	XtAccelerators	
XmNancestorSensitive	dynamic	G
XmCSensitive	Boolean	
XmNbackground	dynamic	CSG
XmCBackground	Pixel	
XmNbackgroundPixmap	XmUNSPECIFIED_PIXMAP	CSG
XmCPixmap	Pixmap	
XmNborderColor	XtDefaultForeground	CSG
XmCBorderColor	Pixel	
XmNborderPixmap	XmUNSPECIFIED_PIXMAP	CSG
XmCPixmap	Pixmap	
XmNborderWidth	1	CSG
XmCBorderWidth	Dimension	
XmNcolormap	dynamic	CG
XmCColormap	Colormap	
XmNdepth	dynamic	CG
XmCDepth	int	
XmNdestroyCallback	NULL	C
XmCCallback	XtCallbackList	
XmNheight	dynamic	CSG
XmCHeight	Dimension	
XmNinitialResourcesPersistent	True	C
XmCInitialResourcesPersistent	Boolean	
XmNmappedWhenManaged	True	CSG
XmCMappedWhenManaged	Boolean	
XmNscreen	dynamic	CG
XmCScreen	Screen *	

Name	Default	Access
Class	Type	
XmNsensitive	True	CSG
XmCSensitive	Boolean	
XmNtranslations	dynamic	CSG
XmCTranslations	XtTranslations	
XmNwidth	dynamic	CSG
XmCWidth	Dimension	
XmNx	0	CSG
XmCPosition	Position	
XmNy	0	CSG
XmCPosition	Position	

Translations

There are no translations for ApplicationShell.

Related Information

Composite(3X), Core(3X), Shell(3X), WMShell(3X), VendorShell(3X), and TopLevelShell(3X).

Composite

Purpose

The Composite widget class

AES Support Level

Full-use

Synopsis

#include <Xm/Xm.h>

Description

Composite widgets are intended to be containers for other widgets and can have an arbitrary number of children. Their responsibilities (implemented either directly by the widget class or indirectly by Intrinsics functions) include:

- Overall management of children from creation to destruction.

- Destruction of descendants when the composite widget is destroyed.

- Physical arrangement (geometry management) of a displayable subset of managed children.

- Mapping and unmapping of a subset of the managed children. Instances of composite widgets need to specify the order in which their children are kept. For example, an application may want a set of command buttons in some logical order grouped by function, and it may want buttons that represent filenames to be kept in alphabetical order.

Classes

Composite inherits behavior and resources from **Core**.

The class pointer is **composite WidgetClass**.

The class name is **Composite**.

New Resources

The following table defines a set of widget resources used by the programmer to specify data. The programmer can also set the resource values for the inherited classes to set attributes for this widget. To reference a resource by name or by class in a .Xdefaults file, remove the **XmN** or **XmC** prefix and use the remaining letters. To specify one of the defined values for a resource in a .Xdefaults file, remove the **Xm** prefix and use the remaining letters (in either lowercase or uppercase, but include any underscores between words). The codes in the access column indicate if the given resource can be set at creation time (**C**), set by using **XtSetValues** (**S**), retrieved by using **XtGetValues** (**G**), or is not applicable (**N/A**).

Composite Resource Set		
Name	**Default**	**Access**
Class	**Type**	
XmNchildren	NULL	G
XmCReadOnly	WidgetList	
XmNinsertPosition	NULL	CSG
XmCInsertPosition	(*)()	
XmNnumChildren	0	G
XmCReadOnly	Cardinal	

XmNchildren

> A read-only list of the children of the widget.

XmNinsertPosition

> Points to the **XtOrderProc** function described below.

XmNnumChildren

> A read-only resource specifying the length of the list of children in **XmNchildren**.

The following procedure pointer in a composite widget instance is of type **XtOrderProc**:

Cardinal (* **XtOrderProc**) (*widget*)
> Widget   *w*;

w   Specifies the widget.

Composite widgets that allow clients to order their children (usually homogeneous boxes) can call their widget instance's insert_position procedure from the class's insert_child procedure to determine where a new child should go in its children array. Thus, a client of a composite class can apply different sorting criteria to widget instances of the class, passing in a different insert_position procedure when it creates each composite widget instance.

The return value of the insert_position procedure indicates how many children should go before the widget. Returning *zero* indicates that the widget should go before all other children; returning num_children indicates that it should go after all other children. The default insert_position function returns num_children and can be overridden by a specific composite widget's resource list or by the argument list provided when the composite widget is created.

Inherited Resources

Composite inherits behavior and resources from the following superclass. For a complete description of each resource, refer to the manual page for that superclass.

Core Resource Set		
Name	**Default**	**Access**
Class	Type	
XmNaccelerators	dynamic	CSG
XmCAccelerators	XtAccelerators	
XmNancestorSensitive	dynamic	G
XmCSensitive	Boolean	
XmNbackground	dynamic	CSG
XmCBackground	Pixel	
XmNbackgroundPixmap	XmUNSPECIFIED_PIXMAP	CSG
XmCPixmap	Pixmap	
XmNborderColor	XtDefaultForeground	CSG
XmCBorderColor	Pixel	
XmNborderPixmap	XmUNSPECIFIED_PIXMAP	CSG
XmCPixmap	Pixmap	
XmNborderWidth	1	CSG
XmCBorderWidth	Dimension	
XmNcolormap	dynamic	CG
XmCColormap	Colormap	
XmNdepth	dynamic	CG
XmCDepth	int	
XmNdestroyCallback	NULL	C
XmCCallback	XtCallbackList	
XmNheight	dynamic	CSG
XmCHeight	Dimension	
XmNinitialResourcesPersistent	True	C
XmCInitialResourcesPersistent	Boolean	
XmNmappedWhenManaged	True	CSG
XmCMappedWhenManaged	Boolean	
XmNscreen	dynamic	CG
XmCScreen	Screen *	

Name	Default	Access
Class	Type	
XmNsensitive	True	CSG
XmCSensitive	Boolean	
XmNtranslations	dynamic	CSG
XmCTranslations	XtTranslations	
XmNwidth	dynamic	CSG
XmCWidth	Dimension	
XmNx	0	CSG
XmCPosition	Position	
XmNy	0	CSG
XmCPosition	Position	

Translations

There are no translations for Composite.

Related Information

Core(3X).

Constraint

Purpose

The Constraint widget class

AES Support Level

Full-use

Synopsis

#include <Xm/Xm.h>

Description

Constraint widgets maintain additional state data for each child. For example, client-defined constraints on the child's geometry may be specified.

When a constrained composite widget defines constraint resources, all of that widget's children inherit all of those resources as their own. These constraint resources are set and read just the same as any other resources defined for the child. This resource inheritance extends exactly one generation down, which means only the first-generation children of a constrained composite widget inherit the parent widget's constraint resources.

Because constraint resources are defined by the parent widgets and not the children, the child widgets never directly use the constraint resource data. Instead, the parents use constraint resource data to attach child-specific data to children.

Classes

Constraint inherits behavior and resources from **Composite** and **Core**.

The class pointer is **constraintWidgetClass**.

The class name is **Constraint**.

New Resources

Constraint defines no new resources.

Inherited Resources

Constraint inherits behavior and resources from **Composite** and **Core**. The following table defines a set of widget resources used by the programmer to specify data. The programmer can also set the resource values for the inherited classes to set attributes for this widget. To reference a resource by name or by class in a .Xdefaults file, remove the **XmN** or **XmC** prefix and use the remaining letters. To specify one of the defined values for a resource in a .Xdefaults file, remove the **Xm** prefix and use the remaining letters (in either lowercase or uppercase, but include any underscores between words). The codes in the access column indicate if the given resource can be set at creation time (**C**), set by using **XtSetValues** (**S**), retrieved by using **XtGetValues** (**G**), or is not applicable (**N/A**).

Core Resource Set		
Name	**Default**	**Access**
Class	**Type**	
XmNaccelerators	dynamic	CSG
XmCAccelerators	XtAccelerators	
XmNancestorSensitive	dynamic	G
XmCSensitive	Boolean	
XmNbackground	dynamic	CSG
XmCBackground	Pixel	
XmNbackgroundPixmap	XmUNSPECIFIED_PIXMAP	CSG
XmCPixmap	Pixmap	
XmNborderColor	XtDefaultForeground	CSG
XmCBorderColor	Pixel	
XmNborderPixmap	XmUNSPECIFIED_PIXMAP	CSG
XmCPixmap	Pixmap	
XmNborderWidth	1	CSG
XmCBorderWidth	Dimension	
XmNcolormap	dynamic	CG
XmCColormap	Colormap	
XmNdepth	dynamic	CG
XmCDepth	int	
XmNdestroyCallback	NULL	C
XmCCallback	XtCallbackList	
XmNheight	dynamic	CSG
XmCHeight	Dimension	
XmNinitialResourcesPersistent	True	C
XmCInitialResourcesPersistent	Boolean	
XmNmappedWhenManaged	True	CSG
XmCMappedWhenManaged	Boolean	
XmNscreen	dynamic	CG
XmCScreen	Screen *	

Name	Default	Access
Class	Type	
XmNsensitive	True	CSG
XmCSensitive	Boolean	
XmNtranslations	dynamic	CSG
XmCTranslations	XtTranslations	
XmNwidth	dynamic	CSG
XmCWidth	Dimension	
XmNx	0	CSG
XmCPosition	Position	
XmNy	0	CSG
XmCPosition	Position	

Translations

There are no translations for Constraint.

Related Information

Composite(3X) and **Core(3X)**.

Core

Purpose

The Core widget class

AES Support Level

Full-use

Synopsis

#include <Xm/Xm.h>

Description

Core is the Xt Intrinsic base class for windowed widgets. The **Object** and **RectObj** classes provide support for windowless widgets.

Classes

All widgets are built from **Core**.

The class pointer is **widgetClass**.

The class name is **Core**.

New Resources

The following table defines a set of widget resources used by the programmer to specify data. The programmer can also set the resource values for the inherited classes to set attributes for this widget. To reference a resource by name or by class in a .Xdefaults file, remove the **XmN** or **XmC** prefix and use the remaining letters. To specify one of the defined values for a resource in a .Xdefaults file, remove the **Xm** prefix and use the remaining letters (in either lowercase or uppercase, but include any underscores between words). The codes in the access column indicate if the given resource can be set at creation time (**C**), set by using **XtSetValues** (**S**), retrieved by using **XtGetValues** (**G**), or is not applicable (**N/A**).

Core Resource Set		

Name
    Class
	Default
	    Type
		Access

XmNaccelerators
    XmCAccelerators
	dynamic
	    XtAccelerators
		CSG

XmNancestorSensitive
    XmCSensitive
	dynamic
	    Boolean
		G

XmNbackground
    XmCBackground
	dynamic
	    Pixel
		CSG

XmNbackgroundPixmap
    XmCPixmap
	XmUNSPECIFIED_PIXMAP
	    Pixmap
		CSG

XmNborderColor
    XmCBorderColor
	XtDefaultForeground
	    Pixel
		CSG

XmNborderPixmap
    XmCPixmap
	XmUNSPECIFIED_PIXMAP
	    Pixmap
		CSG

XmNborderWidth
    XmCBorderWidth
	1
	    Dimension
		CSG

XmNcolormap
    XmCColormap
	dynamic
	    Colormap
		CG

XmNdepth
    XmCDepth
	dynamic
	    int
		CG

XmNdestroyCallback
    XmCCallback
	NULL
	    XtCallbackList
		C

XmNheight
    XmCHeight
	dynamic
	    Dimension
		CSG

XmNinitialResourcesPersistent
    XmCInitialResourcesPersistent
	True
	    Boolean
		C

XmNmappedWhenManaged
    XmCMappedWhenManaged
	True
	    Boolean
		CSG

XmNscreen
    XmCScreen
	dynamic
	    Screen *
		CG

Name	Default	Access
Class	**Type**	
XmNsensitive	True	CSG
XmCSensitive	Boolean	
XmNtranslations	dynamic	CSG
XmCTranslations	XtTranslations	
XmNwidth	dynamic	CSG
XmCWidth	Dimension	
XmNx	0	CSG
XmCPosition	Position	
XmNy	0	CSG
XmCPosition	Position	

XmNaccelerators

Specifies a translation table that is bound with its actions in the context of a particular widget. The accelerator table can then be installed on some destination widget.

XmNancestorSensitive

Specifies whether the immediate parent of the widget receives input events. Use the function **XtSetSensitive** to change the argument to preserve data integrity (see **XmNsensitive** below). For shells, the default is copied from the parent's **XmNancestorSensitive** resource if there is a parent; otherwise, it is True. For other widgets, the default is the bitwise AND of the parent's **XmNsensitive** and **XmNancestorSensitive** resources.

XmNbackground

Specifies the background color for the widget.

XmNbackgroundPixmap

Specifies a pixmap for tiling the background. The first tile is placed at the upper left-hand corner of the widget's window.

XmNborderColor

Specifies the color of the border in a pixel value.

XmNborderPixmap

Specifies a pixmap to be used for tiling the border. The first tile is placed at the upper left-hand corner of the border.

XmNborderWidth

Specifies the width of the border that surrounds the widget's window on all four sides. The width is specified in pixels. A width of zero means that no border shows.

XmNcolormap

Specifies the colormap that is used for conversions to the type **Pixel** for this widget instance. When changed, previously generated pixel values are not affected, but newly generated values are in the new colormap. For shells without parents, the default is the default colormap of the widget's screen. Otherwise, the default is copied from the parent.

XmNdepth Specifies the number of bits that can be used for each pixel in the widget's window. Applications should not change or set the value of this resource as it is set by the Xt Intrinsics when the widget is created. For shells without parents, the default is the default depth of the widget's screen. Otherwise, the default is copied from the parent.

XmNdestroyCallback

Specifies a list of callbacks that is called when the widget is destroyed.

XmNheight Specifies the inside height (excluding the border) of the widget's window.

XmNinitialResourcesPersistent

Specifies whether or not resources are reference counted. If the value is True when the widget is created, the resources referenced by the widget are not reference counted, regardless of how the resource type converter is registered. An application that expects to destroy the widget and wants to have resources deallocated should specify a value of False. The default is True, implying an assumption that the widget will not be destroyed during the life of the application.

XmNmappedWhenManaged

If set to True it maps the widget (makes it visible) as soon as it is both realized and managed. If set to False, the client is responsible for mapping and unmapping the widget. If the value is changed from True to False after the widget has been realized and managed, the widget is unmapped.

XmNscreen Specifies the screen on which a widget instance resides. It is read only. When the Toolkit is initialized, the top-level widget obtains its default value from the default screen of the display. Otherwise, the default is copied from the parent.

XmNsensitive

Determines whether a widget receives input events. If a widget is sensitive, the Xt Intrinsics' Event Manager dispatches to the widget all keyboard, mouse button, motion, window enter/leave, and focus events. Insensitive widgets do not receive these events. Use the function **XtSetSensitive** to change the sensitivity argument. Using **XtSetSensitive** ensures that if a parent widget has **XmNsensitive** set to False, the ancestor-sensitive flag of all its children is appropriately set.

XmNtranslations

Points to a translations list. A translations list is a list of events and actions that are to be performed when the events occur.

XmNwidth Specifies the inside width (excluding the border) of the widget's window.

XmNx Specifies the x-coordinate of the upper left outside corner of the widget's window. The value is relative to the upper left inside corner of the parent window.

XmNy Specifies the y-coordinate of the upper left outside corner of the widget's window. The value is relative to the upper left inside corner of the parent window.

Translations

There are no translations for Core.

Related Information

Object(3X) and **RectObj(3X)**.

MrmCloseHierarchy

Purpose

Closes a UID hierarchy

AES Support Level

Trial-use

Synopsis

#include <Mrm/MrmPublic.h>
Cardinal MrmCloseHierarchy(*hierarchy_id* **)**
   MrmHierarchy *hierarchy_id* **;**

Description

The **MrmCloseHierarchy** function closes a UID hierarchy previously opened by **MrmOpenHierarchy**. All files associated with the hierarchy are closed by the Motif Resource Manager (MRM) and all associated memory is returned.

hierarchy_id Specifies the ID of a previously opened UID hierarchy. The *hierarchy_id* was returned in a previous call to **MrmOpenHierarchy**.

Return Value

This function returns one of these status return constants:

MrmSUCCESS   The function executed successfully.

MrmBAD_HIERARCHY
> The hierarchy ID was invalid.

MrmFAILURE   The function failed.

Related Information

MrmOpenHierarchy(3X)

MrmFetchColorLiteral

Purpose

Fetches a named color literal from a UID file

AES Support Level

Trial-use

Synopsis

#include <Mrm/MrmPublic.h>
int MrmFetchColorLiteral(*hierarchy_id* , *index*, *display*, *colormap_id*, *pixel*)
    MrmHierarchy hierarchy_id;
    String *index*;
    Display *display;
    Colormap *colormap_id*;
    Pixel *pixel;

Description

The **MrmFetchColorLiteral** function fetches a named color literal from a UID file, and converts the color literal to a pixel color value.

hierarchy_id	Specifies the ID of the UID hierarchy that contains the specified literal. The *hierarchy_id* was returned in a previous call to **MrmOpenHierarchy**.
index	Specifies the UIL name of the color literal to fetch. You must define this name in UIL as an exported value.
display	Specifies the display used for the pixmap. The *display* argument specifies the connection to the X server. For more information on the **Display** structure, see the Xlib function **XOpenDisplay**.
colormap_id	Specifies the ID of the color map. If NULL, the default color map is used.
pixel	Returns the ID of the color literal.

Return Value

This function returns one of these status return constants:

MrmSUCCESS   The function executed successfully.

MrmBAD_HIERARCHY
                        The hierarchy ID was invalid.

MrmNOT_FOUND   The color literal was not found in the UIL file.

MrmFAILURE   The function failed.

Related Information

MrmFetchIconLiteral(3X), **MrmFetchLiteral(3X)**, **XOpenDisplay(3X)**

MrmFetchIconLiteral

Purpose

Fetches an icon literal from a hierarchy

AES Support Level

Trial-use

Synopsis

#include <Mrm/MrmPublic.h>
int MrmFetchIconLiteral(*hierarchy_id*, *index*, *screen*, *display*, *fgpix*, *bgpix*, *pixmap*)
    MrmHierarchy *hierarchy_id*;
    String *index*;
    Screen **screen*;
    Display **display*;
    Pixel *fgpix*;
    Pixel *bgpix*;
    Pixmap **pixmap*;

Description

The **MrmFetchIconLiteral** function fetches an icon literal from an MRM
hierarchy, and converts the icon literal to an X pixmap.

hierarchy_id	Specifies the ID of the UID hierarchy that contains the specified icon literal. The *hierarchy_id* was returned in a previous call to **MrmOpenHierarchy**.
index	Specifies the UIL name of the icon literal to fetch.
screen	Specifies the screen used for the pixmap. The *screen* argument specifies a pointer to the Xlib structure **Screen** which contains the information about that screen and is linked to the **Display** structure. For more information on the **Display** and **Screen** structures, see the Xlib function **XOpenDisplay** and the associated screen information macros.
display	Specifies the display used for the pixmap. The *display* argument specifies the connection to the X server. For more information on the **Display** structure, see the Xlib function **XOpenDisplay**.
fgpix	Specifies the foreground color for the pixmap.
bgpix	Specifies the background color for the pixmap.
pixmap	Returns the resulting X pixmap value.

Return Value

This function returns one of these status return constants:

MrmSUCCESS	The function executed successfully.
MrmBAD_HIERARCHY	
	The hierarchy ID was invalid.
MrmNOT_FOUND	The icon literal was not found in the hierarchy.
MrmFAILURE	The function failed.

Related Information

MrmFetchLiteral(3X), MrmFetchColorLiteral(3X), XOpenDisplay(3X)

MrmFetchLiteral

Purpose

Fetches a literal from a UID file

AES Support Level

Trial-use

Synopsis

#include <Mrm/MrmPublic.h>
int MrmFetchLiteral(*hierarchy_id* , *index*, *display*, *value*, *type*)
    MrmHierarchy *hierarchy_id* ;
    String *index* ;
    Display **display* ;
    caddr_t **value* ;
    MrmCode **type* ;

Description

The **MrmFetchLiteral** function reads and returns the value and type of a literal (named value) that is stored as a public resource in a single UID file. This function returns a pointer to the value of the literal. For example, an integer is always returned as a pointer to an integer, and a string is always returned as a pointer to a string.

Applications should not use **MrmmFetchLiteral** for fetching icon or color literals. If this is attempted, **MrmmFetchLiteral** returns an error.

2–81

hierarchy_id	Specifies the ID of the UID hierarchy that contains the specified literal. The *hierarchy_id* was returned in a previous call to **MrmOpenHierarchy**.
index	Specifies the UIL name of the literal (pixmap) to fetch. You must define this name in UIL as an exported value.
display	Specifies the display used for the pixmap. The *display* argument specifies the connection to the X server. For more information on the **Display** structure see the Xlib function **XOpenDisplay**.
value	Returns the ID of the named literal's value.
type	Returns the named literal's data type. Types are defined in the include file **<Mrm/MrmPublic.h>**.

Return Value

This function returns one of these status return constants:

MrmSUCCESS   The function executed successfully.

MrmBAD_HIERARCHY
                  The hierarchy ID was invalid.

MrmNOT_FOUND   The literal was not found in the UIL file.

MrmFAILURE   The function failed.

Related Information

**MrmFetchIconLiteral(3X), MrmFetchColorLiteral(3X),
XOpenDisplay(3X)**

MrmFetchSetValues

Purpose

Fetches the values to be set from literals stored in UID files.

AES Support Level

Trial-use

Synopsis

#include <Mrm/MrmPublic.h>
Cardinal MrmFetchSetValues(*hierarchy_id*, *widget*, *args*, *num_args***)**
    MrmHierarchy *hierarchy_id*;
    Widget *widget*;
    ArgList *args*;
    Cardinal *num_args*;

Description

The **MrmFetchSetValues** function is similar to **XtSetValues**, except that the values to be set are defined by the UIL named values that are stored in the UID hierarchy. **MrmFetchSetValues** fetches the values to be set from literals stored in UID files.

hierarchy_id	Specifies the ID of the UID hierarchy that contains the specified literal. The *hierarchy_id* was returned in a previous call to **MrmOpenHierarchy**.
widget	Specifies the widget that is modified.
args	Specifies an argument list that identifies the widget arguments to be modified as well as the index (UIL name) of the literal that defines the value for that argument. The name part of each argument (args[n].name) must begin with the string **XmN** followed by the name that uniquely identifies this attribute tag. For example, **XmNwidth** is the attribute name associated with the core argument *width*. The value part (args[n].value) must be a string that gives the index (UIL name) of the literal. You must define all literals in UIL as exported values.
num_args	Specifies the number of entries in *args*.

This function sets the values on a widget, evaluating the values as public literal resource references resolvable from a UID hierarchy. Each literal is fetched from the hierarchy, and its value is modified and converted as required. This value is then placed in the argument list and used as the actual value for an **XtSetValues** call. **MrmFetchSetValues** allows a widget to be modified after creation using UID file values exactly as is done for creation values in **MrmFetchWidget**.

As in **MrmFetchWidget**, each argument whose value can be evaluated from the UID hierarchy is set in the widget. Values that are not found or values in which conversion errors occur are not modified.

Each entry in the argument list identifies an argument to be modified in the widget. The name part identifies the tag, which begins with **XmN**. The value part must be a string whose value is the index of the literal. Thus, the following code would modify the label resource of the widget to have the value of the literal accessed by the index OK_button_label in the hierarchy:
args[n].name = XmNlabel; args[n].value = "OK_button_label";

Return Value

This function returns one of these status return constants:

MrmSUCCESS   The function executed successfully.

MrmPARTIAL_SUCCESS
                 At least one literal was successfully fetched.

MrmBAD_HIERARCHY
                 The hierarchy ID was invalid.

MrmFAILURE   The function failed.

Related Information

XtSetValues(3X)

MrmFetchWidget

Purpose

Fetches and creates any indexed (UIL named) application widgets and its children.

AES Support Level

Trial-use

Synopsis

#include <Mrm/MrmPublic.h>
Cardinal MrmFetchWidget(*hierarchy_id*, *index*, *parent_widget*, *widget*, *class***)**
  MrmHierarchy *hierarchy_id*;
  String *index*;
  Widget *parent_widget*;
  Widget **widget*;
  MrmType **class*;

Description

The **MrmFetchWidget** function fetches and creates an indexed application widget and its children. The indexed application widget is any widget that is named in UIL and that is not the child of any other widget in the **uid** hierarchy. In fetch operations, the fetched widget's subtree is also fetched and created. This widget must not appear as the child of a widget within its own subtree. **MrmFetchWidget** does not execute **XtManageChild** for the newly created widget.

hierarchy_id	Specifies the ID of the **uid** hierarchy that contains the interface definition. The *hierarchy_id* was returned in a previous call to **MrmOpenHierarchy**.
index	Specifies the UIL name of the widget to fetch.
parent_widget	Specifies the parent widget ID.
widget	Returns the widget ID of the created widget. If this is not NULL when you call **MrmFetchWidgetOverride**, MRM assumes that the widget has already been created and **MrmFetchWidgetOverride** returns **MrmFAILURE**.
class	Returns the class code identifying MRM's widget class. The widget class code for the main window widget, for example, is **MRMwcMainWindow**. Literals identifying MRM widget class codes are defined in **Mrm.h**.

An application can fetch any named widget in the **uid** hierarchy using **MrmFetchWidget**. **MrmFetchWidget** can be called at any time to fetch a widget that was not fetched at application startup. **MrmFetchWidget** determines if a widget has already been fetched by checking *widget* for a NULL value. Non-NULL values signify that the widget has already been fetched, and **MrmFetchWidget** fails. **MrmFetchWidget** can be used to defer fetching pop-up widgets until they are first referenced (presumably in a callback), and then used to fetch them once.

MrmFetchWidget can also create multiple instances of a widget (and its subtree). In this case, the **uid** definition functions as a template; a widget definition can be fetched any number of times. An application can use this to make multiple instances of a widget, for example, in a dialog box box or menu.

The index (UIL name) that identifies the widget must be known to the application.

Return Value

This function returns one of these status return constants:

MrmSUCCESS   The function executed successfully.

MrmBAD_HIERARCHY
                        The hierarchy ID was invalid.

MrmNOT_FOUND   The widget was not found in UID hierarchy.

MrmFAILURE   The function failed.

Related Information

MrmFetchWidgetOverride(3X)

MrmFetchWidgetOverride

Purpose

Fetches any indexed (UIL named) application widget. It overrides the arguments specified for this application widget in UIL.

AES Support Level

Trial-use

Synopsis

#include <Mrm/MrmPublic.h>
Cardinal MrmFetchWidgetOverride(*hierarchy_id* , *index* , *parent_widget* , *override_name* , *override_args* , *override_num_args* , *widget* , *class* **)**
  MrmHierarchy *hierarchy_id* ;
  String *index* ;
  Widget *parent_widget* ;
  String *override_name* ;
  ArgList *override_args* ;
  Cardinal *override_num_args* ;
  Widget **widget* ;
  MrmType **class* ;

Description

The **MrmFetchWidgetOverride** function is the extended version of **MrmFetchWidget**. It is identical to **MrmFetchWidget**, except that it allows the caller to override the widget's name and any arguments that **MrmFetchWidget** would otherwise retrieve from the UID file or one of the defaulting mechanisms. That is, the override argument list is not limited to those arguments in the UID file.

The override arguments apply only to the widget fetched and returned by this function. Its children (subtree) do not receive any override parameters.

hierarchy_id   Specifies the ID of the UID hierarchy that contains the interface definition. The *hierarchy_id* was returned in a previous call to **MrmOpenHierarchy**.

index   Specifies the UIL name of the widget to fetch.

parent_widget   Specifies the parent widget ID.

override_name   Specifies the name to override the widget name. Use a NULL value if you do not want to override the widget name.

override_args   Specifies the override argument list, exactly as given to **XtCreateWidget** (conversion complete and so forth). Use a NULL value if you do not want to override the argument list.

override_num_args   Specifies the number of arguments in *override_args*.

widget   Returns the widget ID of the created widget. If this is not NULL when you call **MrmFetchWidgetOverride**, MRM assumes that the widget has already been created and **MrmFetchWidgetOverride** returns **MrmFAILURE**.

class   Returns the class code identifying MRM's widget class. Literals identifying MRM widget class codes are defined in the include file **<Mrm/MrmPublic.h>**.

Return Value

This function returns one of these status return constants:

MrmSUCCESS   The function executed successfully.

MrmBAD_HIERARCHY
                        The hierarchy ID was invalid.

MrmNOT_FOUND   The widget was not found in UID hierarchy.

MrmFAILURE   The function failed.

Related Information

MrmFetchWidget(3X)

MrmInitialize

Purpose

Prepares an application to use MRM widget-fetching facilities.

AES Support Level

Trial-use

Synopsis

void MrmInitialize()

Description

The **MrmInitialize** function must be called to prepare an application to use MRM widget-fetching facilities. You must call this function prior to fetching a widget. However, it is good programming practice to call **MrmInitialize** prior to performing any MRM operations.

MrmInitialize initializes the internal data structures that MRM needs to successfully perform type conversion on arguments and to successfully access widget creation facilities. An application must call **MrmInitialize** before it uses other MRM functions.

MrmOpenHierarchy

Purpose

Allocates a hierarchy ID and opens all the UID files in the hierarchy.

AES Support Level

Trial-use

Synopsis

#include <Mrm/MrmPublic.h>
Cardinal MrmOpenHierarchy(*num_files*, *file_names_list*,
ancillary_structures_list , *hierarchy_id*)
    MrmCount *num_files* ;
    String *file_names_list* [];
    MrmOsOpenParamPtr **ancillary_structures_list* ;
    MrmHierarchy **hierarchy_id* ;

Description

The **MrmOpenHierarchy** function allows the user to specify the list of
UID files that MRM searches in subsequent fetch operations. All
subsequent fetch operations return the first occurrence of the named item
encountered while traversing the UID hierarchy from the first list element
(UID file specification) to the last list element. This function also allocates
a hierarchy ID and opens all the UID files in the hierarchy. It initializes the
optimized search lists in the hierarchy. If **MrmOpenHierarchy** encounters
any errors during its execution, any files that were opened are closed.

The application must call **XtAppInitialize** before calling **MrmOpenHierarchy**.

num_files   Specifies the number of files in the name list.

file_names_list   Specifies an array of character strings that identify the UID files.

ancillary_structures_list

A list of operating-system-dependent ancillary structures corresponding to such things as filenames, clobber flag, and so forth. This argument should be NULL for most operations. If you need to reference this structure, see the definition of **MrmOsOpenParamPtr** in **MrmPublic.h** for more information.

hierarchy_id   Returns the search hierarchy ID. The search hierarchy ID identifies the list of UID files that MRM searches (in order) when performing subsequent fetch calls.

Each UID file string in *file_names_list* can specify either a full pathname or a filename. If a UID file string has a leading slash (/), it specifies a full pathname, and MRM opens the file as specified. Otherwise, the UID file string specifies a filename. In this case MRM looks for the file along a search path specified by the **UIDPATH** environment variable or by a default search path, which varies depending on whether or not the **XAPPLRESDIR** environment variable is set. The filename is substituted for each occurrence of %U in the search path.

The **UIDPATH** environment variable specifies a search path and naming conventions associated with UID files. It can contain the substitution field %U, where the UID file string from the *file_names_list* argument to **MrmOpenHierarchy** is substituted for %U. It can also contain the substitution fields accepted by **XtResolvePathname**. For example, the following **UIDPATH** value and **MrmOpenHierarchy** call cause MRM to open two separate UID files:

```
UIDPATH=/uidlib/%L/%U.uid:/uidlib/%U/%L
 static char *uid_files[] = {"/usr/users/me/test.uid", "test2"};
  MrmHierarchy *Hierarchy_id;
  MrmOpenHierarchy((MrmCount)2,uid_files, NULL, Hierarchy_id)
```

MRM opens the first file, **/usr/users/me/test.uid**, as specified in the *file_names_list* argument to **MrmOpenHierarchy**, because the UID file string in the *file_names_list* argument specifies a full pathname. MRM looks for the second file, **test2**, first as **/uidlib/%L/test2.uid** and second as **/uidlib/test2/%L**, where the current setting of the **xnlLanguage** resource or the **LANG** environment variable is substituted for %L.

After **MrmOpenHierarchy** opens the UID hierarchy, you should not delete or modify the UID files until you close the UID hierarchy by calling **MrmCloseHierarchy**.

If **UIDPATH** is not set but the environment variable **XAPPLRESDIR** is set, MRM searches the following pathnames:

```
%U
$XAPPLRESDIR/%L/uid/%N/%U
$XAPPLRESDIR/%l/uid/%N/%U
$XAPPLRESDIR/uid/%N/%U
$XAPPLRESDIR/%L/uid/%U
$XAPPLRESDIR/%l/uid/%U
$XAPPLRESDIR/uid/%U
$HOME/uid/%U
$HOME/%U
/usr/lib/X11/%L/uid/%N/%U
/usr/lib/X11/%l/uid/%N/%U
/usr/lib/X11/uid/%N/%U
/usr/lib/X11/%L/uid/%U
/usr/lib/X11/%l/uid/%U
/usr/lib/X11/uid/%U
/usr/include/X11/uid/%U
```

If neither **UIDPATH** nor **XAPPLRESDIR** is set, MRM searches the following pathnames:

```
%U
$HOME/%L/uid/%N/%U
$HOME/%l/uid/%N/%U
$HOME/uid/%N/%U
$HOME/%L/uid/%U
```

$HOME/%l/uid/%U
$HOME/uid/%U
$HOME/%U
/usr/lib/X11/%L/uid/%N/%U
/usr/lib/X11/%l/uid/%N/%U
/usr/lib/X11/uid/%N/%U
/usr/lib/X11/%L/uid/%U
/usr/lib/X11/%l/uid/%U
/usr/lib/X11/uid/%U
/usr/include/X11/uid/%U

The following substitutions are used in these paths:

%U The UID file string, from the *file_names_list* argument.

%N The class name of the application.

%L The value of the **xnlLanguage** resource or the **LANG** environment variable.

%l The language component of the **xnlLanguage** resource or the **LANG** environment variable.

Return Value

This function returns one of these status return constants:

MrmSUCCESS   The function executed successfully.

MrmNOT_FOUND   File not found.

MrmFAILURE   The function failed.

Related Information

MrmCloseHierarchy(3X)

MrmRegisterClass

Purpose

Saves the information needed for MRM to access the widget creation function for user-defined widgets.

AES Support Level

Trial-use

Synopsis

#include <Mrm/MrmPublic.h>
Cardinal MrmRegisterClass(*class_code*, *class_name*, *create_name*, *create_proc*, *class_record*)
    MrmType *class_code*;
    String *class_name*;
    String *create_name*;
    Widget (* *create_proc*) ();
    WidgetClass *class_record*;

Description

The **MrmRegisterClass** function allows MRM to access user-defined widget classes. This function registers the necessary information for MRM to create widgets of this class. You must call **MrmRegisterClass** prior to fetching any user-defined class widget.

MrmRegisterClass saves the information needed to access the widget creation function and to do type conversion of argument lists by using the information in MRM databases.

class_code This argument is ignored; it is present for compatibility with previous releases.

class_name This argument is ignored; it is present for compatibility with previous releases.

create_name Specifies the case-sensitive name of the low-level widget creation function for the class. An example from the Motif Toolkit is **XmCreateLabel**. Arguments are *parent_widget*, *name*, *override_arglist*, and *override_argcount*.

For user-defined widgets, *create_name* is the creation procedure in the UIL that defines this widget.

create_proc Specifies the address of the creation function that you named in *create_name*.

class_record Specifies a pointer to the class record.

Return Value

This function returns one of these status return constants:

MrmSUCCESS The function executed successfully.

MrmFAILURE The function failed.

MrmRegisterNames

Purpose

Registers the values associated with the names referenced in UIL (for example, UIL callback function names or UIL identifier names).

AES Support Level

Trial-use

Synopsis

#include <Mrm/MrmPublic.h>
Cardinal MrmRegisterNames(*register_list* **,** *register_count* **)**
    MrmRegisterArglist *register_list* **;**
    MrmCount *register_count* **;**

Description

The **MrmRegisterNames** function registers a vector of names and associated values for access in MRM. The values can be callback functions, pointers to user-defined data, or any other values. The information provided is used to resolve symbolic references occurring in UID files to their run-time values. For callbacks, this information provides the procedure address required by the Motif Toolkit. For names used as identifiers in UIL, this information provides any run-time mapping the application needs.

This function is similar to **MrmRegisterNamesInHierarchy**, except that the scope of the names registered by **MrmRegisterNamesInHierarchy** is limited to the hierarchy specified in the call to that function, whereas the names registered by **MrmRegisterNames** have global scope. When MRM looks up a name, it first tries to find the name among those registered for the given hierarchy. If that lookup fails, it tries to find the name among those registered globally.

register_list   Specifies a list of name/value pairs for the names to be registered. Each name is a case-sensitive, NULL-terminated ASCII string. Each value is a 32-bit quantity, interpreted as a procedure address if the name is a callback function, and uninterpreted otherwise.

register_count Specifies the number of entries in *register_list*.

The names in the list are case-sensitive. The list can be either ordered or unordered.

Callback functions registered through **MrmRegisterNames** can be either regular or creation callbacks. Regular callbacks have declarations determined by Motif Toolkit and user requirements. Creation callbacks have the same format as any other callback:

void CallBackProc(*widget_id*, *tag*, *callback_data*)
      Widget *widget_id;
      Opaque *tag*;
      XmAnyCallbackStruct *callback_data;

widget_id   Specifies the widget ID associated with the widget performing the callback (as in any callback function).

tag   Specifies the tag value (as in any callback function).

callback_data   Specifies a widget-specific data structure. This data structure has a minimum of two members: event and reason. The reason member is always set to **MrmCR_CREATE**.

Note that the widget name and parent are available from the widget record accessible through *widget_id*.

Return Value

This function returns one of these status return constants:

MrmSUCCESS   The function executed successfully.

MrmFAILURE   The function failed.

MrmRegisterNamesInHierarchy

Purpose

Registers the values associated with the names referenced in UIL within a single hierarchy (for example, UIL callback function names or UIL identifier names).

AES Support Level

Trial-use

Synopsis

#include <Mrm/MrmPublic.h>
Cardinal MrmRegisterNamesInHierarchy(*hierarchy_id* , *register_list* , *register_count*)
    MrmHierarchy *hierarchy_id* ;
    MrmRegisterArglist *register_list* ;
    MrmCount *register_count* ;

Description

The **MrmRegisterNamesInHierarchy** function registers a vector of names and associated values for access in MRM. The values can be callback functions, pointers to user-defined data, or any other values. The information provided is used to resolve symbolic references occurring in UID files to their run-time values.For callbacks, this information provides the procedure address required by the Motif Toolkit. For names used as identifiers in UIL, this information provides any run-time mapping the application needs.

This function is similar to **MrmRegisterNames**, except that the scope of the names registered by **MrmRegisterNamesInHierarchy** is limited to the hierarchy specified by *hierarchy_id*, whereas the names registered by **MrmRegisterNames** have global scope. When MRM looks up a name, it first tries to find the name among those registered for the given hierarchy. If that lookup fails, it tries to find the name among those registered globally.

hierarchy_id   Specifies the hierarchy with which the names are to be associated.

register_list   Specifies a list of name/value pairs for the names to be registered. Each name is a case-sensitive, NULL-terminated ASCII string. Each value is a 32-bit quantity, interpreted as a procedure address if the name is a callback function, and uninterpreted otherwise.

register_count Specifies the number of entries in *register_list*.

The names in the list are case-sensitive. The list can be either ordered or unordered.

Callback functions registered through **MrmRegisterNamesInHierarchy** can be either regular or creation callbacks. Regular callbacks have declarations determined by Motif Toolkit and user requirements. Creation callbacks have the same format as any other callback:

void CallBackProc(*widget_id*, *tag*, *callback_data*)
        Widget *widget_id;
        Opaque *tag*;
        XmAnyCallbackStruct *callback_data;

widget_id	Specifies the widget ID associated with the widget performing the callback (as in any callback function).
tag	Specifies the tag value (as in any callback function).
callback_data	Specifies a widget-specific data structure. This data structure has a minimum of two members: event and reason. The reason member is always set to **MrmCR_CREATE**.

Note that the widget name and parent are available from the widget record accessible through *widget_id*.

Return Value

This function returns one of these status return constants:

MrmSUCCESS   The function executed successfully.

MrmFAILURE   The function failed.

Object

Purpose

The Object widget class

AES Support Level

Full-use

Synopsis

#include <Xm/Xm.h>

Description

Object is never instantiated. Its sole purpose is as a supporting superclass for other widget classes.

Classes

The class pointer is **objectClass**.

The class name is **Object**.

New Resources

The following table defines a set of widget resources used by the programmer to specify data. The programmer can also set the resource values for the inherited classes to set attributes for this widget. To reference a resource by name or by class in a .Xdefaults file, remove the **XmN** or **XmC** prefix and use the remaining letters. To specify one of the defined values for a resource in a .Xdefaults file, remove the **Xm** prefix and use the remaining letters (in either lowercase or uppercase, but include any underscores between words). The codes in the access column indicate if the given resource can be set at creation time (**C**), set by using **XtSetValues** (**S**), retrieved by using **XtGetValues** (**G**), or is not applicable (**N/A**).

Object Resource Set		
Name	**Default**	**Access**
Class	**Type**	
XmNdestroyCallback	NULL	C
XmCCallback	XtCallbackList	

XmNdestroyCallback
> Specifies a list of callbacks that is called when the gadget is destroyed.

Translations

There are no translation for Object.

OverrideShell

Purpose

The OverrideShell widget class

AES Support Level

Full-use

Synopsis

#include <Xm/Xm.h>
#include <X11/Shell.h>

Description

OverrideShell is used for shell windows that completely bypass the window manager, for example, PopupMenu shells.

Classes

OverrideShell inherits behavior and resources from **Core**, **Composite**, and **Shell**.

The class pointer is **overrideShellWidgetClass**.

The class name is **OverrideShell**.

New Resources

OverrideShell defines no new resources, but overrides the **XmNoverrideRedirect** and **XmNsaveUnder** resources in the **Shell** class.

Inherited Resources

OverrideShell inherits behavior and resources from the following superclasses. For a complete description of each resource, refer to the man page for that superclass.

The following table defines a set of widget resources used by the programmer to specify data. The programmer can also set the resource values for the inherited classes to set attributes for this widget. To reference a resource by name or by class in a .Xdefaults file, remove the **XmN** or **XmC** prefix and use the remaining letters. To specify one of the defined values for a resource in a .Xdefaults file, remove the **Xm** prefix and use the remaining letters (in either lowercase or uppercase, but include any underscores between words). The codes in the access column indicate if the given resource can be set at creation time (**C**), set by using **XtSetValues** (**S**), retrieved by using **XtGetValues** (**G**), or is not applicable (**N/A**).

Shell Resource Set		
Name	**Default**	**Access**
Class	**Type**	
XmNallowShellResize	False	CG
XmCAllowShellResize	Boolean	
XmNcreatePopupChildProc	NULL	CSG
XmCCreatePopupChildProc	(*)()	
XmNgeometry	NULL	CSG
XmCGeometry	String	
XmNoverrideRedirect	True	CSG
XmCOverrideRedirect	Boolean	
XmNpopdownCallback	NULL	C
XmCCallback	XtCallbackList	
XmNpopupCallback	NULL	C
XmCCallback	XtCallbackList	
XmNsaveUnder	True	CSG
XmCSaveUnder	Boolean	
XmNvisual	CopyFromParent	CSG
XmCVisual	Visual *	

Composite Resource Set		
Name	**Default**	**Access**
Class	**Type**	
XmNchildren	NULL	G
XmCReadOnly	WidgetList	
XmNinsertPosition	NULL	CSG
XmCInsertPosition	(*)()	
XmNnumChildren	0	G
XmCReadOnly	Cardinal	

Core Resource Set		
Name	**Default**	**Access**
Class	**Type**	
XmNaccelerators	dynamic	CSG
XmCAccelerators	XtAccelerators	
XmNancestorSensitive	dynamic	G
XmCSensitive	Boolean	
XmNbackground	dynamic	CSG
XmCBackground	Pixel	
XmNbackgroundPixmap	XmUNSPECIFIED_PIXMAP	CSG
XmCPixmap	Pixmap	
XmNborderColor	XtDefaultForeground	CSG
XmCBorderColor	Pixel	
XmNborderPixmap	XmUNSPECIFIED_PIXMAP	CSG
XmCPixmap	Pixmap	
XmNborderWidth	1	CSG
XmCBorderWidth	Dimension	
XmNcolormap	dynamic	CG
XmCColormap	Colormap	
XmNdepth	dynamic	CG
XmCDepth	int	
XmNdestroyCallback	NULL	C
XmCCallback	XtCallbackList	
XmNheight	dynamic	CSG
XmCHeight	Dimension	
XmNinitialResourcesPersistent	True	C
XmCInitialResourcesPersistent	Boolean	
XmNmappedWhenManaged	True	CSG
XmCMappedWhenManaged	Boolean	
XmNscreen	dynamic	CG
XmCScreen	Screen *	

Name	Default	Access
Class	Type	
XmNsensitive	True	CSG
XmCSensitive	Boolean	
XmNtranslations	dynamic	CSG
XmCTranslations	XtTranslations	
XmNwidth	dynamic	CSG
XmCWidth	Dimension	
XmNx	0	CSG
XmCPosition	Position	
XmNy	0	CSG
XmCPosition	Position	

Translations

There are no translations for OverrideShell.

Related Information

Composite(3X), **Core(3X)**, and **Shell(3X)**.

RectObj

Purpose

The RectObj widget class

AES Support Level

Full-use

Synopsis

#include <Xm/Xm.h>

Description

RectObj is never instantiated. Its sole purpose is as a supporting superclass for other widget classes.

Classes

RectObj inherits behavior and a resource from **Object**.

The class pointer is **rectObjClass**.

The class name is **RectObj**.

New Resources

The following table defines a set of widget resources used by the programmer to specify data. The programmer can also set the resource values for the inherited classes to set attributes for this widget. To reference a resource by name or by class in a .Xdefaults file, remove the **XmN** or **XmC** prefix and use the remaining letters. To specify one of the defined values for a resource in a .Xdefaults file, remove the **Xm** prefix and use the remaining letters (in either lowercase or uppercase, but include any underscores between words). The codes in the access column indicate if the given resource can be set at creation time (**C**), set by using **XtSetValues** (**S**), retrieved by using **XtGetValues** (**G**), or is not applicable (**N/A**).

RectObj Resource Set		
Name **Class**	**Default** **Type**	**Access**
XmNancestorSensitive XmCSensitive	dynamic Boolean	G
XmNborderWidth XmCBorderWidth	1 Dimension	CSG
XmNheight XmCHeight	dynamic Dimension	CSG
XmNsensitive XmCSensitive	True Boolean	CSG
XmNwidth XmCWidth	dynamic Dimension	CSG
XmNx XmCPosition	0 Position	CSG
XmNy XmCPosition	0 Position	CSG

XmNancestorSensitive

Specifies whether the immediate parent of the gadget receives input events. Use the function **XtSetSensitive** if you are changing the argument to preserve data integrity (see **XmNsensitive** below). The default is the bitwise AND of the parent's **XmNsensitive** and **XmNancestorSensitive** resources.

XmNborderWidth

Specifies the width of the border placed around the RectObj's rectangular display area.

XmNheight Specifies the inside height (excluding the border) of the RectObj's rectangular display area.

XmNsensitive

Determines whether a RectObj receives input events. If a RectObj is sensitive, the parent dispatches to the gadget all keyboard, mouse button, motion, window enter/leave, and focus events. Insensitive gadgets do not receive these events. Use the function **XtSetSensitive** to change the sensitivity argument. Using **XtSetSensitive** ensures that if a parent widget has **XmNsensitive** set to False, the ancestor-sensitive flag of all its children is appropriately set.

XmNwidth Specifies the inside width (excluding the border) of the RectObj's rectangular display area.

XmNx Specifies the x-coordinate of the upper left outside corner of the RectObj's rectangular display area. The value is relative to the upper left inside corner of the parent window.

XmNy Specifies the y-coordinate of the upper left outside corner of the RectObj's rectangular display area. The value is relative to the upper left inside corner of the parent window.

Inherited Resources

RectObj inherits behavior and a resource from **Object**. For a description of this resource, refer to the **Object** man page.

Object Resource Set		
Name	**Default**	**Access**
Class	**Type**	
XmNdestroyCallback	NULL	C
XmCCallback	XtCallbackList	

Translations

There are no translations for RectObj.

Related Information

Object(3X).

Shell

Purpose

The Shell widget class

AES Support Level

Full-use

Synopsis

#include <Xm/Xm.h>
#include <X11/Shell.h>

Description

Shell is a top-level widget (with only one managed child) that encapsulates the interaction with the window manager.

When the width of both the shell and its child are specified, the larger of the shell's width and the child's width is used for both widgets. When either the shell's width or the child's width, but not the other, is specified, the specified width is used for both widgets. The same relations hold for the height of the shell and its child.

Classes

Shell inherits behavior and resources from **Composite** and **Core**.

The class pointer is **shellWidgetClass**.

The class name is **Shell**.

New Resources

The following table defines a set of widget resources used by the programmer to specify data. The programmer can also set the resource values for the inherited classes to set attributes for this widget. To reference a resource by name or by class in a .Xdefaults file, remove the **XmN** or **XmC** prefix and use the remaining letters. To specify one of the defined values for a resource in a .Xdefaults file, remove the **Xm** prefix and use the remaining letters (in either lowercase or uppercase, but include any underscores between words). The codes in the access column indicate if the given resource can be set at creation time (**C**), set by using **XtSetValues** (**S**), retrieved by using **XtGetValues** (**G**), or is not applicable (**N/A**).

Shell Resource Set		
Name	**Default**	**Access**
Class	**Type**	
XmNallowShellResize	False	CG
XmCAllowShellResize	Boolean	
XmNcreatePopupChildProc	NULL	CSG
XmCCreatePopupChildProc	(*)()	
XmNgeometry	NULL	CSG
XmCGeometry	String	
XmNoverrideRedirect	False	CSG
XmCOverrideRedirect	Boolean	
XmNpopdownCallback	NULL	C
XmCCallback	XtCallbackList	
XmNpopupCallback	NULL	C
XmCCallback	XtCallbackList	
XmNsaveUnder	False	CSG
XmCSaveUnder	Boolean	
XmNvisual	CopyFromParent	CSG
XmCVisual	Visual *	

XmNallowShellResize

Specifies that if this resource is False, the Shell widget instance returns **XtGeometryNo** to all geometry requests from its children.

XmNcreatePopupChildProc

Specifies the pointer to a function that is called when the Shell widget instance is popped up by **XtPopup**. The function creates the child widget when the shell is popped up instead of when the application starts up. This can be used if the child needs to be reconfigured each time the shell is popped up. The function takes one argument, the popup shell, and returns no result. It is called after the popup callbacks specified by **XmNpopupCallback**.

XmNgeometry

Specifies the desired geometry for the widget instance. This resource is examined only when the widget instance is unrealized and the number of its managed children is changed. It is to change the values of the **XmNx**, **XmNy**, **XmNwidth**, and **XmNheight** resources.

XmNoverrideRedirect

Specifies this is True if the widget instance is a temporary window which should be ignored by the window manager. Applications and users should not normally alter this resource.

XmNpopdownCallback

Specifies a list of callbacks that is called when the widget instance is popped down by **XtPopdown**.

XmNpopupCallback

Specifies a list of callbacks that is called when the widget instance is popped up by **XtPopup**.

XmNsaveUnder

Specifies a True value if it is desirable to save the contents of the screen beneath this widget instance, avoiding expose events when the instance is unmapped. This is a hint, and an implementation may save contents whenever it desires, including always or never.

XmNvisual Specifies the visual used in creating the widget.

Inherited Resources

Shell inherits behavior and resources from the following superclass. For a complete description of each resource, refer to the man page for that superclass.

Composite Resource Set		
Name **Class**	**Default** **Type**	**Access**
XmNchildren XmCReadOnly	NULL WidgetList	G
XmNinsertPosition XmCInsertPosition	NULL (*)()	CSG
XmNnumChildren XmCReadOnly	0 Cardinal	G

Core Resource Set		
Name	**Default**	**Access**
Class	**Type**	
XmNaccelerators	dynamic	CSG
XmCAccelerators	XtAccelerators	
XmNancestorSensitive	dynamic	G
XmCSensitive	Boolean	
XmNbackground	dynamic	CSG
XmCBackground	Pixel	
XmNbackgroundPixmap	XmUNSPECIFIED_PIXMAP	CSG
XmCPixmap	Pixmap	
XmNborderColor	XtDefaultForeground	CSG
XmCBorderColor	Pixel	
XmNborderPixmap	XmUNSPECIFIED_PIXMAP	CSG
XmCPixmap	Pixmap	
XmNborderWidth	1	CSG
XmCBorderWidth	Dimension	
XmNcolormap	dynamic	CG
XmCColormap	Colormap	
XmNdepth	dynamic	CG
XmCDepth	int	
XmNdestroyCallback	NULL	C
XmCCallback	XtCallbackList	
XmNheight	dynamic	CSG
XmCHeight	Dimension	
XmNinitialResourcesPersistent	True	C
XmCInitialResourcesPersistent	Boolean	
XmNmappedWhenManaged	True	CSG
XmCMappedWhenManaged	Boolean	
XmNscreen	dynamic	CG
XmCScreen	Screen *	

Name	Default	Access
Class	Type	
XmNsensitive	True	CSG
XmCSensitive	Boolean	
XmNtranslations	dynamic	CSG
XmCTranslations	XtTranslations	
XmNwidth	dynamic	CSG
XmCWidth	Dimension	
XmNx	0	CSG
XmCPosition	Position	
XmNy	0	CSG
XmCPosition	Position	

Translations

There are no translations for Shell.

Related Information

Composite(3X) and **Core(3X)**.

TopLevelShell

Purpose

The TopLevelShell widget class

AES Support Level

Full-use

Synopsis

#include <Xm/Xm.h>
#include <X11/Shell.h>

Description

TopLevelShell is used for normal top-level windows such as any additional top-level widgets an application needs.

Classes

TopLevelShell inherits behavior and resources from **Core**, **Composite**, **Shell**, **WMShell**, and **VendorShell**.

The class pointer is **topLevelShellWidgetClass**.

The class name is **TopLevelShell**.

New Resources

The following table defines a set of widget resources used by the programmer to specify data. The programmer can also set the resource values for the inherited classes to set attributes for this widget. To reference a resource by name or by class in a .Xdefaults file, remove the **XmN** or **XmC** prefix and use the remaining letters. To specify one of the defined values for a resource in a .Xdefaults file, remove the **Xm** prefix and use the remaining letters (in either lowercase or uppercase, but include any underscores between words). The codes in the access column indicate if the given resource can be set at creation time (**C**), set by using **XtSetValues** (**S**), retrieved by using **XtGetValues** (**G**), or is not applicable (**N/A**).

TopLevelShell Resource Set		
Name	**Default**	**Access**
Class	**Type**	
XmNiconic	False	CSG
XmCIconic	Boolean	
XmNiconName	NULL	CSG
XmCIconName	String	
XmNiconNameEncoding	XA_STRING	CSG
XmCIconNameEncoding	Atom	

XmNiconic   Specifies that if this is True when the widget instance is realized, the widget instance indicates to the window manager that the application wishes to start as an icon, irrespective of the **XmNinitialState** resource. This resource is examined by the Intrinsics only during a call to **XtRealize**; it is ignored at all other times.

XmNiconName

Specifies the short form of the application name to be displayed by the window manager when the application is iconified.

XmNiconNameEncoding

Specifies a property type that represents the encoding of the **XmNiconName** string.

Inherited Resources

TopLevelShell inherits behavior and resources from the following superclasses. For a complete description of each resource, refer to the man page for that superclass.

VendorShell Resource Set		

Name
    Class
	Default
	    Type
		Access

XmNdefaultFontList
    XmCDefaultFontList
	dynamic
	    XmFontList
		C

XmNdeleteResponse
    XmCDeleteResponse
	XmDESTROY
	    unsigned char
		CSG

XmNkeyboardFocusPolicy
    XmCKeyboardFocusPolicy
	XmEXPLICIT
	    unsigned char
		CSG

XmNmwmDecorations
    XmCMwmDecorations
	-1
	    int
		CSG

XmNmwmFunctions
    XmCMwmFunctions
	-1
	    int
		CSG

XmNmwmInputMode
    XmCMwmInputMode
	-1
	    int
		CSG

XmNmwmMenu
    XmCMwmMenu
	NULL
	    String
		CSG

WMShell Resource Set		
Name **Class**	**Default** **Type**	**Access**
XmNbaseHeight XmCBaseHeight	XtUnspecifiedShellInt int	CSG
XmNbaseWidth XmCBaseWidth	XtUnspecifiedShellInt int	CSG
XmNheightInc XmCHeightInc	XtUnspecifiedShellInt int	CSG
XmNiconMask XmCIconMask	NULL Pixmap	CSG
XmNiconPixmap XmCIconPixmap	NULL Pixmap	CSG
XmNiconWindow XmCIconWindow	NULL Window	CSG
XmNiconX XmCIconX	-1 int	CSG
XmNiconY XmCIconY	-1 int	CSG
XmNinitialState XmCInitialState	NormalState int	CSG
XmNinput XmCInput	True Boolean	CSG
XmNmaxAspectX XmCMaxAspectX	XtUnspecifiedShellInt int	CSG
XmNmaxAspectY XmCMaxAspectY	XtUnspecifiedShellInt int	CSG
XmNmaxHeight XmCMaxHeight	XtUnspecifiedShellInt int	CSG
XmNmaxWidth XmCMaxWidth	XtUnspecifiedShellInt int	CSG

Name	Default	Access
Class	**Type**	
XmNminAspectX	XtUnspecifiedShellInt	CSG
XmCMinAspectX	int	
XmNminAspectY	XtUnspecifiedShellInt	CSG
XmCMinAspectY	int	
XmNminHeight	XtUnspecifiedShellInt	CSG
XmCMinHeight	int	
XmNminWidth	XtUnspecifiedShellInt	CSG
XmCMinWidth	int	
XmNtitle	dynamic	CSG
XmCTitle	String	
XmNtitleEncoding	XA_STRING	CSG
XmCTitleEncoding	Atom	
XmNtransient	False	CSG
XmCTransient	Boolean	
XmNwaitForWm	True	CSG
XmCWaitForWm	Boolean	
XmNwidthInc	XtUnspecifiedShellInt	CSG
XmCWidthInc	int	
XmNwindowGroup	dynamic	CSG
XmCWindowGroup	Window	
XmNwinGravity	dynamic	CSG
XmCWinGravity	int	
XmNwmTimeout	5000 ms	CSG
XmCWmTimeout	int	

Shell Resource Set		
Name	**Default**	**Access**
Class	**Type**	
XmNallowShellResize	False	CG
XmCAllowShellResize	Boolean	
XmNcreatePopupChildProc	NULL	CSG
XmCCreatePopupChildProc	(*)()	
XmNgeometry	NULL	CSG
XmCGeometry	String	
XmNoverrideRedirect	False	CSG
XmCOverrideRedirect	Boolean	
XmNpopdownCallback	NULL	C
XmCCallback	XtCallbackList	
XmNpopupCallback	NULL	C
XmCCallback	XtCallbackList	
XmNsaveUnder	False	CSG
XmCSaveUnder	Boolean	
XmNvisual	CopyFromParent	CSG
XmCVisual	Visual *	

Composite Resource Set		
Name	**Default**	**Access**
Class	**Type**	
XmNchildren	NULL	G
XmCReadOnly	WidgetList	
XmNinsertPosition	NULL	CSG
XmCInsertPosition	(*)()	
XmNnumChildren	0	G
XmCReadOnly	Cardinal	

Core Resource Set		
Name	**Default**	**Access**
Class	**Type**	
XmNaccelerators	dynamic	CSG
XmCAccelerators	XtAccelerators	
XmNancestorSensitive	dynamic	G
XmCSensitive	Boolean	
XmNbackground	dynamic	CSG
XmCBackground	Pixel	
XmNbackgroundPixmap	XmUNSPECIFIED_PIXMAP	CSG
XmCPixmap	Pixmap	
XmNborderColor	XtDefaultForeground	CSG
XmCBorderColor	Pixel	
XmNborderPixmap	XmUNSPECIFIED_PIXMAP	CSG
XmCPixmap	Pixmap	
XmNborderWidth	1	CSG
XmCBorderWidth	Dimension	
XmNcolormap	dynamic	CG
XmCColormap	Colormap	
XmNdepth	dynamic	CG
XmCDepth	int	
XmNdestroyCallback	NULL	C
XmCCallback	XtCallbackList	
XmNheight	dynamic	CSG
XmCHeight	Dimension	
XmNinitialResourcesPersistent	True	C
XmCInitialResourcesPersistent	Boolean	
XmNmappedWhenManaged	True	CSG
XmCMappedWhenManaged	Boolean	
XmNscreen	dynamic	CG
XmCScreen	Screen *	

Name	Default	Access
Class	Type	
XmNsensitive	True	CSG
XmCSensitive	Boolean	
XmNtranslations	dynamic	CSG
XmCTranslations	XtTranslations	
XmNwidth	dynamic	CSG
XmCWidth	Dimension	
XmNx	0	CSG
XmCPosition	Position	
XmNy	0	CSG
XmCPosition	Position	

Translations

There are no translations for TopLevelShell.

Related Information

Composite(3X), **Core(3X),** **Shell(3X),** **WMShell(3X),** and **VendorShell(3X).**

TransientShell

Purpose

The TransientShell widget class

AES Support Level

Full-use

Synopsis

#include <Xm/Xm.h>
#include <X11/Shell.h>

Description

TransientShell is used for shell windows that can be manipulated by the window manager but are not allowed to be iconified separately. For example, Dialog boxes make no sense without their associated application. They are iconified by the window manager only if the main application shell is iconified.

Classes

TransientShell inherits behavior and resources from **Core**, **Composite**, **Shell**, **WMShell**, and **VendorShell**.

The class pointer is **transientShellWidgetClass**.

The class name is **TransientShell**.

New Resources

The following table defines a set of widget resources used by the programmer to specify data. The programmer can also set the resource values for the inherited classes to set attributes for this widget. To reference a resource by name or by class in a .Xdefaults file, remove the **XmN** or **XmC** prefix and use the remaining letters. To specify one of the defined values for a resource in a .Xdefaults file, remove the **Xm** prefix and use the remaining letters (in either lowercase or uppercase, but include any underscores between words). The codes in the access column indicate if the given resource can be set at creation time (**C**), set by using **XtSetValues** (**S**), retrieved by using **XtGetValues** (**G**), or is not applicable (**N/A**).

In addition to these new resources, new resources, **TransientShell** overrides the **XmNsaveUnder** resource in **Shell** and the **XmNtransient** resource in **WMShell**.

TransientShell Resource Set		
Name	**Default**	**Access**
Class	**Type**	
XmNtransientFor	NULL	CSG
XmCTransientFor	Widget	

XmNtransientFor

Specifies a widget for which the shell acts as a pop-up. If this resource is NULL or is a widget that has not been realized, the **XmNwindowGroup** is used instead.

Inherited Resources

TransientShell inherits behavior and resources from the following superclasses. For a complete description of each resource, refer to the man page for that superclass.

The following table defines a set of widget resources used by the programmer to specify data. The programmer can also set the resource values for the inherited classes to set attributes for this widget. To reference a resource by name or by class in a .Xdefaults file, remove the **XmN** or **XmC** prefix and use the remaining letters. To specify one of the defined values for a resource in a .Xdefaults file, remove the **Xm** prefix and use the remaining letters (in either lowercase or uppercase, but include any underscores between words). The codes in the access column indicate if the given resource can be set at creation time (**C**), set by using **XtSetValues** (**S**), retrieved by using **XtGetValues** (**G**), or is not applicable (**N/A**).

VendorShell Resource Set		
Name	**Default**	**Access**
Class	Type	
XmNdefaultFontList	dynamic	C
XmCDefaultFontList	XmFontList	
XmNdeleteResponse	XmDESTROY	CSG
XmCDeleteResponse	unsigned char	
XmNkeyboardFocusPolicy	XmEXPLICIT	CSG
XmCKeyboardFocusPolicy	unsigned char	
XmNmwmDecorations	-1	CSG
XmCMwmDecorations	int	
XmNmwmFunctions	-1	CSG
XmCMwmFunctions	int	
XmNmwmInputMode	-1	CSG
XmCMwmInputMode	int	
XmNmwmMenu	NULL	CSG
XmCMwmMenu	String	

WMShell Resource Set		
Name	**Default**	**Access**
Class	**Type**	
XmNbaseHeight	XtUnspecifiedShellInt	CSG
XmCBaseHeight	int	
XmNbaseWidth	XtUnspecifiedShellInt	CSG
XmCBaseWidth	int	
XmNheightInc	XtUnspecifiedShellInt	CSG
XmCHeightInc	int	
XmNiconMask	NULL	CSG
XmCIconMask	Pixmap	
XmNiconPixmap	NULL	CSG
XmCIconPixmap	Pixmap	
XmNiconWindow	NULL	CSG
XmCIconWindow	Window	
XmNiconX	-1	CSG
XmCIconX	int	
XmNiconY	-1	CSG
XmCIconY	int	
XmNinitialState	NormalState	CSG
XmCInitialState	int	
XmNinput	True	CSG
XmCInput	Boolean	
XmNmaxAspectX	XtUnspecifiedShellInt	CSG
XmCMaxAspectX	int	
XmNmaxAspectY	XtUnspecifiedShellInt	CSG
XmCMaxAspectY	int	
XmNmaxHeight	XtUnspecifiedShellInt	CSG
XmCMaxHeight	int	
XmNmaxWidth	XtUnspecifiedShellInt	CSG
XmCMaxWidth	int	

Name	Default	Access
Class	**Type**	
XmNminAspectX	XtUnspecifiedShellInt	CSG
XmCMinAspectX	int	
XmNminAspectY	XtUnspecifiedShellInt	CSG
XmCMinAspectY	int	
XmNminHeight	XtUnspecifiedShellInt	CSG
XmCMinHeight	int	
XmNminWidth	XtUnspecifiedShellInt	CSG
XmCMinWidth	int	
XmNtitle	dynamic	CSG
XmCTitle	String	
XmNtitleEncoding	XA_STRING	CSG
XmCTitleEncoding	Atom	
XmNtransient	True	CSG
XmCTransient	Boolean	
XmNwaitForWm	True	CSG
XmCWaitForWm	Boolean	
XmNwidthInc	XtUnspecifiedShellInt	CSG
XmCWidthInc	int	
XmNwindowGroup	dynamic	CSG
XmCWindowGroup	Window	
XmNwinGravity	dynamic	CSG
XmCWinGravity	int	
XmNwmTimeout	5000 ms	CSG
XmCWmTimeout	int	

Shell Resource Set		
Name	**Default**	**Access**
Class	**Type**	
XmNallowShellResize	False	CG
XmCAllowShellResize	Boolean	
XmNcreatePopupChildProc	NULL	CSG
XmCCreatePopupChildProc	(*)()	
XmNgeometry	NULL	CSG
XmCGeometry	String	
XmNoverrideRedirect	False	CSG
XmCOverrideRedirect	Boolean	
XmNpopdownCallback	NULL	C
XmCCallback	XtCallbackList	
XmNpopupCallback	NULL	C
XmCCallback	XtCallbackList	
XmNsaveUnder	True	CSG
XmCSaveUnder	Boolean	
XmNvisual	CopyFromParent	CSG
XmCVisual	Visual *	

Composite Resource Set		
Name	**Default**	**Access**
Class	**Type**	
XmNchildren	NULL	G
XmCReadOnly	WidgetList	
XmNinsertPosition	NULL	CSG
XmCInsertPosition	(*)()	
XmNnumChildren	0	G
XmCReadOnly	Cardinal	

Core Resource Set		
Name Class	**Default** Type	**Access**
XmNaccelerators XmCAccelerators	dynamic XtAccelerators	CSG
XmNancestorSensitive XmCSensitive	dynamic Boolean	G
XmNbackground XmCBackground	dynamic Pixel	CSG
XmNbackgroundPixmap XmCPixmap	XmUNSPECIFIED_PIXMAP Pixmap	CSG
XmNborderColor XmCBorderColor	XtDefaultForeground Pixel	CSG
XmNborderPixmap XmCPixmap	XmUNSPECIFIED_PIXMAP Pixmap	CSG
XmNborderWidth XmCBorderWidth	1 Dimension	CSG
XmNcolormap XmCColormap	dynamic Colormap	CG
XmNdepth XmCDepth	dynamic int	CG
XmNdestroyCallback XmCCallback	NULL XtCallbackList	C
XmNheight XmCHeight	dynamic Dimension	CSG
XmNinitialResourcesPersistent XmCInitialResourcesPersistent	True Boolean	C
XmNmappedWhenManaged XmCMappedWhenManaged	True Boolean	CSG
XmNscreen XmCScreen	dynamic Screen *	CG

Name	Default	Access
Class	Type	
XmNsensitive	True	CSG
XmCSensitive	Boolean	
XmNtranslations	dynamic	CSG
XmCTranslations	XtTranslations	
XmNwidth	dynamic	CSG
XmCWidth	Dimension	
XmNx	0	CSG
XmCPosition	Position	
XmNy	0	CSG
XmCPosition	Position	

Translations

There are no translations for TransientShell.

Related Information

Composite(3X), Core(3X), Shell(3X), VendorShell(3X), and WMShell(3X).

Uil

Purpose

Invokes the UIL compiler from within an application

AES Support Level

Trial-use

Synopsis

#include <uil/UilDef.h>

Uil_status_type Uil (*command_desc, compile_desc, message_cb, message_data, status_cb, status_data*)

Uil_command_type	**command_desc;*
Uil_compile_desc_type	**compile_desc;*
Uil_continue_type	*(*message_cb) ();*
char	**message_data;*
Uil_continue_type	*(*status_cb) ();*
char	**status_data;*

Description

The **Uil** function provides a callable entry point for the UIL compiler. The **Uil** callable interface can be used to process a UIL source file and to generate UID files, as well as return a detailed description of the UIL source module in the form of a symbol table (parse tree).

command_desc   Specifies the **uil** command line.

compile_desc   Returns the results of the compilation.

message_cb   Specifies a callback function that is called when the compiler encounters errors in the UIL source.

message_data   Specifies user data that is passed to the message callback function (message_cb). Note that this argument is not interpreted by UIL, and is used exclusively by the calling application.

status_cb   Specifies a callback function that is called to allow X applications to service X events such as updating the screen. This function is called at various check points, which have been hard coded into the UIL compiler. The status_update_delay argument in command_desc specifies the number of check points to be passed before the status_cb function is invoked.

status_data   Specifies user data that is passed to the status callback function (status_cb). Note that this argument is not interpreted by the UIL compiler, and is used exclusively by the calling application.

The data structures **Uil_command_type** and **Uil_compile_desc_type** are detailed below.

```
typedef struct Uil_command_type {
    char *source_file;
        /* single source to compile */
    char *resource_file; /* name of output file */
    char *listing_file; /* name of listing file */
    unsigned int *include_dir_count;
        /* number of dirs. in include_dir */
```

```
char *((*include_dir) []);
    /* dir. to search for include files */
unsigned listing_file_flag: 1;
    /* produce a listing */
unsigned resource_file_flag: 1;
    /* generate UID output */
unsigned machine_code_flag: 1;
    /* generate machine code */
unsigned report_info_msg_flag: 1;
    /* report info messages */
unsigned report_warn_msg_flag: 1;
    /* report warnings */
unsigned parse_tree_flag: 1;
    /* generate parse tree */
unsigned int status_update_delay;
    /* number of times a status point is */
    /* passed before calling status_cb */
    /* function 0 means called every time */
};

typedef struct Uil_compile_desc_type {
    unsigned int compiler_version;
        /* version number of compiler */
    unsigned int data_version;
        /* version number of structures */
    char *parse_tree_root; /* parse tree output */
    unsigned int message_count [Uil_k_max_status+1];
    /* array of severity counts */
};
```

Following is a description of the message callback function specified by *message_cb*:

Uil_continue_type (**message_cb*) (*message_data, message_number, severity, msg_buffer, src_buffer, ptr_buffer, loc_buffer, message_count*)

char	**message_data*;
int	*message_number*;
int	*severity*;
char	**msg_buffer*, **src_buffer*;
char	**ptr_buffer*, **loc_buffer*;
int	*message_count*[];

Specifies a callback function that UIL invokes instead of printing an error message when the compiler encounters an error in the UIL source. The callback should return one of these values:

Uil_k_terminate   Tells UIL to terminate processing of the source file.

Uil_k_continue   Tells UIL to continue processing the source file.

Following are the arguments:

message_data   Data supplied by the application as the *message_data* argument to the **Uil** function. UIL does not interpret this data in any way; it just passes it to the callback.

message_number   An index into a table of error messages and severities, for internal use by UIL.

severity   An integer that indicates the severity of the error. The possible values are the status constants returned by the **Uil** function. See the "RETURN VALUE" section below.

msg_buffer   A string that describes the error.

src_buffer   A string consisting of the source line where the error occurred. This is not always available; the argument is then NULL.

    ptr_buffer   A string consisting of whitespace and a printing character in the character position corresponding to the column of the source line where the error occurred. This string may be printed beneath the source line to provide a visual indication of the column where the error occurred. This is not always available; the argument is then NULL.

    loc_buffer   A string identifying the line number and file of the source line where the error occurred. This is not always available; the argument is then NULL.

    message_count   An array of integers containing the number of diagnostic messages issued thus far for each severity level. To find the number of messages issued for the current severity level, use the *severity* argument as the index into this array.

Following is a description of the status callback function specified by *status_cb*:

Uil_continue_type (*status_cb) (*status_data, percent_complete, lines_processed, current_file, message_count*)

                     char*status_data;
                     int_percent_complete_;
                     int_lines_processed_;
                     char*current_file;
                     int_message_count_[];

Specifies a callback function that is invoked to allow X applications to service X events such as updating the screen. The callback should return one of these values:

Uil_k_terminate   Tells UIL to terminate processing of the source file.

Uil_k_continue   Tells UIL to continue processing the source file.

Following are the arguments:

status_data   Data supplied by the application as the *status_data* argument to the **Uil** function. UIL does not interpret this data in any way; it just passes it to the callback.

percent_complete   An integer indicating what percentage of the current source file has been processed so far.

lines_processed   An integer indicating how many lines of the current source file have been read so far.

current_file   A string containing the pathname of the current source file.

message_count   An array of integers containing the number of diagnostic messages issued thus far for each severity level. To find the number of messages issued for a given severity level, use the severity level as the index into this array. The possible severity levels are the status constants returned by the **Uil** function. See the "RETURN VALUE" section below.

Return Value

This function returns one of these status return constants:

Uil_k_success_status   The operation succeeded.

Uil_k_info_status   The operation succeeded, and an informational message is returned.

Uil_k_warning_status   The operation succeeded, and a warning message is returned.

Uil_k_error_status   The operation failed due to an error.

Uil_k_severe_status   The operation failed due to an error.

VendorShell

Purpose

The VendorShell widget class

AES Support Level

Full-use

Synopsis

#include <Xm/Xm.h>
#include <X11/Shell.h>

Description

VendorShell is a Motif widget class used as a supporting superclass for all shell classes that are visible to the window manager and that are not override redirect. It contains the subresources that describe the MWM-specific look and feel. It also manages the MWM-specific communication needed by all VendorShell subclasses. See the **mwm**(1X) man page for more information.

Setting **XmNheight**, **XmNwidth**, or **XmNborderWidth** for either a VendorShell or its child sets that resource to the same value in both the parent and the child. An application should always specify these resources for the child, not the parent.

For a child of a VendorShell, setting **XmNx** or **XmNy** sets the corresponding resource of the parent but does not change the child's position relative to the parent. **XtGetValues** for the child's **XmNx** or **XmNy** yields the value of the corresponding resource in the parent. The x and y coordinates of the child's upper left outside corner relative to the parent's upper left inside corner are both zero minus the value of **XmNborderWidth**.

Note that the *Inter-Client Communication Conventions Manual* allows a window manager to change or control the border width of a reparented top-level window.

Classes

VendorShell inherits behavior and resources from **Core**, **Composite**, **Shell**, and **WMShell** classes.

> The class pointer is **vendorShellWidgetClass**.

> The class name is **VendorShell**.

New Resources

The following table defines a set of widget resources used by the programmer to specify data. The programmer can also set the resource values for the inherited classes to set attributes for this widget. To reference a subresource by name or by class in a .Xdefaults file, remove the **XmN** or **XmC** prefix and use the remaining letters. To specify one of the defined values for a subresource in a .Xdefaults file, remove the **Xm** prefix and use the remaining letters (in either lowercase or uppercase, but include any underscores between words). The codes in the access column indicate if the given subresource can be set at creation time (**C**), set by using **XtSetValues** (**S**), retrieved by using **XtGetValues** (**G**), or is not applicable (**N/A**).

VendorShell Resource Set		
Name	**Default**	**Access**
Class	**Type**	
XmNdefaultFontList	dynamic	C
XmCDefaultFontList	XmFontList	
XmNdeleteResponse	XmDESTROY	CSG
XmCDeleteResponse	unsigned char	
XmNkeyboardFocusPolicy	XmEXPLICIT	CSG
XmCKeyboardFocusPolicy	unsigned char	
XmNmwmDecorations	-1	CSG
XmCMwmDecorations	int	
XmNmwmFunctions	-1	CSG
XmCMwmFunctions	int	
XmNmwmInputMode	-1	CSG
XmCMwmInputMode	int	
XmNmwmMenu	NULL	CSG
XmCMwmMenu	String	

XmNdefaultFontList

Specifies a default font list for its children. This font list is used whenever a font list is not specifically set for a Text, Label or Button child of the VendorShell.

XmNdeleteResponse

Determines what action the shell takes in response to a **WM_DELETE_WINDOW** message. The setting can be one of three values: **XmDESTROY**, **XmUNMAP**, and **XmDO_NOTHING**. The resource is scanned, and the appropriate action is taken, after the **WM_DELETE_WINDOW** callback list (if any) that is registered with the Protocol manager has been called.

XmNkeyboardFocusPolicy

Determines allocation of keyboard focus within the widget
hierarchy rooted at this shell. The X keyboard focus must be
directed to somewhere in the hierarchy for this client-side
focus management to take effect. Possible values are
XmEXPLICIT, specifying a click-to-type policy, and
XmPOINTER, specifying a pointer-driven policy.

XmNmwmDecorations

Includes the decoration flags (specific decorations to add or
remove from the window manager frame) for **MWM_HINTS**.

XmNmwmFunctions

Includes the function flags (specific window manager
functions to include or exclude from the system menu) for
MWM_HINTS.

XmNmwmInputMode

Includes the input mode flag (application modal or system
modal input focus constraints) for **MWM_HINTS**.

XmNmwmMenu

Specifies the menu items that the Motif window manager
should add to the end of the system menu. The string contains
a list of items separated by **\n** with the following format:

label [mnemonic] [accelerator] function

If more than one item is specified, the items should be
separated by a newline character.

Inherited Resources

VendorShell inherits behavior and resources from the following
superclasses. For a complete description of each resource, refer to the man
page for that superclass.

WMShell Resource Set		
Name	**Default**	**Access**
Class	**Type**	
XmNbaseHeight	XtUnspecifiedShellInt	CSG
XmCBaseHeight	int	
XmNbaseWidth	XtUnspecifiedShellInt	CSG
XmCBaseWidth	int	
XmNheightInc	XtUnspecifiedShellInt	CSG
XmCHeightInc	int	
XmNiconMask	NULL	CSG
XmCIconMask	Pixmap	
XmNiconPixmap	NULL	CSG
XmCIconPixmap	Pixmap	
XmNiconWindow	NULL	CSG
XmCIconWindow	Window	
XmNiconX	-1	CSG
XmCIconX	int	
XmNiconY	-1	CSG
XmCIconY	int	
XmNinitialState	NormalState	CSG
XmCInitialState	int	
XmNinput	True	CSG
XmCInput	Boolean	
XmNmaxAspectX	XtUnspecifiedShellInt	CSG
XmCMaxAspectX	int	
XmNmaxAspectY	XtUnspecifiedShellInt	CSG
XmCMaxAspectY	int	
XmNmaxHeight	XtUnspecifiedShellInt	CSG
XmCMaxHeight	int	
XmNmaxWidth	XtUnspecifiedShellInt	CSG
XmCMaxWidth	int	

Name
  Class
	Default
	  Type
		Access

XmNminAspectX
  XmCMinAspectX
	XtUnspecifiedShellInt
	  int
		CSG

XmNminAspectY
  XmCMinAspectY
	XtUnspecifiedShellInt
	  int
		CSG

XmNminHeight
  XmCMinHeight
	XtUnspecifiedShellInt
	  int
		CSG

XmNminWidth
  XmCMinWidth
	XtUnspecifiedShellInt
	  int
		CSG

XmNtitle
  XmCTitle
	dynamic
	  String
		CSG

XmNtitleEncoding
  XmCTitleEncoding
	XA_STRING
	  Atom
		CSG

XmNtransient
  XmCTransient
	False
	  Boolean
		CSG

XmNwaitForWm
  XmCWaitForWm
	True
	  Boolean
		CSG

XmNwidthInc
  XmCWidthInc
	XtUnspecifiedShellInt
	  int
		CSG

XmNwindowGroup
  XmCWindowGroup
	dynamic
	  Window
		CSG

XmNwinGravity
  XmCWinGravity
	dynamic
	  int
		CSG

XmNwmTimeout
  XmCWmTimeout
	5000 ms
	  int
		CSG

Shell Resource Set		
Name	**Default**	**Access**
Class	**Type**	
XmNallowShellResize	False	CG
XmCAllowShellResize	Boolean	
XmNcreatePopupChildProc	NULL	CSG
XmCCreatePopupChildProc	(*)()	
XmNgeometry	NULL	CSG
XmCGeometry	String	
XmNoverrideRedirect	False	CSG
XmCOverrideRedirect	Boolean	
XmNpopdownCallback	NULL	C
XmCCallback	XtCallbackList	
XmNpopupCallback	NULL	C
XmCCallback	XtCallbackList	
XmNsaveUnder	False	CSG
XmCSaveUnder	Boolean	
XmNvisual	CopyFromParent	CSG
XmCVisual	Visual *	

Composite Resource Set		
Name	**Default**	**Access**
Class	**Type**	
XmNchildren	NULL	G
XmCReadOnly	WidgetList	
XmNinsertPosition	NULL	CSG
XmCInsertPosition	(*)()	
XmNnumChildren	0	G
XmCReadOnly	Cardinal	

Core Resource Set		

Name
    Class
	Default
	    Type
		Access

XmNaccelerators
    XmCAccelerators
	dynamic
	    XtAccelerators
		CSG

XmNancestorSensitive
    XmCSensitive
	dynamic
	    Boolean
		G

XmNbackground
    XmCBackground
	dynamic
	    Pixel
		CSG

XmNbackgroundPixmap
    XmCPixmap
	XmUNSPECIFIED_PIXMAP
	    Pixmap
		CSG

XmNborderColor
    XmCBorderColor
	XtDefaultForeground
	    Pixel
		CSG

XmNborderPixmap
    XmCPixmap
	XmUNSPECIFIED_PIXMAP
	    Pixmap
		CSG

XmNborderWidth
    XmCBorderWidth
	1
	    Dimension
		CSG

XmNcolormap
    XmCColormap
	dynamic
	    Colormap
		CG

XmNdepth
    XmCDepth
	dynamic
	    int
		CG

XmNdestroyCallback
    XmCCallback
	NULL
	    XtCallbackList
		C

XmNheight
    XmCHeight
	dynamic
	    Dimension
		CSG

XmNinitialResourcesPersistent
    XmCInitialResourcesPersistent
	True
	    Boolean
		C

XmNmappedWhenManaged
    XmCMappedWhenManaged
	True
	    Boolean
		CSG

XmNscreen
    XmCScreen
	dynamic
	    Screen *
		CG

Name	Default	Access
Class	Type	
XmNsensitive	True	CSG
XmCSensitive	Boolean	
XmNtranslations	dynamic	CSG
XmCTranslations	XtTranslations	
XmNwidth	dynamic	CSG
XmCWidth	Dimension	
XmNx	0	CSG
XmCPosition	Position	
XmNy	0	CSG
XmCPosition	Position	

Translations

There are no translations for VendorShell.

Related Information

Composite(3X), Core(3X), mwm(1X), Shell(3X), WMShell(3X), XmActivateProtocol(3X), XmActivateWMProtocol(3X), XmAddProtocolCallback(3X), XmAddWMProtocolCallback(3X), XmAddProtocols(3X), XmAddWMProtocols(3X), XmDeactivateProtocol(3X), XmDeactivateWMProtocol(3X), XmGetAtomName(3X), XmInternAtom(3X), XmIsMotifWMRunning(3X), XmRemoveProtocolCallback(3X), XmRemoveWMProtocolCallback(3X), XmRemoveProtocols(3X), XmRemoveWMProtocols(3X), XmSetProtocolHooks(3X), and XmSetWMProtocolHooks(3X).

WMShell

Purpose

The WMShell widget class

AES Support Level

Full-use

Synopsis

#include <Xm/Xm.h>
#include <X11/Shell.h>

Description

WMShell is a top-level widget that encapsulates the interaction with the window manager.

Classes

WMShell inherits behavior and resources from **Core**, **Composite**, and **Shell** classes.

The class pointer is **wmShellWidgetClass**.

The class name is **WMShell**.

New Resources

The following table defines a set of widget resources used by the programmer to specify data. The programmer can also set the resource values for the inherited classes to set attributes for this widget. To reference a resource by name or by class in a .Xdefaults file, remove the **XmN** or **XmC** prefix and use the remaining letters. To specify one of the defined values for a resource in a .Xdefaults file, remove the **Xm** prefix and use the remaining letters (in either lowercase or uppercase, but include any underscores between words). The codes in the access column indicate if the given resource can be set at creation time (**C**), set by using **XtSetValues** (**S**), retrieved by using **XtGetValues** (**G**), or is not applicable (**N/A**).

WMShell Resource Set		
Name **Class**	**Default** **Type**	**Access**
XmNbaseHeight XmCBaseHeight	XtUnspecifiedShellInt int	CSG
XmNbaseWidth XmCBaseWidth	XtUnspecifiedShellInt int	CSG
XmNheightInc XmCHeightInc	XtUnspecifiedShellInt int	CSG
XmNiconMask XmCIconMask	NULL Pixmap	CSG
XmNiconPixmap XmCIconPixmap	NULL Pixmap	CSG
XmNiconWindow XmCIconWindow	NULL Window	CSG
XmNiconX XmCIconX	-1 int	CSG
XmNiconY XmCIconY	-1 int	CSG
XmNinitialState XmCInitialState	NormalState int	CSG
XmNinput XmCInput	False Boolean	CSG
XmNmaxAspectX XmCMaxAspectX	XtUnspecifiedShellInt int	CSG
XmNmaxAspectY XmCMaxAspectY	XtUnspecifiedShellInt int	CSG
XmNmaxHeight XmCMaxHeight	XtUnspecifiedShellInt int	CSG
XmNmaxWidth XmCMaxWidth	XtUnspecifiedShellInt int	CSG

Name	Default	Access
Class	Type	
XmNminAspectX	XtUnspecifiedShellInt	CSG
XmCMinAspectX	int	
XmNminAspectY	XtUnspecifiedShellInt	CSG
XmCMinAspectY	int	
XmNminHeight	XtUnspecifiedShellInt	CSG
XmCMinHeight	int	
XmNminWidth	XtUnspecifiedShellInt	CSG
XmCMinWidth	int	
XmNtitle	dynamic	CSG
XmCTitle	String	
XmNtitleEncoding	XA_STRING	CSG
XmCTitleEncoding	Atom	
XmNtransient	False	CSG
XmCTransient	Boolean	
XmNwaitForWm	True	CSG
XmCWaitForWm	Boolean	
XmNwidthInc	XtUnspecifiedShellInt	CSG
XmCWidthInc	int	
XmNwindowGroup	dynamic	CSG
XmCWindowGroup	Window	
XmNwinGravity	dynamic	CSG
XmCWinGravity	int	
XmNwmTimeout	5000 ms	CSG
XmCWmTimeout	int	

XmNbaseHeight

Specifies the base for a progression of preferred heights for the window manager to use in sizing the widget. The preferred heights are **XmNbaseHeight** plus integral multiples of **XmNheightInc**, with a minimum of **XmNminHeight** and a maximum of **XmNmaxHeight**. If an initial value is not supplied for **XmNbaseHeight** but is supplied for **XmNbaseWidth**, the value of **XmNbaseHeight** is set to 0 when the widget is realized.

XmNbaseWidth

Specifies the base for a progression of preferred widths for the window manager to use in sizing the widget. The preferred widths are **XmNbaseWidth** plus integral multiples of **XmNwidthInc**, with a minimum of **XmNminWidth** and a maximum of **XmNmaxWidth**. If an initial value is not supplied for **XmNbaseWidth** but is supplied for **XmNbaseHeight**, the value of **XmNbaseWidth** is set to 0 when the widget is realized.

XmNheightInc

Specifies the increment for a progression of preferred heights for the window manager to use in sizing the widget. The preferred heights are **XmNbaseHeight** plus integral multiples of **XmNheightInc**, with a minimum of **XmNminHeight** and a maximum of **XmNmaxHeight**. If an initial value is not supplied for **XmNheightInc** but is supplied for **XmNwidthInc**, the value of **XmNheightInc** is set to 1 when the widget is realized.

XmNiconMask

Specifies a bitmap that could be used by the window manager to clip the **XmNiconPixmap** bitmap to make the icon nonrectangular.

XmNiconPixmap

Specifies a bitmap that could be used by the window manager as the application's icon.

XmNiconWindow

Specifies the ID of a window that could be used by the window manager as the application's icon.

XmNiconX Specifies a suitable place to put the application's icon; this is a hint to the window manager in root window coordinates. Since the window manager controls icon placement policy, this may be ignored. If no initial value is specified, the value is set to -1 when the widget is realized.

XmNiconY   Specifies a suitable place to put the application's icon; this is a hint to the window manager in root window coordinates. Since the window manager controls icon placement policy, this may be ignored. If no initial value is specified, the value is set to -1 when the widget is realized.

XmNinitialState

Specifies the state in which the application wishes the widget instance to start. It must be one of the constants **NormalState** or **IconicState**.

XmNinput   Specifies the application's input model for this widget and its descendants. The meaning of a True or False value for this resource depends on the presence or absence of a **WM_TAKE_FOCUS** atom in the **WM_PROTOCOLS** property:

Input Model	XmNinput	WM_TAKE_FOCUS
No input	False	Absent
Passive	True	Absent
Locally active	True	Present
Globally active	False	Present

For more information on input models, see the X Consortium Standard *Inter-Client Communication Conventions Manual*.

XmNmaxAspectX

Specifies the numerator of the maximum aspect ratio (X/Y) that the application wishes the widget instance to have.

XmNmaxAspectY

Specifies the denominator of the maximum aspect ratio (X/Y) that the application wishes the widget instance to have.

XmNmaxHeight

Specifies the maximum height that the application wishes the widget instance to have. If an initial value is not supplied for **XmNmaxHeight** but is supplied for **XmNmaxWidth**, the value of **XmNmaxHeight** is set to 32767 when the widget is realized.

XmNmaxWidth

Specifies the maximum width that the application wishes the widget instance to have. If an initial value is not supplied for **XmNmaxWidth** but is supplied for **XmNmaxHeight**, the value of **XmNmaxWidth** is set to 32767 when the widget is realized.

XmNminAspectX

Specifies the numerator of the minimum aspect ratio (X/Y) that the application wishes the widget instance to have.

XmNminAspectY

Specifies the denominator of the minimum aspect ratio (X/Y) that the application wishes the widget instance to have.

XmNminHeight

Specifies the minimum height that the application wishes the widget instance to have. If an initial value is not supplied for **XmNminHeight** but is supplied for **XmNminWidth**, the value of **XmNminHeight** is set to 1 when the widget is realized.

XmNminWidth

Specifies the minimum width that the application wishes the widget instance to have. If an initial value is not supplied for **XmNminWidth** but is supplied for **XmNminHeight**, the value of **XmNminWidth** is set to 1 when the widget is realized.

XmNtitle Specifies the application name to be displayed by the window manager. The default is the icon name if specified, otherwise the name of the application.

XmNtitleEncoding

Specifies a property type that represents the encoding of the **XmNtitle** string.

XmNtransient

Specifies a Boolean value that is True if the widget instance is transient, typically a popup on behalf of another widget. The window manager may treat a transient widget's window differently from other windows. For example, a window manager may not iconify a transient window separately from its associated application. Applications and users should not normally alter this resource.

XmNwaitForWm

When True, specifies that the Intrinsics waits the length of time given by the **XmNwmTimeout** resource for the window manager to respond to certain actions before assuming that there is no window manager present. This resource is altered by the Intrinsics as it receives, or fails to receive, responses from the window manager.

XmNwidthInc

Specifies the base for a progression of preferred widths for the window manager to use in sizing the widget. The preferred widths are **XmNbaseWidth** plus integral multiples of **XmNwidthInc**, with a minimum of **XmNminWidth** and a maximum of **XmNmaxWidth**. If an initial value is not supplied for **XmNwidthInc** but is supplied for **XmNheightInc**, the value of **XmNwidthInc** is set to 1 when the widget is realized.

XmNwindowGroup

Specifies the ID of a window with which this widget instance is associated. By convention, this window is the "leader" of a group of windows. A window manager may treat all windows in a group in some way; for example, it may always move or iconify them together.

If no initial value is specified, the value is set to the window of the first realized ancestor widget in the parent hierarchy when the widget is realized. If a value of **XtUnspecifiedWindowGroup** is specified, no window group is set.

XmNwinGravity
> Specifies the window gravity for use by the window manager in positioning the widget. If no initial value is specified, the value is set when the widget is realized. If **XmNgeometry** is not NULL, **XmNwinGravity** is set to the window gravity returned by **XmWMGeometry**. Otherwise, **XmNwinGravity** is set to **NorthWestGravity**.

XmNwmTimeout
> Specifies the length of time that the Intrinsics waits for the window manager to respond to certain actions before assuming that there is no window manager present. The value is in milliseconds and must not be negative.

Inherited Resources

WMShell inherits behavior and resources from the following superclasses. For a complete description of each resource, refer to the man page for that superclass.

Shell Resource Set		
Name	**Default**	**Access**
Class	**Type**	
XmNallowShellResize	False	CG
XmCAllowShellResize	Boolean	
XmNcreatePopupChildProc	NULL	CSG
XmCCreatePopupChildProc	(*)()	
XmNgeometry	NULL	CSG
XmCGeometry	String	
XmNoverrideRedirect	False	CSG
XmCOverrideRedirect	Boolean	
XmNpopdownCallback	NULL	C
XmCCallback	XtCallbackList	
XmNpopupCallback	NULL	C
XmCCallback	XtCallbackList	
XmNsaveUnder	False	CSG
XmCSaveUnder	Boolean	
XmNvisual	CopyFromParent	CSG
XmCVisual	Visual *	

Composite Resource Set		
Name	**Default**	**Access**
Class	**Type**	
XmNchildren	NULL	G
XmCReadOnly	WidgetList	
XmNinsertPosition	NULL	CSG
XmCInsertPosition	(*)()	
XmNnumChildren	0	G
XmCReadOnly	Cardinal	

Core Resource Set		
Name	**Default**	**Access**
Class	**Type**	
XmNaccelerators	dynamic	CSG
XmCAccelerators	XtAccelerators	
XmNancestorSensitive	dynamic	G
XmCSensitive	Boolean	
XmNbackground	dynamic	CSG
XmCBackground	Pixel	
XmNbackgroundPixmap	XmUNSPECIFIED_PIXMAP	CSG
XmCPixmap	Pixmap	
XmNborderColor	XtDefaultForeground	CSG
XmCBorderColor	Pixel	
XmNborderPixmap	XmUNSPECIFIED_PIXMAP	CSG
XmCPixmap	Pixmap	
XmNborderWidth	1	CSG
XmCBorderWidth	Dimension	
XmNcolormap	dynamic	CG
XmCColormap	Colormap	
XmNdepth	dynamic	CG
XmCDepth	int	
XmNdestroyCallback	NULL	C
XmCCallback	XtCallbackList	
XmNheight	dynamic	CSG
XmCHeight	Dimension	
XmNinitialResourcesPersistent	True	C
XmCInitialResourcesPersistent	Boolean	
XmNmappedWhenManaged	True	CSG
XmCMappedWhenManaged	Boolean	
XmNscreen	dynamic	CG
XmCScreen	Screen *	

Name	Default	Access
Class	Type	
XmNsensitive	True	CSG
XmCSensitive	Boolean	
XmNtranslations	dynamic	CSG
XmCTranslations	XtTranslations	
XmNwidth	dynamic	CSG
XmCWidth	Dimension	
XmNx	0	CSG
XmCPosition	Position	
XmNy	0	CSG
XmCPosition	Position	

Translations

There are no translations for WMShell.

Related Information

Composite(3X), Core(3X), and Shell(3X).

XmActivateProtocol

Purpose

A VendorShell function that activates a protocol.

AES Support Level

Trial-use

Synopsis

#include <Xm/Xm.h>
#include <X11/Protocols.h>

void XmActivateProtocol (*shell, property, protocol*)
    Widget   *shell*;
    Atom   *property*;
    Atom   *protocol*;

void XmActivateWMProtocol (*shell, protocol*)
    Widget   *shell*;
    Atom   *protocol*;

Description

XmActivateProtocol activates a protocol. It updates the handlers and the *property* if the *shell* is realized. It is sometimes useful to allow a protocol's state information (callback lists, and so on) to persist, even though the client may choose to temporarily resign from the interaction. This is supported by allowing a *protocol* to be in one of two states: active or inactive. If the *protocol* is active and the *shell* is realized, the *property* contains the *protocol* **Atom**. If the *protocol* is inactive, the **Atom** is not present in the *property*.

XmActivateWMProtocol is a convenience interface. It calls XmActivateProtocol with the property value set to the atom returned by interning **WM_PROTOCOLS**.

shell   Specifies the widget with which the protocol property is associated.

property   Specifies the protocol property.

protocol   Specifies the protocol **Atom** (or an **int** type cast to **Atom**).

For a complete definition of VendorShell and its associated resources, see **VendorShell(3X)**.

Related Information

VendorShell(3X), XmActivateWMProtocol(3X) and XmInternAtom(3X).

XmActivateWMProtocol

Purpose

A VendorShell convenience interface that activates a protocol.

AES Support Level

Trial-use

Synopsis

```
#include <Xm/Xm.h>
#include <X11/Protocols.h>

void XmActivateWMProtocol (shell, protocol)
    Widget      shell;
    Atom        protocol;
```

Description

XmActivateWMProtocol is a convenience interface. It calls **XmActivateProtocol** with the property value set to the atom returned by interning **WM_PROTOCOLS**.

shell   Specifies the widget with which the protocol property is associated.

protocol Specifies the protocol **Atom** (or an **int** type cast to **Atom**).

For a complete definition of VendorShell and its associated resources, see **VendorShell(3X)**.

Related Information

VendorShell(3X), **XmActivateProtocol(3X)**, and **XmInternAtom(3X)**.

XmAddProtocolCallback

Purpose

A VendorShell function that adds client callbacks for a protocol.

AES Support Level

Trial-use

Synopsis

#include <Xm/Xm.h>
#include <X11/Protocols.h>

void   XmAddProtocolCallback (*shell,   property,   protocol,   callback,   closure*)
        Widget   *shell*;
        Atom   *property*;
        Atom   *protocol*;
        XtCallbackProc*callback*;
        caddr_t   *closure*;

void XmAddWMProtocolCallback (*shell, protocol, callback, closure*)
        Widget   *shell*;
        Atom   *protocol*;
        XtCallbackProc*callback*;
        caddr_t   *closure*;

Description

XmAddProtocolCallback adds client callbacks for a protocol. It checks if the protocol is registered, and if it is not, calls **XmAddProtocols**. It then adds the callback to the internal list. These callbacks are called when the corresponding client message is received.

XmAddWMProtocolCallback is a convenience interface. It calls **XmAddProtocolCallback** with the property value set to the atom returned by interning **WM_PROTOCOLS**.

shell   Specifies the widget with which the protocol property is associated.

property Specifies the protocol property.

protocol Specifies the protocol **Atom** (or an **int** type cast to **Atom**).

callback Specifies the procedure to call when a protocol message is received.

closure   Specifies the client data to be passed to the callback when it is invoked.

For a complete definition of VendorShell and its associated resources, see **VendorShell(3X)**.

Related Information

VendorShell(3X), **XmAddProtocols(3X)**,
XmAddWMProtocolCallback(3X), and **XmInternAtom(3X)**.

XmAddProtocols

Purpose

A VendorShell function that adds the protocols to the protocol manager and allocates the internal tables.

AES Support Level

Trial-use

Synopsis

#include <Xm/Xm.h>
#include <X11/Protocols.h>

void XmAddProtocols (*shell, property, protocols, num_protocols*)
    Widget   *shell*;
    Atom   *property*;
    Atom   * *protocols*;
    Cardinal   *num_protocols*;

void XmAddWMProtocols (*shell, protocols, num_protocols*)
    Widget   *shell*;
    Atom   * *protocols*;
    Cardinal   *num_protocols*;

Description

XmAddProtocols adds the protocols to the protocol manager and allocates the internal tables.

XmAddWMProtocols is a convenience interface. It calls **XmAddProtocols** with the property value set to the atom returned by interning **WM_PROTOCOLS**.

shell   Specifies the widget with which the protocol property is associated.

property   Specifies the protocol property.

protocols   Specifies the protocol **Atoms** (or **int** types cast to **Atom**).

num_protocols   Specifies the number of elements in *protocols*.

For a complete definition of VendorShell and its associated resources, see **VendorShell(3X)**.

Related Information

VendorShell(3X), **XmAddWMProtocols(3X)**, and **XmInternAtom(3X)**.

XmAddTabGroup

Purpose

A function that adds a manager or a primitive widget to the list of tab groups.

AES Support Level

Full-use

Synopsis

#include <Xm/Xm.h>

void XmAddTabGroup (*tab_group*)
   Widget   *tab_group*;

Description

When using the keyboard to traverse through a widget hierarchy, primitive or manager widgets are grouped together into what are known as **tab groups**. Any manager or primitive widget can be a tab group. Within a tab group, move the focus to the next widget within the tab group by using the arrow keys. To move to another tab group, use **KNextField** or **KPrevField**.

Tab groups are ordinarily specified by the **XmNnavigationType** resource. **XmAddTabGroup** is called to control the order of traversal of tab groups.The widget specified by *tab_group* is appended to the list of tab groups to be traversed, and the widget's **XmNnavigationType** is set to **XmEXCLUSIVE_TAB_GROUP**.

tab_group
> Specifies the manager or primitive widget ID.

Related Information

XmManager(3X), **XmPrimitive(3X)** and **XmRemoveTabGroup(3X)**.

XmAddWMProtocolCallback

Purpose

A VendorShell convenience interface that adds client callbacks for a protocol.

AES Support Level

Trial-use

Synopsis

#include <Xm/Xm.h>
#include <X11/Protocols.h>

void XmAddWMProtocolCallback (*shell, protocol, callback, closure*)
Widget *shell*;
Atom *protocol*;
XtCallbackProc*callback*;
caddr_t *closure*;

Description

> **XmAddWMProtocolCallback** is a convenience interface. It calls **XmAddProtocolCallback** with the property value set to the atom returned by interning **WM_PROTOCOLS**.

> *shell*   Specifies the widget with which the protocol property is associated.

> *protocol*   Specifies the protocol **Atom** (or an **int** type cast to **Atom**).

> *callback*   Specifies the procedure to call when a protocol message is received.

> *closure*   Specifies the client data to be passed to the callback when it is invoked.

> For a complete definition of VendorShell and its associated resources, see **VendorShell(3X)**.

Related Information

> **VendorShell(3X)**, **XmAddProtocolCallback(3X)**, **XmInternAtom(3X)**.

XmAddWMProtocols

Purpose

A VendorShell convenience interface that adds the protocols to the protocol manager and allocates the internal tables.

AES Support Level

Trial-use

Synopsis

#include <Xm/Xm.h>
#include <X11/Protocols.h>

void XmAddWMProtocols (*shell, protocols, num_protocols*)
    Widget   *shell*;
    Atom   * *protocols*;
    Cardinal   *num_protocols*;

Description

XmAddWMProtocols is a convenience interface. It calls **XmAddProtocols** with the property value set to the atom returned by interning **WM_PROTOCOLS**.

shell   Specifies the widget with which the protocol property is associated.

protocols   Specifies the protocol **Atoms** (or **int** types cast to **Atom**).

num_protocols Specifies the number of elements in *protocols*.

For a complete definition of VendorShell and its associated resources, see **VendorShell(3X)**.

Related Information

VendorShell(3X), **XmAddProtocols(3X)**, and **XmInternAtom(3X)**.

XmArrowButton

Purpose

The ArrowButton widget class

AES Support Level

Full-use

Synopsis

#include <Xm/ArrowB.h>

Description

ArrowButton consists of a directional arrow surrounded by a border shadow. When it is selected, the shadow changes to give the appearance that the ArrowButton has been pressed in. When the ArrowButton is unselected, the shadow reverts to give the appearance that the ArrowButton is released, or out.

Classes

ArrowButton inherits behavior and resources from **Core** and **XmPrimitive** classes.

The class pointer is **xmArrowButtonWidgetClass**.

The class name is **XmArrowButton**.

New Resources

The following table defines a set of widget resources used by the programmer to specify data. The programmer can also set the resource values for the inherited classes to set attributes for this widget. To reference a resource by name or by class in a .Xdefaults file, remove the **XmN** or **XmC** prefix and use the remaining letters. To specify one of the defined values for a resource in a .Xdefaults file, remove the **Xm** prefix and use the remaining letters (in either lowercase or uppercase, but include any underscores between words). The codes in the access column indicate if the given resource can be set at creation time (**C**), set by using **XtSetValues** (**S**), retrieved by using **XtGetValues** (**G**), or is not applicable (**N/A**).

XmArrowButton Resource Set		
Name	**Default**	**Access**
Class	**Type**	
XmNactivateCallback	NULL	C
XmCCallback	XtCallbackList	
XmNarmCallback	NULL	C
XmCCallback	XtCallbackList	
XmNarrowDirection	XmARROW_UP	CSG
XmCArrowDirection	unsigned char	
XmNdisarmCallback	NULL	C
XmCCallback	XtCallbackList	
XmNmultiClick	dynamic	CSG
XmCMultiClick	unsigned char	

XmNactivateCallback

Specifies a list of callbacks that is called when the ArrowButton is activated. To activate the button, press and release **BSelect** while the pointer is inside the ArrowButton widget. Activating the ArrowButton also disarms it. The reason sent by this callback is **XmCR_ACTIVATE**.

XmNarmCallback

Specifies a list of callbacks that is called when the ArrowButton is armed. To arm this widget, press **BSelect** while the pointer is inside the ArrowButton. The reason sent by this callback is **XmCR_ARM**.

XmNarrowDirection

Sets the arrow direction. The following are values for this resource:

- **XmARROW_UP**.

- **XmARROW_DOWN**.

- **XmARROW_LEFT**.

- **XmARROW_RIGHT**.

XmNdisarmCallback

Specifies a list of callbacks that is called when the ArrowButton is disarmed. To disarm this widget, press and release **BSelect** while the pointer is inside the ArrowButton. The reason for this callback is **XmCR_DISARM**.

XmNmultiClick

If a button click is followed by another button click within the time span specified by the display's multi-click time, and this resource is set to **XmMULTICLICK_DISCARD**, do not process the second click. If this resource is set to **XmMULTICLICK_KEEP**, process the event and increment *click_count* in the callback structure. When the button is not in a menu, the default value is **XmMULTICLICK_KEEP**.

Inherited Resources

ArrowButton inherits behavior and resources from the following superclasses. For a complete description of each resource, refer to the man page for that superclass.

XmPrimitive Resource Set		
Name	**Default**	**Access**
Class	Type	
XmNbottomShadowColor	dynamic	CSG
XmCBottomShadowColor	Pixel	
XmNbottomShadowPixmap	XmUNSPECIFIED_PIXMAP	CSG
XmCBottomShadowPixmap	Pixmap	
XmNforeground	dynamic	CSG
XmCForeground	Pixel	
XmNhelpCallback	NULL	C
XmCCallback	XtCallbackList	
XmNhighlightColor	dynamic	CSG
XmCHighlightColor	Pixel	
XmNhighlightOnEnter	False	CSG
XmCHighlightOnEnter	Boolean	
XmNhighlightPixmap	dynamic	CSG
XmCHighlightPixmap	Pixmap	
XmNhighlightThickness	2	CSG
XmCHighlightThickness	Dimension	
XmNnavigationType	XmNONE	G
XmCNavigationType	XmNavigationType	
XmNshadowThickness	2	CSG
XmCShadowThickness	Dimension	
XmNtopShadowColor	dynamic	CSG
XmCTopShadowColor	Pixel	
XmNtopShadowPixmap	dynamic	CSG
XmCTopShadowPixmap	Pixmap	
XmNtraversalOn	True	CSG
XmCTraversalOn	Boolean	
XmNuserData	NULL	CSG
XmCUserData	Pointer	

Core Resource Set		
Name	**Default**	**Access**
Class	**Type**	
XmNaccelerators	dynamic	CSG
XmCAccelerators	XtAccelerators	
XmNancestorSensitive	dynamic	G
XmCSensitive	Boolean	
XmNbackground	dynamic	CSG
XmCBackground	Pixel	
XmNbackgroundPixmap	XmUNSPECIFIED_PIXMAP	CSG
XmCPixmap	Pixmap	
XmNborderColor	XtDefaultForeground	CSG
XmCBorderColor	Pixel	
XmNborderPixmap	XmUNSPECIFIED_PIXMAP	CSG
XmCPixmap	Pixmap	
XmNborderWidth	0	CSG
XmCBorderWidth	Dimension	
XmNcolormap	dynamic	CG
XmCColormap	Colormap	
XmNdepth	dynamic	CG
XmCDepth	int	
XmNdestroyCallback	NULL	C
XmCCallback	XtCallbackList	
XmNheight	dynamic	CSG
XmCHeight	Dimension	
XmNinitialResourcesPersistent	True	C
XmCInitialResourcesPersistent	Boolean	
XmNmappedWhenManaged	True	CSG
XmCMappedWhenManaged	Boolean	
XmNscreen	dynamic	CG
XmCScreen	Screen *	

Name	Default	Access
Class	Type	
XmNsensitive	True	CSG
XmCSensitive	Boolean	
XmNtranslations	dynamic	CSG
XmCTranslations	XtTranslations	
XmNwidth	dynamic	CSG
XmCWidth	Dimension	
XmNx	0	CSG
XmCPosition	Position	
XmNy	0	CSG
XmCPosition	Position	

Callback Information

A pointer to the following structure is passed to each callback:

typedef struct
```
{
    int        reason;
    XEvent     * event;
    int        click_count;
} XmArrowButtonCallbackStruct;
```

reason   Indicates why the callback was invoked.

event   Points to the **XEvent** that triggered the callback.

click_count

This value is valid only when the reason is **XmCR_ACTIVATE**. It contains the number of clicks in the last multiclick sequence if the **XmNmultiClick** resource is set to **XmMULTICLICK_KEEP**; otherwise it contains **1**. The activate callback is invoked for each click if **XmNmultiClick** is set to **XmMULTICLICK_KEEP**.

Translations

XmArrowButton includes translations for XmPrimitive. Additional XmArrowButton translations are listed below. These translations may not directly correspond to a translation table.

BSelect Press:	**Arm()**
BSelect Click:	**Activate()**
	Disarm()
BSelect Release:	**Activate()**
	Disarm()
BSelect Press 2+:	**MultiArm()**
BSelect Release 2+:	**MultiActivate()**
KActivate:	**ArmAndActivate()**
KSelect:	**ArmAndActivate()**
KHelp:	**Help()**

Action Routines

The XmArrowButton action routines are described below:

Activate(): Draws the shadow in the unselected state. If the pointer is within the ArrowButton, calls the callbacks for **XmNactivateCallback**.

Arm(): Draws the shadow in the selected state and calls the callbacks for **XmNarmCallback**.

ArmAndActivate():
Draws the shadow in the selected state and calls the callbacks for **XmNarmCallback**. Arranges for the shadow to be drawn in the unselected state and the callbacks for **XmNactivateCallback** and **XmNdisarmCallback** to be called, either immediately or at a later time.

Disarm(): Draws the shadow in the unselected state and calls the callbacks for **XmNdisarmCallback**.

Help(): Calls the callbacks for **XmNhelpCallback** if any exist. If there are no help callbacks for this widget, this action calls the help callbacks for the nearest ancestor that has them.

MultiActivate():
If **XmNmultiClick** is **XmMULTICLICK_DISCARD**, this action does nothing.

If **XmNmultiClick** is **XmMULTICLICK_KEEP**, this action does the following: Increments *click_count* in the callback structure. Draws the shadow in the unselected state. If the pointer is within the ArrowButton, calls the callbacks for **XmNactivateCallback**. Calls the callbacks for **XmNdisarmCallback**.

MultiArm():
If **XmNmultiClick** is **XmMULTICLICK_DISCARD**, this action does nothing. If **XmNmultiClick** is **XmMULTICLICK_KEEP**, this action draws the shadow in the selected state and calls the callbacks for **XmNarmCallback**.

Additional Behavior

This widget has the additional behavior described below:

<EnterWindow>:

Draws the ArrowButton shadow in its selected state if the pointer leaves and re-enters the window while BSelect is pressed.

<LeaveWindow>:

Draws the ArrowButton shadow in its unselected state if the pointer leaves the window while BSelect is pressed.

Virtual Bindings

The bindings for virtual keys are vendor specific.

Related Information

Core(3X), **XmCreateArrowButton(3X)**, and **XmPrimitive(3X)**.

XmArrowButtonGadget

Purpose

The ArrowButtonGadget widget class

AES Support Level

Full-use

Synopsis

#include <Xm/ArrowBG.h>

Description

ArrowButtonGadget consists of a directional arrow surrounded by a border shadow. When it is selected, the shadow changes to give the appearance that the ArrowButtonGadget has been pressed in. When it is unselected, the shadow reverts to give the appearance that the button is released, or out.

Classes

ArrowButtonGadget inherits behavior and resources from **Object**, **RectObj**, and **XmGadget** classes.

The class pointer is **xmArrowButtonGadgetClass**.

The class name is **XmArrowButtonGadget**.

New Resources

The following table defines a set of widget resources used by the programmer to specify data. The programmer can also set the resource values for the inherited classes to set attributes for this widget. To reference a resource by name or by class in a .Xdefaults file, remove the **XmN** or **XmC** prefix and use the remaining letters. To specify one of the defined values for a resource in a .Xdefaults file, remove the **Xm** prefix and use the remaining letters (in either lowercase or uppercase, but include any underscores between words). The codes in the access column indicate if the given resource can be set at creation time (**C**), set by using **XtSetValues** (**S**), retrieved by using **XtGetValues** (**G**), or is not applicable (**N/A**).

ArrowButtonGadget Resource Set		
Name **Class**	**Default** **Type**	**Access**
XmNactivateCallback XmCCallback	NULL XtCallbackList	C
XmNarmCallback XmCCallback	NULL XtCallbackList	C
XmNarrowDirection XmCArrowDirection	XmARROW_UP unsigned char	CSG
XmNdisarmCallback XmCCallback	NULL XtCallbackList	C
XmNmultiClick XmCMultiClick	dynamic unsigned char	CSG

XmNactivateCallback

Specifies a list of callbacks that is called when the ArrowButtonGadget is activated. To activate the button, press and release **BSelect** while the pointer is inside the ArrowButtonGadget. Activating the ArrowButtonGadget also disarms it. The reason sent by this callback is **XmCR_ACTIVATE**.

XmNarmCallback

Specifies a list of callbacks that is called when the ArrowButtonGadget is armed. To arm this widget, press **BSelect** while the pointer is inside the ArrowButtonGadget. The reason sent by this callback is **XmCR_ARM**.

XmNarrowDirection

Sets the arrow direction. The values for this resource are:

- **XmARROW_UP**.
- **XmARROW_DOWN**.
- **XmARROW_LEFT**.
- **XmARROW_RIGHT**.

XmNdisarmCallback
> Specifies a list of callbacks that is called when the ArrowButtonGadget is disarmed. To disarm this widget, press and release **BSelect** while the pointer is inside the ArrowButtonGadget. The reason sent by this callback is **XmCR_DISARM**.

XmNmultiClick
> If a button click is followed by another button click within the time span specified by the display's multi-click time, and this resource is set to **XmMULTICLICK_DISCARD**, do not process the second click. If this resource is set to **XmMULTICLICK_KEEP**, process the event and increment *click_count* in the callback structure. When the ArrowButtonGadget is not in a menu, the default value is **XmMULTICLICK_KEEP**.

Inherited Resources

ArrowButtonGadget inherits behavior and resources from the following superclasses. For a complete description of each resource, refer to the man page for that superclass.

XmGadget Resource Set		
Name **Class**	**Default** **Type**	**Access**
XmNhelpCallback XmCCallback	NULL XtCallbackList	C
XmNhighlightOnEnter XmCHighlightOnEnter	False Boolean	CSG
XmNhighlightThickness XmCHighlightThickness	2 Dimension	CSG
XmNnavigationType XmCNavigationType	XmNONE XmNavigationType	G
XmNshadowThickness XmCShadowThickness	2 Dimension	CSG
XmNtraversalOn XmCTraversalOn	True Boolean	CSG
XmNuserData XmCUserData	NULL Pointer	CSG

RectObj Resource Set		
Name **Class**	**Default** **Type**	**Access**
XmNancestorSensitive XmCSensitive	dynamic Boolean	G
XmNborderWidth XmCBorderWidth	0 Dimension	CSG
XmNheight XmCHeight	dynamic Dimension	CSG
XmNsensitive XmCSensitive	True Boolean	CSG
XmNwidth XmCWidth	dynamic Dimension	CSG
XmNx XmCPosition	0 Position	CSG
XmNy XmCPosition	0 Position	CSG

Object Resource Set		
Name **Class**	**Default** **Type**	**Access**
XmNdestroyCallback XmCCallback	NULL XtCallbackList	C

Callback Information

A pointer to the following structure is passed to each callback:

typedef struct
{
    int   *reason*;
    XEvent   ** event*;
    int   *click_count*;
} XmArrowButtonCallbackStruct;

reason   Indicates why the callback was invoked.

event   Points to the **XEvent** that triggered the callback.

click_count
             This value is valid only when the reason is **XmCR_ACTIVATE**.
             It contains the number of clicks in the last multiclick sequence if
             the   **XmNmultiClick**   resource   is   set   to
             XmMULTICLICK_KEEP, otherwise it contains **1**. The activate
             callback is invoked for each click if **XmNmultiClick** is set to
             XmMULTICLICK_KEEP.

Behavior

XmArrowButtonGadget includes behavior from XmGadget. Additional
XmArrowButtonGadget behavior is described below:

BSelect Press:
             Draws the shadow in the selected state and calls the callbacks
             for **XmNarmCallback**.

BSelect Click or BSelectRelease:
             Draws the shadow in the unselected state. If the pointer is
             within the ArrowButtonGadget, calls the callbacks for
             XmNactivateCallback.   Calls   the   callbacks   for
             XmNdisarmCallback.

BSelect Press 2+:
             If **XmNmultiClick** is **XmMULTICLICK_DISCARD**, this
             action   does   nothing.   If   **XmNmultiClick**   is
             XmMULTICLICK_KEEP, this action draws the shadow in
             the   selected   state   and   calls   the   callbacks   for
             XmNarmCallback.

BSelect Release 2+:
> If **XmNmultiClick** is **XmMULTICLICK_DISCARD**, this action does nothing.
>
> If **XmNmultiClick** is **XmMULTICLICK_KEEP**, this action does the following: Increments *click_count* in the callback structure. Draws the shadow in the unselected state. If the pointer is within the ArrowButtonGadget, calls the callbacks for **XmNactivateCallback**. Calls the callbacks for **XmNdisarmCallback**.

KActivate or KSelect:
> Draws the shadow in the selected state and calls the callbacks for **XmNarmCallback**. Arranges for the shadow to be drawn in the unselected state and the callbacks for **XmNactivateCallback** and **XmNdisarmCallback** to be called, either immediately or at a later time.

KHelp:
> Calls the callbacks for **XmNhelpCallback** if any exist. If there are no help callbacks for this widget, this calls the help callbacks for the nearest ancestor that has them.

<Enter>:
> Draws the ArrowButtonGadget shadow in its selected state if the pointer leaves and re-enters the gadget while BSelect is pressed.

<Leave>:
> Draws the ArrowButtonGadget shadow in its unselected state if the pointer leaves the gadget while BSelect is pressed.

Virtual Bindings

The bindings for virtual keys are vendor specific.

Related Information

Object(3X), RectObj(3X), XmCreateArrowButtonGadget(3X), and XmGadget(3X).

XmBulletinBoard

Purpose

The BulletinBoard widget class

AES Support Level

Trial-use

History/Direction

The XmNtextTranslations resource is scheduled for removal in revision D.

Synopsis

#include <Xm/BulletinB.h>

Description

BulletinBoard is a composite widget that provides simple geometry management for children widgets. It does not force positioning on its children, but can be set to reject geometry requests that result in overlapping children. BulletinBoard is the base widget for most dialog widgets and is also used as a general container widget.

Modal and modeless dialogs are implemented as collections of widgets that include a DialogShell, a BulletinBoard (or subclass) child of the shell, and various dialog components (buttons, labels, etc.) that are children of BulletinBoard. BulletinBoard defines callbacks useful for dialogs (focus, map, unmap), which are available for application use. If its parent is a DialogShell, BulletinBoard passes title and input mode (based on dialog style) information to the parent, which is responsible for appropriate communication with the window manager.

Classes

BulletinBoard inherits behavior and resources from **Core**, **Composite**, **Constraint**, and **XmManager** classes.

The class pointer is **xmBulletinBoardWidgetClass**.

The class name is **XmBulletinBoard**.

New Resources

The following table defines a set of widget resources used by the programmer to specify data. The programmer can also set the resource values for the inherited classes to set attributes for this widget. To reference a resource by name or by class in a .Xdefaults file, remove the **XmN** or **XmC** prefix and use the remaining letters. To specify one of the defined values for a resource in a .Xdefaults file, remove the **Xm** prefix and use the remaining letters (in either lowercase or uppercase, but include any underscores between words). The codes in the access column indicate if the given resource can be set at creation time (**C**), set by using **XtSetValues** (**S**), retrieved by using **XtGetValues** (**G**), or is not applicable (**N/A**).

XmBulletinBoard Resource Set		
Name Class	**Default** Type	**Access**
XmNallowOverlap XmCAllowOverlap	True Boolean	CSG
XmNautoUnmanage XmCAutoUnmanage	True Boolean	CG
XmNbuttonFontList XmCButtonFontList	dynamic XmFontList	CSG
XmNcancelButton XmCWidget	NULL Widget	SG
XmNdefaultButton XmCWidget	NULL Widget	SG
XmNdefaultPosition XmCDefaultPosition	True Boolean	CSG
XmNdialogStyle XmCDialogStyle	dynamic unsigned char	CSG
XmNdialogTitle XmCDialogTitle	NULL XmString	CSG
XmNfocusCallback XmCCallback	NULL XtCallbackList	C
XmNlabelFontList XmCLabelFontList	dynamic XmFontList	CSG
XmNmapCallback XmCCallback	NULL XtCallbackList	C
XmNmarginHeight XmCMarginHeight	10 Dimension	CSG
XmNmarginWidth XmCMarginWidth	10 Dimension	CSG
XmNnoResize XmCNoResize	False Boolean	CSG

Name	Default	Access
Class	Type	
XmNresizePolicy	XmRESIZE_ANY	CSG
XmCResizePolicy	unsigned char	
XmNshadowType	XmSHADOW_OUT	CSG
XmCShadowType	unsigned char	
XmNtextFontList	dynamic	CSG
XmCTextFontList	XmFontList	
XmNtextTranslations	NULL	C
XmCTranslations	XtTranslations	
XmNunmapCallback	NULL	C
XmCCallback	XtCallbackList	

XmNallowOverlap

Controls the policy for overlapping children widgets. If True, BulletinBoard allows geometry requests that result in overlapping children.

XmNautoUnmanage

Controls whether or not BulletinBoard is automatically unmanaged after a button is activated. If this resource is True on initialization and if the BulletinBoard's parent is a DialogShell, BulletinBoard adds a callback to button children (PushButtons, PushButtonGadgets, and DrawnButtons) that unmanages the BulletinBoard when a button is activated. If this resource is False on initialization or if the BulletinBoard's parent is not a DialogShell, the BulletinBoard is not automatically unmanaged. For BulletinBoard subclasses with Apply or Help buttons, activating those buttons does not automatically unmanage the BulletinBoard.

XmNbuttonFontList

Specifies the font list used for BulletinBoard's button children (PushButtons, PushButtonGadgets, ToggleButtons, and ToggleButtonGadgets). If this value is NULL at initialization, it is initialized by looking up the parent hierarchy of the widget for an ancestor that is a subclass of the XmBulletinBoard, VendorShell, or XmMenuShell widget class. If such an ancestor is found, the font list is initialized to the appropriate default font list of the ancestor widget (XmNdefaultFontList for VendorShell and XmMenuShell, XmNbuttonFontList for XmBulletinBoard).

XmNcancelButton
Specifies the widget ID of the **Cancel** button. BulletinBoard's subclasses, which define a **Cancel** button, set this resource. BulletinBoard does not directly provide any behavior for that button.

XmNdefaultButton
Specifies the widget ID of the default button. Some BulletinBoard subclasses, which define a default button, set this resource. BulletinBoard defines translations and installs accelerators that activate that button when **KActivate** is pressed and the keyboard focus is not in another button.

XmNdefaultPosition
Controls whether or not the BulletinBoard is automatically positioned by its parent. If True, and the parent of the BulletinBoard is a DialogShell, the BulletinBoard is centered within or around the parent of the DialogShell when the BulletinBoard is mapped and managed. If False, the BulletinBoard is not automatically positioned.

XmNdialogStyle
Indicates the dialog style associated with BulletinBoard. If the parent of BulletinBoard is a DialogShell, the parent is configured according to this resource and DialogShell sets the **XmNinputMode** of VendorShell accordingly. This resource can be set only if the BulletinBoard is unmanaged. Possible values for this resource include the following:

- **XmDIALOG_SYSTEM_MODAL** — used for dialogs that must be responded to before any other interaction in any application

- **XmDIALOG_PRIMARY_APPLICATION_MODAL** — used for dialogs that must be responded to before some other interactions in ancestors of the widget

- **XmDIALOG_APPLICATION_MODAL** — used for dialogs that must be responded to before some other interactions in ancestors of the widget. This value is the same as **XmDIALOG_PRIMARY_APPLICATION_MODAL**, and remains for compatibility.

- **XmDIALOG_FULL_APPLICATION_MODAL** — used for dialogs that must be responded to before some other interactions in the same application

- **XmDIALOG_MODELESS** — used for dialogs that do not interrupt interaction of any application. This is the default when the parent of the BulletinBoard is a DialogShell.

- **XmDIALOG_WORK_AREA** — used for BulletinBoard widgets whose parents are not DialogShells. **XmNdialogStyle** is forced to have this value when the parent of the BulletinBoard is not a DialogShell.

XmNdialogTitle

Specifies the dialog title. If this resource is not NULL, and the parent of the BulletinBoard is a subclass of WMShell, BulletinBoard sets the **XmNtitle** and **XmNnameEncoding** of its parent. If the only character set in **XmNdialogTitle** is ISO8859-1, **XmNtitle** is set to the string of the title, and **XmNnameEncoding** is set to **STRING**. If **XmNdialogTitle** contains character sets other than ISO8859-1, **XmNtitle** is set to the string of the title converted to a compound text string, and **XmNnameEncoding** is set to **COMPOUND_TEXT**.

XmNfocusCallback

Specifies the list of callbacks that is called when the BulletinBoard widget or one of its descendants accepts the input focus. The callback reason is **XmCR_FOCUS**.

XmNlabelFontList

Specifies the font list used for BulletinBoard's Label children (Labels and LabelGadgets). If this value is NULL at initialization, it is initialized by looking up the parent hierarchy of the widget for an ancestor that is a subclass of the XmBulletinBoard, VendorShell, or XmMenuShell widget class. If such an ancestor is found, the font list is initialized to the appropriate default font list of the ancestor widget (XmNdefaultFontList for VendorShell and XmMenuShell, XmNlabelFontList for XmBulletinBoard).

XmNmapCallback

Specifies the list of callbacks that is called only when the parent of the BulletinBoard is a DialogShell; in which case, this callback list is invoked when the BulletinBoard widget is mapped. The callback reason is **XmCR_MAP**.

XmNmarginHeight

Specifies the minimum spacing in pixels between the top or bottom edge of BulletinBoard and any child widget.

XmNmarginWidth

Specifies the minimum spacing in pixels between the left or right edge of BulletinBoard and any child widget.

XmNnoResize

Controls whether or not resize controls are included in the window manager frame around the dialog. If set to True, the **mwm** does not include resize controls in the window manager frame containing the DialogShell or TopLevelShell parent of the BulletinBoard. If set to False, the window manager frame does include resize controls. Other controls provided by **mwm** can be included or excluded through the **mwm** resources provided by VendorShell.

XmNresizePolicy

> Controls the policy for resizing BulletinBoard widgets. Possible values include the following:
>
> - **XmRESIZE_NONE** — fixed size
> - **XmRESIZE_ANY** — shrink or grow as needed
> - **XmRESIZE_GROW** — grow only

XmNshadowType

> Describes the shadow drawing style for BulletinBoard. This resource can have the following values:
>
> - **XmSHADOW_IN** — draws the BulletinBoard shadow so that it appears inset. This means that the bottom shadow visuals and top shadow visuals are reversed.
>
> - **XmSHADOW_OUT** — draws the BulletinBoard shadow so that it appears outset
>
> - **XmSHADOW_ETCHED_IN** — draws the BulletinBoard shadow using a double line giving the effect of a line etched into the window, similar to the Separator widget
>
> - **XmSHADOW_ETCHED_OUT** — draws the BulletinBoard shadow using a double line giving the effect of a line coming out of the window, similar to the Separator widget
>
> BulletinBoard widgets draw shadows just within their borders if **XmNshadowThickness** is greater than zero. If the parent of a BulletinBoard widget is a DialogShell, BulletinBoard dynamically changes the default for **XmNshadowThickness** from 0 to 1.

XmNtextFontList

Specifies the font list used for BulletinBoard's Text children. If this value is NULL at initialization, it is initialized by looking up the parent hierarchy of the widget for an ancestor that is a subclass of the XmBulletinBoard, VendorShell, or XmMenuShell widget class. If such an ancestor is found, the font list is initialized to the appropriate default font list of the ancestor widget (XmNdefaultFontList for VendorShell and XmMenuShell, XmNtextFontList for XmBulletinBoard).

XmNtextTranslations

This resource is scheduled for removal in revision D. Adds translations to any Text widget or Text widget subclass that is added as a child of BulletinBoard.

XmNunmapCallback

Specifies the list of callbacks that is called only when the parent of the BulletinBoard is a DialogShell; in which case, this callback list is invoked when the BulletinBoard widget is unmapped. The callback reason is **XmCR_UNMAP**.

Inherited Resources

BulletinBoard inherits behavior and resources from the following superclasses. For a complete description of each resource, refer to the man page for that superclass.

XmManager Resource Set		

Name
    Class
	Default
	    Type
		Access

XmNbottomShadowColor
    XmCBottomShadowColor
	dynamic
	    Pixel
		CSG

XmNbottomShadowPixmap
    XmCBottomShadowPixmap
	XmUNSPECIFIED_PIXMAP
	    Pixmap
		CSG

XmNforeground
    XmCForeground
	dynamic
	    Pixel
		CSG

XmNhelpCallback
    XmCCallback
	NULL
	    XtCallbackList
		C

XmNhighlightColor
    XmCHighlightColor
	dynamic
	    Pixel
		CSG

XmNhighlightPixmap
    XmCHighlightPixmap
	dynamic
	    Pixmap
		CSG

XmNnavigationType
    XmCNavigationType
	XmTAB_GROUP
	    XmNavigationType
		CSG

XmNshadowThickness
    XmCShadowThickness
	dynamic
	    Dimension
		CSG

XmNstringDirection
    XmCStringDirection
	dynamic
	    XmStringDirection
		CG

XmNtopShadowColor
    XmCBackgroundTopShadowColor
	dynamic
	    Pixel
		CSG

XmNtopShadowPixmap
    XmCTopShadowPixmap
	dynamic
	    Pixmap
		CSG

XmNtraversalOn
    XmCTraversalOn
	True
	    Boolean
		CSG

XmNuserData
    XmCUserData
	NULL
	    Pointer
		CSG

Composite Resource Set		
Name	**Default**	**Access**
Class	**Type**	
XmNchildren	NULL	G
XmCReadOnly	WidgetList	
XmNinsertPosition	NULL	CSG
XmCInsertPosition	(*)()	
XmNnumChildren	0	G
XmCReadOnly	Cardinal	

Core Resource Set		
Name	**Default**	**Access**
Class	**Type**	
XmNaccelerators	dynamic	N/A
XmCAccelerators	XtAccelerators	
XmNancestorSensitive	dynamic	G
XmCSensitive	Boolean	
XmNbackground	dynamic	CSG
XmCBackground	Pixel	
XmNbackgroundPixmap⊃	XmUNSPECIFIED_PIXMAP	CSG
XmCPixmap	Pixmap	
XmNborderColor	XtDefaultForeground	CSG
XmCBorderColor	Pixel	
XmNborderPixmap	XmUNSPECIFIED_PIXMAP	CSG
XmCPixmap	Pixmap	
XmNborderWidth	0	CSG
XmCBorderWidth	Dimension	
XmNcolormap	dynamic	CG
XmCColormap	Colormap	
XmNdepth	dynamic	CG
XmCDepth	int	
XmNdestroyCallback	NULL	C
XmCCallback	XtCallbackList	
XmNheight	dynamic	CSG
XmCHeight	Dimension	
XmNinitialResourcesPersistent	True	C
XmCInitialResourcesPersistent	Boolean	
XmNmappedWhenManaged	True	CSG
XmCMappedWhenManaged	Boolean	
XmNscreen	dynamic	CG
XmCScreen	Screen *	

| Name | Default | Access |
Class	Type	
XmNsensitive	True	CSG
XmCSensitive	Boolean	
XmNtranslations	dynamic	CSG
XmCTranslations	XtTranslations	
XmNwidth	dynamic	CSG
XmCWidth	Dimension	
XmNx	0	CSG
XmCPosition	Position	
XmNy	0	CSG
XmCPosition	Position	

Callback Information

A pointer to the following structure is passed to each callback:

typedef struct
{
    int   *reason*;
    XEvent   * *event*;
} XmAnyCallbackStruct;

reason   Indicates why the callback was invoked.

event   Points to the **XEvent** that triggered the callback.

Translations

XmBulletinBoard includes the translations from XmManager.

Additional Behavior

The XmBulletinBoard widget has the additional behavior described below:

MAny KCancel:

Calls the activate callbacks for the cancel button if it is sensitive.

KActivate: Calls the activate callbacks for the button with the keyboard focus. If no button has the keyboard focus, calls the activate callbacks for the default button if it is sensitive. In a List widget or single-line Text widget, the List or Text action associated with **KActivate** is called before the BulletinBoard actions associated with **KActivate**. In a multi-line Text widget, any **KActivate** event except **KEnter** calls the Text action associated with **KActivate**, then the BulletinBoard actions associated with **KActivate**.

<FocusIn>: Calls the callbacks for **XmNfocusCallback**. When the focus policy is **XmPOINTER**, this happens when the pointer enters the window. When the focus policy is **XmEXPLICIT**, this happens when the user traverses to the widget.

<Map>: Calls the callbacks for **XmNmapCallback**.

<Unmap>: Calls the callbacks for **XmNunmapCallback**.

Virtual Bindings

The bindings for virtual keys are vendor specific.

Related Information

Composite(3X), Constraint(3X), Core(3X), XmCreateBulletinBoard(3X), XmCreateBulletinBoardDialog(3X), XmDialogShell(3X), and XmManager(3X).

XmCascadeButton

Purpose

The CascadeButton widget class

AES Support Level

Full-use

Synopsis

#include <Xm/CascadeB.h>

Description

CascadeButton links two MenuPanes or a MenuBar to a MenuPane.

It is used in menu systems and must have a RowColumn parent with its **XmNrowColumnType** resource set to **XmMENU_BAR**, **XmMENU_POPUP** or **XmMENU_PULLDOWN**.

It is the only widget that can have a Pulldown MenuPane attached to it as a submenu. The submenu is displayed when this widget is activated within a MenuBar, a PopupMenu, or a PulldownMenu. Its visuals can include a label or pixmap and a cascading indicator when it is in a Popup or Pulldown MenuPane; or, it can include only a label or a pixmap when it is in a MenuBar.

The default behavior associated with a CascadeButton depends on the type of menu system in which it resides. By default, **BSelect** controls the behavior of the CascadeButton. In addition, **BMenu** controls the behavior of the CascadeButton if it resides in a PopupMenu system. The actual mouse button used is determined by its RowColumn parent.

A CascadeButton's visuals differ from most other button gadgets. When the button becomes armed, its visuals change from a 2-D to a 3-D look, and it displays the submenu that has been attached to it. If no submenu is attached, it simply changes its visuals.

When a CascadeButton within a Pulldown or Popup MenuPane is armed as the result of the user moving the mouse pointer into the widget, it does not immediately display its submenu. Instead, it waits a short amount of time to see if the arming was temporary (that is, the user was simply passing through the widget), or whether the user really wanted the submenu posted. This time delay is configurable via **XmNmappingDelay**.

CascadeButton provides a single mechanism for activating the widget from the keyboard. This mechanism is referred to as a keyboard mnemonic. If a mnemonic has been specified for the widget, the user may activate the CascadeButton by simply typing the mnemonic while the CascadeButton is visible. If the CascadeButton is in a MenuBar and the MenuBar does not have the focus, the **MAlt** modifier must be pressed with the mnemonic. Mnemonics are typically used to interact with a menu via the keyboard interface.

If in a Pulldown or Popup MenuPane and there is a submenu attached, the **XmNmarginBottom**, **XmNmarginLeft**, **XmNmarginRight**, and **XmNmarginTop** resources may enlarge to accommodate **XmNcascadePixmap**. **XmNmarginWidth** defaults to 6 if this resource is in a MenuBar; otherwise, it takes Label's default, which is 2.

Classes

CascadeButton inherits behavior and resources from **Core**, **XmPrimitive**, and **XmLabel** classes.

The class pointer is **xmCascadeButtonWidgetClass**.

The class name is **XmCascadeButton**.

New Resources

The following table defines a set of widget resources used by the programmer to specify data. The programmer can also set the resource values for the inherited classes to set attributes for this widget. To reference a resource by name or by class in a .Xdefaults file, remove the **XmN** or **XmC** prefix and use the remaining letters. To specify one of the defined values for a resource in a .Xdefaults file, remove the **Xm** prefix and use the remaining letters (in either lowercase or uppercase, but include any underscores between words). The codes in the access column indicate if the given resource can be set at creation time (**C**), set by using **XtSetValues** (**S**), retrieved by using **XtGetValues** (**G**), or is not applicable (**N/A**).

XmCascadeButton Resource Set		
Name	**Default**	**Access**
Class	**Type**	
XmNactivateCallback	NULL	C
XmCCallback	XtCallbackList	
XmNcascadePixmap	dynamic	CSG
XmCPixmap	Pixmap	
XmNcascadingCallback	NULL	C
XmCCallback	XtCallbackList	
XmNmappingDelay	180 ms	CSG
XmCMappingDelay	int	
XmNsubMenuId	NULL	CSG
XmCMenuWidget	Widget	

XmNactivateCallback

Specifies the list of callbacks that is called when the user activates the CascadeButton widget, and there is no submenu attached to pop up. The activation occurs by releasing a mouse button or by typing the mnemonic associated with the widget. The specific mouse button depends on information in the RowColumn parent. The reason sent by the callback is **XmCR_ACTIVATE**.

XmNcascadePixmap

Specifies the cascade pixmap displayed on one end of the widget when a CascadeButton is used within a Popup or Pulldown MenuPane and a submenu is attached. The Label class resources **XmNmarginBottom**, **XmNmarginLeft**, **XmNmarginRight**, and **XmNmarginTop** may be modified to ensure that room is left for the cascade pixmap. The default cascade pixmap is an arrow pointing to the side of the menu where the submenu will appear.

XmNcascadingCallback

Specifies the list of callbacks that is called just prior to the mapping of the submenu associated with CascadeButton. The reason sent by the callback is **XmCR_CASCADING**.

XmNmappingDelay

> Specifies the amount of time, in milliseconds, between when a CascadeButton becomes armed and when it maps its submenu. This delay is used only when the widget is within a Popup or Pulldown MenuPane. The value must not be negative.

XmNsubMenuId

> Specifies the widget ID for the Pulldown MenuPane to be associated with this CascadeButton. The specified MenuPane is displayed when the CascadeButton becomes armed. The MenuPane must have been created with the appropriate parentage depending on the type of menu used. See **XmCreateMenuBar(3X)**, **XmCreatePulldownMenu(3X)**, and **XmCreatePopupMenu(3X)** for more information on the menu systems.

Inherited Resources

CascadeButton inherits behavior and resources from the following superclasses. For a complete description of each resource, refer to the man page for that superclass.

XmLabel Resource Set		

Name
  Class
	Default
	  Type
		Access

XmNaccelerator
  XmCAccelerator
	NULL
	  String
		N/A

XmNacceleratorText
  XmCAcceleratorText
	NULL
	  XmString
		N/A

XmNalignment
  XmCAlignment
	dynamic
	  unsigned char
		CSG

XmNfontList
  XmCFontList
	dynamic
	  XmFontList
		CSG

XmNlabelInsensitivePixmap
  XmCLabelInsensitivePixmap
	XmUNSPECIFIED_PIXMAP
	  Pixmap
		CSG

XmNlabelPixmap
  XmCLabelPixmap
	XmUNSPECIFIED_PIXMAP
	  Pixmap
		CSG

XmNlabelString
  XmCXmString
	dynamic
	  XmString
		CSG

XmNlabelType
  XmCLabelType
	XmSTRING
	  unsigned char
		CSG

XmNmarginBottom
  XmCMarginBottom
	dynamic
	  Dimension
		CSG

XmNmarginHeight
  XmCMarginHeight
	2
	  Dimension
		CSG

XmNmarginLeft
  XmCMarginLeft
	0
	  Dimension
		CSG

XmNmarginRight
  XmCMarginRight
	dynamic
	  Dimension
		CSG

XmNmarginTop
  XmCMarginTop
	dynamic
	  Dimension
		CSG

XmNmarginWidth
  XmCMarginWidth
	2
	  Dimension
		CSG

Name	Default	Access
Class	Type	
XmNmnemonic	NULL	CSG
XmCMnemonic	KeySym	
XmNmnemonicCharSet	dynamic	CSG
XmCMnemonicCharSet	String	
XmNrecomputeSize	True	CSG
XmCRecomputeSize	Boolean	
XmNstringDirection	dynamic	CSG
XmCStringDirection	XmStringDirection	

XmPrimitive Resource Set		

Name
    Class
	Default
	    Type
		Access

XmNbottomShadowColor
    XmCBottomShadowColor
	dynamic
	    Pixel
		CSG

XmNbottomShadowPixmap
    XmCBottomShadowPixmap
	XmUNSPECIFIED_PIXMAP
	    Pixmap
		CSG

XmNforeground
    XmCForeground
	dynamic
	    Pixel
		CSG

XmNhelpCallback
    XmCCallback
	NULL
	    XtCallbackList
		C

XmNhighlightColor
    XmCHighlightColor
	dynamic
	    Pixel
		CSG

XmNhighlightOnEnter
    XmCHighlightOnEnter
	False
	    Boolean
		CSG

XmNhighlightPixmap
    XmCHighlightPixmap
	dynamic
	    Pixmap
		CSG

XmNhighlightThickness
    XmCHighlightThickness
	2
	    Dimension
		CSG

XmNnavigationType
    XmCNavigationType
	XmNONE
	    XmNavigationType
		G

XmNshadowThickness
    XmCShadowThickness
	2
	    Dimension
		CSG

XmNtopShadowColor
    XmCTopShadowColor
	dynamic
	    Pixel
		CSG

XmNtopShadowPixmap
    XmCTopShadowPixmap
	dynamic
	    Pixmap
		CSG

XmNtraversalOn
    XmCTraversalOn
	True
	    Boolean
		CSG

XmNuserData
    XmCUserData
	NULL
	    Pointer
		CSG

Core Resource Set		
Name	**Default**	**Access**
Class	**Type**	
XmNaccelerators	dynamic	CSG
XmCAccelerators	XtAccelerators	
XmNancestorSensitive	dynamic	G
XmCSensitive	Boolean	
XmNbackground	dynamic	CSG
XmCBackground	Pixel	
XmNbackgroundPixmap	XmUNSPECIFIED_PIXMAP	CSG
XmCPixmap	Pixmap	
XmNborderColor	XtDefaultForeground	CSG
XmCBorderColor	Pixel	
XmNborderPixmap	XmUNSPECIFIED_PIXMAP	CSG
XmCPixmap	Pixmap	
XmNborderWidth	0	CSG
XmCBorderWidth	Dimension	
XmNcolormap	dynamic	CG
XmCColormap	Colormap	
XmNdepth	dynamic	CG
XmCDepth	int	
XmNdestroyCallback	NULL	C
XmCCallback	XtCallbackList	
XmNheight	dynamic	CSG
XmCHeight	Dimension	
XmNinitialResourcesPersistent	True	C
XmCInitialResourcesPersistent	Boolean	
XmNmappedWhenManaged	True	CSG
XmCMappedWhenManaged	Boolean	
XmNscreen	dynamic	CG
XmCScreen	Screen *	

Name	Default	Access
Class	Type	
XmNsensitive	True	CSG
XmCSensitive	Boolean	
XmNtranslations	dynamic	CSG
XmCTranslations	XtTranslations	
XmNwidth	dynamic	CSG
XmCWidth	Dimension	
XmNx	0	CSG
XmCPosition	Position	
XmNy	0	CSG
XmCPosition	Position	

Callback Information

A pointer to the following structure is passed to each callback:

typedef struct
{
    int   *reason*;
   XEvent   * *event*;
} XmAnyCallbackStruct;

reason   Indicates why the callback was invoked.

event   Points to the **XEvent** that triggered the callback or is NULL if this callback was not triggered due to an **XEvent**.

Translations

XmCascadeButton includes translations from Primitive. XmCascadeButton includes the menu traversal translations from XmLabel. These translations may not directly correspond to a translation table.

Note that altering translations in **#override** or **#augment** mode is undefined.

The translations for a CascadeButton in a MenuBar are listed below. These translations may not directly correspond to a translation table.

BSelect Press:	**MenuBarSelect()**
BSelect Release:	**DoSelect()**
KActivate:	**KeySelect()**
KSelect:	**KeySelect()**
KHelp:	**Help()**
MAny KCancel:	**CleanupMenuBar()**

The translations for a CascadeButton in a PullDown or Popup MenuPane are listed below. In a Popup menu system, **BMenu** also performs the **BSelect** actions. These translations may not directly correspond to a translation table.

BSelect Press:	**StartDrag()**
BSelect Release:	**DoSelect()**
KActivate:	**KeySelect()**
KSelect:	**KeySelect()**
KHelp:	**Help()**
MAny KCancel:	**CleanupMenuBar()**

Action Routines

The XmCascadeButton action routines are described below:

CleanupMenuBar():
>In a MenuBar, disarms the CascadeButton and the menu and restores keyboard focus to the tab group that had the focus before the menu was entered.

In a toplevel Pulldown MenuPane from a MenuBar, unposts the menu, disarms the MenuBar CascadeButton and the MenuBar, and restores keyboard focus to the tab group that had the focus before the MenuBar was entered. In other Pulldown MenuPanes, unposts the menu.

In a Popup MenuPane, unposts the menu and restores keyboard focus to the widget from which the menu was posted.

DoSelect(): Posts the submenu attached to the CascadeButton and enables keyboard traversal within the menu. If the CascadeButton does not have a submenu attached, the CascadeButton is activated and all posted menus in the cascade are unposted.

Help(): Unposts all menus in the menu hierarchy and restores keyboard focus to the tab group that had the focus before the menu system was entered. Calls the callbacks for **XmNhelpCallback** if any exist. If there are no help callbacks for this widget, this action calls the help callbacks for the nearest ancestor that has them.

KeySelect(): Posts the submenu attached to the CascadeButton if keyboard traversal is enabled in the menu. If the CascadeButton does not have a submenu attached, the CascadeButton is activated and all posted menus in the cascade are unposted.

MenuBarSelect():
Unposts any menus posted by the parent menu. Arms both the CascadeButton and the MenuBar, posts the associated submenu, and enables mouse traversal. If the menu is already active, this event disables keyboard traversal for the menu and returns the menu to mouse traversal mode.

StartDrag():
Arms the CascadeButton, posts the associated submenu, and enables mouse traversal. If the menu is already active, this event disables keyboard traversal for the menu and returns the menu to mouse traversal mode.

Additional Behavior

Posting a submenu calls the **XmNcascadingCallback** callbacks. This widget has the additional behavior described below:

<EnterWindow>:
        If keyboard traversal is enabled does nothing. Otherwise, in a MenuBar that is armed, unposts any MenuPanes associated with another MenuBar entry, arms the CascadeButton, and posts the associated submenu. In other menus, arms the CascadeButton and posts the associated submenu after the delay specified by **XmNmappingDelay**.

<LeaveWindow>:
        If keyboard traversal is enabled does nothing. Otherwise, in a MenuBar that is armed, disarms the CascadeButton if the submenu associated with the CascadeButton is not currently posted or if there is no submenu associated with the CascadeButton.

        In other menus, if the pointer moves anywhere except into a submenu associated with the CascadeButton, the CascadeButton is disarmed and its submenu is unposted.

Virtual Bindings

The bindings for virtual keys are vendor specific.

Related Information

Core(3X), **XmCascadeButtonHighlight(3X)**, **XmCreateCascadeButton(3X)**, **XmCreateMenuBar(3X)**, **XmCreatePulldownMenu(3X)**, **XmCreatePopupMenu(3X)**, **XmLabel(3X)**, **XmPrimitive(3X)**, and **XmRowColumn(3X)**.

XmCascadeButtonGadget

Purpose

The CascadeButtonGadget widget class

AES Support Level

Full-use

Synopsis

#include <Xm/CascadeBG.h>

Description

CascadeButtonGadget links two MenuPanes, a MenuBar to a MenuPane, or an OptionMenu to a MenuPane.

It is used in menu systems and must have a RowColumn parent with its **XmNrowColumnType** resource set to **XmMENU_BAR**, **XmMENU_POPUP**, **XmMENU_PULLDOWN**, or **XmMENU_OPTION**.

It is the only gadget that can have a Pulldown MenuPane attached to it as a submenu. The submenu is displayed when this gadget is activated within a PopupMenu, a PulldownMenu, or an OptionMenu. Its visuals can include a label or pixmap and a cascading indicator when it is in a Popup or Pulldown MenuPane; or it can include only a label or a pixmap when it is in an OptionMenu.

The default behavior associated with a CascadeButtonGadget depends on the type of menu system in which it resides. By default, **BSelect** controls the behavior of the CascadeButtonGadget. In addition, **BMenu** controls the behavior of the CascadeButtonGadget if it resides in a PopupMenu system. The actual mouse button used is determined by its RowColumn parent.

A CascadeButtonGadget's visuals differ from most other button gadgets. When the button becomes armed, its visuals change from a 2-D to a 3-D look, and it displays the submenu that has been attached to it. If no submenu is attached, it simply changes its visuals.

When a CascadeButtonGadget within a Pulldown or Popup MenuPane is armed as the result of the user moving the mouse pointer into the gadget, it does not immediately display its submenu. Instead, it waits a short time to see if the arming was temporary (that is, the user was simply passing through the gadget), or the user really wanted the submenu posted. This delay is configurable via **XmNmappingDelay**.

CascadeButtonGadget provides a single mechanism for activating the gadget from the keyboard. This mechanism is referred to as a keyboard mnemonic. If a mnemonic has been specified for the gadget, the user may activate it by simply typing the mnemonic while the CascadeButtonGadget is visible. If the CascadeButtonGadget is in a MenuBar and the MenuBar does not have the focus, the **MAlt** modifier must be pressed with the mnemonic. Mnemonics are typically used to interact with a menu via the keyboard.

If a CascadeButtonGadget is in a Pulldown or Popup MenuPane and there is a submenu attached, the **XmNmarginBottom**, **XmNmarginLeft**, **XmNmarginRight**, and **XmNmarginTop** resources may enlarge to accommodate **XmNcascadePixmap**. **XmNmarginWidth** defaults to 6 if this resource is in a MenuBar; otherwise, it takes LabelGadget's default, which is 2.

Classes

CascadeButtonGadget inherits behavior and resources from **Object**, **RectObj**, **XmGadget**, and **XmLabelGadget** classes.

The class pointer is **xmCascadeButtonGadgetClass**.

The class name is **XmCascadeButtonGadget**.

New Resources

The following table defines a set of widget resources used by the programmer to specify data. The programmer can also set the resource values for the inherited classes to set attributes for this widget. To reference a resource by name or by class in a .Xdefaults file, remove the **XmN** or **XmC** prefix and use the remaining letters. To specify one of the defined values for a resource in a .Xdefaults file, remove the **Xm** prefix and use the remaining letters (in either lowercase or uppercase, but include any underscores between words). The codes in the access column indicate if the given resource can be set at creation time (**C**), set by using **XtSetValues** (**S**), retrieved by using **XtGetValues** (**G**), or is not applicable (**N/A**).

XmCascadeButtonGadget		
Name	**Default**	**Access**
Class	**Type**	
XmNactivateCallback	NULL	C
XmCCallback	XtCallbackList	
XmNcascadePixmap	dynamic	CSG
XmCPixmap	Pixmap	
XmNcascadingCallback	NULL	C
XmCCallback	XtCallbackList	
XmNmappingDelay	180 ms	CSG
XmCMappingDelay	int	
XmNsubMenuId	NULL	CSG
XmCMenuWidget	Widget	

XmNactivateCallback

Specifies the list of callbacks that is called when the user activates the CascadeButtonGadget, and there is no submenu attached to pop up. The activation occurs by releasing a mouse button or by typing the mnemonic associated with the gadget. The specific mouse button depends on information in the RowColumn parent. The reason sent by the callback is **XmCR_ACTIVATE**.

XmNcascadePixmap

Specifies the cascade pixmap displayed on one end of the gadget when a CascadeButtonGadget is used within a Popup or Pulldown MenuPane and a submenu is attached. The LabelGadget class resources **XmNmarginBottom**, **XmNmarginLeft**, **XmNmarginRight**, and **XmNmarginTop** may be modified to ensure that room is left for the cascade pixmap. The default cascade pixmap in menus other than option menus is an arrow pointing to the side of the menu where the submenu will appear. The default for the CascadeButtonGadget in an option menu is **XmUNSPECIFIED_PIXMAP**.

XmNcascadingCallback

Specifies the list of callbacks that is called just prior to the mapping of the submenu associated with the CascadeButtonGadget. The reason sent by the callback is **XmCR_CASCADING**.

XmNmappingDelay

Specifies the amount of time, in milliseconds, between when a CascadeButtonGadget becomes armed and when it maps its submenu. This delay is used only when the gadget is within a Popup or Pulldown MenuPane. The value must not be negative.

XmNsubMenuId

Specifies the widget ID for the Pulldown MenuPane to be associated with this CascadeButtonGadget. The specified MenuPane is displayed when the CascadeButtonGadget becomes armed. The MenuPane must have been created with the appropriate parentage depending on the type of menu used. See **XmCreatePulldownMenu(3X)**, **XmCreatePopupMenu(3X)**, and **XmCreateOptionMenu(3X)** for more information on the menu systems.

Inherited Resources

CascadeButtonGadget inherits behavior and resources from the following superclasses. For a complete description of each resource, refer to the man page for that superclass.

XmLabelGadget Resource Set		
Name Class	**Default** Type	**Access**
XmNaccelerator XmCAccelerator	NULL String	N/A
XmNacceleratorText XmCAcceleratorText	NULL XmString	N/A
XmNalignment XmCAlignment	dynamic unsigned char	CSG
XmNfontList XmCFontList	dynamic XmFontList	CSG
XmNlabelInsensitivePixmap XmCLabelInsensitivePixmap	XmUNSPECIFIED_PIXMAP Pixmap	CSG
XmNlabelPixmap XmCLabelPixmap	XmUNSPECIFIED_PIXMAP Pixmap	CSG
XmNlabelString XmCXmString	dynamic XmString	CSG
XmNlabelType XmCLabelType	XmSTRING unsigned char	CSG
XmNmarginBottom XmCMarginBottom	dynamic Dimension	CSG
XmNmarginHeight XmCMarginHeight	2 Dimension	CSG
XmNmarginLeft XmCMarginLeft	0 Dimension	CSG
XmNmarginRight XmCMarginRight	dynamic Dimension	CSG
XmNmarginTop XmCMarginTop	dynamic Dimension	CSG
XmNmarginWidth XmCMarginWidth	2 Dimension	CSG

Name	Default	Access
Class	Type	
XmNmnemonic	NULL	CSG
XmCMnemonic	KeySym	
XmNmnemonicCharSet	dynamic	CSG
XmCMnemonicCharSet	String	
XmNrecomputeSize	True	CSG
XmCRecomputeSize	Boolean	
XmNstringDirection	dynamic	CSG
XmCStringDirection	XmStringDirection	

XmGadget Resource Set		
Name	Default	Access
Class	Type	
XmNhelpCallback	NULL	C
XmCCallback	XtCallbackList	
XmNhighlightOnEnter	False	CSG
XmCHighlightOnEnter	Boolean	
XmNhighlightThickness	2	CSG
XmCHighlightThickness	Dimension	
XmNnavigationType	XmNONE	G
XmCNavigationType	XmNavigationType	
XmNshadowThickness	2	CSG
XmCShadowThickness	Dimension	
XmNtraversalOn	True	CSG
XmCTraversalOn	Boolean	
XmNuserData	NULL	CSG
XmCUserData	Pointer	

RectObj Resource Set		
Name Class	**Default** Type	**Access**
XmNancestorSensitive XmCSensitive	dynamic Boolean	G
XmNborderWidth XmCBorderWidth	0 Dimension	CSG
XmNheight XmCHeight	dynamic Dimension	CSG
XmNsensitive XmCSensitive	True Boolean	CSG
XmNwidth XmCWidth	dynamic Dimension	CSG
XmNx XmCPosition	0 Position	CSG
XmNy XmCPosition	0 Position	CSG

Object Resource Set		
Name Class	**Default** Type	**Access**
XmNdestroyCallback XmCCallback	NULL XtCallbackList	C

Callback Information

A pointer to the following structure is passed to each callback:

```
typedef struct
{
    int        reason;
    XEvent     * event;
} XmAnyCallbackStruct;
```

reason   Indicates why the callback was invoked.

event   Points to the **XEvent** that triggered the callback or is NULL if this callback was not triggered by an **XEvent**.

Behavior

XmCascadeButtonGadget includes behavior from XmGadget. XmCascadeButton includes the menu traversal behavior from XmLabel. Additional XmCascadeButtonGadget behavior is described below (in a Popup menu sytem, **BMenu** also performs the **BSelect** actions):

BSelect Press:

Unposts any menus posted by the parent menu. Arms the CascadeButtonGadget, posts the associated submenu, enables mouse traversal, and, in a MenuBar, arms the MenuBar. If the menu is already active, this event disables keyboard traversal for the menu and returns the menu to mouse traversal mode.

BSelect Release:

Posts the submenu attached to the CascadeButtonGadget and enables keyboard traversal within the menu. If the CascadeButtonGadget does not have a submenu attached, the CascadeButtonGadget is activated and all posted menus in the cascade are unposted.

KActivate or KSelect:

Posts the submenu attached to the CascadeButtonGadget if keyboard traversal is enabled in the menu. If the CascadeButtonGadget does not have a submenu attached, the CascadeButtonGadget is activated and all posted menus in the cascade are unposted.

KHelp: Unposts all menus in the menu hierarchy and restores keyboard focus to the tab group that had the focus before the menu system was entered. Calls the callbacks for **XmNhelpCallback** if any exist. If there are no help callbacks for this widget, this action calls the help callbacks for the nearest ancestor that has them.

MAny KCancel:

In a MenuBar, disarms the CascadeButtonGadget and the menu and restores keyboard focus to the tab group that had the focus before the menu was entered.

In a toplevel Pulldown MenuPane from a MenuBar, unposts the menu, disarms the MenuBar CascadeButton and the MenuBar, and restores keyboard focus to the tab group that had the focus before the MenuBar was entered. In other Pulldown MenuPanes, unposts the menu.

In a Popup MenuPane, unposts the menu and restores keyboard focus to the widget from which the menu was posted.

<Enter>: If keyboard traversal is enabled does nothing. Otherwise, in a MenuBar, unposts any MenuPanes associated with another MenuBar entry, arms the CascadeButtonGadget, and posts the associated submenu. In other menus, arms the CascadeButtonGadget and posts the associated submenu after the delay specified by **XmNmappingDelay**.

<Leave>: If keyboard traversal is enabled does nothing. Otherwise, in a MenuBar, disarms the CascadeButtonGadget if the submenu associated with the CascadeButtonGadget is not currently posted or if there is no submenu associated with the CascadeButtonGadget.

In other menus, if the pointer moves anywhere except into a submenu associated with the CascadeButtonGadget, the CascadeButtonGadget is disarmed and its submenu is unposted.

Virtual Bindings

The bindings for virtual keys are vendor specific.

Related Information

Object(3X), RectObj(3X), XmCascadeButtonHighlight(3), XmCreateCascadeButtonGadget(3X), XmCreatePulldownMenu(3X), XmCreatePopupMenu(3X), XmCreateOptionMenu(3X), XmGadget(3X), XmLabelGadget(3X), and XmRowColumn(3X).

XmCascadeButtonGadgetHighlight

Purpose

A CascadeButtonGadget function that sets the highlight state.

AES Support Level

Trial-use

Synopsis

#include <Xm/CascadeBG.h>

void   XmCascadeButtonGadgetHighlight   (*cascadeButtonGadget,*
highlight)
> **Widget**   *cascadeButtonGadget*;
> **Boolean**   *highlight*;

Description

XmCascadeButtonGadgetHighlight either draws or erases the shadow highlight around the CascadeButtonGadget.

cascadeButtonGadget
> Specifies the CascadeButtonGadget to be highlighted or unhighlighted.

highlight
> Specifies whether to highlight (True) or to unhighlight (False).

For a complete definition of CascadeButtonGadget and its associated resources, see **XmCascadeButtonGadget(3X)**.

Related Information

XmCascadeButton(3X), **XmCascadeButtonGadget(3X)**, and **XmCascadeButtonHighlight(3X)**.

XmCascadeButtonHighlight

Purpose

A CascadeButton and CascadeButtonGadget function that sets the highlight state.

AES Support Level

Full-use

Synopsis

```
#include <Xm/CascadeB.h>
#include <Xm/CascadeBG.h>

void XmCascadeButtonHighlight (cascadeButton, highlight)
    Widget      cascadeButton;
    Boolean     highlight;
```

Description

XmCascadeButtonHighlight either draws or erases the shadow highlight around the CascadeButton or the CascadeButtonGadget.

cascadeButton	Specifies the CascadeButton or CascadeButtonGadget to be highlighted or unhighlighted.
highlight	Specifies whether to highlight (True) or to unhighlight (False).

For a complete definition of CascadeButton or CascadeButtonGadget and their associated resources, see **XmCascadeButton(3X)** or **XmCascadeButtonGadget(3X)**.

Related Information

XmCascadeButton(3X), **XmCascadeButtonGadget(3X)** and **XmCascadeButtonGadgetHighlight(3X)**.

XmClipboardCancelCopy

Purpose

A clipboard function that cancels a copy to the clipboard.

AES Support Level

Full-use

Synopsis

#include <Xm/Xm.h>
#include <Xm/CutPaste.h>

int XmClipboardCancelCopy (*display, window, item_id*)
    Display   * *display*;
    Window   *window*;
    long   *item_id*;

Description

XmClipboardCancelCopy cancels the copy to clipboard that is in progress
and frees up temporary storage. When a copy is to be performed,
XmClipboardStartCopy allocates temporary storage for the clipboard
data. **XmClipboardCopy** copies the appropriate data into the the
temporary storage. **XmClipboardEndCopy** copies the data to the clipboard
structure and frees up the temporary storage structures. If

XmClipboardCancelCopy is called, the **XmClipboardEndCopy** function does not have to be called. A call to **XmClipboardCancelCopy** is valid only after a call to **XmClipboardStartCopy** and before a call to **XmClipboardEndCopy**.

display   Specifies a pointer to the **Display** structure that was returned in a previous call to **XOpenDisplay** or **XtDisplay**.

window   Specifies a widget's window ID that relates the application window to the clipboard. The widget's window ID can be obtained by using **XtWindow**. The same application instance should pass the same window ID to each of the clipboard functions that it calls.

item_id   Specifies the number assigned to this data item. This number was returned by a previous call to **XmClipboardStartCopy**.

Return Value

ClipboardSuccess
>The function is successful.

ClipboardLocked
>The function failed because the clipboard was locked by another application. The application can continue to call the function again with the same parameters until the lock goes away. This gives the application the opportunity to ask if the user wants to keep trying or to give up on the operation.

ClipboardFail The function failed because **XmClipboardStartCopy** was not called or because the data item contains too many formats.

Related Information

XmClipboardCopy(3X),   XmClipboardEndCopy(3X),   and
XmClipboardStartCopy(3X).

XmClipboardCopy

Purpose

A clipboard function that copies a data item to temporary storage for later copying to clipboard.

AES Support Level

Full-use

Synopsis

#include <Xm/Xm.h>
#include <Xm/CutPaste.h>

int XmClipboardCopy (*display, window, item_id, format_name, buffer, length, private_id, data_id*)
      Display   * *display*;
      Window   *window*;
      long   *item_id*;
      char   * *format_name*;
      char   * *buffer*;
      unsigned long *length*;
      int   *private_id*;
      int   * *data_id*;

Description

XmClipboardCopy copies a data item to temporary storage. The data item is moved from temporary storage to the clipboard data structure when a call to **XmClipboardEndCopy** is made. Additional calls to **XmClipboardCopy** before a call to **XmClipboardEndCopy** add additional data item formats to the same data item or append data to an existing format. Formats are described in the *Inter-Client Communication Conventions Manual* (ICCCM) as targets.

NOTE: Do not call **XmClipboardCopy** before a call to **XmClipboardStartCopy** has been made. The latter function allocates temporary storage required by **XmClipboardCopy**.

If the *buffer* argument is NULL, the data is considered to be passed by name. When data, that has been passed by name is later requested by another application, the application that owns the data receives a callback with a request for the data. The application that owns the data must then transfer the data to the clipboard with the **XmClipboardCopyByName** function. When a data item that was passed by name is deleted from the clipboard, the application that owns the data receives a callback stating that the data is no longer needed.

For information on the callback function, see the callback argument description for **XmClipboardStartCopy**.

display	Specifies a pointer to the **Display** structure that was returned in a previous call to **XOpenDisplay** or **XtDisplay**.
window	Specifies a widget's window ID that relates the application window to the clipboard. The widget's window ID can be obtained by using **XtWindow**. The same application instance should pass the same window ID to each of the clipboard functions that it calls.
item_id	Specifies the number assigned to this data item. This number was returned by a previous call to **XmClipboardStartCopy**.

format_name	Specifies the name of the format in which the data item is stored on the clipboard. Format is known as target in the ICCCM.
buffer	Specifies the buffer from which the clipboard copies the data.
length	Specifies the length of the data being copied to the clipboard.
private_id	Specifies the private data that the application wants to store with the data item.
data_id	Specifies an identifying number assigned to the data item that uniquely identifies the data item and the format. This argument is required only for data that is passed by name.

Return Value

ClipboardSuccess
> The function is successful.

ClipboardLocked
> The function failed because the clipboard was locked by another application. The application can continue to call the function again with the same parameters until the lock goes away. This gives the application the opportunity to ask if the user wants to keep trying or to give up on the operation.

ClipboardFail The function failed because **XmClipboardStartCopy** was not called or because the data item contains too many formats.

Related Information

XmClipboardCopyByName(3X), XmClipboardEndCopy(3X), and
XmClipboardStartCopy(3X).

XmClipboardCopyByName

Purpose

A clipboard function that copies a data item passed by name.

AES Support Level

Full-use

Synopsis

#include <Xm/Xm.h>
#include <Xm/CutPaste.h>

int **XmClipboardCopyByName** (*display, window, data_id, buffer, length, private_id*)
      Display   * *display*;
      Window   *window*;
      int   *data_id*;
      char   * *buffer*;
      unsigned long*length*;
      int   *private_id*;

Description

XmClipboardCopyByName copies the actual data for a data item that was previously passed by name to the clipboard. Data is considered to be passed by name when a call to **XmClipboardCopy** is made with a NULL buffer parameter. Additional calls to this function append new data to the existing data.

display   Specifies a pointer to the **Display** structure that was returned in a previous call to **XOpenDisplay** or **XtDisplay**.

window   Specifies a widget's window ID that relates the application window to the clipboard. The widget's window ID can be obtained by using **XtWindow**. The same application instance should pass the same window ID to each clipboard function it calls.

data_id   Specifies an identifying number assigned to the data item that uniquely identifies the data item and the format. This number was assigned by **XmClipboardCopy** to the data item.

buffer   Specifies the buffer from which the clipboard copies the data.

length   Specifies the number of bytes in the data item.

private_id   Specifies the private data that the application wants to store with the data item.

Return Value

ClipboardSuccess
> The function is successful.

ClipboardLocked
> The function failed because the clipboard was locked by another application. The application can continue to call the function again with the same parameters until the lock goes away. This gives the application the opportunity to ask if the user wants to keep trying or to give up on the operation.

Related Information

XmClipboardCopy(3X), **XmClipboardLock(3X)**, **XmClipboardStartCopy(3X)**, and **XmClipboardUnlock(3X)**.

XmClipboardEndCopy

Purpose

A clipboard function that ends a copy to the clipboard.

AES Support Level

Full-use

Synopsis

#include <Xm/Xm.h>
#include <Xm/CutPaste.h>

int XmClipboardEndCopy (*display, window, item_id*)
    Display   * *display*;
    Window   *window*;
    long   *item_id*;

Description

XmClipboardEndCopy locks the clipboard from access by other applications, places data in the clipboard data structure, and unlocks the clipboard. Data items copied to the clipboard by **XmClipboardCopy** are not actually entered in the clipboard data structure until the call to **XmClipboardEndCopy**.

This function also frees up temporary storage that was allocated by **XmClipboardStartCopy**, which must be called before **XmClipboardEndCopy**. The latter function should not be called if **XmClipboardCancelCopy** has been called.

display Specifies a pointer to the **Display** structure that was returned in a previous call to **XOpenDisplay** or **XtDisplay**.

window Specifies a widget's window ID that relates the application window to the clipboard. The widget's window ID can be obtained by using **XtWindow**. The same application instance should pass the same window ID to each clipboard function it calls.

item_id Specifies the number assigned to this data item. This number was returned by a previous call to **XmClipboardStartCopy**.

Return Value

ClipboardSuccess
> The function is successful.

ClipboardLocked
> The function failed because the clipboard was locked by another application. The application can continue to call the function again with the same parameters until the lock goes away. This gives the application the opportunity to ask if the user wants to keep trying or to give up on the operation.

ClipboardFail The function failed because **XmClipboardStartCopy** was not called.

Related Information

XmClipboardCancelCopy(3X), XmClipboardCopy(3X) and
XmClipboardStartCopy(3X).

XmClipboardEndRetrieve

Purpose

A clipboard function that ends a copy from the clipboard.

AES Support Level

Full-use

Synopsis

```
#include <Xm/Xm.h>
#include <Xm/CutPaste.h>

int XmClipboardEndRetrieve (display, window)
        Display     * display;
        Window      window;
```

Description

XmClipboardEndRetrieve suspends copying data incrementally from the clipboard. It tells the clipboard routines that the application is through copying an item from the clipboard. Until this function is called, data items can be retrieved incrementally from the clipboard by calling **XmClipboardRetrieve**.

display   Specifies a pointer to the **Display** structure that was returned in a previous call to **XOpenDisplay** or **XtDisplay**.

window   Specifies a widget's window ID that relates the application window to the clipboard. The widget's window ID can be obtained by using **XtWindow**. The same application instance should pass the same window ID to each of the clipboard functions that it calls.

Return Value

ClipboardSuccess
> The function is successful.

ClipboardLocked
> The function failed because the clipboard was locked by another application. The application can continue to call the function again with the same parameters until the lock goes away. This gives the application the opportunity to ask if the user wants to keep trying or to give up on the operation.

Related Information

XmClipboardRetrieve(3X), **XmClipboardStartCopy(3X)**, and **XmClipboardStartRetrieve(3X)**.

XmClipboardInquireCount

Purpose

A clipboard function that returns the number of data item formats.

AES Support Level

Full-use

Synopsis

#include <Xm/Xm.h>
#include <Xm/CutPaste.h>

int   **XmClipboardInquireCount**   (*display,*   *window,*   *count,*
max_format_name_length)
    Display   * *display;*
    Window   *window;*
    int   * *count;*
    int   * *max_format_name_length;*

Description

XmClipboardInquireCount returns the number of data item formats available for the data item in the clipboard. This function also returns the maximum name-length for all formats in which the data item is stored.

display   Specifies a pointer to the **Display** structure that was returned in a previous call to **XOpenDisplay** or **XtDisplay**.

window   Specifies a widget's window ID that relates the application window to the clipboard. The widget's window ID can be obtained by using **XtWindow**. The same application instance should pass the same window ID to each of the clipboard functions that it calls.

count   Returns the number of data item formats available for the data item in the clipboard. If no formats are available, this argument equals zero. The count includes the formats that were passed by name.

max_format_name_length
          Specifies the maximum length of all format names for the data item in the clipboard.

Return Value

ClipboardSuccess   The function is successful.

ClipboardLocked   The function failed because the clipboard was locked by another application. The application can continue to call the function again with the same parameters until the lock goes away. This gives the application the opportunity to ask if the user wants to keep trying or to give up on the operation.

ClipboardNoData   The function could not find data on the clipboard corresponding to the format requested. This could occur because the clipboard is empty; there is data on the clipboard but not in the requested format; or the data in the requested format was passed by name and is no longer available.

Related Information

XmClipboardStartCopy(3X).

XmClipboardInquireFormat

Purpose

A clipboard function that returns a specified format name.

AES Support Level

Full-use

Synopsis

#include <Xm/Xm.h>
#include <Xm/CutPaste.h>

int   XmClipboardInquireFormat   (*display*,   *window*,   *index*,
format_name_buf, *buffer_len*, *copied_len*)
        Display   * *display*;
        Window   *window*;
        int   *index*;
        char   * *format_name_buf*;
        unsigned long *buffer_len*;
        unsigned long * *copied_len*;

Description

XmClipboardInquireFormat returns a specified format name for the data item in the clipboard. If the name must be truncated, the function returns a warning status.

display　　　　Specifies a pointer to the **Display** structure that was returned in a previous call to **XOpenDisplay** or **XtDisplay**.

window　　　　Specifies a widget's window ID that relates the application window to the clipboard. The widget's window ID can be obtained by using **XtWindow**. The same application instance should pass the same window ID to each of the clipboard functions that it calls.

index　　　　Specifies which of the ordered format names to obtain. If this index is greater than the number of formats for the data item, this function returns a zero in the *copied_len* argument.

format_name_buf
　　　　Specifies the buffer that receives the format name.

buffer_len　　　Specifies the number of bytes in the format name buffer.

copied_len　　　Specifies the number of bytes in the string copied to the buffer. If this argument equals zero, there is no *nth* format for the data item.

Return Value

ClipboardSuccess
>The function is successful.

ClipboardLocked
>The function failed because the clipboard was locked by another application. The application can continue to call the function again with the same parameters until the lock goes away. This gives the application the opportunity to ask if the user wants to keep trying or to give up on the operation.

ClipboardTruncate
>The data returned is truncated because the user did not provide a buffer large enough to hold the data.

ClipboardNoData
>The function could not find data on the clipboard corresponding to the format requested. This could occur because the clipboard is empty; there is data on the clipboard but not in the requested format; or the data in the requested format was passed by name and is no longer available.

Related Information

XmClipboardStartCopy(3X).

XmClipboardInquireLength

Purpose

A clipboard function that returns the length of the stored data.

AES Support Level

Full-use

Synopsis

#include <Xm/Xm.h>
#include <Xm/CutPaste.h>

int XmClipboardInquireLength (*display, window, format_name, length*)
    Display   * *display*;
    Window   *window*;
    char   * *format_name*;
    unsigned long* *length*;

Description

XmClipboardInquireLength returns the length of the data stored under a specified format name for the clipboard data item. If no data is found for the specified format, or if there is no item on the clipboard, this function returns a value of zero.

Any format passed by name is assumed to have the *length* passed in a call to **XmClipboardCopy**, even though the data has not yet been transferred to the clipboard in that format.

display	Specifies a pointer to the **Display** structure that was returned in a previous call to **XOpenDisplay** or **XtDisplay**.
window	Specifies a widget's window ID that relates the application window to the clipboard. The widget's window ID can be obtained by using **XtWindow**. The same application instance should pass the same window ID to each of the clipboard functions that it calls.
format_name	Specifies the name of the format for the data item.
length	Specifies the length of the next data item in the specified format. This argument equals zero if no data is found for the specified format, or if there is no item on the clipboard.

Return Value

ClipboardSuccess
>The function is successful.

ClipboardLocked
>The function failed because the clipboard was locked by another application. The application can continue to call the function again with the same parameters until the lock goes away. This gives the application the opportunity to ask if the user wants to keep trying or to give up on the operation.

ClipboardNoData
>The function could not find data on the clipboard corresponding to the format requested. This could occur because the clipboard is empty; there is data on the clipboard but not in the requested format; or the data in the requested format was passed by name and is no longer available.

Related Information

XmClipboardCopy(3X) and **XmClipboardStartCopy(3X)**.

XmClipboardInquirePendingItems

Purpose

A clipboard function that returns a list of *data_id*/*private_id* pairs.

AES Support Level

Full-use

Synopsis

```
#include <Xm/Xm.h>
#include <Xm/CutPaste.h>

int XmClipboardInquirePendingItems (display, window, format_name,
item_list, count)
    Display             * display;
    Window              window;
    char                * format_name;
    XmClipboardPendingList* item_list;
    unsigned long       * count;
```

Description

XmClipboardInquirePendingItems returns a list of *data_id*/*private_id* pairs for the specified format name. A data item is considered pending if the application originally passed it by name, the application has not yet copied the data, and the item has not been deleted from the clipboard. The application is responsible for freeing the memory provided by this function to store the list. To free the memory, call **XtFree**.

This function is used by an application when exiting, to determine if the data that is passed by name should be sent to the clipboard.

display	Specifies a pointer to the **Display** structure that was returned in a previous call to **XOpenDisplay** or **XtDisplay**.
window	Specifies a widget's window ID that relates the application window to the clipboard. The widget's window ID can be obtained by using **XtWindow**. The same application instance should pass the same window ID to each of the clipboard functions that it calls.
format_name	Specifies a string that contains the name of the format for which the list of data ID/private ID pairs is to be obtained.
item_list	Specifies the address of the array of data ID/private ID pairs for the specified format name. This argument is a type **XmClipboardPendingList**. The application is responsible for freeing the memory provided by this function for storing the list.
item_count	Specifies the number of items returned in the list. If there is no data for the specified format name, or if there is no item on the clipboard, this argument equals zero.

Return Value

ClipboardSuccess

The function is successful.

ClipboardLocked

The function failed because the clipboard was locked by another application. The application can continue to call the function again with the same parameters until the lock goes away. This gives the application the opportunity to ask if the user wants to keep trying or to give up on the operation.

Related Information

XmClipboardStartCopy(3X).

XmClipboardLock

Purpose

A clipboard function that locks the clipboard

AES Support Level

Full-use

Synopsis

#include <Xm/Xm.h>
#include <Xm/CutPaste.h>

int XmClipboardLock (*display, window*)
    Display   * *display*;
    Window   *window*;

Description

XmClipboardLock locks the clipboard from access by another application until **XmClipboardUnlock** is called. All clipboard functions lock and unlock the clipboard to prevent simultaneous access. This function allows the application to keep the clipboard data from changing between calls to

Inquire and other clipboard functions. The application does not need to lock the clipboard between calls to **XmClipboardStartCopy** and **XmClipboardEndCopy** or to **XmClipboardStartRetrieve** and **XmClipboardEndRetrieve**.

If the clipboard is already locked by another application, **XmClipboardLock** returns an error status. Multiple calls to this function by the same application increases the lock level.

display   Specifies a pointer to the **Display** structure that was returned in a previous call to **XOpenDisplay** or **XtDisplay**.

window   Specifies a widget's window ID that relates the application window to the clipboard. The widget's window ID can be obtained by using **XtWindow**. The same application instance should pass the same window ID to each of the clipboard functions that it calls.

Return Value

ClipboardSuccess
          The function is successful.

ClipboardLocked
          The function failed because the clipboard was locked by another application. The application can continue to call the function again with the same parameters until the lock goes away. This gives the application the opportunity to ask if the user wants to keep trying or to give up on the operation.

Related Information

XmClipboardEndCopy(3X), XmClipboardEndRetrieve(3X),
XmClipboardStartCopy(3X), XmClipboardStartRetrieve(3X), and
XmClipboardUnlock(3X).

XmClipboardRegisterFormat

Purpose

A clipboard function that registers a new format.

AES Support Level

Full-use

Synopsis

#include <Xm/Xm.h>
#include <Xm/CutPaste.h>

int XmClipboardRegisterFormat (*display, format_name, format_length*)
    Display   * *display*;
    char   * *format_name*;
    unsigned long *format_length*;

Description

XmClipboardRegisterFormat registers a new format. Each format stored on the clipboard should have a length associated with it; this length must be known to the clipboard routines. Formats are known as targets in the *Inter-Client Communication Conventions Manual* (ICCCM). All of the formats specified by the ICCCM conventions are preregistered. Any other format that the application wants to use must either be 8-bit data or be registered via this routine. Failure to register the length of the data results in incompatible applications across platforms having different byte-swapping orders.

display	Specifies a pointer to the **Display** structure that was returned in a previous call to **XOpenDisplay** or **XtDisplay**.
format_name	Specifies the string name for the new format (target).
format_length	Specifies the format length in bits (8, 16, or 32).

Return Value

ClipboardBadFormat
The *format_name* must not be NULL, and the *format_length* must be 8, 16, or 32.

ClipboardSuccess The function is successful.

ClipboardLocked The function failed because the clipboard was locked by another application. The application can continue to call the function again with the same parameters until the lock goes away. This gives the application the opportunity to ask if the user wants to keep trying or to give up on the operation.

ClipboardFail The function failed because the format was already registered with this length.

Related Information

XmClipboardStartCopy(3X).

XmClipboardRetrieve

Purpose

A clipboard function that retrieves a data item from the clipboard.

AES Support Level

Full-use

Synopsis

#include <Xm/Xm.h>
#include <Xm/CutPaste.h>

int XmClipboardRetrieve (*display, window, format_name, buffer, length, num_bytes, private_id*)
    Display   * *display*;
    Window   *window*;
    char   * *format_name*;
    char   * *buffer*;
    unsigned long *length*;
    unsigned long * *num_bytes*;
    int   * *private_id*;

Description

> **XmClipboardRetrieve** retrieves the current data item from clipboard storage. It returns a warning if the clipboard is locked; if there is no data on the clipboard; or if the data needs to be truncated because the buffer length is too short.
>
> Between a call to **XmClipboardStartRetrieve** and a call to **XmClipboardEndRetrieve**, multiple calls to **XmClipboardRetrieve** with the same format name result in data being incrementally copied from the clipboard until the data in that format has all been copied.
>
> The return value **ClipboardTruncate** from calls to **XmClipboardRetrieve** indicates that more data remains to be copied in the given format. It is recommended that any calls to the **Inquire** functions that the application needs to make to effect the copy from the clipboard be made between the call to **XmClipboardStartRetrieve** and the first call to **XmClipboardRetrieve**. That way, the application does not need to call **XmClipboardLock** and **XmClipboardUnlock**.

> | | |
> |---|---|
> | *display* | Specifies a pointer to the **Display** structure that was returned in a previous call to **XOpenDisplay** or **XtDisplay**. |
> | *window* | Specifies a widget's window ID that relates the application window to the clipboard. The widget's window ID can be obtained by using **XtWindow**. The same application instance should pass the same window ID to each of the clipboard functions that it calls. |
> | *format_name* | Specifies the name of a format in which the data is stored on the clipboard. |
> | *buffer* | Specifies the buffer to which the application wants the clipboard to copy the data. |

length   Specifies the length of the application buffer.

num_bytes   Specifies the number of bytes of data copied into the application buffer.

private_id   Specifies the private data stored with the data item by the application that placed the data item on the clipboard. If the application did not store private data with the data item, this argument returns zero.

Return Value

ClipboardSuccess
> The function is successful.

ClipboardLocked
> The function failed because the clipboard was locked by another application. The application can continue to call the function again with the same parameters until the lock goes away. This gives the application the opportunity to ask if the user wants to keep trying or to give up on the operation.

ClipboardTruncate
> The data returned is truncated because the user did not provide a buffer large enough to hold the data.

ClipboardNoData
> The function could not find data on the clipboard corresponding to the format requested. This could occur because the clipboard is empty; there is data on the clipboard but not in the requested format; or the data in the requested format was passed by name and is no longer available.

Related Information

XmClipboardEndRetrieve(3X), XmClipboardLock(3X),
XmClipboardStartCopy(3X), XmClipboardStartRetrieve(3X), and
XmClipboardUnlock(3X).

XmClipboardStartCopy

Purpose

A clipboard function that sets up a storage and data structure.

AES Support Level

Full-use

Synopsis

#include <Xm/Xm.h>
#include <Xm/CutPaste.h>

int XmClipboardStartCopy (*display, window, clip_label, timestamp, widget, callback, item_id*)
> **Display**   * *display*;
> **Window**   *window*;
> **XmString**   *clip_label*;
> **Time**   *timestamp*;
> **Widget**   *widget*;
> **VoidProc**   *callback*;
> **long**   * *item_id*;

Description

XmClipboardStartCopy sets up storage and data structures to receive clipboard data. An application calls this function during a cut or copy operation. The data item that these structures receive then becomes the next data item in the clipboard.

Copying a large piece of data to the clipboard can take a long time. It is possible that, once copied, no application will ever request that data. The Motif Toolkit provides a mechanism so that an application does not need to actually pass data to the clipboard until the data has been requested by some application.

Instead, the application passes format and length information in **XmClipboardCopy** to the clipboard functions, along with a widget ID and a callback function address that is passed in **XmClipboardStartCopy**. The widget ID is needed for communications between the clipboard functions in the application that owns the data and the clipboard functions in the application that requests the data.

The callback functions are responsible for copying the actual data to the clipboard via **XmClipboardCopyByName**. The callback function is also called if the data item is removed from the clipboard, and the actual data is therefore no longer needed.

display	Specifies a pointer to the **Display** structure that was returned in a previous call to **XOpenDisplay** or **XtDisplay**.
window	Specifies a widget's window ID that relates the application window to the clipboard. The widget's window ID can be obtained by using **XtWindow**. The same application instance should pass the same window ID to each of the clipboard functions that it calls.
clip_label	Specifies the label to be associated with the data item. This argument is used to identify the data item, for example, in a clipboard viewer. An example of a label is the name of the application that places the data in the clipboard.
timestamp	Specifies the time of the event that triggered the copy. A valid timestamp must be supplied; it is not sufficient to use **CurrentTime**.

widget Specifies the ID of the widget that receives messages requesting data previously passed by name. This argument must be present in order to pass data by name. Any valid widget ID in your application can be used for this purpose and all the message handling is taken care of by the cut and paste functions.

callback Specifies the address of the callback function that is called when the clipboard needs data that was originally passed by name. This is also the callback to receive the **delete** message for items that were originally passed by name. This argument must be present in order to pass data by name.

item_id Specifies the number assigned to this data item. The application uses this number in calls to **XmClipboardCopy**, **XmClipboardEndCopy**, and **XmClipboardCancelCopy**.

For more information on passing data by name, see **XmClipboardCopy(3X)** and **XmClipboardCopyByName(3X)**.

The *widget* and *callback* arguments must be present in order to pass data by name. The callback format is as follows:

function name
    Widget   *widget*;
    int   * *data_id*;
    int   * *private*;
    int   * *reason*;

widget Specifies the ID of the widget passed to this function.

data_id Specifies the identifying number returned by **XmClipboardCopy**, which identifies the pass-by-name data.

private	Specifies the private information passed to **XmClipboardCopy**.
reason	Specifies the reason, which is either **XmCR_CLIPBOARD_DATA_DELETE** or **XmCR_CLIPBOARD_DATA_REQUEST**.

Return Value

ClipboardSuccess
> The function is successful.

ClipboardLocked
> The function failed because the clipboard was locked by another application. The application can continue to call the function again with the same parameters until the lock goes away. This gives the application the opportunity to ask if the user wants to keep trying or to give up on the operation.

Related Information

XmClipboardCancelCopy(3X), XmClipboardCopy(3X), XmClipboardCopyByName(3X), XmClipboardEndCopy(3X), XmClipboardEndRetrieve(3X), XmClipboardInquireCount(3X), XmClipboardInquireFormat(3X), XmClipboardInquireLength(3X), XmClipboardInquirePendingItems(3X), XmClipboardLock(3X), XmClipboardRegisterFormat(3X), XmClipboardRetrieve(3X), XmClipboardStartRetrieve(3X), XmClipboardUndoCopy(3X), XmClipboardUnlock(3X), and XmClipboardWithdrawFormat(3X).

XmClipboardStartRetrieve

Purpose

A clipboard function that starts a copy from the clipboard.

AES Support Level

Full-use

Synopsis

#include <Xm/Xm.h>
#include <Xm/CutPaste.h>

int XmClipboardStartRetrieve (*display, window, timestamp*)
    Display   * *display*;
    Window   *window*;
    Time   *timestamp*;

Description

XmClipboardStartRetrieve tells the clipboard routines that the application is ready to start copying an item from the clipboard. The clipboard is locked by this routine and stays locked until **XmClipboardEndRetrieve** is called. Between a call to **XmClipboardStartRetrieve** and a call to **XmClipboardEndRetrieve**, multiple calls to **XmClipboardRetrieve** with the same format name result in data being incrementally copied from the clipboard until the data in that format has all been copied.

The return value **ClipboardTruncate** from calls to **XmClipboardRetrieve** indicates that more data remains to be copied in the given format. It is recommended that any calls to the **Inquire** functions that the application needs to make to effect the copy from the clipboard be made between the call to **XmClipboardStartRetrieve** and the first call to **XmClipboardRetrieve**. That way, the application does not need to call **XmClipboardLock** and **XmClipboardUnlock**.

display   Specifies a pointer to the **Display** structure that was returned in a previous call to **XOpenDisplay** or **XtDisplay**.

window   Specifies a widget's window ID that relates the application window to the clipboard. The widget's window ID can be obtained by using **XtWindow**. The same application instance should pass the same window ID to each of the clipboard functions that it calls.

timestamp   Specifies the time of the event that triggered the copy. A valid timestamp must be supplied; it is not sufficient to use **CurrentTime**.

Return Value

ClipboardSuccess

> The function is successful.

ClipboardLocked

> The function failed because the clipboard was locked by another application. The application can continue to call the function again with the same parameters until the lock goes away. This gives the application the opportunity to ask if the user wants to keep trying or to give up on the operation.

Related Information

XmClipboardEndRetrieve(3X), XmClipboardInquireCount(3X), XmClipboardInquireFormat(3X), XmClipboardInquireLength(3X), XmClipboardInquirePendingItems(3X), XmClipboardLock(3X), XmClipboardRetrieve(3X), XmClipboardStartCopy(3X), and XmClipboardUnlock(3X).

XmClipboardUndoCopy

Purpose

A clipboard function that deletes the last item placed on the clipboard.

AES Support Level

Full-use

Synopsis

#include <Xm/Xm.h>
#include <Xm/CutPaste.h>

int XmClipboardUndoCopy (*display, window*)
    Display   * *display*;
    Window   *window*;

Description

XmClipboardUndoCopy deletes the last item placed on the clipboard if the item was placed there by an application with the passed *display* and *window* arguments. Any data item deleted from the clipboard by the original call to **XmClipboardCopy** is restored. If the *display* or *window* IDs do not match the last copied item, no action is taken, and this function has no effect.

display   Specifies a pointer to the **Display** structure that was returned in a previous call to **XOpenDisplay** or **XtDisplay**.

window   Specifies a widget's window ID that relates the application window to the clipboard. The widget's window ID can be obtained by using **XtWindow**. The same application instance should pass the same window ID to each clipboard function it calls.

Return Value

ClipboardSuccess
> The function is successful.

ClipboardLocked
> The function failed because the clipboard was locked by another application. The application can continue to call the function again with the same parameters until the lock goes away. This gives the application the opportunity to ask if the user wants to keep trying or to give up on the operation.

Related Information

XmClipboardLock(3X) and **XmClipboardStartCopy(3X)**.

XmClipboardUnlock

Purpose

A clipboard function that unlocks the clipboard

AES Support Level

Full-use

Synopsis

#include <Xm/Xm.h>
#include <Xm/CutPaste.h>

int XmClipboardUnlock (*display, window, remove_all_locks*)
    Display   * *display*;
    Window   *window*;
    Boolean   *remove_all_locks*;

Description

XmClipboardUnlock unlocks the clipboard, enabling it to be accessed by other applications.

If multiple calls to **XmClipboardLock** have occurred, the same number of calls to **XmClipboardUnlock** is necessary to unlock the clipboard, unless *remove_all_locks* is set to True.

display   Specifies a pointer to the **Display** structure that was returned in a previous call to **XOpenDisplay** or **XtDisplay**.

window   Specifies a widget's window ID that relates the application window to the clipboard. The widget's window ID can be obtained by using **XtWindow**. The same application instance should pass the same window ID to each of the clipboard functions that it calls.

remove_all_locks

When True, indicates that all nested locks should be removed. When False, indicates that only one level of lock should be removed.

Return Value

ClipboardSuccess

The function is successful.

ClipboardFail   The function failed because the clipboard was not locked or was locked by another application.

Related Information

XmClipboardCancelCopy(3X), **XmClipboardCopy(3X)**, **XmClipboardEndCopy(3X)**, **XmClipboardEndRetrieve(3X)**, **XmClipboardInquireCount(3X)**, **XmClipboardInquireFormat(3X)**, **XmClipboardInquireLength(3X)**, **XmClipboardInquirePendingItems(3X)**, **XmClipboardLock(3X)**, **XmClipboardRegisterFormat(3X)**, **XmClipboardRetrieve(3X)**, **XmClipboardStartCopy(3X)**, **XmClipboardStartRetrieve(3X)**, **XmClipboardUndoCopy(3X)**, and **XmClipboardWithdrawFormat(3X)**.

XmClipboardWithdrawFormat

Purpose

A clipboard function that indicates that the application no longer wants to supply a data item.

AES Support Level

Full-use

Synopsis

```
#include <Xm/Xm.h>
#include <Xm/CutPaste.h>

int XmClipboardWithdrawFormat (display, window, data_id)
        Display     * display;
        Window      window;
        int         data_id;
```

Description

XmClipboardWithdrawFormat indicates that the application will no longer supply a data item to the clipboard that the application had previously passed by name.

display	Specifies a pointer to the **Display** structure that was returned in a previous call to **XOpenDisplay** or **XtDisplay**.
window	Specifies a widget's window ID that relates the application window to the clipboard. The widget's window ID can be obtained by using **XtWindow**. The same application instance should pass the same window ID to each of the clipboard functions that it calls.
data_id	Specifies an identifying number assigned to the data item that uniquely identifies the data item and the format. This was assigned to the item when it was originally passed by **XmClipboardCopy**.

Return Value

ClipboardSuccess
> The function is successful.

ClipboardLocked
> The function failed because the clipboard was locked by another application. The application can continue to call the function again with the same parameters until the lock goes away. This gives the application the opportunity to ask if the user wants to keep trying or to give up on the operation.

Related Information

XmClipboardCopy(3X) and XmClipboardStartCopy(3X).

XmCommand

Purpose

The Command widget class

AES Support Level

Full-use

Synopsis

#include <Xm/Command.h>

Description

Command is a special-purpose composite widget for command entry that provides a built-in command-history mechanism. Command includes a command-line text-input field, a command-line prompt, and a command-history list region.

One additional **WorkArea** child may be added to the Command after creation.

Whenever a command is entered, it is automatically added to the end of the command-history list and made visible. This does not change the selected item in the list, if there is one.

Many of the new resources specified for Command are actually SelectionBox resources that have been renamed for clarity and ease of use.

Classes

Command inherits behavior and resources from **Core**, **Composite**, **Constraint**, **XmManager**, **XmBulletinBoard**, and **XmSelectionBox** classes.

The class pointer is **xmCommandWidgetClass**.

The class name is **XmCommand**.

New Resources

The following table defines a set of widget resources used by the programmer to specify data. The programmer can also set the resource values for the inherited classes to set attributes for this widget. To reference a resource by name or by class in a .Xdefaults file, remove the **XmN** or **XmC** prefix and use the remaining letters. To specify one of the defined values for a resource in a .Xdefaults file, remove the **Xm** prefix and use the remaining letters (in either lowercase or uppercase, but include any underscores between words). The codes in the access column indicate if the given resource can be set at creation time (**C**), set by using **XtSetValues** (**S**), retrieved by using **XtGetValues** (**G**), or is not applicable (**N/A**).

XmCommand Resource Set		
Name	**Default**	**Access**
Class	**Type**	
XmNcommand	""	CSG
XmCTextString	XmString	
XmNcommandChangedCallback	NULL	C
XmCCallback	XtCallbackList	
XmNcommandEnteredCallback	NULL	C
XmCCallback	XtCallbackList	
XmNhistoryItems	NULL	CSG
XmCItems	XmStringTable	
XmNhistoryItemCount	0	CSG
XmCItemCount	int	
XmNhistoryMaxItems	100	CSG
XmCMaxItems	int	
XmNhistoryVisibleItemCount	dynamic	CSG
XmCVisibleItemCount	int	
XmNpromptString	dynamic	CSG
XmCPromptString	XmString	

XmNcommand

Contains the current command-line text. This is the **XmNtextString** resource in SelectionBox, renamed for Command. This resource can also be modified via **XmCommandSetValue** and **XmCommandAppendValue** functions. The command area is a Text widget.

XmNcommandChangedCallback

Specifies the list of callbacks that is called when the value of the command changes. The callback reason is **XmCR_COMMAND_CHANGED**. This is equivalent to the **XmNvalueChangedCallback** of the Text widget, except that a pointer to an **XmCommandCallbackStructure** is passed, and the structure's *value* member contains the **XmString**.

XmNcommandEnteredCallback

Specifies the list of callbacks that is called when a command is entered in the Command. The callback reason is **XmCR_COMMAND_ENTERED**. A pointer to an **XmCommandCallback** structure is passed.

XmNhistoryItems

Lists **XmString** items that make up the contents of the history list. This is the **XmNlistItems** resource in SelectionBox, renamed for Command.

XmNhistoryItemCount

Specifies the number of **XmStrings** in **XmNhistoryItems**. This is the **XmNlistItemCount** resource in SelectionBox, renamed for Command. The value must not be negative.

XmNhistoryMaxItems

Specifies the maximum number of items allowed in the history list. Once this number is reached, an existing list item must be removed before a new item can be added to the list. For each command entered, the first list item is removed from the list, so the new command can be added to the list. The value must be greater than 0.

XmNhistoryVisibleItemCount

Specifies the number of items in the history list that should be visible at one time. In effect, it sets the height (in lines) of the history list window. This is the **XmNlistVisibleItemCount** resource in SelectionBox, renamed for Command. The value must be greater than 0. The default is dynamic based on the height of the list.

XmNpromptString

Specifies a prompt for the command line. This is the **XmNselectionLabelString** resource in SelectionBox, renamed for Command. The default may vary depending on the value of the **XmNstringDirection** resource.

Inherited Resources

Command inherits behavior and resources from the following superclasses. For a complete description of each resource, refer to the man page for that superclass.

XmSelectionBox Resource Set		
Name	**Default**	**Access**
Class	**Type**	
XmNapplyCallback	NULL	N/A
XmCCallback	XtCallbackList	
XmNapplyLabelString	"Apply"	N/A
XmCApplyLabelString	XmString	
XmNcancelCallback	NULL	N/A
XmCCallback	XtCallbackList	
XmNcancelLabelString	"Cancel"	N/A
XmCCancelLabelString	XmString	
XmNdialogType	XmDIALOG_COMMAND	G
XmCDialogType	unsigned char	
XmNhelpLabelString	"Help"	N/A
XmCHelpLabelString	XmString	
XmNlistItemCount	0	CSG
XmCItemCount	int	
XmNlistItems	NULL	CSG
XmCItems	XmStringTable	
XmNlistLabelString	NULL	N/A
XmCListLabelString	XmString	
XmNlistVisibleItemCount	dynamic	CSG
XmCVisibleItemCount	int	
XmNminimizeButtons	False	N/A
XmCMinimizeButtons	Boolean	
XmNmustMatch	False	N/A
XmCMustMatch	Boolean	
XmNnoMatchCallback	NULL	N/A
XmCCallback	XtCallbackList	

Name	Default	Access
Class	Type	
XmNokCallback	NULL	N/A
XmCCallback	XtCallbackList	
XmNokLabelString	"OK"	N/A
XmCOkLabelString	XmString	
XmNselectionLabelString	">"	CSG
XmCSelectionLabelString	XmString	
XmNtextAccelerators	default	C
XmCTextAccelerators	XtAccelerators	
XmNtextColumns	dynamic	CSG
XmCColumns	short	
XmNtextString	""	CSG
XmCTextString	XmString	

XmBulletinBoard Resource Set		
Name	**Default**	**Access**
Class	Type	
XmNallowOverlap	True	CSG
XmCAllowOverlap	Boolean	
XmNautoUnmanage	False	N/A
XmCAutoUnmanage	Boolean	
XmNbuttonFontList	dynamic	N/A
XmCButtonFontList	XmFontList	
XmNcancelButton	NULL	N/A
XmCWidget	Widget	
XmNdefaultButton	NULL	N/A
XmCWidget	Widget	
XmNdefaultPosition	False	CSG
XmCDefaultPosition	Boolean	
XmNdialogStyle	dynamic	CSG
XmCDialogStyle	unsigned char	
XmNdialogTitle	NULL	CSG
XmCDialogTitle	XmString	
XmNfocusCallback	NULL	C
XmCCallback	XtCallbackList	
XmNlabelFontList	dynamic	CSG
XmCLabelFontList	XmFontList	
XmNmapCallback	NULL	C
XmCCallback	XtCallbackList	
XmNmarginHeight	10	CSG
XmCMarginHeight	Dimension	
XmNmarginWidth	10	CSG
XmCMarginWidth	Dimension	
XmNnoResize	False	CSG
XmCNoResize	Boolean	

Name	Default	Access
Class	Type	
XmNresizePolicy	XmRESIZE_NONE	CSG
XmCResizePolicy	unsigned char	
XmNshadowType	XmSHADOW_OUT	CSG
XmCShadowType	unsigned char	
XmNtextFontList	dynamic	CSG
XmCTextFontList	XmFontList	
XmNtextTranslations	NULL	C
XmCTranslations	XtTranslations	
XmNunmapCallback	NULL	C
XmCCallback	XtCallbackList	

XmManager Resource Set		
Name	**Default**	**Access**
Class	**Type**	
XmNbottomShadowColor	dynamic	CSG
XmCBottomShadowColor	Pixel	
XmNbottomShadowPixmap	XmUNSPECIFIED_PIXMAP	CSG
XmCBottomShadowPixmap	Pixmap	
XmNforeground	dynamic	CSG
XmCForeground	Pixel	
XmNhelpCallback	NULL	C
XmCCallback	XtCallbackList	
XmNhighlightColor	dynamic	CSG
XmCHighlightColor	Pixel	
XmNhighlightPixmap	dynamic	CSG
XmCHighlightPixmap	Pixmap	
XmNnavigationType	dynamic	CSG
XmCNavigationType	XmNavigationType	
XmNshadowThickness	dynamic	CSG
XmCShadowThickness	Dimension	
XmNstringDirection	dynamic	CG
XmCStringDirection	XmStringDirection	
XmNtopShadowColor	dynamic	CSG
XmCBackgroundTopShadowColor	Pixel	
XmNtopShadowPixmap	dynamic	CSG
XmCTopShadowPixmap	Pixmap	
XmNtraversalOn	True	CSG
XmCTraversalOn	Boolean	
XmNuserData	NULL	CSG
XmCUserData	Pointer	

Composite Resource Set		
Name	**Default**	**Access**
Class	**Type**	
XmNchildren	NULL	G
XmCReadOnly	WidgetList	
XmNinsertPosition	NULL	CSG
XmCInsertPosition	(*)()	
XmNnumChildren	0	G
XmCReadOnly	Cardinal	

Core Resource Set		
Name	**Default**	**Access**
Class	**Type**	
XmNaccelerators	dynamic	N/A
XmCAccelerators	XtAccelerators	
XmNancestorSensitive	dynamic	G
XmCSensitive	Boolean	
XmNbackground	dynamic	CSG
XmCBackground	Pixel	
XmNbackgroundPixmap	XmUNSPECIFIED_PIXMAP	CSG
XmCPixmap	Pixmap	
XmNborderColor	XtDefaultForeground	CSG
XmCBorderColor	Pixel	
XmNborderPixmap	XmUNSPECIFIED_PIXMAP	CSG
XmCPixmap	Pixmap	
XmNborderWidth	0	CSG
XmCBorderWidth	Dimension	
XmNcolormap	dynamic	CG
XmCColormap	Colormap	
XmNdepth	dynamic	CG
XmCDepth	int	
XmNdestroyCallback	NULL	C
XmCCallback	XtCallbackList	
XmNheight	dynamic	CSG
XmCHeight	Dimension	
XmNinitialResourcesPersistent	True	C
XmCInitialResourcesPersistent	Boolean	
XmNmappedWhenManaged	True	CSG
XmCMappedWhenManaged	Boolean	
XmNscreen	dynamic	CG
XmCScreen	Screen *	

Name	Default	Access
Class	Type	
XmNsensitive	True	CSG
XmCSensitive	Boolean	
XmNtranslations	dynamic	CSG
XmCTranslations	XtTranslations	
XmNwidth	dynamic	CSG
XmCWidth	Dimension	
XmNx	0	CSG
XmCPosition	Position	
XmNy	0	CSG
XmCPosition	Position	

Callback Information

A pointer to the following structure is passed to each callback:

typedef struct
{
    int   *reason*;
    XEvent   * *event*;
    XmString *value*;
    int   *length*;
} **XmCommandCallbackStruct**;

reason   Indicates why the callback was invoked

event   Points to the **XEvent** that triggered the callback

value   Specifies the **XmString** in the CommandArea

length   Specifies the size of the command in **XmString**

Translations

XmCommand inherits translations from XmSelectionBox.

Accelerators

The **XmNtextAccelerators** from XmSelectionBox are added to the Text descendant of XmCommand.

Action Routines

The XmCommand action routines are described below:

SelectionBoxUpOrDown(0|1|2|3):

> When called with a 0 argument, selects the previous item in the history list and replaces the text with that item.
>
> When called with a 1 argument, selects the next item in the history list and replaces the text with that item.
>
> When called with a 2 argument, selects the first item in the history list and replaces the text with that item.
>
> When called with a 3 argument, selects the last item in the history list and replaces the text with that item.
>
> Calls the callbacks for **XmNcommandChangedCallback**.

Additional Behavior

The Command widget has the additional behavior described below:

<KActivate> in Text:

> Calls the Text widget's **XmNactivateCallback** callbacks. If the text is empty, this action then returns. Otherwise, if the history list has **XmNhistoryMaxItems** items, it removes the

first item in the list. It adds the text to the history list as the last item, clears the text, and calls the **XmNcommandEnteredCallback** callbacks.

\<Key\> in Text:
When any change is made to the text edit widget, this action calls the callbacks for **XmNcommandChangedCallback**.

\<DoubleClick\> or **\<KActivate\>** in List:
Calls the List widget's **XmNdefaultActionCallback** callbacks. If the history list has **XmNhistoryMaxItems** items, this action removes the first item in the list. It adds the selected List item to the history list as the last item, clears the text, and calls the **XmNcommandEnteredCallback** callbacks.

\<FocusIn\>: Calls the callbacks for **XmNfocusCallback**.

\<MapWindow\>:
When a Command that is the child of a DialogShell is mapped, this action calls the callbacks for **XmNmapCallback**.

\<UnmapWindow\>:
When a Command that is the child of a DialogShell is unmapped, this action calls the callbacks for **XmNunmapCallback**.

Virtual Bindings

The bindings for virtual keys are vendor specific.

Related Information

Composite(3X), Constraint(3X), Core(3X), XmBulletinBoard(3X), XmCommandAppendValue(3X), XmCommandError(3X), XmCommandGetChild(3X), XmCommandSetValue(3X), XmCreateCommand(3X), XmManager(3X), and XmSelectionBox(3X).

XmCommandAppendValue

Purpose

A Command function that appends the passed XmString to the end of the string displayed in the command area of the widget.

AES Support Level

Full-use

Synopsis

#include <Xm/Command.h>

void XmCommandAppendValue (*widget, command*)
  Widget   *widget*;
  XmString   *command*;

Description

XmCommandAppendValue appends the passed **XmString** to the end of the string displayed in the command area of the Command widget.

widget   Specifies the Command widget ID

command Specifies the passed **XmString**

For a complete definition of Command and its associated resources, see **XmCommand(3X)**.

Related Information

XmCommand(3X).

XmCommandError

Purpose

A Command function that displays an error message

AES Support Level

Full-use

Synopsis

#include <Xm/Command.h>

void XmCommandError (*widget, error*)
  Widget   *widget*;
  XmString   *error*;

Description

XmCommandError displays an error message in the history area of the Command widget. The **XmString** error is displayed until the next command entered occurs.

widget   Specifies the Command widget ID.

error   Specifies the passed **XmString**.

For a complete definition of Command and its associated resources, see **XmCommand(3X)**.

Related Information

XmCommand(3X).

XmCommandGetChild

Purpose

A Command function that is used to access a component.

AES Support Level

Full-use

Synopsis

#include <Xm/Command.h>

Widget XmCommandGetChild (*widget, child*)
  Widget   *widget*;
  unsigned char   *child*;

Description

XmCommandGetChild is used to access a component within a Command. The parameters given to the function are the Command widget and a value indicating which child to access.

widget Specifies the Command widget ID.

child Specifies a component within the Command. The following are legal values for this parameter:

- **XmDIALOG_COMMAND_TEXT**
- **XmDIALOG_PROMPT_LABEL**
- **XmDIALOG_HISTORY_LIST**

For a complete definition of Command and its associated resources, see **XmCommand(3X)**.

Return Value

Returns the widget ID of the specified Command child. An application should not assume that the returned widget will be of any particular class.

Related Information

XmCommand(3X).

XmCommandSetValue

Purpose

A Command function that replaces a displayed string

AES Support Level

Full-use

Synopsis

#include <Xm/Command.h>

void XmCommandSetValue (*widget, command*)
  Widget   *widget*;
  XmString   *command*;

Description

XmCommandSetValue replaces the string displayed in the command area of the Command widget with the passed **XmString**.

widget   Specifies the Command widget ID.

command Specifies the passed **XmString**.

For a complete definition of Command and its associated resources, see **XmCommand(3X)**.

Related Information

XmCommand(3X).

XmConvertUnits

Purpose

A function that converts a value in one unit type to another unit type.

AES Support Level

Trial-use

Synopsis

#include <Xm/Xm.h>

int **XmConvertUnits** (*widget, orientation, from_unit_type, from_value, to_unit_type*)

Widget	*widget*;
int	*orientation*;
int	*from_unit_type*;
int	*from_value*;
int	*to_unit_type*;

Description

XmConvertUnits converts the value and returns it as the return value from the function.

widget	Specifies the widget for which the data is to be converted
orientation	Specifies whether the converter uses the horizontal or vertical screen resolution when performing the conversions. *orientation* can have values of **XmHORIZONTAL** or **XmVERTICAL**.
from_unit_type	Specifies the current unit type of the supplied value
from_value	Specifies the value to be converted
to_unit_type	Converts the value to the unit type specified

The parameters *from_unit_type* and *to_unit_type* can have the following values:

- **XmPIXELS** — all values provided to the widget are treated as normal pixel values. This is the default for the resource.

- **Xm100TH_MILLIMETERS** — all values provided to the widget are treated as 1/100 millimeter.

- **Xm1000TH_INCHES** — all values provided to the widget are treated as 1/1000 inch.

- **Xm100TH_POINTS** — all values provided to the widget are treated as 1/100 point. A point is a unit typically used in text processing applications and is defined as 1/72 inch.

Return Value

Returns the converted value. If a NULL widget, incorrect *orientation*, or incorrect *unit_type* is supplied as parameter data, 0 is returned.

XmCreateArrowButton

Purpose

The ArrowButton widget creation function

AES Support Level

Full-use

Synopsis

#include <Xm/ArrowB.h>

Widget XmCreateArrowButton (*parent, name, arglist, argcount*)
    Widget   *parent*;
    String   *name*;
    ArgList   *arglist*;
    Cardinal   *argcount*;

Description

> **XmCreateArrowButton** creates an instance of an ArrowButton widget and returns the associated widget ID.

> | | |
> |---|---|
> | *parent* | Specifies the parent widget ID |
> | *name* | Specifies the name of the created widget |
> | *arglist* | Specifies the argument list |
> | *argcount* | Specifies the number of attribute/value pairs in the argument list (*arglist*) |

> For a complete definition of ArrowButton and its associated resources, see **XmArrowButton(3X)**.

Return Value

> Returns the ArrowButton widget ID.

Related Information

> **XmArrowButton(3X)**.

XmCreateArrowButtonGadget

Purpose

The ArrowButtonGadget creation function.

AES Support Level

Full-use

Synopsis

#include <Xm/ArrowBG.h>

Widget **XmCreateArrowButtonGadget** (*parent, name, arglist, argcount*)
      Widget   *parent*;
      String   *name*;
      ArgList   *arglist*;
      Cardinal   *argcount*;

Description

XmCreateArrowButtonGadget creates an instance of an ArrowButtonGadget widget and returns the associated widget ID.

parent   Specifies the parent widget ID

name   Specifies the name of the created widget

arglist   Specifies the argument list

argcount Specifies the number of attribute/value pairs in the argument list (*arglist*)

For a complete definition of ArrowButtonGadget and its associated resources, see **XmArrowButtonGadget(3X)**.

Return Value

Returns the ArrowButtonGadget widget ID.

Related Information

XmArrowButtonGadget(3X).

XmCreateBulletinBoard

Purpose

The BulletinBoard widget creation function

AES Support Level

Full-use

Synopsis

#include <Xm/BulletinB.h>

Widget XmCreateBulletinBoard (*parent, name, arglist, argcount*)
    Widget   *parent*;
    String   *name*;
    ArgList   *arglist*;
    Cardinal *argcount*;

Description

XmCreateBulletinBoard creates an instance of a BulletinBoard widget and returns the associated widget ID.

parent　　Specifies the parent widget ID

name　　Specifies the name of the created widget

arglist　　Specifies the argument list

argcount　Specifies the number of attribute/value pairs in the argument list (*arglist*)

For a complete definition of BulletinBoard and its associated resources, see **XmBulletinBoard(3X)**.

Return Value

Returns the BulletinBoard widget ID.

Related Information

XmBulletinBoard(3X).

XmCreateBulletinBoardDialog

Purpose

The BulletinBoard BulletinBoardDialog convenience creation function.

AES Support Level

Full-use

Synopsis

#include <Xm/BulletinB.h>

Widget XmCreateBulletinBoardDialog (*parent, name, arglist, argcount*)
    Widget   *parent*;
    String   *name*;
    ArgList   *arglist*;
    Cardinal   *argcount*;

Description

XmCreateBulletinBoardDialog is a convenience creation function that creates a DialogShell and an unmanaged BulletinBoard child of the DialogShell. A BulletinBoardDialog is used for interactions not supported by the standard dialog set. This function does not automatically create any labels, buttons, or other dialog components. Such components should be added by the application after the BulletinBoardDialog is created.

Use **XtManageChild** to pop up the BulletinBoardDialog (passing the BulletinBoard as the widget parameter); use **XtUnmanageChild** to pop it down.

parent   Specifies the parent widget ID

name   Specifies the name of the created widget

arglist   Specifies the argument list

argcount Specifies the number of attribute/value pairs in the argument list (*arglist*)

For a complete definition of BulletinBoard and its associated resources, see **XmBulletinBoard(3X)**.

Return Value

Returns the BulletinBoard widget ID.

Related Information

XmBulletinBoard(3X).

XmCreateCascadeButton

Purpose

The CascadeButton widget creation function

AES Support Level

Full-use

Synopsis

#include <Xm/CascadeB.h>

Widget **XmCreateCascadeButton** (*parent, name, arglist, argcount*)
    Widget   *parent*;
    String   *name*;
    ArgList   *arglist*;
    Cardinal *argcount*;

Description

XmCreateCascadeButton creates an instance of a CascadeButton widget and returns the associated widget ID.

parent   Specifies the parent widget ID. The parent must be a RowColumn widget.

name   Specifies the name of the created widget.

arglist   Specifies the argument list.

argcount Specifies the number of attribute/value pairs in the argument list (*arglist*).

For a complete definition of CascadeButton and its associated resources, see **XmCascadeButton(3X)**.

Return Value

Returns the CascadeButton widget ID.

Related Information

XmCascadeButton(3X).

XmCreateCascadeButtonGadget

Purpose

The CascadeButtonGadget creation function.

AES Support Level

Full-use

Synopsis

#include <Xm/CascadeBG.h>

Widget XmCreateCascadeButtonGadget (*parent, name, arglist, argcount*)
    Widget   *parent*;
    String   *name*;
    ArgList   *arglist*;
    Cardinal   *argcount*;

Description

XmCreateCascadeButtonGadget creates an instance of a CascadeButtonGadget and returns the associated widget ID.

parent   Specifies the parent widget ID. The parent must be a RowColumn widget.

name   Specifies the name of the created widget.

arglist   Specifies the argument list.

argcount Specifies the number of attribute/value pairs in the argument list (*arglist*).

For a complete definition of CascadeButtonGadget and its associated resources, see **XmCascadeButtonGadget(3X)**.

Return Value

Returns the CascadeButtonGadget widget ID.

Related Information

XmCascadeButtonGadget(3X).

XmCreateCommand

Purpose

The Command widget creation function

AES Support Level

Full-use

Synopsis

#include <Xm/Command.h>

Widget XmCreateCommand (*parent, name, arglist, argcount*)
    Widget   *parent*;
    String   *name*;
    ArgList   *arglist*;
    Cardinal   *argcount*;

Description

XmCreateCommand creates an instance of a Command widget and returns the associated widget ID.

parent   Specifies the parent widget ID

name   Specifies the name of the created widget

arglist   Specifies the argument list

argcount Specifies the number of attribute/value pairs in the argument list (*arglist*)

For a complete definition of Command and its associated resources, see **XmCommand(3X)**.

Return Value

Returns the Command widget ID.

Related Information

XmCommand(3X).

XmCreateDialogShell

Purpose

The DialogShell widget creation function

AES Support Level

Full-use

Synopsis

#include <Xm/DialogS.h>

Widget XmCreateDialogShell (*parent, name, arglist, argcount*)
    Widget   *parent*;
    String   *name*;
    ArgList   *arglist*;
    Cardinal   *argcount*;

Description

XmCreateDialogShell creates an instance of a DialogShell widget and returns the associated widget ID.

parent   Specifies the parent widget ID

name   Specifies the name of the created widget

arglist   Specifies the argument list

argcount Specifies the number of attribute/value pairs in the argument list (*arglist*)

For a complete definition of DialogShell and its associated resources, see **XmDialogShell(3X)**.

Return Value

Returns the DialogShell widget ID.

Related Information

XmDialogShell(3X).

XmCreateDrawingArea

Purpose

The DrawingArea widget creation function

AES Support Level

Full-use

Synopsis

#include <Xm/DrawingA.h>

Widget XmCreateDrawingArea (*parent, name, arglist, argcount*)
    Widget   *parent*;
    String   *name*;
    ArgList   *arglist*;
    Cardinal   *argcount*;

Description

XmCreateDrawingArea creates an instance of a DrawingArea widget and returns the associated widget ID.

parent   Specifies the parent widget ID

name   Specifies the name of the created widget

arglist   Specifies the argument list

argcount Specifies the number of attribute/value pairs in the argument list (*arglist*)

For a complete definition of DrawingArea and its associated resources, see **XmDrawingArea(3X)**.

Return Value

Returns the DrawingArea widget ID.

Related Information

XmDrawingArea(3X).

XmCreateDrawnButton

Purpose

The DrawnButton widget creation function

AES Support Level

Full-use

Synopsis

#include <Xm/DrawnB.h>

Widget XmCreateDrawnButton (*parent, name, arglist, argcount*)
       Widget   *parent*;
       String   *name*;
       ArgList   *arglist*;
       Cardinal   *argcount*;

Description

> **XmCreateDrawnButton** creates an instance of a DrawnButton widget and returns the associated widget ID.
>
> *parent*   Specifies the parent widget ID
>
> *name*   Specifies the name of the created widget
>
> *arglist*   Specifies the argument list
>
> *argcount* Specifies the number of attribute/value pairs in the argument list (*arglist*)
>
> For a complete definition of DrawnButton and its associated resources, see **XmDrawnButton(3X)**.

Return Value

> Returns the DrawnButton widget ID.

Related Information

> **XmDrawnButton(3X)**.

XmCreateErrorDialog

Purpose

The MessageBox ErrorDialog convenience creation function.

AES Support Level

Full-use

Synopsis

#include <Xm/MessageB.h>

Widget XmCreateErrorDialog (*parent, name, arglist, argcount*)
    Widget   *parent*;
    String   *name*;
    ArgList   *arglist*;
    Cardinal   *argcount*;

Description

XmCreateErrorDialog is a convenience creation function that creates a DialogShell and an unmanaged MessageBox child of the DialogShell. An ErrorDialog warns the user of an invalid or potentially dangerous condition. It includes a symbol, a message, and three buttons. The default symbol is an octagon with a diagonal slash. The default button labels are **OK, Cancel,** and **Help**.

Use **XtManageChild** to pop up the ErrorDialog (passing the MessageBox as the widget parameter); use **XtUnmanageChild** to pop it down.

parent   Specifies the parent widget ID

name   Specifies the name of the created widget

arglist   Specifies the argument list

argcount Specifies the number of attribute/value pairs in the argument list (*arglist*)

For a complete definition of MessageBox and its associated resources, see **XmMessageBox(3X)**.

Return Value

Returns the MessageBox widget ID.

Related Information

XmMessageBox(3X).

XmCreateFileSelectionBox

Purpose

The FileSelectionBox widget creation function

AES Support Level

Full-use

Synopsis

#include <Xm/FileSB.h>

Widget XmCreateFileSelectionBox (*parent, name, arglist, argcount*)
    Widget   *parent*;
    String   *name*;
    ArgList   *arglist*;
    Cardinal   *argcount*;

Description

XmCreateFileSelectionBox creates an unmanaged FileSelectionBox. A FileSelectionBox is used to select a file and includes the following:

- An editable text field for the directory mask
- A scrolling list of filenames

- An editable text field for the selected file
- Labels for the list and text fields
- Four buttons

The default button labels are **OK**, **Filter**, **Cancel**, and **Help**. One additional **WorkArea** child may be added to the FileSelectionBox after creation.

If the parent of the FileSelectionBox is a DialogShell, use **XtManageChild** to pop up the FileSelectionDialog (passing the FileSelectionBox as the widget parameter); use **XtUnmanageChild** to pop it down.

parent	Specifies the parent widget ID
name	Specifies the name of the created widget
arglist	Specifies the argument list
argcount	Specifies the number of attribute/value pairs in the argument list (*arglist*)

For a complete definition of FileSelectionBox and its associated resources, see **XmFileSelectionBox(3X)**.

Return Value

Returns the FileSelectionBox widget ID.

Related Information

XmFileSelectionBox(3X).

XmCreateFileSelectionDialog

Purpose

The FileSelectionBox FileSelectionDialog convenience creation function.

AES Support Level

Full-use

Synopsis

#include <Xm/FileSB.h>

Widget XmCreateFileSelectionDialog (*parent, name, arglist, argcount*)
    Widget   *parent*;
    String   *name*;
    ArgList   *arglist*;
    Cardinal   *argcount*;

Description

XmCreateFileSelectionDialog is a convenience creation function that creates a DialogShell and an unmanaged FileSelectionBox child of the DialogShell. A FileSelectionDialog selects a file. It includes the following:

- An editable text field for the directory mask
- A scrolling list of filenames

- An editable text field for the selected file
- Labels for the list and text fields
- Four buttons

The default button labels are: **OK**, **Filter**, **Cancel**, and **Help**. One additional **WorkArea** child may be added to the FileSelectionBox after creation.

Use **XtManageChild** to pop up the FileSelectionDialog (passing the FileSelectionBox as the widget parameter); use **XtUnmanageChild** to pop it down.

parent   Specifies the parent widget ID

name   Specifies the name of the created widget

arglist   Specifies the argument list

argcount Specifies the number of attribute/value pairs in the argument list (*arglist*)

For a complete definition of FileSelectionBox and its associated resources, see **XmFileSelectionBox(3X)**.

Return Value

Returns the FileSelectionBox widget ID.

Related Information

XmFileSelectionBox(3X).

XmCreateForm

Purpose

The Form widget creation function

AES Support Level

Full-use

Synopsis

#include <Xm/Form.h>

Widget XmCreateForm (*parent, name, arglist, argcount*)
> **Widget**   *parent*;
> **String**   *name*;
> **ArgList**   *arglist*;
> **Cardinal** *argcount*;

Description

>**XmCreateForm** creates an instance of a Form widget and returns the associated widget ID.
>
>*parent*   Specifies the parent widget ID
>
>*name*   Specifies the name of the created widget
>
>*arglist*   Specifies the argument list
>
>*argcount* Specifies the number of attribute/value pairs in the argument list (*arglist*)
>
>For a complete definition of Form and its associated resources, see **XmForm(3X)**.

Return Value

>Returns the Form widget ID.

Related Information

>**XmForm(3X)**.

XmCreateFormDialog

Purpose

A Form FormDialog convenience creation function

AES Support Level

Full-use

Synopsis

#include <Xm/Form.h>

Widget XmCreateFormDialog (*parent, name, arglist, argcount*)
    Widget   *parent*;
    String   *name*;
    ArgList   *arglist*;
    Cardinal   *argcount*;

Description

XmCreateFormDialog is a convenience creation function that creates a DialogShell and an unmanaged Form child of the DialogShell. A FormDialog is used for interactions not supported by the standard dialog set. This function does not automatically create any labels, buttons, or other dialog components. Such components should be added by the application after the FormDialog is created.

Use **XtManageChild** to pop up the FormDialog (passing the Form as the widget parameter); use **XtUnmanageChild** to pop it down.

parent   Specifies the parent widget ID

name   Specifies the name of the created widget

arglist   Specifies the argument list

argcount Specifies the number of attribute/value pairs in the argument list (*arglist*)

For a complete definition of Form and its associated resources, see **XmForm(3X)**.

Return Value

Returns the Form widget ID.

Related Information

XmForm(3X).

XmCreateFrame

Purpose

The Frame widget creation function

AES Support Level

Full-use

Synopsis

#include <Xm/Frame.h>

Widget XmCreateFrame (*parent, name, arglist, argcount*)
       Widget   *parent*;
       String   *name*;
       ArgList   *arglist*;
       Cardinal *argcount*;

Description

XmCreateFrame creates an instance of a Frame widget and returns the associated widget ID.

parent   Specifies the parent widget ID

name   Specifies the name of the created widget

arglist   Specifies the argument list

argcount Specifies the number of attribute/value pairs in the argument list (*arglist*)

For a complete definition of Frame and its associated resources, see **XmFrame(3X)**.

Return Value

Returns the Frame widget ID.

Related Information

XmFrame(3X).

XmCreateInformationDialog

Purpose

The MessageBox InformationDialog convenience creation function.

AES Support Level

Full-use

Synopsis

#include <Xm/MessageB.h>

Widget **XmCreateInformationDialog** (*parent, name, arglist, argcount*)
    Widget   *parent*;
    String   *name*;
    ArgList   *arglist*;
    Cardinal   *argcount*;

Description

XmCreateInformationDialog is a convenience creation function that creates a DialogShell and an unmanaged MessageBox child of the DialogShell. An InformationDialog gives the user information, such as the status of an action. It includes a symbol, a message, and three buttons. The default symbol is a lower case **i**. The default button labels are **OK**, **Cancel**, and **Help**.

Use **XtManageChild** to pop up the InformationDialog (passing the MessageBox as the widget parameter); use **XtUnmanageChild** to pop it down.

parent　　Specifies the parent widget ID

name　　Specifies the name of the created widget

arglist　　Specifies the argument list

argcount Specifies the number of attribute/value pairs in the argument list (*arglist*)

For a complete definition of MessageBox and its associated resources, see **XmMessageBox(3X)**.

Return Value

Returns the MessageBox widget ID.

Related Information

XmMessageBox(3X).

XmCreateLabel

Purpose

The Label widget creation function

AES Support Level

Full-use

Synopsis

#include <Xm/Label.h>

Widget XmCreateLabel (*parent, name, arglist, argcount*)
    Widget   *parent*;
    String   *name*;
    ArgList   *arglist*;
    Cardinal *argcount*;

Description

XmCreateLabel creates an instance of a Label widget and returns the associated widget ID.

parent   Specifies the parent widget ID

name   Specifies the name of the created widget

arglist   Specifies the argument list

argcount Specifies the number of attribute/value pairs in the argument list (*arglist*)

For a complete definition of Label and its associated resources, see **XmLabel(3X)**.

Return Value

Returns the Label widget ID.

Related Information

XmLabel(3X).

XmCreateLabelGadget

Purpose

The LabelGadget creation function

AES Support Level

Full-use

Synopsis

#include <Xm/LabelG.h>

Widget XmCreateLabelGadget (*parent, name, arglist, argcount*)
     Widget   *parent*;
     String   *name*;
     ArgList   *arglist*;
     Cardinal   *argcount*;

Description

XmCreateLabelGadget creates an instance of a LabelGadget widget and returns the associated widget ID.

parent   Specifies the parent widget ID

name   Specifies the name of the created widget

arglist Specifies the argument list

argcount Specifies the number of attribute/value pairs in the argument list (*arglist*)

For a complete definition of LabelGadget and its associated resources, see **XmLabelGadget(3X)**.

Return Value

Returns the LabelGadget widget ID.

Related Information

XmLabelGadget(3X).

XmCreateList

Purpose

The List widget creation function

AES Support Level

Full-use

Synopsis

#include <Xm/List.h>

Widget XmCreateList (*parent, name, arglist, argcount*)
    Widget   *parent*;
    String   *name*;
    ArgList   *arglist*;
    Cardinal   *argcount*;

Description

XmCreateList creates an instance of a List widget and returns the associated widget ID.

parent   Specifies the parent widget ID

name   Specifies the name of the created widget

arglist   Specifies the argument list

argcount Specifies the number of attribute/value pairs in the argument list (*arglist*)

For a complete definition of List and its associated resources, see **XmList(3X)**.

Return Value

Returns the List widget ID.

Related Information

XmList(3X).

XmCreateMainWindow

Purpose

The MainWindow widget creation function

AES Support Level

Full-use

Synopsis

#include <Xm/MainW.h>

Widget XmCreateMainWindow (*parent, name, arglist, argcount*)
    Widget   *parent*;
    String   *name*;
    ArgList   *arglist*;
    Cardinal *argcount*;

Description

XmCreateMainWindow creates an instance of a MainWindow widget and returns the associated widget ID.

parent   Specifies the parent widget ID

name   Specifies the name of the created widget

arglist   Specifies the argument list

argcount Specifies the number of attribute/value pairs in the argument list (*arglist*)

For a complete definition of MainWindow and its associated resources, see **XmMainWindow(3X)**.

Return Value

Returns the MainWindow widget ID.

Related Information

XmMainWindow(3X).

XmCreateMenuBar

Purpose

A RowColumn widget convenience creation function

AES Support Level

Full-use

Synopsis

#include <Xm/RowColumn.h>

Widget **XmCreateMenuBar** (*parent, name, arglist, argcount*)
    Widget   *parent*;
    String   *name*;
    ArgList   *arglist*;
    Cardinal *argcount*;

Description

XmCreateMenuBar creates an instance of a RowColumn widget of type **XmMENU_BAR** and returns the associated widget ID.It is provided as a convenience function for creating RowColumn widgets configured to operate as a MenuBàr and is not implemented as a separate widget class.

The MenuBar widget is generally used for building a Pulldown menu system. Typically, a MenuBar is created and placed along the top of the application window, and several CascadeButtons are inserted as the children. Each of the CascadeButtons has a Pulldown MenuPane associated with it. These Pulldown MenuPanes must have been created as children of the MenuBar. The user interacts with the MenuBar by using either the mouse or the keyboard.

The MenuBar displays a 3-D shadow along its border. The application controls the shadow attributes using the visual-related resources supported by **XmManager**.

The MenuBar widget is homogeneous in that it accepts only children that are a subclass of **XmCascadeButton** or **XmCascadeButtonGadget**. Attempting to insert a child of a different class results in a warning message.

If the MenuBar does not have enough room to fit all of its subwidgets on a single line, the MenuBar attempts to wrap the remaining entries onto additional lines if allowed by the geometry manager of the parent widget.

parent   Specifies the parent widget ID

name   Specifies the name of the created widget

arglist   Specifies the argument list

argcount Specifies the number of attribute/value pairs in the argument list (*arglist*)

For a complete definition of RowColumn and its associated resources, see **XmRowColumn(3X)**.

Return Value

Returns the RowColumn widget ID.

Related Information

XmCascadeButton(3X),
XmCreatePulldownMenu(3X),
XmRowColumn(3X).

XmCascadeButtonGadget(3X),
XmManager(3X), and

XmCreateMenuShell

Purpose

The MenuShell widget creation function

AES Support Level

Full-use

Synopsis

#include <Xm/MenuShell.h>

Widget XmCreateMenuShell (*parent, name, arglist, argcount*)
    Widget   *parent*;
    String   *name*;
    ArgList   *arglist*;
    Cardinal   *argcount*;

Description

XmCreateMenuShell creates an instance of a MenuShell widget and returns the associated widget ID.

parent   Specifies the parent widget ID

name   Specifies the name of the created widget

arglist   Specifies the argument list

argcount Specifies the number of attribute/value pairs in the argument list (*arglist*)

For a complete definition of MenuShell and its associated resources, see **XmMenuShell(3X)**.

Return Value

Returns the MenuShell widget ID.

Related Information

XmMenuShell(3X).

XmCreateMessageBox

Purpose

The MessageBox widget creation function

AES Support Level

Full-use

Synopsis

#include <Xm/MessageB.h>

Widget XmCreateMessageBox (*parent, name, arglist, argcount*)
    Widget   *parent*;
    String   *name*;
    ArgList   *arglist*;
    Cardinal   *argcount*;

Description

XmCreateMessageBox creates an unmanaged MessageBox. A MessageBox is used for common interaction tasks, which include giving information, asking questions, and reporting errors. It includes an optional symbol, a message, and three buttons.

By default, there is no symbol. The default button labels are **OK**, **Cancel**, and **Help**.

If the parent of the MessageBox is a Dialogshell, use **XtManageChild** to pop up the MessageBox (passing the MessageBox as the widget parameter); use **XtUnmanageChild** to pop it down.

parent   Specifies the parent widget ID

name   Specifies the name of the created widget

arglist   Specifies the argument list

argcount Specifies the number of attribute/value pairs in the argument list (*arglist*)

For a complete definition of MessageBox and its associated resources, see **XmMessageBox(3X)**.

Return Value

Returns the MessageBox widget ID.

Related Information

XmMessageBox(3X).

XmCreateMessageDialog

Purpose

The MessageBox MessageDialog convenience creation function.

AES Support Level

Full-use

Synopsis

#include <Xm/MessageB.h>

Widget XmCreateMessageDialog (*parent, name, arglist, argcount*)
      Widget   *parent*;
      String   *name*;
      ArgList   *arglist*;
      Cardinal   *argcount*;

Description

> **XmCreateMessageDialog** is a convenience creation function that creates a DialogShell and an unmanaged MessageBox child of the DialogShell. A MessageDialog is used for common interaction tasks, which include giving information, asking questions, and reporting errors. It includes a symbol, a message, and three buttons. By default, there is no symbol. The default button labels are **OK**, **Cancel**, and **Help**.
>
> Use **XtManageChild** to pop up the MessageDialog (passing the MessageBox as the widget parameter); use **XtUnmanageChild** to pop it down.
>
> *parent*   Specifies the parent widget ID
>
> *name*   Specifies the name of the created widget
>
> *arglist*   Specifies the argument list
>
> *argcount* Specifies the number of attribute/value pairs in the argument list (*arglist*)
>
> For a complete definition of MessageBox and its associated resources, see **XmMessageBox(3X)**.

Return Value

> Returns the MessageBox widget ID.

Related Information

> **XmMessageBox(3X)**.

XmCreateOptionMenu

Purpose

A RowColumn widget convenience creation function

AES Support Level

Full-use

Synopsis

#include <Xm/RowColumn.h>

Widget XmCreateOptionMenu (*parent, name, arglist, argcount*)
  Widget *parent*;
  String   *name*;
  ArgList *arglist*;
  Cardinal *argcount*;

Description

XmCreateOptionMenu creates an instance of a RowColumn widget of type **XmMENU_OPTION** and returns the associated widget ID.

It is provided as a convenience function for creating a RowColumn widget configured to operate as an OptionMenu and is not implemented as a separate widget class.

The OptionMenu widget is a specialized RowColumn manager composed of a label, a selection area, and a single Pulldown MenuPane. When an application creates an OptionMenu widget, it supplies the label string and the Pulldown MenuPane. In order to succeed, there must be a valid **XmNsubMenuId** resource set when calling this function. When the OptionMenu is created, the Pulldown MenuPane must have been created as a child of the OptionMenu's parent and must be specified. The LabelGadget and the selection area (a CascadeButtonGadget) are created by the OptionMenu.

The OptionMenu's Pulldown MenuPane must not contain any ToggleButtons or ToggleButtonGadgets. The results of including CascadeButtons or CascadeButtonGadgets in the OptionMenu's Pulldown MenuPane are undefined.

An OptionMenu is laid out with the label displayed on one side of the widget and the selection area on the other side. The selection area has a dual purpose; it displays the label of the last item selected from the associated Pulldown MenuPane, and it provides the means for posting the Pulldown MenuPane.

The OptionMenu typically does not display any 3-D visuals around itself or the internal LabelGadget. By default, the internal CascadeButtonGadget has a visible 3-D shadow. The application may change this by getting the CascadeButtonGadget ID using **XmOptionButtonGadget**, and then calling **XtSetValues** using the standard visual-related resources.

The Pulldown MenuPane is posted by moving the mouse pointer over the selection area and pressing a mouse button defined by OptionMenu's RowColumn parent. The Pulldown MenuPane is posted and positioned so that the last selected item is directly over the selection area. The mouse is then used to arm the desired menu item. When the mouse button is released, the armed menu item is selected and the label within the selection area is changed to match that of the selected item. By default, **BSelect** is used to interact with an OptionMenu.

The OptionMenu also operates by using the keyboard interface mechanism. If the application has established a mnemonic with the OptionMenu, typing Alt with the mnemonic causes the Pulldown MenuPane to be posted with traversal enabled. The standard traversal keys can then be used to move within the MenuPane. Selection can occur as the result of pressing the Return key or typing a mnemonic or accelerator for one of the menu items.

An application may use the **XmNmenuHistory** resource to indicate which item in the Pulldown MenuPane should be treated as the current choice and have its label displayed in the selection area. By default, the first item in the Pulldown MenuPane is used.

parent   Specifies the parent widget ID

name   Specifies the name of the created widget

arglist   Specifies the argument list

argcount Specifies the number of attribute/value pairs in the argument list (*arglist*)

For a complete definition of RowColumn and its associated resources, see **XmRowColumn(3X)**.

Return Value

Returns the RowColumn widget ID.

Related Information

XmCascadeButtonGadget(3X), **XmCreatePulldownMenu(3X)**, **XmLabelGadget(3X)**, **XmOptionButtonGadget(3X)**, **XmOptionLabelGadget(3X)**, and **XmRowColumn(3X)**.

XmCreatePanedWindow

Purpose

The PanedWindow widget creation function.

AES Support Level

Full-use

Synopsis

#include <Xm/PanedW.h>

Widget XmCreatePanedWindow (*parent, name, arglist, argcount*)
    Widget   *parent*;
    String   *name*;
    ArgList   *arglist*;
    Cardinal   *argcount*;

Description

XmCreatePanedWindow creates an instance of a PanedWindow widget and returns the associated widget ID.

parent   Specifies the parent widget ID

name   Specifies the name of the created widget

arglist   Specifies the argument list

argcount Specifies the number of attribute/value pairs in the argument list (*arglist*)

For a complete definition of PanedWindow and its associated resources, see **XmPanedWindow(3X)**.

Return Value

Returns the PanedWindow widget ID.

Related Information

XmPanedWindow(3X).

XmCreatePopupMenu

Purpose

A RowColumn widget convenience creation function

AES Support Level

Full-use

Synopsis

#include <Xm/RowColumn.h>

Widget XmCreatePopupMenu (*parent, name, arglist, argcount*)
    Widget   *parent*;
    String   *name*;
    ArgList   *arglist*;
    Cardinal   *argcount*;

Description

XmCreatePopupMenu creates an instance of a RowColumn widget of type
XmMENU_POPUP and returns the associated widget ID. When using this
function to create the Popup MenuPane, a MenuShell widget is
automatically created as the parent of the MenuPane. The parent of the
MenuShell widget is the widget indicated by the *parent* parameter.

XmCreatePopupMenu is provided as a convenience function for creating RowColumn widgets configured to operate as Popup MenuPanes and is not implemented as a separate widget class.

The PopupMenu is used as the first MenuPane within a PopupMenu system; all other MenuPanes are of the Pulldown type. A Popup MenuPane displays a 3-D shadow, unless the feature is disabled by the application. The shadow appears around the edge of the MenuPane.

The Popup MenuPane must be created as the child of a MenuShell widget in order to function properly when it is incorporated into a menu. If the application uses this convenience function for creating a Popup MenuPane, the MenuShell is automatically created as the real parent of the MenuPane. If the application does not use this convenience function to create the RowColumn to function as a Popup MenuPane, it is the application's responsibility to create the MenuShell widget.

To access the PopupMenu, the application must first position the widget using the **XmMenuPosition** function and then manage it using **XtManageChild**.

parent   Specifies the parent widget ID

name   Specifies the name of the created widget

arglist   Specifies the argument list

argcount Specifies the number of attribute/value pairs in the argument list (*arglist*)

For a complete definition of RowColumn and its associated resources, see **XmRowColumn(3X)**.

Return Value

Returns the RowColumn widget ID.

Related Information

XmMenuPosition(3X), **XmMenuShell(3X)**, and **XmRowColumn(3X)**.

XmCreatePromptDialog

Purpose

The SelectionBox PromptDialog convenience creation function.

AES Support Level

Full-use

Synopsis

#include <Xm/SelectioB.h>

Widget XmCreatePromptDialog (*parent, name, arglist, argcount*)
    Widget   *parent*;
    String   *name*;
    ArgList   *arglist*;
    Cardinal *argcount*;

Description

XmCreatePromptDialog is a convenience creation function that creates a DialogShell and an unmanaged SelectionBox child of the DialogShell. A PromptDialog prompts the user for text input. It includes a message, a text input region, and three managed buttons. The default button labels are **OK**, **Cancel**, and **Help**. An additional button, with **Apply** as the default label, is created unmanaged; it may be explicitly managed if needed. One additional **WorkArea** child may be added to the SelectionBox after creation.

XmCreatePromptDialog forces the value of the SelectionBox resource **XmNdialogType** to **XmDIALOG_PROMPT**.

Use **XtManageChild** to pop up the PromptDialog (passing the SelectionBox as the widget parameter); use **XtUnmanageChild** to pop it down.

parent   Specifies the parent widget ID

name   Specifies the name of the created widget

arglist   Specifies the argument list

argcount Specifies the number of attribute/value pairs in the argument list (*arglist*)

For a complete definition of SelectionBox and its associated resources, see **XmSelectionBox(3X)**.

Return Value

Returns the SelectionBox widget ID.

Related Information

XmSelectionBox(3X).

XmCreatePulldownMenu

Purpose

A RowColumn widget convenience creation function

AES Support Level

Full-use

Synopsis

#include <Xm/RowColumn.h>

Widget XmCreatePulldownMenu (*parent, name, arglist, argcount*)
    Widget   *parent*;
    String   *name*;
    ArgList   *arglist*;
    Cardinal *argcount*;

Description

XmCreatePulldownMenu creates an instance of a RowColumn widget of type **XmMENU_PULLDOWN** and returns the associated widget ID. When using this function to create the Pulldown MenuPane, a MenuShell widget is automatically created as the parent of the MenuPane. If the widget specified by the *parent* parameter is a Popup or a Pulldown MenuPane, the MenuShell widget is created as a child of the *parent*'s MenuShell; otherwise, it is created as a child of the specified *parent* widget.

XmCreatePulldownMenu is provided as a convenience function for creating RowColumn widgets configured to operate as Pulldown MenuPanes and is not implemented as a separate widget class.

A Pulldown MenuPane displays a 3-D shadow, unless the feature is disabled by the application. The shadow appears around the edge of the MenuPane.

A Pulldown MenuPane is used when creating submenus that are to be attached to a CascadeButton or a CascadeButtonGadget. This is the case for all MenuPanes that are part of a PulldownMenu system (a MenuBar), the MenuPane associated with an OptionMenu, and any MenuPanes that cascade from a Popup MenuPane. Pulldown MenuPanes that are to be associated with an OptionMenu must be created before the OptionMenu is created.

The Pulldown MenuPane must be attached to a CascadeButton or CascadeButtonGadget that resides in a MenuBar, a Popup MenuPane, a Pulldown MenuPane, or an OptionMenu. This is done by using the button resource **XmNsubMenuId**.

A MenuShell widget is required between the Pulldown MenuPane and its parent. If the application uses this convenience function for creating a Pulldown MenuPane, the MenuShell is automatically created as the real parent of the MenuPane; otherwise, it is the application's responsibility to create the MenuShell widget.

To function correctly when incorporated into a menu, the Pulldown MenuPane's hierarchy must be considered; this hierarchy depends on the type of menu system that is being built as follows:

- If the Pulldown MenuPane is to be pulled down from a MenuBar, its *parent* must be the MenuBar.

- If the Pulldown MenuPane is to be pulled down from a Popup or another Pulldown MenuPane, its *parent* must be that Popup or Pulldown MenuPane.

- If the Pulldown MenuPane is to be pulled down from an OptionMenu, its *parent* must be the same as the OptionMenu parent.

parent   Specifies the parent widget ID

name   Specifies the name of the created widget

arglist   Specifies the argument list

argcount   Specifies the number of attribute/value pairs in the argument list (*arglist*)

For a complete definition of RowColumn and its associated resources, see **XmRowColumn(3X)**.

Return Value

Returns the RowColumn widget ID.

Related Information

XmCascadeButton(3X), **XmCascadeButtonGadget(3X)**, **XmCreateOptionMenu(3X)**, **XmCreatePopupMenu(3X)**, **XmMenuShell(3X)**, and **XmRowColumn(3X)**.

XmCreatePushButton

Purpose

The PushButton widget creation function

AES Support Level

Full-use

Synopsis

#include <Xm/PushB.h>

Widget XmCreatePushButton (*parent, name, arglist, argcount*)
    Widget   *parent*;
    String   *name*;
    ArgList   *arglist*;
    Cardinal *argcount*;

Description

XmCreatePushButton creates an instance of a PushButton widget and returns the associated widget ID.

parent Specifies the parent widget ID

name Specifies the name of the created widget

arglist Specifies the argument list

argcount Specifies the number of attribute/value pairs in the argument list (*arglist*)

For a complete definition of PushButton and its associated resources, see **XmPushButton(3X)**.

Return Value

Returns the PushButton widget ID.

Related Information

XmPushButton(3X).

XmCreatePushButtonGadget

Purpose

The PushButtonGadget creation function

AES Support Level

Full-use

Synopsis

#include <Xm/PushBG.h>

Widget XmCreatePushButtonGadget (*parent, name, arglist, argcount*)
    Widget   *parent*;
    String   *name*;
    ArgList   *arglist*;
    Cardinal   *argcount*;

Description

XmCreatePushButtonGadget creates an instance of a PushButtonGadget widget and returns the associated widget ID.

parent   Specifies the parent widget ID

name   Specifies the name of the created widget

arglist   Specifies the argument list

argcount Specifies the number of attribute/value pairs in the argument list (*arglist*)

For a complete definition of PushButtonGadget and its associated resources, see **XmPushButtonGadget(3X)**.

Return Value

Returns the PushButtonGadget widget ID.

Related Information

XmPushButtonGadget(3X).

XmCreateQuestionDialog

Purpose

The MessageBox QuestionDialog convenience creation function.

AES Support Level

Full-use

Synopsis

#include <Xm/MessageB.h>

Widget XmCreateQuestionDialog (*parent, name, arglist, argcount*)
    Widget   *parent*;
    String   *name*;
    ArgList   *arglist*;
    Cardinal *argcount*;

Description

XmCreateQuestionDialog is a convenience creation function that creates a DialogShell and an unmanaged MessageBox child of the DialogShell. A QuestionDialog is used to get the answer to a question from the user. It includes a symbol, a message, and three buttons. The default symbol is a question mark. The default button labels are **OK**, **Cancel**, and **Help**.

Use **XtManageChild** to pop up the QuestionDialog (passing the MessageBox as the widget parameter); use **XtUnmanageChild** to pop it down.

parent   Specifies the parent widget ID

name   Specifies the name of the created widget

arglist   Specifies the argument list

argcount Specifies the number of attribute/value pairs in the argument list (*arglist*)

For a complete definition of MessageBox and its associated resources, see **XmMessageBox(3X)**.

Return Value

Returns the MessageBox widget ID.

Related Information

XmMessageBox(3X).

XmCreateRadioBox

Purpose

A RowColumn widget convenience creation function

AES Support Level

Full-use

Synopsis

#include <Xm/RowColumn.h>

Widget XmCreateRadioBox (*parent, name, arglist, argcount*)
  Widget *parent*;
  String *name*;
  ArgList *arglist*;
  Cardinal *argcount*;

Description

XmCreateRadioBox creates an instance of a RowColumn widget of type **XmWORK_AREA** and returns the associated widget ID. Typically, this is a composite widget that contains multiple ToggleButtonGadgets. The RadioBox arbitrates and ensures that at most one ToggleButtonGadget is on at any time.

Unless the application supplies other values in the *arglist*, this function provides initial values for several RowColumn resources. It initializes **XmNpacking** to **XmPACK_COLUMN**, **XmNradioBehavior** to True, **XmNisHomogeneous** to True, and **XmNentryClass** to **xmToggleButtonGadgetClass**.

In a RadioBox the ToggleButton or ToggleButtonGadget resource **XmNindicatorType** defaults to **XmONE_OF_MANY**, and the ToggleButton or ToggleButtonGadget resource**XmNvisibleWhenOff** defaults to True.

This routine is provided as a convenience function for creating RowColumn widgets.

parent Specifies the parent widget ID

name Specifies the name of the created widget

arglist Specifies the argument list

argcount Specifies the number of attribute/value pairs in the argument list (*arglist*)

For a complete definition of RowColumn and its associated resources, see **XmRowColumn(3X)**.

Return Value

Returns the RowColumn widget ID.

Related Information

XmCreateRowColumn(3X), **XmCreateWorkArea(3X)**, and **XmRowColumn(3X)**.

XmCreateRowColumn

Purpose

The RowColumn widget creation function

AES Support Level

Full-use

Synopsis

#include <Xm/RowColumn.h>

Widget XmCreateRowColumn (*parent, name, arglist, argcount*)
    Widget   *parent*;
    String   *name*;
    ArgList   *arglist*;
    Cardinal *argcount*;

Description

XmCreateRowColumn creates an instance of a RowColumn widget and returns the associated widget ID. If **XmNrowColumnType** is not specified, then it is created with **XmWORK_AREA**, which is the default.

If this function is used to create a Popup Menu of type **XmMENU_POPUP** or a Pulldown Menu of type **XmMENU_PULLDOWN**, a MenuShell widget is not automatically created as the parent of the MenuPane. The application must first create the MenuShell by using either **XmCreateMenuShell** or the standard toolkit create function.

parent   Specifies the parent widget ID

name   Specifies the name of the created widget

arglist   Specifies the argument list

argcount Specifies the number of attribute/value pairs in the argument list (*arglist*)

For a complete definition of RowColumn and its associated resources, see **XmRowColumn(3X)**.

Return Value

Returns the RowColumn widget ID.

Related Information

XmCreateMenuBar(3X), **XmCreateMenuShell(3X)**, **XmCreateOptionMenu(3X)**, **XmCreatePopupMenu(3X)**, **XmCreatePulldownMenu(3X)**, **XmCreateRadioBox(3X)**, **XmCreateWorkArea(3X)**, and **XmRowColumn(3X)**.

XmCreateScale

Purpose

The Scale widget creation function

AES Support Level

Full-use

Synopsis

#include <Xm/Scale.h>

Widget XmCreateScale (*parent, name, arglist, argcount*)
    Widget   *parent*;
    String   *name*;
    ArgList   *arglist*;
    Cardinal *argcount*;

Description

XmCreateScale creates an instance of a Scale widget and returns the associated widget ID.

parent Specifies the parent widget ID

name Specifies the name of the created widget

arglist Specifies the argument list

argcount Specifies the number of attribute/value pairs in the argument list (*arglist*)

For a complete definition of Scale and its associated resources, see **XmScale(3X)**.

Return Value

Returns the Scale widget ID.

Related Information

XmScale(3X).

XmCreateScrollBar

Purpose

The ScrollBar widget creation function

AES Support Level

Full-use

Synopsis

#include <Xm/ScrollBar.h>

Widget XmCreateScrollBar (*parent, name, arglist, argcount*)
    Widget   *parent*;
    String   *name*;
    ArgList   *arglist*;
    Cardinal   *argcount*;

Description

XmCreateScrollBar creates an instance of a ScrollBar widget and returns the associated widget ID.

parent   Specifies the parent widget ID

name   Specifies the name of the created widget

arglist   Specifies the argument list

argcount Specifies the number of attribute/value pairs in the argument list (*arglist*)

For a complete definition of ScrollBar and its associated resources, see **XmScrollBar(3X)**.

Return Value

Returns the ScrollBar widget ID.

Related Information

XmScrollBar(3X).

XmCreateScrolledList

Purpose

The List ScrolledList convenience creation function.

AES Support Level

Full-use

Synopsis

#include <Xm/List.h>

Widget XmCreateScrolledList (*parent, name, arglist, argcount*)
      Widget   *parent*;
      String   *name*;
      ArgList   *arglist*;
      Cardinal *argcount*;

Description

XmCreateScrolledList creates an instance of a List widget that is contained within a ScrolledWindow. All ScrolledWindow subarea widgets are automatically created by this function. The ID returned by this function is that of the List widget. Use this ID for all normal List operations, as well as those that are relevant for the ScrolledList widget.

All arguments to either the List or the ScrolledWindow widget can be specified at creation time using this function. Changes to initial position and size are sent only to the ScrolledWindow widget. Other resources are sent to the List or the ScrolledWindow widget as appropriate.

This function forces the following initial values for ScrolledWindow resources:

- **XmNscrollingPolicy** is set to **XmAPPLICATION_DEFINED**.

- **XmNvisualPolicy** is set to **XmVARIABLE**.

- **XmNscrollBarDisplayPolicy** is set to **XmSTATIC**. (No initial value is forced for the List's **XmNscrollBarDisplayPolicy**.)

- **XmNshadowThickness** is set to 0.

To obtain the ID of the ScrolledWindow widget associated with the ScrolledList, use the Xt Intrinsics **XtParent** function. The name of the ScrolledWindow created by this function is formed by concatenating the letters **SW** onto the end of the *name* specified in the parameter list.

parent	Specifies the parent widget ID
name	Specifies the name of the created widget
arglist	Specifies the argument list
argcount	Specifies the number of attribute/value pairs in the argument list (*arglist*)

For a complete definition of List and its associated resources, see **XmList(3X)**.

Return Value

Returns the List widget ID.

Related Information

XmList(3X) and **XmScrolledWindow(3X)**.

XmCreateScrolledText

Purpose

The Text ScrolledText convenience creation function.

AES Support Level

Full-use

Synopsis

#include <Xm/Text.h>

Widget XmCreateScrolledText (*parent, name, arglist, argcount*)
     Widget   *parent*;
     String   *name*;
     ArgList   *arglist*;
     Cardinal   *argcount*;

Description

XmCreateScrolledText creates an instance of a Text widget that is contained within a ScrolledWindow. All ScrolledWindow subarea widgets are automatically created by this function. The ID returned by this function is that of the Text widget. Use this ID for all normal Text operations, as well as those that are relevant for the ScrolledText widget.

The Text widget defaults to single-line text edit; therefore, no ScrollBars are displayed. The Text resource **XmNeditMode** must be set to **XmMULTI_LINE_EDIT** to display the ScrollBars. The results of placing a Text widget inside a ScrolledWindow when the Text's **XmNeditMode** is **XmSINGLE_LINE_EDIT** are undefined.

All arguments to either the Text or the ScrolledWindow widget can be specified at creation time using this function. Changes to initial position and size are sent only to the ScrolledWindow widget. Other resources are sent to the Text or the ScrolledWindow widget as appropriate.

This function forces the following initial values for ScrolledWindow resources:

- **XmNscrollingPolicy** is set to **XmAPPLICATION_DEFINED**.

- **XmNvisualPolicy** is set to **XmVARIABLE**.

- **XmNscrollBarDisplayPolicy** is set to **XmSTATIC**.

- **XmNshadowThickness** is set to 0.

To obtain the ID of the ScrolledWindow widget associated with the ScrolledText, use the Xt Intrinsics **XtParent** function. The name of the ScrolledWindow created by this function is formed by concatenating the letters **SW** onto the end of the *name* specified in the parameter list.

parent   Specifies the parent widget ID

name   Specifies the name of the created widget

arglist   Specifies the argument list

argcount Specifies the number of attribute/value pairs in the argument list (*arglist*)

For a complete definition of Text and its associated resources, see **XmText(3X)**.

Return Value

Returns the Text widget ID.

Related Information

XmScrolledWindow(3X) and **XmText(3X)**.

XmCreateScrolledWindow

Purpose

The ScrolledWindow widget creation function.

AES Support Level

Full-use

Synopsis

#include <Xm/ScrolledW.h>

Widget XmCreateScrolledWindow (*parent, name, arglist, argcount*)
    Widget   *parent*;
    String   *name*;
    ArgList   *arglist*;
    Cardinal *argcount*;

Description

XmCreateScrolledWindow creates an instance of a ScrolledWindow widget and returns the associated widget ID.

parent Specifies the parent widget ID

name Specifies the name of the created widget

arglist Specifies the argument list

argcount Specifies the number of attribute/value pairs in the argument list (*arglist*)

For a complete definition of ScrolledWindow and its associated resources, see **XmScrolledWindow(3X)**.

Return Value

Returns the ScrolledWindow widget ID.

Related Information

XmScrolledWindow(3X).

XmCreateSelectionBox

Purpose

The SelectionBox widget creation function

AES Support Level

Full-use

Synopsis

#include <Xm/SelectioB.h>

Widget XmCreateSelectionBox (*parent, name, arglist, argcount*)
    Widget   *parent*;
    String   *name*;
    ArgList   *arglist*;
    Cardinal   *argcount*;

Description

XmCreateSelectionBox creates an unmanaged SelectionBox. A SelectionBox is used to get a selection from a list of alternatives from the user and includes the following:

- A scrolling list of alternatives

- An editable text field for the selected alternative

- Labels for the list and text field

- Three or four buttons

The default button labels are **OK**, **Cancel**, and **Help**. By default an **Apply** button is also created; if the parent of the SelectionBox is a DialogShell it is managed, and otherwise it is unmanaged. One additional **WorkArea** child may be added to the SelectionBox after creation.

parent   Specifies the parent widget ID

name   Specifies the name of the created widget

arglist   Specifies the argument list

argcount Specifies the number of attribute/value pairs in the argument list (*arglist*)

For a complete definition of SelectionBox and its associated resources, see **XmSelectionBox(3X)**.

Return Value

Returns the SelectionBox widget ID.

Related Information

XmSelectionBox(3X)

XmCreateSelectionDialog

Purpose

The SelectionBox SelectionDialog convenience creation function.

AES Support Level

Full-use

Synopsis

#include <Xm/SelectioB.h>

Widget XmCreateSelectionDialog (*parent, name, arglist, argcount*)
     Widget   *parent*;
     String   *name*;
     ArgList   *arglist*;
     Cardinal   *argcount*;

Description

XmCreateSelectionDialog is a convenience creation function that creates a DialogShell and an unmanaged SelectionBox child of the DialogShell. A SelectionDialog offers the user a choice from a list of alternatives and gets a selection. It includes the following:

- A scrolling list of alternatives

- An editable text field for the selected alternative

- Labels for the text field

- Four buttons

The default button labels are **OK**, **Cancel**, **Apply**, and **Help**. One additional **WorkArea** child may be added to the SelectionBox after creation.

XmCreateSelectionDialog forces the value of the SelectionBox resource **XmNdialogType** to **XmDIALOG_SELECTION**.

Use **XtManageChild** to pop up the SelectionDialog (passing the SelectionBox as the widget parameter); use **XtUnmanageChild** to pop it down.

parent Specifies the parent widget ID

name Specifies the name of the created widget

arglist Specifies the argument list

argcount Specifies the number of attribute/value pairs in the argument list (*arglist*)

For a complete definition of SelectionBox and its associated resources, see **XmSelectionBox(3X)**.

Return Value

Returns the SelectionBox widget ID.

Related Information

XmSelectionBox(3X).

XmCreateSeparator

Purpose

The Separator widget creation function.

AES Support Level

Full-use

Synopsis

#include <Xm/Separator.h>

Widget XmCreateSeparator (*parent, name, arglist, argcount*)
      Widget   *parent*;
      String   *name*;
      ArgList   *arglist*;
      Cardinal *argcount*;

Description

XmCreateSeparator creates an instance of a Separator widget and returns the associated widget ID.

parent   Specifies the parent widget ID

name   Specifies the name of the created widget

arglist   Specifies the argument list

argcount Specifies the number of attribute/value pairs in the argument list (*arglist*)

For a complete definition of Separator and its associated resources, see **XmSeparator(3X)**.

Return Value

Returns the Separator widget ID.

Related Information

XmSeparator(3X).

XmCreateSeparatorGadget

Purpose

The SeparatorGadget creation function.

AES Support Level

Full-use

Synopsis

#include <Xm/SeparatoG.h>

Widget XmCreateSeparatorGadget (*parent, name, arglist, argcount*)
> **Widget**   *parent*;
> **String**   *name*;
> **ArgList**   *arglist*;
> **Cardinal**   *argcount*;

Description

XmCreateSeparatorGadget creates an instance of a SeparatorGadget widget and returns the associated widget ID.

parent Specifies the parent widget ID

name Specifies the name of the created widget

arglist Specifies the argument list

argcount Specifies the number of attribute/value pairs in the argument list (*arglist*)

For a complete definition of SeparatorGadget and its associated resources, see **XmSeparatorGadget(3X)**.

Return Value

Returns the SeparatorGadget widget ID.

Related Information

XmSeparatorGadget(3X).

XmCreateText

Purpose

The Text widget creation function

AES Support Level

Full-use

Synopsis

#include <Xm/Text.h>

Widget XmCreateText (*parent, name, arglist, argcount*)
    Widget   *parent*;
    String   *name*;
    ArgList   *arglist*;
    Cardinal   *argcount*;

Description

XmCreateText creates an instance of a Text widget and returns the associated widget ID.

parent   Specifies the parent widget ID

name   Specifies the name of the created widget

arglist   Specifies the argument list

argcount Specifies the number of attribute/value pairs in the argument list (*arglist*)

For a complete definition of Text and its associated resources, see **XmText(3X)**.

Return Value

Returns the Text widget ID.

Related Information

XmText(3X).

XmCreateToggleButton

Purpose

The ToggleButton widget creation function

AES Support Level

Full-use

Synopsis

#include <Xm/ToggleB.h>

Widget XmCreateToggleButton (*parent, name, arglist, argcount*)
    Widget   *parent*;
    String   *name*;
    ArgList   *arglist*;
    Cardinal   *argcount*;

Description

> **XmCreateToggleButton** creates an instance of a ToggleButton widget and returns the associated widget ID.
>
> *parent* Specifies the parent widget ID
>
> *name* Specifies the name of the created widget
>
> *arglist* Specifies the argument list
>
> *argcount* Specifies the number of attribute/value pairs in the argument list (*arglist*)
>
> For a complete definition of ToggleButton and its associated resources, see **XmToggleButton(3X)**.

Return Value

> Returns the ToggleButton widget ID.

Related Information

> **XmToggleButton(3X)**.

XmCreateToggleButtonGadget

Purpose

The ToggleButtonGadget creation function.

AES Support Level

Full-use

Synopsis

#include <Xm/ToggleBG.h>

Widget XmCreateToggleButtonGadget (*parent, name, arglist, argcount*)
    Widget   *parent*;
    String   *name*;
    ArgList   *arglist*;
    Cardinal   *argcount*;

Description

XmCreateToggleButtonGadget creates an instance of a ToggleButtonGadget and returns the associated widget ID.

parent   Specifies the parent widget ID

name   Specifies the name of the created widget

arglist   Specifies the argument list

argcount Specifies the number of attribute/value pairs in the argument list (*arglist*)

For a complete definition of ToggleButtonGadget and its associated resources, see **XmToggleButtonGadget(3X)**.

Return Value

Returns the ToggleButtonGadget widget ID.

Related Information

XmToggleButtonGadget(3X).

XmCreateWarningDialog

Purpose

A MessageBox WarningDialog convenience creation function.

AES Support Level

Full-use

Synopsis

#include <Xm/MessageB.h>

Widget XmCreateWarningDialog (*parent, name, arglist, argcount*)
    Widget   *parent*;
    String   *name*;
    ArgList   *arglist*;
    Cardinal   *argcount*;

Description

XmCreateWarningDialog is a convenience creation function that creates a DialogShell and an unmanaged MessageBox child of the DialogShell. A WarningDialog warns users of action consequences and gives them a choice of resolutions. It includes a symbol, a message, and three buttons. The default symbol is an exclamation point. The default button labels are **OK**, **Cancel**, and **Help**.

Use **XtManageChild** to pop up the WarningDialog (passing the MessageBox as the widget parameter); use **XtUnmanageChild** to pop it down.

parent   Specifies the parent widget ID

name   Specifies the name of the created widget

arglist   Specifies the argument list

argcount Specifies the number of attribute/value pairs in the argument list (*arglist*)

For a complete definition of MessageBox and its associated resources, see **XmMessageBox(3X)**.

Return Value

Returns the MessageBox widget ID.

Related Information

XmMessageBox(3X).

XmCreateWorkArea

Purpose

A function that creates a RowColumn work area.

AES Support Level

Trial-use

Synopsis

#include <Xm/RowColumn.h>

Widget XmCreateWorkArea (*parent, name, arglist, argcount*)
    Widget   *parent*;
    String   *name*;
    ArgList   *arglist*;
    Cardinal   *argcount*;

Description

XmCreateWorkArea creates an instance of a RowColumn widget and returns the associated widget ID. The widget is created with **XmNrowColumnType** set to **XmWORK_AREA**.

parent   Specifies the parent widget ID

name   Specifies the name of the created widget

arglist   Specifies the argument list

argcount Specifies the number of attribute/value pairs in the argument list (*arglist*)

For a complete definition of RowColumn and its associated resources, see **XmRowColumn(3X)**.

Return Value

Returns the RowColumn widget ID.

Related Information

XmCreateRadioBox(3X), **XmCreateRowColumn(3X)**, and **XmRowColumn(3X)**.

XmCreateWorkingDialog

Purpose

The MessageBox WorkingDialog convenience creation function.

AES Support Level

Full-use

Synopsis

#include <Xm/MessageB.h>

Widget XmCreateWorkingDialog (*parent, name, arglist, argcount*)
  Widget   *parent*;
  String   *name*;
  ArgList   *arglist*;
  Cardinal   *argcount*;

Description

XmCreateWorkingDialog is a convenience creation function that creates a DialogShell and an unmanaged MessageBox child of the DialogShell. A WorkingDialog informs users that there is a time-consuming operation in progress and allows them to cancel the operation. It includes a symbol, a message, and three buttons. The default symbol is an hourglass. The default button labels are **OK**, **Cancel**, and **Help**.

Use **XtManageChild** to pop up the WorkingDialog (passing the MessageBox as the widget parameter); use **XtUnmanageChild** to pop it down.

parent Specifies the parent widget ID

name Specifies the name of the created widget

arglist Specifies the argument list

argcount Specifies the number of attribute/value pairs in the argument list (*arglist*)

For a complete definition of MessageBox and its associated resources, see **XmMessageBox(3X)**.

Return Value

Returns the MessageBox widget ID.

Related Information

XmMessageBox(3X).

XmCvtCTToXmString

Purpose

A compound string function that converts compound text to a compound string.

AES Support Level

Trial-use

Synopsis

#include <Xm/Xm.h>

XmString XmCvtCTToXmString (*text*)
    char   * *text*;

Description

XmCvtCTToXmString converts a (char *) string in compound text format to a compound string.

text   Specifies a string in compound text format to be converted to a compound string.

Return Value

Returns a compound string derived from the compound text. The compound text is assumed to be NULL-terminated; NULLs within the compound text are handled correctly. The handling of HORIZONTAL TABULATION (HT) control characters within the compound text is undefined. The compound text format is described in the X Consortium Standard *Compound Text Encoding*.

Related Information

XmCvtXmStringToCT(3X).

XmCvtXmStringToCT

Purpose

A compound string function that converts a compound string to compound text.

AES Support Level

Trial-use

Synopsis

#include <Xm/Xm.h>

char * XmCvtXmStringToCT (*string*)
    XmString   *string*;

Description

XmCvtXmStringToCT converts a compound string to a (char *) string in compound text format.

string   Specifies a compound string to be converted to compound text.

Return Value

Returns a (char *) string in compound text format. This format is described in the X Consortium Standard *Compound Text Encoding*.

Related Information

XmCvtCTToXmString(3X).

XmDeactivateProtocol

Purpose

A VendorShell function that deactivates a protocol without removing it.

AES Support Level

Trial-use

Synopsis

#include <Xm/Xm.h>
#include <X11/Protocols.h>

void XmDeactivateProtocol (*shell, property, protocol*)
    Widget   *shell*;
    Atom   *property*;
    Atom   *protocol*;

void XmDeactivateWMProtocol (*shell, protocol*)
    Widget   *shell*;
    Atom   *protocol*;

Description

XmDeactivateProtocol deactivates a protocol without removing it. It updates the handlers and the *property*, if the *shell* is realized. It is sometimes useful to allow a protocol's state information (callback lists, etc.) to persist, even though the client may choose to temporarily resign from the interaction. The main use of this capability is to gray/ungray **f.send_msg** entries in the Mwm system menu. This is supported by allowing a *protocol* to be in one of two states: active or inactive. If the *protocol* is active and the *shell* is realized, the *property* contains the *protocol* **Atom**. If the *protocol* is inactive, the **Atom** is not present in the *property*.

XmDeactivateWMProtocol is a convenience interface. It calls **XmDeactivateProtocol** with the property value set to the atom returned by interning **WM_PROTOCOLS**.

shell   Specifies the widget with which the protocol property is associated

property Specifies the protocol property

protocol Specifies the protocol atom (or an int type cast to Atom)

For a complete definition of VendorShell and its associated resources, see **VendorShell(3X)**.

Related Information

mwm(1X), **VendorShell(3X)**, **XmDeactivateWMProtocol(3X)**, and **XmInternAtom(3X)**.

XmDeactivateWMProtocol

Purpose

A VendorShell convenience interface that deactivates a protocol without removing it.

AES Support Level

Trial-use

Synopsis

#include <Xm/Xm.h>
#include <X11/Protocols.h>

void XmDeactivateWMProtocol (*shell, protocol*)
    Widget   *shell*;
    Atom   *protocol*;

Description

XmDeactivateWMProtocol is a convenience interface. It calls **XmDeactivateProtocol** with the property value set to the atom returned by interning **WM_PROTOCOLS**.

shell   Specifies the widget with which the protocol property is associated

protocol Specifies the protocol atom (or an int type cast to Atom)

For a complete definition of VendorShell and its associated resources, see **VendorShell(3X)**.

Related Information

VendorShell(3X), **XmDeactivateProtocol(3X)**, and **XmInternAtom(3X)**.

XmDestroyPixmap

Purpose

A pixmap caching function that removes a pixmap from the pixmap cache.

AES Support Level

Full-use

Synopsis

#include <Xm/Xm.h>

Boolean XmDestroyPixmap (*screen, pixmap*)
    Screen   * *screen*;
    Pixmap   *pixmap*;

Description

XmDestroyPixmap removes pixmaps that are no longer used. Pixmaps are completely freed only when there is no further reference to them.

screen   Specifies the display screen for which the pixmap was requested

pixmap   Specifies the pixmap to be destroyed

Return Value

Returns True when successful; returns False if there is no matching screen and pixmap in the pixmap cache.

Related Information

XmInstallImage(3X), **XmUninstallImage(3X)**, and **XmGetPixmap(3X)**.

XmDialogShell

Purpose

The DialogShell widget class

AES Support Level

Full-use

Synopsis

#include <Xm/DialogS.h>

Description

Modal and modeless dialogs use DialogShell as the Shell parent. DialogShell widgets cannot be iconified. Instead, all secondary DialogShell widgets associated with an ApplicationShell widget are iconified and de-iconified as a group with the primary widget.

The client indirectly manipulates DialogShell via the convenience interfaces during creation, and it can directly manipulate its BulletinBoard-derived child. Much of the functionality of DialogShell assumes that its child is a BulletinBoard subclass, although it can potentially stand alone.

Setting **XmNheight**, **XmNwidth**, or **XmNborderWidth** for either a DialogShell or its child sets that resource to the same value in both the parent and the child. An application should always specify these resources for the child, not the parent.

For a child of a DialogShell, setting **XmNx** or **XmNy** sets the corresponding resource of the parent but does not change the child's position relative to the parent. **XtGetValues** for the child's **XmNx** or **XmNy** yields the value of the corresponding resource in the parent. The *x* and *y* coordinates of the child's upper left outside corner relative to the parent's upper left inside corner are both zero minus the value of **XmNborderWidth**.

Note that the *Inter-Client Communication Conventions Manual* allows a window manager to change or control the border width of a reparented top-level window.

Classes

DialogShell inherits behavior and resources from **Core**, **Composite**, **Shell**, **WMShell**, **VendorShell**, and **TransientShell** classes.

The class pointer is **xmDialogShellWidgetClass**.

The class name is **XmDialogShell**.

New Resources

DialogShell defines no new resources but overrides the **XmNdeleteResponse** resource in the **VendorShell** class.

Inherited Resources

DialogShell inherits behavior and resources from the following superclasses. For a complete description of each resource, refer to the man page for that superclass.

The following table defines a set of widget resources used by the programmer to specify data. The programmer can also set the resource values for the inherited classes to set attributes for this widget. To reference a resource by name or by class in a .Xdefaults file, remove the **XmN** or **XmC** prefix and use the remaining letters. To specify one of the defined values for a resource in a .Xdefaults file, remove the **Xm** prefix and use the remaining letters (in either lowercase or uppercase, but include any underscores between words). The codes in the access column indicate if the given resource can be set at creation time (**C**), set by using **XtSetValues** (**S**), retrieved by using **XtGetValues** (**G**), or is not applicable (**N/A**).

TransientShell Resource Set		
Name **Class**	**Default** **Type**	**Access**
XmNtransientFor XmCTransientFor	NULL Widget	CSG

VendorShell Resource Set		
Name **Class**	**Default** **Type**	**Access**
XmNdefaultFontList XmCDefaultFontList	dynamic XmFontList	C
XmNdeleteResponse XmCDeleteResponse	XmUNMAP unsigned char	CSG
XmNkeyboardFocusPolicy XmCKeyboardFocusPolicy	XmEXPLICIT unsigned char	CSG
XmNmwmDecorations XmCMwmDecorations	-1 int	CSG
XmNmwmFunctions XmCMwmFunctions	-1 int	CSG
XmNmwmInputMode XmCMwmInputMode	-1 int	CSG
XmNmwmMenu XmCMwmMenu	NULL String	CSG

WMShell Resource Set		
Name Class	**Default** Type	**Access**
XmNbaseHeight XmCBaseHeight	XtUnspecifiedShellInt int	CSG
XmNbaseWidth XmCBaseWidth	XtUnspecifiedShellInt int	CSG
XmNheightInc XmCHeightInc	XtUnspecifiedShellInt int	CSG
XmNiconMask XmCIconMask	NULL Pixmap	CSG
XmNiconPixmap XmCIconPixmap	NULL Pixmap	CSG
XmNiconWindow XmCIconWindow	NULL Window	CSG
XmNiconX XmCIconX	-1 int	CSG
XmNiconY XmCIconY	-1 int	CSG
XmNinitialState XmCInitialState	NormalState int	CSG
XmNinput XmCInput	True Boolean	CSG
XmNmaxAspectX XmCMaxAspectX	XtUnspecifiedShellInt int	CSG
XmNmaxAspectY XmCMaxAspectY	XtUnspecifiedShellInt int	CSG
XmNmaxHeight XmCMaxHeight	XtUnspecifiedShellInt int	CSG
XmNmaxWidth XmCMaxWidth	XtUnspecifiedShellInt int	CSG

Name	Default	Access
Class	Type	
XmNminAspectX	XtUnspecifiedShellInt	CSG
XmCMinAspectX	int	
XmNminAspectY	XtUnspecifiedShellInt	CSG
XmCMinAspectY	int	
XmNminHeight	XtUnspecifiedShellInt	CSG
XmCMinHeight	int	
XmNminWidth	XtUnspecifiedShellInt	CSG
XmCMinWidth	int	
XmNtitle	dynamic	CSG
XmCTitle	String	
XmNtitleEncoding	XA_STRING	CSG
XmCTitleEncoding	Atom	
XmNtransient	True	CSG
XmCTransient	Boolean	
XmNwaitForWm	True	CSG
XmCWaitForWm	Boolean	
XmNwidthInc	XtUnspecifiedShellInt	CSG
XmCWidthInc	int	
XmNwindowGroup	dynamic	CSG
XmCWindowGroup	Window	
XmNwinGravity	dynamic	CSG
XmCWinGravity	int	
XmNwmTimeout	5000 ms	CSG
XmCWmTimeout	int	

Shell Resource Set		
Name **Class**	**Default** **Type**	**Access**
XmNallowShellResize XmCAllowShellResize	False Boolean	CG
XmNcreatePopupChildProc XmCCreatePopupChildProc	NULL (*)()	CSG
XmNgeometry XmCGeometry	NULL String	CSG
XmNoverrideRedirect XmCOverrideRedirect	False Boolean	CSG
XmNpopdownCallback XmCCallback	NULL XtCallbackList	C
XmNpopupCallback XmCCallback	NULL XtCallbackList	C
XmNsaveUnder XmCSaveUnder	True Boolean	CSG
XmNvisual XmCVisual	CopyFromParent Visual *	CSG

Composite Resource Set		
Name **Class**	**Default** **Type**	**Access**
XmNchildren XmCReadOnly	NULL WidgetList	G
XmNinsertPosition XmCInsertPosition	NULL (*)()	CSG
XmNnumChildren XmCReadOnly	0 Cardinal	G

Core Resource Set		
Name	**Default**	**Access**
Class	**Type**	
XmNaccelerators	dynamic	CSG
XmCAccelerators	XtAccelerators	
XmNancestorSensitive	dynamic	G
XmCSensitive	Boolean	
XmNbackground	dynamic	CSG
XmCBackground	Pixel	
XmNbackgroundPixmap	XmUNSPECIFIED_PIXMAP	CSG
XmCPixmap	Pixmap	
XmNborderColor	XtDefaultForeground	CSG
XmCBorderColor	Pixel	
XmNborderPixmap	XmUNSPECIFIED_PIXMAP	CSG
XmCPixmap	Pixmap	
XmNborderWidth	1	CSG
XmCBorderWidth	Dimension	
XmNcolormap	dynamic	CG
XmCColormap	Colormap	
XmNdepth	dynamic	CG
XmCDepth	int	
XmNdestroyCallback	NULL	C
XmCCallback	XtCallbackList	
XmNheight	dynamic	CSG
XmCHeight	Dimension	
XmNinitialResourcesPersistent	True	C
XmCInitialResourcesPersistent	Boolean	
XmNmappedWhenManaged	True	CSG
XmCMappedWhenManaged	Boolean	
XmNscreen	dynamic	CG
XmCScreen	Screen *	

Name	Default	Access
Class	Type	
XmNsensitive	True	CSG
XmCSensitive	Boolean	
XmNtranslations	dynamic	CSG
XmCTranslations	XtTranslations	
XmNwidth	dynamic	CSG
XmCWidth	Dimension	
XmNx	0	CSG
XmCPosition	Position	
XmNy	0	CSG
XmCPosition	Position	

Translations

There are no translations for XmDialogShell.

Related Information

Composite(3X), Core(3X), Shell(3X), TransientShell(3X), WMShell(3X), VendorShell(3X), and XmCreateDialogShell(3X).

XmDrawingArea

Purpose

The DrawingArea widget class

AES Support Level

Full-use

Synopsis

#include <Xm/DrawingA.h>

Description

DrawingArea is an empty widget that is easily adaptable to a variety of purposes. It does no drawing and defines no behavior except for invoking callbacks. Callbacks notify the application when graphics need to be drawn (exposure events or widget resize) and when the widget receives input from the keyboard or mouse.

Applications are responsible for defining appearance and behavior as needed in response to DrawingArea callbacks. Applications must take care not to draw in the shadow and to clear the old shadow when the widget is resized.

DrawingArea is also a composite widget and subclass of **XmManager** that supports minimal geometry management for multiple widget or gadget children.

Classes

DrawingArea inherits behavior and resources from the **Core**, **Composite**, **Constraint**, and **XmManager** classes.

The class pointer is **xmDrawingAreaWidgetClass**.

The class name is **XmDrawingArea**.

New Resources

The following table defines a set of widget resources used by the programmer to specify data. The programmer can also set the resource values for the inherited classes to set attributes for this widget. To reference a resource by name or by class in a .Xdefaults file, remove the **XmN** or **XmC** prefix and use the remaining letters. To specify one of the defined values for a resource in a .Xdefaults file, remove the **Xm** prefix and use the remaining letters (in either lowercase or uppercase, but include any underscores between words). The codes in the access column indicate if the given resource can be set at creation time (**C**), set by using **XtSetValues** (**S**), retrieved by using **XtGetValues** (**G**), or is not applicable (**N/A**).

XmDrawingArea Resource Set		
Name **Class**	**Default** **Type**	**Access**
XmNexposeCallback XmCCallback	NULL XtCallbackList	C
XmNinputCallback XmCCallback	NULL XtCallbackList	C
XmNmarginHeight XmCMarginHeight	10 Dimension	CSG
XmNmarginWidth XmCMarginWidth	10 Dimension	CSG
XmNresizeCallback XmCCallback	NULL XtCallbackList	C
XmNresizePolicy XmCResizePolicy	XmRESIZE_ANY unsigned char	CSG

XmNexposeCallback

Specifies the list of callbacks that is called when DrawingArea receives an exposure event. The callback reason is **XmCR_EXPOSE**. The callback structure also includes the exposure event.

XmNinputCallback

Specifies the list of callbacks that is called when the DrawingArea receives a keyboard or mouse event (key or button, up or down). The callback reason is **XmCR_INPUT**. The callback structure also includes the input event.

XmNmarginHeight

Specifies the minimum spacing in pixels between the top or bottom edge of DrawingArea and any child widget.

XmNmarginWidth

Specifies the minimum spacing in pixels between the left or right edge of DrawingArea and any child widget.

XmNresizeCallback

> Specifies the list of callbacks that is called when the DrawingArea is resized. The callback reason is **XmCR_RESIZE**.

XmNresizePolicy

> Controls the policy for resizing DrawingArea widgets. Possible values include **XmRESIZE_NONE** (fixed size), **XmRESIZE_ANY** (shrink or grow as needed), and **XmRESIZE_GROW** (grow only).

Inherited Resources

DrawingArea inherits behavior and resources from the following superclasses. For a complete description of each resource, refer to the man page for that superclass.

XmManager Resource Set		
Name	**Default**	**Access**
Class	**Type**	
XmNbottomShadowColor	dynamic	CSG
XmCBottomShadowColor	Pixel	
XmNbottomShadowPixmap	XmUNSPECIFIED_PIXMAP	CSG
XmCBottomShadowPixmap	Pixmap	
XmNforeground	dynamic	CSG
XmCForeground	Pixel	
XmNhelpCallback	NULL	C
XmCCallback	XtCallbackList	
XmNhighlightColor	dynamic	CSG
XmCHighlightColor	Pixel	
XmNhighlightPixmap	dynamic	CSG
XmCHighlightPixmap	Pixmap	
XmNnavigationType	XmTAB_GROUP	CSG
XmCNavigationType	XmNavigationType	
XmNshadowThickness	0	CSG
XmCShadowThickness	Dimension	
XmNstringDirection	dynamic	CG
XmCStringDirection	XmStringDirection	
XmNtopShadowColor	dynamic	CSG
XmCBackgroundTopShadowColor	Pixel	
XmNtopShadowPixmap	dynamic	CSG
XmCTopShadowPixmap	Pixmap	
XmNtraversalOn	True	CSG
XmCTraversalOn	Boolean	
XmNuserData	NULL	CSG
XmCUserData	Pointer	

Composite Resource Set		
Name **Class**	**Default** **Type**	**Access**
XmNchildren XmCReadOnly	NULL WidgetList	G
XmNinsertPosition XmCInsertPosition	NULL (*)()	CSG
XmNnumChildren XmCReadOnly	0 Cardinal	G

Core Resource Set		
Name	**Default**	**Access**
Class	**Type**	
XmNaccelerators	dynamic	CSG
XmCAccelerators	XtAccelerators	
XmNancestorSensitive	dynamic	G
XmCSensitive	Boolean	
XmNbackground	dynamic	CSG
XmCBackground	Pixel	
XmNbackgroundPixmap	XmUNSPECIFIED_PIXMAP	CSG
XmCPixmap	Pixmap	
XmNborderColor	XtDefaultForeground	CSG
XmCBorderColor	Pixel	
XmNborderPixmap	XmUNSPECIFIED_PIXMAP	CSG
XmCPixmap	Pixmap	
XmNborderWidth	0	CSG
XmCBorderWidth	Dimension	
XmNcolormap	dynamic	CG
XmCColormap	Colormap	
XmNdepth	dynamic	CG
XmCDepth	int	
XmNdestroyCallback	NULL	C
XmCCallback	XtCallbackList	
XmNheight	dynamic	CSG
XmCHeight	Dimension	
XmNinitialResourcesPersistent	True	C
XmCInitialResourcesPersistent	Boolean	
XmNmappedWhenManaged	True	CSG
XmCMappedWhenManaged	Boolean	
XmNscreen	dynamic	CG
XmCScreen	Screen *	

Name	Default	Access
Class	Type	
XmNsensitive	True	CSG
XmCSensitive	Boolean	
XmNtranslations	dynamic	CSG
XmCTranslations	XtTranslations	
XmNwidth	dynamic	CSG
XmCWidth	Dimension	
XmNx	0	CSG
XmCPosition	Position	
XmNy	0	CSG
XmCPosition	Position	

Callback Information

A pointer to the following structure is passed to each callback:

typedef struct
{
    int   *reason*;
    XEvent   * *event*;
    Window *window*;
} **XmDrawingAreaCallbackStruct**;

reason   Indicates why the callback was invoked

event   Points to the **XEvent** that triggered the callback. This is NULL for the **XmNresizeCallback**.

window   Is set to the widget window

Translations

XmDrawingArea inherits translations from XmManager. Before calling the XmManager actions, all events in the inherited translations except **<BtnMotion>**, **<EnterWindow>**, **<LeaveWindow>**, **<FocusIn>**, and **<FocusOut>** also call the **DrawingAreaInput()** action.

XmDrawingArea has the additional translations listed below. These translations may not directly correspond to a translation table.

MAny BAny Press: DrawingAreaInput()
MAny BAny Release:DrawingAreaInput()

MAny KAny Press:DrawingAreaInput()
                      ManagerGadgetKeyInput()
MAny KAny Release:DrawingAreaInput()

Action Routines

The XmDrawingArea action routines are described below:

DrawingAreaInput():
        Unless the event takes place in a gadget, calls the callbacks for **XmNinputCallback**.

ManagerGadgetKeyInput():
        Causes the current gadget to process a keyboard event.

Additional Behavior

The XmDrawingArea widget has the additional behavior described below:

<Expose>:   Calls the callbacks for **XmNexposeCallback**.

<Widget Resize>:
        Calls the callbacks for **XmNresizeCallback**.

Virtual Bindings

The bindings for virtual keys are vendor specific.

Related Information

Composite(3X), **Constraint(3X)**, **Core(3X)**, **XmCreateDrawingArea(3X)**, and **XmManager(3X)**.

XmDrawnButton

Purpose

The DrawnButton widget class

AES Support Level

Full-use

Synopsis

#include <Xm/DrawnB.h>

Description

The DrawnButton widget consists of an empty widget window surrounded by a shadow border. It provides the application developer with a graphics area that can have PushButton input semantics.

Callback types are defined for widget exposure and widget resize to allow the application to redraw or reposition its graphics. If the DrawnButton widget has a highlight and shadow thickness, the application should not draw in that area. To avoid drawing in the highlight and shadow area, create the graphics context with a clipping rectangle for drawing in the widget. The clipping rectangle should take into account the size of the widget's highlight thickness and shadow.

Classes

DrawnButton inherits behavior and resources from **Core**, **XmPrimitive**, and **XmLabel** Classes.

The class pointer is **xmDrawnButtonWidgetClass**.

The class name is **XmDrawnButton**.

New Resources

The following table defines a set of widget resources used by the programmer to specify data. The programmer can also set the resource values for the inherited classes to set attributes for this widget. To reference a resource by name or by class in a .Xdefaults file, remove the **XmN** or **XmC** prefix and use the remaining letters. To specify one of the defined values for a resource in a .Xdefaults file, remove the **Xm** prefix and use the remaining letters (in either lowercase or uppercase, but include any underscores between words). The codes in the access column indicate if the given resource can be set at creation time (**C**), set by using **XtSetValues** (**S**), retrieved by using **XtGetValues** (**G**), or is not applicable (**N/A**).

XmDrawnButton Resource Set		
Name **Class**	**Default** **Type**	**Access**
XmNactivateCallback XmCCallback	NULL XtCallbackList	C
XmNarmCallback XmCCallback	NULL XtCallbackList	C
XmNdisarmCallback XmCCallback	NULL XtCallbackList	C
XmNexposeCallback XmCCallback	NULL XtCallbackList	C
XmNmultiClick XmCMultiClick	dynamic unsigned char	CSG
XmNpushButtonEnabled XmCPushButtonEnabled	False Boolean	CSG
XmNresizeCallback XmCCallback	NULL XtCallbackList	C
XmNshadowType XmCShadowType	XmSHADOW_ETCHED_IN unsigned char	CSG

XmNactivateCallback

Specifies the list of callbacks that is called when the widget becomes selected. The reason sent by the callback is **XmCR_ACTIVATE**.

XmNarmCallback

Specifies the list of callbacks that is called when the widget becomes armed. The reason sent by the callback is **XmCR_ARM**.

XmNdisarmCallback

Specifies the list of callbacks that is called when the widget becomes disarmed. The reason sent by the callback is **XmCR_DISARM**.

XmNexposeCallback
>Specifies the list of callbacks that is called when the widget receives an exposure event. The reason sent by the callback is **XmCR_EXPOSE**.

XmNmultiClick
>If a button click is followed by another button click within the time span specified by the display's multi-click time, and this resource is set to **XmMULTICLICK_DISCARD**, do not process the second click. If this resource is set to **XmMULTICLICK_KEEP**, process the event and increment *click_count* in the callback structure. When the button is not in a menu, the default value is **XmMULTICLICK_KEEP**.

XmNpushButtonEnabled
>Enables or disables the three-dimensional shadow drawing as in PushButton.

XmNresizeCallback
>Specifies the list of callbacks that is called when the widget receives a resize event. The reason sent by the callback is **XmCR_RESIZE**. The event returned for this callback is NULL.

XmNshadowType
>Describes the drawing style for the DrawnButton. This resource can have the following values:

>- **XmSHADOW_IN** — draws the DrawnButton so that the shadow appears inset. This means that the bottom shadow visuals and top shadow visuals are reversed.

>- **XmSHADOW_OUT** — draws the DrawnButton so that the shadow appears outset.

- **XmSHADOW_ETCHED_IN** — draws the DrawnButton using a double line. This gives the effect of a line etched into the window. The thickness of the double line is equal to the value of **XmNshadowThickness**.

- **XmSHADOW_ETCHED_OUT** — draws the DrawnButton using a double line. This gives the effect of a line coming out of the window. The thickness of the double line is equal to the value of **XmNshadowThickness**.

Inherited Resources

DrawnButton inherits behavior and resources from the following superclasses. For a complete description of each resource, refer to the man page for that superclass.

XmLabel Resource Set		
Name	**Default**	**Access**
Class	Type	
XmNaccelerator	NULL	N/A
XmCAccelerator	String	
XmNacceleratorText	NULL	N/A
XmCAcceleratorText	XmString	
XmNalignment	dynamic	CSG
XmCAlignment	unsigned char	
XmNfontList	dynamic	CSG
XmCFontList	XmFontList	
XmNlabelInsensitivePixmap	XmUNSPECIFIED_PIXMAP	CSG
XmCLabelInsensitivePixmap	Pixmap	
XmNlabelPixmap	XmUNSPECIFIED_PIXMAP	CSG
XmCLabelPixmap	Pixmap	
XmNlabelString	"\0"	CSG
XmCXmString	XmString	
XmNlabelType	XmSTRING	CSG
XmCLabelType	unsigned char	
XmNmarginBottom	0	CSG
XmCMarginBottom	Dimension	
XmNmarginHeight	2	CSG
XmCMarginHeight	Dimension	
XmNmarginLeft	0	CSG
XmCMarginLeft	Dimension	
XmNmarginRight	0	CSG
XmCMarginRight	Dimension	
XmNmarginTop	0	CSG
XmCMarginTop	Dimension	
XmNmarginWidth	2	CSG
XmCMarginWidth	Dimension	

Name	Default	Access
Class	Type	
XmNmnemonic	NULL	N/A
XmCMnemonic	KeySym	
XmNmnemonicCharSet	dynamic	N/A
XmCMnemonicCharSet	String	
XmNrecomputeSize	True	CSG
XmCRecomputeSize	Boolean	
XmNstringDirection	dynamic	CSG
XmCStringDirection	XmStringDirection	

XmPrimitive Resource Set		
Name Class	**Default** Type	**Access**
XmNbottomShadowColor XmCBottomShadowColor	dynamic Pixel	CSG
XmNbottomShadowPixmap XmCBottomShadowPixmap	XmUNSPECIFIED_PIXMAP Pixmap	CSG
XmNforeground XmCForeground	dynamic Pixel	CSG
XmNhelpCallback XmCCallback	NULL XtCallbackList	C
XmNhighlightColor XmCHighlightColor	dynamic Pixel	CSG
XmNhighlightOnEnter XmCHighlightOnEnter	False Boolean	CSG
XmNhighlightPixmap XmCHighlightPixmap	dynamic Pixmap	CSG
XmNhighlightThickness XmCHighlightThickness	2 Dimension	CSG
XmNnavigationType XmCNavigationType	XmNONE XmNavigationType	G
XmNshadowThickness XmCShadowThickness	2 Dimension	CSG
XmNtopShadowColor XmCTopShadowColor	dynamic Pixel	CSG
XmNtopShadowPixmap XmCTopShadowPixmap	dynamic Pixmap	CSG
XmNtraversalOn XmCTraversalOn	True Boolean	CSG
XmNuserData XmCUserData	NULL Pointer	CSG

Core Resource Set		

Name
    Class
	Default
	    Type
		Access

XmNaccelerators
   XmCAccelerators
	dynamic
	   XtAccelerators
		CSG

XmNancestorSensitive
   XmCSensitive
	dynamic
	   Boolean
		G

XmNbackground
   XmCBackground
	dynamic
	   Pixel
		CSG

XmNbackgroundPixmap
   XmCPixmap
	XmUNSPECIFIED_PIXMAP
	   Pixmap
		CSG

XmNborderColor
   XmCBorderColor
	XtDefaultForeground
	   Pixel
		CSG

XmNborderPixmap
   XmCPixmap
	XmUNSPECIFIED_PIXMAP
	   Pixmap
		CSG

XmNborderWidth
   XmCBorderWidth
	0
	   Dimension
		CSG

XmNcolormap
   XmCColormap
	dynamic
	   Colormap
		CG

XmNdepth
   XmCDepth
	dynamic
	   int
		CG

XmNdestroyCallback
   XmCCallback
	NULL
	   XtCallbackList
		C

XmNheight
   XmCHeight
	dynamic
	   Dimension
		CSG

XmNinitialResourcesPersistent
   XmCInitialResourcesPersistent
	True
	   Boolean
		C

XmNmappedWhenManaged
   XmCMappedWhenManaged
	True
	   Boolean
		CSG

XmNscreen
   XmCScreen
	dynamic
	   Screen *
		CG

Name	Default	Access
Class	Type	
XmNsensitive	True	CSG
XmCSensitive	Boolean	
XmNtranslations	dynamic	CSG
XmCTranslations	XtTranslations	
XmNwidth	dynamic	CSG
XmCWidth	Dimension	
XmNx	0	CSG
XmCPosition	Position	
XmNy	0	CSG
XmCPosition	Position	

Callback Information

A pointer to the following structure is passed to each callback:

typedef struct
{
    int   *reason*;
    XEvent   * *event*;
    Window *window*;
    int   *click_count*;
} XmDrawnButtonCallbackStruct;

reason   Indicates why the callback was invoked.

event   Points to the **XEvent** that triggered the callback. This is NULL for **XmNresizeCallback**.

window Is set to the window ID in which the event occurred.

click_count

    Contains the number of clicks in the last multiclick sequence if the **XmNmultiClick** resource is set to **XmMULTICLICK_KEEP**, otherwise it contains **1**. The activate callback is invoked for each click if **XmNmultiClick** is set to **XmMULTICLICK_KEEP**.

Translations

XmDrawnButton includes translations from Primitive. The XmDrawnButton translations are listed below. These translations may not directly correspond to a translation table.

BSelect Press:	**Arm()**
BSelect Click:	**Activate()**
	Disarm()
BSelect Release:	**Activate()**
	Disarm()
BSelect Press 2+:	**MultiArm()**
BSelect Release 2+:	**MultiActivate()**
KActivate:	**ArmAndActivate()**
KSelect:	**ArmAndActivate()**
KHelp:	**Help()**

Action Routines

The XmDrawnButton action routines are described below:

Activate(): If **XmNpushButtonEnabled** is True, redraws the shadow in the unselected state; otherwise, redraws the shadow according to **XmNshadowType**. If the pointer is within the DrawnButton, calls the **XmNactivateCallback** callbacks.

Arm(): If **XmNpushButtonEnabled** is True, redraws the shadow in the selected state; otherwise, redraws the shadow according to **XmNshadowType**. Calls the callbacks for **XmNarmCallback**.

ArmAndActivate():
If **XmNpushButtonEnabled** is True, redraws the shadow in the selected state; otherwise, redraws the shadow according to **XmNshadowType**. Calls the callbacks for **XmNarmCallback**.

Arranges for the following to happen, either immediately or at a later time: If **XmNpushButtonEnabled** is True, the shadow is redrawn in the unselected state; otherwise, the shadow is redrawn according to **XmNshadowType**. The callbacks for **XmNactivateCallback** and **XmNdisarmCallback** are called.

Disarm(): Marks the DrawnButton as unselected and calls the callbacks for **XmNdisarmCallback**.

Help(): Calls the callbacks for **XmNhelpCallback** if any exist. If there are no help callbacks for this widget, this action calls the help callbacks for the nearest ancestor that has them.

MultiActivate():
If **XmNmultiClick** is **XmMULTICLICK_DISCARD**, this action does nothing.

If **XmNmultiClick** is **XmMULTICLICK_KEEP**, this action does the following: Increments *click_count* in the callback structure. If **XmNpushButtonEnabled** is True, redraws the shadow in the unselected state; otherwise, redraws the shadow according to **XmNshadowType**. If the pointer is within the DrawnButton, calls the **XmNactivateCallback** callbacks. Calls the callbacks for **XmNdisarmCallback**.

MultiArm():

If **XmNmultiClick** is **XmMULTICLICK_DISCARD**, this action does nothing.

If **XmNmultiClick** is **XmMULTICLICK_KEEP**, this action does the following: If **XmNpushButtonEnabled** is True, redraws the shadow in the selected state; otherwise, redraws the shadow according to **XmNshadowType**. Calls the callbacks for **XmNarmCallback**.

Additional Behavior

This widget has the additional behavior described below:

<EnterWindow>:

Draws the shadow in its selected state if **XmNpushButtonEnabled** is True and if the cursor leaves and re-enters the window while **BSelect** is pressed.

<LeaveWindow>:

Draws the shadow in its unselected state if **XmNpushButtonEnabled** is True and if the cursor leaves the window while **BSelect** is pressed.

Virtual Bindings

The bindings for virtual keys are vendor specific.

Related Information

Core(3X), **XmCreateDrawnButton**, **XmLabel(3X)**, **XmPrimitive(3X)**, **XmPushButton**, and **XmSeparator(3X)**.

XmFileSelectionBox

Purpose

The FileSelectionBox widget class

AES Support Level

Full-use

Synopsis

#include <Xm/FileSB.h>

Description

FileSelectionBox traverses through directories, views the files and subdirectories in them, and then selects files.

A FileSelectionBox has five main areas:

- A text input field for displaying and editing a directory mask used to select the files to be displayed

- A scrollable list of filenames

- A scrollable list of subdirectories

- A text input field for displaying and editing a filename

- A group of PushButtons, labeled **OK**, **Filter**, **Cancel**, and **Help**

One additional **WorkArea** child may be added to the FileSelectionBox after creation. The list of filenames, the list of subdirectories, or both can be removed from the FileSelectionBox after creation by unmanaging the appropriate widgets and their labels. The list and label widgets are obtained by calling the function **XmFileSelectionBoxGetChild**. To remove either the directory list or the file list, unmanage the parent of the appropriate list widget and unmanage the corresponding label.

The directory mask is a string specifying the base directory to be examined and a search pattern. Ordinarily, the directory list displays the subdirectories of the base directory, as well as the base directory itself and its parent directory. The file list ordinarily displays all files and/or subdirectories in the base directory that match the search pattern.

A procedure specified by the **XmNqualifySearchDataProc** resource extracts the base directory and search pattern from the directory mask. If the directory specification is empty, the current working directory is used. If the search pattern is empty, a pattern that matches all files is used.

An application can supply its own **XmNqualifySearchDataProc** as well as its own procedures to search for subdirectories and files. The default **XmNqualifySearchDataProc** works as follows: The directory mask is a pathname that can contain zero or more *wildcard* characters in its directory portion, its file portion, or both. The directory components of the directory mask up to, but not including, the first component with a wildcard character specify the directory to be searched, relative to the current working directory. The remaining components specify the search pattern. If the directory mask is empty or if its first component contains a wildcard character, the current working directory is searched. If no component of the directory mask contains a wildcard character, the entire directory mask is the directory specification, and all files in that directory are matched.

The user can select a new directory to examine by scrolling through the list of directories and selecting the desired directory or by editing the directory mask. Selecting a new directory from the directory list does not change the search pattern. A user can select a new search pattern by editing the directory mask. Double clicking or pressing **KActivate** on a directory in the directory list initiates a search for files and subdirectories in the new directory, using the current search pattern.

The user can select a file by scrolling through the list of filenames and selecting the desired file or by entering the filename directly into the text edit area. Selecting a file from the list causes that filename to appear in the file selection text edit area.

The user may select a new file as many times as desired. The application is not notified until the user takes one of these actions:

- Selects the **OK** PushButton

- Presses **KActivate** while the selection text edit area has the keyboard focus.

- Double clicks or presses **KActivate** on an item in the file list

FileSelectionBox initiates a directory and file search when any of the following occurs:

- The FileSelectionBox is initialized

- The function **XtSetValues** is used to change **XmNdirMask**, **XmNdirectory**, **XmNpattern**, or **XmNfileTypeMask**

- The user activates the **Filter** PushButton

- The user double clicks or presses **KActivate** on an item in the directory list

- The application calls **XmFileSelectionDoSearch**

- The user presses **KActivate** while the directory mask text edit area has the keyboard focus

When a file search is initiated, the FileSelectionBox takes the following actions:

- Constructs an **XmFileSelectionBoxCallbackStruct** structure with values appropriate for the action that initiated the search

- Calls the **XmNqualifySearchDataProc** with the callback structure as the data input argument

- Sets **XmNdirectoryValid** and **XmNlistUpdated** to False

- Calls the **XmNdirSearchProc** with the qualified data returned by the **XmNqualifySearchDataProc**

If **XmNdirectoryValid** is True, the FileSelectionBox takes these additional actions:

- Sets **XmNlistUpdated** to False

- Calls the **XmNfileSearchProc** with the qualified data returned by the **XmNqualifySearchDataProc** (and possibly modified by the **XmNdirSearchProc**)

- If **XmNlistUpdated** is True and the file list is empty, displays the **XmNnoMatchString** in the file list and clears the selection text and **XmNdirSpec**

- If **XmNlistUpdated** is True and the file list is not empty, sets the selection text and **XmNdirSpec** to the qualified *dir* returned by the **XmNqualifySearchDataProc** (and possibly modified by the **XmNdirSearchProc**)

- Sets the directory mask text and **XmNdirMask** to the qualified *mask* returned by the **XmNqualifySearchDataProc** (and possibly modified by the **XmNdirSearchProc**)

- Sets **XmNdirectory** to the qualified *dir* returned by the **XmNqualifySearchDataProc** (and possibly modified by the **XmNdirSearchProc**)

- Sets **XmNpattern** to the qualified *pattern* returned by the **XmNqualifySearchDataProc** (and possibly modified by the **XmNdirSearchProc**)

Classes

FileSelectionBox inherits behavior and resources from **Core**, **Composite**, **Constraint**, **XmManager**, **XmBulletinBoard**, and **XmSelectionBox**.

The class pointer is **xmFileSelectionBoxWidgetClass**. The class name is **XmFileSelectionBox**.

New Resources

The following table defines a set of widget resources used by the programmer to specify data. The programmer can also set the resource values for the inherited classes to set attributes for this widget. To reference a resource by name or by class in a .Xdefaults file, remove the **XmN** or **XmC** prefix and use the remaining letters. To specify one of the defined values for a resource in a .Xdefaults file, remove the **Xm** prefix and use the remaining letters (in either lowercase or uppercase, but include any underscores between words). The codes in the access column indicate if the given resource can be set at creation time (**C**), set by using **XtSetValues** (**S**), retrieved by using **XtGetValues** (**G**), or is not applicable (**N/A**).

XmFileSelectionBox Resource Set		
Name	**Default**	**Access**
Class	**Type**	
XmNdirectory	dynamic	CSG
XmCDirectory	XmString	
XmNdirectoryValid	dynamic	SG
XmCDirectoryValid	Boolean	
XmNdirListItems	dynamic	SG
XmCDirListItems	XmStringTable	
XmNdirListItemCount	dynamic	SG
XmCDirListItemCount	int	
XmNdirListLabelString	"Directories"	CSG
XmCDirListLabelString	XmString	
XmNdirMask	dynamic	CSG
XmCDirMask	XmString	
XmNdirSearchProc	default procedure	CSG
XmCDirSearchProc	(*)()	
XmNdirSpec	dynamic	CSG
XmCDirSpec	XmString	
XmNfileListItems	dynamic	SG
XmCItems	XmStringTable	
XmNfileListItemCount	dynamic	SG
XmCItemCount	int	
XmNfileListLabelString	"Files"	CSG
XmCFileListLabelString	XmString	
XmNfileSearchProc	default procedure	CSG
XmCFileSearchProc	(*)()	
XmNfileTypeMask	XmFILE_REGULAR	CSG
XmCFileTypeMask	unsigned char	
XmNfilterLabelString	"Filter"	CSG
XmCFilterLabelString	XmString	

Name	Default	Access
Class	Type	
XmNlistUpdated	dynamic	SG
XmCListUpdated	Boolean	
XmNnoMatchString	" [ ] "	CSG
XmCNoMatchString	XmString	
XmNpattern	dynamic	CSG
XmCPattern	XmString	
XmNqualifySearchDataProc	default procedure	CSG
XmCQualifySearchDataProc	(*)()	

XmNdirectory

Specifies the base directory used in combination with **XmNpattern** in determining the files and directories to be displayed. The default value is determined by the **XmNqualifySearchDataProc** and depends on the initial values of **XmNdirMask**, **XmNdirectory**, and **XmNpattern**. If the default is NULL or empty, the current working directory is used.

XmNdirectoryValid

Specifies an attribute that is set only by the directory search procedure. The value is set to True if the directory passed to the directory search procedure can actually be searched. If this value is False the file search procedure is not called, and **XmNdirMask**, **XmNdirectory**, and **XmNpattern** are not changed.

XmNdirListItems

Specifies the items in the directory list.

XmNdirListItemCount

Specifies the number of items in the directory list. The value must not be negative.

XmNdirListLabelString

Specifies the label string of the directory list.

XmNdirMask

Specifies the directory mask used in determining the files and directories to be displayed. The default value is determined by the **XmNqualifySearchDataProc** and depends on the initial values of **XmNdirMask**, **XmNdirectory**, and **XmNpattern**.

XmNdirSearchProc

Specifies a directory search procedure to replace the default directory-search procedure. FileSelectionBox's default directory-search procedure fulfills the needs of most applications. Because it is impossible to cover the requirements of all applications, you can replace the default search procedure.

The directory search procedure is called with two arguments: the FileSelectionBox widget and a pointer to an **XmFileSelectionBoxCallbackStruct** structure. The callback structure is generated by the **XmNqualifySearchDataProc** and contains all information required to conduct a directory search, including the directory mask and a qualified base directory and search pattern. Once called, it is up to the search routine to generate a new list of directories and update the FileSelectionBox widget by using **XtSetValues**.

The search procedure must set **XmNdirectoryValid** and **XmNlistUpdated**. If it generates a new list of directories, it must also set **XmNdirListItems** and **XmNdirListItemCount**.

If the search procedure cannot search the specified directory, it must warn the user and set **XmNdirectoryValid** and **XmNlistUpdated** to False, unless it prompts and subsequently obtains a valid directory. If the directory is valid but is the same as the current **XmNdirectory**, the search procedure must set **XmNdirectoryValid** to True, but it may elect not to generate a new list of directories. In this case is must set **XmNlistUpdated** to False.

If the search procedure generates a new list of directories, it must set **XmNdirListItems** to the new list of directories and **XmNdirListItemCount** to the number of items in the list. If there are no directories, it sets **XmNdirListItems** to NULL and **XmNdirListItemCount** to 0. In either case it must set **XmNdirectoryValid** and **XmNlistUpdated** to True.

The search procedure ordinarily should not change the callback struct. But if the original directory is not valid, the search procedure may obtain a new directory from the user. In this case it should set the *dir* member of the callback struct to the new directory, call the **XmNqualifySearchDataProc** with the callback struct as the input argument, and copy the qualified data returned by the **XmNqualifySearchDataProc** into the callback struct.

XmNdirSpec

Specifies the full file path specification. This is the **XmNtextString** resource in SelectionBox, renamed for FileSelectionBox. The default value is determined by the FileSelectionBox after conducting the initial directory and file search.

XmNfileListItems

Specifies the items in the file list. This is the **XmNlistItems** resource in SelectionBox, renamed for FileSelectionBox.

XmNfileListItemCount

Specifies the number of items in the file list. This is the **XmNlistItemCount** resource in SelectionBox, renamed for FileSelectionBox. The value must not be negative.

XmNfileListLabelString

Specifies the label string of the file list. This is the **XmNlistLabelString** resource in SelectionBox, renamed for FileSelectionBox.

XmNfileSearchProc

Specifies a file search procedure to replace the default file-search procedure. FileSelectionBox's default file-search procedure fulfills the needs of most applications. Because it is impossible to cover the requirements of all applications, you can replace the default search procedure.

The file search procedure is called with two arguments: the FileSelectionBox widget and a pointer to an **XmFileSelectionBoxCallbackStruct** structure. The callback structure is generated by the **XmNqualifySearchDataProc** (and possibly modified by the **XmNdirSearchProc**). It contains all information required to conduct a file search, including the directory mask and a qualified base directory and search pattern. Once called, it is up to the search routine to generate a new list of files and update the FileSelectionBox widget by using **XtSetValues**.

The search procedure must set **XmNlistUpdated**. If it generates a new list of files, it must also set **XmNfileListItems** and **XmNfileListItemCount**.

The search procedure is recommended always to generate a new list of files. If the *mask* member of the callback struct is the same as the *mask* member of the callback struct in the preceding call to the search procedure, the procedure may elect not to generate a new list of files. In this case it must set **XmNlistUpdated** to False.

If the search procedure generates a new list of files, it must set **XmNfileListItems** to the new list of files and **XmNfileListItemCount** to the number of items in the list. If there are no files, it sets **XmNfileListItems** to NULL and **XmNfileListItemCount** to 0. In either case it must set **XmNlistUpdated** to True.

In constructing the list of files, the search procedure should include only files of the types specified by the widget's **XmNfileTypeMask**.

Setting **XmNdirSpec** is optional, but recommended. Set this attribute to the full file specification of the directory searched. The directory specification is displayed below the directory and file lists.

XmNfileTypeMask

Specifies the type of files listed in the file list. Following are the possible values:

- **XmFILE_REGULAR** restricts the file list to contain only regular files.

- **XmFILE_DIRECTORY** restricts the file list to contain only directories.

- **XmFILE_ANY_TYPE** allows the list to contain all file types including directories.

XmNfilterLabelString

Specifies the label string for the text entry field for the directory mask.

XmNlistUpdated

Specifies an attribute that is set only by the directory and file search procedures. Set to True if the search procedure updated the directory or file list.

XmNnoMatchString

Specifies a string to be displayed in the file list if the list of files is empty.

XmNpattern

Specifies the search pattern used in combination with **XmNdirectory** in determining the files and directories to be displayed. The default value is determined by the **XmNqualifySearchDataProc** and depends on the initial values of **XmNdirMask**, **XmNdirectory**, and **XmNpattern**. If the default is NULL or empty, a pattern that matches all files is used.

XmNqualifySearchDataProc

Specifies a search data qualification procedure to replace the default data qualification procedure. FileSelectionBox's default data qualification procedure fulfills the needs of most applications. Because it is impossible to cover the requirements of all applications, you can replace the default procedure.

The data qualification procedure is called to generate a qualified directory mask, base directory, and search pattern for use by the directory and file search procedures. It is called with three arguments: the FileSelectionBox widget and pointers to two **XmFileSelectionBoxCallbackStruct** structures. The first callback struct contains the input data. The second callback struct contains the output data, to be filled in by the data qualification procedure.

If the input *dir* and *pattern* members are not NULL, the procedure must copy them to the corresponding members of the output callback struct.

If the input *dir* is NULL, the procedure constructs the output *dir* as follows: If the input *mask* member is NULL, the procedure uses the widget's **XmNdirectory** as the output *dir*; otherwise, it extracts the output *dir* from the input *mask*. If the resulting output *dir* is empty, the procedure uses the current working directory instead.

If the input *pattern* is NULL, the procedure constructs the output *pattern* as follows: If the input *mask* member is NULL, the procedure uses the widget's **XmNpattern** as the output *pattern*; otherwise, it extracts the output *pattern* from the input *mask*. If the resulting output *pattern* is empty, the procedure uses a pattern that matches all files instead.

The data qualification procedure constructs the output *mask* from the output *dir* and *pattern*. The procedure must ensure that the output *dir*, *pattern*, and *mask* are fully qualified.

If the input *value* member is not NULL, the procedure must copy it to the output *value* member; otherwise, the procedure must copy the widget's **XmNdirSpec** to the output *value*.

The data qualification procedure must calculate the lengths of the output *value*, *mask*, *dir*, and *pattern* members and must fill in the corresponding length members of the output callback struct.

The data qualification procedure must copy the input *reason* and *event* members to the corresponding output members.

Inherited Resources

FileSelectionBox inherits behavior and resources from the following superclasses. For a complete description of each resource, refer to the man page for that superclass.

XmSelectionBox Resource Set		
Name	**Default**	**Access**
Class	**Type**	
XmNapplyCallback	NULL	C
XmCCallback	XtCallbackList	
XmNapplyLabelString	"Filter"	CSG
XmCApplyLabelString	XmString	
XmNcancelCallback	NULL	C
XmCCallback	XtCallbackList	
XmNcancelLabelString	"Cancel"	CSG
XmCCancelLabelString	XmString	
XmNdialogType	XmDIALOG_FILE_SELECTION	G
XmCDialogType	unsigned char	
XmNhelpLabelString	"Help"	CSG
XmCHelpLabelString	XmString	
XmNlistItemCount	dynamic	CSG
XmCItemCount	int	
XmNlistItems	dynamic	CSG
XmCItems	XmStringTable	
XmNlistLabelString	"Files"	CSG
XmCListLabelString	XmString	
XmNlistVisibleItemCount	dynamic	CSG
XmCVisibleItemCount	int	
XmNminimizeButtons	False	CSG
XmCMinimizeButtons	Boolean	
XmNmustMatch	False	CSG
XmCMustMatch	Boolean	
XmNnoMatchCallback	NULL	C
XmCCallback	XtCallbackList	

Name	Default	Access
Class	Type	
XmNokCallback	NULL	C
XmCCallback	XtCallbackList	
XmNokLabelString	"OK"	CSG
XmCOkLabelString	XmString	
XmNselectionLabelString	"Selection"	CSG
XmCSelectionLabelString	XmString	
XmNtextAccelerators	default	C
XmCTextAccelerators	XtAccelerators	
XmNtextColumns	dynamic	CSG
XmCColumns	short	
XmNtextString	dynamic	CSG
XmCTextString	XmString	

XmBulletinBoard Resource Set		
Name	**Default**	**Access**
Class	Type	
XmNallowOverlap	True	CSG
XmCAllowOverlap	Boolean	
XmNautoUnmanage	False	CG
XmCAutoUnmanage	Boolean	
XmNbuttonFontList	dynamic	CSG
XmCButtonFontList	XmFontList	
XmNcancelButton	Cancel button	SG
XmCWidget	Widget	
XmNdefaultButton	OK button	SG
XmCWidget	Widget	
XmNdefaultPosition	True	CSG
XmCDefaultPosition	Boolean	
XmNdialogStyle	dynamic	CSG
XmCDialogStyle	unsigned char	
XmNdialogTitle	NULL	CSG
XmCDialogTitle	XmString	
XmNfocusCallback	NULL	C
XmCCallback	XtCallbackList	
XmNlabelFontList	dynamic	CSG
XmCLabelFontList	XmFontList	
XmNmapCallback	NULL	C
XmCCallback	XtCallbackList	
XmNmarginHeight	10	CSG
XmCMarginHeight	Dimension	
XmNmarginWidth	10	CSG
XmCMarginWidth	Dimension	
XmNnoResize	False	CSG
XmCNoResize	Boolean	

Name	Default	Access
Class	Type	
XmNresizePolicy	XmRESIZE_ANY	CSG
XmCResizePolicy	unsigned char	
XmNshadowType	XmSHADOW_OUT	CSG
XmCShadowType	unsigned char	
XmNtextFontList	dynamic	CSG
XmCTextFontList	XmFontList	
XmNtextTranslations	NULL	C
XmCTranslations	XtTranslations	
XmNunmapCallback	NULL	C
XmCCallback	XtCallbackList	

XmManager Resource Set		
Name	**Default**	**Access**
Class	**Type**	
XmNbottomShadowColor	dynamic	CSG
XmCBottomShadowColor	Pixel	
XmNbottomShadowPixmap	XmUNSPECIFIED_PIXMAP	CSG
XmCBottomShadowPixmap	Pixmap	
XmNforeground	dynamic	CSG
XmCForeground	Pixel	
XmNhelpCallback	NULL	C
XmCCallback	XtCallbackList	
XmNhighlightColor	dynamic	CSG
XmCHighlightColor	Pixel	
XmNhighlightPixmap	dynamic	CSG
XmCHighlightPixmap	Pixmap	
XmNnavigationType	dynamic	CSG
XmCNavigationType	XmNavigationType	
XmNshadowThickness	dynamic	CSG
XmCShadowThickness	Dimension	
XmNstringDirection	dynamic	CG
XmCStringDirection	XmStringDirection	
XmNtopShadowColor	dynamic	CSG
XmCBackgroundTopShadowColor	Pixel	
XmNtopShadowPixmap	dynamic	CSG
XmCTopShadowPixmap	Pixmap	
XmNtraversalOn	True	CSG
XmCTraversalOn	Boolean	
XmNuserData	NULL	CSG
XmCUserData	Pointer	

Composite Resource Set		
Name	**Default**	**Access**
Class	**Type**	
XmNchildren	NULL	G
XmCReadOnly	WidgetList	
XmNinsertPosition	NULL	CSG
XmCInsertPosition	(*)()	
XmNnumChildren	0	G
XmCReadOnly	Cardinal	

Core Resource Set		
Name	**Default**	**Access**
Class	**Type**	
XmNaccelerators	dynamic	N/A
XmCAccelerators	XtAccelerators	
XmNancestorSensitive	dynamic	G
XmCSensitive	Boolean	
XmNbackground	dynamic	CSG
XmCBackground	Pixel	
XmNbackgroundPixmap	XmUNSPECIFIED_PIXMAP	CSG
XmCPixmap	Pixmap	
XmNborderColor	XtDefaultForeground	CSG
XmCBorderColor	Pixel	
XmNborderPixmap	XmUNSPECIFIED_PIXMAP	CSG
XmCPixmap	Pixmap	
XmNborderWidth	0	CSG
XmCBorderWidth	Dimension	
XmNcolormap	dynamic	CG
XmCColormap	Colormap	
XmNdepth	dynamic	CG
XmCDepth	int	
XmNdestroyCallback	NULL	C
XmCCallback	XtCallbackList	
XmNheight	dynamic	CSG
XmCHeight	Dimension	
XmNinitialResourcesPersistent	True	C
XmCInitialResourcesPersistent	Boolean	
XmNmappedWhenManaged	True	CSG
XmCMappedWhenManaged	Boolean	
XmNscreen	dynamic	CG
XmCScreen	Screen *	

Name	Default	Access
Class	Type	
XmNsensitive	True	CSG
XmCSensitive	Boolean	
XmNtranslations	dynamic	CSG
XmCTranslations	XtTranslations	
XmNwidth	dynamic	CSG
XmCWidth	Dimension	
XmNx	0	CSG
XmCPosition	Position	
XmNy	0	CSG
XmCPosition	Position	

Callback Information

A pointer to the following structure is passed to each callback:

```
typedef struct
{
    int       reason;
    XEvent    * event;
    XmString  value;
    int       length;
    XmString  mask;
    int       mask_length;
    XmString  dir;
    int       dir_length;
    XmString  pattern;
    int       pattern_length;
} XmFileSelectionBoxCallbackStruct;
```

reason   Indicates why the callback was invoked

event   Points to the **XEvent** that triggered the callback

value   Specifies the current value of **XmNdirSpec**

length   Specifies the number of bytes in *value*

mask   Specifies the current value of **XmNdirMask**

mask_length   Specifies the number of bytes in *mask*

dir   Specifies the current base directory

dir_length   Specifies the number of bytes in *dir*

pattern   Specifies the current search pattern

pattern_length
                Specifies the number of bytes in *pattern*

Translations

XmFileSelectionBox inherits translations from XmSelectionBox.

Accelerators

The **XmNtextAccelerators** from XmSelectionBox are added to the selection and directory mask (filter) Text descendants of XmFileSelectionBox.

Action Routines

The XmFileSelectionBox action routines are described below:

SelectionBoxUpOrDown(0|1|2|3):
                If neither the selection text nor the directory mask (filter) text has the focus, this action does nothing.

If the selection text has the focus, the term *list* in the following description refers to the file list, and the term *text* refers to the selection text. If the directory mask text has the focus, *list* refers to the directory list, and *text* refers to the directory mask text.

When called with a 0 argument, selects the previous item in the list and replaces the text with that item.

When called with a 1 argument, selects the next item in the list and replaces the text with that item.

When called with a 2 argument, selects the first item in the list and replaces the text with that item.

When called with a 3 argument, selects the last item in the list and replaces the text with that item.

SelectionBoxRestore():

If neither the selection text nor the directory mask (filter) text has the focus, this action does nothing.

If the selection text has the focus, replaces the selection text with the selected item in the file list. If no item in the file list is selected, clears the selection text.

If the directory mask text has the focus, replaces the directory mask text with a new directory mask constructed from the **XmNdirectory** and **XmNpattern** resources.

Additional Behavior

The FileSelectionBox widget has the additional behavior described below:

MAny KCancel:

Calls the activate callbacks for the cancel button if it is sensitive.

<KActivate> in Selection Text:

Calls the selection text widget's **XmNactivateCallback** callbacks. If **XmNmustMatch** is True and the selection text does not match an item in the file list, calls the

XmNnoMatchCallback callbacks with reason **XmCR_NO_MATCH**. Otherwise, calls the **XmNokCallback** callbacks with reason **XmCR_OK**.

<KActivate> in Directory Mask Text:

Calls the directory mask text widget's **XmNactivateCallback** callbacks. Initiates a directory and file search. Calls the **XmNapplyCallback** callbacks with reason **XmCR_APPLY**.

<DoubleClick> or **<KActivate>** in Directory List:

Calls the directory list widget's **XmNdefaultActionCallback** callbacks. Initiates a directory and file search. Calls the **XmNapplyCallback** callbacks with reason **XmCR_APPLY**.

<DoubleClick> or **<KActivate>** in File List:

Calls the file list widget's **XmNdefaultActionCallback** callbacks. Calls the **XmNokCallback** callbacks with reason **XmCR_OK**.

<Single Select> or **<Browse Select>** in Directory List:

Generates a new directory mask, using the selected list item as the directory and the pattern extracted from the current directory mask text as the search pattern. If the search pattern is empty, uses a pattern that matches all files in the directory. Replaces the directory mask text with the new directory mask.

<Single Select> or **<Browse Select>** in File List:

Replaces the selection text with the selected list item.

<Apply Button Activated>:

Initiates a directory and file search. Calls the **XmNapplyCallback** callbacks with reason **XmCR_APPLY**.

<OK Button Activated>:

If **XmNmustMatch** is True and the selection text does not match an item in the file list, calls the **XmNnoMatchCallback** callbacks with reason **XmCR_NO_MATCH**. Otherwise, calls the **XmNokCallback** callbacks with reason **XmCR_OK**.

<Cancel Button Activated>:
> Calls the **XmNcancelCallback** callbacks with reason **XmCR_CANCEL**.

<Help Button Activated>:
> Calls the **XmNhelpCallback** callbacks with reason **XmCR_HELP**.

<KActivate>:
> If no button, list widget, or text widget has the keyboard focus: If **XmNmustMatch** is True and the selection text does not match an item in the file list, calls the **XmNnoMatchCallback** callbacks with reason **XmCR_NO_MATCH**. Otherwise, calls the **XmNokCallback** callbacks with reason **XmCR_OK**.

Virtual Bindings

The bindings for virtual keys are vendor specific.

Related Information

Composite(3X), Constraint(3X), Core(3X), XmBulletinBoard(3X), XmCreateFileSelectionBox(3X), XmCreateFileSelectionDialog(3X), XmFileSelectionBoxGetChild(3X), XmFileSelectionDoSearch(3X), XmManager(3X), and XmSelectionBox(3X),

XmFileSelectionBoxGetChild

Purpose

A FileSelectionBox function that is used to access a component.

AES Support Level

Full-use

Synopsis

#include <Xm/FileSB.h>

Widget XmFileSelectionBoxGetChild (*widget, child*)
    Widget   *widget*;
    unsigned char*child*;

Description

XmFileSelectionBoxGetChild is used to access a component within a FileSelectionBox. The parameters given to the function are the FileSelectionBox widget and a value indicating which child to access.

widget   Specifies the FileSelectionBox widget ID.

child   Specifies a component within the FileSelectionBox. The following are legal values for this parameter:

- **XmDIALOG_APPLY_BUTTON**
- **XmDIALOG_CANCEL_BUTTON**
- **XmDIALOG_DEFAULT_BUTTON**
- **XmDIALOG_DIR_LIST**
- **XmDIALOG_DIR_LIST_LABEL**
- **XmDIALOG_FILTER_LABEL**
- **XmDIALOG_FILTER_TEXT**
- **XmDIALOG_HELP_BUTTON**
- **XmDIALOG_LIST**
- **XmDIALOG_LIST_LABEL**
- **XmDIALOG_OK_BUTTON**
- **XmDIALOG_SELECTION_LABEL**
- **XmDIALOG_SEPARATOR**
- **XmDIALOG_TEXT**
- **XmDIALOG_WORK_AREA**

For a complete definition of FileSelectionBox and its associated resources, see **XmFileSelectionBox(3X)**.

Return Value

Returns the widget ID of the specified FileSelectionBox child. An application should not assume that the returned widget will be of any particular class.

Related Information

XmFileSelectionBox(3X).

XmFileSelectionDoSearch

Purpose

A FileSelectionBox function that initiates a directory search.

AES Support Level

Full-use

Synopsis

#include <Xm/FileSB.h>

void XmFileSelectionDoSearch (*widget, dirmask*)
    Widget   *widget*;
    XmString   *dirmask*;

Description

XmFileSelectionDoSearch initiates a directory and file search in a FileSelectionBox widget. For a description of the actions that the FileSelectionBox takes when doing a search, see **XmFileSelectionBox(3X)**.

widget Specifies the FileSelectionBox widget ID.

dirmask Specifies the directory mask used in determining the directories and files displayed in the FileSelectionBox lists. This value is used as the *mask* member of the input data **XmFileSelectionBoxCallbackStruct** structure passed to the FileSelectionBox's **XmNqualifySearchDataProc**. The *dir* and *pattern* members of that structure are NULL.

For a complete definition of FileSelectionBox and its associated resources, see **XmFileSelectionBox(3X)**.

Related Information

XmFileSelectionBox(3X).

XmFontList

Purpose

Data type for a font list

AES Support Level

Trial-use

Synopsis

#include <Xm/Xm.h>

Description

XmFontList is the data type for a font list. Font lists contain information corresponding to one or more fonts. Each element of the font list includes a font and a corresponding character set. When a compound string is displayed, the character sets in the compound string are matched with the character sets in the font list, and the corresponding fonts in the font list are used to display the string. If the character set in a compound string segment does not match any character set in the font list, the first font in the font list is used to display that segment. The font list interface consists of the routines listed under "Related Information."

Font lists are specified in resource files using the following syntax:

resource_spec : *font_name* [= *charset*] [, *font_name* [= *charset*]]+

The resource value string consists of one or more font list elements separated by commas. Each font list element is a font name and an optional character set. If a character set is specified for a font list element, it follows the font name and is separated from the font name by =. If no character set is specified, the character set is derived from the current language environment.

Related Information

XmFontListAdd(3X), **XmFontListCreate(3X)**, and **XmFontListFree(3X)**.

XmFontListAdd

Purpose

A compound string function that creates a new font list

AES Support Level

Trial-use

Synopsis

#include <Xm/Xm.h>

XmFontList XmFontListAdd (*oldlist, font, charset*)
    XmFontList   *oldlist*;
    XFontStruct   * *font*;
    XmStringCharSet*charset*;

Description

XmFontListAdd creates a new font list consisting of the contents of the *oldlist* and the new font-list element being added. This function deallocates the *oldlist* after extracting the required information; therefore, do not reference *oldlist* thereafter.

oldlist   Specifies a pointer to the font list to which an entry will be added.

font   Specifies a pointer to a font structure for which the new font list is generated. This is the structure returned by the XLib **XLoadQueryFont** function.

charset   Specifies the character set identifier for the font.

Return Value

Returns NULL if *oldlist* is NULL; returns *oldlist* if *font* or *charset* is NULL; otherwise, returns a new font list.

Related Information

XmFontListCreate(3X).

XmFontListCreate

Purpose

A compound string function that creates a font list

AES Support Level

Trial-use

Synopsis

#include <Xm/Xm.h>

XmFontList XmFontListCreate (*font, charset*)
  XFontStruct * *font*;
  XmStringCharSet*charset*;

Description

XmFontListCreate creates a new font list with a single element specified by the provided font and character set. It also allocates the space for the font list.

font Specifies a pointer to a font structure for which the new font list is generated. This is the structure returned by the XLib **XLoadQueryFont** function.

charset Specifies the character set identifier for the font.

Return Value

Returns NULL if *font* or *charset* is NULL; otherwise, returns a new font list.

Related Information

**XmFontList(3X), XmFontListAdd(3X), XmFontListFree(3X),
XmString(3X), XmStringBaseline(3X), XmStringByteCompare(3X),
XmStringCompare(3X), XmStringConcat(3X), XmStringCopy(3X),
XmStringCreate(3X), XmStringCreateSimple(3X), XmStringDraw(3X),
XmStringDrawImage(3X), XmStringDrawUnderline(3X),
XmStringEmpty(3X), XmStringExtent(3X), XmStringFree(3X),
XmStringHasSubstring(3X), XmStringHeight(3X),
XmStringLength(3X), XmStringLineCount(3X),
XmStringNConcat(3X), XmStringNCopy(3X),
XmStringSeparatorCreate(3X), XmStringTable(3X),** and
XmStringWidth(3X).

XmFontListFree

Purpose

A compound string function that recovers memory used by a font list.

AES Support Level

Trial-use

Synopsis

#include <Xm/Xm.h>

void XmFontListFree (*list*)
    XmFontList *list*;

Description

XmFontListFree recovers memory used by a font list.

list   Specifies the font list to be freed

Related Information

XmFontListCreate(3X).

XmForm

Purpose

The Form widget class

AES Support Level

Full-use

Synopsis

#include <Xm/Form.h>

Description

Form is a container widget with no input semantics of its own. Constraints are placed on children of the Form to define attachments for each of the child's four sides. These attachments can be to the Form, to another child widget or gadget, to a relative position within the Form, or to the initial position of the child. The attachments determine the layout behavior of the Form when resizing occurs.

Following are some important considerations in using a Form:

- Every child must have an attachment on either the left or the right. If initialization or **XtSetValues** leaves a widget without such an attachment, the result depends upon the value of **XmNrubberPositioning**.

  If **XmNrubberPositioning** is False, the child is given an **XmNleftAttachment** of **XmATTACH_FORM** and an **XmNleftOffset** equal to its current x value.

  If **XmNrubberPositioning** is True, the child is given an **XmNleftAttachment** of **XmATTACH_POSITION** and an **XmNleftPosition** proportional to the current x value divided by the width of the Form.

  In either case, if the child has not been previously given an x value, its x value is taken to be 0, which places the child at the left side of the Form.

- If you want to create a child without any attachments, and then later (e.g., after creating and managing it, but before realizing it) give it a right attachment via **XtSetValues**, you must set its **XmNleftAttachment** to **XmATTACH_NONE** at the same time.

- The **XmNresizable** resource controls only whether a geometry request by the child will be granted. It has no effect on whether the child's size can be changed because of changes in geometry of the Form or of other children.

- Every child has a preferred width, based on geometry requests it makes (whether they are granted or not).

- If a child has attachments on both the left and the right sides, its size is completely controlled by the Form. It can be shrunk below its preferred width or enlarged above it, if necessary, due to other constraints. In addition, the child's geometry requests to change its own width may be refused.

- If a child has attachments on only its left or right side, it will always be at its preferred width (if resizable, otherwise at is current width). This may cause it to be clipped by the Form or by other children.

- If a child's left (or right) attachment is set to **XmATTACH_SELF**, its corresponding left (or right) offset is forced to 0. The attachment is then changed to **XmATTACH_POSITION**, with a position that corresponds to x value of the child's left (or right) edge. To fix the position of a side at a specific x value use **XmATTACH_FORM** or **XmATTACH_OPPOSITE_FORM** with the x value as the left (or right) offset.

- Unmapping a child has no effect on the Form except that the child is not mapped.

- Unmanaging a child unmaps it. If no other child is attached to it, or if all children attached to it and all children recursively attached to them are also all unmanaged, all of those children are treated as if they did not exist in determining the size of the Form.

- When using **XtSetValues** to change the **XmNx** resource of a child, you must simultaneously set its left attachment to either **XmATTACH_SELF** or **XmATTACH_NONE**. Otherwise, the request is not granted. If **XmNresizable** is False, the request is granted only if the child's size can remain the same.

- A left (or right) attachment of **XmATTACH_WIDGET**, where **XmNleftWidget** (or **XmNrightWidget**) is NULL, acts like an attachment of **XmATTACH_FORM**.

- If an attachment is made to a widget that is not a child of the Form, but an ancestor of the widget is a child of the Form, the attachment is made to the ancestor.

All these considerations are true of top and bottom attachments as well, with top acting like left, bottom acting like right, y acting like x, and height acting like width.

Classes

Form inherits behavior and resources from **Core**, **Composite**, **Constraint**, **XmManager**, and **XmBulletinBoard** classes.

The class pointer is **xmFormWidgetClass**.

The class name is **XmForm**.

New Resources

The following table defines a set of widget resources used by the programmer to specify data. The programmer can also set the resource values for the inherited classes to set attributes for this widget. To reference a resource by name or by class in a .Xdefaults file, remove the **XmN** or **XmC** prefix and use the remaining letters. To specify one of the defined values for a resource in a .Xdefaults file, remove the **Xm** prefix and use the remaining letters (in either lowercase or uppercase, but include any underscores between words). The codes in the access column indicate if the given resource can be set at creation time (**C**), set by using **XtSetValues** (**S**), retrieved by using **XtGetValues** (**G**), or is not applicable (**N/A**).

XmForm Resource Set		
Name	**Default**	**Access**
Class	**Type**	
XmNfractionBase	100	CSG
XmCMaxValue	int	
XmNhorizontalSpacing	0	CSG
XmCSpacing	Dimension	
XmNrubberPositioning	False	CSG
XmCRubberPositioning	Boolean	
XmNverticalSpacing	0	CSG
XmCSpacing	Dimension	

XmNfractionBase

Specifies the denominator used in calculating the relative position of a child widget using **XmATTACH_POSITION** constraints. The value must not be 0.

If the value of a child's **XmNleftAttachment** (or **XmNrightAttachment**) is **XmATTACH_POSITION**, the position of the left (or right) side of the child is relative to the left side of the Form and is a fraction of the width of the Form. This fraction is the value of the child's **XmNleftPosition** (or **XmNrightPosition**) resource divided by the value of the Form's **XmNfractionBase**.

If the value of a child's **XmNtopAttachment** (or **XmNbottomAttachment**) is **XmATTACH_POSITION**, the position of the top (or bottom) side of the child is relative to the top side of the Form and is a fraction of the height of the Form. This fraction is the value of the child's **XmNtopPosition** (or **XmNbottomPosition**) resource divided by the value of the Form's **XmNfractionBase**.

XmNhorizontalSpacing

Specifies the offset for right and left attachments.

XmNrubberPositioning

Indicates the default near (left) and top attachments for a child of the Form. (**Note:** Whether this resource actually applies to the left or right side of the child and its attachment may depend on the value of the **XmNstringDirection** resource.)

The default left attachment is applied whenever initialization or **XtSetValues** leaves the child without either a left or right attachment. The default top attachment is applied whenever initialization or **XtSetValues** leaves the child without either a top or bottom attachment.

If this Boolean resource is set to False, **XmNleftAttachment** and **XmNtopAttachment** default to **XmATTACH_FORM**, **XmNleftOffset** defaults to the current x value of the left side of the child, and **XmNtopOffset** defaults to the current y value of the child. The effect is to position the child according to its absolute distance from the left or top side of the Form.

If this resource is set to True, **XmNleftAttachment** and **XmNtopAttachment** default to **XmATTACH_POSITION**, **XmNleftPosition** defaults to a value proportional to the current x value of the left side of the child divided by the width of the Form, and **XmNtopPosition** defaults to a value proportional to the current y value of the child divided by the height of the Form. The effect is to position the child relative to the left or top side of the Form and in proportion to the width or height of the Form.

XmNverticalSpacing
Specifies the offset for top and bottom attachments.

XmForm Constraint Resource Set		
Name **Class**	**Default** **Type**	**Access**
XmNbottomAttachment XmCAttachment	XmATTACH_NONE unsigned char	CSG
XmNbottomOffset XmCOffset	0 int	CSG
XmNbottomPosition XmCAttachment	0 int	CSG
XmNbottomWidget XmCWidget	NULL Widget	CSG
XmNleftAttachment XmCAttachment	XmATTACH_NONE unsigned char	CSG
XmNleftOffset XmCOffset	0 int	CSG
XmNleftPosition XmCAttachment	0 int	CSG
XmNleftWidget XmCWidget	NULL Widget	CSG
XmNresizable XmCBoolean	True Boolean	CSG
XmNrightAttachment XmCAttachment	XmATTACH_NONE unsigned char	CSG
XmNrightOffset XmCOffset	0 int	CSG
XmNrightPosition XmCAttachment	0 int	CSG
XmNrightWidget XmCWidget	NULL Widget	CSG
XmNtopAttachment XmCAttachment	XmATTACH_NONE unsigned char	CSG

Name	Default	Access
Class	Type	
XmNtopOffset	0	CSG
XmCOffset	int	
XmNtopPosition	0	CSG
XmCAttachment	int	
XmNtopWidget	NULL	CSG
XmCWidget	Widget	

XmNbottomAttachment

Specifies attachment of the bottom side of the child. It can have the following values:

- **XmATTACH_NONE** — Do not attach the bottom side of the child.

- **XmATTACH_FORM** — Attach the bottom side of the child to the bottom side of the Form.

- **XmATTACH_OPPOSITE_FORM** — Attach the bottom side of the child to the top side of the Form. **XmNbottomOffset** can be used to determine the visibility of the child.

- **XmATTACH_WIDGET** — Attach the bottom side of the child to the top side of the widget or gadget specified in the **XmNbottomWidget** resource. If **XmNbottomWidget** is NULL, **XmATTACH_WIDGET** is replaced by **XmATTACH_FORM**, and the child is attached to the bottom side of the Form.

- **XmATTACH_OPPOSITE_WIDGET** — Attach the bottom side of the child to the bottom side of the widget or gadget specified in the **XmNbottomWidget** resource.

- **XmATTACH_POSITION** — Attach the bottom side of the child to a position that is relative to the top side of the Form and in proportion to the height of the Form. This position is determined by the **XmNbottomPosition** and **XmNfractionBase** resources.

- **XmATTACH_SELF** — Attach the bottom side of the child to a position that is proportional to the current y value of the bottom of the child divided by the height of the Form. This position is determined by the **XmNbottomPosition** and **XmNfractionBase** resources. **XmNbottomPosition** is set to a value proportional to the current y value of the bottom of the child divided by the height of the Form.

XmNbottomOffset

Specifies the constant offset between the bottom side of the child and the object to which it is attached. The effect of a nonzero value for this resource is undefined if **XmNbottomAttachment** is set to **XmATTACH_POSITION**. The relationship established remains, regardless of any resizing operations that occur.

XmNbottomPosition

This resource is used to determine the position of the bottom side of the child when the child's **XmNbottomAttachment** is set to **XmATTACH_POSITION**. In this case the position of the bottom side of the child is relative to the top side of the Form and is a fraction of the height of the Form. This fraction is the value of the child's **XmNbottomPosition** resource divided by the value of the Form's **XmNfractionBase**. For example, if the child's **XmNbottomPosition** is 50, the Form's **XmNfractionBase** is 100, and the Form's height is 200, the position of the bottom side of the child is 100.

XmNbottomWidget

Specifies the widget or gadget to which the bottom side of the child is attached. This resource is used if **XmNbottomAttachment** is set to either **XmATTACH_WIDGET** or **XmATTACH_OPPOSITE_WIDGET**.

XmNleftAttachment

Specifies attachment of the near (left) side of the child. (**Note:** Whether this resource actually applies to the left or right side of the child and its attachment may depend on the value of the **XmNstringDirection** resource.) It can have the following values:

- **XmATTACH_NONE** — Do not attach the left side of the child. If **XmNrightAttachment** is also **XmATTACH_NONE**, this value is ignored and the child is given a default left attachment.

- **XmATTACH_FORM** — Attach the left side of the child to the left side of the Form.

- **XmATTACH_OPPOSITE_FORM** — Attach the left side of the child to the right side of the Form. **XmNleftOffset** can be used to determine the visibility of the child.

- **XmATTACH_WIDGET** — Attach the left side of the child to the right side of the widget or gadget specified in the **XmNleftWidget** resource. If **XmNleftWidget** is NULL, **XmATTACH_WIDGET** is replaced by **XmATTACH_FORM**, and the child is attached to the left side of the Form.

- **XmATTACH_OPPOSITE_WIDGET** — Attach the left side of the child to the left side of the widget or gadget specified in the **XmNleftWidget** resource.

- **XmATTACH_POSITION** — Attach the left side of the child to a position that is relative to the left side of the Form and in proportion to the width of the Form. This position is determined by the **XmNleftPosition** and **XmNfractionBase** resources.

- **XmATTACH_SELF** — Attach the left side of the child to a position that is proportional to the current x value of the left side of the child divided by the width of the Form. This position is determined by the **XmNleftPosition** and **XmNfractionBase** resources. **XmNleftPosition** is set to a value proportional to the current x value of the left side of the child divided by the width of the Form.

XmNleftOffset

Specifies the constant offset between the near (left) side of the child and the object to which it is attached. (**Note:** Whether this resource actually applies to the left or right side of the child and its attachment may depend on the value of the **XmNstringDirection** resource.) The effect of a nonzero value for this resource is undefined if **XmNleftAttachment** is set to **XmATTACH_POSITION**. The relationship established remains, regardless of any resizing operations that occur.

XmNleftPosition

This resource is used to determine the position of the near (left) side of the child when the child's **XmNleftAttachment** is set to **XmATTACH_POSITION**. (**Note:** Whether this resource actually applies to the left or right side of the child and its attachment may depend on the value of the **XmNstringDirection** resource.)

In this case the position of the left side of the child is relative to the left side of the Form and is a fraction of the width of the Form. This fraction is the value of the child's **XmNleftPosition** resource divided by the value of the Form's **XmNfractionBase**. For example, if the child's **XmNleftPosition** is 50, the Form's **XmNfractionBase** is 100, and the Form's width is 200, the position of the left side of the child is 100.

XmNleftWidget

> Specifies the widget or gadget to which the near (left) side of the child is attached. (**Note:** Whether this resource actually applies to the left or right side of the child and its attachment may depend on the value of the **XmNstringDirection** resource.) This resource is used if **XmNleftAttachment** is set to either **XmATTACH_WIDGET** or **XmATTACH_OPPOSITE_WIDGET**.

XmNresizable

> This Boolean resource specifies whether or not a child's request for a new size is (conditionally) granted by the Form. If this resource is set to True the request is granted if possible. If this resource is set to False the request is always refused.

> If a child has both left and right attachments, its width is completely controlled by the Form, regardless of the value of the child's **XmNresizable** resource. If a child has a left or right attachment but not both, the child's **XmNwidth** is used in setting its width if the value of the child's **XmNresizable** resource is True. These conditions are also true for top and bottom attachments, with height acting like width.

XmNrightAttachment

> Specifies attachment of the far (right) side of the child. (**Note:** Whether this resource actually applies to the left or right side of the child and its attachment may depend on the value of the **XmNstringDirection** resource.) It can have the following values:

> - **XmATTACH_NONE** — Do not attach the right side of the child.

> - **XmATTACH_FORM** — Attach the right side of the child to the right side of the Form.

> - **XmATTACH_OPPOSITE_FORM** — Attach the right side of the child to the left side of the Form. **XmNrightOffset** can be used to determine the visibility of the child.

- **XmATTACH_WIDGET** — Attach the right side of the child to the left side of the widget or gadget specified in the **XmNrightWidget** resource. If **XmNrightWidget** is NULL, **XmATTACH_WIDGET** is replaced by **XmATTACH_FORM**, and the child is attached to the right side of the Form.

- **XmATTACH_OPPOSITE_WIDGET** — Attach the right side of the child to the right side of the widget or gadget specified in the **XmNrightWidget** resource.

- **XmATTACH_POSITION** — Attach the right side of the child to a position that is relative to the left side of the Form and in proportion to the width of the Form. This position is determined by the **XmNrightPosition** and **XmNfractionBase** resources.

- **XmATTACH_SELF** — Attach the right side of the child to a position that is proportional to the current x value of the right side of the child divided by the width of the Form. This position is determined by the **XmNrightPosition** and **XmNfractionBase** resources. **XmNrightPosition** is set to a value proportional to the current x value of the right side of the child divided by the width of the Form.

XmNrightOffset

Specifies the constant offset between the far (right) side of the child and the object to which it is attached. (**Note:** Whether this resource actually applies to the left or right side of the child and its attachment may depend on the value of the **XmNstringDirection** resource.) The effect of a nonzero value for this resource is undefined if **XmNrightAttachment** is set to **XmATTACH_POSITION**. The relationship established remains, regardless of any resizing operations that occur.

XmNrightPosition

This resource is used to determine the position of the far (right) side of the child when the child's **XmNrightAttachment** is set to **XmATTACH_POSITION**. (**Note:** Whether this resource actually applies to the left or right side of the child and its attachment may depend on the value of the **XmNstringDirection** resource.)

In this case the position of the right side of the child is relative to the left side of the Form and is a fraction of the width of the Form. This fraction is the value of the child's **XmNrightPosition** resource divided by the value of the Form's **XmNfractionBase**. For example, if the child's **XmNrightPosition** is 50, the Form's **XmNfractionBase** is 100, and the Form's width is 200, the position of the right side of the child is 100.

XmNrightWidget

Specifies the widget or gadget to which the far (right) side of the child is attached. (**Note:** Whether this resource actually applies to the left or right side of the child and its attachment may depend on the value of the **XmNstringDirection** resource.) This resource is used if **XmNrightAttachment** is set to either **XmATTACH_WIDGET** or **XmATTACH_OPPOSITE_WIDGET**.

XmNtopAttachment

Specifies attachment of the top side of the child. It can have following values:

- **XmATTACH_NONE** — Do not attach the top side of the child. If **XmNbottomAttachment** is also **XmATTACH_NONE**, this value is ignored and the child is given a default top attachment.

- **XmATTACH_FORM** — Attach the top side of the child to the top side of the Form.

- **XmATTACH_OPPOSITE_FORM** — Attach the top side of the child to the bottom side of the Form. **XmNtopOffset** can be used to determine the visibility of the child.

- **XmATTACH_WIDGET** — Attach the top side of the child to the bottom side of the widget or gadget specified in the **XmNtopWidget** resource. If **XmNtopWidget** is NULL, **XmATTACH_WIDGET** is replaced by **XmATTACH_FORM**, and the child is attached to the top side of the Form.

- **XmATTACH_OPPOSITE_WIDGET** — Attach the top side of the child to the top side of the widget or gadget specified in the **XmNtopWidget** resource.

- **XmATTACH_POSITION** — Attach the top side of the child to a position that is relative to the top side of the Form and in proportion to the height of the Form. This position is determined by the **XmNtopPosition** and **XmNfractionBase** resources.

- **XmATTACH_SELF** — Attach the top side of the child to a position that is proportional to the current y value of the child divided by the height of the Form. This position is determined by the **XmNtopPosition** and **XmNfractionBase** resources. **XmNtopPosition** is set to a value proportional to the current y value of the child divided by the height of the Form.

XmNtopOffset
> Specifies the constant offset between the top side of the child and the object to which it is attached. The effect of a nonzero value for this resource is undefined if **XmNtopAttachment** is set to **XmATTACH_POSITION**. The relationship established remains, regardless of any resizing operations that occur.

XmNtopPosition
> This resource is used to determine the position of the top side of the child when the child's **XmNtopAttachment** is set to **XmATTACH_POSITION**. In this case the position of the top side of the child is relative to the top side of the Form and is a fraction of the height of the Form. This fraction is the value of the child's **XmNtopPosition** resource divided by the value of the Form's **XmNfractionBase**. For example, if the child's **XmNtopPosition** is 50, the Form's **XmNfractionBase** is 100, and the Form's height is 200, the position of the top side of the child is 100.

XmNtopWidget
> Specifies the widget or gadget to which the top side of the child is attached. This resource is used if **XmNtopAttachment** is set to either **XmATTACH_WIDGET** or **XmATTACH_OPPOSITE_WIDGET**.

Inherited Resources

Form inherits behavior and resources from the following superclasses. For a complete description of each resource, refer to the man page for that superclass.

XmBulletinBoard Resource Set		
Name	**Default**	**Access**
Class	**Type**	
XmNallowOverlap	True	CSG
XmCAllowOverlap	Boolean	
XmNautoUnmanage	True	CG
XmCAutoUnmanage	Boolean	
XmNbuttonFontList	dynamic	CSG
XmCButtonFontList	XmFontList	
XmNcancelButton	NULL	SG
XmCWidget	Widget	
XmNdefaultButton	NULL	SG
XmCWidget	Widget	
XmNdefaultPosition	True	CSG
XmCDefaultPosition	Boolean	
XmNdialogStyle	dynamic	CSG
XmCDialogStyle	unsigned char	
XmNdialogTitle	NULL	CSG
XmCDialogTitle	XmString	
XmNfocusCallback	NULL	C
XmCCallback	XtCallbackList	
XmNlabelFontList	dynamic	CSG
XmCLabelFontList	XmFontList	
XmNmapCallback	NULL	C
XmCCallback	XtCallbackList	
XmNmarginHeight	0	CSG
XmCMarginHeight	Dimension	
XmNmarginWidth	0	CSG
XmCMarginWidth	Dimension	
XmNnoResize	False	CSG
XmCNoResize	Boolean	

Name	Default	Access
Class	Type	
XmNresizePolicy	XmRESIZE_ANY	CSG
XmCResizePolicy	unsigned char	
XmNshadowType	XmSHADOW_OUT	CSG
XmCShadowType	unsigned char	
XmNtextFontList	dynamic	CSG
XmCTextFontList	XmFontList	
XmNtextTranslations	NULL	C
XmCTranslations	XtTranslations	
XmNunmapCallback	NULL	C
XmCCallback	XtCallbackList	

XmManager Resource Set		
Name Class	**Default** Type	**Access**
XmNbottomShadowColor XmCBottomShadowColor	dynamic Pixel	CSG
XmNbottomShadowPixmap XmCBottomShadowPixmap	XmUNSPECIFIED_PIXMAP Pixmap	CSG
XmNforeground XmCForeground	dynamic Pixel	CSG
XmNhelpCallback XmCCallback	NULL XtCallbackList	C
XmNhighlightColor XmCHighlightColor	dynamic Pixel	CSG
XmNhighlightPixmap XmCHighlightPixmap	dynamic Pixmap	CSG
XmNnavigationType XmCNavigationType	XmTAB_GROUP XmNavigationType	CSG
XmNshadowThickness XmCShadowThickness	dynamic Dimension	CSG
XmNstringDirection XmCStringDirection	dynamic XmStringDirection	CG
XmNtopShadowColor XmCBackgroundTopShadowColor	dynamic Pixel	CSG
XmNtopShadowPixmap XmCTopShadowPixmap	dynamic Pixmap	CSG
XmNtraversalOn XmCTraversalOn	True Boolean	CSG
XmNuserData XmCUserData	NULL Pointer	CSG

Composite Resource Set		
Name	**Default**	**Access**
Class	**Type**	
XmNchildren	NULL	G
XmCReadOnly	WidgetList	
XmNinsertPosition	NULL	CSG
XmCInsertPosition	(*)()	
XmNnumChildren	0	G
XmCReadOnly	Cardinal	

Core Resource Set		
Name	**Default**	**Access**
Class	**Type**	
XmNaccelerators	dynamic	N/A
XmCAccelerators	XtAccelerators	
XmNancestorSensitive	dynamic	G
XmCSensitive	Boolean	
XmNbackground	dynamic	CSG
XmCBackground	Pixel	
XmNbackgroundPixmap	XmUNSPECIFIED_PIXMAP	CSG
XmCPixmap	Pixmap	
XmNborderColor	XtDefaultForeground	CSG
XmCBorderColor	Pixel	
XmNborderPixmap	XmUNSPECIFIED_PIXMAP	CSG
XmCPixmap	Pixmap	
XmNborderWidth	0	CSG
XmCBorderWidth	Dimension	
XmNcolormap	dynamic	CG
XmCColormap	Colormap	
XmNdepth	dynamic	CG
XmCDepth	int	
XmNdestroyCallback	NULL	C
XmCCallback	XtCallbackList	
XmNheight	dynamic	CSG
XmCHeight	Dimension	
XmNinitialResourcesPersistent	True	C
XmCInitialResourcesPersistent	Boolean	
XmNmappedWhenManaged	True	CSG
XmCMappedWhenManaged	Boolean	
XmNscreen	dynamic	CG
XmCScreen	Screen *	

Name	Default	Access
Class	Type	
XmNsensitive	True	CSG
XmCSensitive	Boolean	
XmNtranslations	dynamic	CSG
XmCTranslations	XtTranslations	
XmNwidth	dynamic	CSG
XmCWidth	Dimension	
XmNx	0	CSG
XmCPosition	Position	
XmNy	0	CSG
XmCPosition	Position	

Translations

XmForm inherits translations from XmBulletinBoard.

Related Information

Composite(3X), Constraint(3X), Core(3X), XmBulletinBoard(3X), XmCreateForm, XmCreateFormDialog(3X), and XmManager(3X).

XmFrame

Purpose

The Frame widget class

AES Support Level

Full-use

Synopsis

#include <Xm/Frame.h>

Description

Frame is a very simple manager used to enclose a single child in a border drawn by Frame. It uses the Manager class resources for border drawing and performs geometry management so that its size always matches its child's outer size plus the Frame's margins and shadow thickness.

Frame is most often used to enclose other managers when the application developer desires the manager to have the same border appearance as the primitive widgets. Frame can also be used to enclose primitive widgets that do not support the same type of border drawing. This gives visual consistency when you develop applications using diverse widget sets.

If the Frame's parent is a Shell widget, **XmNshadowType** defaults to **XmSHADOW_OUT**, and Manager's resource **XmNshadowThickness** defaults to 1.

If the Frame's parent is not a Shell widget, **XmNshadowType** defaults to **XmSHADOW_ETCHED_IN**, and Manager's resource **XmNshadowThickness** defaults to 2.

Classes

Frame inherits behavior and resources from the **Core**, **Composite**, **Constraint**, and **XmManager** classes.

The class pointer is **xmFrameWidgetClass**.

The class name is **XmFrame**.

New Resources

The following table defines a set of widget resources used by the programmer to specify data. The programmer can also set the resource values for the inherited classes to set attributes for this widget. To reference a resource by name or by class in a .Xdefaults file, remove the **XmN** or **XmC** prefix and use the remaining letters. To specify one of the defined values for a resource in a .Xdefaults file, remove the **Xm** prefix and use the remaining letters (in either lowercase or uppercase, but include any underscores between words). The codes in the access column indicate if the given resource can be set at creation time (**C**), set by using **XtSetValues** (**S**), retrieved by using **XtGetValues** (**G**), or is not applicable (**N/A**).

XmFrame Resource Set		
Name **Class**	**Default** **Type**	**Access**
XmNmarginWidth XmCMarginWidth	0 Dimension	CSG
XmNmarginHeight XmCMarginHeight	0 Dimension	CSG
XmNshadowType XmCShadowType	dynamic unsigned char	CSG

XmNmarginWidth
Specifies the padding space on the left and right sides between Frame's child and Frame's shadow drawing.

XmNmarginHeight
Specifies the padding space on the top and bottom sides between Frame's child and Frame's shadow drawing.

XmNshadowType
Describes the drawing style for Frame. This resource can have the following values:

• **XmSHADOW_IN** — draws Frame so that it appears inset. This means that the bottom shadow visuals and top shadow visuals are reversed.

• **XmSHADOW_OUT** — draws Frame so that it appears outset. This is the default if Frame's parent is a Shell widget.

• **XmSHADOW_ETCHED_IN** — draws Frame using a double line giving the effect of a line etched into the window. The thickness of the double line is equal to the value of **XmNshadowThickness**. This is the default when Frame's parent is not a Shell widget.

• **XmSHADOW_ETCHED_OUT** — draws Frame using a double line giving the effect of a line coming out of the window. The thickness of the double line is equal to the value of **XmNshadowThickness**.

Inherited Resources

Frame inherits behavior and resources from the following superclasses. For a complete description of each resource, refer to the man page for that superclass.

XmManager Resource Set		
Name / Class	**Default** / Type	**Access**
XmNbottomShadowColor XmCBottomShadowColor	dynamic Pixel	CSG
XmNbottomShadowPixmap XmCBottomShadowPixmap	XmUNSPECIFIED_PIXMAP Pixmap	CSG
XmNforeground XmCForeground	dynamic Pixel	CSG
XmNhelpCallback XmCCallback	NULL XtCallbackList	C
XmNhighlightColor XmCHighlightColor	dynamic Pixel	CSG
XmNhighlightPixmap XmCHighlightPixmap	dynamic Pixmap	CSG
XmNnavigationType XmCNavigationType	XmTAB_GROUP XmNavigationType	CSG
XmNshadowThickness XmCShadowThickness	dynamic Dimension	CSG
XmNstringDirection XmCStringDirection	dynamic XmStringDirection	CG
XmNtopShadowColor XmCBackgroundTopShadowColor	dynamic Pixel	CSG
XmNtopShadowPixmap XmCTopShadowPixmap	dynamic Pixmap	CSG
XmNtraversalOn XmCTraversalOn	True Boolean	CSG
XmNuserData XmCUserData	NULL Pointer	CSG

Composite Resource Set		
Name	**Default**	**Access**
Class	**Type**	
XmNchildren	NULL	G
XmCReadOnly	WidgetList	
XmNinsertPosition	NULL	CSG
XmCInsertPosition	(*)()	
XmNnumChildren	0	G
XmCReadOnly	Cardinal	

Core Resource Set		
Name	**Default**	**Access**
Class	**Type**	
XmNaccelerators	dynamic	CSG
XmCAccelerators	XtAccelerators	
XmNancestorSensitive	dynamic	G
XmCSensitive	Boolean	
XmNbackground	dynamic	CSG
XmCBackground	Pixel	
XmNbackgroundPixmap	XmUNSPECIFIED_PIXMAP	CSG
XmCPixmap	Pixmap	
XmNborderColor	XtDefaultForeground	CSG
XmCBorderColor	Pixel	
XmNborderPixmap	XmUNSPECIFIED_PIXMAP	CSG
XmCPixmap	Pixmap	
XmNborderWidth	0	CSG
XmCBorderWidth	Dimension	
XmNcolormap	dynamic	CG
XmCColormap	Colormap	
XmNdepth	dynamic	CG
XmCDepth	int	
XmNdestroyCallback	NULL	C
XmCCallback	XtCallbackList	
XmNheight	dynamic	CSG
XmCHeight	Dimension	
XmNinitialResourcesPersistent	True	C
XmCInitialResourcesPersistent	Boolean	
XmNmappedWhenManaged	True	CSG
XmCMappedWhenManaged	Boolean	
XmNscreen	dynamic	CG
XmCScreen	Screen *	

Name	Default	Access
Class	Type	
XmNsensitive	True	CSG
XmCSensitive	Boolean	
XmNtranslations	dynamic	CSG
XmCTranslations	XtTranslations	
XmNwidth	dynamic	CSG
XmCWidth	Dimension	
XmNx	0	CSG
XmCPosition	Position	
XmNy	0	CSG
XmCPosition	Position	

Translations

XmFrame inherits translations from XmManager.

Related Information

Composite(3X), **Constraint(3X)**, **Core(3X)**, **XmCreateFrame(3X)**, and **XmManager(3X)**.

XmGadget

Purpose

The Gadget widget class

AES Support Level

Full-use

Synopsis

#include <Xm/Xm.h>

Description

Gadget is a widget class used as a supporting superclass for other gadget classes. It handles shadow-border drawing and highlighting, traversal activation and deactivation, and various callback lists needed by gadgets.

The color and pixmap resources defined by XmManager are directly used by gadgets. If **XtSetValues** is used to change one of the resources for a manager widget, all of the gadget children within the manager also change.

Classes

Gadget inherits behavior and resources from **Object** and **RectObj** classes.

The class pointer is **xmGadgetClass**.

The class name is **XmGadget**.

New Resources

The following table defines a set of widget resources used by the programmer to specify data. The programmer can also set the resource values for the inherited classes to set attributes for this widget. To reference a resource by name or by class in a .Xdefaults file, remove the **XmN** or **XmC** prefix and use the remaining letters. To specify one of the defined values for a resource in a .Xdefaults file, remove the **Xm** prefix and use the remaining letters (in either lowercase or uppercase, but include any underscores between words). The codes in the access column indicate if the given resource can be set at creation time (**C**), set by using **XtSetValues** (**S**), retrieved by using **XtGetValues** (**G**), or is not applicable (**N/A**).

XmGadget Resource Set		
Name	**Default**	**Access**
Class	**Type**	
XmNhelpCallback	NULL	C
XmCCallback	XtCallbackList	
XmNhighlightOnEnter	False	CSG
XmCHighlightOnEnter	Boolean	
XmNhighlightThickness	2	CSG
XmCHighlightThickness	Dimension	
XmNnavigationType	XmNONE	G
XmCNavigationType	XmNavigationType	
XmNshadowThickness	2	CSG
XmCShadowThickness	Dimension	
XmNtraversalOn	True	CSG
XmCTraversalOn	Boolean	
XmNuserData	NULL	CSG
XmCUserData	Pointer	

XmNhelpCallback

Specifies the list of callbacks that is called when the help key sequence is pressed. The reason sent by the callback is **XmCR_HELP**.

XmNhighlightOnEnter

Specifies if the highlighting rectangle is drawn when the cursor moves into the widget. If the shell's focus policy is **XmEXPLICIT**, this resource is ignored, and the widget is highlighted when it has the focus. If the shell's focus policy is **XmPOINTER** and if this resource is True, the highlighting rectangle is drawn when the the cursor moves into the widget. If the shell's focus policy is **XmPOINTER** and if this resource is False, the highlighting rectangle is not drawn when the the cursor moves into the widget. The default is False.

XmNhighlightThickness

Specifies the thickness of the highlighting rectangle.

XmNnavigationType

Controls whether the Widget is a navigation group.

- **XmNONE** indicates that the Widget is not a navigation group.

- **XmTAB_GROUP** indicates that the Widget is included automatically in keyboard navigation, unless **XmAddTabGroup** has been called.

- **XmSTICKY_TAB_GROUP** indicates that the Widget is included automatically in keyboard navigation, even if **XmAddTabGroup** has been called.

- **XmEXCLUSIVE_TAB_GROUP** indicates that the Widget is included explicitly in keyboard navigation by the application. With **XmEXCLUSIVE_TAB_GROUP**, traversal of widgets within the group is based on the order of children.

If the gadget's parent is a shell, the default is **XmTAB_GROUP**; otherwise, the default is **XmNONE**.

XmNshadowThickness

Specifies the size of the drawn border shadow.

XmNtraversalOn

Specifies traversal activation for this gadget.

XmNuserData

Allows the application to attach any necessary specific data to the gadget. This is an internally unused resource.

Inherited Resources

Gadget inherits the following resources from the named superclass. For a complete description of each resource, refer to the man page for that superclass.

RectObj Resource Set		
Name	**Default**	**Access**
Class	**Type**	
XmNancestorSensitive	dynamic	G
XmCSensitive	Boolean	
XmNborderWidth	0	CSG
XmCBorderWidth	Dimension	
XmNheight	dynamic	CSG
XmCHeight	Dimension	
XmNsensitive	True	CSG
XmCSensitive	Boolean	
XmNwidth	dynamic	CSG
XmCWidth	Dimension	
XmNx	0	CSG
XmCPosition	Position	
XmNy	0	CSG
XmCPosition	Position	

Object Resource Set		
Name	**Default**	**Access**
Class	**Type**	
XmNdestroyCallback	NULL	C
XmCCallback	XtCallbackList	

Related Information

Object(3X), RectObj(3X), and XmManager(3X).

XmGetAtomName

Purpose

A function that returns the string representation for an atom.

AES Support Level

Full-use

History/Direction

The include file **AtomMgr.h** moved from the **X11** directory to the **Xm** directory. In revision B this include file will be accessible from either directory. In future revisions it will only be accessible from the **Xm** directory.

Synopsis

```
#include <Xm/Xm.h>
#include <Xm/AtomMgr.h>

String XmGetAtomName (display, atom)
    Display     * display;
    Atom        atom;
```

Description

XmGetAtomName returns the string representation for an atom. It mirrors the **Xlib** interfaces for atom management but provides client-side caching. When and where caching is provided in **Xlib**, the routines will become pseudonyms for the **Xlib** routines.

display   Specifies the connection to the X server

atom   Specifies the atom for the property name you want returned

Return Value

Returns a string.

XmGetColors

Purpose

A function that generates foreground, select, and shadow colors.

AES Support Level

Trial-use

Synopsis

#include <Xm/Xm.h>

void   XmGetColors (*screen,   colormap,   background,   foreground, top_shadow, bottom_shadow, select*)
Screen	* *screen*;
Colormap	*colormap*;
Pixel	*background*;
Pixel	* *foreground*;
Pixel	* *top_shadow*;
Pixel	* *bottom_shadow*;
Pixel	* *select*;

Description

XmGetColors takes a screen, a colormap, and a background pixel, and it returns pixel values for foreground, select, and shadow colors.

screen   Specifies the screen for which these colors should be allocated

colormap Specifies the colormap from which these colors should be allocated

background
            Specifies the background on which the colors should be based

foreground
            Specifies a pointer to the returned foreground pixel value. If this argument is NULL no value is returned for this color.

top_shadow
            Specifies a pointer to the returned top shadow pixel value. If this argument is NULL no value is returned for this color.

bottom_shadow
            Specifies a pointer to the returned bottom shadow pixel value. If this argument is NULL no value is returned for this color.

select   Specifies a pointer to the returned select pixel value. If this argument is NULL no value is returned for this color.

XmGetMenuCursor

Purpose

A RowColumn function that returns the cursor ID for the current menu cursor.

AES Support Level

Full-use

Synopsis

Cursor XmGetMenuCursor (*display*)
    Display   * *display*;

Description

XmGetMenuCursor queries the menu cursor currently being used by this client on the specified display and returns the cursor ID.

display   Specifies the display whose menu cursor is to be queried

For a complete definition of the menu cursor resource, see **XmRowColumn(3X)**.

Return Value

Returns the cursor ID for the current menu cursor or the value None if a cursor is not yet defined. A cursor will not be defined if the application makes this call before the client has created any menus on the specified display.

Related Information

XmRowColumn(3X).

XmGetPixmap

Purpose

A pixmap caching function that generates a pixmap, stores it in a pixmap cache, and returns the pixmap.

AES Support Level

Full-use

Synopsis

#include <Xm/Xm.h>

Pixmap XmGetPixmap (*screen, image_name, foreground, background*)
    Screen   * *screen*;
    char   * *image_name*;
    Pixel   *foreground*;
    Pixel   *background*;

Description

XmGetPixmap uses the parameter data to perform a lookup in the pixmap cache to see if a pixmap has already been generated that matches the data.

If one is found, a reference count is incremented and the pixmap is returned. Applications should use **XmDestroyPixmap** when the pixmap is no longer needed.

If a pixmap is not found, *image_name* is used to perform a lookup in the image cache. If an image is found, it is used to generate the pixmap, which is then cached and returned.

If an image is not found, the *image_name* is used as a filename, and a search is made for an **X10** or **X11** bitmap file. If it is found, the file is read, converted into an image, and cached in the image cache. The image is then used to generate a pixmap, which is cached and returned.

If *image_name* begins with a slash character (/), it is taken to be a full pathname specification and is the only pathname searched to find the file. Otherwise, several paths are searched. The user can specify an environment variable **XBMLANGPATH**, which is used to generate one set of paths. If **XBMLANGPATH** is not set but the environment variable **XAPPLRESDIR** is set, the following path names are searched:

> **%B**
> **$XAPPLRESDIR/%L/bitmaps/%N/%B**
> **$XAPPLRESDIR/%l/bitmaps/%N/%B**
> **$XAPPLRESDIR/bitmaps/%N/%B**
> **$XAPPLRESDIR/%L/bitmaps/%B**
> **$XAPPLRESDIR/%l/bitmaps/%B**
> **$XAPPLRESDIR/bitmaps/%B**
> **$HOME/%B**
> **/usr/lib/X11/%L/bitmaps/%N/%B**
> **/usr/lib/X11/%l/bitmaps/%N/%B**
> **/usr/lib/X11/bitmaps/%N/%B**
> **/usr/lib/X11/%L/bitmaps/%B**
> **/usr/lib/X11/%l/bitmaps/%B**
> **/usr/lib/X11/bitmaps/%B**
> **/usr/include/X11/bitmaps/%B**

If neither **XBMLANGPATH** nor **XAPPLRESDIR** is set, the following path names are searched:

> **%B**
> **$HOME/%L/bitmaps/%N/%B**
> **$HOME/%l/bitmaps/%N/%B**
> **$HOME/bitmaps/%N/%B**
> **$HOME/%L/bitmaps/%B**
> **$HOME/%l/bitmaps/%B**
> **$HOME/bitmaps/%B**
> **$HOME/%B**
> **/usr/lib/X11/%L/bitmaps/%N/%B**
> **/usr/lib/X11/%l/bitmaps/%N/%B**
> **/usr/lib/X11/bitmaps/%N/%B**
> **/usr/lib/X11/%L/bitmaps/%B**
> **/usr/lib/X11/%l/bitmaps/%B**
> **/usr/lib/X11/bitmaps/%B**
> **/usr/include/X11/bitmaps/%B**

The following substitutions are used in these paths:

%B   The image name, from the *image_name* argument.

%N   The class_name of the application.

%L   The value of the **LANG** environment variable.

%l   The language component of the **LANG** environment variable.

Parameter descriptions are listed below:

screen   Specifies the display screen on which the pixmap is to be drawn. The depth of the pixmap is the default depth for this screen.

image_name   Specifies the name of the image to be used to generate the pixmap

foreground   Combines the image with the *foreground* color to create the pixmap if the image referenced is a bit-per-pixel image

> *background*   Combines the image with the *background* color to create the pixmap if the image referenced is a bit-per-pixel image

Return Value

Returns a pixmap when successful; returns **XmUNSPECIFIED_PIXMAP** if the image corresponding to the *image_name* cannot be found.

Related Information

XmDestroyPixmap(3X),   **XmInstallImage(3X)**,   and
XmUninstallImage(3X).

XmGetPostedFromWidget

Purpose

A RowColumn function that returns the widget from which a menu was posted.

AES Support Level

Trial-use

Synopsis

#include <Xm/RowColumn.h>

Widget XmGetPostedFromWidget (*menu*)
    Widget   *menu*;

Description

XmGetPostedFromWidget returns the widget from which a menu was posted. An application can use this routine during the activate callback to determine the context in which the menu callback should be interpreted.

menu   Specifies the widget ID of the menu

For a complete definition of RowColumn and its associated resources, see
XmRowColumn(3X).

Return Value

Returns the widget ID of the widget from which the menu was posted. If the
menu is a Popup Menu, the returned widget is the widget from which the
menu was popped up. If the menu is a Pulldown Menu, the returned widget
is the MenuBar or OptionMenu from which the widget was pulled down.

Related Information

XmRowColumn(3X).

XmInstallImage

Purpose

A pixmap caching function that adds an image to the pixmap cache.

AES Support Level

Full-use

Synopsis

#include <Xm/Xm.h>

Boolean XmInstallImage (*image, image_name*)
    XImage   * *image*;
    char   * *image_name*;

Description

XmInstallImage stores an image in an image cache that can later be used to generate a pixmap. Part of the installation process is to extend the resource converter used to reference these images. The resource converter is given the image name so that the image can be referenced in a .Xdefaults file. Since an image can be referenced by a widget through its pixmap resources, it is up to the application to ensure that the image is installed before the widget is created.

     image   Points to the image structure to be installed. The installation process does not make a local copy of the image. Therefore, the application should not destroy the image until it is uninstalled from the caching functions.

     image_name Specifies a string that the application uses to name the image. After installation, this name can be used in .Xdefaults for referencing the image. A local copy of the name is created by the image caching functions.

The image caching functions provide a set of eight preinstalled images. These names can be used within a **.Xdefaults** file for generating pixmaps for the resource for which they are provided.

Image Name	Description
background	A tile of solid background
25_foreground	A tile of 25% foreground, 75% background
50_foreground	A tile of 50% foreground, 50% background
75_foreground	A tile of 75% foreground, 25% background
horizontal	A tile of horizontal lines of the two colors
vertical	A tile of vertical lines of the two colors
slant_right	A tile of slanting lines of the two colors
slant_left	A tile of slanting lines of the two colors

Return Value

Returns True when successful; returns False if NULL *image*, NULL *image_name*, or duplicate *image_name* are used as parameter values.

Related Information

XmUninstallImage(3X), **XmGetPixmap(3X)**, and **XmDestroyPixmap(3X)**.

XmInternAtom

Purpose

A function that returns an atom for a given name

AES Support Level

Full-use

History/Direction

The include file **AtomMgr.h** moved from the **X11** directory to the **Xm** directory. In revision B this include file will be accessible from either directory. In future revisions it will only be accessible from the **Xm** directory.

Synopsis

#include <Xm/Xm.h>
#include <Xm/AtomMgr.h>

Atom XmInternAtom (*display, name, only_if_exists*)
    Display   * *display*;
    String   *name*;
    Boolean   *only_if_exists*;

Description

XmInternAtom returns an atom for a given name. It mirrors the **Xlib** interfaces for atom management, but provides client-side caching. When and where caching is provided in **Xlib**, the routines will become pseudonyms for the **Xlib** routines.

display   Specifies the connection to the X server

name   Specifies the name associated with the atom you want returned

only_if_exists

     Specifies a Boolean value that indicates whether **XInternAtom** creates the atom

Return Value

Returns an atom.

XmIsMotifWMRunning

Purpose

A function that specifies if the window manager is running.

AES Support Level

Full-use

History/Direction

This include file for this function has changed from **X11/Shell.h** to **Xm/Xm.h**. Since all motif applications must include **Xm/Xm.h** this change requires no change to existing applications.

Synopsis

#include <Xm/Xm.h>

Boolean XmIsMotifWMRunning (*shell*)
    Widget   *shell*;

Description

XmIsMotifWMRunning lets a user know if the Motif Window Manager is running on a screen that contains a specific widget hierarchy. This function first sees whether the **_MOTIF_WM_INFO** property is present on the root window of the shell's screen. If it is, its window field is used to query for the presence of the specified window as a child of root.

shell   Specifies the shell whose screen will be tested for **mwm**'s presence.

Return Value

Returns True if MWM is running.

XmLabel

Purpose

The Label widget class

AES Support Level

Full-use

Synopsis

#include <Xm/Label.h>

Description

Label is an instantiable widget and is also used as a superclass for other button widgets, such as PushButton and ToggleButton. The Label widget does not accept any button or key input, and the help callback is the only callback defined. Label also receives enter and leave events.

Label can contain either text or a pixmap. Label text is a compound string. Refer to the *OSF/Motif Programmer's Guide* for more information on compound strings. The text can be multilingual, multiline, and/or multifont. When a Label is insensitive, its text is stippled, or the user-supplied insensitive pixmap is displayed.

Label supports both accelerators and mnemonics primarily for use in Label subclass widgets that are contained in menus. Mnemonics are available in a menu system when the button is visible. Accelerators in a menu system are accessible even when the button is not visible. The Label widget displays the mnemonic by underlining the first matching character in the text string. The accelerator is displayed as a text string to the side of the label text or pixmap.

Label consists of many margin fields surrounding the text or pixmap. These margin fields are resources that may be set by the user, but Label subclasses also modify some of these fields. The subclasses tend to modify the **XmNmarginLeft**, **XmNmarginRight**, **XmNmarginTop**, and **XmNmarginBottom** resources and leave the **XmNmarginWidth** and **XmNmarginHeight** resources as set by the application.

In a Label **XmNtraversalOn** and **XmNhighlightOnEnter** are forced to False inside Popup MenuPanes, Pulldown MenuPanes, and OptionMenus. Otherwise these resources default to False.

Classes

Label inherits behavior and resources from **Core** and **XmPrimitive** Classes.

The class pointer is **xmLabelWidgetClass**.

The class name is **XmLabel**.

New Resources

The following table defines a set of widget resources used by the programmer to specify data. The programmer can also set the resource values for the inherited classes to set attributes for this widget. To reference a resource by name or by class in a .Xdefaults file, remove the **XmN** or **XmC** prefix and use the remaining letters. To specify one of the defined values for a resource in a .Xdefaults file, remove the **Xm** prefix and use the remaining letters (in either lowercase or uppercase, but include any underscores between words). The codes in the access column indicate if the given resource can be set at creation time (**C**), set by using **XtSetValues** (**S**), retrieved by using **XtGetValues** (**G**), or is not applicable (**N/A**).

XmLabel Resource Set		
Name	**Default**	**Access**
Class	**Type**	
XmNaccelerator	NULL	CSG
XmCAccelerator	String	
XmNacceleratorText	NULL	CSG
XmCAcceleratorText	XmString	
XmNalignment	dynamic	CSG
XmCAlignment	unsigned char	
XmNfontList	dynamic	CSG
XmCFontList	XmFontList	
XmNlabelInsensitivePixmap	XmUNSPECIFIED_PIXMAP	CSG
XmCLabelInsensitivePixmap	Pixmap	
XmNlabelPixmap	XmUNSPECIFIED_PIXMAP	CSG
XmCLabelPixmap	Pixmap	
XmNlabelString	dynamic	CSG
XmCXmString	XmString	
XmNlabelType	XmSTRING	CSG
XmCLabelType	unsigned char	
XmNmarginBottom	0	CSG
XmCMarginBottom	Dimension	
XmNmarginHeight	2	CSG
XmCMarginHeight	Dimension	
XmNmarginLeft	0	CSG
XmCMarginLeft	Dimension	
XmNmarginRight	0	CSG
XmCMarginRight	Dimension	
XmNmarginTop	0	CSG
XmCMarginTop	Dimension	
XmNmarginWidth	2	CSG
XmCMarginWidth	Dimension	

Name	Default	Access
Class	Type	
XmNmnemonic	NULL	CSG
XmCMnemonic	KeySym	
XmNmnemonicCharSet	dynamic	CSG
XmCMnemonicCharSet	String	
XmNrecomputeSize	True	CSG
XmCRecomputeSize	Boolean	
XmNstringDirection	dynamic	CSG
XmCStringDirection	XmStringDirection	

XmNaccelerator

Sets the accelerator on a button widget in a menu, which activates a visible or invisible button from the keyboard. This resource is a string that describes a set of modifiers and the key that may be used to select the button. The format of this string is identical to that used by the translations manager, with the exception that only a single event may be specified and only **KeyPress** events are allowed.

Accelerators for buttons are supported only for PushButton and ToggleButton in Pulldown and Popup MenuPanes.

XmNaccelerator Text

Specifies the text displayed for the accelerator. The text is displayed to the side of the label string or pixmap. Accelerator text for buttons is displayed only for PushButtons and ToggleButtons in Pulldown and Popup Menus.

XmNalignment

Specifies the label alignment for text or pixmap.

- **XmALIGNMENT_BEGINNING** (left alignment) — causes the left sides of the lines of text to be vertically aligned with the left edge of the widget window. For a pixmap, its left side is vertically aligned with the left edge of the widget window. **XmALIGNMENT_CENTER** (center alignment) — causes the centers of the lines of text to be vertically aligned in the center of the widget window.

For a pixmap, its center is vertically aligned with the center of the widget window.

- **XmALIGNMENT_END** (right alignment) — causes the right sides of the lines of text to be vertically aligned with the right edge of the widget window. For a pixmap, its right side is vertically aligned with the right edge of the widget window.

The above descriptions for text are correct when **XmNstringDirection** is **XmSTRING_DIRECTION_L_TO_R**. When that resource is **XmSTRING_DIRECTION_R_TO_L**, the descriptions for **XmALIGNMENT_BEGINNING** and **XmALIGNMENT_END** are switched.

If the parent is a RowColumn whose **XmNisAligned** resource is True, **XmNalignment** is forced to the same value as the RowColumn's **XmNentryAlignment** if the RowColumn's **XmNrowColumnType** is **XmWORK_AREA** or if the widget is a subclass of XmLabel. Otherwise, the default is **XmALIGNMENT_CENTER**.

XmNfontList

Specifies the font of the text used in the widget. If this value is NULL at initialization, it is initialized by looking up the parent hierarchy of the widget for an ancestor that is a subclass of the XmBulletinBoard, VendorShell, or XmMenuShell widget class. If such an ancestor is found, the font list is initialized to the appropriate default font list of the ancestor widget (XmNdefaultFontList for VendorShell and XmMenuShell, XmNlabelFontList or XmNbuttonFontList for XmBulletinBoard). Refer to **XmFontList(3X)** for more information on the creation and structure of a font list.

XmNlabelInsensitivePixmap

Specifies a pixmap used as the button face if **XmNlabelType** is **XmPIXMAP** and the button is insensitive.

XmNlabelPixmap

Specifies the pixmap when **XmNlabelType** is **XmPIXMAP**.

XmNlabelString

Specifies the compound string when the **XmNlabelType** is **XmSTRING**. If this value is NULL, it is initialized by converting the name of the widget to a compound string. Refer to **XmString(3X)** for more information on the creation and structure of compound strings.

XmNlabelType

Specifies the label type.

- **XmSTRING** — text displays **XmNlabelString**.

- **XmPIXMAP** — icon data in pixmap displays **XmNlabelPixmap** or **XmNlabelInsensitivePixmap**.

XmNmarginBottom

Specifies the amount of spacing between the bottom of the label text and the top of the bottom margin (specified by **XmNmarginHeight**). This may be modified by Label's subclasses. For example, CascadeButton may increase this field to make room for the cascade pixmap.

XmNmarginHeight

Specifies the amount of spacing between the top of the label (specified by **XmNmarginTop**) and the bottom edge of the top shadow, and the amount of spacing between the bottom of the label (specified by **XmNmarginBottom**) and the top edge of the bottom shadow.

XmNmarginLeft

Specifies the amount of spacing between the left edge of the label text and the right side of the left margin (specified by **XmNmarginWidth**). This may be modified by Label's subclasses. For example, ToggleButton may increase this field to make room for the toggle indicator and for spacing between the indicator and label. Whether this actually applies to the left or right side of the label may depend on the value of **XmNstringDirection**.

XmNmarginRight

Specifies the amount of spacing between the right edge of the label text and the left side of the right margin (specified by **XmNmarginWidth**). This may be modified by Label's subclasses. For example, CascadeButton may increase this field to make room for the cascade pixmap. Whether this actually applies to the left or right side of the label may depend on the value of **XmNstringDirection**.

XmNmarginTop

Specifies the amount of spacing between the top of the label text and the bottom of the top margin (specified by **XmNmarginHeight**). This may be modified by Label's subclasses. For example, CascadeButton may increase this field to make room for the cascade pixmap.

XmNmarginWidth

Specifies the amount of spacing between the left side of the label (specified by **XmNmarginLeft**) and the right edge of the left shadow, and the amount of spacing between the right side of the label (specified by **XmNmarginRight**) and the left edge of the right shadow.

XmNmnemonic

Provides the user with an alternate means of selecting a button. A button in a MenuBar, a Popup MenuPane, or a Pulldown MenuPane can have a mnemonic.

This resource contains a keysym as listed in the X11 keysym table. The first character in the label string that exactly matches the mnemonic in the character set specified in **XmNmnemonicCharSet** is underlined when the button is displayed.

When a mnemonic has been specified, the user activates the button by pressing the mnemonic key while the button is visible. If the button is a CascadeButton in a MenuBar and the MenuBar does not have the focus, the user must use the **MAlt** modifier while pressing the mnemonic. The user can activate the button by pressing either the shifted or the unshifted mnemonic key.

XmNmnemonicCharSet

Specifies the character set of the mnemonic for the label. The default is determined dynamically depending on the current language environment.

XmNrecomputeSize

Specifies a Boolean value that indicates whether the widget attempts to be big enough to contain the label. If True, an **XtSetValues** with a resource value that would change the size of the widget causes the widget to shrink or expand to exactly fit the label string or pixmap. If False, the widget never attempts to change size on its own.

XmNstringDirection

Specifies the direction in which the string is to be drawn. The following are the values:

- **XmSTRING_DIRECTION_L_TO_R** — left to right
- **XmSTRING_DIRECTION_R_TO_L** — right to left

The default for this resource is determined at creation time. If no value is specified for this resource and the widget's parent is a manager, the value is inherited from the parent; otherwise, it defaults to **XmSTRING_DIRECTION_L_TO_R**.

Inherited Resources

Label inherits behavior and resources from the following superclasses. For a complete description of each resource, refer to the man page for that superclass.

XmPrimitive Resource Set		
Name	**Default**	**Access**
Class	**Type**	
XmNbottomShadowColor	dynamic	CSG
XmCBottomShadowColor	Pixel	
XmNbottomShadowPixmap	XmUNSPECIFIED_PIXMAP	CSG
XmCBottomShadowPixmap	Pixmap	
XmNforeground	dynamic	CSG
XmCForeground	Pixel	
XmNhelpCallback	NULL	C
XmCCallback	XtCallbackList	
XmNhighlightColor	dynamic	CSG
XmCHighlightColor	Pixel	
XmNhighlightOnEnter	False	CSG
XmCHighlightOnEnter	Boolean	
XmNhighlightPixmap	dynamic	CSG
XmCHighlightPixmap	Pixmap	
XmNhighlightThickness	0	CSG
XmCHighlightThickness	Dimension	
XmNnavigationType	XmNONE	G
XmCNavigationType	XmNavigationType	
XmNshadowThickness	0	CSG
XmCShadowThickness	Dimension	
XmNtopShadowColor	dynamic	CSG
XmCTopShadowColor	Pixel	
XmNtopShadowPixmap	dynamic	CSG
XmCTopShadowPixmap	Pixmap	
XmNtraversalOn	False	CSG
XmCTraversalOn	Boolean	
XmNuserData	NULL	CSG
XmCUserData	Pointer	

Core Resource Set		
Name	**Default**	**Access**
Class	**Type**	
XmNaccelerators	dynamic	CSG
XmCAccelerators	XtAccelerators	
XmNancestorSensitive	dynamic	G
XmCSensitive	Boolean	
XmNbackground	dynamic	CSG
XmCBackground	Pixel	
XmNbackgroundPixmap	XmUNSPECIFIED_PIXMAP	CSG
XmCPixmap	Pixmap	
XmNborderColor	XtDefaultForeground	CSG
XmCBorderColor	Pixel	
XmNborderPixmap	XmUNSPECIFIED_PIXMAP	CSG
XmCPixmap	Pixmap	
XmNborderWidth	0	CSG
XmCBorderWidth	Dimension	
XmNcolormap	dynamic	CG
XmCColormap	Colormap	
XmNdepth	dynamic	CG
XmCDepth	int	
XmNdestroyCallback	NULL	C
XmCCallback	XtCallbackList	
XmNheight	dynamic	CSG
XmCHeight	Dimension	
XmNinitialResourcesPersistent	True	C
XmCInitialResourcesPersistent	Boolean	
XmNmappedWhenManaged	True	CSG
XmCMappedWhenManaged	Boolean	
XmNscreen	dynamic	CG
XmCScreen	Screen *	

Name Class	Default Type	Access
XmNsensitive XmCSensitive	True Boolean	CSG
XmNtranslations XmCTranslations	dynamic XtTranslations	CSG
XmNwidth XmCWidth	dynamic Dimension	CSG
XmNx XmCPosition	0 Position	CSG
XmNy XmCPosition	0 Position	CSG

Callback Information

A pointer to the following structure is passed to each callback:

typedef struct
{
    int   *reason*;
    XEvent   * *event*;
} XmAnyCallbackStruct;

reason   Indicates why the callback was invoked. For this callback, *reason* is set to **XmCR_HELP**.

event   Points to the **XEvent** that triggered the callback.

Translations

XmLabel includes translations from Primitive. The XmLabel translations are listed below. These translations may not directly correspond to a translation table.

KHelp: **Help()**

The translations used by subclasses of XmLabel for menu traversal are listed below. These translations may not directly correspond to a translation table.

KLeft: **MenuTraverseLeft()**
KRight: **MenuTraverseRight()**
KUp: **MenuTraverseUp()**
KDown: **MenuTraverseDown()**
MAny KCancel: **MenuEscape()**

Action Routines

The XmLabel action routines are described below:

Help():   In a Popup or Pulldown MenuPane, unposts all menus in the menu hierarchy and, when the shell's keyboard focus policy is **XmEXPLICIT**, restores keyboard focus to the tab group that had the focus before the menu system was entered. Calls the callbacks for **XmNhelpCallback** if any exist. If there are no help callbacks for this widget, this action calls the help callbacks for the nearest ancestor that has them.

MenuEscape():
In a MenuBar, disarms the CascadeButton and the menu and, when the shell's keyboard focus policy is **XmEXPLICIT**, restores keyboard focus to the tab group that had the focus before the menu was entered.

In a toplevel Pulldown MenuPane from a MenuBar, unposts the menu, disarms the MenuBar CascadeButton and the MenuBar, and, when the shell's keyboard focus policy is **XmEXPLICIT**, restores keyboard focus to the tab group that had the focus before the MenuBar was entered. In other Pulldown MenuPanes, unposts the menu.

In a Popup MenuPane, unposts the menu and, when the shell's keyboard focus policy is **XmEXPLICIT**, restores keyboard focus to the widget from which the menu was posted.

MenuTraverseDown():

In a vertical menu, disarms the current menu entry and arms the entry just below it in the MenuPane. This action wraps within the MenuPane.

In a horizontal menu, if the menu entry is a CascadeButton with a submenu, posts the MenuPane associated with the CascadeButton. Otherwise, this action searches for an ancestor menu that is vertical. If it finds one, it unposts the cascade from the vertical menu and traverses to the next entry toward the bottom in the vertical menu. If this entry is a CascadeButton with a submenu, posts the MenuPane associated with the CascadeButton. This action wraps within the vertical menu.

MenuTraverseLeft():

In a vertical menu, if the menu's parent is a horizontal menu, this action unposts the current MenuPane and traverses to the next entry to the left in the parent menu. If this entry is a CascadeButton with a submenu, posts the MenuPane associated with the CascadeButton. This action wraps within the horizontal menu. If the menu's parent is a vertical menu, this action unposts the current MenuPane.

In a horizontal menu, disarms the current menu entry and arms the entry just to the left of it in the menu. This action wraps within the menu.

MenuTraverseRight():

In a vertical menu, if the menu entry is a CascadeButton with a submenu, posts the MenuPane associated with the CascadeButton. Otherwise, this action searches for an ancestor menu that is horizontal. If it finds one, it unposts the cascade from the horizontal menu and traverses to the next entry to the right in the horizontal menu. If this entry is a CascadeButton with a submenu, posts the MenuPane associated with the CascadeButton. This action wraps within the horizontal menu.

In a horizontal menu, disarms the current menu entry and arms the entry just to the right of it in the menu. This action wraps within the menu.

MenuTraverseUp():

In a vertical menu, disarms the current menu entry and arms the entry just above it in the MenuPane. This action wraps within the MenuPane.

In a horizontal menu, if the menu's parent is a vertical menu, this action unposts the current MenuPane and traverses to the next entry toward the top in the parent menu. If this entry is a CascadeButton with a submenu, posts the MenuPane associated with the CascadeButton. This action wraps within the vertical menu. If the menu's parent is a horizontal menu, this action unposts the current MenuPane.

Virtual Bindings

The bindings for virtual keys are vendor specific.

Related Information

Core(3X), **XmCreateLabel(3X)**, and **XmPrimitive(3X)**.

XmLabelGadget

Purpose

The LabelGadget widget class

AES Support Level

Full-use

Synopsis

#include <Xm/LabelG.h>

Description

LabelGadget is an instantiable widget and is also used as a superclass for other button gadgets, such as PushButtonGadget and ToggleButtonGadget.

LabelGadget can contain either text or a pixmap. LabelGadget text is a compound string. Refer to the *OSF/Motif Programmer's Guide* for more information on compound strings. The text can be multilingual, multiline, and/or multifont. When a LabelGadget is insensitive, its text is stippled, or the user-supplied insensitive pixmap is displayed.

LabelGadget supports both accelerators and mnemonics primarily for use in LabelGadget subclass widgets that are contained in menus. Mnemonics are available in a menu system when the button is visible. Accelerators in a menu system are accessible even when the button is not visible. The LabelGadget displays the mnemonic by underlining the first matching character in the text string. The accelerator is displayed as a text string to the side of the label text or pixmap.

LabelGadget consists of many margin fields surrounding the text or pixmap. These margin fields are resources that may be set by the user, but LabelGadget subclasses also modify some of these fields. The subclasses tend to modify the **XmNmarginLeft**, **XmNmarginRight**, **XmNmarginTop**, and **XmNmarginBottom** resources and leave the **XmNmarginWidth** and **XmNmarginHeight** resources as set by the application.

In a LabelGadget **XmNtraversalOn** and **XmNhighlightOnEnter** are forced to False inside Popup MenuPanes, Pulldown MenuPanes, and OptionMenus. Otherwise these resources default to False.

Classes

LabelGadget inherits behavior and resources from **Object**, **RectObj** and **XmGadget** classes.

The class pointer is **xmLabelGadgetClass**.

The class name is **XmLabelGadget**.

New Resources

The following table defines a set of widget resources used by the programmer to specify data. The programmer can also set the resource values for the inherited classes to set attributes for this widget. To reference a resource by name or by class in a .Xdefaults file, remove the **XmN** or **XmC** prefix and use the remaining letters. To specify one of the defined values for a resource in a .Xdefaults file, remove the **Xm** prefix and use the remaining letters (in either lowercase or uppercase, but include any underscores between words). The codes in the access column indicate if the given resource can be set at creation time (**C**), set by using **XtSetValues** (**S**), retrieved by using **XtGetValues** (**G**), or is not applicable (**N/A**).

XmLabelGadget Resource Set		
Name **Class**	**Default** **Type**	**Access**
XmNaccelerator XmCAccelerator	NULL String	CSG
XmNacceleratorText XmCAcceleratorText	NULL XmString	CSG
XmNalignment XmCAlignment	dynamic unsigned char	CSG
XmNfontList XmCFontList	dynamic XmFontList	CSG
XmNlabelInsensitivePixmap XmCLabelInsensitivePixmap	XmUNSPECIFIED_PIXMAP Pixmap	CSG
XmNlabelPixmap XmCLabelPixmap	XmUNSPECIFIED_PIXMAP Pixmap	CSG
XmNlabelString XmCXmString	dynamic XmString	CSG
XmNlabelType XmCLabelType	XmSTRING unsigned char	CSG
XmNmarginBottom XmCMarginBottom	0 Dimension	CSG
XmNmarginHeight XmCMarginHeight	2 Dimension	CSG
XmNmarginLeft XmCMarginLeft	0 Dimension	CSG
XmNmarginRight XmCMarginRight	0 Dimension	CSG
XmNmarginTop XmCMarginTop	0 Dimension	CSG
XmNmarginWidth XmCMarginWidth	2 Dimension	CSG

Name	Default	Access
Class	Type	
XmNmnemonic	NULL	CSG
XmCMnemonic	KeySym	
XmNmnemonicCharSet	dynamic	CSG
XmCMnemonicCharSet	String	
XmNrecomputeSize	True	CSG
XmCRecomputeSize	Boolean	
XmNstringDirection	dynamic	CSG
XmCStringDirection	XmStringDirection	

XmNaccelerator

Sets the accelerator on a button widget in a menu, which activates a visible or invisible button from the keyboard. This resource is a string that describes a set of modifiers and the key that may be used to select the button. The format of this string is identical to that used by the translations manager, with the exception that only a single event may be specified and only **KeyPress** events are allowed.

Accelerators for buttons are supported only for PushButtonGadget and ToggleButtonGadget in Pulldown and Popup menus.

XmNacceleratorText

Specifies the text displayed for the accelerator. The text is displayed to the side of the label string or pixmap. Accelerator text for buttons is displayed only for PushButtonGadgets and ToggleButtonGadgets in Pulldown and Popup Menus.

XmNalignment

Specifies the label alignment for text or pixmap.

- **XmALIGNMENT_BEGINNING** (left alignment) — causes the left sides of the lines of text to be vertically aligned with the left edge of the gadget. For a pixmap, its left side is vertically aligned with the left edge of the gadget.

- **XmALIGNMENT_CENTER** (center alignment) — causes the centers of the lines of text to be vertically aligned in the center of the gadget. For a pixmap, its center is vertically aligned with the center of the gadget.

- **XmALIGNMENT_END** (right alignment) — causes the right sides of the lines of text to be vertically aligned with the right edge of the gadget. For a pixmap, its right side is vertically aligned with the right edge of the gadget.

The above descriptions for text are correct when **XmNstringDirection** is **XmSTRING_DIRECTION_L_TO_R**; the descriptions for **XmALIGNMENT_BEGINNING** and **XmALIGNMENT_END** are switched When the resource is **XmSTRING_DIRECTION_R_TO_L**.

If the parent is a RowColumn whose **XmNisAligned** resource is True, **XmNalignment** is forced to the same value as the RowColumn's **XmNentryAlignment** if the RowColumn's **XmNrowColumnType** is **XmWORK_AREA** or if the gadget is a subclass of XmLabelGadget. Otherwise, the default is **XmALIGNMENT_CENTER**.

XmNfontList
Specifies the font of the text used in the gadget. If this value is NULL at initialization, it is initialized by looking up the parent hierarchy of the widget for an ancestor that is a subclass of the XmBulletinBoard, VendorShell, or XmMenuShell widget class. If such an ancestor is found, the font list is initialized to the appropriate default font list of the ancestor widget (XmNdefaultFontList for VendorShell and XmMenuShell, XmNlabelFontList or XmNbuttonFontList for XmBulletinBoard). Refer to **XmFontList(3X)** for more information on the creation and the structure of a font list.

XmNlabelInsensitivePixmap
Specifies a pixmap used as the button face if **XmNlabelType** is **XmPIXMAP** and the button is insensitive.

XmNlabelPixmap
Specifies the pixmap when **XmNlabelType** is **XmPIXMAP**.

XmNlabelString

Specifies the compound string when **XmNlabelType** is **XmSTRING**. If this value is NULL, it is initialized by converting the name of the gadget to a compound string. Refer to **XmString(3X)** for more information on the creation and the structure of compound strings.

XmNlabelType

Specifies the label type.

- **XmSTRING** — text displays **XmNlabelString**

- **XmPIXMAP** — icon data in pixmap displays **XmNlabelPixmap** or **XmNlabelInsensitivePixmap**

XmNmarginBottom

Specifies the amount of spacing between the bottom of the label text and the top of the bottom margin (specified by **XmNmarginHeight**). This may be modified by LabelGadget's subclasses. For example, CascadeButtonGadget may increase this field to make room for the cascade pixmap.

XmNmarginHeight

Specifies the amount of spacing between the top of the label (specified by **XmNmarginTop**) and the bottom edge of the top shadow, and the amount of spacing between the bottom of the label (specified by **XmNmarginBottom**) and the top edge of the bottom shadow.

XmNmarginLeft

Specifies the amount of spacing between the left edge of the label text and the right side of the left margin (specified by **XmNmarginWidth**). This may be modified by LabelGadget's subclasses. For example, ToggleButtonGadget may increase this field to make room for the toggle indicator and for spacing between the indicator and label. Whether this actually applies to the left or right side of the label may depend on the value of **XmNstringDirection**.

XmNmarginRight

Specifies the amount of spacing between the right edge of the label text and the left side of the right margin (specified by

XmNmarginWidth). This may be modified by LabelGadget's subclasses. For example, CascadeButtonGadget may increase this field to make room for the cascade pixmap. Whether this actually applies to the left or right side of the label may depend on the value of **XmNstringDirection**.

XmNmarginTop

Specifies the amount of spacing between the top of the label text and the bottom of the top margin (specified by **XmNmarginHeight**). This may be modified by LabelGadget's subclasses. For example, CascadeButtonGadget may increase this field to make room for the cascade pixmap.

XmNmarginWidth

Specifies the amount of spacing between the left side of the label (specified by **XmNmarginLeft**) and the right edge of the left shadow, and the amount of spacing between the right side of the label (specified by **XmNmarginRight**) and the left edge of the right shadow.

XmNmnemonic

Provides the user with an alternate means of selecting a button. A button in a MenuBar, a Popup MenuPane, or a Pulldown MenuPane can have a mnemonic.

This resource contains a keysym as listed in the X11 keysym table. The first character in the label string that exactly matches the mnemonic in the character set specified in **XmNmnemonicCharSet** is underlined when the button is displayed.

When a mnemonic has been specified, the user activates the button by pressing the mnemonic key while the button is visible. If the button is a CascadeButtonGadget in a MenuBar and the MenuBar does not have the focus, the user must use the **MAlt** modifier while pressing the mnemonic. The user can activate the button by pressing either the shifted or the unshifted mnemonic key.

XmNmnemonicCharSet
Specifies the character set of the mnemonic for the label. The default is determined dynamically depending on the locale of the widget.

XmNrecomputeSize
Specifies a Boolean value that indicates whether the gadget attempts to be big enough to contain the label. If True, an **XtSetValues** with a resource value that would change the size of the gadget causes the gadget to shrink or expand to exactly fit the label string or pixmap. If False, the gadget never attempts to change size on its own.

XmNstringDirection
Specifies the direction in which the string is to be drawn. The following are the values:

- **XmSTRING_DIRECTION_L_TO_R** — left to right

- **XmSTRING_DIRECTION_R_TO_L** — right to left

The default for this resource is determined at creation time. If no value is specified for this resource and the widget's parent is a manager, the value is inherited from the parent; otherwise, it defaults to **XmSTRING_DIRECTION_L_TO_R**.

Inherited Resources

LabelGadget inherits behavior and resources from the following superclasses. For a complete description of each resource, refer to the man page for that superclass.

XmGadget Resource Set		
Name Class	**Default** Type	**Access**
XmNhelpCallback XmCCallback	NULL XtCallbackList	C
XmNhighlightOnEnter XmCHighlightOnEnter	False Boolean	CSG
XmNhighlightThickness XmCHighlightThickness	0 Dimension	CSG
XmNnavigationType XmCNavigationType	XmNONE XmNavigationType	G
XmNshadowThickness XmCShadowThickness	0 Dimension	CSG
XmNtraversalOn XmCTraversalOn	False Boolean	CSG
XmNuserData XmCUserData	NULL Pointer	CSG

RectObj Resource Set		
Name	**Default**	**Access**
Class	**Type**	
XmNancestorSensitive	dynamic	G
XmCSensitive	Boolean	
XmNborderWidth	0	CSG
XmCBorderWidth	Dimension	
XmNheight	dynamic	CSG
XmCHeight	Dimension	
XmNsensitive	True	CSG
XmCSensitive	Boolean	
XmNwidth	dynamic	CSG
XmCWidth	Dimension	
XmNx	0	CSG
XmCPosition	Position	
XmNy	0	CSG
XmCPosition	Position	

Object Resource Set		
Name	**Default**	**Access**
Class	**Type**	
XmNdestroyCallback	NULL	C
XmCCallback	XtCallbackList	

Behavior

XmLabelGadget includes behavior from XmGadget. Additional XmLabelGadget behavior is described below:

KHelp: In a Popup or Pulldown MenuPane, unposts all menus in the menu hierarchy and, when the shell's keyboard focus policy is **XmEXPLICIT**, restores keyboard focus to the tab group that had the focus before the menu system was entered. Calls the callbacks for **XmNhelpCallback** if any exist. If there are no help callbacks for this widget, this action calls the help callbacks for the nearest ancestor that has them.

MAny KCancel:

In a MenuBar, disarms the CascadeButton and the menu and, when the shell's keyboard focus policy is **XmEXPLICIT**, restores keyboard focus to the tab group that had the focus before the menu was entered.

In a toplevel Pulldown MenuPane from a MenuBar, unposts the menu, disarms the MenuBar CascadeButton and the MenuBar, and, when the shell's keyboard focus policy is **XmEXPLICIT**, restores keyboard focus to the tab group that had the focus before the MenuBar was entered. In other Pulldown MenuPanes, unposts the menu.

In a Popup MenuPane, unposts the menu and, when the shell's keyboard focus policy is **XmEXPLICIT**, restores keyboard focus to the widget from which the menu was posted.

KDown:

In a vertical menu, disarms the current menu entry and arms the entry just below it in the MenuPane. This action wraps within the MenuPane.

In a horizontal menu, if the menu entry is a CascadeButton with a submenu, posts the MenuPane associated with the CascadeButton. Otherwise, this action searches for an ancestor menu that is vertical. If it finds one, it unposts the cascade from the vertical menu and traverses to the next entry toward the bottom in the vertical menu. If this entry is a CascadeButton with a submenu, posts the MenuPane associated with the Cascadeutton. This action wraps within the vertical menu.

KLeft:

In a vertical menu, if the menu's parent is a horizontal menu, this action unposts the current MenuPane and traverses to the next entry to the left in the parent menu. If this entry is a CascadeButton with a submenu, posts the MenuPane associated with the CascadeButton. This action wraps within the horizontal menu. If the menu's parent is a vertical menu, this action unposts the current MenuPane.

> In a horizontal menu, disarms the current menu entry and arms the entry just to the left of it in the menu. This action wraps within the menu.

KRight: In a vertical menu, if the menu entry is a CascadeButton with a submenu, posts the MenuPane associated with the CascadeButton. Otherwise, this action searches for an ancestor menu that is horizontal. If it finds one, it unposts the cascade from the horizontal menu and traverses to the next entry to the right in the horizontal menu. If this entry is a CascadeButton with a submenu, posts the MenuPane associated with the CascadeButton. This action wraps within the horizontal menu.

> In a horizontal menu, disarms the current menu entry and arms the entry just to the right of it in the menu. This action wraps within the menu.

KUp: In a vertical menu, disarms the current menu entry and arms the entry just above it in the MenuPane. This action wraps within the MenuPane.

> In a horizontal menu, if the menu's parent is a vertical menu, this action unposts the current MenuPane and traverses to the next entry toward the top in the parent menu. If this entry is a CascadeButton with a submenu, posts the MenuPane associated with the CascadeButton. This action wraps within the vertical menu. If the menu's parent is a horizontal menu, this action unposts the current MenuPane.

Virtual Bindings

The bindings for virtual keys are vendor specific.

Related Information

Object(3X), **RectObj(3X)**, **XmCreateLabelGadget(3X)**, **XmFontListCreate(3X)**, **XmStringCreate(3X)**, and **XmGadget(3X)**.

XmList

Purpose

The List widget class

AES Support Level

Full-use

Synopsis

#include <Xm/List.h>

Description

List allows a user to select one or more items from a group of choices. Items are selected from the list in a variety of ways, using both the pointer and the keyboard.

List operates on an array of strings that are defined by the application. Each string becomes an item in the List, with the first string becoming the item in position 1, the second string becoming the item in position 2, and so on.

The size of the List is set by specifying the number of items that are visible. To create a list that allows the user to scroll easily through a large number of items, use the **XmCreateScrolledList** convenience function.

If the List has no items at initialization or as a result of **XtSetValues**, it saves the current value of **XmNtraversalOn** and forces **XmNtraversalOn** to False. If **XtSetValues** is called for **XmNtraversalOn** while the List has no items, the List updates the saved value but does not change the **XmNtraversalOn** resource. If the List later has items as a result of **XtSetValues**, it sets **XmNtraversalOn** to the saved value.

To select items, move the pointer or cursor to the desired item and press the **BSelect** mouse button or the key defined as **KSelect**. There are several styles of selection behavior, and they all highlight the selected item or items by displaying them in inverse colors. An appropriate callback is invoked to notify the application of the user's choice. The application then takes whatever action is required for the specified selection.

Selection

Each list has one of four selection models:

- Single Select
- Browse Select
- Multiple Select
- Extended Select

In Single Select and Browse Select, at most one item is selected at a time. In Single Select, pressing **BSelect** on an item toggles its selection state and deselects any other selected item. In Browse Select, pressing **BSelect** on an item selects it and deselects any other selected item; dragging **BSelect** moves the selection along with the cursor.

In Multiple Select, any number of items can be selected at a time. Pressing **BSelect** on an item toggles its selection state but does not deselect any other selected items.

In Extended Select, any number of items can be selected at a time, and the user can easily select ranges of items. Pressing **BSelect** on an item selects it and deselects any other selected item. Dragging **BSelect** or pressing or dragging **BExtend** following a **BSelect** action selects all items between the item under the pointer and the item on which **BSelect** was pressed. This action also deselects any other selected items outside that range.

Extended Select also allows the user to select and deselect discontiguous ranges of items. Pressing **BToggle** on an item toggles its selection state but does not deselect any other selected items. Dragging **BToggle** or pressing or dragging **BExtend** following a **BToggle** action sets the selection state of all items between the item under the pointer and the item on which **BToggle** was pressed to the state of the item on which **BToggle** was pressed. This action does not deselect any other selected items outside that range.

All selection operations available from the mouse are also available from the keyboard. List has two keyboard selection modes, Normal Mode and Add Mode. In Normal Mode, navigation operations and **KSelect** select the item at the location cursor and deselect any other selected items. In Add Mode, navigation operations have no effect on selection, and **KSelect** toggles the selection state of the item at the location cursor without deselecting any other selected items.

Single and Multiple Select use Add Mode, and Browse Select uses Normal Mode.

Extended Select can use either mode; the user changes modes by pressing **KAddMode**. In Extended Select Normal Mode, pressing **KSelect** has the same effect as pressing **BSelect**; **KExtend** and shifted navigation have the same effect as pressing **BExtend** following a **BSelect** action. In Extended Select Add Mode, pressing **KSelect** has the same effect as pressing **BToggle**; **KExtend** and shifted navigation have the same effect as pressing **BExtend** following a **BToggle** action.

Normal Mode is indicated by a solid location cursor, and Add Mode is indicated by a dashed location cursor.

Classes

List inherits behavior and resources from **Core** and **XmPrimitive** classes.

The class pointer is **xmListWidgetClass**.

The class name is **XmList**.

New Resources

The following table defines a set of widget resources used by the programmer to specify data. The programmer can also set the resource values for the inherited classes to set attributes for this widget. To reference a resource by name or by class in a .Xdefaults file, remove the **XmN** or **XmC** prefix and use the remaining letters. To specify one of the defined values for a resource in a .Xdefaults file, remove the **Xm** prefix and use the remaining letters (in either lowercase or uppercase, but include any underscores between words). The codes in the access column indicate if the given resource can be set at creation time (**C**), set by using **XtSetValues** (**S**), retrieved by using **XtGetValues** (**G**), or is not applicable (**N/A**).

XmList Resource Set		
Name	**Default**	**Access**
Class	**Type**	
XmNautomaticSelection	False	CSG
XmCAutomaticSelection	Boolean	
XmNbrowseSelectionCallback	NULL	C
XmCCallback	XtCallbackList	
XmNdefaultActionCallback	NULL	C
XmCCallback	XtCallbackList	
XmNextendedSelectionCallback	NULL	C
XmCCallback	XtCallbackList	
XmNfontList	dynamic	CSG
XmCFontList	XmFontList	
XmNitemCount	0	CSG
XmCItemCount	int	
XmNitems	NULL	CSG
XmCItems	XmStringTable	
XmNlistMarginHeight	0	CSG
XmCListMarginHeight	Dimension	
XmNlistMarginWidth	0	CSG
XmCListMarginWidth	Dimension	
XmNlistSizePolicy	XmVARIABLE	CG
XmCListSizePolicy	unsigned char	
XmNlistSpacing	0	CSG
XmCListSpacing	Dimension	
XmNmultipleSelectionCallback	NULL	C
XmCCallback	XtCallbackList	
XmNscrollBarDisplayPolicy	XmAS_NEEDED	CSG
XmCScrollBarDisplayPolicy	unsigned char	

Name	Default	Access
Class	Type	
XmNselectedItemCount	0	CSG
XmCSelectedItemCount	int	
XmNselectedItems	NULL	CSG
XmCSelectedItems	XmStringTable	
XmNselectionPolicy	XmBROWSE_SELECT	CSG
XmCSelectionPolicy	unsigned char	
XmNsingleSelectionCallback	NULL	C
XmCCallback	XtCallbackList	
XmNstringDirection	dynamic	CSG
XmCStringDirection	XmStringDirection	
XmNtopItemPosition	1	CSG
XmCTopItemPosition	int	
XmNvisibleItemCount	1	CSG
XmCVisibleItemCount	int	

XmNautomaticSelection

Invokes **XmNsingleSelectionCallback** when the user moves into a new item if the value is True and the selection mode is either **XmBROWSE_SELECT** or **XmEXTENDED_SELECT**. If False, no selection callbacks are invoked until the user releases the mouse button. See the Behavior section for further details on the interaction of this resource with the selection modes.

XmNbrowseSelectionCallback

Specifies a list of callbacks that is called when an item is selected in the browse selection mode. The reason is **XmCR_BROWSE_SELECT**.

XmNdefaultActionCallback

Specifies a list of callbacks that is called when an item is double clicked. The reason is **XmCR_DEFAULT_ACTION**.

XmNextendedSelectionCallback

Specifies a list of callbacks that is called when items are selected using the extended selection mode. The reason is **XmCR_EXTENDED_SELECT**.

XmNfontList

Specifies the font list associated with the list items. This is used in conjunction with the **XmNvisibleItemCount** resource to determine the height of the List widget. If this value is NULL at initialization, it is initialized by looking up the parent hierarchy of the widget for an ancestor that is a subclass of the XmBulletinBoard, VendorShell, or XmMenuShell widget class. If such an ancestor is found, the font list is initialized to the appropriate default font list of the ancestor widget (XmNdefaultFontList for VendorShell and XmMenuShell, XmNtextFontList for XmBulletinBoard).

XmNitemCount

Specifies the total number of items. The value must be the number of items in **XmNitems** and must not be negative. It is automatically updated by the list whenever an item is added to or deleted from the list.

XmNitems   Points to an array of compound strings that are to be displayed as the list items. Refer to **XmString(3X)** for more information on the creation and structure of compound strings.

XmNlistMarginHeight

Specifies the height of the margin between the list border and the items.

XmNlistMarginWidth

Specifies the width of the margin between the list border and the items.

XmNlistSizePolicy

Controls the reaction of the List when an item grows horizontally beyond the current size of the list work area. If the value is **XmCONSTANT**, the list viewing area does not grow, and a horizontal ScrollBar is added for a ScrolledList. If this resource is set to **XmVARIABLE**, the List grows to match the size of the longest item, and no horizontal ScrollBar appears.

When the value of this resource is **XmRESIZE_IF_POSSIBLE**, the List attempts to grow or shrink to match the width of the widest item. If it cannot grow to match the widest size, a horizontal ScrollBar is added for a ScrolledList if the longest item is wider than the list viewing area.

The size policy must be set at the time the List widget is created. It cannot be changed at a later time through **XtSetValues**.

XmNlistSpacing

Specifies the spacing between list items. This spacing increases by the value of the **XmNhighlightThickness** resource in Primitive.

XmNmultipleSelectionCallback

Specifies a list of callbacks that is called when an item is selected in multiple selection mode. The reason is **XmCR_MULTIPLE_SELECT**.

XmNscrollBarDisplayPolicy
> Controls the display of vertical ScrollBars in a ScrolledList. When the value of this resource is **XmAS_NEEDED**, a vertical ScrollBar is displayed only when the number of items in the List exceeds the number of Visible items. When the value is **XmSTATIC**, a vertical ScrollBar is always displayed.

XmNselectedItemCount
> Specifies the number of strings in the selected items list. The value must be the number of items in **XmNselectedItems** and must not be negative.

XmNselectedItems
> Points to an array of compound strings that represents the list items that are currently selected, either by the user or by the application.

XmNselectionPolicy
> Defines the interpretation of the selection action. This can be one of the following:
>
> - **XmSINGLE_SELECT** — allows only single selections
> - **XmMULTIPLE_SELECT** — allows multiple selections
> - **XmEXTENDED_SELECT** — allows extended selections
> - **XmBROWSE_SELECT** — allows PM "drag and browse" functionality

XmNsingleSelectionCallback
> Specifies a list of callbacks that is called when an item is selected in single selection mode. The reason is **XmCR_SINGLE_SELECT**.

XmNstringDirection

Specifies the initial direction to draw the string. The values are **XmSTRING_DIRECTION_L_TO_R** and **XmSTRING_DIRECTION_R_TO_L**. The value of this resource is determined at creation time. If the widget's parent is a manager, this value is inherited from the widget's parent, otherwise it is set to XmSTRING_DIRECTION_L_TO_R.

XmNtopItemPosition

Specifies the position of the item that is the first visible item in the list. Setting this resource is equivalent to calling the **XmListSetPos** function. The position of the first item in the list is 1; the position of the second item is 2; and so on. A position of 0 specifies the last item in the list. The value must not be negative.

XmNvisibleItemCount

Specifies the number of items that can fit in the visible space of the list work area. The List uses this value to determine its height. The value must be greater than 0.

Inherited Resources

List inherits behavior and resources from the following superclasses. For a complete description of each resource, refer to the man page for that superclass.

XmPrimitive Resource Set		
Name	**Default**	**Access**
Class	**Type**	
XmNbottomShadowColor	dynamic	CSG
XmCBottomShadowColor	Pixel	
XmNbottomShadowPixmap	XmUNSPECIFIED_PIXMAP	CSG
XmCBottomShadowPixmap	Pixmap	
XmNforeground	dynamic	CSG
XmCForeground	Pixel	
XmNhelpCallback	NULL	C
XmCCallback	XtCallbackList	
XmNhighlightColor	dynamic	CSG
XmCHighlightColor	Pixel	
XmNhighlightOnEnter	False	CSG
XmCHighlightOnEnter	Boolean	
XmNhighlightPixmap	dynamic	CSG
XmCHighlightPixmap	Pixmap	
XmNhighlightThickness	2	CSG
XmCHighlightThickness	Dimension	
XmNnavigationType	XmTAB_GROUP	G
XmCNavigationType	XmNavigationType	
XmNshadowThickness	2	CSG
XmCShadowThickness	Dimension	
XmNtopShadowColor	dynamic	CSG
XmCTopShadowColor	Pixel	
XmNtopShadowPixmap	dynamic	CSG
XmCTopShadowPixmap	Pixmap	
XmNtraversalOn	dynamic	CSG
XmCTraversalOn	Boolean	
XmNuserData	NULL	CSG
XmCUserData	Pointer	

Core Resource Set		
Name	**Default**	**Access**
Class	**Type**	
XmNaccelerators	dynamic	CSG
XmCAccelerators	XtAccelerators	
XmNancestorSensitive	dynamic	G
XmCSensitive	Boolean	
XmNbackground	dynamic	CSG
XmCBackground	Pixel	
XmNbackgroundPixmap	XmUNSPECIFIED_PIXMAP	CSG
XmCPixmap	Pixmap	
XmNborderColor	XtDefaultForeground	CSG
XmCBorderColor	Pixel	
XmNborderPixmap	XmUNSPECIFIED_PIXMAP	CSG
XmCPixmap	Pixmap	
XmNborderWidth	0	CSG
XmCBorderWidth	Dimension	
XmNcolormap	dynamic	CG
XmCColormap	Colormap	
XmNdepth	dynamic	CG
XmCDepth	int	
XmNdestroyCallback	NULL	C
XmCCallback	XtCallbackList	
XmNheight	dynamic	CSG
XmCHeight	Dimension	
XmNinitialResourcesPersistent	True	C
XmCInitialResourcesPersistent	Boolean	
XmNmappedWhenManaged	True	CSG
XmCMappedWhenManaged	Boolean	
XmNscreen	dynamic	CG
XmCScreen	Screen *	

Name	Default	Access
Class	Type	
XmNsensitive	True	CSG
XmCSensitive	Boolean	
XmNtranslations	dynamic	CSG
XmCTranslations	XtTranslations	
XmNwidth	dynamic	CSG
XmCWidth	Dimension	
XmNx	0	CSG
XmCPosition	Position	
XmNy	0	CSG
XmCPosition	Position	

Callback Information

List defines a new callback structure. The application must first look at the reason field and use only the structure members that are valid for that particular reason, because not all fields are relevant for every possible reason. The callback structure is defined as follows:

```
typedef struct
{
    int             reason;
    XEvent          *event;
    XmString        item;
    int             item_length;
    int             item_position;
    XmString        *selected_items;
    int             selected_item_count;
    int             *selected_item_positions;
    int             selection_type;
} XmListCallbackStruct;
```

reason	Indicates why the callback was invoked.
event	Points to the **XEvent** that triggered the callback. It can be NULL.
item	Is the last item selected at the time of the *event* that caused the callback. *item* points to a temporary storage space that is reused after the callback is finished. Therefore, if an application needs to save the item, it should copy the item into its own data space.
item_length	Is the length in bytes of *item*.
item_position	Is the position of *item* in the List's **XmNitems** array.
selected_items	Is a list of items selected at the time of the *event* that caused the callback. *selected_items* points to a temporary storage space that is reused after the callback is finished. Therefore, if an application needs to save the selected list, it should copy the list into its own data space.

selected_item_count

Is the number of items in the *selected_items* list.

selected_item_positions

Is an array of integers, one for each selected item, representing the position of each selected item in the List's **XmNitems** array. *selected_item_positions* points to a temporary storage space that is reused after the callback is finished. Therefore, if an application needs to save this array, it should copy the array into its own data space.

selection_type — Indicates that the most recent extended selection was the initial selection (**XmINITIAL**), a modification of an existing selection (**XmMODIFICATION**), or an additional noncontiguous selection (**XmADDITION**).

The following table describes the reasons for which the individual callback structure fields are valid:

Reason	Valid Fields
XmCR_SINGLE_SELECT	*reason, event, item, item_length, item_position*
XmCR_DEFAULT_ACTION	*reason, event, item, item_length, item_position*
XmCR_BROWSE_SELECT	*reason, event, item, item_length, item_position*
XmCR_MULTIPLE_SELECT	*reason, event, item, item_length, item_position, selected_items, selected_item_count, selected_item_positions*
XmCR_EXTENDED_SELECT	*reason, event, item, item_length, item_position, selected_items, selected_item_count, selected_item_positions, selection_type*

Translations

XmList includes translations from Primitive. The XmList translations are listed below. These translations may not directly correspond to a translation table.

BSelect Press:	**ListBeginSelect()**
BSelect Motion:	**ListButtonMotion()**
BSelect Release:	**ListEndSelect()**
BExtend Press:	**ListBeginExtend()**
BExtend Motion:	**ListButtonMotion()**
BExtend Release:	**ListEndExtend()**
BToggle Press:	**ListBeginToggle()**
BToggle Motion:	**ListButtonMotion()**
BToggle Release:	**ListEndToggle()**
KUp:	**ListPrevItem()**
MShift KUp:	**ListExtendPrevItem()**
KDown:	**ListNextItem()**

MShift KDown:	**ListExtendNextItem()**
KLeft:	**ListLeftChar()**
MCtrl KLeft:	**ListLeftPage()**
KRight:	**ListRightChar()**
MCtrl KRight:	**ListRightPage()**
KPageUp:	**ListPrevPage()**
KPageDown:	**ListNextPage()**
KPageLeft:	**ListLeftPage()**
KPageRight:	**ListRightPage()**
KBeginLine:	**ListBeginLine()**
KEndLine:	**ListEndLine()**
KBeginData:	**ListBeginData()**
MShift KBeginData:	**ListBeginDataExtend()**
KEndData:	**ListEndData()**
MShift KEndData:	**ListEndDataExtend()**
KAddMode:	**ListAddMode()**
KActivate:	**ListKbdActivate()**
KSelect Press:	**ListKbdBeginSelect()**
KSelect Release:	**ListKbdEndSelect()**
KExtend Press:	**ListKbdBeginExtend()**
KExtend Release:	**ListKbdEndExtend()**
MAny KCancel:	**ListKbdCancel()**
KSelectAll:	**ListKbdSelectAll()**
KDeselectAll:	**ListKbdDeSelectAll()**
KHelp:	**PrimitiveHelp()**
KNextField	**PrimitiveNextTabGroup()**
KPrevField	**PrimitivePrevTabGroup()**

Action Routines

The XmList action routines are described below. The current selection is always shown with inverted colors.

ListAddMode():
> Toggles the state of Add Mode for keyboard selection.

ListBeginData():
> Moves the location cursor to the first item in the list. In Normal Mode, this also deselects any current selection, selects the first item in the list, and calls the appropriate selection callbacks (**XmNbrowseSelectionCallback** when **XmNselectionPolicy** is set to **XmBROWSE_SELECT**, **XmNextendedSelectionCallback** when **XmNselectionPolicy** is set to **XmEXTENDED_SELECT**).

ListBeginDataExtend():
> If the **XmNselectionPolicy** is set to **XmMULTIPLE_SELECT** or **XmEXTENDED_SELECT**, moves the location cursor to the first item in the list.
>
> If the **XmNselectionPolicy** is set to **XmEXTENDED_SELECT**, does the following: If an extended selection has been made from the current anchor point, restores the selection state of the items in that range to their state before the extended selection was done. Changes the selection state of the first item and all items between it and the current anchor point to the state of the item at the current anchor point. Calls the **XmNextendedSelectionCallback** callbacks.

ListBeginExtend():
> If the **XmNselectionPolicy** is set to **XmEXTENDED_SELECT**, does the following: If an extended selection has been made from the current anchor point, restores the selection state of the items in that range to their state before the extended selection was done. Changes the selection state of the item under the pointer and all items

between it and the current anchor point to the state of the item at the current anchor point. If **XmNautomaticSelection** is set to True, calls the **XmNextendedSelectionCallback** callbacks.

ListBeginLine():
Moves the horizontal scroll region to the beginning of the line.

ListBeginSelect():
If the **XmNselectionPolicy** is set to **XmSINGLE_SELECT**, deselects any current selection and toggles the selection state of the item under the pointer.

If the **XmNselectionPolicy** is set to **XmBROWSE_SELECT**, deselects any current selection and selects the item under the pointer. If **XmNautomaticSelection** is set to True, calls the **XmNbrowseSelectionCallback** callbacks.

If the **XmNselectionPolicy** is set to **XmMULTIPLE_SELECT**, toggles the selection state of the item under the pointer. Any previous selections remain.

If the **XmNselectionPolicy** is set to **XmEXTENDED_SELECT**, deselects any current selection, selects the item under the pointer, and sets the current anchor at that item. If **XmNautomaticSelection** is set to True, calls the **XmNextendedSelectionCallback** callbacks.

ListBeginToggle():
If the **XmNselectionPolicy** is set to **XmEXTENDED_SELECT**, does the following: Moves the current anchor to the item under the pointer without changing the current selection. If the item is unselected, it is selected; if the item is selected, it is unselected. If **XmNautomaticSelection** is set to True, calls the **XmNextendedSelectionCallback** callbacks.

ListButtonMotion():
If the **XmNselectionPolicy** is set to **XmBROWSE_SELECT**, deselects any current selection and selects the item under the pointer. If **XmNautomaticSelection** is set to True and the pointer has entered a new list item, calls the **XmNbrowseSelectionCallback** callbacks.

If the **XmNselectionPolicy** is set to **XmEXTENDED_SELECT**, does the following: If an extended selection is being made and an extended selection has previously been made from the current anchor point, restores the selection state of the items in that range to their state before the previous extended selection was done. Changes the selection state of the item under the pointer and all items between it and the current anchor point to the state of the item at the current anchor point. If **XmNautomaticSelection** is set to True and the pointer has entered a new list item, calls the **XmNextendedSelectionCallback** callbacks.

If the pointer leaves a scrolled list, this action scrolls the list in the direction of the pointer motion.

ListEndData():

Moves the location cursor to the last item in the list. In Normal Mode, this also deselects any current selection, selects the last item in the list, and calls the appropriate selection callbacks (**XmNbrowseSelectionCallback** when **XmNselectionPolicy** is set to **XmBROWSE_SELECT**, **XmNextendedSelectionCallback** when **XmNselectionPolicy** is set to **XmEXTENDED_SELECT**).

ListEndDataExtend():

If the **XmNselectionPolicy** is set to **XmMULTIPLE_SELECT** or **XmEXTENDED_SELECT**, moves the location cursor to the last item in the list.

If the **XmNselectionPolicy** is set to **XmEXTENDED_SELECT**, does the following: If an extended selection has been made from the current anchor point, restores the selection state of the items in that range to their state before the extended selection was done. Changes the selection state of the last item and all items between it and the current anchor point to the state of the item at the current anchor point. Calls the **XmNextendedSelectionCallback** callbacks.

ListEndExtend():

> If the **XmNselectionPolicy** is set to **XmEXTENDED_SELECT**, moves the location cursor to the last item selected or deselected and, if **XmNautomaticSelection** is set to False, calls the **XmNextendedSelectionCallback** callbacks.

ListEndLine():

> Moves the horizontal scroll region to the end of the line.

ListEndSelect():

> If the **XmNselectionPolicy** is set to **XmSINGLE_SELECT** or **XmMULTIPLE_SELECT**, moves the location cursor to the last item selected or deselected and calls the appropriate selection callbacks (**XmNsingleSelectionCallback** when **XmNselectionPolicy** is set to **XmSINGLE_SELECT**, **XmNmultipleSelectionCallback** when **XmNselectionPolicy** is set to **XmMULTIPLE_SELECT**).
>
> If the **XmNselectionPolicy** is set to **XmBROWSE_SELECT** or **XmEXTENDED_SELECT**, moves the location cursor to the last item selected or deselected and, if **XmNautomaticSelection** is set to False, calls the appropriate selection callbacks (**XmNbrowseSelectionCallback** when **XmNselectionPolicy** is set to **XmBROWSE_SELECT**, **XmNextendedSelectionCallback** when **XmNselectionPolicy** is set to **XmEXTENDED_SELECT**).

ListEndToggle():

> If the **XmNselectionPolicy** is set to **XmEXTENDED_SELECT**, moves the location cursor to the last item selected or deselected and, if **XmNautomaticSelection** is set to False, calls the **XmNextendedSelectionCallback** callbacks.

ListExtendNextItem():

> If the **XmNselectionPolicy** is set to **XmEXTENDED_SELECT**, does the following: If an extended selection has been made from the current anchor point, restores the selection state of the items in that range to their state before the extended selection was done. Moves the

location cursor to the next item and changes the selection state of the item and all items between it and the current anchor point to the state of the item at the current anchor point. Calls the **XmNextendedSelectionCallback** callbacks.

ListExtendPrevItem():

If the **XmNselectionPolicy** is set to **XmEXTENDED_SELECT**, does the following: If an extended selection has been made from the current anchor point, restores the selection state of the items in that range to their state before the extended selection was done. Moves the location cursor to the previous item and changes the selection state of the item and all items between it and the current anchor point to the state of the item at the current anchor point. Calls the **XmNextendedSelectionCallback** callbacks.

ListKbdActivate():

Calls the callbacks for **XmNdefaultActionCallback**.

ListKbdBeginExtend():

If the **XmNselectionPolicy** is set to **XmEXTENDED_SELECT**, does the following: If an extended selection has been made from the current anchor point, restores the selection state of the items in that range to their state before the extended selection was done. Changes the selection state of the item at the location cursor and all items between it and the current anchor point to the state of the item at the current anchor point.

ListKbdBeginSelect():

If the **XmNselectionPolicy** is set to **XmSINGLE_SELECT**, deselects any current selection and toggles the state of the item at the location cursor.

If the **XmNselectionPolicy** is set to **XmBROWSE_SELECT**, deselects any current selection and selects the item at the location cursor. If **XmNautomaticSelection** is set to True, calls the **XmNbrowseSelectionCallback** callbacks.

If the **XmNselectionPolicy** is set to **XmMULTIPLE_SELECT**, toggles the selection state of the item at the location cursor. Any previous selections remain.

If the **XmNselectionPolicy** is set to **XmEXTENDED_SELECT**, moves the current anchor to the item at the location cursor. In Normal Mode, deselects any current selection and selects the item at the location cursor. In Add Mode, toggles the selection state of the item at the location cursor and leaves the current selection unchanged. If **XmNautomaticSelection** is set to True, calls the **XmNextendedSelectionCallback** callbacks.

ListKbdCancel():

If the **XmNselectionPolicy** is set to **XmEXTENDED_SELECT** and an extended selection is being made from the current anchor point, cancels the new selection and restores the selection state of the items in that range to their state before the extended selection was done.

ListKbdDeSelectAll():

If the **XmNselectionPolicy** is set to **XmSINGLE_SELECT**, **XmMULTIPLE_SELECT**, or **XmEXTENDED_SELECT** in Add Mode, deselects all items in the list. If the **XmNselectionPolicy** is set to **XmEXTENDED_SELECT** in Normal Mode, deselects all items in the list (except the item at the location cursor if the shell's **XmNkeyboardFocusPolicy** is **XmEXPLICIT**). Calls the appropriate selection callbacks (**XmNsingleSelectionCallback** when **XmNselectionPolicy** is set to **XmSINGLE_SELECT**, **XmNmultipleSelectionCallback** when **XmNselectionPolicy** is set to **XmMULTIPLE_SELECT**, **XmNextendedSelectionCallback** when **XmNselectionPolicy** is set to **XmEXTENDED_SELECT**).

ListKbdEndExtend():

If the **XmNselectionPolicy** is set to **XmEXTENDED_SELECT** and if **XmNautomaticSelection** is set to False, calls the **XmNextendedSelectionCallback** callbacks.

ListKbdEndSelect():

> If the **XmNselectionPolicy** is set to **XmSINGLE_SELECT** or **XmMULTIPLE_SELECT** or if **XmNautomaticSelection** is set to False, calls the appropriate selection callbacks (**XmNsingleSelectionCallback** when **XmNselectionPolicy** is set to **XmSINGLE_SELECT**, **XmNbrowseSelectionCallback** when **XmNselectionPolicy** is set to **XmBROWSE_SELECT**, **XmNmultipleSelectionCallback** when **XmNselectionPolicy** is set to **XmMULTIPLE_SELECT**, **XmNextendedSelectionCallback** when **XmNselectionPolicy** is set to **XmEXTENDED_SELECT**).

ListKbdSelectAll():

> If the **XmNselectionPolicy** is set to **XmSINGLE_SELECT** or **XmBROWSE_SELECT**, selects the item at the location cursor. If the **XmNselectionPolicy** is set to **XmEXTENDED_SELECT** or **XmMULTIPLE_SELECT**, selects all items in the list. Calls the appropriate selection callbacks (**XmNsingleSelectionCallback** when **XmNselectionPolicy** is set to **XmSINGLE_SELECT**, **XmNbrowseSelectionCallback** when **XmNselectionPolicy** is set to **XmBROWSE_SELECT**, **XmNmultipleSelectionCallback** when **XmNselectionPolicy** is set to **XmMULTIPLE_SELECT**, **XmNextendedSelectionCallback** when **XmNselectionPolicy** is set to **XmEXTENDED_SELECT**).

ListLeftChar():
> Scrolls the list one character to the left.

ListLeftPage():
> Scrolls the list one page to the left.

ListNextItem():
> Moves the location cursor to the next item in the list.

> If the **XmNselectionPolicy** is set to **XmBROWSE_SELECT**, this action also selects the next item, deselects any current selection, and calls the **XmNbrowseSelectionCallback** callbacks.

If the **XmNselectionPolicy** is set to **XmEXTENDED_SELECT**, this action in Normal Mode also selects the next item, deselects any current selection, moves the current anchor to the next item, and calls the **XmNextendedSelectionCallback** callbacks. In Add Mode this action does not affect the selection or the anchor.

ListNextPage():

Scrolls the list to the next page, moving the location cursor to a new item.

If the **XmNselectionPolicy** is set to **XmBROWSE_SELECT**, this action also selects the new item, deselects any current selection, and calls the **XmNbrowseSelectionCallback** callbacks.

If the **XmNselectionPolicy** is set to **XmEXTENDED_SELECT**, this action in Normal Mode also selects the new item, deselects any current selection, moves the current anchor to the new item, and calls the **XmNextendedSelectionCallback** callbacks. In Add Mode this action does not affect the selection or the anchor.

ListPrevItem():

Moves the location cursor to the previous item in the list.

If the **XmNselectionPolicy** is set to **XmBROWSE_SELECT**, this action also selects the previous item, deselects any current selection, and calls the **XmNbrowseSelectionCallback** callbacks.

If the **XmNselectionPolicy** is set to **XmEXTENDED_SELECT**, this action in Normal Mode also selects the previous item, deselects any current selection, moves the current anchor to the previous item, and calls the **XmNextendedSelectionCallback** callbacks. In Add Mode this action does not affect the selection or the anchor.

ListPrevPage():
> Scrolls the list to the previous page, moving the location cursor to a new item.
>
> If the **XmNselectionPolicy** is set to **XmBROWSE_SELECT**, this action also selects the new item, deselects any current selection, and calls the **XmNbrowseSelectionCallback** callbacks.
>
> If the **XmNselectionPolicy** is set to **XmEXTENDED_SELECT**, this action in Normal Mode also selects the new item, deselects any current selection, moves the current anchor to the new item, and calls the **XmNextendedSelectionCallback** callbacks. In Add Mode this action does not affect the selection or the anchor.

ListRightChar():
> Scrolls the list one character to the right.

ListRightPage():
> Scrolls the list one page to the right.

PrimitiveHelp():
> Calls the callbacks for **XmNhelpCallback** if any exist. If there are no help callbacks for this widget, this action calls the help callbacks for the nearest ancestor that has them.

PrimitiveNextTabGroup():
> Moves the focus to the first item contained within the next tab group. If the current tab group is the last entry in the tab group list, it wraps to the beginning of the tab group list.

PrimitivePrevTabGroup():
> Moves the focus to the first item contained within the previous tab group. If the beginning of the tab group list is reached, it wraps to the end of the tab group list.

Additional Behavior

The List widget has the additional behavior described below:

<Double Click>
> If a button click is followed by another button click within the time span specified by the display's multi-click time, the List interprets that as a double click and calls the callbacks for **XmNdefaultActionCallback**. The item's colors invert to indicate that it is selected.

<FocusIn>: If the focus policy is Explicit, sets the focus and draw the location cursor.

<FocusOut>:
> If the focus policy is Explicit, removes the focus and erase the location cursor.

Virtual Bindings

The bindings for virtual keys are vendor specific.

Related Information

Core(3X), XmCreateList(3X), XmCreateScrolledList(3X), XmListAddItem(3X), XmListAddItemUnselected(3X), XmListDeleteItem(3X), XmListDeletePos(3X), XmListDeselectItem(3X), XmListDeselectAllItems(3X), XmListSelectItem(3X), XmListSetHorizPos(3X), XmListSetItem(3X), XmListSetPos(3X), XmListSetBottomItem(3X), XmListSetBottomPos(3X), XmListSelectPos(3X), XmListDeselectPos(3X), XmListItemExists(3X), and XmPrimitive(3X).

XmListAddItem

Purpose

A List function that adds an item to the list

AES Support Level

Full-use

Synopsis

#include <Xm/List.h>

void XmListAddItem (*widget, item, position*)
    Widget   *widget*;
    XmString   *item*;
    int   *position*;

Description

XmListAddItem adds an item to the list at the given position. When the item is inserted into the list, it is compared with the current **XmNselectedItems** list. If the new item matches an item on the selected list, it appears selected.

     widget   Specifies the ID of the List to which an item is added.

     item   Specifies the item to be added to the list.

     position   Specifies the position of the new item in the list. A value of 1 makes the new item the first item in the list; a value of 2 makes it the second item; and so on. A value of 0 makes the new item the last item in the list.

For a complete definition of List and its associated resources, see **XmList(3X)**.

Related Information

XmList(3X).

XmListAddItems

Purpose

A List function that adds items to the list

AES Support Level

Trial-use

Synopsis

#include <Xm/List.h>

void XmListAddItems (*widget, items, item_count, position*)
    Widget   *widget*;
    XmString **items*;
    int   *item_count*;
    int   *position*;

Description

XmListAddItems adds the specified items to the list at the given position. The first *item_count* items of the *items* array are added to the list. When the items are inserted into the list, they are compared with the current **XmNselectedItems** list. If the any of the new items matches an item on the selected list, it appears selected.

widget   Specifies the ID of the **XmList**.

items   Specifies a pointer to the items to be added to the list.

item_count
        Specifies the number of items in *items*.

position   Specifies the position of the first new item in the list. A value of 1 makes the first new item the first item in the list; a value of 2 makes it the second item; and so on. A value of 0 makes the first new item follow the last item in the list.

For a complete definition of List and its associated resources, see **XmList(3X)**.

Related Information

XmList(3X).

XmListAddItemUnselected

Purpose

A List function that adds an item to the list

AES Support Level

Full-use

Synopsis

#include <Xm/List.h>

void XmListAddItemUnselected (*widget, item, position*)
    Widget   *widget*;
    XmString   *item*;
    int   *position*;

Description

XmListAddItemUnselected adds an item to the list at the given position. The item does not appear selected, even if it matches an item in the current **XmNselectedItems** list.

widget   Specifies the ID of the List from whose list an item is added.

item   Specifies the item to be added to the list.

position   Specifies the position of the new item in the list. A value of 1 makes the new item the first item in the list; a value of 2 makes it the second item; and so on. A value of 0 makes the new item the last item in the list.

For a complete definition of List and its associated resources, see **XmList(3X)**.

Related Information

XmList(3X).

XmListDeleteAllItems

Purpose

A List function that deletes all items from the list

AES Support Level

Trial-use

Synopsis

#include <Xm/List.h>

void XmListDeleteAllItems (*widget*)
   Widget   *widget*;

Description

XmListDeleteAllItems deletes all items from the list.

widget   Specifies the ID of the List from whose list the items are deleted

For a complete definition of List and its associated resources, see **XmList(3X)**.

Related Information

XmList(3X).

XmListDeleteItem

Purpose

A List function that deletes an item from the list

AES Support Level

Full-use

Synopsis

#include <Xm/List.h>

void **XmListDeleteItem** (*widget, item*)
    Widget   *widget*;
    XmString   *item*;

Description

XmListDeleteItem deletes a specified item from the list. A warning message appears if the item does not exist.

widget   Specifies the ID of the List from whose list an item is deleted

item   Specifies the text of the item to be deleted from the list

For a complete definition of List and its associated resources, see **XmList(3X)**.

Related Information

XmList(3X).

XmListDeleteItems

Purpose

A List function that deletes items from the list

AES Support Level

Full-use

Synopsis

#include <Xm/List.h>

void **XmListDeleteItems** (*widget, items, item_count*)
    Widget   *widget*;
    XmString **items*;
    int   *item_count*;

Description

XmListDeleteItems deletes the specified items from the list. A warning message appears if any of the items do not exist.

widget   Specifies the ID of the List from whose list an item is deleted

items   Specifies a pointer to items to be deleted from the list

item_count
          Specifies the number of elements in *items*

For a complete definition of List and its associated resources, see
XmList(3X).

Related Information

XmList(3X).

XmListDeleteItemsPos

Purpose

A List function that deletes items from the list starting at the given position.

AES Support Level

Full-use

Synopsis

#include <Xm/List.h>

void **XmListDeleteItemsPos** (*widget, item_count, position*)
    Widget   *widget*;
    int   *item_count*;
    int   *position*;

Description

XmListDeleteItemsPos deletes the specified number of items from the list starting at the specified position.

widget   Specifies the ID of the List from whose list an item is deleted.

item_count
        Specifies the number of items to be deleted.

position   Specifies the position in the list of the first item to be deleted. A value of 1 indicates that the first deleted item is the first item in the list; a value of 2 indicates that it is the second item; and so on.

For a complete definition of List and its associated resources, see **XmList(3X)**.

Related Information

XmList(3X).

XmListDeletePos

Purpose

A List function that deletes an item from a list at a specified position.

AES Support Level

Full-use

Synopsis

#include <Xm/List.h>

void XmListDeletePos (*widget, position*)
    Widget   *widget*;
    int   *position*;

Description

XmListDeletePos deletes an item at a specified position. A warning message appears if the position does not exist.

widget   Specifies the ID of the List from which an item is to be deleted.

position   Specifies the position of the item to be deleted. A value of 1 indicates that the first item in the list is deleted; a value of 2 indicates that the second item is deleted; and so on. A value of 0 indicates that the last item in the list is deleted.

For a complete definition of List and its associated resources, see **XmList(3X)**.

Related Information

XmList(3X).

XmListDeselectAllItems

Purpose

A List function that unhighlights and removes all items from the selected list.

AES Support Level

Full-use

Synopsis

#include <Xm/List.h>

void XmListDeselectAllItems (*widget*)
    Widget   *widget*;

Description

XmListDeselectAllItems unhighlights and removes all items from the selected list.

widget   Specifies the ID of the List widget from whose list all selected items are deselected

For a complete definition of List and its associated resources, see **XmList(3X)**.

Related Information

XmList(3X).

XmListDeselectItem

Purpose

A List function that deselects the specified item from the selected list.

AES Support Level

Full-use

Synopsis

#include <Xm/List.h>

void **XmListDeselectItem** (*widget, item*)
    Widget   *widget*;
    XmString   *item*;

Description

XmListDeselectItem unhighlights and removes the specified item from the selected list.

widget   Specifies the ID of the List from whose list an item is deselected

item   Specifies the item to be deselected from the list

For a complete definition of List and its associated resources, see **XmList(3X)**.

Related Information

XmList(3X).

XmListDeselectPos

Purpose

A List function that deselects an item at a specified position in the list.

AES Support Level

Full-use

Synopsis

#include <Xm/List.h>

void XmListDeselectPos (*widget, position*)
    Widget   *widget*;
    int   *position*;

Description

XmListDeselectPos unhighlights the item at the specified position and deletes it from the list of selected items.

widget   Specifies the ID of the List widget

position   Specifies the position of the item to be deselected. A value of 1 indicates that the first item in the list is deselected; a value of 2 indicates that the second item is deselected; and so on. A value of 0 indicates that the last item in the list is deselected.

For a complete definition of List and its associated resources, see **XmList(3X)**.

Related Information

XmList(3X).

XmListGetMatchPos

Purpose

A List function that returns all instances of an item in the list.

AES Support Level

Trial-use

Synopsis

#include <Xm/List.h>

Boolean XmListGetMatchPos (*widget, item, position_list, position_count*)
    Widget   *widget*;
    XmString   *item*;
    int   ***position_list**;
    int   **position_count*;

Description

XmListGetMatchPos is a Boolean function that returns an array of positions where a specified item is found in a List.

widget   Specifies the ID of the List widget.

item   Specifies the item to search for.

position_list

Returns an array of positions at which the item occurs in the List. The position of the first item in the list is 1; the position of the second item is 2; and so on. When the return value is TRUE, **XmListGetMatchPos** allocates memory for this array. The caller is responsible for freeing this memory.

position_count

Returns the number of elements in the *position_list*.

For a complete definition of List and its associated resources, see **XmList(3X)**.

Return Value

Returns TRUE if the specified item is present in the list, and FALSE if it is not.

Related Information

XmList(3X).

XmListGetSelectedPos

Purpose

A List function that returns the position of every selected item in the list.

AES Support Level

Trial-use

Synopsis

#include <Xm/List.h>

Boolean XmListGetSelectedPos (*widget, position_list, position_count*)
    Widget   *widget*;
    int   *******position_list*;
    int   ******position_count*;

Description

XmListGetSelectedPos is a Boolean function that returns an array of the positions of the selected items in a List.

widget   Specifies the ID of the List widget.

position_list

        Returns an array of the positions of the selected items in the List. The position of the first item in the list is 1; the position of the second item is 2; and so on. When the return value is TRUE,

XmListGetSelectedPos allocates memory for this array. The caller is responsible for freeing this memory.

position_count
Returns the number of elements in the *position_list*.

For a complete definition of List and its associated resources, see **XmList(3X)**.

Return Value

Returns TRUE if the list has any selected items, and FALSE if it does not.

Related Information

XmList(3X).

XmListItemExists

Purpose

A List function that checks if a specified item is in the list.

AES Support Level

Full-use

Synopsis

#include <Xm/List.h>

Boolean XmListItemExists (*widget, item*)
    Widget   *widget*;
    XmString *item*;

Description

XmListItemExists is a Boolean function that checks if a specified item is present in the list.

widget   Specifies the ID of the List widget

item   Specifies the item whose presence is checked

For a complete definition of List and its associated resources, see **XmList(3X)**.

Return Value

Returns True if the specified item is present in the list.

Related Information

XmList(3X).

XmListItemPos

Purpose

A List function that returns the position of an item in the list.

AES Support Level

Trial-use

Synopsis

#include <Xm/List.h>

int XmListItemPos (*widget, item*)
    Widget   *widget*;
    XmString *item*;

Description

XmListItemPos returns the position of the first instance of the specified item in a List.

widget   Specifies the ID of the List widget

item   Specifies the item whose position is returned

For a complete definition of List and its associated resources, see **XmList(3X)**.

Return Value

Returns the position in the list of the first instance of the specified item. The position of the first item in the list is 1; the position of the second item is 2; and so on. This function returns 0 if the item is not found.

Related Information

XmList(3X).

XmListReplaceItems

Purpose

A List function that replaces the specified elements in the list.

AES Support Level

Trial-use

Synopsis

#include <Xm/List.h>

void XmListReplaceItems (*widget, old_items, item_count, new_items*)
    Widget   *widget*;
    XmString   **old_items*;
    int   *item_count*;
    XmString   **new_items*;

Description

XmListReplaceItems replaces each specified item of the list with a corresponding new item.

widget   Specifies the ID of the List widget

old_items

          Specifies the items to be replaced

item_count
>   Specifies the number of items in *old_items* and *new_items*

new_items
>   Specifies the replacement items

Every occurrence of each element of *old_items* is replaced with the corresponding element from *new_items*.

For a complete definition of List and its associated resources, see **XmList(3X)**.

Related Information

XmList(3X).

XmListReplaceItemsPos

Purpose

A List function that replaces the specified elements in the list.

AES Support Level

Trial-use

Synopsis

#include <Xm/List.h>

void XmListReplaceItemsPos (*widget, new_items, item_count, position*)
    Widget   *widget*;
    XmString   *new_items*;
    int   *item_count*;
    int   *position*;

Description

XmListReplaceItemsPos replaces the specified number of items of the List with new items, starting at the specified position in the List.

widget   Specifies the ID of the List widget.

new_items
         Specifies the replacement items.

item_count
> Specifies the number of items in *new_items* and the number of items in the list to replace.

position Specifies the position of the first item in the list to be replaced. A value of 1 indicates that the first item replaced is the first item in the list; a value of 2 indicates that it is the second item; and so on.

Beginning with the item specified in *position*, *item_count* items in the list are replaced with the corresponding elements from *new_items*.

For a complete definition of List and its associated resources, see **XmList(3X)**.

Related Information

XmList(3X).

XmListSelectItem

Purpose

A List function that selects an item in the list

AES Support Level

Full-use

Synopsis

#include <Xm/List.h>

void XmListSelectItem (*widget, item, notify*)
    Widget   *widget*;
    XmString *item*;
    Boolean   *notify*;

Description

> **XmListSelectItem** highlights and adds the specified item to the current selected list.

> *widget* Specifies the ID of the List widget from whose list an item is selected
>
> *item* Specifies the item to be added to the List widget
>
> *notify* Specifies a Boolean value that when True invokes the selection callback for the current mode. From an application interface view, calling this function with *notify* True is indistinguishable from a user-initiated selection action.

> For a complete definition of List and its associated resources, see **XmList(3X)**.

Related Information

> **XmList(3X)**.

XmListSelectPos

Purpose

A List function that selects an item at a specified position in the list.

AES Support Level

Full-use

Synopsis

#include <Xm/List.h>

void XmListSelectPos (*widget, position, notify*)
    Widget   *widget*;
    int   *position*;
    Boolean   *notify*;

Description

XmListSelectPos highlights a List item at the specified position and adds it to the list of selected items.

widget   Specifies the ID of the List widget.

position Specifies the position of the item to be selected. A value of 1 indicates that the first item in the list is selected; a value of 2 indicates that the second item is selected; and so on. A value of 0 indicates that the last item in the list is selected.

notify   Specifies a Boolean value that when True invokes the selection callback for the current mode. From an application interface view, calling this function with *notify* True is indistinguishable from a user-initiated selection action.

For a complete definition of List and its associated resources, see **XmList(3X)**.

Related Information

XmList(3X).

XmListSetAddMode

Purpose

A List function that sets add mode in the list

AES Support Level

Trial-use

Synopsis

#include <Xm/List.h>

void XmListSetAddMode (*widget, mode*)
    Widget   *widget*;
    Boolean   *mode*;

Description

XmListSetAddMode allows applications control over Add Mode in the extended selection model.

widget   Specifies the ID of the List widget

item   Specifies whether to activate or deactivate Add Mode. If *item* is True, Add Mode is activated. If *item* is False, Add Mode is deactivated.

For a complete definition of List and its associated resources, see
XmList(3X).

Related Information

XmList(3X).

XmListSetBottomItem

Purpose

A List function that makes an existing item the last visible item in the list.

AES Support Level

Full-use

Synopsis

#include <Xm/List.h>

void XmListSetBottomItem (*widget, item*)
    Widget   *widget*;
    XmString   *item*;

Description

XmListSetBottomItem makes an existing item the last visible item in the list. The item can be any valid item in the list.

widget   Specifies the ID of the List widget from whose list an item is made the last visible

item   Specifies the given item

For a complete definition of List and its associated resources, see
XmList(3X).

Related Information

XmList(3X).

XmListSetBottomPos

Purpose

A List function that makes a specified item the last visible item in the list.

AES Support Level

Full-use

Synopsis

#include <Xm/List.h>

void **XmListSetBottomPos** (*widget, position*)
    Widget   *widget*;
    int   *position*;

Description

XmListSetBottomPos makes the item at the specified position the last visible item in the List.

widget   Specifies the ID of the List widget.

position Specifies the position of the item to be made the last visible item in the list. A value of 1 indicates that the first item in the list is the last visible item; a value of 2 indicates that the second item is the last visible item; and so on. A value of 0 indicates that the last item in the list is the last visible item.

For a complete definition of List and its associated resources, see **XmList(3X)**.

Related Information

XmList(3X).

XmListSetHorizPos

Purpose

A List function that scrolls to the specified position in the list.

AES Support Level

Full-use

Synopsis

#include <Xm/List.h>

void XmListSetHorizPos (*widget, position*)
    Widget   *widget*;
    int   *position*;

Description

XmListSetHorizPos sets the **XmNvalue** resource of the horizontal ScrollBar to the specified position and updates the visible portion of the list with the new value if the List widget's **XmNlistSizePolicy** is set to **XmCONSTANT** or **XmRESIZE_IF_POSSIBLE** and the horizontal ScrollBar is currently visible. This is equivalent to moving the horizontal ScrollBar to the specified position.

widget   Specifies the ID of the List widget

position   Specifies the horizontal position

For a complete definition of List and its associated resources, see **XmList(3X)**.

Related Information

XmList(3X).

XmListSetItem

Purpose

A List function that makes an existing item the first visible item in the list.

AES Support Level

Full-use

Synopsis

#include <Xm/List.h>

void XmListSetItem (*widget, item*)
    Widget   *widget*;
    XmString *item*;

Description

XmListSetItem makes an existing item the first visible item in the list. The item can be any valid item in the list.

widget   Specifies the ID of the List widget from whose list an item is made the first visible

item   Specifies the item

For a complete definition of List and its associated resources, see **XmList(3X)**.

Related Information

XmList(3X).

XmListSetPos

Purpose

A List function that makes the item at the given position the first visible position in the list.

AES Support Level

Full-use

Synopsis

#include <Xm/List.h>

void XmListSetPos (*widget, position*)
    Widget   *widget*;
    int   *position*;

Description

XmListSetPos makes the item at the given position the first visible position in the List.

widget   Specifies the ID of the List widget.

position   Specifies the position of the item to be made the first visible item in the list. A value of 1 indicates that the first item in the list is the first visible item; a value of 2 indicates that the second item is the first visible item; and so on. A value of 0 indicates that the last item in the list is the first visible item.

For a complete definition of List and its associated resources, see **XmList(3X)**.

Related Information

XmList(3X).

XmMainWindow

Purpose

The MainWindow widget class

AES Support Level

Full-use

Synopsis

#include <Xm/MainW.h>

Description

MainWindow provides a standard layout for the primary window of an application. This layout includes a MenuBar, a CommandWindow, a work region, a MessageWindow, and ScrollBars. Any or all of these areas are optional. The work region and ScrollBars in the MainWindow behave identically to the work region and ScrollBars in the ScrolledWindow widget. The user can think of the MainWindow as an extended ScrolledWindow with an optional MenuBar and optional CommandWindow and MessageWindow.

In a fully-loaded MainWindow, the MenuBar spans the top of the window horizontally. The CommandWindow spans the MainWindow horizontally just below the MenuBar, and the work region lies below the CommandWindow. The MessageWindow is is below the work region. Any space remaining below the MessageWindow is managed in a manner identical to ScrolledWindow. The behavior of ScrolledWindow can be controlled by the ScrolledWindow resources. To create a MainWindow, first create the work region elements, a MenuBar, a CommandWindow, a MessageWindow, a horizontal ScrollBar, and a vertical ScrollBar widget, and then call **XmMainWindowSetAreas** with those widget IDs.

MainWindow can also create three Separator widgets that provide a visual separation of MainWindow's four components.

Classes

MainWindow inherits behavior and resources from **Core**, **Composite**, **Constraint**, **XmManager**, and **ScrolledWindow** classes.

The class pointer is **xmMainWindowWidgetClass.**

The class name is **XmMainWindow**.

New Resources

The following table defines a set of widget resources used by the programmer to specify data. The programmer can also set the resource values for the inherited classes to set attributes for this widget. To reference a resource by name or by class in a .Xdefaults file, remove the **XmN** or **XmC** prefix and use the remaining letters. To specify one of the defined values for a resource in a .Xdefaults file, remove the **Xm** prefix and use the remaining letters (in either lowercase or uppercase, but include any underscores between words). The codes in the access column indicate if the given resource can be set at creation time (**C**), set by using **XtSetValues** (**S**), retrieved by using **XtGetValues** (**G**), or is not applicable (**N/A**).

XmMainWindow Resource Set		

Name
    Class
	Default
	    Type
		Access

XmNcommandWindow
    XmCCommandWindow
	NULL
	    Widget
		CSG

XmNcommandWindowLocation
    XmCCommandWindowLocation
	ABOVE (SeeDesc.)
	    unsigned char
		CG

XmNmainWindowMarginHeight
    XmCMainWindowMarginHeight
	0
	    Dimension
		CSG

XmNmainWindowMarginWidth
    XmCMainWindowMarginWidth
	0
	    Dimension
		CSG

XmNmenuBar
    XmCMenuBar
	NULL
	    Widget
		CSG

XmNmessageWindow
    XmCMessageWindow
	NULL
	    Widget
		CSG

XmNshowSeparator
    XmCShowSeparator
	False
	    Boolean
		CSG

XmNcommandWindow
> Specifies the widget to be laid out as the CommandWindow. This widget must have been previously created and managed as a child of MainWindow.

XmNcommandWindowLocation
> Controls the position of the command window. **XmCOMMAND_ABOVE_WORKSPACE** locates the command window between the menu bar and the work window. **XmCOMMAND_BELOW_WORKSPACE** locates the command window between the work window and the message window.

XmNmainWindowMarginHeight
> Specifies the margin height on the top and bottom of MainWindow. This resource overrides any setting of the **XmNscrolledWindowMarginHeight**.

XmNmainWindowMarginWidth

Specifies the margin width on the right and left sides of MainWindow. This resource overrides any setting of the ScrolledWindow resource **XmNscrolledWindowMarginWidth**.

XmNmenuBar

Specifies the widget to be laid out as the MenuBar. This widget must have been previously created and managed as a child of MainWindow.

XmNmessageWindow

Specifies the widget to be laid out as the MessageWindow. This widget must have been previously created and managed as a child of MainWindow. The MessageWindow is positioned at the bottom of the MainWindow. If this value is NULL, no message window is included in the MainWindow.

XmNshowSeparator

Displays separators between the components of the MainWindow when set to True. If set to False, no separators are displayed.

Inherited Resources

MainWindow inherits behavior and resources from the following superclasses. For a complete description of each resource, refer to the man page for that superclass.

XmScrolledWindow Resource Set		
Name	**Default**	**Access**
Class	**Type**	
XmNclipWindow	dynamic	G
XmCClipWindow	Widget	
XmNhorizontalScrollBar	dynamic	CSG
XmCHorizontalScrollBar	Widget	
XmNscrollBarDisplayPolicy	dynamic	CSG
XmCScrollBarDisplayPolicy	unsigned char	
XmNscrollBarPlacement	XmBOTTOM_RIGHT	CSG
XmCScrollBarPlacement	unsigned char	
XmNscrolledWindowMarginHeight	0	N/A
XmCScrolledWindowMarginHeight	Dimension	
XmNscrolledWindowMarginWidth	0	N/A
XmCScrolledWindowMarginWidth	Dimension	
XmNscrollingPolicy	XmAPPLICATION_DEFINED	CG
XmCScrollingPolicy	unsigned char	
XmNspacing	4	CSG
XmCSpacing	Dimension	
XmNverticalScrollBar	dynamic	CSG
XmCVerticalScrollBar	Widget	
XmNvisualPolicy	dynamic	CG
XmCVisualPolicy	unsigned char	
XmNworkWindow	NULL	CSG
XmCWorkWindow	Widget	

XmManager Resource Set		

Name
    Class
	Default
	    Type
		Access

XmNbottomShadowColor
    XmCBottomShadowColor
	dynamic
	    Pixel
		CSG

XmNbottomShadowPixmap
    XmCBottomShadowPixmap
	XmUNSPECIFIED_PIXMAP
	    Pixmap
		CSG

XmNforeground
    XmCForeground
	dynamic
	    Pixel
		CSG

XmNhelpCallback
    XmCCallback
	NULL
	    XtCallbackList
		C

XmNhighlightColor
    XmCHighlightColor
	dynamic
	    Pixel
		CSG

XmNhighlightPixmap
    XmCHighlightPixmap
	dynamic
	    Pixmap
		CSG

XmNnavigationType
    XmCNavigationType
	XmTAB_GROUP
	    XmNavigationType
		CSG

XmNshadowThickness
    XmCShadowThickness
	0
	    Dimension
		CSG

XmNstringDirection
    XmCStringDirection
	dynamic
	    XmStringDirection
		CG

XmNtopShadowColor
    XmCBackgroundTopShadowColor
	dynamic
	    Pixel
		CSG

XmNtopShadowPixmap
    XmCTopShadowPixmap
	dynamic
	    Pixmap
		CSG

XmNtraversalOn
    XmCTraversalOn
	True
	    Boolean
		CSG

XmNuserData
    XmCUserData
	NULL
	    Pointer
		CSG

Composite Resource Set		
Name	**Default**	**Access**
Class	**Type**	
XmNchildren	NULL	G
XmCReadOnly	WidgetList	
XmNinsertPosition	NULL	CSG
XmCInsertPosition	(*)()	
XmNnumChildren	0	G
XmCReadOnly	Cardinal	

Core Resource Set		
Name **Class**	**Default** **Type**	**Access**
XmNaccelerators XmCAccelerators	dynamic XtAccelerators	CSG
XmNancestorSensitive XmCSensitive	dynamic Boolean	G
XmNbackground XmCBackground	dynamic Pixel	CSG
XmNbackgroundPixmap XmCPixmap	XmUNSPECIFIED_PIXMAP Pixmap	CSG
XmNborderColor XmCBorderColor	XtDefaultForeground Pixel	CSG
XmNborderPixmap XmCPixmap	XmUNSPECIFIED_PIXMAP Pixmap	CSG
XmNborderWidth XmCBorderWidth	0 Dimension	CSG
XmNcolormap XmCColormap	dynamic Colormap	CG
XmNdepth XmCDepth	dynamic int	CG
XmNdestroyCallback XmCCallback	NULL XtCallbackList	C
XmNheight XmCHeight	dynamic Dimension	CSG
XmNinitialResourcesPersistent XmCInitialResourcesPersistent	True Boolean	C
XmNmappedWhenManaged XmCMappedWhenManaged	True Boolean	CSG
XmNscreen XmCScreen	dynamic Screen *	CG

Name	Default	Access
Class	Type	
XmNsensitive	True	CSG
XmCSensitive	Boolean	
XmNtranslations	dynamic	CSG
XmCTranslations	XtTranslations	
XmNwidth	dynamic	CSG
XmCWidth	Dimension	
XmNx	0	CSG
XmCPosition	Position	
XmNy	0	CSG
XmCPosition	Position	

Translations

MainWindow inherits translations from ScrolledWindow.

Related Information

Composite(3X), Constraint(3X), Core(3X), XmCreateMainWindow(3X), XmMainWindowSep1(3X), XmMainWindowSep2(3X), XmMainWindowSep3(3X), XmMainWindowSetAreas(3X), XmManager(3X), and XmScrolledWindow(3X)

XmMainWindowSep1

Purpose

A MainWindow function that returns the widget ID of the first Separator widget.

AES Support Level

Full-use

Synopsis

#include <Xm/MainW.h>

Widget XmMainWindowSep1 (*widget*)
    Widget   *widget*;

Description

XmMainWindowSep1 returns the widget ID of the first Separator widget in the MainWindow. The first Separator widget is located between the MenuBar and the Command widget. This Separator is visible only when **XmNshowSeparator** is True.

widget   Specifies the MainWindow widget ID

For a complete definition of MainWindow and its associated resources, see **XmMainWindow(3X)**.

Return Value

Returns the widget ID of the first Separator.

Related Information

XmMainWindow(3X).

XmMainWindowSep2

Purpose

A MainWindow function that returns the widget ID of the second Separator widget.

AES Support Level

Full-use

Synopsis

#include <Xm/MainW.h>

Widget XmMainWindowSep2 (*widget*)
    Widget   *widget*;

Description

XmMainWindowSep2 returns the widget ID of the second Separator widget in the MainWindow. The second Separator widget is located between the Command widget and the ScrolledWindow. This Separator is visible only when **XmNshowSeparator** is True.

widget   Specifies the MainWindow widget ID

For a complete definition of MainWindow and its associated resources, see **XmMainWindow(3X)**.

Return Value

Returns the widget ID of the second Separator.

Related Information

XmMainWindow(3X).

XmMainWindowSep3

Purpose

A MainWindow function that returns the widget ID of the third Separator widget.

AES Support Level

Full-use

Synopsis

#include <Xm/MainW.h>

Widget XmMainWindowSep3 (*widget*)
    Widget   *widget*;

Description

XmMainWindowSep3 returns the widget ID of the third Separator widget in the MainWindow. The third Separator widget is located between the message window and the widget above it. This Separator is visible only when **XmNshowSeparator** is True.

widget   Specifies the MainWindow widget ID

For a complete definition of MainWindow and its associated resources, see **XmMainWindow(3X)**.

Return Value

Returns the widget ID of the third Separator.

Related Information

XmMainWindow(3X).

XmMainWindowSetAreas

Purpose

A MainWindow function that identifies manageable children for each area.

AES Support Level

Full-use

Synopsis

#include <Xm/MainW.h>

void XmMainWindowSetAreas (*widget, menu_bar, command_window,*
horizontal_scrollbar, vertical_scrollbar, work_region)
    Widget   *widget*;
    Widget   *menu_bar*;
    Widget   *command_window*;
    Widget   *horizontal_scrollbar*;
    Widget   *vertical_scrollbar*;
    Widget   *work_region*;

Description

XmMainWindowSetAreas identifies which of the valid children for each area (such as the MenuBar and work region) are to be actively managed by MainWindow. This function also sets up or adds the MenuBar, work window, command window, and ScrollBar widgets to the application's main window widget.

Each area is optional; therefore, the user can pass NULL to one or more of the following arguments. The window manager provides the title bar.

widget   Specifies the MainWindow widget ID.

menu_bar   Specifies the widget ID for the MenuBar to be associated with the MainWindow widget. Set this ID only after creating an instance of the MainWindow widget. The attribute name associated with this argument is **XmNmenuBar**.

command_window
          Specifies the widget ID for the command window to be associated with the MainWindow widget. Set this ID only after creating an instance of the MainWindow widget. The attribute name associated with this argument is **XmNcommandWindow**.

horizontal_scrollbar
          Specifies the ScrollBar widget ID for the horizontal ScrollBar to be associated with the MainWindow widget. Set this ID only after creating an instance of the MainWindow widget. The attribute name associated with this argument is **XmNhorizontalScrollBar**.

vertical_scrollbar
          Specifies the ScrollBar widget ID for the vertical ScrollBar to be associated with the MainWindow widget. Set this ID only after creating an instance of the MainWindow widget. The attribute name associated with this argument is **XmNverticalScrollBar**.

work_region   Specifies the widget ID for the work window to be associated with the MainWindow widget. Set this ID only after creating an instance of the MainWindow widget. The attribute name associated with this argument is **XmNworkWindow**.

For a complete definition of MainWindow and its associated resources, see **XmMainWindow(3X)**.

Related Information

XmMainWindow(3X).

XmManager

Purpose

The Manager widget class

AES Support Level

Full-use

Synopsis

#include <Xm/Xm.h>

Description

Manager is a widget class used as a supporting superclass for other widget classes. It supports the visual resources, graphics contexts, and traversal resources necessary for the graphics and traversal mechanisms.

Classes

Manager inherits behavior and resources from **Core**, **Composite**, and **Constraint** classes.

The class pointer is **xmManagerWidgetClass**.

The class name is **XmManager**.

New Resources

The following table defines a set of widget resources used by the programmer to specify data. The programmer can also set the resource values for the inherited classes to set attributes for this widget. To reference a resource by name or by class in a .Xdefaults file, remove the **XmN** or **XmC** prefix and use the remaining letters. To specify one of the defined values for a resource in a .Xdefaults file, remove the **Xm** prefix and use the remaining letters (in either lowercase or uppercase, but include any underscores between words). The codes in the access column indicate if the given resource can be set at creation time (**C**), set by using **XtSetValues** (**S**), retrieved by using **XtGetValues** (**G**), or is not applicable (**N/A**).

XmManager Resource Set		
Name	**Default**	**Access**
Class	**Type**	
XmNbottomShadowColor	dynamic	CSG
XmCBottomShadowColor	Pixel	
XmNbottomShadowPixmap	XmUNSPECIFIED_PIXMAP	CSG
XmCBottomShadowPixmap	Pixmap	
XmNforeground	dynamic	CSG
XmCForeground	Pixel	
XmNhelpCallback	NULL	C
XmCCallback	XtCallbackList	
XmNhighlightColor	dynamic	CSG
XmCHighlightColor	Pixel	
XmNhighlightPixmap	dynamic	CSG
XmCHighlightPixmap	Pixmap	
XmNnavigationType	XmTAB_GROUP	CSG
XmCNavigationType	XmNavigationType	
XmNshadowThickness	0	CSG
XmCShadowThickness	Dimension	
XmNstringDirection	dynamic	CG
XmCStringDirection	XmStringDirection	
XmNtopShadowColor	dynamic	CSG
XmCBackgroundTopShadowColor	Pixel	
XmNtopShadowPixmap	dynamic	CSG
XmCTopShadowPixmap	Pixmap	
XmNtraversalOn	True	CSG
XmCTraversalOn	Boolean	
XmNuserData	NULL	CSG
XmCUserData	Pointer	

XmNbottomShadowColor
>Specifies the color to use to draw the bottom and right sides of the border shadow. This color is used if the **XmNbottomShadowPixmap** resource is NULL.

XmNbottomShadowPixmap
>Specifies the pixmap to use to draw the bottom and right sides of the border shadow.

XmNforeground
>Specifies the foreground drawing color used by manager widgets.

XmNhelpCallback
>Specifies the list of callbacks that are called when the help key sequence is pressed. The reason sent by this callback is **XmCR_HELP**. No translation is bound to this resource. It is up to the application to install a translation for help.

XmNhighlightColor
>Specifies the color of the highlighting rectangle. This color is used if the highlight pixmap resource is **XmUNSPECIFIED_PIXMAP**.

XmNhighlightPixmap
>Specifies the pixmap used to draw the highlighting rectangle.

XmNnavigationType
>Controls whether the Widget is a navigation group.

>- **XmNONE** indicates that the Widget is not a navigation group.

>- **XmTAB_GROUP** indicates that the Widget is included automatically in keyboard navigation, unless **XmAddTabGroup** has been called.

>- **XmSTICKY_TAB_GROUP** indicates that the Widget is included automatically in keyboard navigation, even if **XmAddTabGroup** has been called.

>- **XmEXCLUSIVE_TAB_GROUP** indicates that the Widget is included explicitly in keyboard navigation by

the application. With **XmEXCLUSIVE_TAB_GROUP**, traversal of widgets within the group is based on the order of children.

XmNshadowThickness
Specifies the thickness of the drawn border shadow. **XmBulletinBoard** and its descendants set this value dynamically. If the widget is a top level window, this value is set to 1. If it is not a top level window, this value is set to 0.

XmNstringDirection
Specifies the initial direction to draw strings. The values are **XmSTRING_DIRECTION_L_TO_R** and **XmSTRING_DIRECTION_R_TO_L**. The value of this resource is determined at creation time. If the widget's parent is a manager, this value is inherited from the widget's parent, otherwise it is set to XmSTRING_DIRECTION_L_TO_R.

XmNtopShadowColor
Specifies the color to use to draw the top and left sides of the border shadow. This color is used if the **XmNtopShadowPixmap** resource is NULL.

XmNtopShadowPixmap
Specifies the pixmap to use to draw the top and left sides of the border shadow.

XmNtraversalOn
Specifies whether traversal is activated for this widget.

XmNuserData
Allows the application to attach any necessary specific data to the widget. This is an internally unused resource.

Dynamic Color Defaults

The foreground, background, top shadow, and bottom shadow resources are dynamically defaulted. If no color data is specified, the colors are automatically generated. On a single-plane system, a black and white color scheme is generated. Otherwise, four colors are generated, which display the correct shading for the 3-D visuals. If the background is the only color specified for a widget, the top shadow, bottom shadow, and foreground colors are generated to give the 3-D appearance.

Colors are generated only at creation. Resetting the background through **XtSetValues** does not regenerate the other colors.

Inherited Resources

Manager inherits the following resources from the named superclasses. For a complete description of each resource, refer to the man page for that superclass.

Composite Resource Set		
Name	**Default**	**Access**
Class	**Type**	
XmNchildren	NULL	G
XmCReadOnly	WidgetList	
XmNinsertPosition	NULL	CSG
XmCInsertPosition	(*)()	
XmNnumChildren	0	G
XmCReadOnly	Cardinal	

Core Resource Set		

Name
  Class
	Default
	  Type
		Access

XmNaccelerators
  XmCAccelerators
	dynamic
	  XtAccelerators
		CSG

XmNancestorSensitive
  XmCSensitive
	dynamic
	  Boolean
		G

XmNbackground
  XmCBackground
	dynamic
	  Pixel
		CSG

XmNbackgroundPixmap
  XmCPixmap
	XmUNSPECIFIED_PIXMAP
	  Pixmap
		CSG

XmNborderColor
  XmCBorderColor
	XtDefaultForeground
	  Pixel
		CSG

XmNborderPixmap
  XmCPixmap
	XmUNSPECIFIED_PIXMAP
	  Pixmap
		CSG

XmNborderWidth
  XmCBorderWidth
	0
	  Dimension
		CSG

XmNcolormap
  XmCColormap
	dynamic
	  Colormap
		CG

XmNdepth
  XmCDepth
	dynamic
	  int
		CG

XmNdestroyCallback
  XmCCallback
	NULL
	  XtCallbackList
		C

XmNheight
  XmCHeight
	dynamic
	  Dimension
		CSG

XmNinitialResourcesPersistent
  XmCInitialResourcesPersistent
	True
	  Boolean
		C

XmNmappedWhenManaged
  XmCMappedWhenManaged
	True
	  Boolean
		CSG

XmNscreen
  XmCScreen
	dynamic
	  Screen *
		CG

Name Class	Default Type	Access
XmNsensitive XmCSensitive	True Boolean	CSG
XmNtranslations XmCTranslations	dynamic XtTranslations	CSG
XmNwidth XmCWidth	dynamic Dimension	CSG
XmNx XmCPosition	0 Position	CSG
XmNy XmCPosition	0 Position	CSG

Translations

The following set of translations are used by Manager widgets that have Gadget children. Since Gadgets cannot have translations associated with them, it is the responsibility of the Manager widget to intercept the events of interest and pass them to any Gadget child with focus. These events are ignored if no Gadget child has the focus. These translations may not directly correspond to a translation table.

BAny Motion: **ManagerGadgetButtonMotion()**
BSelect Press: **ManagerGadgetArm()**
BSelect Click: **ManagerGadgetActivate()**
BSelect Release: **ManagerGadgetActivate()**
BSelect Press 2+:   **ManagerGadgetMultiArm()**
BSelect Release 2+:ManagerGadgetMultiActivate()

KSelect: **ManagerGadgetSelect()**
KActivate: **ManagerGadgetSelect()**

KPrevField: **ManagerGadgetPrevTabGroup()**
KNextField: **ManagerGadgetNextTabGroup()**

KUp:	**ManagerGadgetTraverseUp()**
KDown:	**ManagerGadgetTraverseDown()**
KLeft:	**ManagerGadgetTraverseLeft()**
KRight:	**ManagerGadgetTraverseRight()**
KBeginLine:	**ManagerGadgetTraverseHome()**
KHelp:	**ManagerGadgetHelp()**
KAny:	**ManagerGadgetKeyInput()**

Action Routines

The XmManager action routines are described below:

ManagerGadgetActivate():
Causes the current gadget to be activated.

ManagerGadgetArm():
Causes the current gadget to be armed.

ManagerGadgetButtonMotion():
Causes the current gadget to process a mouse motion event.

ManagerGadgetHelp():
Calls the callbacks for the current gadget's **XmNhelpCallback** if any exist. If there are no help callbacks for this widget, this action calls the help callbacks for the nearest ancestor that has them.

ManagerGadgetKeyInput():
Causes the current gadget to process a keyboard event.

ManagerGadgetMultiActivate():
Causes the current gadget to process a multiple mouse click.

ManagerGadgetMultiArm():
Causes the current gadget to process a multiple mouse button press.

ManagerGadgetNextTabGroup():

Traverses to the first item in the next tab group. If the current tab group is the last entry in the tab group list, it wraps to the beginning of the tab group list.

ManagerGadgetPrevTabGroup():

Traverses to the first item in the previous tab group. If the beginning of the tab group list is reached, it wraps to the end of the tab group list.

ManagerGadgetSelect():

Causes the current gadget to be armed and activated.

ManagerGadgetTraverseDown():

Traverses to the next item below the current gadget in the current tab group, wrapping if necessary.

ManagerGadgetTraverseHome():

Traverses to the first widget or gadget in the current tab group.

ManagerGadgetTraverseLeft():

Traverses to the next item to the left of the current gadget in the current tab group, wrapping if necessary.

ManagerGadgetTraverseNext():

Traverses to the next item in the current tab group, wrapping if necessary.

ManagerGadgetTraversePrev():

Traverses to the previous item in the current tab group, wrapping if necessary.

ManagerGadgetTraverseRight():

Traverses to the next item to the right of the current gadget in the current tab group, wrapping if necessary.

ManagerGadgetTraverseUp():

Traverses to the next item above the current gadget in the current tab group, wrapping if necessary.

Additional Behavior

This widget has the additional behavior described below:

<FocusIn>: If the shell's keyboard focus policy is **XmEXPLICIT** and the event occurs in a gadget, causes the gadget to be highlighted and to take the focus.

<FocusOut>:
If the shell's keyboard focus policy is **XmEXPLICIT** and the event occurs in a gadget, causes the gadget to be unhighlighted and to lose the focus.

Virtual Bindings

The bindings for virtual keys are vendor specific.

Related Information

Composite(3X), **Constraint(3X)**, **Core(3X)**, and **XmGadget3X)**.

XmMenuPosition

Purpose

A RowColumn function that positions a Popup MenuPane

AES Support Level

Full-use

Synopsis

#include <Xm/RowColumn.h>

void XmMenuPosition (*menu, event*)
    Widget   *menu*;
    XButtonPressedEvent* *event*;

Description

XmMenuPosition positions a Popup MenuPane using the information in the specified event. Unless an application is positioning the MenuPane itself, it must first invoke this function before managing the PopupMenu. The *x_root* and *y_root* values in the specified event are used to determine the menu position.

menu   Specifies the PopupMenu to be positioned

event   Specifies the event passed to the action procedure which manages the PopupMenu

For a complete definition of RowColumn and its associated resources, see **XmRowColumn(3X)**.

Related Information

XmRowColumn(3X).

XmMenuShell

Purpose

The MenuShell widget class

AES Support Level

Full-use

Synopsis

#include <Xm/MenuShell.h>

Description

The MenuShell widget is a custom OverrideShell widget. An OverrideShell widget bypasses **mwm** when displaying itself. It is designed specifically to contain Popup or Pulldown MenuPanes.

Most application writers never encounter this widget if they use the menu-system convenience functions, **XmCreatePopupMenu** or **XmCreatePulldown Menu**, to create a Popup or Pulldown MenuPane. The convenience functions automatically create a MenuShell widget as the parent of the MenuPane. However, if the convenience functions are not used, the application programmer must create the required MenuShell. In this case, it is important to note that the parent of the MenuShell depends on the type of menu system being built.

- If the MenuShell is for the top-level Popup MenuPane, the MenuShell's parent must be the widget from which the Popup MenuPane is popped up.

- If the MenuShell is for a MenuPane that is pulled down from a Popup or another Pulldown MenuPane, the MenuShell's parent must be the Popup or Pulldown MenuPane.

- If the MenuShell is for a MenuPane that is pulled down from a MenuBar, the MenuShell's parent must be the MenuBar.

- If the MenuShell is for a Pulldown MenuPane in an OptionMenu, the MenuShell's parent must be the OptionMenu.

Setting **XmNheight**, **XmNwidth**, or **XmNborderWidth** for either a MenuShell or its child sets that resource to the same value in both the parent and the child. An application should always specify these resources for the child, not the parent.

For a child of a MenuShell, setting **XmNx** or **XmNy** sets the corresponding resource of the parent but does not change the child's position relative to the parent. **XtGetValues** for the child's **XmNx** or **XmNy** yields the value of the corresponding resource in the parent. The x and y coordinates of the child's upper left outside corner relative to the parent's upper left inside corner are both zero minus the value of **XmNborderWidth**.

Classes

MenuShell inherits behavior and resources from **Core**, **Composite**, **Shell**, and **OverrideShell** classes.

The class pointer is **xmMenuShellWidgetClass**.

The class name is **XmMenuShell**.

New Resources

MenuShell overrides the **XmNallowShellResize** resource in Shell. The following table defines a set of widget resources used by the programmer to specify data. The programmer can also set the resource values for the inherited classes to set attributes for this widget. To reference a resource by name or by class in a .Xdefaults file, remove the **XmN** or **XmC** prefix and use the remaining letters. To specify one of the defined values for a resource in a .Xdefaults file, remove the **Xm** prefix and use the remaining letters (in either lowercase or uppercase, but include any underscores between words). The codes in the access column indicate if the given resource can be set at creation time (**C**), set by using **XtSetValues** (**S**), retrieved by using **XtGetValues** (**G**), or is not applicable (**N/A**).

XmMenuShell Resource Set		
Name	**Default**	**Access**
Class	**Type**	
XmNdefaultFontList	dynamic	C
XmCDefaultFontList	XmFontList	

XmNdefaultFontList
> Specifies a default font list for its children. This font list is used whenever a font list is not specifically set for a Text, Label or Button child of the MenuShell.

Inherited Resources

MenuShell inherits behavior and resources from the following superclasses. For a complete description of each resource, refer to the man page for that superclass. The following tables define a set of widget resources used by the programmer to specify data. The programmer can set the resource values for these inherited classes to set attributes for this widget. To reference a resource by name or by class in a .Xdefaults file, remove the **XmN** or **XmC** prefix and use the remaining letters. To specify one of the defined values for a resource in a .Xdefaults file, remove the **Xm** prefix and use the remaining letters (in either lowercase or uppercase, but include any underscores between words). The codes in the access column indicate if the given resource can be set at creation time (**C**), set by using **XtSetValues** (**S**), retrieved by using **XtGetValues** (**G**), or is not applicable (**N/A**).

Shell Resource Set		

Name
   Class
	Default
	   Type
		Access

XmNallowShellResize
   XmCAllowShellResize
	True
	   Boolean
		G

XmNcreatePopupChildProc
   XmCCreatePopupChildProc
	NULL
	   (*)()
		CSG

XmNgeometry
   XmCGeometry
	NULL
	   String
		CSG

XmNoverrideRedirect
   XmCOverrideRedirect
	True
	   Boolean
		CSG

XmNpopdownCallback
   XmCCallback
	NULL
	   XtCallbackList
		C

XmNpopupCallback
   XmCCallback
	NULL
	   XtCallbackList
		C

XmNsaveUnder
   XmCSaveUnder
	True
	   Boolean
		CSG

XmNvisual
   XmCVisual
	CopyFromParent
	   Visual *
		CSG

Composite Resource Set		

Name
   Class
	Default
	   Type
		Access

XmNchildren
   XmCReadOnly
	NULL
	   WidgetList
		G

XmNinsertPosition
   XmCInsertPosition
	NULL
	   (*)()
		CSG

XmNnumChildren
   XmCReadOnly
	0
	   Cardinal
		G

Core Resource Set		
Name	**Default**	**Access**
Class	**Type**	
XmNaccelerators	dynamic	CSG
XmCAccelerators	XtAccelerators	
XmNancestorSensitive	dynamic	G
XmCSensitive	Boolean	
XmNbackground	dynamic	CSG
XmCBackground	Pixel	
XmNbackgroundPixmap	XmUNSPECIFIED_PIXMAP	CSG
XmCPixmap	Pixmap	
XmNborderColor	XtDefaultForeground	CSG
XmCBorderColor	Pixel	
XmNborderPixmap	XmUNSPECIFIED_PIXMAP	CSG
XmCPixmap	Pixmap	
XmNborderWidth	1	CSG
XmCBorderWidth	Dimension	
XmNcolormap	dynamic	CG
XmCColormap	Colormap	
XmNdepth	dynamic	CG
XmCDepth	int	
XmNdestroyCallback	NULL	C
XmCCallback	XtCallbackList	
XmNheight	dynamic	CSG
XmCHeight	Dimension	
XmNinitialResourcesPersistent	True	C
XmCInitialResourcesPersistent	Boolean	
XmNmappedWhenManaged	True	CSG
XmCMappedWhenManaged	Boolean	
XmNscreen	dynamic	CG
XmCScreen	Screen *	

Name	Default	Access
Class	Type	
XmNsensitive	True	CSG
XmCSensitive	Boolean	
XmNtranslations	dynamic	CSG
XmCTranslations	XtTranslations	
XmNwidth	dynamic	CSG
XmCWidth	Dimension	
XmNx	0	CSG
XmCPosition	Position	
XmNy	0	CSG
XmCPosition	Position	

Translations

The XmMenuShell translations are listed below. These translations may not directly correspond to a translation table.

BSelect Press: **ClearTraversal()**
BSelect Release: **MenuShellPopdownDone()**

Action Routines

The XmMenuShell action routines are described below:

ClearTraversal():
Disables keyboard traversal for the menu, enables mouse traversal, and unposts any menus posted by this menu.

2–693

MenuShellPopdownDone():

> Unposts the menu hierarchy and restores focus to the tab group that had the focus before the menu system was entered.

MenuShellPopdownOne():

> In a toplevel Pulldown MenuPane from a MenuBar, unposts the menu, disarms the MenuBar CascadeButton and the MenuBar, and restores keyboard focus to the tab group that had the focus before the MenuBar was entered. In other Pulldown MenuPanes, unposts the menu.
>
> In a Popup MenuPane, unposts the menu and restores keyboard focus to the widget from which the menu was posted.

Virtual Bindings

The bindings for virtual keys are vendor specific.

Related Information

Composite(3X), Core(3X), OverrideShell(3X), Shell(3X), XmCreateMenuShell(3X), XmCreatePopupMenu(3X), XmCreatePulldown(3X), and XmRowColumn(3X).

XmMessageBox

Purpose

The MessageBox widget class

AES Support Level

Full-use

Synopsis

#include <Xm/MessageB.h>

Description

MessageBox is a dialog class used for creating simple message dialogs. Convenience dialogs based on MessageBox are provided for several common interaction tasks, which include giving information, asking questions, and reporting errors.

A MessageBox dialog is typically transient in nature, displayed for the duration of a single interaction. MessageBox is a subclass of XmBulletinBoard and depends on it for much of its general dialog behavior.

A MessageBox can contain a message symbol, a message, and up to three standard default PushButtons: **OK, Cancel**, and **Help**. It is laid out with the symbol and message on top and the PushButtons on the bottom. The help button is positioned to the side of the other push buttons. You can localize the default symbols and button labels for MessageBox convenience dialogs.

At initialization, MessageBox looks for the following bitmap files:

- xm_error
- xm_information
- xm_question
- xm_working
- xm_warning

See **XmGetPixmap(3X)** for a list of the paths that are searched for these files.

Classes

MessageBox inherits behavior and resources from **Core**, **Composite**, **Constraint**, **XmManager**, and **XmBulletinBoard**.

The class pointer is **xmMessageBoxWidgetClass**.

The class name is **XmMessageBox**.

New Resources

The following table defines a set of widget resources used by the programmer to specify data. The programmer can also set the resource values for the inherited classes to set attributes for this widget. To reference a resource by name or by class in a .Xdefaults file, remove the **XmN** or **XmC** prefix and use the remaining letters. To specify one of the defined values for a resource in a .Xdefaults file, remove the **Xm** prefix and use the remaining letters (in either lowercase or uppercase, but include any underscores between words). The codes in the access column indicate if the given resource can be set at creation time (**C**), set by using **XtSetValues** (**S**), retrieved by using **XtGetValues** (**G**), or is not applicable (**N/A**).

XmMessageBox Resource Set		
Name **Class**	**Default** **Type**	**Access**
XmNcancelCallback XmCCallback	NULL XtCallbackList	C
XmNcancelLabelString XmCCancelLabelString	"Cancel" XmString	CSG
XmNdefaultButtonType XmCDefaultButtonType	XmDIALOG_OK_BUTTON unsigned char	CSG
XmNdialogType XmCDialogType	XmDIALOG_MESSAGE unsigned char	CSG
XmNhelpLabelString XmCHelpLabelString	"Help" XmString	CSG
XmNmessageAlignment XmCAlignment	XmALIGNMENT_BEGINNING unsigned char	CSG
XmNmessageString XmCMessageString	"" XmString	CSG
XmNminimizeButtons XmCMinimizeButtons	False Boolean	CSG
XmNokCallback XmCCallback	NULL XtCallbackList	C
XmNokLabelString XmCOkLabelString	"OK" XmString	CSG
XmNsymbolPixmap XmCPixmap	dynamic Pixmap	CSG

XmNcancelCallback

Specifies the list of callbacks that is called when the user clicks on the cancel button. The reason sent by the callback is **XmCR_CANCEL**.

XmNcancelLabelString

Specifies the string label for the cancel button.

XmNdefaultButtonType

Specifies the default PushButton. The following are valid types:

- **XmDIALOG_CANCEL_BUTTON**

- **XmDIALOG_OK_BUTTON**

- **XmDIALOG_HELP_BUTTON**

XmNdialogType

Specifies the type of MessageBox dialog, which determines the default message symbol. The following are the possible values for this resource:

- **XmDIALOG_ERROR** — indicates an ErrorDialog

- **XmDIALOG_INFORMATION** — indicates an InformationDialog

- **XmDIALOG_MESSAGE** — indicates a MessageDialog. This is the default MessageBox dialog type. The default message symbol is NULL.

- **XmDIALOG_QUESTION** — indicates a QuestionDialog

- **XmDIALOG_WARNING** — indicates a WarningDialog

- **XmDIALOG_WORKING** — indicates a WorkingDialog

If this resource is changed via **XtSetValues**, the symbol bitmap is modified to the new **XmdialogType** bitmap unless **XmNsymbolPixmap** is also being set in **XtSetValues**.

XmNhelpLabelString

Specifies the string label for the help button.

XmNmessageAlignment
> Controls the alignment of the message Label. Possible values include the following:

> - **XmALIGNMENT_BEGINNING** — the default
> - **XmALIGNMENT_CENTER**
> - **XmALIGNMENT_END**

XmNmessageString
> Specifies the string to be used as the message.

XmNminimizeButtons
> Sets the buttons to the width of the widest button and height of the tallest button if False. If True, button width and height are set to the preferred size of each button.

XmNokCallback
> Specifies the list of callbacks that is called when the user clicks on the OK button. The reason sent by the callback is **XmCR_OK**.

XmNokLabelString
> Specifies the string label for the OK button.

XmNsymbolPixmap
> Specifies the pixmap label to be used as the message symbol.

Inherited Resources

MessageBox inherits behavior and resources from the following superclasses. For a complete description of each resource, refer to the man page for that superclass.

XmBulletinBoard Resource Set		
Name	**Default**	**Access**
Class	**Type**	
XmNallowOverlap	True	CSG
XmCAllowOverlap	Boolean	
XmNautoUnmanage	True	CG
XmCAutoUnmanage	Boolean	
XmNbuttonFontList	dynamic	CSG
XmCButtonFontList	XmFontList	
XmNcancelButton	Cancel button	SG
XmCWidget	Widget	
XmNdefaultButton	dynamic	SG
XmCWidget	Widget	
XmNdefaultPosition	True	CSG
XmCDefaultPosition	Boolean	
XmNdialogStyle	dynamic	CSG
XmCDialogStyle	unsigned char	
XmNdialogTitle	NULL	CSG
XmCDialogTitle	XmString	
XmNfocusCallback	NULL	C
XmCCallback	XtCallbackList	
XmNlabelFontList	dynamic	CSG
XmCLabelFontList	XmFontList	
XmNmapCallback	NULL	C
XmCCallback	XtCallbackList	
XmNmarginHeight	10	CSG
XmCMarginHeight	Dimension	
XmNmarginWidth	10	CSG
XmCMarginWidth	Dimension	
XmNnoResize	False	CSG
XmCNoResize	Boolean	

Name Class	Default Type	Access
XmNresizePolicy XmCResizePolicy	XmRESIZE_ANY unsigned char	CSG
XmNshadowType XmCShadowType	XmSHADOW_OUT unsigned char	CSG
XmNtextFontList XmCTextFontList	dynamic XmFontList	CSG
XmNtextTranslations XmCTranslations	NULL XtTranslations	C
XmNunmapCallback XmCCallback	NULL XtCallbackList	C

XmManager Resource Set		
Name Class	**Default** Type	**Access**
XmNbottomShadowColor XmCBottomShadowColor	dynamic Pixel	CSG
XmNbottomShadowPixmap XmCBottomShadowPixmap	XmUNSPECIFIED_PIXMAP Pixmap	CSG
XmNforeground XmCForeground	dynamic Pixel	CSG
XmNhelpCallback XmCCallback	NULL XtCallbackList	C
XmNhighlightColor XmCHighlightColor	dynamic Pixel	CSG
XmNhighlightPixmap XmCHighlightPixmap	dynamic Pixmap	CSG
XmNnavigationType XmCNavigationType	dynamic XmNavigationType	CSG
XmNshadowThickness XmCShadowThickness	dynamic Dimension	CSG
XmNstringDirection XmCStringDirection	dynamic XmStringDirection	CG
XmNtopShadowColor XmCBackgroundTopShadowColor	dynamic Pixel	CSG
XmNtopShadowPixmap XmCTopShadowPixmap	dynamic Pixmap	CSG
XmNtraversalOn XmCTraversalOn	True Boolean	CSG
XmNuserData XmCUserData	NULL Pointer	CSG

Composite Resource Set		
Name	**Default**	**Access**
Class	**Type**	
XmNchildren	NULL	G
XmCReadOnly	WidgetList	
XmNinsertPosition	NULL	CSG
XmCInsertPosition	(*)()	
XmNnumChildren	0	G
XmCReadOnly	Cardinal	

Core Resource Set		
Name	**Default**	**Access**
Class	**Type**	
XmNaccelerators	dynamic	N/A
XmCAccelerators	XtAccelerators	
XmNancestorSensitive	dynamic	G
XmCSensitive	Boolean	
XmNbackground	dynamic	CSG
XmCBackground	Pixel	
XmNbackgroundPixmap	XmUNSPECIFIED_PIXMAP	CSG
XmCPixmap	Pixmap	
XmNborderColor	XtDefaultForeground	CSG
XmCBorderColor	Pixel	
XmNborderPixmap	XmUNSPECIFIED_PIXMAP	CSG
XmCPixmap	Pixmap	
XmNborderWidth	0	CSG
XmCBorderWidth	Dimension	
XmNcolormap	dynamic	CG
XmCColormap	Colormap	
XmNdepth	dynamic	CG
XmCDepth	int	
XmNdestroyCallback	NULL	C
XmCCallback	XtCallbackList	
XmNheight	dynamic	CSG
XmCHeight	Dimension	
XmNinitialResourcesPersistent	True	C
XmCInitialResourcesPersistent	Boolean	
XmNmappedWhenManaged	True	CSG
XmCMappedWhenManaged	Boolean	
XmNscreen	dynamic	CG
XmCScreen	Screen *	

Name Class	Default Type	Access
XmNsensitive XmCSensitive	True Boolean	CSG
XmNtranslations XmCTranslations	dynamic XtTranslations	CSG
XmNwidth XmCWidth	dynamic Dimension	CSG
XmNx XmCPosition	0 Position	CSG
XmNy XmCPosition	0 Position	CSG

Callback Information

A pointer to the following structure is passed to each callback:

```
typedef struct
{
    int             reason;
    XEvent          * event;
} XmAnyCallbackStruct;
```

reason   Indicates why the callback was invoked

event   Points to the **XEvent** that triggered the callback

Translations

XmMessageBox includes the translations from XmManager.

Additional Behavior

The XmMessageBox widget has the additional behavior described below:

MAny KCancel:
Calls the activate callbacks for the cancel button if it is sensitive.

KActivate: Calls the activate callbacks for the button with the keyboard focus. If no button has the keyboard focus, calls the activate callbacks for the default button if it is sensitive.

<Ok Button Activated>:
Calls the callbacks for **XmNokCallback**.

<Cancel Button Activated>:
Calls the callbacks for **XmNcancelCallback**.

<Help Button Activated>:
Calls the callbacks for **XmNhelpCallback**.

<FocusIn>: Calls the callbacks for **XmNfocusCallback**.

<Map>: Calls the callbacks for **XmNmapCallback** if the parent is a DialogShell.

<Unmap>: Calls the callbacks for **XmNunmapCallback** if the parent is a DialogShell.

Virtual Bindings

The bindings for virtual keys are vendor specific.

Related Information

Composite(3X), Constraint(3X), Core(3X), XmBulletinBoard(3X),
XmCreateErrorDialog(3X), XmCreateInformationDialog(3X),
XmCreateMessageBox(3X), XmCreateMessageDialog(3X),
XmCreateQuestionDialog(3X), XmCreateWarningDialog(3X),
XmCreateWorkingDialog(3X), XmManager(3X), and
XmMessageBoxGetChild(3X).

XmMessageBoxGetChild

Purpose

A MessageBox function that is used to access a component.

AES Support Level

Full-use

Synopsis

#include <Xm/MessageB.h>

Widget XmMessageBoxGetChild (*widget, child*)
    Widget   *widget*;
    unsigned char*child*;

Description

XmMessageBoxGetChild is used to access a component within a MessageBox. The parameters given to the function are the MessageBox widget and a value indicating which child to access.

widget   Specifies the MessageBox widget ID.

child   Specifies a component within the MessageBox. The following are legal values for this parameter:

- **XmDIALOG_CANCEL_BUTTON**
- **XmDIALOG_DEFAULT_BUTTON**
- **XmDIALOG_HELP_BUTTON**
- **XmDIALOG_MESSAGE_LABEL**
- **XmDIALOG_OK_BUTTON**
- **XmDIALOG_SEPARATOR**
- **XmDIALOG_SYMBOL_LABEL**

For a complete definition of MessageBox and its associated resources, see **XmMessageBox(3X)**.

Return Value

Returns the widget ID of the specified MessageBox child. An application should not assume that the returned widget will be of any particular class.

Related Information

XmMessageBox(3X).

XmOptionButtonGadget

Purpose

A RowColumn function that obtains the widget ID for the CascadeButtonGadget in an OptionMenu.

AES Support Level

Full-use

Synopsis

#include <Xm/RowColumn.h>

Widget XmOptionButtonGadget (*option_menu*)
   Widget   *option_menu*;

Description

XmOptionButtonGadget provides the application with the means for obtaining the widget ID for the internally created CascadeButtonGadget. Once the application has obtained the widget ID, it can adjust the visuals for the CascadeButtonGadget, if desired.

When an application creates an instance of the OptionMenu widget, the widget creates two internal gadgets. One is a LabelGadget that is used to display RowColumn's **XmNlabelString** resource. The other is a CascadeButtonGadget that displays the current selection and provides the means for posting the OptionMenu's submenu.

option_menu Specifies the OptionMenu widget ID

For a complete definition of RowColumn and its associated resources, see **XmRowColumn(3X)**.

Return Value

Returns the widget ID for the internal button.

Related Information

XmCreateOptionMenu(3X), XmCascadeButtonGadget(3X), XmOptionLabelGadget(3X), and XmRowColumn(3X).

XmOptionLabelGadget

Purpose

A RowColumn function that obtains the widget ID for the LabelGadget in an OptionMenu.

AES Support Level

Full-use

Synopsis

#include <Xm/RowColumn.h>

Widget XmOptionLabelGadget (*option_menu*)
    Widget   *option_menu*;

Description

XmOptionLabelGadget provides the application with the means for obtaining the widget ID for the internally created LabelGadget. Once the application has obtained the widget ID, it can adjust the visuals for the LabelGadget, if desired.

When an application creates an instance of the OptionMenu widget, the widget creates two internal gadgets. One is a LabelGadget that is used to display RowColumn's **XmNlabelString** resource. The other is a CascadeButtonGadget that displays the current selection and provides the means for posting the OptionMenu's submenu.

option_menu Specifies the OptionMenu widget ID

For a complete definition of RowColumn and its associated resources, see **XmRowColumn(3X)**.

Return Value

Returns the widget ID for the internal label.

Related Information

XmCreateOptionMenu(3X), XmLabelGadget(3X), XmOptionButtonGadget(3X), and **XmRowColumn(3X)**.

XmPanedWindow

Purpose

The PanedWindow widget class

AES Support Level

Full-use

Synopsis

#include <Xm/PanedW.h>

Description

PanedWindow is a composite widget that lays out children in a vertically tiled format. Children appear in top-to-bottom fashion, with the first child inserted appearing at the top of the PanedWindow and the last child inserted appearing at the bottom. The PanedWindow grows to match the width of its widest child and all other children are forced to this width. The height of the PanedWindow is equal to the sum of the heights of all its children, the spacing between them, and the size of the top and bottom margins.

The user can also adjust the size of the panes. To facilitate this adjustment, a pane control sash is created for most children. The sash appears as a square box positioned on the bottom of the pane that it controls. The user can adjust the size of a pane by using the mouse or keyboard.

The PanedWindow is also a constraint widget, which means that it creates and manages a set of constraints for each child. You can specify a minimum and maximum size for each pane. The PanedWindow does not allow a pane to be resized below its minimum size or beyond its maximum size. Also, when the minimum size of a pane is equal to its maximum size, no control sash is presented for that pane or for the lowest pane.

The default **XmNinsertPosition** procedure for PanedWindow causes sashes to be inserted at the end of the list of children and causes non-sash widgets to be inserted after other non-sash children but before any sashes.

Classes

PanedWindow inherits behavior and resources from the **Core**, **Composite**, **Constraint**, and **XmManager** classes.

The class pointer is **xmPanedWindowWidgetClass**.

The class name is **XmPanedWindow**.

New Resources

The following table defines a set of widget resources used by the programmer to specify data. The programmer can also set the resource values for the inherited classes to set attributes for this widget. To reference a resource by name or by class in a .Xdefaults file, remove the **XmN** or **XmC** prefix and use the remaining letters. To specify one of the defined values for a resource in a .Xdefaults file, remove the **Xm** prefix and use the remaining letters (in either lowercase or uppercase, but include any underscores between words). The codes in the access column indicate if the given resource can be set at creation time (**C**), set by using **XtSetValues** (**S**), retrieved by using **XtGetValues** (**G**), or is not applicable (**N/A**).

XmPanedWindow Resource Set		
Name	**Default**	**Access**
Class	Type	
XmNmarginHeight	3	CSG
XmCMarginHeight	Dimension	
XmNmarginWidth	3	CSG
XmCMarginWidth	Dimension	
XmNrefigureMode	True	CSG
XmCBoolean	Boolean	
XmNsashHeight	10	CSG
XmCSashHeight	Dimension	
XmNsashIndent	-10	CSG
XmCSashIndent	Position	
XmNsashShadowThickness	dynamic	CSG
XmCShadowThickness	Dimension	
XmNsashWidth	10	CSG
XmCSashWidth	Dimension	
XmNseparatorOn	True	CSG
XmCSeparatorOn	Boolean	
XmNspacing	8	CSG
XmCSpacing	Dimension	

XmNmarginHeight

Specifies the distance between the top and bottom edges of the PanedWindow and its children.

XmNmarginWidth

Specifies the distance between the left and right edges of the PanedWindow and its children.

XmNrefigureMode

Determines whether the panes' positions are recomputed and repositioned when programmatic changes are being made to the PanedWindow. Setting this resource to True resets the children to their appropriate positions.

XmNsashHeight

Specifies the height of the sash.

XmNsashIndent

Specifies the horizontal placement of the sash along each pane. A positive value causes the sash to be offset from the near (left) side of the PanedWindow, and a negative value causes the sash to be offset from the far (right) side of the PanedWindow. If the offset is greater than the width of the PanedWindow minus the width of the sash, the sash is placed flush against the near side of the PanedWindow.

Whether the placement actually corresponds to the left or right side of the PanedWindow may depend on the value of the **XmNstringDirection** resource.

XmNsashShadowThickness

Specifies the thickness of the shadows of the sashes.

XmNsashWidth

Specifies the width of the sash.

XmNseparatorOn

Determines whether a separator is created between each of the panes. Setting this resource to True creates a Separator at the midpoint between each of the panes.

XmNspacing

Specifies the distance between each child pane.

XmPanedWindow Constraint Resource Set		
Name Class	Default Type	Access
XmNallowResize XmCBoolean	False Boolean	CSG
XmNpaneMaximum XmCPaneMaximum	1000 Dimension	CSG
XmNpaneMinimum XmCPaneMinimum	1 Dimension	CSG
XmNskipAdjust XmCBoolean	False Boolean	CSG

XmNallowResize

Allows an application to specify whether the PanedWindow should allow a pane to request to be resized. This flag has an effect only after the PanedWindow and its children have been realized. If this flag is set to True, the PanedWindow tries to honor requests to alter the height of the pane. If False, it always denies pane requests to resize.

XmNpaneMaximum

Allows an application to specify the maximum size to which a pane may be resized. This value must be greater than the specified minimum.

XmNpaneMinimum

Allows an application to specify the minimum size to which a pane may be resized. This value must be greater than 0.

XmNskipAdjust

When set to True, this Boolean resource allows an application to specify that the PanedWindow should not automatically resize this pane.

Inherited Resources

PanedWindow inherits behavior and resources from the following superclasses. For a complete description of each resource, refer to the man page for that superclass.

XmManager Resource Set		
Name	**Default**	**Access**
Class	**Type**	
XmNbottomShadowColor	dynamic	CSG
XmCBottomShadowColor	Pixel	
XmNbottomShadowPixmap	XmUNSPECIFIED_PIXMAP	CSG
XmCBottomShadowPixmap	Pixmap	
XmNforeground	dynamic	CSG
XmCForeground	Pixel	
XmNhelpCallback	NULL	C
XmCCallback	XtCallbackList	
XmNhighlightColor	dynamic	CSG
XmCHighlightColor	Pixel	
XmNhighlightPixmap	dynamic	CSG
XmCHighlightPixmap	Pixmap	
XmNnavigationType	XmTAB_GROUP	CSG
XmCNavigationType	XmNavigationType	
XmNshadowThickness	2	CSG
XmCShadowThickness	Dimension	
XmNstringDirection	dynamic	CG
XmCStringDirection	XmStringDirection	
XmNtopShadowColor	dynamic	CSG
XmCBackgroundTopShadowColor	Pixel	
XmNtopShadowPixmap	dynamic	CSG
XmCTopShadowPixmap	Pixmap	
XmNtraversalOn	True	CSG
XmCTraversalOn	Boolean	
XmNuserData	NULL	CSG
XmCUserData	Pointer	

Core Resource Set		

Name
     Class
	Default
	     Type
		Access

XmNaccelerators
   XmCAccelerators
	dynamic
	   XtAccelerators
		CSG

XmNancestorSensitive
   XmCSensitive
	dynamic
	   Boolean
		G

XmNbackground
   XmCBackground
	dynamic
	   Pixel
		CSG

XmNbackgroundPixmap
   XmCPixmap
	XmUNSPECIFIED_PIXMAP
	   Pixmap
		CSG

XmNborderColor
   XmCBorderColor
	XtDefaultForeground
	   Pixel
		CSG

XmNborderPixmap
   XmCPixmap
	XmUNSPECIFIED_PIXMAP
	   Pixmap
		CSG

XmNborderWidth
   XmCBorderWidth
	0
	   Dimension
		CSG

XmNcolormap
   XmCColormap
	dynamic
	   Colormap
		CG

XmNdepth
   XmCDepth
	dynamic
	   int
		CG

XmNdestroyCallback
   XmCCallback
	NULL
	   XtCallbackList
		C

XmNheight
   XmCHeight
	dynamic
	   Dimension
		CSG

XmNinitialResourcesPersistent
   XmCInitialResourcesPersistent
	True
	   Boolean
		C

XmNmappedWhenManaged
   XmCMappedWhenManaged
	True
	   Boolean
		CSG

XmNscreen
   XmCScreen
	dynamic
	   Screen *
		CG

Name	Default	Access
Class	Type	
XmNsensitive	True	CSG
XmCSensitive	Boolean	
XmNtranslations	dynamic	CSG
XmCTranslations	XtTranslations	
XmNwidth	dynamic	CSG
XmCWidth	Dimension	
XmNx	0	CSG
XmCPosition	Position	
XmNy	0	CSG
XmCPosition	Position	

Composite Resource Set		
Name	Default	Access
Class	Type	
XmNchildren	NULL	G
XmCReadOnly	WidgetList	
XmNinsertPosition	default procedure	CSG
XmCInsertPosition	(*)()	
XmNnumChildren	0	G
XmCReadOnly	Cardinal	

Translations

XmPanedWindow inherits translations from XmManager.

The translations for sashes within the PanedWindow are listed below. These translations may not directly correspond to a translation table.

BSelect Press:	**SashAction(Start)**
BSelect Motion:	**SashAction(Move)**
BSelect Release:	**SashAction(Commit)**

BDrag Press:	SashAction(Start)
BDrag Motion:	SashAction(Move)
BDrag Release:	SashAction(Commit)
KUp:	SashAction(Key,DefaultIncr,Up)
MCtrl KUp:	SashAction(Key,LargeIncr,Up)
KDown:	SashAction(Key,DefaultIncr,Down)
MCtrl KDown:	SashAction(Key,LargeIncr,Down)
KNextField:	NextTabGroup()
KPrevField:	PrevTabGroup()
KHelp:	Help()

Action Routines

The XmPanedWindow action routines are described below:

Help(): Calls the callbacks for **XmNhelpCallback** if any exist. If there are no help callbacks for this widget, this action calls the help callbacks for the nearest ancestor that has them.

NextTabGroup():
Moves the keyboard focus to the next tab group. By default each pane and sash is a tab group.

PrevTabGroup():
Moves the keyboard focus to the previous tab group. By default each pane and sash is a tab group.

SashAction(*action*) or **SashAction**(**Key**,*increment*,*direction*):
The **Start** action activates the interactive placement of the pane's borders. The **Move** action causes the sash to track the position of the pointer. If one of the panes reaches its minimum or maximum size, adjustment continues with the next adjustable pane. The **Commit** action ends sash motion.

When sash action is caused by a keyboard event, the sash with the keyboard focus is moved according to the *increment* and *direction* specified. **DefaultIncr** adjusts the sash by one line. **LargeIncr** adjusts the sash by one view region. The *direction* is specified as either **Up** or **Down**.

Additional Behavior

This widget has the additional behavior described below:

<FocusIn>: Moves the keyboard focus to the sash and highlights it.

<FocusOut>:
Unsets the keyboard focus in the sash and unhighlights it.

Virtual Bindings

The bindings for virtual keys are vendor specific.

Related Information

Composite(3X),   Constraint(3X),   Core(3X), XmCreatePanedWindow(3X), and XmManager(3X).

XmPrimitive

Purpose

The Primitive widget class

AES Support Level

Full-use

Synopsis

#include <Xm/Xm.h>

Description

Primitive is a widget class used as a supporting superclass for other widget classes. It handles border drawing and highlighting, traversal activation and deactivation, and various callback lists needed by Primitive widgets.

Classes

Primitive inherits behavior and resources from **Core** class.

The class pointer is **xmPrimitiveWidgetClass**.

The class name is **XmPrimitive**.

New Resources

The following table defines a set of widget resources used by the programmer to specify data. The programmer can also set the resource values for the inherited classes to set attributes for this widget. To reference a resource by name or by class in a .Xdefaults file, remove the **XmN** or **XmC** prefix and use the remaining letters. To specify one of the defined values for a resource in a .Xdefaults file, remove the **Xm** prefix and use the remaining letters (in either lowercase or uppercase, but include any underscores between words). The codes in the access column indicate if the given resource can be set at creation time (**C**), set by using **XtSetValues** (**S**), retrieved by using **XtGetValues** (**G**), or is not applicable (**N/A**).

XmPrimitive Resource Set		
Name	**Default**	**Access**
Class	**Type**	
XmNbottomShadowColor	dynamic	CSG
XmCBottomShadowColor	Pixel	
XmNbottomShadowPixmap	XmUNSPECIFIED_PIXMAP	CSG
XmCBottomShadowPixmap	Pixmap	
XmNforeground	dynamic	CSG
XmCForeground	Pixel	
XmNhelpCallback	NULL	C
XmCCallback	XtCallbackList	
XmNhighlightColor	dynamic	CSG
XmCHighlightColor	Pixel	
XmNhighlightOnEnter	False	CSG
XmCHighlightOnEnter	Boolean	
XmNhighlightPixmap	dynamic	CSG
XmCHighlightPixmap	Pixmap	
XmNhighlightThickness	2	CSG
XmCHighlightThickness	Dimension	
XmNnavigationType	XmNONE	G
XmCNavigationType	XmNavigationType	
XmNshadowThickness	2	CSG
XmCShadowThickness	Dimension	
XmNtopShadowColor	dynamic	CSG
XmCTopShadowColor	Pixel	
XmNtopShadowPixmap	dynamic	CSG
XmCTopShadowPixmap	Pixmap	
XmNtraversalOn	True	CSG
XmCTraversalOn	Boolean	
XmNuserData	NULL	CSG
XmCUserData	Pointer	

XmNbottomShadowColor

Specifies the color to use to draw the bottom and right sides of the border shadow. This color is used if the **XmNtopShadowPixmap** resource is unspecified.

XmNbottomShadowPixmap

Specifies the pixmap to use to draw the bottom and right sides of the border shadow.

XmNforeground

Specifies the foreground drawing color used by Primitive widgets.

XmNhelpCallback

Specifies the list of callbacks that is called when the help key is pressed. The reason sent by the callback is **XmCR_HELP**.

XmNhighlightColor

Specifies the color of the highlighting rectangle. This color is used if the highlight pixmap resource is **XmUNSPECIFIED_PIXMAP**.

XmNhighlightOnEnter

Specifies if the highlighting rectangle is drawn when the cursor moves into the widget. If the shell's focus policy is **XmEXPLICIT**, this resource is ignored, and the widget is highlighted when it has the focus. If the shell's focus policy is **XmPOINTER** and if this resource is True, the highlighting rectangle is drawn when the the cursor moves into the widget. If the shell's focus policy is **XmPOINTER** and if this resource is False, the highlighting rectangle is not drawn when the the cursor moves into the widget. The default is False.

XmNhighlightPixmap

Specifies the pixmap used to draw the highlighting rectangle.

XmNhighlightThickness

Specifies the thickness of the highlighting rectangle.

XmNnavigationType

Controls whether the Widget is a navigation group.

- **XmNONE** indicates that the Widget is not a navigation group.

- **XmTAB_GROUP** indicates that the Widget is included automatically in keyboard navigation, unless **XmAddTabGroup** has been called.

- **XmSTICKY_TAB_GROUP** indicates that the Widget is included automatically in keyboard navigation, even if **XmAddTabGroup** has been called.

- **XmEXCLUSIVE_TAB_GROUP** indicates that the Widget is included explicitly in keyboard navigation by the application. With **XmEXCLUSIVE_TAB_GROUP**, traversal of widgets within the group is based on the order of children.

If the widget's parent is a shell, the default is **XmTAB_GROUP**; otherwise, the default is **XmNONE**.

XmNshadowThickness

Specifies the size of the drawn border shadow.

XmNtopShadowColor

Specifies the color to use to draw the top and left sides of the border shadow. This color is used if the **XmNtopShadowPixmap** resource is unspecified.

XmNtopShadowPixmap

Specifies the pixmap to use to draw the top and left sides of the border shadow.

XmNtraversalOn

Specifies if traversal is activated for this widget.

XmNuserData

Allows the application to attach any necessary specific data to the widget. It is an internally unused resource.

Dynamic Color Defaults

The foreground, background, top shadow, and bottom shadow resources are dynamically defaulted. If no color data is specified, the colors are automatically generated. On a single-plane system, a black and white color scheme is generated. Otherwise, four colors are generated, which display the correct shading for the 3-D visuals. If the background is the only color specified for a widget, the top shadow, bottom shadow, and foreground colors are generated to give the 3-D appearance.

Colors are generated only at creation. Resetting the background through **XtSetValues** does not regenerate the other colors.

Inherited Resources

Primitive inherits behavior and resources from the following superclass. For a complete description of each resource, refer to the man page for that superclass.

Core Resource Set		
Name	**Default**	**Access**
Class	**Type**	
XmNaccelerators	dynamic	CSG
XmCAccelerators	XtAccelerators	
XmNancestorSensitive	dynamic	G
XmCSensitive	Boolean	
XmNbackground	dynamic	CSG
XmCBackground	Pixel	
XmNbackgroundPixmap	XmUNSPECIFIED_PIXMAP	CSG
XmCPixmap	Pixmap	
XmNborderColor	XtDefaultForeground	CSG
XmCBorderColor	Pixel	
XmNborderPixmap	XmUNSPECIFIED_PIXMAP	CSG
XmCPixmap	Pixmap	
XmNborderWidth	0	CSG
XmCBorderWidth	Dimension	
XmNcolormap	dynamic	CG
XmCColormap	Colormap	
XmNdepth	dynamic	CG
XmCDepth	int	
XmNdestroyCallback	NULL	C
XmCCallback	XtCallbackList	
XmNheight	dynamic	CSG
XmCHeight	Dimension	
XmNinitialResourcesPersistent	True	C
XmCInitialResourcesPersistent	Boolean	
XmNmappedWhenManaged	True	CSG
XmCMappedWhenManaged	Boolean	
XmNscreen	dynamic	CG
XmCScreen	Screen *	

Name	Default	Access
Class	Type	
XmNsensitive	True	CSG
XmCSensitive	Boolean	
XmNtranslations	dynamic	CSG
XmCTranslations	XtTranslations	
XmNwidth	dynamic	CSG
XmCWidth	Dimension	
XmNx	0	CSG
XmCPosition	Position	
XmNy	0	CSG
XmCPosition	Position	

Translations

The XmPrimitive translations are listed below. These translations may not directly correspond to a translation table.

Note that for buttons in menus, altering translations in **#override** or **#augment** mode is undefined.

KUp:	**PrimitiveTraverseUp()**
KDown:	**PrimitiveTraverseDown()**
KLeft:	**PrimitiveTraverseLeft()**
KRight:	**PrimitiveTraverseRight()**
KBeginLine:	**PrimitiveTraverseHome()**
KNextField:	**PrimitiveNextTabGroup()**
KPrevField:	**PrimitivePrevTabGroup()**
KHelp:	**PrimitiveHelp()**

Action Routines

The XmPrimitive action routines are described below:

PrimitiveHelp():
Calls the callbacks for **XmNhelpCallback** if any exist. If there are no help callbacks for this widget, this action calls the help callbacks for the nearest ancestor that has them.

PrimitiveNextTabGroup():
Traverses to the first item in the next tab group. If the current tab group is the last entry in the tab group list, it wraps to the beginning of the tab group list.

PrimitivePrevTabGroup():
Traverses to the first item in the previous tab group. If the beginning of the tab group list is reached, it wraps to the end of the tab group list.

PrimitiveTraverseDown():
Traverses to the next item below the current widget in the current tab group, wrapping if necessary.

PrimitiveTraverseHome():
Traverses to the first widget or gadget in the current tab group.

PrimitiveTraverseLeft():
Traverses to the next item to the left of the current widget in the current tab group, wrapping if necessary.

PrimitiveTraverseNext():
Traverses to the next item in the current tab group, wrapping if necessary.

PrimitiveTraversePrev():
Traverses to the previous item in the current tab group, wrapping if necessary.

PrimitiveTraverseRight():
Traverses to the next item to the right of the current gadget in the current tab group, wrapping if necessary.

PrimitiveTraverseUp():
Traverses to the next item above the current gadget in the current tab group, wrapping if necessary.

Additional Behavior

This widget has the additional behavior described below:

<FocusIn>: If the shell's keyboard focus policy is **XmEXPLICIT**, highlights the widget and gives it the focus.

<FocusOut>:
If the shell's keyboard focus policy is **XmEXPLICIT**, unhighlights the widget and removes the focus.

Virtual Bindings

The bindings for virtual keys are vendor specific.

Related Information

Core(3X).

XmProcessTraversal

Purpose

A function that determines which component receives keyboard events when a widget has the focus.

AES Support Level

Trial-use

Synopsis

#include <Xm/Xm.h>

Boolean XmProcessTraversal (*widget, direction*)
    Widget   *widget*;
    int   *direction*;

Description

XmProcessTraversal determines which component of a hierarchy receives keyboard events when the hierarchy that contains the given widget has keyboard focus. It is not possible to use **XmProcessTraversal** to traverse to MenuBars, Pulldown MenuPanes, or Popup MenuPanes.

widget   Specifies the widget ID of the widget whose hierarchy is to be traversed

direction   Specifies the direction of traversal

The *direction* parameter can have the following values, which cause the routine to take the corresponding actions:

- **XmTRAVERSE_CURRENT** — Finds the hierarchy and the tab group that contain *widget*. If this tab group is not the active tab group, makes it the active tab group. If *widget* is an item in the active tab group, makes it the active item. If *widget* is the active tab group, makes the first traversable item in the tab group the active item.

- **XmTRAVERSE_DOWN** — Finds the hierarchy that contains *widget*. Finds the active item in the active tab group and makes the item below it the active item. If there is no item below, wraps.

- **XmTRAVERSE_HOME** — Finds the hierarchy that contains *widget*. Finds the active item in the active tab group and makes the first traversable item in the tab group the active item.

- **XmTRAVERSE_LEFT** — Finds the hierarchy that contains *widget*. Finds the active item in the active tab group and makes the item to the left the active item. If there is no item to the left, wraps.

- **XmTRAVERSE_NEXT** — Finds the hierarchy that contains *widget*. Finds the active item in the active tab group and makes the next item the active item.

- **XmTRAVERSE_NEXT_TAB_GROUP** — Finds the hierarchy that contains *widget*. Finds the active tab group (if any) and makes the next tab group the active tab group in the hierarchy.

- **XmTRAVERSE_PREV** — Finds the hierarchy that contains *widget*. Finds the active item in the active tab group and makes the previous item the active item.

- **XmTRAVERSE_PREV_TAB_GROUP** — Finds the hierarchy that contains *widget*. Finds the active tab group (if any) and makes the previous tab group the active tab group in the hierarchy.

- **XmTRAVERSE_RIGHT** — Finds the hierarchy that contains *widget*. Finds the active item in the active tab group and makes the item to the right the active item. If there is no item to the right, wraps.

- **XmTRAVERSE_UP** — Finds the hierarchy that contains *widget*. Finds the active item in the active tab group and makes the item above it the active item. If there is no item above, wraps.

Return Value

Returns True if the setting succeeded. Returns False if the keyboard focus policy is not **XmEXPLICIT**, if there are no traversable items, or if the call to the routine has invalid parameters.

XmPushButton

Purpose

The PushButton widget class

AES Support Level

Full-use

Synopsis

#include <Xm/PushB.h>

Description

PushButton issues commands within an application. It consists of a text label or pixmap surrounded by a border shadow. When a PushButton is selected, the shadow changes to give the appearance that it has been pressed in. When a PushButton is unselected, the shadow changes to give the appearance that it is out.

The default behavior associated with a PushButton in a menu depends on the type of menu system in which it resides. By default, **BSelect** controls the behavior of the PushButton. In addition, **BMenu** controls the behavior of the PushButton if it resides in a PopupMenu system. The actual mouse button used is determined by its RowColumn parent.

Thickness for a second shadow, used when the PushButton is the default button, may be specified by using the **XmNshowAsDefault** resource. If it has a non-zero value, the Label's resources **XmNmarginLeft**, **XmNmarginRight**, **XmNmarginTop**, and **XmNmarginBottom** may be modified to accommodate the second shadow.

If an initial value is specified for **XmNarmPixmap** but not for **XmNlabelPixmap**, the **XmNarmPixmap** value is used for **XmNlabelPixmap**.

Classes

PushButton inherits behavior and resources from **Core**, **XmPrimitive**, and **XmLabel** Classes.

The class pointer is **xmPushButtonWidgetClass**.

The class name is **XmPushButton**.

New Resources

The following table defines a set of widget resources used by the programmer to specify data. The programmer can also set the resource values for the inherited classes to set attributes for this widget. To reference a resource by name or by class in a .Xdefaults file, remove the **XmN** or **XmC** prefix and use the remaining letters. To specify one of the defined values for a resource in a .Xdefaults file, remove the **Xm** prefix and use the remaining letters (in either lowercase or uppercase, but include any underscores between words). The codes in the access column indicate if the given resource can be set at creation time (**C**), set by using **XtSetValues** (**S**), retrieved by using **XtGetValues** (**G**), or is not applicable (**N/A**).

XmPushButton Resource Set		
Name	**Default**	**Access**
Class	**Type**	
XmNactivateCallback	NULL	C
XmCCallback	XtCallbackList	
XmNarmCallback	NULL	C
XmCCallback	XtCallbackList	
XmNarmColor	dynamic	CSG
XmCArmColor	Pixel	
XmNarmPixmap	XmUNSPECIFIED_PIXMAP	CSG
XmCArmPixmap	Pixmap	
XmNdefaultButtonShadowThickness	dynamic	CSG
XmCDefaultButtonShadowThickness	Dimension	
XmNdisarmCallback	NULL	C
XmCCallback	XtCallbackList	
XmNfillOnArm	True	CSG
XmCFillOnArm	Boolean	
XmNmultiClick	dynamic	CSG
XmCMultiClick	unsigned char	
XmNshowAsDefault	0	CSG
XmCShowAsDefault	Dimension	

XmNactivateCallback

Specifies the list of callbacks that is called when PushButton is activated. PushButton is activated when the user presses and releases the active mouse button while the pointer is inside that widget. Activating the PushButton also disarms it. For this callback the reason is **XmCR_ACTIVATE**.

XmNarmCallback

Specifies the list of callbacks that is called when PushButton is armed. PushButton is armed when the user presses the active mouse button while the pointer is inside that widget. For this callback the reason is **XmCR_ARM**.

XmNarmColor

Specifies the color with which to fill the armed button. **XmNfillOnArm** must be set to True for this resource to have an effect. The default for a color display is a color between the background and the bottom shadow color. For a monochrome display, the default is set to the foreground color, and any text in the label appears in the background color when the button is armed.

XmNarmPixmap

Specifies the pixmap to be used as the button face if **XmNlabelType** is **XmPIXMAP** and PushButton is armed. This resource is disabled when the PushButton is in a menu.

XmNdefaultButtonShadowThickness

This resource specifies the width of the default button indicator shadow. If this resource is zero, the width of the shadow comes from the value of the **XmNshowAsDefault** resource. If this resource is greater than zero, the **XmNshowAsDefault** resource is only used to specify whether this button is the default. The default value is the initial value of **XmNshowAsDefault**.

XmNdisarmCallback

Specifies the list of callbacks that is called when PushButton is disarmed. PushButton is disarmed when the user presses and releases the active mouse button while the pointer is inside that widget. For this callback, the reason is **XmCR_DISARM**.

XmNfillOnArm

Forces the PushButton to fill the background of the button with the color specified by **XmNarmColor** when the button is armed and when this resource is set to True. If False, only the top and bottom shadow colors are switched. When the PushButton is in a menu, this resource is ignored and assumed to be False.

XmNmultiClick

If a button click is followed by another button click within the time span specified by the display's multi-click time, and this resource is set to **XmMULTICLICK_DISCARD**, do not process the second click. If this resource is set to **XmMULTICLICK_KEEP**, process the event and increment *click_count* in the callback structure. When the button is not in a menu, the default value is **XmMULTICLICK_KEEP**.

XmNshowAsDefault

If **XmNdefaultButtonShadowThickness** is greater than zero, a value greater than zero in this resource specifies to mark this button as the default button. If **XmNdefaultButtonShadowThickness** is zero, a value greater than zero in this resource specifies to mark this button as the default button with the shadow thickness specified by this resource. The space between the shadow and the default shadow is equal to the sum of both shadows. The default value is zero. When this value is not zero, the Label resources **XmNmarginLeft**, **XmNmarginRight**, **XmNmarginTop**, and **XmNmarginBottom** may be modified to accommodate the second shadow. This resource is disabled when the PushButton is in a menu.

Inherited Resources

PushButton inherits behavior and resources from the following superclasses. For a complete description of each resource, refer to the man page for that superclass.

XmLabel Resource Set		
Name Class	**Default** Type	**Access**
XmNaccelerator XmCAccelerator	NULL String	CSG
XmNacceleratorText XmCAcceleratorText	NULL XmString	CSG
XmNalignment XmCAlignment	dynamic unsigned char	CSG
XmNfontList XmCFontList	dynamic XmFontList	CSG
XmNlabelInsensitivePixmap XmCLabelInsensitivePixmap	XmUNSPECIFIED_PIXMAP Pixmap	CSG
XmNlabelPixmap XmCLabelPixmap	dynamic Pixmap	CSG
XmNlabelString XmCXmString	dynamic XmString	CSG
XmNlabelType XmCLabelType	XmSTRING unsigned char	CSG
XmNmarginBottom XmCMarginBottom	dynamic Dimension	CSG
XmNmarginHeight XmCMarginHeight	2 Dimension	CSG
XmNmarginLeft XmCMarginLeft	dynamic Dimension	CSG
XmNmarginRight XmCMarginRight	dynamic Dimension	CSG
XmNmarginTop XmCMarginTop	dynamic Dimension	CSG
XmNmarginWidth XmCMarginWidth	2 Dimension	CSG

Name	Default	Access
Class	Type	
XmNmnemonic	NULL	CSG
XmCMnemonic	KeySym	
XmNmnemonicCharSet	dynamic	CSG
XmCMnemonicCharSet	String	
XmNrecomputeSize	True	CSG
XmCRecomputeSize	Boolean	
XmNstringDirection	dynamic	CSG
XmCStringDirection	XmStringDirection	

XmPrimitive Resource Set		
Name	**Default**	**Access**
Class	**Type**	
XmNbottomShadowColor	dynamic	CSG
XmCBottomShadowColor	Pixel	
XmNbottomShadowPixmap	XmUNSPECIFIED_PIXMAP	CSG
XmCBottomShadowPixmap	Pixmap	
XmNforeground	dynamic	CSG
XmCForeground	Pixel	
XmNhelpCallback	NULL	C
XmCCallback	XtCallbackList	
XmNhighlightColor	dynamic	CSG
XmCHighlightColor	Pixel	
XmNhighlightOnEnter	False	CSG
XmCHighlightOnEnter	Boolean	
XmNhighlightPixmap	dynamic	CSG
XmCHighlightPixmap	Pixmap	
XmNhighlightThickness	2	CSG
XmCHighlightThickness	Dimension	
XmNnavigationType	XmNONE	G
XmCNavigationType	XmNavigationType	
XmNshadowThickness	2	CSG
XmCShadowThickness	Dimension	
XmNtopShadowColor	dynamic	CSG
XmCTopShadowColor	Pixel	
XmNtopShadowPixmap	dynamic	CSG
XmCTopShadowPixmap	Pixmap	
XmNtraversalOn	True	CSG
XmCTraversalOn	Boolean	
XmNuserData	NULL	CSG
XmCUserData	Pointer	

Core Resource Set		
Name	**Default**	**Access**
Class	**Type**	
XmNaccelerators	dynamic	CSG
XmCAccelerators	XtAccelerators	
XmNancestorSensitive	dynamic	G
XmCSensitive	Boolean	
XmNbackground	dynamic	CSG
XmCBackground	Pixel	
XmNbackgroundPixmap	XmUNSPECIFIED_PIXMAP	CSG
XmCPixmap	Pixmap	
XmNborderColor	XtDefaultForeground	CSG
XmCBorderColor	Pixel	
XmNborderPixmap	XmUNSPECIFIED_PIXMAP	CSG
XmCPixmap	Pixmap	
XmNborderWidth	0	CSG
XmCBorderWidth	Dimension	
XmNcolormap	dynamic	CG
XmCColormap	Colormap	
XmNdepth	dynamic	CG
XmCDepth	int	
XmNdestroyCallback	NULL	C
XmCCallback	XtCallbackList	
XmNheight	dynamic	CSG
XmCHeight	Dimension	
XmNinitialResourcesPersistent	True	C
XmCInitialResourcesPersistent	Boolean	
XmNmappedWhenManaged	True	CSG
XmCMappedWhenManaged	Boolean	
XmNscreen	dynamic	CG
XmCScreen	Screen *	

Name	Default	Access
Class	Type	
XmNsensitive	True	CSG
XmCSensitive	Boolean	
XmNtranslations	dynamic	CSG
XmCTranslations	XtTranslations	
XmNwidth	dynamic	CSG
XmCWidth	Dimension	
XmNx	0	CSG
XmCPosition	Position	
XmNy	0	CSG
XmCPosition	Position	

Callback Information

A pointer to the following structure is passed to each callback:

typedef struct
{
    int   *reason*;
    XEvent   * *event*;
    int   *click_count*;
} **XmPushButtonCallbackStruct**;

reason   Indicates why the callback was invoked.

event   Points to the **XEvent** that triggered the callback.

click_count
        This value is valid only when the reason is **XmCR_ACTIVATE**.
        It contains the number of clicks in the last multiclick sequence if
        the **XmNmultiClick** resource is set to
        XmMULTICLICK_KEEP, otherwise it contains **1**. The activate
        callback is invoked for each click if **XmNmultiClick** is set to
        XmMULTICLICK_KEEP.

Translations

XmPushButton includes translations from Primitive.

Note that altering translations in **#override** or **#augment** mode is undefined.

The XmPushButton translations for XmPushButtons not in a menu system are listed below. These translations may not directly correspond to a translation table.

BSelect Press:	**Arm()**
BSelect Click:	**Activate()**
	Disarm()
BSelect Release:	**Activate()**
	Disarm()
BSelect Press 2+:	**MultiArm()**
BSelect Release 2+:	**MultiActivate()**
	Disarm()
KActivate:	**ArmAndActivate()**
KSelect:	**ArmAndActivate()**
KHelp:	**Help()**

XmPushButton inherits menu traversal translations from XmLabel. Additional XmPushButton translations for PushButtons in a menu system are listed below. In a Popup menu system, **BMenu** also performs the **BSelect** actions. These translations may not directly correspond to a translation table.

BSelect Press:	**BtnDown()**
BSelect Release:	**BtnUp()**
KActivate:	**ArmAndActivate()**
KSelect:	**ArmAndActivate()**
MAny KCancel:	**MenuShellPopdownOne()**

Action Routines

The XmPushButton action routines are described below:

Activate():   This action draws the shadow in the unarmed state. If the button is not in a menu and if **XmNfillOnArm** is set to True, the background color reverts to the unarmed color. If **XmNlabelType** is **XmPIXMAP**, the **XmNlabelPixmap** is used for the button face. If the pointer is still within the button, this action calls the callbacks for **XmNactivateCallback**.

Arm():   This action arms the PushButton. It draws the shadow in the armed state. If the button is not in a menu and if **XmNfillOnArm** is set to True, it fills the button with the color specified by **XmNarmColor**. If **XmNlabelType** is **XmPIXMAP**, the **XmNarmPixmap** is used for the button face. It calls the **XmNarmCallback** callbacks.

ArmAndActivate():

In a menu, does the following: Unposts all menus in the menu hierarchy. Unless the button is already armed, calls the **XmNarmCallback** callbacks. Calls the **XmNactivateCallback** and **XmNdisarmCallback** callbacks.

Outside a menu, does the following: Draws the shadow in the armed state and, if **XmNfillOnArm** is set to True, fills the button with the color specified by **XmNarmColor**. If **XmNlabelType** is **XmPIXMAP**, the **XmNarmPixmap** is used for the button face. Calls the **XmNarmCallback** callbacks.

Outside a menu, this action also arranges for the following to happen, either immediately or at a later time: The shadow is drawn in the unarmed state and, if **XmNfillOnArm** is set to True, the background color reverts to the unarmed color. If **XmNlabelType** is **XmPIXMAP**, the **XmNlabelPixmap** is used for the button face. The **XmNactivateCallback** and **XmNdisarmCallback** callbacks are called.

BtnDown(): This action unposts any menus posted by the PushButton's parent menu, disables keyboard traversal for the menu, and enables mouse traversal for the menu. It draws the shadow in the armed state and, unless the button is already armed, calls the **XmNarmCallback** callbacks.

BtnUp(): This action unposts all menus in the menu hierarchy and activates the PushButton. It calls the **XmNactivateCallback** callbacks and then the **XmNdisarmCallback** callbacks.

Disarm(): Calls the callbacks for **XmNdisarmCallback**.

Help(): In a Pulldown or Popup MenuPane, unposts all menus in the menu hierarchy and restores keyboard focus to the tab group that had the focus before the menu system was entered. Calls the callbacks for **XmNhelpCallback** if any exist. If there are no help callbacks for this widget, this action calls the help callbacks for the nearest ancestor that has them.

MenuShellPopdownOne():

In a toplevel Pulldown MenuPane from a MenuBar, unposts the menu, disarms the MenuBar CascadeButton and the MenuBar, and restores keyboard focus to the tab group that had the focus before the MenuBar was entered. In other Pulldown MenuPanes, unposts the menu.

In a Popup MenuPane, unposts the menu and restores keyboard focus to the widget from which the menu was posted.

MultiActivate():

If **XmNmultiClick** is **XmMULTICLICK_DISCARD**, this action does nothing.

If **XmNmultiClick** is **XmMULTICLICK_KEEP**, this action does the following: Increments *click_count* in the callback structure. Draws the shadow in the unarmed state. If the button is not in a menu and if **XmNfillOnArm** is set to True, the background color reverts to the unarmed color. If **XmNlabelType** is **XmPIXMAP**, the **XmNlabelPixmap** is used for the button face. If the pointer is within the PushButton, calls the callbacks for **XmNactivateCallback**. Calls the callbacks for **XmNdisarmCallback**.

MultiArm():

If **XmNmultiClick** is **XmMULTICLICK_DISCARD**, this action does nothing.

If **XmNmultiClick** is **XmMULTICLICK_KEEP**, this action does the following: Draws the shadow in the armed state. If the button is not in a menu and if **XmNfillOnArm** is set to True, fills the button with the color specified by **XmNarmColor**. If **XmNlabelType** is **XmPIXMAP**, the **XmNarmPixmap** is used for the button face. Calls the **XmNarmCallback** callbacks.

Additional Behavior

This widget has the additional behavior described below:

<EnterWindow>:

In a menu, if keyboard traversal is enabled, this action does nothing. Otherwise, it draws the shadow in the armed state and calls the **XmNarmCallback** callbacks.

If the PushButton is not in a menu and the cursor leaves and then reenters the PushButton's window while the button is pressed, this action draws the shadow in the armed state. If **XmNfillOnArm** is set to True, it also fills the button with the color specified by **XmNarmColor**. If **XmNlabelType** is **XmPIXMAP**, the **XmNarmPixmap** is used for the button face.

<LeaveWindow>:

In a menu, if keyboard traversal is enabled, this action does nothing. Otherwise, it draws the shadow in the unarmed state and calls the **XmNdisarmCallback** callbacks.

If the PushButton is not in a menu and the cursor leaves the PushButton's window while the button is pressed, this action draws the shadow in the unarmed state. If **XmNfillOnArm** is set to True, the background color reverts to the unarmed color. If **XmNlabelType** is **XmPIXMAP**, the **XmNlabelPixmap** is used for the button face.

Virtual Bindings

The bindings for virtual keys are vendor specific.

Related Information

Core(3X), **XmCreatePushButton(3X)**, **XmLabel(3X)**, **XmPrimitive(3X)**, and **XmRowColumn(3X)**.

XmPushButtonGadget

Purpose

The PushButtonGadget widget class

AES Support Level

Full-use

Synopsis

#include <Xm/PushBG.h>

Description

PushButtonGadget issues commands within an application. It consists of a text label or pixmap surrounded by a border shadow. When PushButtonGadget is selected, the shadow changes to give the appearance that the PushButtonGadget has been pressed in. When PushButtonGadget is unselected, the shadow changes to give the appearance that the PushButtonGadget is out.

The default behavior associated with a PushButtonGadget in a menu depends on the type of menu system in which it resides. By default, **BSelect** controls the behavior of the PushButtonGadget. In addition, **BMenu** controls the behavior of the PushButtonGadget if it resides in a PopupMenu system. The actual mouse button used is determined by its RowColumn parent.

Thickness for a second shadow may be specified by using the **XmNshowAsDefault** resource. If it has a non-zero value, the Label's resources **XmNmarginLeft**, **XmNmarginRight**, **XmNmarginTop**, and **XmNmarginBottom** may be modified to accommodate the second shadow.

If an initial value is specified for **XmNarmPixmap** but not for **XmNlabelPixmap**, the **XmNarmPixmap** value is used for **XmNlabelPixmap**.

Classes

PushButtonGadget inherits behavior and resources from **Object**, **RectObj**, **XmGadget** and **XmLabelGadget** classes.

The class pointer is **xmPushButtonGadgetClass**.

The class name is **XmPushButtonGadget**.

New Resources

The following table defines a set of widget resources used by the programmer to specify data. The programmer can also set the resource values for the inherited classes to set attributes for this widget. To reference a resource by name or by class in a .Xdefaults file, remove the **XmN** or **XmC** prefix and use the remaining letters. To specify one of the defined values for a resource in a .Xdefaults file, remove the **Xm** prefix and use the remaining letters (in either lowercase or uppercase, but include any underscores between words). The codes in the access column indicate if the given resource can be set at creation time (**C**), set by using **XtSetValues** (**S**), retrieved by using **XtGetValues** (**G**), or is not applicable (**N/A**).

XmPushButtonGadget		

Name
    Class
	Default
	    Type
		Access

XmNactivateCallback
    XmCCallback
	NULL
	    XtCallbackList
		C

XmNarmCallback
    XmCCallback
	NULL
	    XtCallbackList
		C

XmNarmColor
    XmCArmColor
	dynamic
	    Pixel
		CSG

XmNarmPixmap
    XmCArmPixmap
	XmUNSPECIFIED_PIXMAP
	    Pixmap
		CSG

XmNdefaultButtonShadowThickness
    XmCdefaultButtonShadowThickness
	dynamic
	    Dimension
		CSG

XmNdisarmCallback
    XmCCallback
	NULL
	    XtCallbackList
		C

XmNfillOnArm
    XmCFillOnArm
	True
	    Boolean
		CSG

XmNmultiClick
    XmCMultiClick
	dynamic
	    unsigned char
		CSG

XmNshowAsDefault
    XmCShowAsDefault
	0
	    Dimension
		CSG

XmNactivateCallback

Specifies the list of callbacks that is called when the PushButtonGadget is activated. It is activated when the user presses and releases the active mouse button while the pointer is inside the PushButtonGadget. Activating PushButtonGadget also disarms it. For this callback the reason is **XmCR_ACTIVATE**.

XmNarmCallback

Specifies the list of callbacks that is called when PushButtonGadget is armed. It is armed when the user presses the active mouse button while the pointer is inside the PushButtonGadget. For this callback the reason is **XmCR_ARM**.

XmNarmColor

Specifies the color with which to fill the armed button. **XmNfillOnArm** must be set to True for this resource to have an effect. The default for a color display is a color between the background and the bottom shadow color. For a monochrome display, the default is set to the foreground color, and any text in the label appears in the background color when the button is armed.

XmNarmPixmap

Specifies the pixmap to be used as the button face if **XmNlabeltype** is **XmPIXMAP** and PushButtonGadget is armed. This resource is disabled when the PushButtonGadget is in a menu.

XmNdefaultButtonShadowThickness

This resource specifies the width of the default button indicator shadow. If this resource is zero, the width of the shadow comes from the value of the **XmNshowAsDefault** resource. If this resource is greater than zero, the **XmNshowAsDefault** resource is only used to specify whether this button is the default. The default value is the initial value of **XmNshowAsDefault**.

XmNdisarmCallback

Specifies the list of callbacks that is called when the PushButtonGadget is disarmed. PushButtonGadget is disarmed when the user presses and releases the active mouse button while the pointer is inside that gadget. For this callback, the reason is **XmCR_DISARM**.

XmNfillOnArm

Forces the PushButtonGadget to fill the background of the button with the color specified by **XmNarmColor** when the button is armed and when this resource is set to True. If False, only the top and bottom shadow colors are switched. When the PushButtonGadget is in a menu, this resource is ignored and assumed to be False.

XmNmultiClick

If a button click is followed by another button click within the
time span specified by the display's multi-click time, and this
resource is set to **XmMULTICLICK_DISCARD**, do not
process the second click. If this resource is set to
XmMULTICLICK_KEEP, process the event and increment
click_count in the callback structure. When the
PushButtonGadget is not in a menu, the default value is
XmMULTICLICK_KEEP.

XmNshowAsDefault

If **XmNdefaultButtonShadowThickness** is greater than zero,
a value greater than zero in this resource specifes to mark this
button as the default button. If
XmNdefaultButtonShadowThickness is zero, a value greater
than zero in this resource specifies to mark this button as the
default button with the shadow thickness specified by this
resource. The space between the shadow and the default
shadow is equal to the sum of both shadows. The default value
is zero. When this value is not zero, the Label resources
XmNmarginLeft, **XmNmarginRight**, **XmNmarginTop**, and
XmNmarginBottom may be modified to accommodate the
second shadow. This resource is disabled when the
PushButton is in a menu.

Inherited Resources

PushButtonGadget inherits behavior and resources from the following
superclasses. For a complete description of each resource, refer to the man
page for that superclass.

XmLabelGadget Resource Set		
Name Class	**Default** Type	**Access**
XmNaccelerator XmCAccelerator	NULL String	CSG
XmNacceleratorText XmCAcceleratorText	NULL XmString	CSG
XmNalignment XmCAlignment	dynamic unsigned char	CSG
XmNfontList XmCFontList	dynamic XmFontList	CSG
XmNlabelInsensitivePixmap XmCLabelInsensitivePixmap	XmUNSPECIFIED_PIXMAP Pixmap	CSG
XmNlabelPixmap XmCLabelPixmap	dynamic Pixmap	CSG
XmNlabelString XmCXmString	dynamic XmString	CSG
XmNlabelType XmCLabelType	XmSTRING unsigned char	CSG
XmNmarginBottom XmCMarginBottom	dynamic Dimension	CSG
XmNmarginHeight XmCMarginHeight	2 Dimension	CSG
XmNmarginLeft XmCMarginLeft	dynamic Dimension	CSG
XmNmarginRight XmCMarginRight	dynamic Dimension	CSG
XmNmarginTop XmCMarginTop	dynamic Dimension	CSG
XmNmarginWidth XmCMarginWidth	2 Dimension	CSG

Name	Default	Access
Class	Type	
XmNmnemonic	NULL	CSG
XmCMnemonic	KeySym	
XmNmnemonicCharSet	dynamic	CSG
XmCMnemonicCharSet	String	
XmNrecomputeSize	True	CSG
XmCRecomputeSize	Boolean	
XmNstringDirection	dynamic	CSG
XmCStringDirection	XmStringDirection	

XmGadget Resource Set		
Name	**Default**	**Access**
Class	Type	
XmNhelpCallback	NULL	C
XmCCallback	XtCallbackList	
XmNhighlightOnEnter	False	CSG
XmCHighlightOnEnter	Boolean	
XmNhighlightThickness	2	CSG
XmCHighlightThickness	Dimension	
XmNnavigationType	XmNONE	G
XmCNavigationType	XmNavigationType	
XmNshadowThickness	2	CSG
XmCShadowThickness	Dimension	
XmNtraversalOn	True	CSG
XmCTraversalOn	Boolean	
XmNuserData	NULL	CSG
XmCUserData	Pointer	

RectObj Resource Set		
Name	**Default**	**Access**
Class	**Type**	
XmNancestorSensitive	dynamic	G
XmCSensitive	Boolean	
XmNborderWidth	0	CSG
XmCBorderWidth	Dimension	
XmNheight	dynamic	CSG
XmCHeight	Dimension	
XmNsensitive	True	CSG
XmCSensitive	Boolean	
XmNwidth	dynamic	CSG
XmCWidth	Dimension	
XmNx	0	CSG
XmCPosition	Position	
XmNy	0	CSG
XmCPosition	Position	

Object Resource Set		
Name	**Default**	**Access**
Class	**Type**	
XmNdestroyCallback	NULL	C
XmCCallback	XtCallbackList	

Callback Information

A pointer to the following structure is passed to each callback:

typedef struct
{
    int   *reason*;
    XEvent   * *event*;
    int   *click_count*;
} **XmPushButtonCallbackStruct**;

reason   Indicates why the callback was invoked.

event   Points to the **XEvent** that triggered the callback.

click_count

This value is valid only when the reason is **XmCR_ACTIVATE**. It contains the number of clicks in the last multiclick sequence if the **XmNmultiClick** resource is set to **XmMULTICLICK_KEEP**, otherwise it contains **1**. The activate callback is invoked for each click if **XmNmultiClick** is set to **XmMULTICLICK_KEEP**.

Behavior

XmPushButtonGadget includes behavior from XmGadget. XmPushButtonGadget includes menu traversal behavior from XmLabelGadget. Additional behavior for XmPushButtonGadget is described below:

BSelect Press:

This action arms the PushButtonGadget.

In a menu, this action unposts any menus posted by the PushButtonGadget's parent menu, disables keyboard traversal for the menu, and enables mouse traversal for the menu. It draws the shadow in the armed state. Unless the button is already armed, it calls the **XmNarmCallback** callbacks.

If the button is not in a menu, this action draws the shadow in the armed state. If **XmNfillOnArm** is set to True, it fills the button with the color specified by **XmNarmColor**. If **XmNlabelType** is **XmPIXMAP**, the **XmNarmPixmap** is used for the button face. It calls the **XmNarmCallback** callbacks.

BSelect Press 2+:

If **XmNmultiClick** is **XmMULTICLICK_DISCARD**, this action does nothing.

If **XmNmultiClick** is **XmMULTICLICK_KEEP**, this action does the following: Draws the shadow in the armed state. If the button is not in a menu and if **XmNfillOnArm** is set to True, fills the button with the color specified by **XmNarmColor**. If **XmNlabelType** is **XmPIXMAP**, the **XmNarmPixmap** is used for the button face. Calls the **XmNarmCallback** callbacks.

BSelect Click or BSelect Release:

In a menu, this action unposts all menus in the menu hierarchy and activates the PushButtonGadget. It calls the **XmNactivateCallback** callbacks and then the **XmNdisarmCallback** callbacks.

If the PushButtonGadget is not in a menu, this action draws the shadow in the unarmed state. If **XmNfillOnArm** is set to True, the background color reverts to the unarmed color. If **XmNlabelType** is **XmPIXMAP**, the **XmNlabelPixmap** is used for the button face. If the pointer is still within the button, this action calls the callbacks for **XmNactivateCallback**. Calls the callbacks for **XmNdisarmCallback**.

BSelect Release 2+:

If **XmNmultiClick** is **XmMULTICLICK_DISCARD**, this action does nothing.

If **XmNmultiClick** is **XmMULTICLICK_KEEP**, this action does the following: Increments *click_count* in the callback structure. Draws the shadow in the unarmed state. If the button is not in a menu and if **XmNfillOnArm** is set to True, the background color reverts to the unarmed color. If **XmNlabelType** is **XmPIXMAP**, the **XmNlabelPixmap** is used for the button face. If the pointer is within the PushButtonGadget, calls the callbacks for **XmNactivateCallback**. Calls the callbacks for **XmNdisarmCallback**.

KActivate or KSelect:

In a menu, does the following: Unposts all menus in the menu hierarchy. Unless the button is already armed, calls the **XmNarmCallback** callbacks. Calls the **XmNactivateCallback** and **XmNdisarmCallback** callbacks.

Outside a menu, does the following: Draws the shadow in the armed state and, if **XmNfillOnArm** is set to True, fills the button with the color specified by **XmNarmColor**. If **XmNlabelType** is **XmPIXMAP**, the **XmNarmPixmap** is used for the button face. Calls the **XmNarmCallback** callbacks.

Outside a menu, this action also arranges for the following to happen, either immediately or at a later time: The shadow is drawn in the unarmed state and, if **XmNfillOnArm** is set to True, the background color reverts to the unarmed color. If **XmNlabelType** is **XmPIXMAP**, the **XmNlabelPixmap** is used for the button face. The **XmNactivateCallback** and **XmNdisarmCallback** callbacks are called.

KHelp: In a Pulldown or Popup MenuPane, unposts all menus in the menu hierarchy and restores keyboard focus to the tab group that had the focus before the menu system was entered. Calls the callbacks for **XmNhelpCallback** if any exist. If there are no help callbacks for this widget, this action calls the help callbacks for the nearest ancestor that has them.

MAny KCancel:

In a toplevel Pulldown MenuPane from a MenuBar, unposts the menu, disarms the MenuBar CascadeButton and the MenuBar, and restores keyboard focus to the tab group that had the focus before the MenuBar was entered. In other Pulldown MenuPanes, unposts the menu.

In a Popup MenuPane, unposts the menu and restores keyboard focus to the widget from which the menu was posted.

<Enter>: In a menu, if keyboard traversal is enabled, this action does nothing. Otherwise, it draws the shadow in the armed state and calls the **XmNarmCallback** callbacks.

If the PushButtonGadget is not in a menu and the cursor leaves and then reenters the PushButtonGadget while the button is pressed, this action draws the shadow in the armed state. If **XmNfillOnArm** is set to True, it also fills the button with the color specified by **XmNarmColor**. If **XmNlabelType** is **XmPIXMAP**, the **XmNarmPixmap** is used for the button face.

<Leave>: In a menu, if keyboard traversal is enabled, this action does nothing. Otherwise, it draws the shadow in the unarmed state and calls the **XmNdisarmCallback** callbacks.

If the PushButtonGadget is not in a menu and the cursor leaves the PushButtonGadget while the button is pressed, this action draws the shadow in the unarmed state. If **XmNfillOnArm** is set to True, the background color reverts to the unarmed color. If **XmNlabelType** is **XmPIXMAP**, the **XmNlabelPixmap** is used for the button face.

Virtual Bindings

The bindings for virtual keys are vendor specific.

Related Information

Object(3X), RectObj(3X), XmCreatePushButtonGadget(3X), XmGadget(3X), XmLabelGadget(3X), and XmRowColumn(3X).

XmRemoveProtocolCallback

Purpose

A VendorShell function that removes a callback from the internal list.

AES Support Level

Trial-use

Synopsis

#include <Xm/Xm.h>
#include <X11/Protocols.h>

void XmRemoveProtocolCallback (*shell, property, protocol, callback, closure*)
    Widget   *shell*;
    Atom   *property*;
    Atom   *protocol*;
    XtCallbackProc*callback*;
    caddr_t   *closure*;

void XmRemoveWMProtocolCallback (*shell, protocol, callback, closure*)
    Widget   *shell*;
    Atom   *protocol*;
    XtCallbackProc*callback*;
    caddr_t   *closure*;

Description

XmRemoveProtocolCallback removes a callback from the internal list.

XmRemoveWMProtocolCallback is a convenience interface. It calls **XmRemoveProtocolCallback** with the property value set to the atom returned by interning **WM_PROTOCOLS**.

shell   Specifies the widget with which the protocol property is associated

property   Specifies the protocol property

protocol   Specifies the protocol atom (or an int cast to Atom)

callback   Specifies the procedure to call when a protocol message is received

closure   Specifies the client data to be passed to the callback when it is invoked

For a complete definition of VendorShell and its associated resources, see **VendorShell(3X)**.

Related Information

VendorShell(3X), **XmInternAtom(3X)**, and **XmRemoveWMProtocolCallback(3X)**.

XmRemoveProtocols

Purpose

A VendorShell function that removes the protocols from the protocol manager and deallocates the internal tables.

AES Support Level

Trial-use

Synopsis

#include <Xm/Xm.h>
#include <X11/Protocols.h>

void XmRemoveProtocols (*shell, property, protocols, num_protocols*)
    Widget   *shell*;
    Atom   *property*;
    Atom   * *protocols*;
    Cardinal   *num_protocols*;

void XmRemoveWMProtocols (*shell, protocols, num_protocols*)
    Widget   *shell*;
    Atom   * *protocols*;
    Cardinal   *num_protocols*;

Description

XmRemoveProtocols removes the protocols from the protocol manager and deallocates the internal tables. If any of the protocols are active, it will update the handlers and update the property if *shell* is realized.

XmRemoveWMProtocols is a convenience interface. It calls **XmRemoveProtocols** with the property value set to the atom returned by interning **WM_PROTOCOLS**.

shell   Specifies the widget with which the protocol property is associated

property   Specifies the protocol property

protocols   Specifies the protocol atoms (or ints cast to Atom)

num_protocols Specifies the number of elements in protocols

For a complete definition of VendorShell and its associated resources, see **VendorShell(3X)**.

Related Information

VendorShell(3X), **XmInternAtom(3X)**, and **XmRemoveWMProtocols(3X)**.

XmRemoveTabGroup

Purpose

A function that removes a tab group

AES Support Level

Full-use

Synopsis

#include <Xm/Xm.h>

void XmRemoveTabGroup (*tab_group*)
    Widget   *tab_group*;

Description

XmRemoveTabGroup removes a widget from the list of tab groups associated with a particular widget hierarchy and sets the widget's **XmNnavigationType** to **XmNONE**.

tab_group   Specifies the widget ID

Related Information

XmAddTabGroup(3X), XmManager(3X), and XmPrimitive(3X).

XmRemoveWMProtocolCallback

Purpose

A VendorShell convenience interface that removes a callback from the internal list.

AES Support Level

Trial-use

Synopsis

```
#include <Xm/Xm.h>
#include <X11/Protocols.h>
```

void XmRemoveWMProtocolCallback (*shell, protocol, callback, closure*)
    Widget   *shell*;
    Atom   *protocol*;
    XtCallbackProc*callback*;
    caddr_t   *closure*;

Description

XmRemoveWMProtocolCallback is a convenience interface. It calls **XmRemoveProtocolCallback** with the property value set to the atom returned by interning **WM_PROTOCOLS**.

shell Specifies the widget with which the protocol property is associated

protocol Specifies the protocol atom (or an int type cast to Atom)

callback Specifies the procedure to call when a protocol message is received

closure Specifies the client data to be passed to the callback when it is invoked

For a complete definition of VendorShell and its associated resources, see **VendorShell(3X)**.

Related Information

VendorShell(3X), **XmInternAtom(3X)**, and **XmRemoveProtocolCallback(3X)**.

XmRemoveWMProtocols

Purpose

A VendorShell convenience interface that removes the protocols from the protocol manager and deallocates the internal tables.

AES Support Level

Trial-use

Synopsis

```
#include <Xm/Xm.h>
#include <X11/Protocols.h>

void XmRemoveWMProtocols (shell, protocols, num_protocols)
    Widget      shell;
    Atom        * protocols;
    Cardinal    num_protocols;
```

Description

XmRemoveWMProtocols is a convenience interface. It calls **XmRemoveProtocols** with the property value set to the atom returned by interning **WM_PROTOCOLS**.

shell　　　　Specifies the widget with which the protocol property is associated

protocols　　Specifies the protocol atoms (or ints cast to Atom)

num_protocols　Specifies the number of elements in protocols

For a complete definition of VendorShell and its associated resources, see **VendorShell(3X)**.

Related Information

VendorShell(3X), XmInternAtom(3X), and **XmRemoveProtocols(3X)**.

XmResolvePartOffsets

Purpose

A function that allows writing of upward-compatible applications and widgets.

AES Support Level

Full-use

Synopsis

#include <Xm/XmP.h>

void **XmResolvePartOffsets** (*widget_class, offset*)
    WidgetClass *widget_class*;
    XmOffsetPtr * *offset*;

Description

The use of offset records requires one extra global variable per widget class. The variable consists of a pointer to an array of offsets into the widget record for each part of the widget structure. The **XmResolvePartOffsets** function allocates the offset records needed by an application to guarantee upward-compatible access to widget instance records by applications and widgets. These offset records are used by the widget to access all of the widget's variables. A widget needs to take the following steps:

- Instead of creating a resource list, the widget creates an offset resource list. To help you accomplish this, use the **XmPartResource** structure and the **XmPartOffset** macro. The **XmPartResource** data structure looks just like a resource list, but instead of having one integer for its offset, it has two shorts. This is put into the class record as if it were a normal resource list. Instead of using **XtOffset** for the offset, the widget uses **XmPartOffset**.

```
XmPartResource resources[] = {
  { BarNxyz, BarCXyz, XmRBoolean,
    sizeof(Boolean), XmPartOffset(Bar,xyz),
    XmRImmediate, (caddr_t)False }
};
```

- Instead of putting the widget size in the class record, the widget puts the widget part size in the same field.

- Instead of putting **XtVersion** in the class record, the widget puts **XtVersionDontCheck** in the class record.

- The widget defines a variable, of type **XmOffsetPtr**, to point to the offset record. This can be part of the widget's class record or a separate global variable.

- In class initialization, the widget calls **XmResolvePartOffsets**, passing it a pointer to contain the address of the offset record and the class record. This does several things:

  Adds the superclass (which, by definition, has already been initialized) size field to the part size field

  Allocates an array based upon the number of superclasses

  Fills in the offsets of all the widget parts with the appropriate values, determined by examining the size fields of all superclass records

  Uses the part offset array to modify the offset entries in the resource list to be real offsets, in place

- The widget defines a constant which will be the index to its part structure in the offsets array. The value should be 1 greater than the index of the widget's superclass. Constants defined for all Xm widgets can be found in **XmP.h**.

```
#define BarIndex (XmBulletinBIndex + 1)
```

- Instead of accessing fields directly, the widget must always go through the offset table. The **XmField** macro helps you access these fields. Because the **XmPartOffset** and **XmField** macros concatenate things together, you must ensure that there is no space after the part argument. For example, the following macros do not work because of the space after the part (Label) argument:

```
XmField(w, offset, Label , text, char *)
XmPartOffset(Label , text)
```

Therefore, you must not have any spaces after the part (Label) argument, as illustrated here:

```
XmField(w, offset, Label, text, char *)
```

You can define macros for each field to make this easier. Assume an integer field *xyz*:

```
#define BarXyz(w) (*(int *)(((char *) w) + \
    offset[BarIndex] + XtOffset(BarPart,xyz)))
```

The parameters for **XmResolvePartOffsets** are defined below:

widget_class Specifies the widget class pointer for the created widget.

offset   Returns the offset record.

XmRowColumn

Purpose

The RowColumn widget class

AES Support Level

Full-use

Synopsis

#include <Xm/RowColumn.h>

Description

The RowColumn widget is a general purpose RowColumn manager capable of containing any widget type as a child. In general, it requires no special knowledge about how its children function and provides nothing beyond support for several different layout styles. However, it can be configured as a menu, in which case, it expects only certain children, and it configures to a particular layout. The menus supported are: MenuBar, Pulldown or Popup MenuPanes, and OptionMenu.

The type of layout performed is controlled by how the application has set the various layout resources. It can be configured to lay out its children in either rows or columns. In addition, the application can specify how the children are laid out, as follows:

- the children are packed tightly together into either rows or columns

- each child is placed in an identically sized box (producing a symmetrical look)

- a specific layout (the current x and y positions of the children control their location)

In addition, the application has control over both the spacing that occurs between each row and column and the margin spacing present between the edges of the RowColumn widget and any children that are placed against it.

In a MenuBar, Pulldown MenuPane, or Popup MenuPane the default for the **XmNshadowThickness** resource is 2. In an OptionMenu or a WorkArea (such as a RadioBox or CheckBox) this resource is not applicable and its use is undefined. If an application wishes to place a 3-D shadow around an OptionMenu or WorkArea, it can create the RowColumn as a child of a Frame widget.

In a MenuBar, Pulldown MenuPane, or Popup MenuPane the **XmNnavigationType** resource is not applicable and its use is undefined. In a WorkArea the default for **XmNnavigationType** is **XmTAB_GROUP**. In an OptionMenu the default for **XmNnavigationType** is **XmNONE**.

In a MenuBar, Pulldown MenuPane, or Popup MenuPane the **XmNtraversalOn** resource is not applicable and its use is undefined. In an OptionMenu or WorkArea the default for **XmNtraversalOn** is True.

If the parent of the RowColumn is a MenuShell, the **XmNmappedWhenManaged** resource is forced to False when the widget is realized.

Classes

RowColumn inherits behavior and resources from **Core**, **Composite**, **Constraint**, and **XmManager** classes.

The class pointer is **xmRowColumnWidgetClass**.

The class name is **XmRowColumn**.

New Resources

The following table defines a set of widget resources used by the programmer to specify data. The programmer can also set the resource values for the inherited classes to set attributes for this widget. To reference a resource by name or by class in a .Xdefaults file, remove the **XmN** or **XmC** prefix and use the remaining letters. To specify one of the defined values for a resource in a .Xdefaults file, remove the **Xm** prefix and use the remaining letters (in either lowercase or uppercase, but include any underscores between words). The codes in the access column indicate if the given resource can be set at creation time (**C**), set by using **XtSetValues** (**S**), retrieved by using **XtGetValues** (**G**), or is not applicable (**N/A**).

XmRowColumn Resource Set		
Name	**Default**	**Access**
Class	Type	
XmNadjustLast	True	CSG
XmCAdjustLast	Boolean	
XmNadjustMargin	True	CSG
XmCAdjustMargin	Boolean	
XmNentryAlignment	XmALIGNMENT_BEGINNING	CSG
XmCAlignment	unsigned char	
XmNentryBorder	0	CSG
XmCEntryBorder	Dimension	
XmNentryCallback	NULL	C
XtCCallback	XtCallbackList	
XmNentryClass	dynamic	CSG
XmCEntryClass	WidgetClass	
XmNisAligned	True	CSG
XmCIsAligned	Boolean	
XmNisHomogeneous	dynamic	CG
XmCIsHomogeneous	Boolean	
XmNlabelString	NULL	C
XmCXmString	XmString	
XmNmapCallback	NULL	C
XmCCallback	XtCallbackList	
XmNmarginHeight	dynamic	CSG
XmCMarginHeight	Dimension	
XmNmarginWidth	dynamic	CSG
XmCMarginWidth	Dimension	
XmNmenuAccelerator	dynamic	CSG
XmCAccelerators	String	

Name	Default	Access
Class	Type	
XmNmenuHelpWidget	NULL	CSG
XmCMenuWidget	Widget	
XmNmenuHistory	NULL	CSG
XmCMenuWidget	Widget	
XmNmnemonic	NULL	CSG
XmCMnemonic	KeySym	
XmNmnemonicCharSet	dynamic	CSG
XmCMnemonicCharSet	String	
XmNnumColumns	1	CSG
XmCNumColumns	short	
XmNorientation	dynamic	CSG
XmCOrientation	unsigned char	
XmNpacking	dynamic	CSG
XmCPacking	unsigned char	
XmNpopupEnabled	True	CSG
XmCPopupEnabled	Boolean	
XmNradioAlwaysOne	True	CSG
XmCRadioAlwaysOne	Boolean	
XmNradioBehavior	False	CSG
XmCRadioBehavior	Boolean	
XmNresizeHeight	True	CSG
XmCResizeHeight	Boolean	
XmNresizeWidth	True	CSG
XmCResizeWidth	Boolean	
XmNrowColumnType	XmWORK_AREA	CG
XmCRowColumnType	unsigned char	

Name	Default	Access
Class	Type	
XmNspacing	dynamic	CSG
XmCSpacing	Dimension	
XmNsubMenuId	NULL	CSG
XmCMenuWidget	Widget	
XmNunmapCallback	NULL	C
XmCCallback	XtCallbackList	

XmNadjustLast

Extends the last row of children to the bottom edge of RowColumn (when **XmOrientation** is **XmHORIZONTAL**) or extends the last column to the right edge of RowColumn (when **XmOrientation** is **XmVERTICAL**). This feature is disabled by setting **XmNadjustLast** to False.

XmNadjustMargin

Specifies whether the inner minor margins of all items contained within the RowColumn widget are forced to the same value. The inner minor margin corresponds to the **XmNmarginLeft**, **XmNmarginRight**, **XmNmarginTop**, and **XmNmarginBottom** resources supported by **XmLabel** and **XmLabelGadget**.

A horizontal orientation causes **XmNmarginTop** and **XmNmarginBottom** for all items in a particular row to be forced to the same value; the value is the largest margin specified for one of the Label items.

A vertical orientation causes **XmNmarginLeft** and **XmNmarginRight** for all items in a particular column to be forced to the same value; the value is the largest margin specified for one of the Label items.

This keeps all text within each row or column lined up with all other text in its row or column. If the **XmNrowColumnType** is either **XmMENU_POPUP** or **XmMENU_PULLDOWN** and this resource is True, only button children have their margins adjusted.

XmNentryAlignment

> Specifies the alignment type for children that are subclasses of **XmLabel** or **XmLabelGadget** when **XmNisAligned** is enabled. The following are textual alignment types:

> **XmALIGNMENT_BEGINNING** — the default

> **XmALIGNMENT_CENTER**

> **XmALIGNMENT_END**

> See the description of **XmNalignment** in the **XmLabel(3X)** man page for an explanation of these actions.

XmNentryBorder

> Imposes a uniform border width upon all RowColumn's children. The default value is 0, which disables the feature.

XmNentryCallback

> Disables the **XmNactivateCallback** and **XmNvalueChangedCallback** callbacks for all CascadeButton, DrawnButton, PushButton, and ToggleButton widgets and gadgets contained within the RowColumn widget. If the application supplies this resource, the **XmNactivateCallback** and **XmNvalueChangedCallback** callbacks are then revectored to the **XmNentryCallback** callbacks. This allows an application to supply a single callback routine for handling all items contained in a RowColumn widget. The callback reason is **XmCR_ACTIVATE**. If the application does not supply this resource, the **XmNactivateCallback** and **XmNvalueChangedCallback** callbacks for each item in the RowColumn widget work as normal.

> The application must supply this resource when this widget is created. Changing this resource using the **XtSetValues** is not supported.

XmNentryClass

Specifies the only widget class that can be added to the RowColumn widget; this resource is meaningful only when the **XmNisHomogeneous** resource is set to True. Both widget and gadget variants of the specified class may be added to the widget.

When **XmNrowColumnType** is set to **XmWORK_AREA** and **XmNradioBehavior** is True, the default value for **XmNentryClass** is **xmToggleButtonGadgetClass**. When **XmNrowColumnType** is set to **XmMENU_BAR**, the value of **XmNentryClass** is forced to **xmCascadeButtonWidgetClass**.

XmNisAligned

Specifies text alignment for each item within the RowColumn widget; this applies only to items that are subclasses of **XmLabel** or **XmLabelGadget**. However, if the item is a Label widget or gadget and its parent is either a Popup MenuPane or a Pulldown MenuPane, alignment is not performed; the Label is treated as the title within the MenuPane, and the alignment set by the application is not overridden. **XmNentryAlignment** controls the type of textual alignment.

XmNisHomogeneous

Indicates if the RowColumn widget should enforce exact homogeneity among the items it contains; if True, only the widgets that are of the class indicated by **XmNentryClass** are allowed as children of the RowColumn widget. This is most often used when creating a MenuBar or a RadioBox widget.

Attempting to insert a child that is not a member of the specified class generates a warning message. The default value is False, except when creating a MenuBar or a RadioBox, when the value is forced to True. The value is forced to False in an OptionMenu.

XmNlabelString

> Points to a text string, which displays the label to one side of the selection area when **XmNrowColumnType** is set to **XmMENU_OPTION**. This resource is not meaningful for all other RowColumn types. If the application wishes to change the label after creation, it must get the LabelGadget ID (**XmOptionLabelGadget**) and call **XtSetValues** on the LabelGadget directly. The default value is no label.

XmNmapCallback

> Specifies a widget-specific callback function that is invoked when the window associated with the RowColumn widget is about to be mapped. The callback reason is **XmCR_MAP**.

XmNmarginHeight

> Specifies the amount of blank space between the top edge of the RowColumn widget and the first item in each column, and the bottom edge of the RowColumn widget and the last item in each column. The default value is 0 for Pulldown and Popup MenuPanes, and three pixels for other RowColumn types.

XmNmarginWidth

> Specifies the amount of blank space between the left edge of the RowColumn widget and the first item in each row, and the right edge of the RowColumn widget and the last item in each row. The default value is 0 for Pulldown and Popup MenuPanes, and three pixels for other RowColumn types.

XmNmenuAccelerator

> This resource is useful only when the RowColumn widget has been configured to operate as a Popup MenuPane or a MenuBar. The format of this resource is similar to the left side specification of a translation string, with the limitation that it must specify a key event. For a Popup MenuPane, when the accelerator is typed by the user, the Popup MenuPane is posted. For a MenuBar, when the accelerator is typed by the user, the first item in the MenuBar is highlighted, and traversal is enabled in the MenuBar. The default for a Popup MenuPane is **KMenu**. The default for a MenuBar is **KMenuBar**. The accelerator can be disabled by setting the **XmNpopupEnabled** resource to False.

Reference Pages

XmRowColumn(3X)

XmNmenuHelpWidget

Specifies the widget ID for the CascadeButton, which is treated as the Help widget if **XmNrowColumnType** is set to **XmMENU_BAR**. The MenuBar always places the Help widget at a lower corner of the menu. If the RowColumn widget is any type other than **XmMENU_BAR**, this resource is not meaningful.

XmNmenuHistory

Specifies the widget ID of the last menu entry to be activated. It is also useful for specifying the current selection for an OptionMenu. If **XmNrowColumnType** is set to **XmMENU_OPTION**, the specified menu item is positioned under the cursor when the menu is displayed.

If the RowColumn widget has the **XmNradioBehavior** resource set to True, the widget field associated with this resource contains the widget ID of the last ToggleButton or ToggleButtonGadget to change from unselected to selected. The default value is the widget ID of the first child in the widget.

XmNmnemonic

This resource is useful only when **XmNrowColumnType** is set to **XmMENU_OPTION**. Specifies a keysym for a key that, when pressed by the user along with the **MAlt** modifier, posts the associated Pulldown MenuPane. The first character in the OptionMenu label string that exactly matches the mnemonic in the character set specified in **XmNmnemonicCharSet** is underlined. The user can post the menu by pressing either the shifted or the unshifted mnemonic key. The default is no mnemonic.

XmNmnemonicCharSet

Specifies the character set of the mnemonic for an OptionMenu. The default is determined dynamically depending on the current language environment.

2–787

XmNnumColumns

Specifies the number of minor dimension extensions that are made to accommodate the entries; this attribute is meaningful only when **XmNpacking** is set to **XmPACK_COLUMN**.

For vertically oriented RowColumn widgets, this attribute indicates how many columns are built; the number of entries per column is adjusted to maintain this number of columns, if possible.

For horizontally oriented RowColumn widgets, this attribute indicates how many rows are built.

The default value is 1. In an OptionMenu the value is initialized to 1. The value must be greater than 0.

XmNorientation

Determines whether RowColumn layouts are row-major or column-major. In a column-major layout, the children of the RowColumn are laid out in columns top to bottom within the widget. In a row-major layout the children of the RowColumn are laid out in rows. **XmVERTICAL** resource value selects a column-major layout. **XmHORIZONTAL** resource value selects a row-major layout.

When creating a MenuBar or an OptionMenu, the default is **XmHORIZONTAL**. Otherwise, the default value is **XmVERTICAL**. The results of specifying a value of **XmVERTICAL** for a MenuBar are undefined.

XmNpacking

Specifies how to pack the items contained within a RowColumn widget. This can be set to **XmPACK_TIGHT, XmPACK_COLUMN** or **XmPACK_NONE**. When a RowColumn widget packs the items it contains, it determines its major dimension using the value of the **XmNorientation** resource.

XmPACK_TIGHT indicates that given the current major dimension (for example, vertical if **XmNorientation** is **XmVERTICAL**), entries are placed one after the other until the RowColumn widget must wrap. RowColumn wraps when there is no room left for a complete child in that dimension. Wrapping occurs by beginning a new row or column in the next available space. Wrapping continues, as often as necessary, until all of the children are laid out. In the vertical dimension (columns), boxes are set to the same width; in the horizontal dimension (rows), boxes are set to the same depth. Each entry's position in the major dimension is left unaltered (for example, **XmNy** is left unchanged when **XmNorientation** is **XmVERTICAL**); its position in the minor dimension is set to the same value as the greatest entry in that particular row or column. The position in the minor dimension of any particular row or column is independent of all other rows or columns.

XmPACK_COLUMN indicates that all entries are placed in identically sized boxes. The box is based on the largest height and width values of all the children widgets. The value of the **XmNnumColumns** resource determines how many boxes are placed in the major dimension, before extending in the minor dimension.

XmPACK_NONE indicates that no packing is performed. The x and y attributes of each entry are left alone, and the RowColumn widget attempts to become large enough to enclose all entries.

The default value is **XmPACK_TIGHT** except when building a RadioBox, when the default is **XmPACK_COLUMN**. In an OptionMenu the value is initialized to **XmPACK_TIGHT**.

XmNpopupEnabled

Allows the menu system to enable keyboard input (accelerators and mnemonics) defined for the Popup MenuPane and any of its submenus. The Popup MenuPane needs to be informed whenever its accessibility to the user changes because posting of the Popup MenuPane is controlled by the application. The default value for this resource is True (keyboard input — accelerators and mnemonics — defined for the Popup MenuPane and any of its submenus is enabled).

XmNradioAlwaysOne

If True, forces the active ToggleButton or ToggleButtonGadget to be automatically selected after having been unselected (if no other toggle was activated). If False, the active toggle may be unselected. The default value is True. This resource is important only when **XmNradioBehavior** is True.

The application can always add and subtract toggles from RowColumn regardless of the selected/unselected state of the toggle. The application can also manage and unmanage toggle children of RowColumn at any time regardless of state. Therefore, the application can sometimes create a RowColumn that has **XmNradioAlwaysOne** set to True and none of the toggle children selected. The result is undefined if the value of this resource is True and the application sets more than one ToggleButton at a time.

XmNradioBehavior

Specifies a Boolean value that when True, indicates that the RowColumn widget should enforce a RadioBox-type behavior on all of its children that are ToggleButtons or ToggleButtonGadgets.

When the value of this resource is True, the defaults for two resources for ToggleButton and ToggleButtonGadget children change: **XmNindicatorType** defaults to **XmONE_OF_MANY** and **XmNvisibleWhenOff** defaults to True.

RadioBox behavior dictates that when one toggle is selected and the user selects another toggle, the first toggle is unselected automatically. The RowColumn usually does not enforce this behavior if the application, rather than the user, changes the state of a toggle. The RowColumn does enforce this behavior if a toggle child is selected using **XmToggleButtonSetState** or **XmToggleButtonGadgetSetState** with a *notify* argument of True.

The default value is False, except that **XmCreateRadioBox** sets it to true.

XmNresizeHeight

Requests a new height if necessary, when set to True. When set to False, the widget does not request a new height regardless of any changes to the widget or its children.

XmNresizeWidth

Requests a new width if necessary, when set to True. When set to False, the widget does not request a new width regardless of any changes to the widget or its children.

XmNrowColumnType

Specifies the type of RowColumn widget to be created. It is a non-standard resource that cannot be changed after it is set. If an application uses any of the convenience routines, except **XmCreateRowColumn**, this resource is automatically forced to the appropriate value by the convenience routine. If an application uses the Xt Intrinsics API to create its RowColumn widgets, it must specify this resource itself. The set of possible settings for this resource are:

XmWORK_AREA — the default

XmMENU_BAR

XmMENU_PULLDOWN

XmMENU_POPUP

XmMENU_OPTION

This resource cannot be changed after the RowColumn widget is created. Any changes attempted through **XtSetValues** are ignored.

The value of this resource is used to determine the value of a number of other resources. The descriptions of RowColumn resources explain this when it is the case. The resource **XmNnavigationType**, inherited from **XmManager**, is changed to **XmNONE** if **XmNrowColumnType** is **XmMENU_OPTION**.

XmNspacing

Specifies the horizontal and vertical spacing between items contained within the RowColumn widget. The default value is three pixels for **XmOPTION_MENU** and **XmWORK_AREA** and 0 for other RowColumn types.

XmNsubMenuId

Specifies the widget ID for the Pulldown MenuPane to be associated with an OptionMenu. This resource is useful only when **XmNrowColumnType** is set to **XmMENU_OPTION**. The default value is NULL.

XmNunmapCallback

Specifies a list of callbacks that is called after the window associated with the RowColumn widget has been unmapped. The callback reason is **XmCR_UNMAP**. The default value is NULL.

Display Resource		
Name	**Default**	**Access**
Class	**Type**	
XmNmenuCursor	arrow	C
XmCCursor	String	

XmNmenuCursor

Sets a variable that controls the cursor used whenever this application posts a menu. This resource can be specified only once at application startup time, either by placing it within a defaults file or by using the **-xrm** command line argument.

Example: myProg -xrm "*menuCursor: arrow"

The menu cursor can also be selected programmatically by using the function **XmSetMenuCursor**. The following is a list of acceptable cursor names. If the application does not specify a cursor or if an invalid name is supplied, the default cursor (an arrow pointing up and to the right) is used.

X_cursor	dotbox	man	sizing
arrow	double_arrow	middlebutton	spider
based_arrow_down	draft_large	mouse	spraycan
based_arrow_up	draft_small	pencil	star
boat	draped_box	pirate	target
bogosity	exchange	plus	tcross
bottom_left_corner	fleur	question_arrow	top_left_arrow
bottom_right_corner	gobbler	right_ptr	top_left_corner
bottom_side	gumby	right_side	top_right_corner
bottom_tee	hand1	right_tee	top_side
box_spiral	hand2	rightbutton	top_tee
center_ptr	heart	rtl_logo	trek
circle	icon	sailboat	ul_angle
clock	iron_cross	sb_down_arrow	umbrella
coffee_mug	left_ptr	sb_h_double_arrow	ur_angle
cross	left_side	sb_left_arrow	watch
cross_reverse	left_tee	sb_right_arrow	xterm
crosshair	leftbutton	sb_up_arrow	
diamond_cross	ll_angle	sb_v_double_arrow	
dot	lr_angle	shuttle	

Inherited Resources

RowColumn inherits behavior and resources from the following named superclasses. For a complete description of each resource, refer to the man page for that superclass.

XmManager Resource Set		

Name
    Class
	Default
	    Type
		Access

XmNbottomShadowColor
   XmCBottomShadowColor
	dynamic
	   Pixel
		CSG

XmNbottomShadowPixmap
   XmCBottomShadowPixmap
	XmUNSPECIFIED_PIXMAP
	   Pixmap
		CSG

XmNforeground
   XmCForeground
	dynamic
	   Pixel
		CSG

XmNhelpCallback
   XmCCallback
	NULL
	   XtCallbackList
		C

XmNhighlightColor
   XmCHighlightColor
	dynamic
	   Pixel
		CSG

XmNhighlightPixmap
   XmCHighlightPixmap
	dynamic
	   Pixmap
		CSG

XmNnavigationType
   XmCNavigationType
	dynamic
	   XmNavigationType
		CSG

XmNshadowThickness
   XmCShadowThickness
	dynamic
	   Dimension
		CSG

XmNstringDirection
   XmCStringDirection
	dynamic
	   XmStringDirection
		CG

XmNtopShadowColor
   XmCBackgroundTopShadowColor
	dynamic
	   Pixel
		CSG

XmNtopShadowPixmap
   XmCTopShadowPixmap
	dynamic
	   Pixmap
		CSG

XmNtraversalOn
   XmCTraversalOn
	dynamic
	   Boolean
		CSG

XmNuserData
   XmCUserData
	NULL
	   Pointer
		CSG

Composite Resource Set		
Name	**Default**	**Access**
Class	**Type**	
XmNchildren	NULL	G
XmCReadOnly	WidgetList	
XmNinsertPosition	NULL	CSG
XmCInsertPosition	(*)()	
XmNnumChildren	0	G
XmCReadOnly	Cardinal	

Core Resource Set		
Name	**Default**	**Access**
Class	**Type**	
XmNaccelerators	dynamic	CSG
XmCAccelerators	XtAccelerators	
XmNancestorSensitive	dynamic	G
XmCSensitive	Boolean	
XmNbackground	dynamic	CSG
XmCBackground	Pixel	
XmNbackgroundPixmap	XmUNSPECIFIED_PIXMAP	CSG
XmCPixmap	Pixmap	
XmNborderColor	XtDefaultForeground	CSG
XmCBorderColor	Pixel	
XmNborderPixmap	XmUNSPECIFIED_PIXMAP	CSG
XmCPixmap	Pixmap	
XmNborderWidth	0	CSG
XmCBorderWidth	Dimension	
XmNcolormap	dynamic	CG
XmCColormap	Colormap	
XmNdepth	dynamic	CG
XmCDepth	int	
XmNdestroyCallback	NULL	C
XmCCallback	XtCallbackList	
XmNheight	dynamic	CSG
XmCHeight	Dimension	
XmNinitialResourcesPersistent	True	C
XmCInitialResourcesPersistent	Boolean	
XmNmappedWhenManaged	True	CSG
XmCMappedWhenManaged	Boolean	
XmNscreen	dynamic	CG
XmCScreen	Screen *	

Name	Default	Access
Class	Type	
XmNsensitive	True	CSG
XmCSensitive	Boolean	
XmNtranslations	dynamic	CSG
XmCTranslations	XtTranslations	
XmNwidth	dynamic	CSG
XmCWidth	Dimension	
XmNx	0	CSG
XmCPosition	Position	
XmNy	0	CSG
XmCPosition	Position	

Callback Information

A pointer to the following structure is passed to each callback:

typedef struct
{
    int   *reason*;
    XEvent   * *event*;
    Widget   *widget*;
    char   * *data*;
    char   * *callbackstruct*;
} XmRowColumnCallbackStruct;

reason   Indicates why the callback was invoked

event   Points to the **XEvent** that triggered the callback

The following fields apply only when the callback reason is **XmCR_ACTIVATE**; for all other callback reasons, these fields are set to NULL. The **XmCR_ACTIVATE** callback reason is generated only when the application has supplied an entry callback, which overrides any activation callbacks registered with the individual RowColumn items.

widget   Is set to the widget ID of the RowColumn item that has been activated

data   Contains the client-data value supplied by the application when the RowColumn item's activation callback was registered

callbackstruct
        Points to the callback structure generated by the RowColumn item's activation callback

Translations

XmRowColumn translations depend on the value of the **XmNrowColumnType** resource.

If **XmNrowColumnType** is set to **XmWORK_AREA**, XmRowColumn inherits traversal translations from XmManager.

If **XmNrowColumnType** is set to **XmMENU_OPTION**, XmRowColumn inherits traversal translations from XmManager and has the additional translations listed below. These translations may not directly correspond to a translation table.

BSelect Press:	**MenuBtnDown()**
BSelect Release:	**MenuBtnUp()**
KActivate:	**ManagerGadgetSelect()**
KSelect:	**ManagerGadgetSelect()**
KHelp:	**Help()**

The translations for XmRowColumn if **XmNrowColumnType** is set to **XmMENU_BAR XmMENU_PULLDOWN**, or **XmMENU_POPUP** are listed below. In a Popup menu system, **BMenu** also performs the **BSelect** actions. These translations may not directly correspond to a translation table.

BSelect Press:	**MenuBtnDown()**
BSelect Release:	**MenuBtnUp()**

KActivate:	**ManagerGadgetSelect()**
KSelect:	**ManagerGadgetSelect()**
MAny KCancel:	**MenuGadgetEscape()**
KHelp:	**Help()**
KLeft:	**MenuGadgetTraverseLeft()**
KRight:	**MenuGadgetTraverseRight()**
KUp:	**MenuGadgetTraverseUp()**
KDown:	**MenuGadgetTraverseDown()**

Action Routines

The XmRowColumn action routines are described below:

Help(): Calls the callbacks for **XmNhelpCallback** if any exist. If there are no help callbacks for this widget, this action calls the help callbacks for the nearest ancestor that has them.

ManagerGadgetSelect():
When a gadget child of the menu has the focus, invokes the gadget child's behavior associated with **KActivate** or **KSelect**. This generally has the effect of unposting the menu hierarchy and arming and activating the gadget, except that for a CascadeButtonGadget with a submenu, it posts the submenu.

MenuBtnDown():
When a gadget child of the menu has the focus, invokes the gadget child's behavior associated with **BSelect Press**. This generally has the effect of unposting any menus posted by the parent menu, enabling mouse traversal in the menu, and arming the gadget. For a CascadeButtonGadget with a submenu, it also posts the associated submenu.

MenuBtnUp():
> When a gadget child of the menu has the focus, invokes the gadget child's behavior associated with **BSelect Release**. This generally has the effect of unposting the menu hierarchy and activating the gadget, except that for a CascadeButtonGadget with a submenu, it posts the submenu and enables keyboard traversal in the menu.

MenuGadgetEscape():
> In a toplevel Pulldown MenuPane from a MenuBar, unposts the menu, disarms the MenuBar CascadeButton and the MenuBar, and, when the shell's keyboard focus policy is **XmEXPLICIT**, restores keyboard focus to the tab group that had the focus before the MenuBar was entered. In other Pulldown MenuPanes, unposts the menu.

> In a Popup MenuPane, unposts the menu and, when the shell's keyboard focus policy is **XmEXPLICIT**, restores keyboard focus to the widget from which the menu was posted.

MenuGadgetTraverseDown():
> In a vertical menu, disarms the current menu entry and arms the entry just below it in the MenuPane. This action wraps within the MenuPane.

> In a horizontal menu, if the menu entry is a CascadeButton with a submenu, posts the MenuPane associated with the CascadeButton. Otherwise, this action searches for an ancestor menu that is vertical. If it finds one, it unposts the cascade from the vertical menu and traverses to the next entry toward the bottom in the vertical menu. If this entry is a CascadeButton with a submenu, posts the MenuPane associated with the Cascadeutton. This action wraps within the vertical menu.

MenuGadgetTraverseLeft():

> In a vertical menu, if the menu's parent is a horizontal menu, this action unposts the current MenuPane and traverses to the next entry to the left in the parent menu. If this entry is a CascadeButton with a submenu, posts the MenuPane associated with the CascadeButton. This action wraps within the horizontal menu. If the menu's parent is a vertical menu, this action unposts the current MenuPane.

> In a horizontal menu, disarms the current menu entry and arms the entry just to the left of it in the menu. This action wraps within the menu.

MenuGadgetTraverseRight():

> In a vertical menu, if the menu entry is a CascadeButton with a submenu, posts the MenuPane associated with the CascadeButton. Otherwise, this action searches for an ancestor menu that is horizontal. If it finds one, it unposts the cascade from the horizontal menu and traverses to the next entry to the right in the horizontal menu. If this entry is a CascadeButton with a submenu, posts the MenuPane associated with the CascadeButton. This action wraps within the horizontal menu.

> In a horizontal menu, disarms the current menu entry and arms the entry just to the right of it in the menu. This action wraps within the menu.

MenuGadgetTraverseUp():

> In a vertical menu, disarms the current menu entry and arms the entry just above it in the MenuPane. This action wraps within the MenuPane.

> In a horizontal menu, if the menu's parent is a vertical menu, this action unposts the current MenuPane and traverses to the next entry toward the top in the parent menu. If this entry is a CascadeButton with a submenu, posts the MenuPane associated with the CascadeButton. This action wraps within the vertical menu. If the menu's parent is a horizontal menu, this action unposts the current MenuPane.

Related Behavior

The following menu functions are available.

KMenuBar: In any non-popup descendant of a MenuBar's parent, excluding the MenuBar itself, this action enables keyboard traversal and moves keyboard focus to the first item in the MenuBar.In the MenuBar or any menu cascaded from it, this action unposts the menu hierarchy and, when the shell's keyboard focus policy is **XmEXPLICIT**, restores focus to the tab group that had the focus when the menu system was entered.

KMenu: Pops up the menu associated with the control that has the keyboard focus. Enables keyboard traversal in the menu. In the Popup menu system or any menu cascaded from it, this action unposts the menu hierarchy and, when the shell's keyboard focus policy is **XmEXPLICIT**, restores focus to the tab group that had the focus when the menu system was entered.

Virtual Bindings

The bindings for virtual keys are vendor specific.

Related Information

Composite(3X), Constraint(3X), Core(3X), XmCreateMenuBar(3X), XmCreateOptionMenu(3X), XmCreatePopupMenu(3X), XmCreatePulldownMenu(3X), XmCreateRadioBox(3X), XmCreateRowColumn(3X), XmCreateWorkArea(3X), XmGetMenuCursor(3X), XmGetPostedFromWidget(3X), XmLabel(3X), XmManager(3X), XmMenuPosition(3X), XmOptionButtonGadget(3X), XmOptionLabelGadget(3X), XmSetMenuCursor(3X), and XmUpdateDisplay(3X).

XmScale

Purpose

The Scale widget class

AES Support Level

Full-use

Synopsis

#include <Xm/Scale.h>

Description

Scale is used by an application to indicate a value from within a range of values, and it allows the user to input or modify a value from the same range.

A Scale has an elongated rectangular region similar to a ScrollBar. A slider inside this region indicates the current value along the Scale. The user can also modify the Scale's value by moving the slider within the rectangular region of the Scale. A Scale can also include a label set located outside the Scale region. These can indicate the relative value at various positions along the scale.

A Scale can be either input/output or output only. An input/output Scale's value can be set by the application and also modified by the user with the slider. An output-only Scale is used strictly as an indicator of the current value of something and cannot be modified interactively by the user.

Classes

Scale inherits behavior and resources from **Core**, **Composite**, **Constraint**, and **XmManager** classes.

The class pointer is **xmScaleWidgetClass**.

The class name is **XmScale**.

New Resources

The following table defines a set of widget resources used by the programmer to specify data. The programmer can also set the resource values for the inherited classes to set attributes for this widget. To reference a resource by name or by class in a .Xdefaults file, remove the **XmN** or **XmC** prefix and use the remaining letters. To specify one of the defined values for a resource in a .Xdefaults file, remove the **Xm** prefix and use the remaining letters (in either lowercase or uppercase, but include any underscores between words). The codes in the access column indicate if the given resource can be set at creation time (**C**), set by using **XtSetValues** (**S**), retrieved by using **XtGetValues** (**G**), or is not applicable (**N/A**).

XmScale Resource Set		
Name	**Default**	**Access**
Class	**Type**	
XmNdecimalPoints	0	CSG
XmCDecimalPoints	short	
XmNdragCallback	NULL	C
XmCCallback	XtCallbackList	
XmNfontList	dynamic	CSG
XmCFontList	XmFontList	
XmNhighlightOnEnter	False	CSG
XmCHighlightOnEnter	Boolean	
XmNhighlightThickness	2	CSG
XmCHighlightThickness	Dimension	
XmNmaximum	100	CSG
XmCMaximum	int	
XmNminimum	0	CSG
XmCMinimum	int	
XmNorientation	XmVERTICAL	CSG
XmCOrientation	unsigned char	
XmNprocessingDirection	dynamic	CSG
XmCProcessingDirection	unsigned char	
XmNscaleHeight	0	CSG
XmCScaleHeight	Dimension	
XmNscaleMultiple	dynamic	CSG
XmCScaleMultiple	int	
XmNscaleWidth	0	CSG
XmCScaleWidth	Dimension	
XmNshowValue	False	CSG
XmCShowValue	Boolean	

Name	Default	Access
Class	Type	
XmNtitleString	NULL	CSG
XmCTitleString	XmString	
XmNvalue	0	CSG
XmCValue	int	
XmNvalueChangedCallback	NULL	C
XmCCallback	XtCallbackList	

XmNdecimalPoints

Specifies the number of decimal points to shift the slider value when displaying it. For example, a slider value of 2,350 and an **XmdecimalPoints** value of 2 results in a display value of 23.50. The value must not be negative.

XmNdragCallback

Specifies the list of callbacks that is called when the slider position changes as the slider is being dragged. The reason sent by the callback is **XmCR_DRAG**.

XmNfontList

Specifies the font list to use for the title text string specified by **XmNtitleString**. If this value is NULL at initialization, it is initialized by looking up the parent hierarchy of the widget for an ancestor that is a subclass of the XmBulletinBoard, VendorShell, or XmMenuShell widget class. If such an ancestor is found, the font list is initialized to the appropriate default font list of the ancestor widget (XmNdefaultFontList for VendorShell and XmMenuShell, XmNlabelFontList for XmBulletinBoard).

XmNhighlightOnEnter

Specifies whether the highlighting rectangle is drawn when the cursor moves into the widget. If the shell's focus policy is **XmEXPLICIT**, this resource is ignored, and the widget is

highlighted when it has the focus. If the shell's focus policy is
XmPOINTER and if this resource is True, the highlighting
rectangle is drawn when the the cursor moves into the widget.
If the shell's focus policy is **XmPOINTER** and if this resource
is False, the highlighting rectangle is not drawn when the the
cursor moves into the widget. The default is False.

XmNhighlightThickness

Specifies the size of the slider's border drawing rectangle used
for enter window and traversal highlight drawing.

XmNmaximum

Specifies the slider's maximum value.

XmNminimum

Specifies the slider's minimum value.

XmNorientation

Displays Scale vertically or horizontally. This resource can
have values of **XmVERTICAL and XmHORIZONTAL**.

XmNprocessingDirection

Specifies whether the value for **XmNmaximum** is on the right
or left side of **XmNminimum** for horizontal Scales or above
or below **XmNminimum** for vertical Scales. This resource
can   have   values   of   **XmMAX_ON_TOP,
XmMAX_ON_BOTTOM,   XmMAX_ON_LEFT**,   and
XmMAX_ON_RIGHT. If the XmScale is oriented vertically,
the default value is **XmMAX_ON_TOP**. If the XmScale is
oriented horizontally, the default value may depend on the
value of the **XmNstringDirection** resource.

XmNscaleHeight

Specifies the height of the slider area. The value should be in
the specified unit type (the default is pixels). If no value is
specified a default height is computed.

XmNscaleMultiple

Specifies the amount to move the slider when the user takes an
action that moves the slider by a multiple increment. The
default is (**XmNmaximum** - **XmNminimum**) divided by 10,
with a minimum of 1.

XmNscaleWidth

> Specifies the width of the slider area. The value should be in the specified unit type (the default is pixels). If no value is specified a default width is computed.

XmNshowValue

> Specifies whether a label for the current slider value should be displayed next to the slider. If the value is True, the current slider value is displayed.

XmNtitleString

> Specifies the title text string to appear in the Scale widget window.

XmNvalue Specifies the slider's current position along the scale, between **XmNminimum** and **XmNmaximum**. The value is constrained to be within these inclusive bounds.

XmNvalueChangedCallback

> Specifies the list of callbacks that is called when the value of the slider has changed. The reason sent by the callback is **XmCR_VALUE_CHANGED**.

Inherited Resources

Scale inherits behavior and resources from the following superclasses. For a complete description of each resource, refer to the man page for that superclass.

XmManager Resource Set		
Name	**Default**	**Access**
Class	**Type**	
XmNbottomShadowColor	dynamic	CSG
XmCBottomShadowColor	Pixel	
XmNbottomShadowPixmap	XmUNSPECIFIED_PIXMAP	CSG
XmCBottomShadowPixmap	Pixmap	
XmNforeground	dynamic	CSG
XmCForeground	Pixel	
XmNhelpCallback	NULL	C
XmCCallback	XtCallbackList	
XmNhighlightColor	dynamic	CSG
XmCHighlightColor	Pixel	
XmNhighlightPixmap	dynamic	CSG
XmCHighlightPixmap	Pixmap	
XmNnavigationType	XmTAB_GROUP	G
XmCNavigationType	XmNavigationType	
XmNshadowThickness	2	CSG
XmCShadowThickness	Dimension	
XmNstringDirection	dynamic	CG
XmCStringDirection	XmStringDirection	
XmNtopShadowColor	dynamic	CSG
XmCBackgroundTopShadowColor	Pixel	
XmNtopShadowPixmap	dynamic	CSG
XmCTopShadowPixmap	Pixmap	
XmNtraversalOn	True	CSG
XmCTraversalOn	Boolean	
XmNuserData	NULL	CSG
XmCUserData	Pointer	

Composite Resource Set		
Name	**Default**	**Access**
Class	**Type**	
XmNchildren	NULL	G
XmCReadOnly	WidgetList	
XmNinsertPosition	NULL	CSG
XmCInsertPosition	(*)()	
XmNnumChildren	0	G
XmCReadOnly	Cardinal	

Core Resource Set		
Name	**Default**	**Access**
Class	**Type**	
XmNaccelerators	dynamic	CSG
XmCAccelerators	XtAccelerators	
XmNancestorSensitive	dynamic	G
XmCSensitive	Boolean	
XmNbackground	dynamic	CSG
XmCBackground	Pixel	
XmNbackgroundPixmap	XmUNSPECIFIED_PIXMAP	CSG
XmCPixmap	Pixmap	
XmNborderColor	XtDefaultForeground	CSG
XmCBorderColor	Pixel	
XmNborderPixmap	XmUNSPECIFIED_PIXMAP	CSG
XmCPixmap	Pixmap	
XmNborderWidth	0	CSG
XmCBorderWidth	Dimension	
XmNcolormap	dynamic	CG
XmCColormap	Colormap	
XmNdepth	dynamic	CG
XmCDepth	int	
XmNdestroyCallback	NULL	C
XmCCallback	XtCallbackList	
XmNheight	dynamic	CSG
XmCHeight	Dimension	
XmNinitialResourcesPersistent	True	C
XmCInitialResourcesPersistent	Boolean	
XmNmappedWhenManaged	True	CSG
XmCMappedWhenManaged	Boolean	
XmNscreen	dynamic	CG
XmCScreen	Screen *	

Name	Default	Access
Class	Type	
XmNsensitive	True	CSG
XmCSensitive	Boolean	
XmNtranslations	dynamic	CSG
XmCTranslations	XtTranslations	
XmNwidth	dynamic	CSG
XmCWidth	Dimension	
XmNx	0	CSG
XmCPosition	Position	
XmNy	0	CSG
XmCPosition	Position	

Callback Information

A pointer to the following structure is passed to each callback:

typedef struct
{
    int   *reason*;
    XEvent * *event*;
    int   *value*;
} **XmScaleCallbackStruct**;

reason   Indicates why the callback was invoked

event   Points to the **XEvent** that triggered the callback

value   Is the new slider value

Behavior

XmScale behavior is described below:

BSelect Press or **BDrag Press**:
 (in region between an end of the Scale and the slider): Moves the slider by one multiple increment in the direction of the end of the Scale and calls the **XmNvalueChangedCallback** callbacks. If **XmNprocessingDirection** is **XmMAX_ON_RIGHT** or **XmMAX_ON_BOTTOM**, movement toward the right or bottom increments the Scale value, and movement toward the left or top decrements the Scale value. If **XmNprocessingDirection** is **XmMAX_ON_LEFT** or **XmMAX_ON_TOP**, movement toward the right or bottom decrements the Scale value, and movement toward the left or top increments the Scale value. If the button is held down longer than a delay period, the slider is moved again by the same increment and the same callbacks are called.

 (in slider): Activates the interactive dragging of the slider.

BSelect Motion or **BDrag Motion**:
 If the button press occurs within the slider, the subsequent motion events move the slider to the position of the pointer and call the callbacks for **XmNdragCallback**.

BSelect Release or **BDrag Release**:
 If the button press occurs within the slider and the slider position is changed, the callbacks for **XmNvalueChangedCallback** are called.

MCtrl BSelect Press:
 (in region between an end of the Scale and the slider): Moves the slider to that end of the Scale and calls the **XmNvalueChangedCallback** callbacks. If **XmNprocessingDirection** is **XmMAX_ON_RIGHT** or

XmMAX_ON_BOTTOM, movement toward the right or bottom increments the Scale value, and movement toward the left or top decrements the Scale value. If **XmNprocessingDirection** is **XmMAX_ON_LEFT** or **XmMAX_ON_TOP**, movement toward the right or bottom decrements the Scale value, and movement toward the left or top increments the Scale value.

KUp: For vertical Scales, moves the slider up one increment and calls the **XmNvalueChangedCallback** callbacks. If **XmNprocessingDirection** is **XmMAX_ON_TOP**, movement toward the top increments the Scale value. If **XmNprocessingDirection** is **XmMAX_ON_BOTTOM**, movement toward the top decrements the Scale value.

KDown: For vertical Scales, moves the slider down one increment and calls the **XmNvalueChangedCallback** callbacks. If **XmNprocessingDirection** is **XmMAX_ON_BOTTOM**, movement toward the bottom increments the Scale value. If **XmNprocessingDirection** is **XmMAX_ON_TOP**, movement toward the bottom decrements the Scale value.

KLeft: For horizontal Scales, moves the slider one increment to the left and calls the **XmNvalueChangedCallback** callbacks. If **XmNprocessingDirection** is **XmMAX_ON_LEFT**, movement toward the left increments the Scale value. If **XmNprocessingDirection** is **XmMAX_ON_RIGHT**, movement toward the left decrements the Scale value.

KRight: For horizontal Scales, moves the slider one increment to the right and calls the **XmNvalueChangedCallback** callbacks. If **XmNprocessingDirection** is **XmMAX_ON_RIGHT**, movement toward the right increments the Scale value. If **XmNprocessingDirection** is **XmMAX_ON_LEFT**, movement toward the right decrements the Scale value.

MCtrl KUp or **KPageUp**:

For vertical Scales, moves the slider up one multiple increment and calls the **XmNvalueChangedCallback** callbacks. If **XmNprocessingDirection** is **XmMAX_ON_TOP**, movement toward the top increments the Scale value. If **XmNprocessingDirection** is **XmMAX_ON_BOTTOM**, movement toward the top decrements the Scale value.

MCtrl KDown or **KPageDown**:

For vertical Scales, moves the slider down one multiple increment and calls the **XmNvalueChangedCallback** callbacks. If **XmNprocessingDirection** is **XmMAX_ON_BOTTOM**, movement toward the bottom increments the Scale value. If **XmNprocessingDirection** is **XmMAX_ON_TOP**, movement toward the bottom decrements the Scale value.

MCtrl KLeft or **KPageLeft**:

For horizontal Scales, moves the slider one multiple increment to the left and calls the **XmNvalueChangedCallback** callbacks. If **XmNprocessingDirection** is **XmMAX_ON_LEFT**, movement toward the left increments the Scale value. If **XmNprocessingDirection** is **XmMAX_ON_RIGHT**, movement toward the left decrements the Scale value.

MCtrl KRight or **KPageRight**:

For horizontal Scales, moves the slider one multiple increment to the right and calls the **XmNvalueChangedCallback** callbacks. If **XmNprocessingDirection** is **XmMAX_ON_RIGHT**, movement toward the right increments the Scale value. If **XmNprocessingDirection** is **XmMAX_ON_LEFT**, movement toward the right decrements the Scale value.

KBeginLine or **KBeginData**:

Moves the slider to the minimum value and calls the **XmNvalueChangedCallback** callbacks.

KEndLine or **KEndData**:
> Moves the slider to the maximum value and calls the **XmNvalueChangedCallback** callbacks.

KNextField: Traverses to the first item in the next tab group. If the current tab group is the last entry in the tab group list, it wraps to the beginning of the tab group list.

KPrevField: Traverses to the first item in the previous tab group. If the beginning of the tab group list is reached, it wraps to the end of the tab group list.

KHelp: Calls the callbacks for **XmNhelpCallback** if any exist. If there are no help callbacks for this widget, this action calls the help callbacks for the nearest ancestor that has them.

Virtual Bindings

The bindings for virtual keys are vendor specific.

Related Information

Composite(3X), Constraint(3X), Core(3X), XmCreateScale(3X), XmManager(3X), XmScaleGetValue(3X), and XmScaleSetValue(3X).

XmScaleGetValue

Purpose

A Scale function that returns the current slider position.

AES Support Level

Full-use

Synopsis

#include <Xm/Scale.h>

void XmScaleGetValue (*widget, value_return*)
    Widget   *widget*;
    int   * *value_return*;

Description

XmScaleGetValue returns the current slider position value displayed in the scale.

widget   Specifies the Scale widget ID

value_return Returns the current slider position value

For a complete definition of Scale and its associated resources, see **XmScale(3X)**.

Related Information

XmScale(3X).

XmScaleSetValue

Purpose

A Scale function that sets a slider value

AES Support Level

Full-use

Synopsis

#include <Xm/Scale.h>

void XmScaleSetValue (*widget, value*)
     Widget   *widget*;
     int   *value*;

Description

XmScaleSetValue sets the slider *value* within the Scale widget.

widget   Specifies the Scale widget ID.

value   Specifies the slider position along the scale. This sets the **XmNvalue** resource.

For a complete definition of Scale and its associated resources, see **XmScale(3X)**.

Related Information

XmScale(3X).

XmScrollBar

Purpose

The ScrollBar widget class

AES Support Level

Full-use

Synopsis

#include <Xm/ScrollBar.h>

Description

The ScrollBar widget allows the user to view data that is too large to be displayed all at once. ScrollBars are usually located inside a ScrolledWindow and adjacent to the widget that contains the data to be viewed. When the user interacts with the ScrollBar, the data within the other widget scrolls.

A ScrollBar consists of two arrows placed at each end of a rectangle. The rectangle is called the scroll region. A smaller rectangle, called the slider, is placed within the scroll region. The data is scrolled by clicking either arrow, selecting on the scroll region, or dragging the slider. When an arrow is selected, the slider within the scroll region is moved in the direction of the arrow by an amount supplied by the application. If the mouse button is held down, the slider continues to move at a constant rate.

The ratio of the slider size to the scroll region size typically corresponds to the relationship between the size of the visible data and the total size of the data. For example, if 10 percent of the data is visible, the slider typically occupies 10 percent of the scroll region. This provides the user with a visual clue to the size of the invisible data.

Classes

ScrollBar inherits behavior and resources from the **Core** and **XmPrimitive** classes.

The class pointer is **xmScrollBarWidgetClass**.

The class name is **XmScrollBar**.

New Resources

The following table defines a set of widget resources used by the programmer to specify data. The programmer can also set the resource values for the inherited classes to set attributes for this widget. To reference a resource by name or by class in a .Xdefaults file, remove the **XmN** or **XmC** prefix and use the remaining letters. To specify one of the defined values for a resource in a .Xdefaults file, remove the **Xm** prefix and use the remaining letters (in either lowercase or uppercase, but include any underscores between words). The codes in the access column indicate if the given resource can be set at creation time (**C**), set by using **XtSetValues** (**S**), retrieved by using **XtGetValues** (**G**), or is not applicable (**N/A**).

XmScrollBar Resource Set		

Name
  Class
	Default
	  Type
		Access

XmNdecrementCallback
  XmCCallback
	NULL
	  XtCallbackList
		C

XmNdragCallback
  XmCCallback
	NULL
	  XtCallbackList
		C

XmNincrement
  XmCIncrement
	1
	  int
		CSG

XmNincrementCallback
  XmCCallback
	NULL
	  XtCallbackList
		C

XmNinitialDelay
  XmCInitialDelay
	250 ms
	  int
		CSG

XmNmaximum
  XmCMaximum
	100
	  int
		CSG

XmNminimum
  XmCMinimum
	0
	  int
		CSG

XmNorientation
  XmCOrientation
	XmVERTICAL
	  unsigned char
		CSG

XmNpageDecrementCallback
  XmCCallback
	NULL
	  XtCallbackList
		C

XmNpageIncrement
  XmCPageIncrement
	10
	  int
		CSG

XmNpageIncrementCallback
  XmCCallback
	NULL
	  XtCallbackList
		C

XmNprocessingDirection
  XmCProcessingDirection
	dynamic
	  unsigned char
		CSG

XmNrepeatDelay
  XmCRepeatDelay
	50 ms
	  int
		CSG

XmNshowArrows
  XmCShowArrows
	True
	  Boolean
		CSG

Name	Default	Access
Class	Type	
XmNsliderSize	dynamic	CSG
XmCSliderSize	int	
XmNtoBottomCallback	NULL	C
XmCCallback	XtCallbackList	
XmNtoTopCallback	NULL	C
XmCCallback	XtCallbackList	
XmNtroughColor	dynamic	CSG
XmCTroughColor	Pixel	
XmNvalue	0	CSG
XmCValue	int	
XmNvalueChangedCallback	NULL	C
XmCCallback	XtCallbackList	

XmNdecrementCallback

Specifies the list of callbacks that is called when the user takes an action that moves the ScrollBar by one increment and the value decreases. The reason passed to the callback is **XmCR_DECREMENT**.

XmNdragCallback

Specifies the list of callbacks that is called on each incremental change of position when the slider is being dragged. The reason sent by the callback is **XmCR_DRAG**.

XmNincrement

Specifies the amount by which the value increases or decreases when the user takes an action that moves the slider by one increment. The actual change in value is the lesser of **XmNincrement** and (previous **XmNvalue** - **XmNminimum**) when the slider moves to the end of the ScrollBar with the minimum value, and the lesser of**XmNincrement** and (**XmNmaximum**- **XmNsliderSize** - previous **XmNvalue**) when the slider moves to the end of the ScrollBar with the maximum value. The value of this resource must be greater than 0.

XmNincrementCallback

Specifies the list of callbacks that is called when the user takes an action that moves the ScrollBar by one increment and the value increases. The reason passed to the callback is **XmCR_INCREMENT**.

XmNinitialDelay

Specifies the amount of time in milliseconds to wait before starting continuous slider movement while a button is pressed in an arrow or the scroll region. The value of this resource must be greater than 0.

XmNmaximum

Specifies the slider's maximum value.

XmNminimum

Specifies the slider's minimum value.

XmNorientation

Specifies whether the ScrollBar is displayed vertically or horizontally. This resource can have values of **XmVERTICAL** and **XmHORIZONTAL**.

XmNpageDecrementCallback

Specifies the list of callbacks that is called when the user takes an action that moves the ScrollBar by one page increment and the value decreases. The reason passed to the callback is **XmCR_PAGE_DECREMENT**.

XmNpageIncrement

Specifies the amount by which the value increases or decreases when the user takes an action that moves the slider by one page increment. The actual change in value is the lesser of **XmNpageIncrement** and (previous **XmNvalue** - **XmNminimum**) when the slider moves to the end of the

ScrollBar with the minimum value, and the lesser of **XmNpageIncrement** and (**XmNmaximum**- **XmNsliderSize** - previous **XmNvalue**) when the slider moves to the end of the ScrollBar with the maximum value. The value of this resource must be greater than 0.

XmNpageIncrementCallback

Specifies the list of callbacks that is called when the user takes an action that moves the ScrollBar by one page increment and the value increases. The reason passed to the callback is **XmCR_PAGE_INCREMENT**.

XmNprocessingDirection

Specifies whether the value for **XmNmaximum** should be on the right or left side of **XmNminimum** for horizontal ScrollBars or above or below **XmNminimum** for vertical ScrollBars. This resource can have values of **XmMAX_ON_TOP,** **XmMAX_ON_BOTTOM,** **XmMAX_ON_LEFT**, and **XmMAX_ON_RIGHT**. If the XmScrollBar is oriented vertically, the default value is **XmMAX_ON_BOTTOM**. If the XmScrollBar is oriented horizontally, the default value may depend on the value of the **XmNstringDirection** resource.

XmNrepeatDelay

Specifies the amount of time in milliseconds to wait between subsequent slider movements after the **XmNinitialDelay** has been processed. The value of this resource must be greater than 0.

XmNshowArrows

Specifies whether the arrows are displayed.

XmNsliderSize

Specifies the length of the slider between the values of 1 and (**XmNmaximum** - **XmNminimum**). The value is constrained to be within these inclusive bounds. The default value is (**XmNmaximum** - **XmNminimum**) divided by 10, with a minimum of 1.

XmNtoBottomCallback

Specifies the list of callbacks that is called when the user takes an action that moves the slider to the end of the ScrollBar with the maximum value. The reason passed to the callback is **XmCR_TO_BOTTOM**.

XmNtoTopCallback

Specifies the list of callbacks that is called when the user takes an action that moves the slider to the end of the ScrollBar with the minimum value. The reason passed to the callback is **XmCR_TO_TOP**.

XmNtroughColor

Specifies the color of the slider trough.

XmNvalue Specifies the slider's position, between **XmNminimum** and (**XmNmaximum** - **XmNsliderSize**). The value is constrained to be within these inclusive bounds.

XmNvalueChangedCallback

Specifies the list of callbacks that is called when the slider is released after being dragged. These callbacks are also called in place of **XmNincrementCallback**, **XmNdecrementCallback**, **XmNpageIncrementCallback**, **XmNpageDecrementCallback**, **XmNtoTopCallback**, or **XmNtoBottomCallback** when one of these callback lists would normally be called but the value of the corresponding resource is NULL. The reason passed to the callback is **XmCR_VALUE_CHANGED**.

Inherited Resources

ScrollBar inherits behavior and resources from the following superclasses. For a complete description of each resource, refer to the man page for that superclass.

XmPrimitive Resource Set		
Name	**Default**	**Access**
Class	**Type**	
XmNbottomShadowColor	dynamic	CSG
XmCBottomShadowColor	Pixel	
XmNbottomShadowPixmap	XmUNSPECIFIED_PIXMAP	CSG
XmCBottomShadowPixmap	Pixmap	
XmNforeground	dynamic	CSG
XmCForeground	Pixel	
XmNhelpCallback	NULL	C
XmCCallback	XtCallbackList	
XmNhighlightColor	dynamic	CSG
XmCHighlightColor	Pixel	
XmNhighlightOnEnter	False	CSG
XmCHighlightOnEnter	Boolean	
XmNhighlightPixmap	dynamic	CSG
XmCHighlightPixmap	Pixmap	
XmNhighlightThickness	dynamic	CSG
XmCHighlightThickness	Dimension	
XmNnavigationType	XmSTICKY_TAB_GROUP	G
XmCNavigationType	XmNavigationType	
XmNshadowThickness	2	CSG
XmCShadowThickness	Dimension	
XmNtopShadowColor	dynamic	CSG
XmCTopShadowColor	Pixel	
XmNtopShadowPixmap	dynamic	CSG
XmCTopShadowPixmap	Pixmap	
XmNtraversalOn	dynamic	CSG
XmCTraversalOn	Boolean	
XmNuserData	NULL	CSG
XmCUserData	Pointer	

Core Resource Set		
Name	**Default**	**Access**
Class	**Type**	
XmNaccelerators	dynamic	CSG
XmCAccelerators	XtAccelerators	
XmNancestorSensitive	dynamic	G
XmCSensitive	Boolean	
XmNbackground	dynamic	CSG
XmCBackground	Pixel	
XmNbackgroundPixmap	XmUNSPECIFIED_PIXMAP	CSG
XmCPixmap	Pixmap	
XmNborderColor	XtDefaultForeground	CSG
XmCBorderColor	Pixel	
XmNborderPixmap	XmUNSPECIFIED_PIXMAP	CSG
XmCPixmap	Pixmap	
XmNborderWidth	0	CSG
XmCBorderWidth	Dimension	
XmNcolormap	dynamic	CG
XmCColormap	Colormap	
XmNdepth	dynamic	CG
XmCDepth	int	
XmNdestroyCallback	NULL	C
XmCCallback	XtCallbackList	
XmNheight	dynamic	CSG
XmCHeight	Dimension	
XmNinitialResourcesPersistent	True	C
XmCInitialResourcesPersistent	Boolean	
XmNmappedWhenManaged	True	CSG
XmCMappedWhenManaged	Boolean	
XmNscreen	dynamic	CG
XmCScreen	Screen *	

Name	Default	Access
Class	Type	
XmNsensitive	True	CSG
XmCSensitive	Boolean	
XmNtranslations	dynamic	CSG
XmCTranslations	XtTranslations	
XmNwidth	dynamic	CSG
XmCWidth	Dimension	
XmNx	0	CSG
XmCPosition	Position	
XmNy	0	CSG
XmCPosition	Position	

Callback Information

A pointer to the following structure is passed to each callback:

typedef struct
{
   int   *reason*;
   XEvent * *event*;
   int   *value*;
   int   *pixel*;
} **XmScrollBarCallbackStruct**;

reason   Indicates why the callback was invoked.

event   Points to the **XEvent** that triggered the callback.

value   Contains the new slider location value.

pixel   Is used only for **XmNtoTopCallback** and **XmNtoBottomCallback**. For horizontal ScrollBars, it contains the *x* coordinate of where the mouse button selection occurred. For vertical ScrollBars, it contains the *y* coordinate.

Translations

XmScrollBar includes translations from Primitive. The XmScrollBar translations are listed below. These translations may not directly correspond to a translation table.

BSelect Press: Select()
BSelect Release: Release()
BSelect Press Moved:Moved()

BDrag Press: Select()
BDrag Release: Release()
BDrag Press Moved:Moved()

MCtrl BSelect Press:TopOrBottom()
MCtrl BSelect Release:Release()

KUp:	**IncrementUpOrLeft(0)**
MCtrl KUp:	**PageUpOrLeft(0)**
KDown:	**IncrementDownOrRight(0)**
MCtrl KDown:	**PageDownOrRight(0)**
KLeft:	**IncrementUpOrLeft(1)**
MCtrl KLeft:	**PageUpOrLeft(1)**
KRight:	**IncrementDownOrRight(1)**
MCtrl KRight:	**PageDownOrRight(1)**
KPageUp:	**PageUpOrLeft(0)**
KPageDown:	**PageDownOrRight(0)**
KPageLeft:	**PageUpOrLeft(1)**
KPageRight:	**PageDownOrRight(1)**
KBeginLine:	**TopOrBottom()**
KEndLine:	**TopOrBottom()**
KBeginData:	**TopOrBottom()**

KEndData:	**TopOrBottom()**
KNextField:	**PrimitiveNextTabGroup()**
KPrevField:	**PrimitivePrevTabGroup()**
KHelp:	**PrimitiveHelp()**

Action Routines

The ScrollBar action routines are described below:

IncrementDownOrRight(0|1):

With an argument of 0, moves the slider down by one increment. With an argument of 1, moves the slider right by one increment. If **XmNprocessingDirection** is **XmMAX_ON_RIGHT** or **XmMAX_ON_BOTTOM**, movement toward the right or bottom calls the callbacks for **XmNincrementCallback**. If **XmNprocessingDirection** is **XmMAX_ON_LEFT** or **XmMAX_ON_TOP**, movement toward the right or bottom calls the callbacks for **XmNdecrementCallback**. The **XmNvalueChangedCallback** is called if the **XmNincrementCallback** or **XmNdecrementCallback** is NULL.

IncrementUpOrLeft(0|1):

With an argument of 0, moves the slider up by one increment. With an argument of 1, moves the slider left by one increment. If **XmNprocessingDirection** is **XmMAX_ON_RIGHT** or **XmMAX_ON_BOTTOM**, movement to the left or top calls the callbacks for **XmNdecrementCallback**. If **XmNprocessingDirection** is **XmMAX_ON_LEFT** or **XmMAX_ON_TOP**, movement to the left or top calls the callbacks for **XmNincrementCallback**. The **XmNvalueChangedCallback** is called if the **XmNincrementCallback** or **XmNdecrementCallback** is NULL.

Moved():   If the button press occurs within the slider, the subsequent motion events move the slider to the position of the pointer and call the callbacks for **XmNdragCallback**.

PageDownOrRight(0|1):

With an argument of 0, moves the slider down by one page increment. With an argument of 1, moves the slider right by one page increment. If **XmNprocessingDirection** is **XmMAX_ON_RIGHT** or **XmMAX_ON_BOTTOM**, movement toward the right or bottom calls the callbacks for **XmNpageIncrementCallback**. If **XmNprocessingDirection** is **XmMAX_ON_LEFT** or **XmMAX_ON_TOP**, movement toward the right or bottom calls the callbacks for **XmNpageDecrementCallback**. The **XmNvalueChangedCallback** is called if the **XmNpageIncrementCallback** or **XmNpageDecrementCallback** is NULL.

PageUpOrLeft(0|1):

With an argument of 0, moves the slider up by one page increment. With an argument of 1, moves the slider left by one page increment. If **XmNprocessingDirection** is **XmMAX_ON_RIGHT** or **XmMAX_ON_BOTTOM**, movement to the left or top calls the callbacks for **XmNpageDecrementCallback**. If **XmNprocessingDirection** is **XmMAX_ON_LEFT** or **XmMAX_ON_TOP**, movement to the left or top calls the callbacks for **XmNpageIncrementCallback**. The **XmNvalueChangedCallback** is called if the **XmNpageIncrementCallback** or **XmNpageDecrementCallback** is NULL.

PrimitiveHelp():

Calls the callbacks for **XmNhelpCallback** if any exist. If there are no help callbacks for this widget, this action calls the help callbacks for the nearest ancestor that has them.

PrimitiveNextTabGroup():

Traverses to the first item in the next tab group. If the current tab group is the last entry in the tab group list, it wraps to the beginning of the tab group list.

PrimitivePrevTabGroup():
Traverses to the first item in the previous tab group. If the beginning of the tab group list is reached, it wraps to the end of the tab group list.

Release(): If the button press occurs within the slider and the slider position is changed, the callbacks for **XmNvalueChangedCallback** are called.

Select(): **(in arrow)**: Moves the slider by one increment in the direction of the arrow. If **XmNprocessingDirection** is **XmMAX_ON_RIGHT** or **XmMAX_ON_BOTTOM**, movement toward the right or bottom calls the callbacks for **XmNincrementCallback**, and movement to the left or top calls the callbacks for **XmNdecrementCallback**. If **XmNprocessingDirection** is **XmMAX_ON_LEFT** or **XmMAX_ON_TOP**, movement toward the right or bottom calls the callbacks for **XmNdecrementCallback**, and movement to the left or top calls the callbacks for **XmNincrementCallback**. The **XmNvalueChangedCallback** is called if the **XmNincrementCallback** or **XmNdecrementCallback** is NULL.

(in scroll region between an arrow and the slider): Moves the slider by one page increment in the direction of the arrow. If **XmNprocessingDirection** is **XmMAX_ON_RIGHT** or **XmMAX_ON_BOTTOM**, movement toward the right or bottom calls the callbacks for **XmNpageIncrementCallback**, and movement to the left or top calls the callbacks for **XmNpageDecrementCallback**. If **XmNprocessingDirection** is **XmMAX_ON_LEFT** or **XmMAX_ON_TOP**, movement toward the right or bottom calls the callbacks for **XmNpageDecrementCallback**, and movement to the left or top calls the callbacks for **XmNpageIncrementCallback**. The **XmNvalueChangedCallback** is called if the **XmNpageIncrementCallback** or **XmNpageDecrementCallback** is NULL.

(in slider): Activates the interactive dragging of the slider.

If the button is held down in either the arrows or the scroll region longer than the **XmNinitialDelay** resource, the slider is moved again by the same increment and the same callbacks are called. After the initial delay has been used, the time delay changes to the time defined by the resource **XmNrepeatDelay**.

TopOrBottom():

MCtrl BSelect Press in an arrow or in the scroll region between an arrow and the slider moves the slider as far as possible in the direction of the arrow. If **XmNprocessingDirection** is **XmMAX_ON_RIGHT** or **XmMAX_ON_BOTTOM**, movement toward the right or bottom calls the callbacks for **XmNtoBottomCallback**, and movement to the left or top calls the callbacks for **XmNtoTopCallback**. If **XmNprocessingDirection** is **XmMAX_ON_LEFT** or **XmMAX_ON_TOP**, movement toward the right or bottom calls the callbacks for **XmNtoTopCallback**, and movement to the left or top calls the callbacks for **XmNtoBottomCallback**. The **XmNvalueChangedCallback** is called if the **XmNtoTopCallback** or **XmNtoBottomCallback** is NULL. Pressing **KBeginLine** or **KBeginData** moves the slider to the minimum value and invokes the **XmNtoTopCallback**. Pressing **KEndLine** or **KEndData** moves the slider to the maximum value and invokes the **XmNtoBottomCallback**.

Virtual Bindings

The bindings for virtual keys are vendor specific.

Related Information

Core(3X), **XmCreateScrollBar(3X)**, **XmPrimitive(3X)**, **XmScrollBarGetValues(3X)**, and **XmScrollBarSetValues(3X)**.

XmScrollBarGetValues

Purpose

A ScrollBar function that returns the ScrollBar's increment values.

AES Support Level

Full-use

Synopsis

#include <Xm/ScrollBar.h>

void XmScrollBarGetValues (*widget, value_return, slider_size_return, increment_return,*
                    page_increment_return)
        Widget   *widget*;
        int   * *value_return*;
        int   * *slider_size_return*;
        int   * *increment_return*;
        int   * *page_increment_return*;

Description

XmScrollBarGetValues returns the the ScrollBar's increment values. The scroll region is overlaid with a slider bar that is adjusted in size and position using the main ScrollBar or set slider function attributes.

widget	Specifies the ScrollBar widget ID.
value_return	Returns the ScrollBar's slider position between the **XmNminimum** and **XmNmaximum** resources.
slider_size_return	Returns the size of the slider as a value between zero and the absolute value of **XmNmaximum** minus **XmNminimum**. The size of the slider varies, depending on how much of the slider scroll area it represents.
increment_return	Returns the amount of increment and decrement.
page_increment_return	
	Returns the amount of page increment and decrement.

For a complete definition of ScrollBar and its associated resources, see **XmScrollBar(3X)**.

Return Value

Returns the ScrollBar's increment values.

Related Information

XmScrollBar(3X).

XmScrollBarSetValues

Purpose

A ScrollBar function that changes ScrollBar's increment values and the slider's size and position.

AES Support Level

Full-use

Synopsis

#include <Xm/ScrollBar.h>

void XmScrollBarSetValues (*widget, value, slider_size, increment, page_increment, notify*)
        Widget   *widget*;
        int   *value*;
        int   *slider_size*;
        int   *increment*;
        int   *page_increment*;
        Boolean   *notify*;

Description

XmSetScrollBarValues changes the ScrollBar's increment values and the slider's size and position. The scroll region is overlaid with a slider bar that is adjusted in size and position using the main ScrollBar or set slider function attributes.

widget	Specifies the ScrollBar widget ID.
value	Specifies the ScrollBar's slider position between **XmNminimum** and **XmNmaximum**. The resource name associated with this argument is **XmNvalue**.
slider_size	Specifies the size of the slider as a value between zero and the absolute value of **XmNmaximum** minus **XmNminimum**. The size of the slider varies, depending on how much of the slider scroll area it represents. This sets the **XmNsliderSize** resource associated with ScrollBar.
increment	Specifies the amount of button increment and decrement. If this argument is not zero, the ScrollBar widget automatically adjusts the slider when an increment or decrement action occurs. This sets the **XmNincrement** resource associated with ScrollBar.
page_increment	Specifies the amount of page increment and decrement. If this argument is not zero, the ScrollBar widget automatically adjusts the slider when an increment or decrement action occurs. This sets the **XmNpageIncrement** resource associated with ScrollBar.
notify	Specifies a Boolean value that when True, indicates a change in the ScrollBar value and also specifies that the ScrollBar widget automatically activates the **XmNvalueChangedCallback** with the recent change. If False, no change has occurred in the ScrollBar's value and **XmNvalueChangedCallback** is not activated.

For a complete definition of ScrollBar and its associated resources, see **XmScrollBar(3X)**.

Related Information

XmScrollBar(3X).

XmScrolledWindow

Purpose

The ScrolledWindow widget class

AES Support Level

Full-use

Synopsis

#include <Xm/ScrolledW.h>

Description

The ScrolledWindow widget combines one or two ScrollBar widgets and a viewing area to implement a visible window onto some other (usually larger) data display. The visible part of the window can be scrolled through the larger display by the use of ScrollBars.

To use ScrolledWindow, an application first creates a ScrolledWindow widget, any needed ScrollBar widgets, and a widget capable of displaying any desired data as the work area of ScrolledWindow. ScrolledWindow positions the work area widget and display the ScrollBars if so requested. When the user performs some action on the ScrollBar, the application is notified through the normal ScrollBar callback interface.

ScrolledWindow can be configured to operate automatically so that it performs all scrolling and display actions with no need for application program involvement. It can also be configured to provide a minimal support framework in which the application is responsible for processing all user input and making all visual changes to the displayed data in response to that input.

When ScrolledWindow is performing automatic scrolling it creates a clipping window. Conceptually, this window becomes the viewport through which the user examines the larger underlying data area. The application simply creates the desired data, then makes that data the work area of the ScrolledWindow. When the user moves the slider to change the displayed data, the workspace is moved under the viewing area so that a new portion of the data becomes visible.

Sometimes it is impractical for an application to create a large data space and simply display it through a small clipping window. For example, in a text editor, creating a single data area that consisted of a large file would involve an undesirable amount of overhead. The application needs to use a ScrolledWindow (a small viewport onto some larger data), but needs to be notified when the user scrolled the viewport so it could bring in more data from storage and update the display area. For these cases the ScrolledWindow can be configured so that it provides only visual layout support. No clipping window is created, and the application must maintain the data displayed in the work area, as well as respond to user input on the ScrollBars.

Classes

ScrolledWindow inherits behavior and resources from **Core**, **Composite**, **Constraint**, and **XmManager** Classes.

The class pointer is **xmScrolledWindowWidgetClass**.

The class name is **XmScrolledWindow**.

New Resources

The following table defines a set of widget resources used by the programmer to specify data. The programmer can also set the resource values for the inherited classes to set attributes for this widget. To reference a resource by name or by class in a .Xdefaults file, remove the **XmN** or **XmC** prefix and use the remaining letters. To specify one of the defined values for a resource in a .Xdefaults file, remove the **Xm** prefix and use the remaining letters (in either lowercase or uppercase, but include any underscores between words). The codes in the access column indicate if the given resource can be set at creation time (**C**), set by using **XtSetValues** (**S**), retrieved by using **XtGetValues** (**G**), or is not applicable (**N/A**).

XmScrolledWindow Resource Set		
Name	**Default**	**Access**
Class	**Type**	
XmNclipWindow	dynamic	G
XmCClipWindow	Widget	
XmNhorizontalScrollBar	dynamic	CSG
XmCHorizontalScrollBar	Widget	
XmNscrollBarDisplayPolicy	dynamic	CSG
XmCScrollBarDisplayPolicy	unsigned char	
XmNscrollBarPlacement	XmBOTTOM_RIGHT	CSG
XmCScrollBarPlacement	unsigned char	
XmNscrolledWindowMarginHeight	0	CSG
XmCScrolledWindowMarginHeight	Dimension	
XmNscrolledWindowMarginWidth	0	CSG
XmCScrolledWindowMarginWidth	Dimension	
XmNscrollingPolicy	XmAPPLICATION_DEFINED	CG
XmCScrollingPolicy	unsigned char	
XmNspacing	4	CSG
XmCSpacing	Dimension	
XmNverticalScrollBar	dynamic	CSG
XmCVerticalScrollBar	Widget	
XmNvisualPolicy	dynamic	CG
XmCVisualPolicy	unsigned char	
XmNworkWindow	NULL	CSG
XmCWorkWindow	Widget	

XmNclipWindow

Specifies the widget ID of the clipping area. This is automatically created by ScrolledWindow when the **XmNvisualPolicy** resource is set to **XmCONSTANT** and can only be read by the application. Any attempt to set this resource to a new value causes a warning message to be printed by the scrolled window. If the **XmNvisualPolicy** resource is set to **XmVARIABLE**, this resource is set to NULL, and no clipping window is created.

XmNhorizontalScrollBar

Specifies the widget ID of the horizontal ScrollBar. This is automatically created by ScrolledWindow when the **XmNscrollingPolicy** is initialized to **XmAUTOMATIC**; otherwise, the default is NULL.

XmNscrollBarDisplayPolicy

Controls the automatic placement of the ScrollBars. If it is set to **XmAS_NEEDED** and if **XmNscrollingPolicy** is set to **XmAUTOMATIC**, ScrollBars are displayed only if the workspace exceeds the clip area in one or both dimensions. A resource value of **XmSTATIC** causes the ScrolledWindow to display the ScrollBars whenever they are managed, regardless of the relationship between the clip window and the work area. This resource must be **XmSTATIC** when **XmNscrollingPolicy** is **XmAPPLICATION_DEFINED**. The default is **XmAS_NEEDED** when **XmNscrollingPolicy** is **XmAUTOMATIC**, and **XmSTATIC** otherwise.

XmNscrollBarPlacement

Specifies the positioning of the ScrollBars in relation to the work window. The following are the values:

- **XmTOP_LEFT** — The horizontal ScrollBar is placed above the work window; the vertical ScrollBar to the left.

- **XmBOTTOM_LEFT** — The horizontal ScrollBar is placed below the work window; the vertical ScrollBar to the left.

- **XmTOP_RIGHT** — The horizontal ScrollBar is placed above the work window; the vertical ScrollBar to the right.

- **XmBOTTOM_RIGHT** — The horizontal ScrollBar is placed below the work window; the vertical ScrollBar to the right.

The default value may depend on the value of the **XmNstringDirection** resource.

XmNscrolledWindowMarginHeight

Specifies the margin height on the top and bottom of the ScrolledWindow.

XmNscrolledWindowMarginWidth
> Specifies the margin width on the right and left sides of the ScrolledWindow.

XmNscrollingPolicy
> Performs automatic scrolling of the work area with no application interaction. If the value of this resource is **XmAUTOMATIC**, ScrolledWindow automatically creates the ScrollBars; attaches callbacks to the ScrollBars; sets the visual policy to **XmCONSTANT**; and automatically moves the work area through the clip window in response to any user interaction with the ScrollBars. An application can also add its own callbacks to the ScrollBars. This allows the application to be notified of a scroll event without having to perform any layout procedures.
>
> **NOTE**: Since the ScrolledWindow adds callbacks to the ScrollBars, an application should not perform an **XtRemoveAllCallbacks** on any of the ScrollBar widgets.
>
> When **XmNscrollingPolicy** is set to **XmAPPLICATION_DEFINED**, the application is responsible for all aspects of scrolling. The ScrollBars must be created by the application, and it is responsible for performing any visual changes in the work area in response to user input.
>
> This resource must be set to the desired policy at the time the ScrolledWindow is created. It cannot be changed through **SetValues**.

XmNspacing
> Specifies the distance that separates the ScrollBars from the work window.

XmNverticalScrollBar
> Specifies the widget ID of the vertical ScrollBar. This is automatically created by ScrolledWindow when the **XmNscrollingPolicy** is initialized to **XmAUTOMATIC**; otherwise, the default is NULL.

XmNvisualPolicy

Grows the ScrolledWindow to match the size of the work area, or it can be used as a static viewport onto a larger data space. If the visual policy is **XmVARIABLE**, the ScrolledWindow forces the ScrollBar display policy to **XmSTATIC** and allow the work area to grow or shrink at any time and adjusts its layout to accommodate the new size. When the policy is **XmCONSTANT**, the work area grows or shrinks as requested, but a clipping window forces the size of the visible portion to remain constant. The only time the viewing area can grow is in response to a resize from the ScrolledWindow's parent. The default is **XmCONSTANT** when **XmNscrollingPolicy** is **XmAUTOMATIC**, and **XmVARIABLE** otherwise.

NOTE: This resource must be set to the desired policy at the time the ScrolledWindow is created. It cannot be changed through **SetValues**.

XmNworkWindow

Specifies the widget ID of the viewing area.

Inherited Resources

ScrolledWindow inherits behavior and resources from the following superclasses. For a complete description of each resource, refer to the man page for that superclass.

XmManager Resource Set		
Name Class	**Default** Type	**Access**
XmNbottomShadowColor XmCBottomShadowColor	dynamic Pixel	CSG
XmNbottomShadowPixmap XmCBottomShadowPixmap	XmUNSPECIFIED_PIXMAP Pixmap	CSG
XmNforeground XmCForeground	dynamic Pixel	CSG
XmNhelpCallback XmCCallback	NULL XtCallbackList	C
XmNhighlightColor XmCHighlightColor	dynamic Pixel	CSG
XmNhighlightPixmap XmCHighlightPixmap	dynamic Pixmap	CSG
XmNnavigationType XmCNavigationType	XmTAB_GROUP XmNavigationType	CSG
XmNshadowThickness XmCShadowThickness	dynamic Dimension	CSG
XmNstringDirection XmCStringDirection	dynamic XmStringDirection	CG
XmNtopShadowColor XmCBackgroundTopShadowColor	dynamic Pixel	CSG
XmNtopShadowPixmap XmCTopShadowPixmap	dynamic Pixmap	CSG
XmNtraversalOn XmCTraversalOn	True Boolean	CSG
XmNuserData XmCUserData	NULL Pointer	CSG

Composite Resource Set		
Name	**Default**	**Access**
Class	**Type**	
XmNchildren	NULL	G
XmCReadOnly	WidgetList	
XmNinsertPosition	NULL	CSG
XmCInsertPosition	(*)()	
XmNnumChildren	0	G
XmCReadOnly	Cardinal	

Core Resource Set		
Name	**Default**	**Access**
Class	**Type**	
XmNaccelerators	dynamic	CSG
XmCAccelerators	XtAccelerators	
XmNancestorSensitive	dynamic	G
XmCSensitive	Boolean	
XmNbackground	dynamic	CSG
XmCBackground	Pixel	
XmNbackgroundPixmap	XmUNSPECIFIED_PIXMAP	CSG
XmCPixmap	Pixmap	
XmNborderColor	XtDefaultForeground	CSG
XmCBorderColor	Pixel	
XmNborderPixmap	XmUNSPECIFIED_PIXMAP	CSG
XmCPixmap	Pixmap	
XmNborderWidth	0	CSG
XmCBorderWidth	Dimension	
XmNcolormap	dynamic	CG
XmCColormap	Colormap	
XmNdepth	dynamic	CG
XmCDepth	int	
XmNdestroyCallback	NULL	C
XmCCallback	XtCallbackList	
XmNheight	dynamic	CSG
XmCHeight	Dimension	
XmNinitialResourcesPersistent	True	C
XmCInitialResourcesPersistent	Boolean	
XmNmappedWhenManaged	True	CSG
XmCMappedWhenManaged	Boolean	
XmNscreen	dynamic	CG
XmCScreen	Screen *	

Name	Default	Access
Class	Type	
XmNsensitive	True	CSG
XmCSensitive	Boolean	
XmNtranslations	dynamic	CSG
XmCTranslations	XtTranslations	
XmNwidth	dynamic	CSG
XmCWidth	Dimension	
XmNx	0	CSG
XmCPosition	Position	
XmNy	0	CSG
XmCPosition	Position	

Callback Information

ScrolledWindow defines no new callback structures. The application must use the ScrollBar callbacks to be notified of user input.

Translations

XmScrolledWindow includes the translations from XmManager.

Additional Behavior

This widget has the additional behavior described below:

KPageUp: If **XmNscrollingPolicy** is **XmAUTOMATIC**, scrolls the window up the height of the viewport. The distance scrolled my be reduced to provide some overlap. The actual distance scrolled depends on the **XmNpageIncrement** resource of the vertical ScrollBar.

KPageDown:
If **XmNscrollingPolicy** is **XmAUTOMATIC**, scrolls the window down the height of the viewport. The distance scrolled my be reduced to provide some overlap. The actual distance scrolled depends on the **XmNpageIncrement** resource of the vertical ScrollBar.

KPageLeft: If **XmNscrollingPolicy** is **XmAUTOMATIC**, scrolls the window left the width of the viewport. The distance scrolled my be reduced to provide some overlap. The actual distance scrolled depends on the **XmNpageIncrement** resource of the horizontal ScrollBar.

KPageRight:
If **XmNscrollingPolicy** is **XmAUTOMATIC**, scrolls the window right the width of the viewport. The distance scrolled my be reduced to provide some overlap. The actual distance scrolled depends on the **XmNpageIncrement** resource of the horizontal ScrollBar.

KBeginLine:
If **XmNscrollingPolicy** is **XmAUTOMATIC**, scrolls the window horizontally to the edge corresponding to the horizontal ScrollBar's minimum value.

KEndLine: If **XmNscrollingPolicy** is **XmAUTOMATIC**, scrolls the window horizontally to the edge corresponding to the horizontal ScrollBar's maximum value.

KBeginData:
If **XmNscrollingPolicy** is **XmAUTOMATIC**, scrolls the window vertically to the edge corresponding to the vertical ScrollBar's minimum value.

KEndData: If **XmNscrollingPolicy** is **XmAUTOMATIC**, scrolls the window vertically to the edge corresponding to the vertical ScrollBar's maximum value.

Virtual Bindings

The bindings for virtual keys are vendor specific.

Related Information

Composite(3X), **Constraint(3X)**, **Core(3X)**, **XmCreateScrolledWindow(3X)**, **XmManager(3X)**, and **XmScrolledWindowSetAreas(3X)**.

XmScrolledWindowSetAreas

Purpose

A ScrolledWindow function that adds or changes a window work region and a horizontal or vertical ScrollBar widget to the ScrolledWindow widget.

AES Support Level

Full-use

Synopsis

#include <Xm/ScrolledW.h>

void   XmScrolledWindowSetAreas   (*widget,   horizontal_scrollbar, vertical_scrollbar, work_region*)
      Widget   *widget*;
      Widget   *horizontal_scrollbar*;
      Widget   *vertical_scrollbar*;
      Widget   *work_region*;

Description

XmScrolledWindowSetAreas adds or changes a window work region and a horizontal or vertical ScrollBar widget to the ScrolledWindow widget for the application. Each widget is optional and may be passed as NULL.

widget   Specifies the ScrolledWindow widget ID.

horizontal_scrollbar

Specifies the ScrollBar widget ID for the horizontal ScrollBar to be associated with the ScrolledWindow widget. Set this ID only after creating an instance of the ScrolledWindow widget. The resource name associated with this argument is **XmNhorizontalScrollBar**.

vertical_scrollbar   Specifies the ScrollBar widget ID for the vertical ScrollBar to be associated with the ScrolledWindow widget. Set this ID only after creating an instance of the ScrolledWindow widget. The resource name associated with this argument is **XmNverticalScrollBar**.

work_region   Specifies the widget ID for the work window to be associated with the ScrolledWindow widget. Set this ID only after creating an instance of the ScrolledWindow widget. The attribute name associated with this argument is **XmNworkWindow**.

For a complete definition of ScrolledWindow and its associated resources, see **XmScrolledWindow(3X)**.

Related Information

XmScrolledWindow(3X).

XmSelectionBox

Purpose

The SelectionBox widget class

AES Support Level

Full-use

Synopsis

#include <Xm/SelectioB.h>

Description

SelectionBox is a general dialog widget that allows the user to select one item from a list. By default a SelectionBox includes the following:

- A scrolling list of alternatives

- An editable text field for the selected alternative

- Labels for the list and text field

- Three or four buttons

The default button labels are **OK**, **Cancel**, and **Help**. By default an **Apply** button is also created; if the parent of the SelectionBox is a DialogShell it is managed, and otherwise it is unmanaged. One additional **WorkArea** child may be added to the SelectionBox after creation.

The user can select an item in two ways: by scrolling through the list and selecting the desired item or by entering the item name directly into the text edit area. Selecting an item from the list causes that item name to appear in the selection text edit area.

The user may select a new item as many times as desired. The item is not actually selected until the user presses the **OK** PushButton.

The default value for the **XmBulletinBoard** resource **XmNcancelButton** is the Cancel button unless **XmNdialogType** is **XmDIALOG_COMMAND**, when the default is NULL. The default value for the **XmBulletinBoard** resource **XmNdefaultButton** is the OK button unless **XmNdialogType** is **XmDIALOG_COMMAND**, when the default is NULL.

Classes

SelectionBox inherits behavior and resources from **Core**, **Composite**, **Constraint**, **XmManager**, and **XmBulletinBoard** Classes.

The class pointer is **xmSelectionBoxWidgetClass**.

The class name is **XmSelectionBox**.

New Resources

The following table defines a set of widget resources used by the programmer to specify data. The programmer can also set the resource values for the inherited classes to set attributes for this widget. To reference a resource by name or by class in a .Xdefaults file, remove the **XmN** or **XmC** prefix and use the remaining letters. To specify one of the defined values for a resource in a .Xdefaults file, remove the **Xm** prefix and use the remaining letters (in either lowercase or uppercase, but include any underscores between words). The codes in the access column indicate if the given resource can be set at creation time (**C**), set by using **XtSetValues** (**S**), retrieved by using **XtGetValues** (**G**), or is not applicable (**N/A**).

XmSelectionBox Resource Set		
Name **Class**	**Default** **Type**	**Access**
XmNapplyCallback XmCCallback	NULL XtCallbackList	C
XmNapplyLabelString XmCApplyLabelString	"Apply" XmString	CSG
XmNcancelCallback XmCCallback	NULL XtCallbackList	C
XmNcancelLabelString XmCCancelLabelString	"Cancel" XmString	CSG
XmNdialogType XmCDialogType	dynamic unsigned char	CG
XmNhelpLabelString XmCHelpLabelString	"Help" XmString	CSG
XmNlistItemCount XmCItemCount	0 int	CSG
XmNlistItems XmCItems	NULL XmStringTable	CSG
XmNlistLabelString XmCListLabelString	"Items" XmString	CSG
XmNlistVisibleItemCount XmCVisibleItemCount	dynamic int	CSG
XmNminimizeButtons XmCMinimizeButtons	False Boolean	CSG
XmNmustMatch XmCMustMatch	False Boolean	CSG
XmNnoMatchCallback XmCCallback	NULL XtCallbackList	C

Name	Default	Access
Class	Type	
XmNokCallback	NULL	C
XmCCallback	XtCallbackList	
XmNokLabelString	"OK"	CSG
XmCOkLabelString	XmString	
XmNselectionLabelString	"Selection"	CSG
XmCSelectionLabelString	XmString	
XmNtextAccelerators	default	C
XmCTextAccelerators	XtAccelerators	
XmNtextColumns	dynamic	CSG
XmCColumns	short	
XmNtextString	""	CSG
XmCTextString	XmString	

XmNapplyCallback

> Specifies the list of callbacks called when the user activates the **Apply** button. The callback reason is **XmCR_APPLY**.

XmNapplyLabelString

> Specifies the string label for the **Apply** button.

XmNcancelCallback

> Specifies the list of callbacks called when the user activates the **Cancel** button. The callback reason is **XmCR_CANCEL**.

XmNcancelLabelString

> Specifies the string label for the **Cancel** button.

XmNdialogType

> Determines the set of SelectionBox children widgets that are created and managed at initialization. The following are possible values:

> - **XmDIALOG_PROMPT** — all standard children except the list and list label are created, and all except the **Apply** button are managed

> - **XmDIALOG_COMMAND** — only the list, the selection label, and the text field are created and managed

- **XmDIALOG_SELECTION** — all standard children are created and managed

- **XmDIALOG_FILE_SELECTION** — all standard children are created and managed

- **XmDIALOG_WORK_AREA** — all standard children are created, and all except the **Apply** button are managed

If the parent of the SelectionBox is a DialogShell, the default is **XmDIALOG_SELECTION**; otherwise, the default is **XmDIALOG_WORK_AREA**. **XmCreatePromptDialog** and **XmCreateSelectionDialog** set and append this resource to the creation *arglist* supplied by the application. This resource cannot be modified after creation.

XmNhelpLabelString
Specifies the string label for the **Help** button.

XmNlistItems
Specifies the items in the SelectionBox list.

XmNlistItemCount
Specifies the number of items in the SelectionBox list. The value must not be negative.

XmNlistLabelString
Specifies the string label to appear above the SelectionBox list containing the selection items.

XmNlistVisibleItemCount
Specifies the number of items displayed in the SelectionBox list. The value must be greater than 0. The default is dynamic based on the height of the list.

XmNminimizeButtons
Sets the buttons to the width of the widest button and height of the tallest button if False. If True, button width and height are not modified.

XmNmustMatch

Specifies whether the selection widget should check if the
user's selection in the text edit field has an exact match in the
SelectionBox list when the BOK button is activated. If the
selection does not have an exact match, and **XmNmustMatch**
is True, the **XmNnoMatchCallback** callbacks are called. If
the selection does have an exact match or if **XmNmustMatch**
is False, **XmNokCallback** callbacks are called.

XmNnoMatchCallback

Specifies the list of callbacks called when the user makes a
selection from the text edit field that does not have an exact
match with any of the items in the list box. The callback
reason is **XmCR_NO_MATCH**. Callbacks in this list are
called only if **XmNmustMatch** is true.

XmNokCallback

Specifies the list of callbacks called when the user activates
the **OK** button. The callback reason is **XmCR_OK**. If the
selection text does not match a list item, and **XmNmustMatch**
is True, the **XmNnoMatchCallback** callbacks are called
instead.

XmNokLabelString

Specifies the string label for the **OK** button.

XmNselectionLabelString

Specifies the string label for the selection text edit field.

XmNtextAccelerators

Specifies translations added to the Text widget child of the
SelectionBox. The default includes bindings for the up and
down keys for auto selection of list items. This resource is
ignored if **XmNaccelerators** is initialized to a nondefault
value.

XmNtextColumns

Specifies the number of columns in the Text widget. The value must be greater than 0.

XmNtextString

Specifies the text in the text edit selection field.

Inherited Resources

SelectionBox inherits behavior and resources from the following superclasses. For a complete description of each resource, refer to the man page for that superclass.

XmBulletinBoard Resource Set		

Name
    Class
	Default
	    Type
		Access

XmNallowOverlap
    XmCAllowOverlap
	True
	    Boolean
		CSG

XmNautoUnmanage
    XmCAutoUnmanage
	True
	    Boolean
		CG

XmNbuttonFontList
    XmCButtonFontList
	dynamic
	    XmFontList
		CSG

XmNcancelButton
    XmCWidget
	dynamic
	    Widget
		SG

XmNdefaultButton
    XmCWidget
	dynamic
	    Widget
		SG

XmNdefaultPosition
    XmCDefaultPosition
	True
	    Boolean
		CSG

XmNdialogStyle
    XmCDialogStyle
	dynamic
	    unsigned char
		CSG

XmNdialogTitle
    XmCDialogTitle
	NULL
	    XmString
		CSG

XmNfocusCallback
    XmCCallback
	NULL
	    XtCallbackList
		C

XmNlabelFontList
    XmCLabelFontList
	dynamic
	    XmFontList
		CSG

XmNmapCallback
    XmCCallback
	NULL
	    XtCallbackList
		C

XmNmarginHeight
    XmCMarginHeight
	10
	    Dimension
		CSG

XmNmarginWidth
    XmCMarginWidth
	10
	    Dimension
		CSG

XmNnoResize
    XmCNoResize
	False
	    Boolean
		CSG

Name	Default	Access
Class	Type	
XmNresizePolicy	XmRESIZE_ANY	CSG
XmCResizePolicy	unsigned char	
XmNshadowType	XmSHADOW_OUT	CSG
XmCShadowType	unsigned char	
XmNtextFontList	dynamic	CSG
XmCTextFontList	XmFontList	
XmNtextTranslations	NULL	C
XmCTranslations	XtTranslations	
XmNunmapCallback	NULL	C
XmCCallback	XtCallbackList	

XmManager Resource Set		

Name
    Class
	Default
	    Type
		Access

XmNbottomShadowColor
    XmCBottomShadowColor
	dynamic
	    Pixel
		CSG

XmNbottomShadowPixmap
    XmCBottomShadowPixmap
	XmUNSPECIFIED_PIXMAP
	    Pixmap
		CSG

XmNforeground
    XmCForeground
	dynamic
	    Pixel
		CSG

XmNhelpCallback
    XmCCallback
	NULL
	    XtCallbackList
		C

XmNhighlightColor
    XmCHighlightColor
	dynamic
	    Pixel
		CSG

XmNhighlightPixmap
    XmCHighlightPixmap
	dynamic
	    Pixmap
		CSG

XmNnavigationType
    XmCNavigationType
	dynamic
	    XmNavigationType
		CSG

XmNshadowThickness
    XmCShadowThickness
	dynamic
	    Dimension
		CSG

XmNstringDirection
    XmCStringDirection
	dynamic
	    XmStringDirection
		CG

XmNtopShadowColor
    XmCBackgroundTopShadowColor
	dynamic
	    Pixel
		CSG

XmNtopShadowPixmap
    XmCTopShadowPixmap
	dynamic
	    Pixmap
		CSG

XmNtraversalOn
    XmCTraversalOn
	True
	    Boolean
		CSG

XmNuserData
    XmCUserData
	NULL
	    Pointer
		CSG

Composite Resource Set		
Name	**Default**	**Access**
Class	**Type**	
XmNchildren	NULL	G
XmCReadOnly	WidgetList	
XmNinsertPosition	NULL	CSG
XmCInsertPosition	(*)()	
XmNnumChildren	0	G
XmCReadOnly	Cardinal	

Core Resource Set		
Name	**Default**	**Access**
Class	**Type**	
XmNaccelerators	dynamic	N/A
XmCAccelerators	XtAccelerators	
XmNancestorSensitive	dynamic	G
XmCSensitive	Boolean	
XmNbackground	dynamic	CSG
XmCBackground	Pixel	
XmNbackgroundPixmap	XmUNSPECIFIED_PIXMAP	CSG
XmCPixmap	Pixmap	
XmNborderColor	XtDefaultForeground	CSG
XmCBorderColor	Pixel	
XmNborderPixmap	XmUNSPECIFIED_PIXMAP	CSG
XmCPixmap	Pixmap	
XmNborderWidth	0	CSG
XmCBorderWidth	Dimension	
XmNcolormap	dynamic	CG
XmCColormap	Colormap	
XmNdepth	dynamic	CG
XmCDepth	int	
XmNdestroyCallback	NULL	C
XmCCallback	XtCallbackList	
XmNheight	dynamic	CSG
XmCHeight	Dimension	
XmNinitialResourcesPersistent	True	C
XmCInitialResourcesPersistent	Boolean	
XmNmappedWhenManaged	True	CSG
XmCMappedWhenManaged	Boolean	
XmNscreen	dynamic	CG
XmCScreen	Screen *	

Name	Default	Access
Class	Type	
XmNsensitive	True	CSG
XmCSensitive	Boolean	
XmNtranslations	dynamic	CSG
XmCTranslations	XtTranslations	
XmNwidth	dynamic	CSG
XmCWidth	Dimension	
XmNx	0	CSG
XmCPosition	Position	
XmNy	0	CSG
XmCPosition	Position	

Callback Information

A pointer to the following structure is passed to each callback:

```
typedef struct
{
    int         reason;
    XEvent      * event;
    XmString    value;
    int         length;
} XmSelectionBoxCallbackStruct;
```

reason   Indicates why the callback was invoked

event   Points to the **XEvent** that triggered the callback

value   Indicates the **XmString** value selected by the user from the SelectionBox list or entered into the SelectionBox text field

length   Indicates the size in bytes of the **XmString** value

Translations

XmSelectionBox inherits translations from XmBulletinBoard.

Accelerators

The **XmNtextAccelerators** are added to the Text descendant of XmSelectionBox. The default accelerators are listed below. These accelerators may not directly correspond to a translation table.

KUp:	**SelectionBoxUpOrDown(0)**
KDown:	**SelectionBoxUpOrDown(1)**
KBeginData:	**SelectionBoxUpOrDown(2)**
KEndData:	**SelectionBoxUpOrDown(3)**
KRestore:	**SelectionBoxRestore()**

Action Routines

The XmSelectionBox action routines are described below:

SelectionBoxUpOrDown(0|1|2|3):
When called with a 0 argument, selects the previous item in the list and replaces the text with that item.

When called with a 1 argument, selects the next item in the list and replaces the text with that item.

When called with a 2 argument, selects the first item in the list and replaces the text with that item.

When called with a 3 argument, selects the last item in the list and replaces the text with that item.

SelectionBoxRestore():
Replaces the text value with the list selection. If no item in the list is selected, clears the text.

Additional Behavior

The SelectionBox widget has the additional behavior described below:

MAny KCancel:
Calls the activate callbacks for the cancel button if it is sensitive.

KActivate: Calls the activate callbacks for the button with the keyboard focus. If no button has the keyboard focus, calls the activate callbacks for the default button if it is sensitive. In a List widget or single-line Text widget, the List or Text action associated with **KActivate** is called before the SelectionBox actions associated with **KActivate**. In a multi-line Text widget, any **KActivate** event except **KEnter** calls the Text action associated with **KActivate**, then the SelectionBox actions associated with **KActivate**.

<OK Button Activated>:
If **XmNmustMatch** is True and the text does not match an item in the file list, calls the **XmNnoMatchCallback** callbacks with reason **XmCR_NO_MATCH**. Otherwise, calls the **XmNokCallback** callbacks with reason **XmCR_OK**.

<Apply Button Activated>:
Calls the **XmNapplyCallback** callbacks with reason **XmCR_APPLY**.

<Cancel Button Activated>:
Calls the **XmNcancelCallback** callbacks with reason **XmCR_CANCEL**.

<Help Button Activated>:
Calls the **XmNhelpCallback** callbacks with reason **XmCR_HELP**.

<MapWindow>:
Calls the callbacks for **XmNmapCallback** if the SelectionBox is a child of a Dialog shell.

<UnmapWindow>:
Calls the callbacks for **XmNunmapCallback** if the SelectionBox is the child of a DialogShell.

Virtual Bindings

The bindings for virtual keys are vendor specific.

Related Information

Composite(3X), **Constraint(3X),** **Core(3X),** **XmBulletinBoard(3X),** **XmCreateSelectionBox(3X),** **XmCreateSelectionDialog(3X),** **XmCreatePromptDialog(3X),** **XmManager(3X),** and **XmSelectionBoxGetChild(3X).**

XmSelectionBoxGetChild

Purpose

A SelectionBox function that is used to access a component.

AES Support Level

Full-use

Synopsis

#include <Xm/SelectioB.h>

Widget XmSelectionBoxGetChild (*widget, child*)

    Widget   *widget*;
    unsigned char*child*;

Description

XmSelectionBoxGetChild is used to access a component within a SelectionBox. The parameters given to the function are the SelectionBox widget and a value indicating which child to access.

widget   Specifies the SelectionBox widget ID.

child   Specifies a component within the SelectionBox. The following are legal values for this parameter:

- **XmDIALOG_APPLY_BUTTON**
- **XmDIALOG_CANCEL_BUTTON**
- **XmDIALOG_DEFAULT_BUTTON**
- **XmDIALOG_HELP_BUTTON**
- **XmDIALOG_LIST**
- **XmDIALOG_LIST_LABEL**
- **XmDIALOG_OK_BUTTON**
- **XmDIALOG_SELECTION_LABEL**
- **XmDIALOG_SEPARATOR**
- **XmDIALOG_TEXT**
- **XmDIALOG_WORK_AREA**

For a complete definition of SelectionBox and its associated resources, see **XmSelectionBox(3X)**.

Return Value

Returns the widget ID of the specified SelectionBox child. An application should not assume that the returned widget will be of any particular class.

Related Information

XmSelectionBox(3X).

XmSeparator

Purpose

The Separator widget class

AES Support Level

Full-use

Synopsis

#include <Xm/Separator.h>

Description

Separator is a primitive widget that separates items in a display. Several different line drawing styles are provided, as well as horizontal or vertical orientation.

The Separator line drawing is automatically centered within the height of the widget for a horizontal orientation and centered within the width of the widget for a vertical orientation. An **XtSetValues** with a new **XmNseparatorType** resizes the widget to its minimal height (for horizontal orientation) or its minimal width (for vertical orientation) unless height or width is explicitly set in the **XtSetValues** call.

Separator does not draw shadows around the separator. The Primitive resource **XmNshadowThickness** is used for the Separator's thickness when **XmNseparatorType** is **XmSHADOW_ETCHED_IN** or **XmSHADOW_ETCHED_OUT**.

Separator does not highlight and allows no traversing. The primitive resource **XmNtraversalOn** is forced to False.

The **XmNseparatorType** of **XmNO_LINE** provides an escape to the application programmer who needs a different style of drawing. A pixmap the height of the widget can be created and used as the background pixmap by building an argument list using the **XmNbackgroundPixmap** argument type as defined by **Core**. Whenever the widget is redrawn, its background is displayed containing the desired separator drawing.

Classes

Separator inherits behavior and resources from **Core** and **XmPrimitive** Classes.

The class pointer is **xmSeparatorWidgetClass**.

The class name is **XmSeparator**.

New Resources

The following table defines a set of widget resources used by the programmer to specify data. The programmer can also set the resource values for the inherited classes to set attributes for this widget. To reference a resource by name or by class in a .Xdefaults file, remove the **XmN** or **XmC** prefix and use the remaining letters. To specify one of the defined values for a resource in a .Xdefaults file, remove the **Xm** prefix and use the remaining letters (in either lowercase or uppercase, but include any underscores between words). The codes in the access column indicate if the given resource can be set at creation time (**C**), set by using **XtSetValues** (**S**), retrieved by using **XtGetValues** (**G**), or is not applicable (**N/A**).

XmSeparator Resource Set		
Name **Class**	**Default** **Type**	**Access**

XmNmargin
    XmCMargin
	0
	    Dimension
		CSG

XmNorientation
    XmCOrientation
	XmHORIZONTAL
	    unsigned char
		CSG

XmNseparatorType
    XmCSeparatorType
	XmSHADOW_ETCHED_IN
	    unsigned char
		CSG

XmNmargin

For horizontal orientation, specifies the space on the left and right sides between the border of the Separator and the line drawn. For vertical orientation, specifies the space on the top and bottom between the border of the Separator and the line drawn.

XmNorientation

Displays Separator vertically or horizontally. This resource can have values of **XmVERTICAL** and **XmHORIZONTAL**.

XmNseparatorType

Specifies the type of line drawing to be done in the Separator widget.

- **XmSINGLE_LINE** — single line.

- **XmDOUBLE_LINE** — double line.

- **XmSINGLE_DASHED_LINE** — single-dashed line.

- **XmDOUBLE_DASHED_LINE** — double-dashed line.

- **XmNO_LINE** — no line.

- **XmSHADOW_ETCHED_IN** — double line giving the effect of a line etched into the window. The thickness of the double line is equal to the value of **XmNshadowThickness**. For horizontal orientation, the top line is drawn in **XmNtopShadowColor** and the bottom line is drawn in **XmNbottomShadowColor**. For vertical orientation, the left line is drawn in **XmNtopShadowColor** and the right line is drawn in **XmNbottomShadowColor**.

- **XmSHADOW_ETCHED_OUT** — double line giving the effect of an etched line coming out from the window. The thickness of the double line is equal to the value of **XmNshadowThickness**. For horizontal orientation, the top line is drawn in **XmNbottomShadowColor** and the bottom line is drawn in **XmNtopShadowColor**. For vertical orientation, the left line is drawn in **XmNbottomShadowColor** and the right line is drawn in **XmNtopShadowColor**.

Inherited Resources

Separator inherits behavior and resources from the following superclasses. For a complete description of each resource, refer to the man page for that superclass.

XmPrimitive Resource Set		
Name	**Default**	**Access**
Class	**Type**	
XmNbottomShadowColor	dynamic	CSG
XmCBottomShadowColor	Pixel	
XmNbottomShadowPixmap	XmUNSPECIFIED_PIXMAP	CSG
XmCBottomShadowPixmap	Pixmap	
XmNforeground	dynamic	CSG
XmCForeground	Pixel	
XmNhelpCallback	NULL	C
XmCCallback	XtCallbackList	
XmNhighlightColor	dynamic	CSG
XmCHighlightColor	Pixel	
XmNhighlightOnEnter	False	CSG
XmCHighlightOnEnter	Boolean	
XmNhighlightPixmap	dynamic	CSG
XmCHighlightPixmap	Pixmap	
XmNhighlightThickness	0	CSG
XmCHighlightThickness	Dimension	
XmNnavigationType	XmNONE	G
XmCNavigationType	XmNavigationType	
XmNshadowThickness	2	CSG
XmCShadowThickness	Dimension	
XmNtopShadowColor	dynamic	CSG
XmCTopShadowColor	Pixel	
XmNtopShadowPixmap	dynamic	CSG
XmCTopShadowPixmap	Pixmap	
XmNtraversalOn	False	G
XmCTraversalOn	Boolean	
XmNuserData	NULL	CSG
XmCUserData	Pointer	

Core Resource Set		
Name	**Default**	**Access**
Class	**Type**	
XmNaccelerators	dynamic	CSG
XmCAccelerators	XtAccelerators	
XmNancestorSensitive	dynamic	G
XmCSensitive	Boolean	
XmNbackground	dynamic	CSG
XmCBackground	Pixel	
XmNbackgroundPixmap	XmUNSPECIFIED_PIXMAP	CSG
XmCPixmap	Pixmap	
XmNborderColor	XtDefaultForeground	CSG
XmCBorderColor	Pixel	
XmNborderPixmap	XmUNSPECIFIED_PIXMAP	CSG
XmCPixmap	Pixmap	
XmNborderWidth	0	CSG
XmCBorderWidth	Dimension	
XmNcolormap	dynamic	CG
XmCColormap	Colormap	
XmNdepth	dynamic	CG
XmCDepth	int	
XmNdestroyCallback	NULL	C
XmCCallback	XtCallbackList	
XmNheight	dynamic	CSG
XmCHeight	Dimension	
XmNinitialResourcesPersistent	True	C
XmCInitialResourcesPersistent	Boolean	
XmNmappedWhenManaged	True	CSG
XmCMappedWhenManaged	Boolean	
XmNscreen	dynamic	CG
XmCScreen	Screen *	

Name	Default	Access
Class	Type	
XmNsensitive	True	CSG
XmCSensitive	Boolean	
XmNtranslations	dynamic	CSG
XmCTranslations	XtTranslations	
XmNwidth	dynamic	CSG
XmCWidth	Dimension	
XmNx	0	CSG
XmCPosition	Position	
XmNy	0	CSG
XmCPosition	Position	

Behavior

   XmSeparatorGadget has no behavior.

Related Information

   Core(3X), **XmCreateSeparator(3X)**, and **XmPrimitive(3X)**.

XmSeparatorGadget

Purpose

The SeparatorGadget widget class

AES Support Level

Full-use

Synopsis

#include <Xm/SeparatoG.h>

Description

SeparatorGadget separates items in a display. Several line drawing styles are provided, as well as horizontal or vertical orientation.

Lines drawn within the SeparatorGadget are automatically centered within the height of the gadget for a horizontal orientation and centered within the width of the gadget for a vertical orientation. An **XtSetValues** with a new **XmNseparatorType** resizes the widget to its minimal height (for horizontal orientation) or its minimal width (for vertical orientation) unless height or width is explicitly set in the **XtSetValues** call.

SeparatorGadget does not draw shadows around the separator. The Gadget resource **XmNshadowThickness** is used for the SeparatorGadget's thickness when **XmNseparatorType** is **XmSHADOW_ETCHED_IN** or **XmSHADOW_ETCHED_OUT**.

SeparatorGadget does not highlight and allows no traversing. The Gadget resource **XmNtraversalOn** is forced to False.

Classes

SeparatorGadget inherits behavior and resources from **Object**, **RectObj**, and **XmGadget** Classes.

The class pointer is **xmSeparatorGadgetClass**.

The class name is **XmSeparatorGadget**.

New Resources

The following table defines a set of widget resources used by the programmer to specify data. The programmer can also set the resource values for the inherited classes to set attributes for this widget. To reference a resource by name or by class in a .Xdefaults file, remove the **XmN** or **XmC** prefix and use the remaining letters. To specify one of the defined values for a resource in a .Xdefaults file, remove the **Xm** prefix and use the remaining letters (in either lowercase or uppercase, but include any underscores between words). The codes in the access column indicate if the given resource can be set at creation time (**C**), set by using **XtSetValues** (**S**), retrieved by using **XtGetValues** (**G**), or is not applicable (**N/A**).

XmSeparatorGadget Resource Set		
Name Class	Default Type	Access
XmNmargin XmCMargin	0 Dimension	CSG
XmNorientation XmCOrientation	XmHORIZONTAL unsigned char	CSG
XmNseparatorType XmCSeparatorType	XmSHADOW_ETCHED_IN unsigned char	CSG

XmNmargin

For horizontal orientation, specifies the space on the left and right sides between the border of SeparatorGadget and the line drawn. For vertical orientation, specifies the space on the top and bottom between the border of SeparatorGadget and the line drawn.

XmNorientation

Specifies whether SeparatorGadget is displayed vertically or horizontally. This resource can have values of **XmVERTICAL** and **XmHORIZONTAL**.

XmNseparatorType

Specifies the type of line drawing to be done in the Separator widget.

- **XmSINGLE_LINE** — single line.

- **XmDOUBLE_LINE** — double line.

- **XmSINGLE_DASHED_LINE** — single-dashed line.

- **XmDOUBLE_DASHED_LINE** — double-dashed line.

- **XmNO_LINE** — no line.

- **XmSHADOW_ETCHED_IN** — double line giving the effect of a line etched into the window. The thickness of the double line is equal to the value of **XmNshadowThickness**. For horizontal orientation, the top line is drawn in **XmNtopShadowColor** and the bottom line is drawn in **XmNbottomShadowColor**. For vertical orientation, the left line is drawn in **XmNtopShadowColor** and the right line is drawn in **XmNbottomShadowColor**.

- **XmSHADOW_ETCHED_OUT** — double line giving the effect of an etched line coming out from the window. The thickness of the double line is equal to the value of **XmNshadowThickness**. For horizontal orientation, the top line is drawn in **XmNbottomShadowColor** and the bottom line is drawn in **XmNtopShadowColor**. For vertical orientation, the left line is drawn in **XmNbottomShadowColor** and the right line is drawn in **XmNtopShadowColor**.

Inherited Resources

SeparatorGadget inherits behavior and resources from the following superclasses. For a complete description of each resource, refer to the man page for that superclass.

XmGadget Resource Set		
Name	**Default**	**Access**
Class	**Type**	
XmNhelpCallback	NULL	C
XmCCallback	XtCallbackList	
XmNhighlightOnEnter	False	CSG
XmCHighlightOnEnter	Boolean	
XmNhighlightThickness	0	CSG
XmCHighlightThickness	Dimension	
XmNnavigationType	XmNONE	G
XmCNavigationType	XmNavigationType	
XmNshadowThickness	2	CSG
XmCShadowThickness	Dimension	
XmNtraversalOn	False	G
XmCTraversalOn	Boolean	
XmNuserData	NULL	CSG
XmCUserData	Pointer	

RectObj Resource Set		
Name	**Default**	**Access**
Class	**Type**	
XmNancestorSensitive	dynamic	G
XmCSensitive	Boolean	
XmNborderWidth	0	CSG
XmCBorderWidth	Dimension	
XmNheight	dynamic	CSG
XmCHeight	Dimension	
XmNsensitive	True	CSG
XmCSensitive	Boolean	
XmNwidth	dynamic	CSG
XmCWidth	Dimension	
XmNx	0	CSG
XmCPosition	Position	
XmNy	0	CSG
XmCPosition	Position	

Object Resource Set		
Name	**Default**	**Access**
Class	**Type**	
XmNdestroyCallback	NULL	C
XmCCallback	XtCallbackList	

Behavior

XmSeparatorGadget has no behavior.

Related Information

Object(3X), **RectObject(3X)**, **XmCreateSeparatorGadget(3X)**, and **XmGadget(3X)**.

XmSetMenuCursor

Purpose

A RowColumn function that modifies the menu cursor for a client.

AES Support Level

Full-use

Synopsis

```
void XmSetMenuCursor (display, cursorId)
        Display     * display;
        Cursor      cursorId;
```

Description

XmSetMenuCursor programmatically modifies the menu cursor for a client; after the cursor has been created by the client, this function registers the cursor with the menu system. After calling this function, the specified cursor is displayed whenever this client displays a Motif menu on the indicated display. The client can then specify different cursors on different displays.

display   Specifies the display to which the cursor is to be associated

cursorId   Specifies the **X** cursor ID

For a complete definition of the menu cursor resource, see **XmRowColumn(3X)**.

Related Information

XmRowColumn(3X).

XmSetProtocolHooks

Purpose

A VendorShell function that allows pre and post actions to be executed when a protocol message is received from MWM.

AES Support Level

Trial-use

Synopsis

#include <Xm/Xm.h>
#include <X11/Protocols.h>

void   XmSetProtocolHooks (*shell,   property,   protocol,   prehook, pre_closure, posthook, post_closure*)
    Widget   *shell*;
    Atom   *property*;
    Atom   *protocol*;
    XtCallbackProc   *prehook*;
    caddr_t   *pre_closure*;
    XtCallbackProc   *posthook*;
    caddr_t   *post_closure*;

void XmSetWMProtocolHooks (*shell, protocol, prehook, pre_closure, posthook, post_closure*)
    Widget   *shell*;
    Atom   *protocol*;

> **XtCallbackProc**   *prehook*;
> **caddr_t**   *pre_closure*;
> **XtCallbackProc**   *posthook*;
> **caddr_t**   *post_closure*;

Description

XmSetProtocolHooks is used by shells that want to have pre and post actions executed when a protocol message is received from MWM. Since there is no guaranteed ordering in execution of event handlers or callback lists, this allows the shell to control the flow while leaving the protocol manager structures opaque.

XmSetWMProtocolHooks is a convenience interface. It calls **XmSetProtocolHooks** with the property value set to the atom returned by interning **WM_PROTOCOLS**.

shell   Specifies the widget with which the protocol property is associated

property   Specifies the protocol property

protocol   Specifies the protocol atom (or an int cast to Atom)

prehook   Specifies the procedure to call before calling entries on the client callback-list

pre_closure Specifies the client data to be passed to the prehook when it is invoked

posthook   Specifies the procedure to call after calling entries on the client callback-list

post_closure Specifies the client data to be passed to the posthook when it is invoked

For a complete definition of VendorShell and its associated resources, see **VendorShell(3X)**.

Related Information

VendorShell(3X),   XmInternAtom(3X),   and
XmSetWMProtocolHooks(3X).

XmSetWMProtocolHooks

Purpose

A VendorShell convenience interface that allows pre and post actions to be executed when a protocol message is received from the window manager.

AES Support Level

Trial-use

Synopsis

#include <Xm/Xm.h>
#include <X11/Protocols.h>

void XmSetWMProtocolHooks (*shell, protocol, prehook, pre_closure, posthook, post_closure*)
      Widget   *shell*;
      Atom   *protocol*;
      XtCallbackProc*prehook*;
      caddr_t   *pre_closure*;
      XtCallbackProc*posthook*;
      caddr_t   *post_closure*;

Description

XmSetWMProtocolHooks is a convenience interface. It calls **XmSetProtocolHooks** with the property value set to the atom returned by interning **WM_PROTOCOLS**.

shell　　　Specifies the widget with which the protocol property is associated

protocol　　Specifies the protocol atom (or an int cast to Atom)

prehook　　Specifies the procedure to call before calling entries on the client callback-list

pre_closure　Specifies the client data to be passed to the prehook when it is invoked

posthook　　Specifies the procedure to call after calling entries on the client callback-list

post_closure　Specifies the client data to be passed to the posthook when it is invoked

For a complete definition of VendorShell and its associated resources, see **VendorShell(3X)**.

Related Information

VendorShell(3X), **XmInternAtom(3X)**, and **XmSetProtocolHooks(3X)**.

XmString

Purpose

Data type for a compound string

AES Support Level

Trial-use

Synopsis

#include <Xm/Xm.h>

Description

XmString is the data type for a compound string. Compound strings include one or more segments, each of which contains text, character set, and string direction. When a compound string is displayed, the character set and direction are used to determine how to display the text. The compound string interface consists of the routines listed under "Related Information."

Calling **XtGetValues** for a resource whose type is XmString yields a copy of the compound string resource value. The application is responsible for using **XmStringFree** to free the memory allocated for the copy.

Related Information

XmStringBaseline(3X),   XmStringByteCompare(3X),
XmStringCompare(3X),   XmStringConcat(3X),   XmStringCopy(3X),
XmStringCreate(3X), XmStringCreateSimple(3X), XmStringDraw(3X),
XmStringDrawImage(3X),   XmStringDrawUnderline(3X),
XmStringEmpty(3X),   XmStringExtent(3X),   XmStringFree(3X),
XmStringHasSubstring(3X),   XmStringHeight(3X),
XmStringLength(3X),   XmStringLineCount(3X),
XmStringNConcat(3X),   XmStringNCopy(3X),
XmStringSeparatorCreate(3X),   XmStringTable(3X),   and
XmStringWidth(3X).

XmStringBaseline

Purpose

A compound string function that returns the number of pixels between the top of the character box and the baseline of the first line of text.

AES Support Level

Trial-use

Synopsis

#include <Xm/Xm.h>

Dimension XmStringBaseline (*fontlist, string*)
    XmFontList *fontlist*;
    XmString   *string*;

Description

XmStringBaseline returns the number of pixels between the top of the character box and the baseline of the first line of text in the provided compound string.

When *string* has been created with **XmStringCreateSimple**, the font associated with the character set derived from the current language environment must appear at the front of *fontlist*. Otherwise, the result of the function is undefined.

fontlist   Specifies the font list

string   Specifies the string

Return Value

Returns the number of pixels between the top of the character box and the baseline of the first line of text.

Related Information

XmStringCreate(3X) and **XmStringCreateSimple(3X)**.

XmStringByteCompare

Purpose

A compound string function that indicates the results of a byte-by-byte comparison.

AES Support Level

Trial-use

Synopsis

> **#include <Xm/Xm.h>**
>
> **Boolean XmStringByteCompare** (*s1, s2*)
>   **XmString**   *s1*;
>   **XmString**   *s2*;

Description

XmStringByteCompare returns a Boolean indicating the results of a byte-by-byte comparison of two compound strings.

In general, if two compound strings are created with the same (char *) string using **XmStringCreateSimple** in the same language environment, the compound strings compare as equal. If two compound strings are created with the same (char *) string and the same character set using

XmStringCreate, the strings compare as equal. The result of comparing a compound string created with **XmStringCreate** against a compound string created with **XmStringCreateSimple** is undefined.

In some cases, once a compound string is put into a widget, that string is converted into an internal form to allow faster processing. Part of the conversion process strips out unnecessary or redundant information. If an application then does an **XtGetValues** to retrieve a compound string from a widget (specifically, Label and all of its subclasses), it is not guaranteed that the compound string returned is byte-for-byte the same as the string given to the widget originally.

s1   Specifies a compound string to be compared with *s2*

s2   Specifies a compound string to be compared with *s1*

Return Value

Returns True if two compound strings are identical byte-by-byte.

Related Information

XmStringCreate(3X) and **XmStringCreateSimple(3X)**.

XmStringCompare

Purpose

A compound string function that compares two strings

AES Support Level

Trial-use

Synopsis

#include <Xm/Xm.h>

Boolean XmStringCompare (*s1, s2*)
>**XmString**   *s1*;
>**XmString**   *s2*;

Description

XmStringCompare returns a Boolean value indicating the results of a semantically equivalent comparison of two compound strings.

Semantically equivalent means that the strings have the same text components, directions, and separators. If character sets are specified, they must be equal as well. In general, if two compound strings are created with the same (char *) string using **XmStringCreateSimple** in the same language environment, the compound strings compare as equal. If two compound strings are created with the same (char *) string and the same character set using **XmStringCreate**, the strings compare as equal. The result of comparing a compound string created with **XmStringCreate** against a compound string created with **XmStringCreateSimple** is undefined.

s1   Specifies a compound string to be compared with *s2*

s2   Specifies a compound string to be compared with *s1*

Return Value

Returns True if two compound strings are equivalent.

Related Information

XmStringCreate(3X) and **XmStringCreateSimple(3X)**.

XmStringConcat

Purpose

A compound string function that appends one string to another.

AES Support Level

Trial-use

Synopsis

#include <Xm/Xm.h>

XmString XmStringConcat (*s1, s2*)
    XmString   *s1*;
    XmString   *s2*;

Description

XmStringConcat copies *s2* to the end of *s1* and returns a copy of the resulting compound string. The original strings are preserved. The space for the resulting compound string is allocated within the function. After using this function, free this space by calling **XmStringFree**.

s1   Specifies the compound string to which a copy of *s2* is appended

s2   Specifies the compound string that is appended to the end of *s1*

Return Value

Returns a new compound string.

Related Information

XmStringCreate(3X) and **XmStringFree(3X)**.

XmStringCopy

Purpose

A compound string function that makes a copy of a string.

AES Support Level

Trial-use

Synopsis

#include <Xm/Xm.h>

XmString XmStringCopy (*s1*)
    XmString   *s1*;

Description

XmStringCopy makes a copy of a compound string. The space for the resulting compound string is allocated within the function. The application is responsible for managing the allocated space. The memory can be recovered by calling **XmStringFree**.

s1   Specifies the compound string to be copied

Return Value

Returns a new compound string.

Related Information

XmStringCreate(3X) and **XmStringFree(3X)**.

XmStringCreate

Purpose

A compound string function that creates a compound string.

AES Support Level

Temporary-use

Synopsis

#include <Xm/Xm.h>

XmString XmStringCreate (*text, charset*)
    char   * *text*;
    XmStringCharSet*charset*;

Description

XmStringCreate creates a compound string with two components: text and a character set.

    text   Specifies a null-terminated string to be used as the text component of the compound string.

    charset Specifies the character set identifier to be associated with the given text.

Return Value

Returns a new compound string.

Related Information

XmFontList(3X), **XmFontListAdd(3X)**, **XmFontListCreate(3X)**, **XmFontListFree(3X)**, **XmString(3X)**, **XmStringBaseline(3X)**, **XmStringByteCompare(3X)**, **XmStringCompare(3X)**, **XmStringConcat(3X)**, **XmStringCopy(3X)**, **XmStringCreateSimple(3X)**, **XmStringDraw(3X)**, **XmStringDrawImage(3X)**, **XmStringDrawUnderline(3X)**, **XmStringEmpty(3X)**, **XmStringExtent(3X)**, **XmStringFree(3X)**, **XmStringHasSubstring(3X)**, **XmStringHeight(3X)**, **XmStringLength(3X)**, **XmStringLineCount(3X)**, **XmStringNConcat(3X)**, **XmStringNCopy(3X)**, **XmStringSeparatorCreate(3X)**, **XmStringTable(3X)**, and **XmStringWidth(3X)**.

XmStringCreateSimple

Purpose

A compound string function that creates a compound string in the language environment of a widget.

AES Support Level

Temporary-use

Synopsis

#include <Xm/Xm.h>

XmString XmStringCreateSimple (*text*)
    char   * *text*;

Description

XmStringCreateSimple creates a compound string with two components: text and a character set. It derives the character set from the current language environment.

text   Specifies a null-terminated string to be used as the text component of the compound string.

Return Value

Returns a new compound string.

Related Information

XmStringCreate(3X).

XmStringDirection

Purpose

Data type for the direction of display in a string

AES Support Level

Trial-use

Synopsis

#include <Xm/Xm.h>

Description

XmStringDirection is the data type for specifying the direction in which the system displays characters of a string, or characters of a segment of a compound string. This is an enumeration with two possible values:

XmSTRING_DIRECTION_L_TO_R
          Specifies left to right display

XmSTRING_DIRECTION_R_TO_L
          Specifies right to left display

Related Information

XmString(3X).

XmStringDraw

Purpose

A compound string function that draws a compound string in an X window.

AES Support Level

Trial-use

Synopsis

#include <Xm/Xm.h>

void XmStringDraw (*d, w, fontlist, string, gc, x, y, width, alignment, layout_direction, clip*)

Display	** d*;
Window	*w*;
XmFontList	*fontlist*;
XmString	*string*;
GC	*gc*;
Position	*x*;
Position	*y*;
Dimension	*width*;
unsigned char	*alignment*;
unsigned char	*layout_direction*;
XRectangle	** clip*;

Description

XmStringDraw draws a compound string in an X Window.

When *string* has been created with **XmStringCreateSimple**, the font associated with the character set derived from the current language environment must appear at the front of *fontlist*. Otherwise, the result of the function is undefined.

d	Specifies the display.
w	Specifies the window.
fontlist	Specifies the font list.
string	Specifies the string.
gc	Specifies the graphics context to use.
x	Specifies a coordinate of the rectangle that will contain the displayed compound string.
y	Specifies a coordinate of the rectangle that will contain the displayed compound string.
width	Specifies the width of the rectangle that will contain the displayed compound string.
alignment	Specifies how the string will be aligned within the specified rectangle. It is either **XmALIGNMENT_BEGINNING**, **XmALIGNMENT_CENTER**, or **XmALIGNMENT_END**.
layout_direction	Controls the direction in which the segments of the compound string will be laid out. It also determines the meaning of the *alignment* parameter.
clip	Allows the application to restrict the area into which the compound string will be drawn. If NULL, no clipping will be done.

Related Information

XmStringCreate(3X) and **XmStringCreateSimple(3X)**.

XmStringDrawImage

Purpose

A compound string function that draws a compound string in an X Window and creates an image.

AES Support Level

Trial-use

Synopsis

#include <Xm/Xm.h>

void XmStringDrawImage (*d, w, fontlist, string, gc, x, y, width, alignment, layout_direction, clip*)
      Display   * *d*;
      Window   *w*;
      XmFontList *fontlist*;
      XmString   *string*;
      GC   *gc*;
      Position   *x*;
      Position   *y*;
      Dimension *width*;
      unsigned char*alignment*;
      unsigned char*layout_direction*;
      XRectangle * *clip*;

Description

XmStringDrawImage draws a compound string in an X Window and paints both the foreground and background bits of each character.

When *string* has been created with **XmStringCreateSimple**, the font associated with the character set derived from the current language environment must appear at the front of *fontlist*. Otherwise, the result of the function is undefined.

d	Specifies the display.
w	Specifies the window.
fontlist	Specifies the font list.
string	Specifies the string.
gc	Specifies the graphics context to use.
x	Specifies a coordinate of the rectangle that will contain the displayed compound string.
y	Specifies a coordinate of the rectangle that will contain the displayed compound string.
width	Specifies the width of the rectangle that will contain the displayed compound string.
alignment	Specifies how the string will be aligned within the specified rectangle. It is either **XmALIGNMENT_BEGINNING**, **XmALIGNMENT_CENTER**, or **XmALIGNMENT_END**.
layout_direction	Controls the direction in which the segments of the compound string will be laid out. It also determines the meaning of the *alignment* parameter.
clip	Allows the application to restrict the area into which the compound string will be drawn. If NULL, no clipping will be done.

Related Information

XmStringCreate(3X) and **XmStringCreateSimple(3X)**.

XmStringDrawUnderline

Purpose

A compound string function that underlines a string drawn in an X Window.

AES Support Level

Trial-use

Synopsis

#include <Xm/Xm.h>

void XmStringDrawUnderline (*d, w, fontlist, string, gc, x, y, width, alignment, layout_direction, clip, underline*)
    Display   * *d*;
    Window   *w*;
    XmFontList *fontlist*;
    XmString   *string*;
    GC   *gc*;
    Position   *x*;
    Position   *y*;
    Dimension *width*;
    unsigned char*alignment*;
    unsigned char*layout_direction*;
    XRectangle * *clip*;
    XmString   *underline*;

Description

XmStringDrawUnderline draws a compound string in an X Window. If the substring identified by *underline* can be matched in *string*, the substring will be underlined. Once a match has occurred, no further matches or underlining will be done.

When *string* has been created with **XmStringCreateSimple**, the font associated with the character set derived from the current language environment must appear at the front of *fontlist*. Otherwise, the result of the function is undefined.

d	Specifies the display.
w	Specifies the window.
fontlist	Specifies the font list.
string	Specifies the string.
gc	Specifies the graphics context to use.
x	Specifies a coordinate of the rectangle that will contain the displayed compound string.
y	Specifies a coordinate of the rectangle that will contain the displayed compound string.
width	Specifies the width of the rectangle that will contain the displayed compound string.
alignment	Specifies how the string will be aligned within the specified rectangle. It is one of **XmALIGNMENT_BEGINNING**, **XmALIGNMENT_CENTER**, or **XmALIGNMENT_END**.
layout_direction	Controls the direction in which the segments of the compound string will be laid out. It also determines the meaning of the *alignment* parameter.

clip	Allows the application to restrict the area into which the compound string will be drawn. If NULL, no clipping will be done.
underline	Specifies the substring to be underlined.

Related Information

XmStringCreate(3X) and **XmStringCreateSimple(3X)**.

XmStringEmpty

Purpose

A compound string function that provides information on the existence of non-zero length text components.

AES Support Level

Trial-use

Synopsis

#include <Xm/Xm.h>

Boolean XmStringEmpty (*s1*)
    XmString   *s1*;

Description

XmStringEmpty returns a Boolean value indicating whether any non-zero length text components exist in the provided compound string. It returns True if there are no text segments in the string. If this routine is passed NULL as the string, it returns True.

s1   Specifies the compound string

Return Value

Returns True if there are no text segments in the string. If this routine is passed NULL as the string, it returns True.

Related Information

XmStringCreate(3X).

XmStringExtent

Purpose

A compound string function that determines the size of the smallest rectangle that will enclose the compound string.

AES Support Level

Trial-use

Synopsis

#include <Xm/Xm.h>

void XmStringExtent (*fontlist, string, width, height*)
    XmFontList *fontlist*;
    XmString   *string*;
    Dimension   **width*;
    Dimension   **height*;

Description

XmStringExtent determines the width and height, in pixels, of the smallest rectangle that will enclose the provided compound string.

When *string* has been created with **XmStringCreateSimple**, the font associated with the character set derived from the current language environment must appear at the front of *fontlist*. Otherwise, the result of the function is undefined.

fontlist   Specifies the font list

string   Specifies the string

width   Specifies a pointer to the width of the rectangle

height   Specifies a pointer to the height of the rectangle

Related Information

XmStringCreate(3X) and **XmStringCreateSimple(3X)**.

XmStringFree

Purpose

A compound string function that recovers memory

AES Support Level

Trial-use

Synopsis

#include <Xm/Xm.h>

void XmStringFree (*string*)
    XmString   *string*;

Description

XmStringFree recovers memory used by a compound string.

string   Specifies the compound string to be freed

Related Information

XmStringCreate(3X).

XmStringHasSubstring

Purpose

A compound string function that indicates whether one compound string is contained within another.

AES Support Level

Trial-use

Synopsis

#include <Xm/Xm.h>

Boolean XmStringHasSubstring (*string, substring*)
    XmString   *string*;
    XmString   *substring*;

Description

XmStringHasSubstring indicates whether or not one compound string is contained within another.

string   Specifies the compound string to be searched

string   Specifies the compound string to be searched for

Return Value

Returns True if *substring* has a single segment and if its text is completely contained within any single segment of *string*; otherwise, returns False. If two compound strings created using **XmStringCreateSimple** in the same language environment satisfy this condition, the function returns True. If two compound strings created with the same character set using **XmStringCreate** satisfy this condition, the function returns True. The result of comparing a compound string created with **XmStringCreate** against a compound string created with **XmStringCreateSimple** is undefined.

Related Information

XmStringCreate(3X) and **XmStringCreateSimple(3X)**.

XmStringHeight

Purpose

A compound string function that returns the line height of the given compound string.

AES Support Level

Trial-use

Synopsis

#include <Xm/Xm.h>

Dimension XmStringHeight (*fontlist, string*)
    XmFontList *fontlist*;
    XmString   *string*;

Description

XmStringHeight returns the height, in pixels, of the sum of all the line heights of the given compound string. Separator components delimit lines.

When *string* has been created with **XmStringCreateSimple**, the font associated with the character set derived from the current language environment must appear at the front of *fontlist*. Otherwise, the result of the function is undefined.

fontlist   Specifies the font list

string   Specifies the string

Return Value

Returns the height of the specified string.

Related Information

XmStringCreate(3X) and **XmStringCreateSimple(3X)**.

XmStringLength

Purpose

A compound string function that obtains the length of a compound string.

AES Support Level

Trial-use

Synopsis

#include <Xm/Xm.h>

int XmStringLength (*s1*)
  XmString *s1*;

Description

XmStringLength obtains the length of a compound string. It returns the number of bytes in *s1* including all tags, direction indicators, and separators. If the compound string has an invalid structure, zero is returned.

 s1 Specifies the compound string

Return Value

Returns the length of the compound string.

Related Information

XmStringCreate(3X).

XmStringLineCount

Purpose

A compound string function that returns the number of separators plus one in the provided compound string.

AES Support Level

Trial-use

Synopsis

#include <Xm/Xm.h>

int XmStringLineCount (*string*)
    XmString   *string*;

Description

XmStringLineCount returns the number of separators plus one in the provided compound string. In effect, it counts the lines of text.

string   Specifies the string.

Return Value

Returns the number of lines in the compound string

Related Information

XmStringCreate(3X).

XmStringNConcat

Purpose

A compound string function that appends a specified number of bytes to a compound string.

AES Support Level

Trial-use

Synopsis

#include <Xm/Xm.h>

XmString XmStringNConcat (*s1, s2, num_bytes*)
      XmString   *s1*;
      XmString   *s2*;
      int   *num_bytes*;

Description

XmStringNConcat appends a specified number of bytes from *s2* to the end of *s1*, including tags, directional indicators, and separators. It then returns the resulting compound string. The original strings are preserved. The space for the resulting compound string is allocated within the function. The application is responsible for managing the allocated space. The memory can be recovered by calling **XmStringFree**.

s1   Specifies the compound string to which a copy of *s2* is appended.

s2   Specifies the compound string that is appended to the end of *s1*.

num_bytes

Specifies the number of bytes of *s2* to append to *s1*. If this value is less than the length of *s2*, as many bytes as possible, but possibly fewer than this value, will be appended to *s1* such that the resulting string is still a valid compound string.

Return Value

Returns a new compound string.

Related Information

XmStringCreate(3X) and **XmStringFree(3X)**.

XmStringNCopy

Purpose

A compound string function that creates a copy of a compound string.

AES Support Level

Trial-use

Synopsis

#include <Xm/Xm.h>

XmString XmStringNCopy (*s1, num_bytes*)
    XmString   *s1*;
    int   *num_bytes*;

Description

XmStringNCopy creates a copy of *s1* that contains a specified number of bytes, including tags, directional indicators, and separators. It then returns the resulting compound string. The original strings are preserved. The space for the resulting compound string is allocated within the function. The application is responsible for managing the allocated space. The memory can be recovered by calling **XmStringFree**.

s1   Specifies the compound string.

num_bytes

Specifies the number of bytes of *s1* to copy. If this value is less than the length of *s1*, as many bytes as possible, but possibly fewer than this value, will be appended to *s1* such that the resulting string is still a valid compound string.

Return Value

Returns a new compound string.

Related Information

XmStringCreate(3X) and **XmStringFree(3X)**.

XmStringSeparatorCreate

Purpose

A compound string function that creates a compound string.

AES Support Level

Trial-use

Synopsis

#include <Xm/Xm.h>

XmString XmStringSeparatorCreate ()

Description

XmStringSeparatorCreate creates a compound string with a single component, a separator.

Return Value

Returns a new compound string.

Related Information

XmStringCreate(3X).

XmStringTable

Purpose

Data type for an array of compound strings

AES Support Level

Trial-use

Synopsis

#include <Xm/Xm.h>

Description

XmStringTable is the data type for an array of compound strings (objects of type **XmString**).

Related Information

XmString(3X).

XmStringWidth

Purpose

A compound string function that returns the width of the longest sequence of text components in a compound string.

AES Support Level

Trial-use

Synopsis

#include <Xm/Xm.h>

Dimension XmStringWidth (*fontlist, string*)
  XmFontList *fontlist*;
  XmString   *string*;

Description

XmStringWidth returns the width, in pixels, of the longest sequence of text components in the provided compound string. Separator components are used to delimit sequences of text components.

When *string* has been created with **XmStringCreateSimple**, the font associated with the character set derived from the current language environment must appear at the front of *fontlist*. Otherwise, the result of the function is undefined.

fontlist   Specifies the font list

string   Specifies the string

Return Value

Returns the width of the compound string.

Related Information

XmStringCreate(3X) and **XmStringCreateSimple(3X).**

XmText

Purpose

The Text widget class

AES Support Level

Full-use

Synopsis

#include <Xm/Text.h>

Description

Text provides a single-line and multiline text editor for customizing both user and programmatic interfaces. It can be used for single-line string entry, forms entry with verification procedures, and full-window editing. It provides an application with a consistent editing system for textual data. The screen's textual data adjusts to the application writer's needs.

Text provides separate callback lists to verify movement of the insert cursor, modification of the text, and changes in input focus. Each of these callbacks provides the verification function with the widget instance, the event that caused the callback, and a data structure specific to the verification type. From this information the function can verify if the application considers this to be a legitimate state change and can signal the widget whether to continue with the action.

The user interface tailors a new set of translations. The default translations provide key bindings for insert cursor movement, deletion, insertion, and selection of text.

Text allows the user to select regions of text. Selection is based on the model specified in the *Inter-Client Communication Conventions Manual* (ICCCM). Text supports primary and secondary selection.

Mouse Selection

The Text widget allows text to be edited, inserted, and selected. The user can cut, copy, and paste text using the clipboard, primary transfer, or secondary transfer.

The insertion cursor, displayed as an I-beam, shows where input is inserted. Clicking **BSelect** moves the insertion cursor and deselects the current selection if it is in the Text widget. Clicking **BToggle** moves the insertion cursor but does not change the current selection.

The Text widget allows the user to select a range of text. Pressing **BSelect** starts a new primary selection. Dragging **BSelect** selects all text between the position of the pointer and the position where **BSelect** was pressed.

BExtend extends a selection using the balance-beam method. When the user presses **BExtend**, the selection becomes anchored at the edge of the selection farthest from the pointer position. When the user releases **BExtend**, the selection extends from the anchor to the position where **BExtend** is released, and any text outside that range is deselected.

Clicking **BDrag** copies the current selection to the insertion cursor, whether the current selection is in the same widget or a different widget. Clicking **MAlt BDrag** cuts the current selection to the insertion cursor.

The destination cursor shows the last place that text was inserted, edited, or selected. When it is separate from the insertion cursor, it is shown as a caret. When the user pastes data from the clipboard, the data go to the destination cursor. Clicking **BSelect** moves the destination cursor. Clicking **BToggle** also moves the destination cursor, but only if no text is selected in the widget.

Pressing **BDrag** starts a new secondary selection. Dragging **BDrag** makes a secondary selection consisting of all text between the position of the pointer and the position where **BDrag** was pressed. Releasing **BDrag** copies the secondary selection to the destination cursor, whether the destination cursor is in the same widget or a different widget. Dragging **MAlt BDrag** also makes a secondary selection, and releasing **MAlt BDrag** cuts the secondary selection to the destination cursor.

Keyboard Selection

All selection operations available from the mouse are also available from the keyboard. Text has two keyboard selection modes, Normal Mode and Add Mode. In Normal Mode, if text is selected, a navigation operation deselects the selected text and moves the destination cursor to the insertion cursor before navigating. In Add Mode, navigation operations have no effect other than navigation. In both modes, pressing **KSelect** has the same effect as pressing **BSelect** at that position.

Pressing **KExtend** extends the current selection to the insertion cursor using the balance-beam method. The current selection becomes anchored at the edge of the selection farthest from the insertion cursor. The selection then extends from the anchor to the insertion cursor, and any text outside that range is deselected. If no text is selected, **KExtend** selects the text between the destination cursor and the insertion cursor.

Shifted navigation operations also extend a selection. In Normal Mode, if no text is selected or if the selection is disjoint from the insertion cursor, a shifted navigation operation selects the navigated text and deselects any text outside that range. In Add Mode, if no text is selected, a shifted navigation operation first navigates and then selects the text between the destination cursor and the insertion cursor.

In the remaining cases — Normal Mode with the insertion cursor at or inside a selection, and Add Mode with any selection — a shifted navigation operation extends the selection using the balance-beam method. Before navigation, the current selection becomes anchored at the edge of the selection farthest from the insertion cursor. After navigation, the selection extends from the anchor to the insertion cursor, and any text outside that range is deselected.

KPrimaryCopy copies the current selection to the insertion cursor. **KPrimaryCut** cuts the current selection to the insertion cursor.

KQuickCopy and **KQuickCut** start a secondary selection at the insertion cursor. Navigation operations extend the secondary selection. **KQuickExtend** then copies or cuts the secondary selection to the destination cursor.

Classes

Text inherits behavior and resources from **Core** and **Primitive** classes.

The class pointer is **xmTextWidgetClass**.

The class name is **XmText**.

New Resources

The following table defines a set of widget resources used by the programmer to specify data. The programmer can also set the resource values for the inherited classes to set attributes for this widget. To reference a resource by name or by class in a .Xdefaults file, remove the **XmN** or **XmC** prefix and use the remaining letters. To specify one of the defined values for a resource in a .Xdefaults file, remove the **Xm** prefix and use the remaining letters (in either lowercase or uppercase, but include any underscores between words). The codes in the access column indicate if the given resource can be set at creation time (**C**), set by using **XtSetValues** (**S**), retrieved by using **XtGetValues** (**G**), or is not applicable (**N/A**).

XmText Resource Set		

Name
    Class
	Default
	    Type
		Access

XmNactivateCallback
   XmCCallback
	NULL
	   XtCallbackList
		C

XmNautoShowCursorPosition
   XmCAutoShowCursorPosition
	True
	   Boolean
		CSG

XmNcursorPosition
   XmCCursorPosition
	0
	   XmTextPosition
		CSG

XmNeditable
   XmCEditable
	True
	   Boolean
		CSG

XmNeditMode
   XmCEditMode
	XmSINGLE_LINE_EDIT
	   int
		CSG

XmNfocusCallback
   XmCCallback
	NULL
	   XtCallbackList
		C

XmNgainPrimaryCallback
   XmCCallback
	NULL
	   XtCallbackList
		C

XmNlosePrimaryCallback
   XmCCallback
	NULL
	   XtCallbackList
		C

XmNlosingFocusCallback
   XmCCallback
	NULL
	   XtCallbackList
		C

XmNmarginHeight
   XmCMarginHeight
	5
	   Dimension
		CSG

XmNmarginWidth
   XmCMarginWidth
	5
	   Dimension
		CSG

XmNmaxLength
   XmCMaxLength
	largest integer
	   int
		CSG

XmNmodifyVerifyCallback
   XmCCallback
	NULL
	   XtCallbackList
		C

Name	Default	Access
Class	Type	
XmNmotionVerifyCallback	NULL	C
XmCCallback	XtCallbackList	
XmNsource	Default source	CSG
XmCSource	XmTextSource	
XmNtopCharacter	0	CSG
XmCTextPosition	XmTextPosition	
XmNvalue	""	CSG
XmCValue	String	
XmNvalueChangedCallback	NULL	C
XmCCallback	XtCallbackList	
XmNverifyBell	True	CSG
XmCVerifyBell	Boolean	

XmNactivateCallback

Specifies the list of callbacks that is called when the user invokes an event that calls the **Activate()** function. The type of the structure whose address is passed to this callback is **XmAnyCallbackStruct**. The reason sent by the callback is **XmCR_ACTIVATE**.

XmNautoShowCursorPosition

Ensures that the visible text contains the insert cursor when set to True. If the insert cursor changes, the contents of Text may scroll in order to bring the insertion point into the window.

XmNcursorPosition

Indicates the position in the text where the current insert cursor is to be located. Position is determined by the number of characters from the beginning of the text. The first character position is 0.

XmNeditable

Indicates that the user can edit the text string when set to True. Prohibits the user from editing the text when set to False.

XmNeditMode

Specifies the set of keyboard bindings used in Text. The default keyboard bindings (**XmSINGLE_LINE_EDIT**) provides the set of key bindings to be used in editing single-line text. The multiline bindings (**XmMULTI_LINE_EDIT**) provides the set of key bindings to be used in editing multiline text.

The results of placing a Text widget inside a ScrolledWindow when the Text's **XmNeditMode** is **XmSINGLE_LINE_EDIT** are undefined.

XmNfocusCallback

Specifies the list of callbacks called before Text has accepted input focus. The type of the structure whose address is passed to this callback is **XmAnyCallbackStruct**. The reason sent by the callback is **XmCR_FOCUS**.

XmNgainPrimaryCallback

Specifies the list of callbacks called when an event causes the Text widget to gain ownership of the primary selection. The reason sent by the callback is **XmCR_GAIN_PRIMARY**.

XmNlosePrimaryCallback

Specifies the list of callbacks called when an event causes the Text widget to lose ownership of the primary selection. The reason sent by the callback is **XmCR_LOSE_PRIMARY**.

XmNlosingFocusCallback

Specifies the list of callbacks called before Text loses input focus. The type of the structure whose address is passed to this callback is **XmTextVerifyCallbackStruct**. The reason sent by the callback is **XmCR_LOSING_FOCUS**.

XmNmarginHeight

Specifies the distance between the top edge of the widget window and the text, and between the bottom edge of the widget window and the text.

XmNmarginWidth

Specifies the distance between the left edge of the widget window and the text, and between the right edge of the widget window and the text.

XmNmaxLength

Specifies the maximum length of the text string that can be entered into text from the keyboard. Strings that are entered using the **XmNvalue** resource or the **XmTextSetString** function ignore this resource.

XmNmodifyVerifyCallback

Specifies the list of callbacks called before text is deleted from or inserted into Text. The type of the structure whose address is passed to this callback is **XmTextVerifyCallbackStruct**. The reason sent by the callback is **XmCR_MODIFYING_TEXT_VALUE**.

XmNmotionVerifyCallback

Specifies the list of callbacks called before the insert cursor is moved to a new position. The type of the structure whose address is passed to this callback is **XmTextVerifyCallbackStruct**. The reason sent by the callback is **XmCR_MOVING_INSERT_CURSOR**.

XmNsource Specifies the source with which the widget displays text. If no source is specified, the widget creates a default string source. This resource can be used to share text sources between Text widgets.

XmNtopCharacter

Displays the position of text at the top of the window. Position is determined by the number of characters from the beginning of the text. The first character position is 0.

If the **XmNeditMode** is **XmMULTI_LINE_EDIT**, the line of text that contains the top character is displayed at the top of the widget without shifting the text left or right. **XtGetValues** for **XmNtopCharacter** returns the position of the first character in the line that is displayed at the top of the widget.

XmNvalue Displays the string value. **XtGetValues** returns the value of the internal buffer and **XtSetValues** copies the string values into the internal buffer.

XmNvalueChangedCallback

Specifies the list of callbacks called after text is deleted from or inserted into Text. The type of the structure whose address is passed to this callback is **XmAnyCallbackStruct**. The reason sent by the callback is **XmCR_VALUE_CHANGED**.

XmNverifyBell

Specifies whether the bell should sound when the verification returns without continuing the action. The default is True, indicating that the bell should sound.

XmText Input Resource Set		
Name	**Default**	**Access**
Class	**Type**	
XmNpendingDelete	True	CSG
XmCPendingDelete	Boolean	
XmNselectionArray	default array	CSG
XmCSelectionArray	Pointer	
XmNselectionArrayCount	4	CSG
XmCSelectionArrayCount	int	
XmNselectThreshold	5	CSG
XmCSelectThreshold	int	

XmNpendingDelete

Indicates that pending delete mode is on when the Boolean value is True. Pending deletion is defined as deletion of the selected text when an insertion is made.

XmNselectionArray

Defines the actions for multiple mouse clicks. The value of the resource is an array of **XmTextScanType** elements. **XmTextScanType** is an enumeration indicating possible actions. Each mouse click performed within half a second of the previous mouse click increments the index into this array and performs the defined action for that index. The possible actions in the order they occur in the default array are:

- **XmSELECT_POSITION** — resets the insert cursor position
- **XmSELECT_WORD** — selects a word
- **XmSELECT_LINE** — selects a line of text
- **XmSELECT_ALL** — selects all of the text

XmNselectionArrayCount

Indicates the number of elements in the **XmNselectionArray** resource. The value must not be negative.

XmNselectThreshold

Specifies the number of pixels of motion that is required to select the next character when selection is performed using the click-drag mode of selection. The value must not be negative.

XmText Output Resource Set		
Name Class	**Default** Type	**Access**
XmNblinkRate XmCBlinkRate	500 int	CSG
XmNcolumns XmCColumns	dynamic short	CSG
XmNcursorPositionVisible XmCCursorPositionVisible	True Boolean	CSG
XmNfontList XmCFontList	dynamic XmFontList	CSG
XmNresizeHeight XmCResizeHeight	False Boolean	CSG
XmNresizeWidth XmCResizeWidth	False Boolean	CSG
XmNrows XmCRows	dynamic short	CSG
XmNwordWrap XmCWordWrap	False Boolean	CSG

XmNblinkRate

Specifies the blink rate of the text cursor in milliseconds. The time indicated in the blink rate relates to the time the cursor is visible and the time the cursor is invisible (that is, the time it takes to blink the insertion cursor on and off is twice the blink rate). The cursor does not blink when the blink rate is set to zero. The value must not be negative.

XmNcolumns

Specifies the initial width of the text window measured in character spaces. The value must be greater than 0. The default value depends on the value of the **XmNwidth** resource. If no width is specified the default is 20.

XmNcursorPositionVisible

Indicates that the insert cursor position is marked by a blinking text cursor when the Boolean value is True.

XmNfontList

Specifies the font list to be used for Text. If this value is NULL at initialization, it is initialized by looking up the parent hierarchy of the widget for an ancestor that is a subclass of the XmBulletinBoard, VendorShell, or XmMenuShell widget class. If such an ancestor is found, the font list is initialized to the appropriate default font list of the ancestor widget (XmNdefaultFontList for VendorShell and XmMenuShell, XmNtextFontList for XmBulletinBoard). See **XmFontListCreate(3X)** to create a font list.

XmNresizeHeight

Indicates that Text attempts to resize its height to accommodate all the text contained in the widget when the Boolean value is True. If the Boolean value is set to True, the text is always displayed starting from the first position in the source, even if instructed otherwise. This attribute is ignored when the application uses a ScrolledText widget and when **XmNscrollVertical** is True.

XmNresizeWidth

Indicates that Text attempts to resize its width to accommodate all the text contained in the widget when the Boolean value is True. This attribute is ignored if **XmNwordWrap** is True.

XmNrows Specifies the initial height of the text window measured in character heights. This attribute is ignored if the text widget resource **XmNeditMode** is **XmSINGLE_LINE_EDIT**. The value must be greater than 0. The default value depends on the value of the **XmNheight** resource. If no height is specified the default is 1.

XmNwordWrap
Indicates that lines are to be broken at word breaks (that is, the text does not go off the right edge of the window) when the Boolean value is True. Words are defined as a sequence of characters separated by white space. White space is defined as a space, tab, or newline. This attribute is ignored if the text widget resource **XmNeditMode** is **XmSINGLE_LINE_EDIT**.

The following resources are used only when text is created in a ScrolledWindow. See the man page for **XmCreateScrolledText.**

XmText ScrolledText Resource Set		
Name Class	Default Type	Access
XmNscrollHorizontal XmCScroll	True Boolean	CG
XmNscrollLeftSide XmCScrollSide	dynamic Boolean	CG
XmNscrollTopSide XmCScrollSide	False Boolean	CG
XmNscrollVertical XmCScroll	True Boolean	CG

XmNscrollHorizontal

Adds a ScrollBar that allows the user to scroll horizontally through text when the Boolean value is True. This attribute is ignored if the Text resource **XmNeditMode** is **XmSINGLE_LINE_EDIT**. This resource is forced to False when the Text widget is placed in a ScrolledWindow with **XmNscrollingPolicy** set to **XmAUTOMATIC**.

XmNscrollLeftSide

Indicates that the vertical ScrollBar should be placed on the left side of the scrolled text window when the Boolean value is True. This attribute is ignored if **XmNscrollVertical** is False or the Text resource **XmNeditMode** is **XmSINGLE_LINE_EDIT**. The default value may depend on the value of the **XmNstringDirection** resource.

XmNscrollTopSide

Indicates that the horizontal ScrollBar should be placed on the top side of the scrolled text window when the Boolean value is True.

XmNscrollVertical

Adds a ScrollBar that allows the user to scroll vertically through text when the Boolean value is True. This resource is forced to False when the Text widget is placed in a ScrolledWindow with **XmNscrollingPolicy** set to **XmAUTOMATIC**.

Inherited Resources

Text inherits behavior and resources from the following superclasses. For a complete description of each resource, refer to the man page for that superclass.

XmPrimitive Resource Set		

Name
   Class
	Default
	   Type
		Access

XmNbottomShadowColor
   XmCBottomShadowColor
	dynamic
	   Pixel
		CSG

XmNbottomShadowPixmap
   XmCBottomShadowPixmap
	XmUNSPECIFIED_PIXMAP
	   Pixmap
		CSG

XmNforeground
   XmCForeground
	dynamic
	   Pixel
		CSG

XmNhelpCallback
   XmCCallback
	NULL
	   XtCallbackList
		C

XmNhighlightColor
   XmCHighlightColor
	dynamic
	   Pixel
		CSG

XmNhighlightOnEnter
   XmCHighlightOnEnter
	False
	   Boolean
		CSG

XmNhighlightPixmap
   XmCHighlightPixmap
	dynamic
	   Pixmap
		CSG

XmNhighlightThickness
   XmCHighlightThickness
	2
	   Dimension
		CSG

XmNnavigationType
   XmCNavigationType
	dynamic
	   XmNavigationType
		CSG

XmNshadowThickness
   XmCShadowThickness
	2
	   Dimension
		CSG

XmNtopShadowColor
   XmCTopShadowColor
	dynamic
	   Pixel
		CSG

XmNtopShadowPixmap
   XmCTopShadowPixmap
	dynamic
	   Pixmap
		CSG

XmNtraversalOn
   XmCTraversalOn
	True
	   Boolean
		CSG

XmNuserData
   XmCUserData
	NULL
	   Pointer
		CSG

Core Resource Set		
Name	**Default**	**Access**
Class	**Type**	
XmNaccelerators	dynamic	CSG
XmCAccelerators	XtAccelerators	
XmNancestorSensitive	dynamic	G
XmCSensitive	Boolean	
XmNbackground	dynamic	CSG
XmCBackground	Pixel	
XmNbackgroundPixmap	XmUNSPECIFIED_PIXMAP	CSG
XmCPixmap	Pixmap	
XmNborderColor	XtDefaultForeground	CSG
XmCBorderColor	Pixel	
XmNborderPixmap	XmUNSPECIFIED_PIXMAP	CSG
XmCPixmap	Pixmap	
XmNborderWidth	0	CSG
XmCBorderWidth	Dimension	
XmNcolormap	dynamic	CG
XmCColormap	Colormap	
XmNdepth	dynamic	CG
XmCDepth	int	
XmNdestroyCallback	NULL	C
XmCCallback	XtCallbackList	
XmNheight	dynamic	CSG
XmCHeight	Dimension	
XmNinitialResourcesPersistent	True	C
XmCInitialResourcesPersistent	Boolean	
XmNmappedWhenManaged	True	CSG
XmCMappedWhenManaged	Boolean	
XmNscreen	dynamic	CG
XmCScreen	Screen *	

Name	Default	Access
Class	Type	
XmNsensitive	True	CSG
XmCSensitive	Boolean	
XmNtranslations	dynamic	CSG
XmCTranslations	XtTranslations	
XmNwidth	dynamic	CSG
XmCWidth	Dimension	
XmNx	0	CSG
XmCPosition	Position	
XmNy	0	CSG
XmCPosition	Position	

Callback Information

A pointer to the following structure is passed to each callback:

```
typedef struct
{
    int          reason;
    XEvent       * event;
} XmAnyCallbackStruct;
```

reason   Indicates why the callback was invoked

event   Points to the **XEvent** that triggered the callback

The Text widget defines a new callback structure for use with verification callbacks. Note that not all fields are relevant for every callback reason. The application must first look at the reason field and use only the structure members that are valid for the particular reason. A pointer to the following structure is passed to callbacks for **XmNlosingFocusCallback**, **XmNmodifyVerifyCallback**, and **XmNmotionVerifyCallback**.

typedef struct

```
{
    int             reason;
    XEvent          * event;
    Boolean         doit;
    XmTextPosition currInsert, newInsert;
    XmTextPosition startPos, endPos;
    XmTextBlock     text;
} XmTextVerifyCallbackStruct, *XmTextVerifyPtr;
```

reason   Indicates why the callback was invoked.

event   Points to the **XEvent** that triggered the callback.

doit   Indicates whether the action that invoked the callback is performed. Setting *doit* to False negates the action.

currInsert
           Indicates the current position of the insert cursor.

newInsert
           Indicates the position at which the user attempts to position the insert cursor.

startPos Indicates the starting position of the text to modify. If the callback is not a modify verification callback, this value is the same as *currInsert*.

endPos   Indicates the ending position of the text to modify. If no text is replaced or deleted, the value is the same as *startPos*. If the callback is not a modify verification callback, this value is the same as *currInsert*.

text   Points to a structure of type **XmTextBlockRec**. This structure holds the textual information to be inserted.

typedef struct
```
{
    char            * ptr;
    int             length;
    XmTextFormat format;
} XmTextBlockRec, *XmTextBlock;
```

ptr   Points to the text to be inserted.

length   Specifies the length of the text to be inserted.

format   Specifies the format of the text (for example, **FMT8BIT**).

The following table describes the reasons why the individual verification callback structure fields are valid:

Reason	Valid Fields
XmCR_LOSING_FOCUS	*reason, event, doit, currInsert, newInsert, startPos, endPos*
XmCR_MODIFYING_TEXT_VALUE	*reason, event, doit, currInsert, newInsert, startPos, endPos, text*
XmCR_MOVING_INSERT_CURSOR	*reason, event, doit, currInsert, newInsert*

Translations

XmText includes translations from XmPrimitive. The XmText translations are listed below. These translations may not directly correspond to a translation table. The actions represent the effective behavior of the associated events, and they may differ in a right-to-left language environment.

BSelect Press: **grab-focus()**
BSelect Motion: **extend-adjust()**
BSelect Release: **extend-end()**

BExtend Press: **extend-start()**
BExtend Motion: **extend-adjust()**
BExtend Release: **extend-end()**

BToggle Press: **move-destination()**

BDrag Press: secondary-start()
BDrag Motion: secondary-adjust()
BDrag Release: copy-to()

MCtrl BDrag Press:secondary-start()
MCtrl BDrag Motion:secondary-adjust()
MCtrl BDrag Release:copy-to()

MAlt BDrag Press:secondary-start()
MAlt BDrag Motion:secondary-adjust()
MAlt BDrag Release:move-to()

KUp: process-up()
MShift KUp: process-shift-up()
MCtrl KUp: backward-paragraph()
MShift MCtrl KUp:backward-paragraph(extend)

KDown: process-down()
MShift KDown: process-shift-down()
MCtrl KDown: forward-paragraph()
MShift MCtrl KDown:forward-paragraph(extend)

KLeft: backward-character()
MShift KLeft: key-select(left)
MCtrl KLeft: backward-word()
MShift MCtrl KLeft:backward-word(extend)

KRight: forward-character()
MShift KRight: key-select(right)
MCtrl KRight: forward-word()
MShift MCtrl KRight:forward-word(extend)

KPageUp: previous-page()
MShift KPageUp: previous-page(extend)

KPageDown: next-page()
MShift KPageDown:next-page(extend)

KPageLeft:	**page-left()**
KPageRight:	**page-right()**
KBeginLine:	**beginning-of-line()**
MShift KBeginLine:	**beginning-of-line(extend)**
KEndLine:	**end-of-line()**
MShift KEndLine:	**end-of-line(extend)**
KBeginData:	**beginning-of-file()**
MShift KBeginData:	**beginning-of-file(extend)**
KEndData:	**end-of-file()**
MShift KEndData:	**end-of-file(extend)**
KTab:	**process-tab()**
KNextField:	**next-tab-group()**
KPrevField:	**prev-tab-group()**
KEnter:	**process-return()**
KActivate:	**activate()**
KDelete:	**delete-next-character()**
KBackSpace:	**delete-previous-character()**
KAddMode:	**toggle-add-mode()**
KSpace:	**self-insert()**
KSelect:	**set-anchor()**
KExtend:	**key-select()**
MAny KCancel:	**process-cancel()**
KClear:	**clear-selection()**
KSelectAll:	**select-all()**
KDeselectAll:	**deselect-all()**
KCut:	**cut-clipboard()**
KCopy:	**copy-clipboard()**
KPaste:	**paste-clipboard()**

KPrimaryCut:	**cut-primary()**
KPrimaryCopy:	**copy-primary()**
KPrimaryPaste:	**copy-primary()**
KQuickCut:	**quick-cut-set()**
KQuickCopy:	**quick-copy-set()**
KQuickPaste:	**quick-copy-set()**
KQuickExtend:	**do-quick-action()**
KHelp:	**Help()**
KAny:	**self-insert()**

Action Routines

The XmText action routines are described below:

activate(): Calls the callbacks for **XmNactivateCallback**.

backward-character():

Moves the insertion cursor one character to the left. For other effects, see the description of navigation operations in the "Keyboard Selection" section. This action may have different behavior in a right-to-left language environment.

backward-paragraph(*extend*):

If **XmNeditMode** is **XmMULTI_LINE_EDIT** and this action is called with no argument, moves the insertion cursor to the first non-whitespace character following the first previous blank line or beginning of the text. If the insertion cursor is already at the beginning of a paragraph, moves the insertion cursor to the beginning of the previous paragraph. For other effects, see the description of navigation operations in the "Keyboard Selection" section.

If **XmNeditMode** is **XmMULTI_LINE_EDIT** and this action is called with an argument of **extend**, moves the insertion cursor as in the case of no argument and extends the selection.

2-967

For other effects, see the description of shifted navigation operations in the "Keyboard Selection" section.

backward-word(*extend*):

If this action is called with no argument, moves the insertion cursor to the first non-whitespace character after the first whitespace character to the left or the beginning of the line. If the insertion cursor is already at the beginning of a word, moves the insertion cursor to the beginning of the previous word. For other effects, see the description of navigation operations in the "Keyboard Selection" section. This action may have different behavior in a right-to-left language environment.

If called with an argument of **extend**, moves the insertion cursor as in the case of no argument and extends the selection. For other effects, see the description of shifted navigation operations in the "Keyboard Selection" section.

beep():   Causes the terminal to beep.

beginning-of-file(*extend*):

If this action is called with no argument, moves the insertion cursor to the beginning of the text. For other effects, see the description of navigation operations in the "Keyboard Selection" section.

If called with an argument of **extend**, moves the insertion cursor as in the case of no argument and extends the selection. For other effects, see the description of shifted navigation operations in the "Keyboard Selection" section.

beginning-of-line(*extend*):

If this action is called with no argument, moves the insertion cursor to the beginning of the line. For other effects, see the description of navigation operations in the "Keyboard Selection" section.

If called with an argument of **extend**, moves the insertion cursor as in the case of no argument and extends the selection. For other effects, see the description of shifted navigation operations in the "Keyboard Selection" section.

clear-selection():
> Clears the current selection by replacing each character except **<Return>** with a **<space>** character.

copy-clipboard():
> Copies the current selection to the clipboard.

copy-primary():
> Copies the primary selection to the insertion cursor.

copy-to(): If a secondary selection exists, copies the secondary selection to the insertion cursor. If no secondary selection exists, copies the primary selection to the pointer location.

cut-clipboard():
> Cuts the current selection to the clipboard.

cut-primary():
> Cuts the primary selection to the insertion cursor.

delete-next-character():
> If **XmNpendingDelete** is True and the cursor is inside the selection, deletes the entire selection; otherwise, deletes the character following the insertion cursor.

delete-next-word():
> If **XmNpendingDelete** is True and the cursor is inside the selection, deletes the entire selection; otherwise, deletes the characters following the insertion cursor to the next space, tab or end of line character.

delete-previous-character():
> If **XmNpendingDelete** is True and the cursor is inside the selection, deletes the entire selection; otherwise, deletes the character of text immediately preceding the insertion cursor.

delete-previous-word():
> If **XmNpendingDelete** is True and the cursor is inside the selection, deletes the entire selection; otherwise, deletes the characters preceding the insertion cursor to the next space, tab or beginning of line character.

delete-selection():
> Deletes the current selection.

delete-to-end-of-line():

> Deletes the characters following the insertion cursor to the next end of line character.

delete-to-start-of-line():

> Deletes the characters preceding the insertion cursor to the previous beginning of line character.

deselect-all():

> Deselects the current selection.

do-quick-action():

> Marks the end of a secondary selection. Performs the quick action initiated by the **quick-copy-set** or **quick-cut-set** action.

end-of-file(*extend*):

> If this action is called with no argument, moves the insertion cursor to the end of the text. For other effects, see the description of navigation operations in the "Keyboard Selection" section.
>
> If called with an argument of **extend**, moves the insertion cursor as in the case of no argument and extends the selection. For other effects, see the description of shifted navigation operations in the "Keyboard Selection" section.

end-of-line(*extend*):

> If this action is called with no argument, moves the insertion cursor to the end of the line. For other effects, see the description of navigation operations in the "Keyboard Selection" section. If called with an argument of **extend**, moves the insertion cursor as in the case of no argument and extends the selection. For other effects, see the description of shifted navigation operations in the "Keyboard Selection" section.

extend-adjust():

> Selects text from the anchor to the pointer position and deselects text outside that range. Moving the pointer over several lines selects text from the anchor to the end of each line the pointer moves over and up to the pointer position on the current line.

extend-end():
> Moves the insertion cursor to the position of the pointer.

extend-start():
> Adjusts the anchor using the balance-beam method. Selects text from the anchor to the pointer position and deselects text outside that range.

forward-character():
> Moves the insertion cursor one character to the right. For other effects, see the description of navigation operations in the "Keyboard Selection" section. This action may have different behavior in a right-to-left language environment.

forward-paragraph(*extend*):
> If **XmNeditMode** is **XmMULTI_LINE_EDIT**, and this action is called with no argument, moves the insertion cursor to the first non-whitespace character following the next blank line. If the insertion cursor is already at the beginning of a paragraph, moves the insertion cursor to the beginning of the next paragraph. For other effects, see the description of navigation operations in the "Keyboard Selection" section.
>
> If **XmNeditMode** is **XmMULTI_LINE_EDIT** and this action is called with an argument of **extend**, moves the insertion cursor as in the case of no argument and extends the selection. For other effects, see the description of shifted navigation operations in the "Keyboard Selection" section.

forward-word(*extend*):
> If this action is called with no argument, moves the insertion cursor to the first whitespace character or end of line following the next non-whitespace character. If the insertion cursor is already at the end of a word, moves the insertion cursor to the end of the next word. For other effects, see the description of navigation operations in the "Keyboard Selection" section. This action may have different behavior in a right-to-left language environment.

If called with an argument of **extend**, moves the insertion cursor as in the case of no argument and extends the selection. For other effects, see the description of shifted navigation operations in the "Keyboard Selection" section.

grab-focus():

This key binding performs the action defined in the **XmNselectionArray**, depending on the number of multiple mouse clicks. The default selection array ordering is one click to move the insertion cursor to the pointer position, two clicks to select a word, three clicks to select a line of text, and four clicks to select all text. A single click also deselects any selected text and sets the anchor at the pointer position.

Help(): Calls the callbacks for **XmNhelpCallback** if any exist. If there are no help callbacks for this widget, this action calls the help callbacks for the nearest ancestor that has them.

insert-string(*string*):

If **XmNpendingDelete** is True and the cursor is inside the selection, deletes the entire selection. Inserts *string* at the insertion cursor.

key-select(*direction*):

If called with an argument of **right**, moves the insertion cursor one character to the right and extends the selection. If called with an argument of **left**, moves the insertion cursor one character to the left and extends the selection. If called with no argument, extends the selection. For other effects, see the description of shifted navigation operations and **KExtend** in the "Keyboard Selection" section.

kill-next-character():

If **XmNpendingDelete** is True and the cursor is inside the selection, deletes the entire selection. Otherwise, kills the character following the insertion cursor and stores the character in the cut buffer.

kill-next-word():
>   If **XmNpendingDelete** is True and the cursor is inside the
>   selection, deletes the entire selection. Otherwise, kills the
>   characters following the insertion cursor to the next space, tab
>   or end of line character, and stores the characters in the cut
>   buffer.

kill-previous-character():
>   If **XmNpendingDelete** is True and the cursor is inside the
>   selection, deletes the entire selection. Otherwise, kills the
>   character of text immediately preceding the insertion cursor
>   and stores the character in the cut buffer.

kill-previous-word():
>   If **XmNpendingDelete** is True and the cursor is inside the
>   selection, deletes the entire selection. Otherwise, kills the
>   characters preceding the insertion cursor to the next space, tab
>   or beginning of line character, and stores the characters in the
>   cut buffer.

kill-selection():
>   Kills the currently selected text and stores the text in the cut
>   buffer.

kill-to-end-of-line():
>   Kills the characters following the insertion cursor to the next
>   end of line character and stores the characters in the cut buffer.

kill-to-start-of-line():
>   Kills the characters preceding the insertion cursor to the next
>   beginning of line character and stores the characters in the cut
>   buffer.

move-destination():
>   Moves the insertion cursor to the pointer position without
>   changing any existing selection. If no selection exists, also
>   moves the destination cursor to the pointer position.

move-to():   If a secondary selection exists, cuts the secondary selection to
>   the insertion cursor. If no secondary selection exists, cuts the
>   primary selection to the pointer location.

newline(): If **XmNpendingDelete** is True and the cursor is inside the selection, deletes the entire selection. Inserts a newline at the insertion cursor.

newline-and-backup():
   If **XmNpendingDelete** is True and the cursor is inside the selection, deletes the entire selection. Inserts a newline and repositions the insertion cursor to the end of the line before the newline.

newline-and-indent():
   If **XmNpendingDelete** is True and the cursor is inside the selection, deletes the entire selection. Inserts a newline and then the same number of whitespace characters as at the beginning of the previous line.

next-line(): Moves the insertion cursor to the next line. For other effects, see the description of navigation operations in the "Keyboard Selection" section.

next-page(*extend***)**:
   If this action is called with no argument, moves the insertion cursor forward one page. For other effects, see the description of navigation operations in the "Keyboard Selection" section.

   If called with an argument of **extend**, moves the insertion cursor as in the case of no argument and extends the selection. For other effects, see the description of shifted navigation operations in the "Keyboard Selection" section.

next-tab-group():
   Traverses to the next tab group.

page-left(): Scrolls the viewing window left one page of text.

page-right():
   Scrolls the viewing window right one page of text.

paste-clipboard():
   Pastes the contents of the clipboard before the insertion cursor.

prev-tab-group():
   Traverses to the previous tab group.

previous-line():

> Moves the insertion cursor to the previous line. For other effects, see the description of navigation operations in the "Keyboard Selection" section.

previous-page(*extend***)**:

> If this action is called with no argument, moves the insertion cursor back one page. For other effects, see the description of navigation operations in the "Keyboard Selection" section.
>
> If called with an argument of **extend**, moves the insertion cursor as in the case of no argument and extends the selection. For other effects, see the description of shifted navigation operations in the "Keyboard Selection" section.

process-cancel():

> Cancels the current **extend-adjust()** or **secondary-adjust()** operation and leaves the selection state as it was before the operation.

process-down():

> If **XmNeditMode** is **XmSINGLE_LINE_EDIT** and **XmNnavigationType** is **XmNONE**, traverses to the widget below the current one in the tab group.
>
> If **XmNeditMode** is **XmMULTI_LINE_EDIT**, moves the insertion cursor down one line. For other effects, see the description of navigation operations in the "Keyboard Selection" section.

process-home():

> Moves the insertion cursor to the beginning of the line. For other effects, see the description of navigation operations in the "Keyboard Selection" section.

process-return():

> If **XmNeditMode** is **XmSINGLE_LINE_EDIT**, calls the callbacks for **XmNactivateCallback**. If **XmNeditMode** is **XmMULTI_LINE_EDIT**, inserts a newline.

process-shift-down():
> If **XmNeditMode** is **XmMULTI_LINE_EDIT**, moves the insertion cursor down one line. For other effects, see the description of navigation operations in the "Keyboard Selection" section.

process-shift-up():
> If **XmNeditMode** is **XmMULTI_LINE_EDIT**, moves the insertion cursor up one line. For other effects, see the description of navigation operations in the "Keyboard Selection" section.

process-tab():
> If **XmNeditMode** is **XmSINGLE_LINE_EDIT**, traverses to the next tab group. If **XmNeditMode** is **XmMULTI_LINE_EDIT**, inserts a tab.

process-up():
> If **XmNeditMode** is **XmSINGLE_LINE_EDIT** and **XmNnavigationType** is **XmNONE**, traverses to the widget above the current one in the tab group.
>
> If **XmNeditMode** is **XmMULTI_LINE_EDIT**, moves the insertion cursor up one line. For other effects, see the description of navigation operations in the "Keyboard Selection" section.

quick-copy-set():
> Marks the beginning of a secondary selection for use in quick copy.

quick-cut-set():
> Marks the beginning of a secondary selection for use in quick cut.

redraw-display():
> Redraws the contents of the text window.

scroll-one-line-down():
> Scrolls the text area down one line.

scroll-one-line-up():
> Scrolls the text area up one line.

secondary-adjust():
>Extends the secondary selection to the pointer position.

secondary-notify():
>Copies the secondary selection to the destination cursor.

secondary-start():
>Marks the beginning of a secondary selection.

select-adjust():
>Extends the selection. The amount of text selected depends on the number of mouse clicks, as specified by the **XmNselectionArray** resource.

select-all(): Selects all text.

select-end(): Extends the selection. The amount of text selected depends on the number of mouse clicks, as specified by the **XmNselectionArray** resource.

select-start():
>Marks the beginning of a new selection region.

self-insert(): If **XmNpendingDelete** is True and the cursor is inside the selection, deletes the entire selection. Inserts the character associated with the key pressed at the insertion cursor.

set-anchor():
>Resets the anchor point for extended selections. Resets the destination of secondary selection actions.

set-insertion-point():
>Sets the insertion position.

set-selection-hint():
>Sets the text source and location of the selection.

toggle-add-mode():
>Toggles the state of Add Mode.

traverse-home():
>Traverses to the first widget in the tab group.

traverse-next():
>Traverses to the next widget in the tab group.

traverse-prev():
Traverses to the previous widget in the tab group.

unkill(): Restores last killed text to the position of the insertion cursor.

Additional Behavior

This widget has the additional behavior described below:

<FocusIn>: Draws the insertion cursor and starts blinking the cursor.

<FocusOut>:
Stops blinking the cursor.

Virtual Bindings

The bindings for virtual keys are vendor specific.

Related Information

**Core(3X), XmCreateScrolledText(3X), XmCreateText(3X),
XmFontListCreate(3X), XmPrimitive(3X), XmTextClearSelection(3X),
XmTextCopy(3X), XmTextCut(3X), XmTextField(3X),
XmTextGetBaseline(3X), XmTextGetEditable(3X),
XmTextGetInsertionPosition(3X), XmTextGetLastPosition(3X),
XmTextGetMaxLength(3X), XmTextGetSelection(3X),
XmTextGetSelectionPosition(3X), XmTextGetSource(3X),
XmTextGetString(3X), XmTextGetTopCharacter(3X),
XmTextInsert(3X), XmTextPaste(3X), XmTextPosToXY(3X),
XmTextPosition(3X), XmTextRemove(3X), XmTextReplace(3X),
XmTextScroll(3X), XmTextSetAddMode(3X), XmTextSetEditable(3X),
XmTextSetHighlight(3X), XmTextSetInsertionPosition(3X),
XmTextSetMaxLength(3X), XmTextSetSelection(3X),
XmTextSetSource(3X), XmTextSetString(3X),
XmTextSetTopCharacter(3X), XmTextShowPosition(3X), and
XmTextXYToPos(3X).**

XmTextClearSelection

Purpose

A Text function that clears the primary selection

AES Support Level

Full-use

Synopsis

#include <Xm/Text.h>

void XmTextClearSelection (*widget, time*)
    Widget   *widget*;
    Time   *time*;

Description

XmTextClearSelection clears the primary selection in the Text widget.

widget   Specifies the Text widget ID.

time   Specifies the time at which the selection value is desired. This should be the time of the event which triggered this request.

For a complete definition of Text and its associated resources, see
XmText(3X).

Related Information

XmText(3X).

XmTextCopy

Purpose

A Text function that copies the primary selection to the clipboard

AES Support Level

Trial-use

Synopsis

#include <Xm/Text.h>

Boolean XmTextCopy (*widget, time*)
    Widget   *widget*;
    Time   *time*;

Description

XmTextCopy copies the primary selected text to the clipboard.

widget   Specifies the Text widget ID.

time   Specifies the time at which the selection value is to be modified. This should be the time of the event which triggered this request.

For a complete definition of Text and its associated resources, see **XmText(3X)**.

Return Value

This function returns False if the primary selection is NULL, if the *widget* doesn't own the primary selection, or if the function is unable to gain ownership of the clipboard selection. Otherwise, it returns True.

Related Information

XmText(3X).

XmTextCut

Purpose

A Text function that copies the primary selection to the clipboard and deletes the selected text

AES Support Level

Trial-use

Synopsis

#include <Xm/Text.h>

Boolean XmTextCut (*widget, time*)
    Widget   *widget*;
    Time   *time*;

Description

XmTextCut copies the primary selected text to the clipboard and then deletes the primary selected text. This routine also calls the widget's **XmNmodifyVerifyCallback** and **XmNvalueChangedCallback** callbacks.

widget	Specifies the Text widget ID.
time	Specifies the time at which the selection value is to be modified. This should be the time of the event which triggered this request.

For a complete definition of Text and its associated resources, see **XmText(3X)**.

Return Value

This function returns False if the primary selection is NULL, if the *widget* doesn't own the primary selection, or if the function is unable to gain ownership of the clipboard selection. Otherwise, it returns True.

Related Information

XmText(3X).

XmTextGetBaseline

Purpose

A Text function that accesses the *x* position of the first baseline

Synopsis

#include <Xm/Text.h>

int XmTextGetBaseline (*widget*)
    Widget   *widget*;

Description

XmTextGetBaseline accesses the *x* position of the first baseline in the Text widget, relative to the *x* position of the top of the widget.

widget   Specifies the Text widget ID

For a complete definition of Text and its associated resources, see **XmText(3X)**.

Return Value

Returns an integer value that indicates the x position of the first baseline in the Text widget. The calculation takes into account the margin height, shadow thickness, highlight thickness, and font ascent of the first font in the fontlist. In this calculation the x position of the top of the widget is 0.

Related Information

XmText(3X).

XmTextGetEditable

Purpose

A Text function that accesses the edit permission state.

AES Support Level

Full-use

Synopsis

#include <Xm/Text.h>

Boolean XmTextGetEditable (*widget*)
    Widget   *widget*;

Description

XmTextGetEditable accesses the edit permission state of the Text widget.

widget   Specifies the Text widget ID

For a complete definition of Text and its associated resources, see
XmText(3X).

Return Value

Returns a Boolean value that indicates the state of the **XmNeditable** resource.

Related Information

XmText(3X).

XmTextGetInsertionPosition

Purpose

A Text function that accesses the position of the insert cursor

AES Support Level

Trial-use

Synopsis

#include <Xm/Text.h>

XmTextPosition XmTextGetInsertionPosition (*widget*)
  Widget *widget*;

Description

XmTextGetInsertionPosition accesses the insertion cursor position of the Text widget.

widget Specifies the Text widget ID

For a complete definition of Text and its associated resources, see **XmText(3X)**.

Return Value

Returns an XmTextPosition value that indicates the state of the **XmNcursorPosition** resource. This is an integer number of characters from the beginning of the text buffer. The first character position is 0.

Related Information

XmText(3X).

XmTextGetLastPosition

Purpose

A Text function that accesses the position of the last text character

AES Support Level

Trial-use

Synopsis

#include <Xm/Text.h>

XmTextPosition XmTextGetLastPosition (*widget*)
  Widget   *widget*;

Description

XmTextGetLastPosition accesses the position of the last character in the text buffer of the Text widget.

widget   Specifies the Text widget ID

For a complete definition of Text and its associated resources, see **XmText(3X)**.

Return Value

Returns an XmTextPosition value that indicates the position of the last character in the text buffer. This is an integer number of characters from the beginning of the buffer. The first character position is 0.

Related Information

XmText(3X).

XmTextGetMaxLength

Purpose

A Text function that accesses the value of the current maximum allowable length of a text string entered from the keyboard.

AES Support Level

Full-use

Synopsis

#include <Xm/Text.h>

int XmTextGetMaxLength (*widget*)
    Widget   *widget*;

Description

XmTextGetMaxLength accesses the value of the current maximum allowable length of the text string in the Text widget entered from the keyboard. The maximum allowable length prevents the user from entering a text string larger than this limit.

widget   Specifies the Text widget ID

For a complete definition of Text and its associated resources, see **XmText(3X)**.

Return Value

Returns the integer value that indicates the string's maximum allowable length that can be entered from the keyboard.

Related Information

XmText(3X).

XmTextGetSelection

Purpose

A Text function that retrieves the value of the primary selection.

AES Support Level

Full-use

Synopsis

#include <Xm/Text.h>

char * XmTextGetSelection (*widget*)
    Widget   *widget*;

Description

XmTextGetSelection retrieves the value of the primary selection. It returns a NULL pointer if no text is selected in the widget. The application is responsible for freeing the storage associated with the string by calling **XtFree**.

widget   Specifies the Text widget ID

For a complete definition of Text and its associated resources, see
XmText(3X).

Return Value

Returns a character pointer to the string that is associated with the primary
selection.

Related Information

XmText(3X).

XmTextGetSelectionPosition

Purpose

A Text function that accesses the position of the primary selection

AES Support Level

Trial-use

Synopsis

#include <Xm/Text.h>

Boolean XmTextGetSelectionPosition (*widget, left, right*)
    Widget   *widget*;
    XmTextPosition*left;
    XmTextPosition*right;

Description

XmTextGetSelectionPosition accesses the left and right position of the primary selection in the text buffer of the Text widget.

widget   Specifies the Text widget ID

left   Specifies the pointer in which the position of the left boundary of the primary selection is returned. This is an integer number of characters from the beginning of the buffer. The first character position is 0.

right   Specifies the pointer in which the position of the right boundary of the primary selection is returned. This is an integer number of characters from the beginning of the buffer. The first character position is 0.

For a complete definition of Text and its associated resources, see **XmText(3X)**.

Return Value

This function returns True if the widget owns the primary selection; otherwise, it returns False.

Related Information

XmText(3X).

XmTextGetSource

Purpose

A Text function that accesses the source of the widget

AES Support Level

Trial-use

Synopsis

#include <Xm/Text.h>

XmTextSource XmTextGetSource (*widget*)
    Widget   *widget*;

Description

XmTextGetSource accesses the source of the Text widget. Text widgets can share sources of text so that editing in one widget is reflected in another. This function accesses the source of one widget so that it can be made the source of another widget, using the function **XmTextSetSource(3X)**.

Setting a new text source destroys the old text source if no other Text widgets are using that source. To replace a text source but keep it for later use, create an unmanaged Text widget and set its source to the text source you want to keep.

widget   Specifies the Text widget ID

For a complete definition of Text and its associated resources, see **XmText(3X)**.

Return Value

Returns an XmTextSource value that represents the source of the Text widget.

Related Information

XmText(3X).

XmTextGetString

Purpose

A Text function that accesses the string value

AES Support Level

Full-use

Synopsis

#include <Xm/Text.h>

char * XmTextGetString (*widget*)
    Widget   *widget*;

Description

XmTextGetString accesses the string value of the Text widget. The application is responsible for freeing the storage associated with the string by calling **XtFree**.

widget   Specifies the Text widget ID

For a complete definition of Text and its associated resources, see **XmText(3X)**.

Return Value

Returns a character pointer to the string value of the text widget. Returns an empty string if the length of the Text widget's string is 0.

Related Information

XmText(3X).

XmTextGetTopCharacter

Purpose

A Text function that accesses the position of the first character displayed

AES Support Level

Trial-use

Synopsis

#include <Xm/Text.h>

XmTextPosition XmTextGetTopCharacter (*widget*)
    Widget   *widget*;

Description

XmTextGetTopCharacter accesses the position of the text at the top of the Text widget.

widget   Specifies the Text widget ID

For a complete definition of Text and its associated resources, see **XmText(3X)**.

Return Value

Returns an XmTextPosition value that indicates the state of the **XmNtopCharacter** resource. This is an integer number of characters from the beginning of the text buffer. The first character position is 0.

Related Information

XmText(3X).

XmTextInsert

Purpose

A Text function that inserts a character string into a text string

AES Support Level

Trial-use

Synopsis

#include <Xm/Text.h>

void XmTextInsert(*widget, position, value*)
    Widget   *widget*;
    XmTextPosition *position*;
    char   * *value*;

Description

XmTextInsert inserts a character string into the text string in the Text
widget. The character positions begin at zero and are numbered
sequentially from the beginning of the text. For example, to insert a string
after the fourth character, the parameter *position* must be 4.

This routine also calls the widget's **XmNmodifyVerifyCallback** and **XmNvalueChangedCallback** callbacks.

widget   Specifies the Text widget ID.

position   Specifies the position in the text string where the character string is to be inserted.

value   Specifies the character string value to be added to the text widget.

For a complete definition of Text and its associated resources, see **XmText(3X)**.

Related Information

XmText(3X).

XmTextPaste

Purpose

A Text function that inserts the clipboard selection

AES Support Level

Trial-use

Synopsis

#include <Xm/Text.h>

Boolean XmTextPaste (*widget*)
    Widget   *widget*;

Description

XmTextPaste inserts the clipboard selection at the destination cursor. If **XmNpendingDelete** is True and the destination cursor is inside the current selection, the clipboard selection replaces the selected text. This routine also calls the widget's **XmNmodifyVerifyCallback** and **XmNvalueChangedCallback** callbacks if there is a clipboard selection.

widget   Specifies the Text widget ID.

For a complete definition of Text and its associated resources, see **XmText(3X)**.

Return Value

This function returns False if the *widget* doesn't own the primary selection. Otherwise, it returns True.

Related Information

XmText(3X).

XmTextPosToXY

Purpose

A Text function that accesses the x and y position of a character position

AES Support Level

Trial-use

Synopsis

#include <Xm/Text.h>

Boolean XmTextPosToXY (*widget, position, x, y*)
    Widget   *widget*;
    XmTextPosition*position*;
    Position   **x*;
    Position   **y*;

Description

XmTextPosToXY accesses the x and y position, relative to the upper left corner of the Text widget, of a given character position in the text buffer.

widget   Specifies the Text widget ID

position   Specifies the character position in the text for which the x and y position is accessed. This is an integer number of characters from the beginning of the buffer. The first character position is 0.

x   Specifies the pointer in which the x position, relative to the upper left corner of the widget, is returned. This value is meaningful only if the function returns True.

y   Specifies the pointer in which the y position, relative to the upper left corner of the widget, is returned. This value is meaningful only if the function returns True.

For a complete definition of Text and its associated resources, see **XmText(3X)**.

Return Value

This function returns True if the character position is displayed in the Text widget; otherwise, it returns False, and no *x* or *y* value is returned.

Related Information

XmText(3X).

XmTextPosition

Purpose

Data type for a character position within a text string

AES Support Level

Trial-use

Synopsis

#include <Xm/Xm.h>

Description

XmTextPosition is the data type for a character position within a text string. The text position is an integer representing the number of characters from the beginning of the string. The first character position in the string is 0.

Related Information

XmText(3X).

XmTextRemove

Purpose

A Text function that deletes the primary selection

AES Support Level

Trial-use

Synopsis

#include <Xm/Text.h>

Boolean XmTextRemove (*widget*)
    Widget   *widget*;

Description

XmTextRemove deletes the primary selected text. This routine also calls the widget's **XmNmodifyVerifyCallback** and **XmNvalueChangedCallback** callbacks if there is a selection.

widget   Specifies the Text widget ID.

For a complete definition of Text and its associated resources, see **XmText(3X)**.

Return Value

This function returns False if the primary selection is NULL or if the *widget* doesn't own the primary selection. Otherwise, it returns True.

Related Information

XmText(3X).

XmTextReplace

Purpose

A Text function that replaces part of a text string

AES Support Level

Full-use

Synopsis

#include <Xm/Text.h>

void XmTextReplace (*widget, from_pos, to_pos, value*)
    Widget   *widget*;
    XmTextPosition*from_pos*;
    XmTextPosition*to_pos*;
    char   * *value*;

Description

XmTextReplace replaces part of the text string in the Text widget. The character positions begin at zero and are numbered sequentially from the beginning of the text.

An example text replacement would be to replace the second and third characters in the text string. To accomplish this, the parameter *from_pos* must be 1 and *to_pos* must be 3. To insert a string after the fourth character, both parameters, *from_pos* and *to_pos*, must be 4.

This routine also calls the widget's **XmNmodifyVerifyCallback** and **XmNvalueChangedCallback** callbacks.

widget   Specifies the Text widget ID

from_pos Specifies the start position of the text to be replaced

to_pos   Specifies the end position of the text to be replaced

value   Specifies the character string value to be added to the text widget

For a complete definition of Text and its associated resources, see **XmText(3X)**.

Related Information

XmText(3X).

XmTextScroll

Purpose

A Text function that scrolls text

AES Support Level

Trial-use

Synopsis

#include <Xm/Text.h>

void XmTextScroll (*widget, lines*)
    Widget   *widget*;
    int   *lines*;

Description

XmTextScroll scrolls text in a Text widget.

widget   Specifies the Text widget ID

lines   Specifies the number of lines of text to scroll. A positive value causes text to scroll upward; a negative value causes text to scroll downward.

For a complete definition of Text and its associated resources, see
XmText(3X).

Related Information

XmText(3X).

XmTextSetAddMode

Purpose

A Text function that sets the state of Add Mode

AES Support Level

Trial-use

Synopsis

#include <Xm/Text.h>

void XmTextSetAddMode (*widget, state*)
    Widget   *widget*;
    Boolean   *state*;

Description

XmTextSetAddMode controls whether or not the Text widget is in Add Mode. When the widget is in Add Mode, the insert cursor can be moved without disturbing the primary selection.

widget   Specifies the Text widget ID

state   Specifies whether or not the widget is in Add Mode. A value of True turns on Add Mode; a value of False turns off Add Mode.

For a complete definition of Text and its associated resources, see
XmText(3X).

Related Information

XmText(3X).

XmTextSetEditable

Purpose

A Text function that sets the edit permission

AES Support Level

Full-use

Synopsis

#include <Xm/Text.h>

void XmTextSetEditable (*widget, editable*)
    Widget   *widget*;
    Boolean   *editable*;

Description

XmTextSetEditable sets the edit permission state of the Text widget. When set to True, the text string can be edited.

widget   Specifies the Text widget ID

editable Specifies a Boolean value that when True allows text string edits

For a complete definition of Text and its associated resources, see **XmText(3X)**.

Related Information

XmText(3X).

XmTextSetHighlight

Purpose

A Text function that highlights text

AES Support Level

Trial-use

Synopsis

#include <Xm/Text.h>

void XmTextSetHighlight (*widget, left, right, mode*)
    Widget   *widget*;
    XmTextPosition*left*;
    XmTextPosition*right*;
    XmHighlightMode*mode*;

Description

XmTextSetHighlight highlights text between the two specified character positions. The *mode* parameter determines the type of highlighting. Highlighting text merely changes the visual appearance of the text; it does not set the selection.

widget   Specifies the Text widget ID

left   Specifies the position of the left boundary of text to be highlighted. This is an integer number of characters from the beginning of the text buffer. The first character position is 0.

right   Specifies the position of the right boundary of text to be highlighted. This is an integer number of characters from the beginning of the text buffer. The first character position is 0.

mode   Specifies the type of highlighting to be done. A value of **XmHIGHLIGHT_NORMAL** removes highlighting. A value of **XmHIGHLIGHT_SELECTED** highlights the text using reverse video. A value of **XmHIGHLIGHT_SECONDARY_SELECTED** highlights the text using underlining.

For a complete definition of Text and its associated resources, see **XmText(3X)**.

Related Information

XmText(3X).

XmTextSetInsertionPosition

Purpose

A Text function that sets the position of the insert cursor

AES Support Level

Trial-use

Synopsis

#include <Xm/Text.h>

void XmTextSetInsertionPosition (*widget, position*)
Widget   *widget*;
XmTextPosition*position*;

Description

XmTextSetInsertionPosition sets the insertion cursor position of the Text widget. This routine also calls the widget's **XmNmotionVerifyCallback** callbacks if the insertion cursor position changes.

widget   Specifies the Text widget ID

position Specifies the position of the insertion cursor. This is an integer number of characters from the beginning of the text buffer. The first character position is 0.

For a complete definition of Text and its associated resources, see **XmText(3X)**.

Related Information

XmText(3X).

XmTextSetMaxLength

Purpose

A Text function that sets the value of the current maximum allowable length of a text string entered from the keyboard.

AES Support Level

Full-use

Synopsis

#include <Xm/Text.h>

void XmTextSetMaxLength (*widget, max_length*)
    Widget   *widget*;
    int   *max_length*;

Description

XmTextSetMaxLength sets the value of the current maximum allowable length of the text string in the Text widget. The maximum allowable length prevents the user from entering a text string from the keyboard that is larger than this limit. Strings that are entered using the **XmNvalue** resource or the **XmTextSetString** function ignore this resource.

widget   Specifies the Text widget ID

max_length
            Specifies the maximum allowable length of the text string

For a complete definition of Text and its associated resources, see
XmText(3X).

Related Information

XmText(3X) and **XmTextSetString(3X)**.

XmTextSetSelection

Purpose

A Text function that sets the primary selection of the text.

AES Support Level

Full-use

Synopsis

#include <Xm/Text.h>

void XmTextSetSelection (*widget, first, last, time*)
    Widget   *widget*;
    XmTextPosition*first*;
    XmTextPosition*last*;
    Time   *time*;

Description

XmTextSetSelection sets the primary selection of the text in the widget. It also sets the insertion cursor position to the last position of the selection and calls the widget's **XmNmotionVerifyCallback** callbacks.

widget   Specifies the Text widget ID

first   Marks the first character position of the text to be selected

last   Marks the last position of the text to be selected

time   Specifies the time at which the selection value is desired. This should be the same as the time of the event that triggered this request.

For a complete definition of Text and its associated resources, see **XmText(3X)**.

Related Information

XmText(3X).

XmTextSetSource

Purpose

A Text function that sets the source of the widget

AES Support Level

Trial-use

Synopsis

#include <Xm/Text.h>

void XmTextSetSource (*widget, source, top_character, cursor_position*)
Widget *widget*;
XmTextSource*source*;
XmTextPosition*top_character*;
XmTextPosition*cursor_position*;

Description

XmTextSetSource sets the source of the Text widget. Text widgets can share sources of text so that editing in one widget is reflected in another. This function sets the source of one widget so that it can share the source of another widget.

Setting a new text source destroys the old text source if no other Text widgets are using that source. To replace a text source but keep it for later use, create an unmanaged Text widget and set its source to the text source you want to keep.

widget   Specifies the Text widget ID

source   Specifies the source with which the widget displays text. This can be a value returned by the **XmTextGetSource(3X)** function. If no source is specified, the widget creates a default string source.

top_character

Specifies the position in the text to display at the top of the widget. This is an integer number of characters from the beginning of the text buffer. The first character position is 0.

cursor_position

Specifies the position in the text at which the insert cursor is located. This is an integer number of characters from the beginning of the text buffer. The first character position is 0.

For a complete definition of Text and its associated resources, see **XmText(3X)**.

Related Information

XmText(3X).

XmTextSetString

Purpose

A Text function that sets the string value

AES Support Level

Full-use

Synopsis

#include <Xm/Text.h>

void XmTextSetString (*widget, value*)
    Widget   *widget*;
    char   ** value*;

Description

XmTextSetString sets the string value of the Text widget. This routine calls the widget's **XmNmodifyVerifyCallback** and **XmNvalueChangedCallback** callbacks. It also sets the insertion cursor position to the beginning of the string and calls the widget's **XmNmotionVerifyCallback** callbacks.

widget   Specifies the Text widget ID

value   Specifies the character pointer to the string value and places the string into the text edit window

For a complete definition of Text and its associated resources, see **XmText(3X)**.

Related Information

XmText(3X).

XmTextSetTopCharacter

Purpose

A Text function that sets the position of the first character displayed

AES Support Level

Trial-use

Synopsis

#include <Xm/Text.h>

void XmTextSetTopCharacter (*widget, top_character*)
    Widget   *widget*;
    XmTextPosition*top_character*;

Description

XmTextSetTopCharacter sets the position of the text at the top of the Text widget. If the **XmNeditMode** is **XmMULTI_LINE_EDIT**, the line of text that contains *top_character* is displayed at the top of the widget without shifting the text left or right.

widget   Specifies the Text widget ID

top_character

> Specifies the position in the text to display at the top of the widget. This is an integer number of characters from the beginning of the text buffer. The first character position is 0.

For a complete definition of Text and its associated resources, see **XmText(3X)**.

Related Information

XmText(3X).

XmTextShowPosition

Purpose

A Text function that forces text at a given position to be displayed

AES Support Level

Trial-use

Synopsis

#include <Xm/Text.h>

void XmTextShowPosition (*widget, position*)
    Widget   *widget*;
    XmTextPosition*position*;

Description

XmTextShowPosition forces text at the specified position to be displayed.
If the **XmNautoShowCursorPosition** resource is True, the application
should also set the insert cursor to this position.

widget   Specifies the Text widget ID

position   Specifies the character position to be displayed. This is an integer number of characters from the beginning of the text buffer. The first character position is 0.

For a complete definition of Text and its associated resources, see **XmText(3X)**.

Related Information

XmText(3X).

XmTextXYToPos

Purpose

A Text function that accesses the character position nearest an x and y position

AES Support Level

Trial-use

Synopsis

#include <Xm/Text.h>

XmTextPosition XmTextXYToPos (*widget, x, y*)
    Widget   *widget*;
    Position   *x*;
    Position   *y*;

Description

XmTextXYToPos accesses the character position nearest to the specified x and y position, relative to the upper left corner of the Text widget.

widget   Specifies the Text widget ID

x   Specifies the x position, relative to the upper left corner of the widget.

y   Specifies the y position, relative to the upper left corner of the widget.

For a complete definition of Text and its associated resources, see **XmText(3X)**.

Return Value

Returns the character position in the text nearest the x and y position specified. This is an integer number of characters from the beginning of the buffer. The first character position is 0.

Related Information

XmText(3X).

XmToggleButton

Purpose

The ToggleButton widget class

AES Support Level

Full-use

Synopsis

#include <Xm/ToggleB.h>

Description

ToggleButton sets nontransitory state data within an application. Usually this widget consists of an indicator (square or diamond) with either text or a pixmap on one side of it. However, it can also consist of just text or a pixmap without the indicator.

The toggle graphics display a **1-of-many** or **N-of-many** selection state. When a toggle indicator is displayed, a square indicator shows an **N-of-many** selection state and a diamond indicator shows a **1-of-many** selection state.

ToggleButton implies a selected or unselected state. In the case of a label and an indicator, an empty indicator (square or diamond shaped) indicates that ToggleButton is unselected, and a filled indicator shows that it is selected. In the case of a pixmap toggle, different pixmaps are used to display the selected/unselected states.

The default behavior associated with a ToggleButton in a menu depends on the type of menu system in which it resides. By default, **BSelect** controls the behavior of the ToggleButton. In addition, **BMenu** controls the behavior of the ToggleButton if it resides in a PopupMenu system. The actual mouse button used is determined by its RowColumn parent.

To accommodate the toggle indicator when created, Label's resource **XmNmarginLeft** may be increased.

Classes

ToggleButton inherits behavior and resources from **Core**, **XmPrimitive**, and **XmLabel** Classes.

The class pointer is **xmToggleButtonWidgetClass**.

The class name is **XmToggleButton**.

New Resources

The following table defines a set of widget resources used by the programmer to specify data. The programmer can also set the resource values for the inherited classes to set attributes for this widget. To reference a resource by name or by class in a .Xdefaults file, remove the **XmN** or **XmC** prefix and use the remaining letters. To specify one of the defined values for a resource in a .Xdefaults file, remove the **Xm** prefix and use the remaining letters (in either lowercase or uppercase, but include any underscores between words). The codes in the access column indicate if the given resource can be set at creation time (**C**), set by using **XtSetValues** (**S**), retrieved by using **XtGetValues** (**G**), or is not applicable (**N/A**).

XmToggleButton Resource Set		
Name **Class**	**Default** **Type**	**Access**
XmNarmCallback XmCArmCallback	NULL XtCallbackList	C
XmNdisarmCallback XmCDisarmCallback	NULL XtCallbackList	C
XmNfillOnSelect XmCFillOnSelect	True Boolean	CSG
XmNindicatorOn XmCIndicatorOn	True Boolean	CSG
XmNindicatorSize XmCIndicatorSize	dynamic Dimension	CSG
XmNindicatorType XmCIndicatorType	dynamic unsigned char	CSG
XmNselectColor XmCSelectColor	dynamic Pixel	CSG
XmNselectInsensitivePixmap XmCSelectInsensitivePixmap	XmUNSPECIFIED_PIXMAP Pixmap	CSG
XmNselectPixmap XmCSelectPixmap	XmUNSPECIFIED_PIXMAP Pixmap	CSG
XmNset XmCSet	False Boolean	CSG
XmNspacing XmCSpacing	4 Dimension	CSG
XmNvalueChangedCallback XmCValueChangedCallback	NULL XtCallbackList	C
XmNvisibleWhenOff XmCVisibleWhenOff	dynamic Boolean	CSG

XmNarmCallback

Specifies the list of callbacks called when the ToggleButton is armed. To arm this widget, press the active mouse button while the pointer is inside the ToggleButton. For this callback, the reason is **XmCR_ARM**.

XmNdisarmCallback

Specifies the list of callbacks called when ToggleButton is disarmed. To disarm this widget, press and release the active mouse button while the pointer is inside the ToggleButton. This widget is also disarmed when the user moves out of the widget and releases the mouse button when the pointer is outside the widget. For this callback, the reason is **XmCR_DISARM**.

XmNfillOnSelect

Fills the indicator with the color specified in **XmNselectColor** and switches the top and bottom shadow colors when set to True. Otherwise, it switches only the top and bottom shadow colors.

XmNindicatorOn

Specifies that a toggle indicator is drawn to one side of the toggle text or pixmap when set to True. When set to False, no space is allocated for the indicator, and it is not displayed. If **XmNindicatorOn** is True, the indicator shadows are switched when the button is selected or unselected, but, any shadows around the entire widget are not switched. However, if **XmNindicatorOn** is False, any shadows around the entire widget are switched when the toggle is selected or unselected.

XmNindicatorSize

Sets the size of the indicator. If no value is specified, the size of the indicator is based on the size of the label string or pixmap. If the label string or pixmap changes, the size of the indicator is recomputed based on the size of the label string or pixmap. Once a value has been specified for **XmNindicatorSize**, the indicator has that size, regardless of the size of the label string or pixmap, until a new value is specified.

XmNindicatorType

Specifies if the indicator is a **1-of** or **N-of** indicator. For the **1-of** indicator, the value is **XmONE_OF_MANY**. For the **N-of** indicator, the value is **XmN_OF_MANY**. The **N-of-many** indicator is square. The **1-of-many** indicator is diamond shaped. This resource specifies only the visuals and does not enforce the behavior. When the ToggleButton is in a RadioBox, the default is **XmONE_OF_MANY**; otherwise, the default is **XmN_OF_MANY**.

XmNselectColor

Allows the application to specify what color fills the center of the square or diamond-shaped indicator when it is set. If this color is the same as either the top or the bottom shadow color of the indicator, a one-pixel-wide margin is left between the shadows and the fill; otherwise, it is filled completely. This resource's default for a color display is a color between the background and the bottom shadow color. For a monochrome display, the default is set to the foreground color. The meaning of this resource is undefined when **XmNindicatorOn** is False.

XmNselectInsensitivePixmap

Specifies a pixmap used as the button face when the ToggleButton is selected and the button is insensitive if the Label resource **XmNlabelType** is set to **XmPIXMAP**. If the ToggleButton is unselected and the button is insensitive, the pixmap in **XmNlabelInsensitivePixmap** is used as the button face. If no value is specified for **XmNlabelInsensitivePixmap**, that resource is set to the value specified for **XmNselectInsensitivePixmap**.

XmNselectPixmap

Specifies the pixmap to be used as the button face if **XmNlabelType** is **XmPIXMAP** and the ToggleButton is selected. When the ToggleButton is unselected, the pixmap specified in Label's **XmNlabelPixmap** is used. If no value is specified for **XmNlabelPixmap**, that resource is set to the value specified for **XmNselectPixmap**.

XmNset   Displays the button in its selected state if set to True. This shows some conditions as active when a set of buttons first appears.

XmNspacing

Specifies the amount of spacing between the toggle indicator and the toggle label (text or pixmap).

XmNvalueChangedCallback
> Specifies the list of callbacks called when the ToggleButton value is changed. To change the value, press and release the active mouse button while the pointer is inside the ToggleButton. This action also causes this widget to be disarmed. For this callback, the reason is **XmCR_VALUE_CHANGED**.

XmNvisibleWhenOff
> Indicates that the toggle indicator is visible in the unselected state when the Boolean value is True. When the ToggleButton is in a menu, the default value is False. When the ToggleButton is in a RadioBox, the default value is True.

Inherited Resources

ToggleButton inherits behavior and resources from the following superclasses. For a complete description of each resource, refer to the man page for that superclass.

XmLabel Resource Set		
Name **Class**	**Default** **Type**	**Access**
XmNaccelerator XmCAccelerator	NULL String	CSG
XmNacceleratorText XmCAcceleratorText	NULL XmString	CSG
XmNalignment XmCAlignment	dynamic unsigned char	CSG
XmNfontList XmCFontList	dynamic XmFontList	CSG
XmNlabelInsensitivePixmap XmCLabelInsensitivePixmap	XmUNSPECIFIED_PIXMAP Pixmap	CSG
XmNlabelPixmap XmCLabelPixmap	XmUNSPECIFIED_PIXMAP Pixmap	CSG
XmNlabelString XmCXmString	dynamic XmString	CSG
XmNlabelType XmCLabelType	XmSTRING unsigned char	CSG
XmNmarginBottom XmCMarginBottom	dynamic Dimension	CSG
XmNmarginHeight XmCMarginHeight	2 Dimension	CSG
XmNmarginLeft XmCMarginLeft	dynamic Dimension	CSG
XmNmarginRight XmCMarginRight	0 Dimension	CSG
XmNmarginTop XmCMarginTop	dynamic Dimension	CSG
XmNmarginWidth XmCMarginWidth	2 Dimension	CSG

Name	Default	Access
Class	Type	
XmNmnemonic	NULL	CSG
XmCMnemonic	KeySym	
XmNmnemonicCharSet	dynamic	CSG
XmCMnemonicCharSet	String	
XmNrecomputeSize	True	CSG
XmCRecomputeSize	Boolean	
XmNstringDirection	dynamic	CSG
XmCStringDirection	XmStringDirection	

XmPrimitive Resource Set		
Name Class	**Default** Type	**Access**
XmNbottomShadowColor XmCBottomShadowColor	dynamic Pixel	CSG
XmNbottomShadowPixmap XmCBottomShadowPixmap	XmUNSPECIFIED_PIXMAP Pixmap	CSG
XmNforeground XmCForeground	dynamic Pixel	CSG
XmNhelpCallback XmCCallback	NULL XtCallbackList	C
XmNhighlightColor XmCHighlightColor	dynamic Pixel	CSG
XmNhighlightOnEnter XmCHighlightOnEnter	False Boolean	CSG
XmNhighlightPixmap XmCHighlightPixmap	dynamic Pixmap	CSG
XmNhighlightThickness XmCHighlightThickness	2 Dimension	CSG
XmNnavigationType XmCNavigationType	XmNONE XmNavigationType	G
XmNshadowThickness XmCShadowThickness	dynamic Dimension	CSG
XmNtopShadowColor XmCTopShadowColor	dynamic Pixel	CSG
XmNtopShadowPixmap XmCTopShadowPixmap	dynamic Pixmap	CSG
XmNtraversalOn XmCTraversalOn	True Boolean	CSG
XmNuserData XmCUserData	NULL Pointer	CSG

Core Resource Set		
Name **Class**	**Default** **Type**	**Access**
XmNaccelerators XmCAccelerators	dynamic XtAccelerators	CSG
XmNancestorSensitive XmCSensitive	dynamic Boolean	G
XmNbackground XmCBackground	dynamic Pixel	CSG
XmNbackgroundPixmap XmCPixmap	XmUNSPECIFIED_PIXMAP Pixmap	CSG
XmNborderColor XmCBorderColor	XtDefaultForeground Pixel	CSG
XmNborderPixmap XmCPixmap	XmUNSPECIFIED_PIXMAP Pixmap	CSG
XmNborderWidth XmCBorderWidth	0 Dimension	CSG
XmNcolormap XmCColormap	dynamic Colormap	CG
XmNdepth XmCDepth	dynamic int	CG
XmNdestroyCallback XmCCallback	NULL XtCallbackList	C
XmNheight XmCHeight	dynamic Dimension	CSG
XmNinitialResourcesPersistent XmCInitialResourcesPersistent	True Boolean	C
XmNmappedWhenManaged XmCMappedWhenManaged	True Boolean	CSG
XmNscreen XmCScreen	dynamic Screen *	CG

Name	Default	Access
Class	Type	
XmNsensitive	True	CSG
XmCSensitive	Boolean	
XmNtranslations	dynamic	CSG
XmCTranslations	XtTranslations	
XmNwidth	dynamic	CSG
XmCWidth	Dimension	
XmNx	0	CSG
XmCPosition	Position	
XmNy	0	CSG
XmCPosition	Position	

Callback Information

A pointer to the following structure is passed to each callback:

typedef struct
{
    int   *reason*;
    XEvent   ** event*;
    int   *set*;
} XmToggleButtonCallbackStruct;

reason   Indicates why the callback was invoked

event   Points to the **XEvent** that triggered the callback

set   Reflects the ToggleButton's current state when the callback occurred, either True (selected) or False (unselected)

Translations

XmToggleButton includes translations from Primitive. The XmToggleButton translations for buttons not in a menu system are listed below. These translations may not directly correspond to a translation table.

Note that altering translations in **#override** or **#augment** mode is undefined.

BSelect Press: **Arm()**
BSelect Release: **Select()**
                              Disarm()
KHelp: **Help()**
KActivate: **ArmAndActivate()**
KSelect: **ArmAndActivate()**

XmToggleButton inherits menu traversal translations from XmLabel. Additional XmToggleButton translations for ToggleButtons in a menu system are listed below. In a Popup menu system, **BMenu** also performs the **BSelect** actions. These translations may not directly correspond to a translation table.

BSelect Press: **BtnDown()**
BSelect Release: **BtnUp()**
KHelp: **Help()**
KActivate: **ArmAndActivate()**
KSelect: **ArmAndActivate()**
MAny KCancel: **MenuShellPopdownOne()**

Action Routines

The XmToggleButton action routines are described below:

Arm(): If the button was previously unset, this action does the following: If **XmNindicatorOn** is True, it draws the indicator shadow so that the indicator looks pressed; if **XmNfillOnSelect** is True, it fills the indicator with the color specified by **XmNselectColor**. If **XmNindicatorOn** is False, it draws the button shadow so that the button looks pressed. If **XmNlabelType** is **XmPIXMAP**, the **XmNselectPixmap** is used as the button face. Calls the **XmNarmCallback** callbacks.

If the button was previously set, this action does the following: If both **XmNindicatorOn** and **XmNvisibleWhenOff** are True, it draws the indicator shadow so that the indicator looks raised; if **XmNfillOnSelect** is True, it fills the indicator with the background color. If **XmNindicatorOn** is False, it draws the button shadow so that the button looks raised. If **XmNlabelType** is **XmPIXMAP**, the **XmNlabelPixmap** is used as the button face. Calls the **XmNarmCallback** callbacks.

ArmAndActivate():
If the ToggleButton was previously set, unsets it; if the ToggleButton was previously unset, sets it.

In a menu, does the following: Unposts all menus in the menu hierarchy. Unless the button is already armed, calls the **XmNarmCallback** callbacks. Calls the **XmNvalueChangedCallback** and **XmNdisarmCallback** callbacks.

Outside a menu, if the button was previously unset, this action does the following: If **XmNindicatorOn** is True, it draws the indicator shadow so that the indicator looks pressed; if **XmNfillOnSelect** is True, it fills the indicator with the color specified by **XmNselectColor**. If **XmNindicatorOn** is False, it draws the button shadow so that the button looks pressed. If **XmNlabelType** is **XmPIXMAP**, the **XmNselectPixmap** is used as the button face. Calls the **XmNarmCallback**, **XmNvalueChangedCallback**, and **XmNdisarmCallback** callbacks.

Outside a menu, if the button was previously set, this action does the following: If both **XmNindicatorOn** and **XmNvisibleWhenOff** are True, it draws the indicator shadow so that the indicator looks raised; if **XmNfillOnSelect** is True, it fills the indicator with the background color. If **XmNindicatorOn** is False, it draws the button shadow so that the button looks raised. If **XmNlabelType** is **XmPIXMAP**, the **XmNlabelPixmap** is used as the button face. Calls the **XmNarmCallback**, **XmNvalueChangedCallback**, and **XmNdisarmCallback** callbacks.

BtnDown(): This action unposts any menus posted by the ToggleButton's parent menu, disables keyboard traversal for the menu, and enables mouse traversal for the menu. It draws the shadow in the armed state and, unless the button is already armed, calls the **XmNarmCallback** callbacks.

BtnUp(): This action unposts all menus in the menu hierarchy. If the ToggleButton was previously set, unsets it; if the ToggleButton was previously unset, sets it. It calls the **XmNvalueChangedCallback** callbacks and then the **XmNdisarmCallback** callbacks.

Disarm(): Calls the callbacks for **XmNdisarmCallback**.

Help(): In a Pulldown or Popup MenuPane, unposts all menus in the menu hierarchy and restores keyboard focus to the tab group that had the focus before the menu system was entered. Calls the callbacks for **XmNhelpCallback** if any exist. If there are no help callbacks for this widget, this action calls the help callbacks for the nearest ancestor that has them.

MenuShellPopdownOne():

In a toplevel Pulldown MenuPane from a MenuBar, unposts the menu, disarms the MenuBar CascadeButton and the MenuBar, and restores keyboard focus to the tab group that had the focus before the MenuBar was entered. In other Pulldown MenuPanes, unposts the menu.

In a Popup MenuPane, unposts the menu and restores keyboard focus to the widget from which the menu was posted.

Select(): If the pointer is within the button, takes the following actions: If the button was previously unset, sets it; if the button was previously set, unsets it. Calls the **XmNvalueChangedCallback** callbacks.

Additional Behavior

This widget has the additional behavior described below:

<EnterWindow>:

In a menu, if keyboard traversal is enabled, this action does nothing. Otherwise, it draws the shadow in the armed state and calls the **XmNarmCallback** callbacks.

If the ToggleButton is not in a menu and the cursor leaves and then reenters the ToggleButton's window while the button is pressed, this action restores the button's armed appearance.

<LeaveWindow>:

> In a menu, if keyboard traversal is enabled, this action does nothing. Otherwise, it draws the shadow in the unarmed state and calls the **XmNdisarmCallback** callbacks.

> If the ToggleButton is not in a menu and the cursor leaves the ToggleButton's window while the button is pressed, this action restores the button's unarmed appearance.

Virtual Bindings

The bindings for virtual keys are vendor specific.

Related Information

Core(3X), XmCreateRadioBox(3X), XmCreateToggleButton(3X), XmLabel(3X), XmPrimitive(3X), XmRowColumn(3X), XmToggleButtonGetState(3X), and XmToggleButtonSetState(3X).

XmToggleButtonGadget

Purpose

The ToggleButtonGadget widget class

AES Support Level

Full-use

Synopsis

#include <Xm/ToggleBG.h>

Description

ToggleButtonGadget sets nontransitory state data within an application. Usually this gadget consists of an indicator (square or diamond-shaped) with either text or a pixmap on one side of it. However, it can also consist of just text or a pixmap without the indicator.

The toggle graphics display a **1-of-many** or **N-of-many** selection state. When a toggle indicator is displayed, a square indicator shows an **N-of-many** selection state and a diamond-shaped indicator shows a **1-of-many** selection state.

ToggleButtonGadget implies a selected or unselected state. In the case of a label and an indicator, an empty indicator (square or diamond-shaped) indicates that ToggleButtonGadget is unselected, and a filled indicator shows that it is selected. In the case of a pixmap toggle, different pixmaps are used to display the selected/unselected states.

The default behavior associated with a ToggleButtonGadget in a menu depends on the type of menu system in which it resides. By default, **BSelect** controls the behavior of the ToggleButtonGadget. In addition, **BMenu** controls the behavior of the ToggleButtonGadget if it resides in a PopupMenu system. The actual mouse button used is determined by its RowColumn parent.

To accommodate the toggle indicator when created, Label's resource **XmNmarginLeft** may be increased.

Classes

ToggleButtonGadget inherits behavior and resources from **Object**, **RectObj**, **XmGadget** and **XmLabelGadget** classes.

The class pointer is **xmToggleButtonGadgetClass**.

The class name is **XmToggleButtonGadget**.

New Resources

The following table defines a set of widget resources used by the programmer to specify data. The programmer can also set the resource values for the inherited classes to set attributes for this widget. To reference a resource by name or by class in a .Xdefaults file, remove the **XmN** or **XmC** prefix and use the remaining letters. To specify one of the defined values for a resource in a .Xdefaults file, remove the **Xm** prefix and use the remaining letters (in either lowercase or uppercase, but include any underscores between words). The codes in the access column indicate if the given resource can be set at creation time (**C**), set by using **XtSetValues** (**S**), retrieved by using **XtGetValues** (**G**), or is not applicable (**N/A**).

XmToggleButtonGadget Resource Set		
Name	**Default**	**Access**
Class	**Type**	
XmNarmCallback	NULL	C
XmCArmCallback	XtCallbackList	
XmNdisarmCallback	NULL	C
XmCDisarmCallback	XtCallbackList	
XmNfillOnSelect	True	CSG
XmCFillOnSelect	Boolean	
XmNindicatorOn	True	CSG
XmCIndicatorOn	Boolean	
XmNindicatorSize	dynamic	CSG
XmCIndicatorSize	Dimension	
XmNindicatorType	dynamic	CSG
XmCIndicatorType	unsigned char	
XmNselectColor	dynamic	CSG
XmCSelectColor	Pixel	
XmNselectInsensitivePixmap	XmUNSPECIFIED_PIXMAP	CSG
XmCSelectInsensitivePixmap	Pixmap	
XmNselectPixmap	XmUNSPECIFIED_PIXMAP	CSG
XmCSelectPixmap	Pixmap	
XmNset	False	CSG
XmCSet	Boolean	
XmNspacing	4	CSG
XmCSpacing	Dimension	
XmNvalueChangedCallback	NULL	C
XmCValueChangedCallback	XtCallbackList	
XmNvisibleWhenOff	dynamic	CSG
XmCVisibleWhenOff	Boolean	

XmNarmCallback
>   Specifies a list of callbacks that is called when the
>   ToggleButtonGadget is armed. To arm this gadget, press the
>   active mouse button while the pointer is inside the
>   ToggleButtonGadget. For this callback, the reason is
>   **XmCR_ARM**.

XmNdisarmCallback
>   Specifies a list of callbacks called when ToggleButtonGadget
>   is disarmed. To disarm this gadget, press and release the active
>   mouse button while the pointer is inside the
>   ToggleButtonGadget. The gadget is also disarmed when the
>   user moves out of the gadget and releases the mouse button
>   when the pointer is outside the gadget. For this callback, the
>   reason is **XmCR_DISARM**.

XmNfillOnSelect
>   Fills the indicator with the color specified in **XmNselectColor**
>   and switches the top and bottom shadow colors when set to
>   True. Otherwise, it only switches the top and bottom shadow
>   colors.

XmNindicatorOn
>   Specifies that a toggle indicator is drawn to one side of the
>   toggle text or pixmap when set to True. When set to False, no
>   space is allocated for the indicator, and it is not displayed. If
>   **XmNindicatorOn** is True, the indicator shadows are switched
>   when the button is selected or unselected, but any shadows
>   around the entire gadget are not switched. However, if
>   **XmNindicatorOn** is False, any shadows around the entire
>   gadget are switched when the toggle is selected or unselected.

XmNindicatorSize
>   Sets the size of the indicator. If no value is specified, the size
>   of the indicator is based on the size of the label string or
>   pixmap. If the label string or pixmap changes, the size of the
>   indicator is recomputed based on the size of the label string or

pixmap. Once a value has been specified for **XmNindicatorSize**, the indicator has that size, regardless of the size of the label string or pixmap, until a new value is specified.

XmNindicatorType

Specifies if the indicator is a **1-of** or an **N-of** indicator. For the **1-of** indicator, the value is **XmONE_OF_MANY**. For the **N-of** indicator, the value is **XmN_OF_MANY**. The **N-of-many** indicator is square. The **1-of-many** indicator is diamond-shaped. This resource specifies only the visuals and does not enforce the behavior. When the ToggleButtonGadget is in a RadioBox, the default is **XmONE_OF_MANY**; otherwise, the default is **XmN_OF_MANY**.

XmNselectColor

Allows the application to specify what color fills the center of the square or diamond-shaped indicator when it is set. If this color is the same as either the top or the bottom shadow color of the indicator, a one-pixel-wide margin is left between the shadows and the fill; otherwise, it is filled completely. This resource's default for a color display is a color between the background and the bottom shadow color. For a monochrome display, the default is set to the foreground color. The meaning of this resource is undefined when **XmNindicatorOn** is False.

XmNselectInsensitivePixmap

Specifies a pixmap used as the button face when the ToggleButtonGadget is selected and the button is insensitive if the LabelGadget resource **XmNlabelType** is **XmPIXMAP**. If the ToggleButtonGadget is unselected and the button is insensitive, the pixmap in **XmNlabelInsensitivePixmap** is used as the button face. If no value is specified for **XmNlabelInsensitivePixmap**, that resource is set to the value specified for **XmNselectInsensitivePixmap**.

XmNselectPixmap
> Specifies the pixmap to be used as the button face if **XmNlabelType** is **XmPIXMAP** and the ToggleButtonGadget is selected. When the ToggleButtonGadget is unselected, the pixmap specified in LabelGadget's **XmNlabelPixmap** is used. If no value is specified for **XmNlabelPixmap**, that resource is set to the value specified for **XmNselectPixmap**.

XmNset Displays the button in its selected state if set to True. This shows some conditions as active when a set of buttons first appears.

XmNspacing
> Specifies the amount of spacing between the toggle indicator and the toggle label (text or pixmap).

XmNvalueChangedCallback
> Specifies a list of callbacks called when the ToggleButtonGadget value is changed. To change the value, press and release the active mouse button while the pointer is inside the ToggleButtonGadget. This action also causes the gadget to be disarmed. For this callback, the reason is **XmCR_VALUE_CHANGED**.

XmNvisibleWhenOff
> Indicates that the toggle indicator is visible in the unselected state when the Boolean value is True. When the ToggleButtonGadget is in a menu, the default value is False. When the ToggleButtonGadget is in a RadioBox, the default value is True.

Inherited Resources

ToggleButtonGadget inherits behavior and resources from the following superclasses. For a complete description of each resource, refer to the man page for that superclass.

XmLabelGadget Resource Set		
Name	**Default**	**Access**
Class	**Type**	
XmNaccelerator	NULL	CSG
XmCAccelerator	String	
XmNacceleratorText	NULL	CSG
XmCAcceleratorText	XmString	
XmNalignment	dynamic	CSG
XmCAlignment	unsigned char	
XmNfontList	dynamic	CSG
XmCFontList	XmFontList	
XmNlabelInsensitivePixmap	XmUNSPECIFIED_PIXMAP	CSG
XmCLabelInsensitivePixmap	Pixmap	
XmNlabelPixmap	XmUNSPECIFIED_PIXMAP	CSG
XmCLabelPixmap	Pixmap	
XmNlabelString	dynamic	CSG
XmCXmString	XmString	
XmNlabelType	XmSTRING	CSG
XmCLabelType	unsigned char	
XmNmarginBottom	dynamic	CSG
XmCMarginBottom	Dimension	
XmNmarginHeight	2	CSG
XmCMarginHeight	Dimension	
XmNmarginLeft	dynamic	CSG
XmCMarginLeft	Dimension	
XmNmarginRight	0	CSG
XmCMarginRight	Dimension	
XmNmarginTop	dynamic	CSG
XmCMarginTop	Dimension	
XmNmarginWidth	2	CSG
XmCMarginWidth	Dimension	

Name	Default	Access
Class	Type	
XmNmnemonic	NULL	CSG
XmCMnemonic	KeySym	
XmNmnemonicCharSet	dynamic	CSG
XmCMnemonicCharSet	String	
XmNrecomputeSize	True	CSG
XmCRecomputeSize	Boolean	
XmNstringDirection	dynamic	CSG
XmCStringDirection	XmStringDirection	

XmGadget Resource Set		
Name	Default	Access
Class	Type	
XmNhelpCallback	NULL	C
XmCCallback	XtCallbackList	
XmNhighlightOnEnter	False	CSG
XmCHighlightOnEnter	Boolean	
XmNhighlightThickness	2	CSG
XmCHighlightThickness	Dimension	
XmNnavigationType	XmNONE	G
XmCNavigationType	XmNavigationType	
XmNshadowThickness	dynamic	CSG
XmCShadowThickness	Dimension	
XmNtraversalOn	True	CSG
XmCTraversalOn	Boolean	
XmNuserData	NULL	CSG
XmCUserData	Pointer	

RectObj Resource Set		
Name	**Default**	**Access**
Class	**Type**	
XmNancestorSensitive	dynamic	G
XmCSensitive	Boolean	
XmNborderWidth	0	CSG
XmCBorderWidth	Dimension	
XmNheight	dynamic	CSG
XmCHeight	Dimension	
XmNsensitive	True	CSG
XmCSensitive	Boolean	
XmNwidth	dynamic	CSG
XmCWidth	Dimension	
XmNx	0	CSG
XmCPosition	Position	
XmNy	0	CSG
XmCPosition	Position	

Callback Information

A pointer to the following structure is passed to each callback:

typedef struct
{
    int   *reason*;
    XEvent   * *event*;
    int   *set*;
} **XmToggleButtonCallbackStruct;**

reason   Indicates why the callback was invoked

event   Points to the **XEvent** that triggered the callback

set   Reflects the ToggleButtonGadget's current state when the callback occurred, either True (selected) or False (unselected)

Behavior

XmToggleButtonGadget includes behavior from XmGadget. XmToggleButtonGadget includes menu traversal behavior from XmLabelGadget. Additional XmToggleButtonGadget behavior is described below:

BSelect Press:

In a menu, this action unposts any menus posted by the ToggleButtonGadget's parent menu, disables keyboard traversal for the menu, and enables mouse traversal for the menu. It draws the shadow in the armed state and, unless the button is already armed, calls the **XmNarmCallback** callbacks.

Outside a menu, if the button was previously unset, this action does the following: If **XmNindicatorOn** is True, it draws the indicator shadow so that the indicator looks pressed; if **XmNfillOnSelect** is True, it fills the indicator with the color specified by **XmNselectColor**. If **XmNindicatorOn** is False, it draws the button shadow so that the button looks pressed. If **XmNlabelType** is **XmPIXMAP**, the **XmNselectPixmap** is used as the button face. Calls the **XmNarmCallback** callbacks.

Outside a menu, if the button was previously set, this action does the following: If both **XmNindicatorOn** and **XmNvisibleWhenOff** are True, it draws the indicator shadow so that the indicator looks raised; if **XmNfillOnSelect** is True, it fills the indicator with the background color. If **XmNindicatorOn** is False, it draws the button shadow so that the button looks raised. If **XmNlabelType** is **XmPIXMAP**, the **XmNlabelPixmap** is used as the button face. Calls the **XmNarmCallback** callbacks.

BSelect Release:
In a menu, this action does the following: It unposts all menus in the menu hierarchy. If the ToggleButtonGadget was previously set, unsets it; if the ToggleButtonGadget was previously unset, sets it. It calls the **XmNvalueChangedCallback** callbacks and then the **XmNdisarmCallback** callbacks.

If the button is outside a menu and the pointer is within the button, this action does the following: If the button was previously unset, sets it; if the button was previously set, unsets it. Calls the **XmNvalueChangedCallback** callbacks.

If the button is outside a menu, calls the **XmNdisarmCallback** callbacks.

KHelp:
In a Pulldown or Popup MenuPane, unposts all menus in the menu hierarchy and restores keyboard focus to the tab group that had the focus before the menu system was entered. Calls the callbacks for **XmNhelpCallback** if any exist. If there are no help callbacks for this widget, this action calls the help callbacks for the nearest ancestor that has them.

KActivate or KSelect:
If the ToggleButtonGadget was previously set, unsets it; if the ToggleButtonGadget was previously unset, sets it.

In a menu, does the following: Unposts all menus in the menu hierarchy. Unless the button is already armed, calls the **XmNarmCallback** callbacks. Calls the **XmNvalueChangedCallback** and **XmNdisarmCallback** callbacks.

Outside a menu, if the button was previously unset, this action does the following: If **XmNindicatorOn** is True, it draws the indicator shadow so that the indicator looks pressed; if **XmNfillOnSelect** is True, it fills the indicator with the color specified by **XmNselectColor**. If **XmNindicatorOn** is False, it draws the button shadow so that the button looks pressed. If **XmNlabelType** is **XmPIXMAP**, the **XmNselectPixmap** is used as the button face. Calls the **XmNarmCallback**, **XmNvalueChangedCallback**, **XmNdisarmCallback** callbacks.

Outside a menu, if the button was previously set, this action does the following: If both **XmNindicatorOn** and **XmNvisibleWhenOff** are True, it draws the indicator shadow so that the indicator looks raised; if **XmNfillOnSelect** is True, it fills the indicator with the background color. If **XmNindicatorOn** is False, it draws the button shadow so that the button looks raised. If **XmNlabelType** is **XmPIXMAP**, the **XmNlabelPixmap** is used as the button face. Calls the **XmNarmCallback**, **XmNvalueChangedCallback**, and **XmNdisarmCallback** callbacks.

MAny KCancel:

In a toplevel Pulldown MenuPane from a MenuBar, unposts the menu, disarms the MenuBar CascadeButton and the MenuBar, and restores keyboard focus to the tab group that had the focus before the MenuBar was entered. In other Pulldown MenuPanes, unposts the menu.

In a Popup MenuPane, unposts the menu and restores keyboard focus to the widget from which the menu was posted.

\<Enter\>: In a menu, if keyboard traversal is enabled, this action does nothing. Otherwise, it draws the shadow in the armed state and calls the **XmNarmCallback** callbacks.

If the ToggleButtonGadget is not in a menu and the cursor leaves and then reenters the ToggleButtonGadget while the button is pressed, this action restores the button's armed appearance.

\<Leave\>: In a menu, if keyboard traversal is enabled, this action does nothing. Otherwise, it draws the shadow in the unarmed state and calls the **XmNdisarmCallback** callbacks.

If the ToggleButtonGadget is not in a menu and the cursor leaves the ToggleButtonGadget while the button is pressed, this action restores the button's unarmed appearance.

Virtual Bindings

The bindings for virtual keys are vendor specific.

Related Information

Object(3X), **RectObj(3X)**, **XmCreateRadioBox(3X)**, **XmCreateToggleButtonGadget(3X)**, **XmGadget(3X)**, **XmLabelGadget(3X)**, **XmRowColumn(3X)**, **XmToggleButtonGadgetGetState(3X)**, and **XmToggleButtonGadgetSetState(3X)**.

XmToggleButtonGadgetGetState

Purpose

A ToggleButtonGadget function that obtains the state of a ToggleButtonGadget.

AES Support Level

Full-use

Synopsis

#include <Xm/ToggleBG.h>

Boolean XmToggleButtonGadgetGetState (*widget*)
    Widget   *widget*;

Description

XmToggleButtonGadgetGetState obtains the state of a ToggleButtonGadget.

widget   Specifies the ToggleButtonGadget ID

For a complete definition of ToggleButtonGadget and its associated resources, see **XmToggleButtonGadget(3X)**.

Return Value

Returns True if the button is selected and False if the button is unselected.

Related Information

XmToggleButtonGadget(3X).

XmToggleButtonGadgetSetState

Purpose

A ToggleButtonGadget function that sets or changes the current state.

AES Support Level

Full-use

Synopsis

#include <Xm/ToggleBG.h>

void XmToggleButtonGadgetSetState (*widget, state, notify*)
    Widget   *widget*;
    Boolean   *state*;
    Boolean   *notify*;

Description

XmToggleButtonGadgetSetState   sets   or   changes   the ToggleButtonGadget's current state.

widget   Specifies the ToggleButtonGadget widget ID.

state   Specifies a Boolean value that indicates whether the ToggleButtonGadget state is selected or unselected. If True, the button state is selected; if False, the button state is unselected.

notify   Indicates whether **XmNvalueChangedCallback** is called; it can be either True or False. When this argument is True and the ToggleButtonGadget is a child of a RowColumn widget whose **XmNradioBehavior** is True, selecting the ToggleButtonGadget causes other ToggleButton and ToggleButtonGadget children of the RowColumn to be unselected.

For a complete definition of ToggleButtonGadget and its associated resources, see **XmToggleButtonGadget(3X)**.

Related Information

XmToggleButtonGadget(3X).

XmToggleButtonGetState

Purpose

A ToggleButton function that obtains the state of a ToggleButton.

AES Support Level

Full-use

Synopsis

#include <Xm/ToggleB.h>

Boolean XmToggleButtonGetState (*widget*)
    Widget   *widget*;

Description

XmToggleButtonGetState obtains the state of a ToggleButton.

widget   Specifies the ToggleButton widget ID

For a complete definition of ToggleButton and its associated resources, see
XmToggleButton(3X).

Return Value

Returns True if the button is selected and False if the button is unselected.

Related Information

XmToggleButton(3X).

XmToggleButtonSetState

Purpose

A ToggleButton function that sets or changes the current state.

AES Support Level

Full-use

Synopsis

#include <Xm/ToggleB.h>

void XmToggleButtonSetState (*widget, state, notify*)
    Widget   *widget*;
    Boolean   *state*;
    Boolean   *notify*;

Description

XmToggleButtonSetState sets or changes the ToggleButton's current state.

widget   Specifies the ToggleButton widget ID.

state   Specifies a Boolean value that indicates whether the ToggleButton state is selected or unselected. If True, the button state is selected; if False, the button state is unselected.

notify   Indicates whether **XmNvalueChangedCallback** is called; it can be either True or False. When this argument is True and the ToggleButton is a child of a RowColumn widget whose **XmNradioBehavior** is True, selecting the ToggleButton causes other ToggleButton and ToggleButtonGadget children of the RowColumn to be unselected.

For a complete definition of ToggleButton and its associated resources, see **XmToggleButton(3X)**.

Related Information

XmToggleButton(3X).

XmTrackingLocate

Purpose

A Toolkit function that provides a modal interaction.

AES Support Level

Trial-use

Synopsis

#include <Xm/Xm.h>

Widget XmTrackingLocate (*widget, cursor, confine_to*)
    Widget   *widget*;
    Cursor   *cursor*;
    Boolean   *confine_to*;

Description

XmTrackingLocate provides a modal interface for selection of a component. It is intended to support context help. The function grabs the pointer and returns the widget in which a button press occurs.

widget   Specifies the widget ID of a widget to use as the basis of the modal interaction. That is, the widget within which the interaction must occur, usually a top level shell.

cursor   Specifies the cursor to be used for the pointer during the interaction. This is a standard X cursor name.

confine_to
        Specifies whether or not the cursor should be confined to *widget*

Return Value

Returns the widget in which a button press occurs. If the window in which a button press occurs is not a widget, the function returns NULL.

XmUninstallImage

Purpose

A pixmap caching function that removes an image from the image cache.

AES Support Level

Full-use

Synopsis

#include <Xm/Xm.h>

Boolean XmUninstallImage (*image*)
    XImage   * *image*;

Description

XmUninstallImage removes an image from the image cache.

image   Points to the image structure given to the **XmInstallImage**()
            routine

Return Value

Returns True when successful; returns False if the *image* is NULL, or if it cannot be found to be uninstalled.

Related Information

XmInstallImage(3X), **XmGetPixmap(3X)**, and **XmDestroyPixmap(3X)**.

XmUpdateDisplay

Purpose

A function that processes all pending exposure events immediately.

AES Support Level

Full-use

Synopsis

> void **XmUpdateDisplay** (*widget*)
>   Widget   *widget*;

Description

XmUpdateDisplay provides the application with a mechanism for forcing all pending exposure events to be removed from the input queue and processed immediately.

When a user selects a button within a MenuPane, the MenuPanes are unposted and then any activation callbacks registered by the application are invoked. If one of the callbacks performs a time-consuming action, the portion of the application window that was covered by the MenuPanes is not redrawn; normal exposure processing does not occur until all of the callbacks have been invoked. If the application writer suspects that a callback will take a long time, then the callback may choose to invoke **XmUpdateDisplay** before starting its time-consuming operation.

This function is also useful any time a transient window, such as a dialog box, is unposted; callbacks are invoked before normal exposure processing can occur.

widget   Specifies any widget or gadget.

Index

D

E

L

R

real estate, 2-8, 2-23
RectObj, 2-112
resize borders, 2-5
resource description file, 2-18,
        2-35
resources, 2-8, 2-9, 2-10, 2-11,
        2-12, 2-13, 2-14, 2-17,
        2-18, 2-20, 2-21, 2-22,
        2-23, 2-24, 2-26, 2-27,
        2-28, 2-30, 2-31, 2-32,
        2-34
RowColumn functions
        XmGetMenuCursor,
            2-541
        XmGetPostedFromWidget,
            2-547
        XmMenuPosition, 2-686
        XmOptionButtonGadget,
            2-710
        XmOptionLabelGadget,
            2-712
        XmSetMenuCursor,
            2-889

S

Scale functions
        XmScaleGetValue,
            2-818
        XmScaleSetValue,
        2-820
ScrollBar functions
        XmScrollBarGetValues,
            2-837
        XmScrollBarSetValues,
        2-839

ScrolledWindow functions,
        XmScrolledWindowSetAreas,
        2-855
SelectionBox functions,
        XmSelectionBoxGetChild,
        2-873
service outline, 1-11
        1, 1-10
session manager, 2-2
Shell, 2-116
support levels, 1-8, 1-12, 1-13,
        1-14, 1-15, 1-16
        1, 1-8

T

temporary use, 1-12, 1-14
        1, 1-14
Text functions
        XmTextClearSelection,
            2-979
        XmTextCopy, 2-981
        XmTextCut, 2-983
        XmTextGetBaseline,
            2-985
        XmTextGetEditable,
            2-987
        XmTextGetInsertionPosition,
            2-989
        XmTextGetLastPosition,
            2-991
        XmTextGetMaxLength,
            2-993
        XmTextGetSelection,
            2-995
        XmTextGetSelectionPosition,
            2-997
        XmTextGetSource,

U

X

Notes

Notes

Notes

Notes

OPEN SOFTWARE FOUNDATION

INFORMATION REQUEST FORM

Please send me the following:

( ) OSF Membership Information

( ) OSF/Motif™ License Materials

( ) OSF/Motif™ Training Information

Contact Name   _____

Company Name   _____

Street Address   _____

Mail Stop   _____

City   _____ State _____ Zip _____

Phone   _____ FAX _____

Electronic Mail   _____

MAIL TO:

Open Software Foundation
11 Cambridge Center
Cambridge, MA 02142

Attn: OSF/Motif™

For more information about OSF/Motif™, call 617-621-8755.